ROUTLEDGE LIBR
BRITISH IN INDIA

Volume 21

THE SOCIAL SYSTEM AND CULTURE OF MODERN INDIA

THE SOCIAL SYSTEM AND CULTURE OF MODERN INDIA

A Research Bibliography

Edited with an Introduction by
DANESH A. CHEKKI

Routledge
Taylor & Francis Group

LONDON AND NEW YORK

First published in 1975 by Garland Publishing, Inc.

This edition first published in 2017
by Routledge
2 Park Square, Milton Park, Abingdon, Oxon OX14 4RN

and by Routledge
711 Third Avenue, New York, NY 10017

Routledge is an imprint of the Taylor & Francis Group, an informa business

British Library Cataloguing in Publication Data
A catalogue record for this book is available from the British Library

ISBN: 978-1-138-22929-7 (Set)
ISBN: 978-1-315-20179-5 (Set) (ebk)
ISBN: 978-1-138-28406-7 (Volume 21) (hbk)
ISBN: 978-1-138-28409-8 (Volume 21) (pbk)
ISBN: 978-1-315-26981-8 (Volume 21) (ebk)

Publisher's Note
The publisher has gone to great lengths to ensure the quality of this reprint but
points out that some imperfections in the original copies may be apparent.

Disclaimer
The publisher has made every effort to trace copyright holders and would welcome
correspondence from those they have been unable to trace.

The Social System
and
Culture of Modern India:
A Research Bibliography

Edited with an Introduction by
Danesh A. Chekki

Garland Publishing, Inc., New York & London

1975

Library of Congress Cataloging in Publication Data

Chekki, Danesh A
    The social system and culture of modern India.

    1. India--Social conditions--1947-   --Bibliography.
I. Title.
Z7165.I6C5   016.3091'54'04   74-19226
ISBN 0-8240-1056-6

Printed in the United States of America

To Sheela

Contents

CONTENTS

CONTENTS

Introduction

I

According to Arnold J. Toynbee, "India is a world in itself; it is a society of the same immensity and importance as is our Western society." In global perspective, the immensity, diversity, and unique importance of Indian society and culture can hardly be underestimated. India's cultural diversity is evident in her various religious, caste, class, linguistic and regional characteristics. Despite its diversity, what strikes us most is the underlying similarity of cultural traits – a common 'ethos' that pervades the Indian sociocultural system.[1] This reference volume encompasses studies that reflect both the unity and diversity of India's culture and social system.

As the flood of sociological research on India continues to rise at a tremendous rate, the significance of documentation and keeping an inventory of research on Indian society and culture amounts to almost that of research itself. The two academic disciplines represented here are sociology, and social and cultural anthropology (it excludes physical anthropology and archeology) in their broad connotation as conceived by Talcott Parsons.[2] Specifically, sociology is concerned with the analysis of social systems, with special but by no means exclusive reference to the type of social system we call a society, whereas, anthropology is the analytical study of phenomena of culture,[3] of the patterned symbolic meaning systems in and by which social systems and personalities are oriented and guided.

INTRODUCTION

II

This book can be considered as an important indicator of the nature of sociological research output on India during the last quarter of a century or so, since the founding of the modern state of India. We believe, however, that this volume is representative of the numerous studies on Indian society and culture undertaken and/or published during 1947-1972. It was further updated to include studies made in 1973 and 1974, and includes some scheduled to appear in 1975.

An effort to demarcate boundaries of academic disciplines is often difficult and at times this problem becomes insurmountable. An overwhelming majority of the studies documented in this volume fall under the various branches of sociology as manifested in the subject classification used here. Speaking of sociology as an academic discipline, Parsons observes: "Not only is there no 'official' sociological point of view, but there is no authoritative catalog, to say nothing of logically symmetrical classification, of sectors and subdivisions of the discipline."[4] The scheme of subject classification adopted here is a modified version of the one used by *Sociological Abstracts*.

Boundaries of academic disciplines are blurred especially when studies emerging from fields such as agriculture, communication, criminology, demography, economics, education, geography, history, health and medicine, industry, indology, law, political science, psychology, religion and social work have been included because of their sociological relevance. The purists may argue for clear-cut demarcation of academic disciplines. Our overriding concern in this volume, however, has been the adherence to an interdisciplinary social science approach.

This bibliography has emerged primarily as a result of my preoccupation with analyses of Indian sociological research since India gained political independence in 1947. In order to review trends of research during the last quarter of a century in India a large body of data was collected. Initially 5,226 entries that were considered contributions to Indian sociology were prepared in bibliographic form. This process involved reading and browsing through a large number of original and secondary sources, which included books, journals, doctoral dissertations, abstracts, bibliographies, reports, papers submitted to conferences and symposia, etc.

The resultant data were not the product of a statistically designed sample but were assumed to be a fairly accurate representation of research that has been undertaken from 1947 to 1972. An effort is made to include a large variety and number of sources with a view to reduce possible biases.

Some types of entries have been excluded from this bibliography because of several problems encountered in the process. For instance, a considerable number of government reports were not examined because of lack of ready access. However, such entries found in other sources were included in this bibliography. The coverage of government reports which contribute to sociology in India is hardly representative. Furthermore, sociological studies published in Indian languages (such as Hindi, Bengali, Gujarati, Marathi, Kannada, Tamil, etc.) were not included because of problems of translation. In this volume about ninety-eight percent of the citations are in English and the remaining are in European languages, viz. Dutch, Finnish, French, German, Hungarian, Italian, Japanese, Norwegian, Polish, Russian, Serbian and Spanish.

Since this bibliography is about studies on India conducted by both Indian and foreign scholars, several studies carried out by Indians solely on societies other than Indian were obviously excluded except a few on Nepal, Bhutan, Sikkim, Ceylon, Pakistan and Bangladesh which had cross-national relevance to the understanding of Indian society. Many studies which transcend Indian national boundaries have been

INTRODUCTION

included in this bibliography because of their cross-national content and relevance to Indian society and culture.

III

The subject classification and code chosen was from *Sociological Abstracts* (refer: vol. XX, 1972). This classification system was selected because it is fairly comprehensive and well-organized, using major subject categories and subcategories that have been fairly well established in sociology since the days of Emile Durkheim's periodical publication *l'Année Sociologique.* Approximately one third of the data collected for this bibliography were from *Sociological Abstracts.* Such entries bear reference to the source (for eg. SA, XVII, 1, D5426).

This classification system was modified to render it more suitable to the kinds of entries being included as well as to separate more distinctly particular subject areas. A category was added for general works in social psychology (300) that were mainly of the text-book variety. An addition of a subcategory containing entries that dealt with attitudes, prejudices, sentiments, and motives (0308) was also made to the major subject category of social psychology (0300), providing a more specific classification for these kinds of studies.

Likewise, another subcategory was added for entries that attempted to focus on social problems broadly (2101) and as a result could not be included in the more restricted category under social problems and social welfare (2100). A subcategory was created in the category of demography and human biology (1800) for studies on family planning (1835), since this subject area appeared to form, using the number of entries as the criterion, a definite body of research.

Research on the adoption process and innovations, if

INTRODUCTION

unrelated to family planning, was classified under the subcategory of communication (0828) under the major subject category mass phenomena (0800). In most cases these entries had been classified under rural sociology (1116) by *Sociological Abstracts*. Judging by the number of entries collected and giving precedence to the process of adoption and innovation over the nature of innovation, that is, agricultural, it appeared useful to classify these entries more distinctly.

Sociological Abstracts have only one subcategory under community development (2300); that refers to the sociology of communities and regions (2317). This subject classification seemed to be cumbersome and insufficiently differentiated. For this bibliography, regional and community studies were deleted from the category of community development and reclassified under rural sociology (1116) or urban sociology (1218) depending on the nature of the study. By this method, community development as a process of planned change became a distinct subject category with no extraneous materials.

Tribal studies were classified under the subcategory social anthropology (& ethnology) (0514). The resultant subject classification scheme used in this bibliography includes twenty-eight major subject categories and sixty subcategories (see table of contents). This volume contains entries in all subject categories except mass culture (0850) and radical sociology (2500).

IV

In the process of classifying entries into various branches of sociology a series of difficulties were encountered. Firstly, as the *Sociological Abstracts* classification system has expanded in recent years, some entries from earlier years had to be reclassified. More important, however, was the problem encountered in attempting to classify entries from sources other than *Sociological Abstracts* into subject areas, in several cases based only on the information provided by the titles. Titles of books and articles need not, of course, necessarily indicate conclusively the main intention or aim of the author or the nature of the study. The problem was partially solved by locating and examining the original sources, by relying on familiarity with the work in question from past usage, and by noting the nature of the source from which the entry was drawn. For example, a study drawn from a bibliography on tribal ethnography may have had an ambiguous title but the topic with which the bibliography dealt provided necessary information to make a logical decision regarding subject classification.

It is doubtful whether or not the time spent painstakingly obtaining over five thousand books, journal articles, reports, doctoral dissertations, and papers presented at conferences, etc. and then researching each study to permit careful classification would be worth the added accuracy. It must also be borne in mind that any classification scheme of the kind employed here contains some degree of arbitrariness as to where lines can be drawn between two seemingly overlapping subject subcategories. After all, our general objective is to reduce information into generalizations of varying degrees in the form of major subject categories and subcategories in order that a general overview of trends of research through time can be discerned.

During the process of subject classification operational definitions for each subject area were derived by examining the nature of studies classified into various subject categories by *Sociological Abstracts*. In an attempt to be consistent in considering similar studies, decisions were made by example or precedence as indicated in *Sociological Abstracts*. Ideally the task of classification should have taken place accompanied by lists of characteristics for each subject area. The possibility of deriving such clear-cut delineation of subject areas, however, seems to be remote due to the ambiguity that presently prevails in sociology relating to the exact nature of its specialized branches. One researcher who experienced similar problems noted, "Obstacles which stand in the way of (scientific journals) use in analyzing developments in the field of sociology largely derive from the somewhat amorphous state of the field itself and the consequent lack of clearly defined analytical categories."[5]

The lack of clear-cut lines of demarcation between subject areas poses another question regarding classification of studies that appear to belong to more than one subject area. Other researchers[6] who have had similar questions have examined the study to assess the author's main intention or more concisely stated, the dependent variable in the study was identified and given more weight than the independent variable.[7] Because of the large number involved and the lack of ready accessibility of many studies, we cross-classified those studies that seemed to contribute to more than one subject area.

V

The bibliography includes studies which have emerged in several published or unpublished forms such as book, chapter in a book, journal article, doctoral dissertation (completed), doctoral dissertation (in progress), papers submitted to conferences, studies in languages other than English, etc. Each entry is given a serial number. Within each subject subcategory all entries are arranged alphabetically according to the author's name. For instance, the entry of books follows the following format:

2481   Lynch, Owen M.
The Politics of Untouchability:
Social Mobility and Social Change
In a City of India
New York, Columbia U. Press, 1970

A chapter in a book is documented in the following way:

3222   Thirumalai, S.
Trends in Rural Change
in: *Rural Sociology in India*
ed. A.R. Desai, Bombay,
Popular, 1969, pp. 691-693

Journal articles have certain set of characteristics which need to be recorded for purposes of research reference. Besides author and title of study, such entry would include name of the journal in which it appears, year of publication, volume and issue number and pagination. Most journal article entries also include *Sociological Abstracts* (SA) numbers of volume, issue, and serial of abstract of the article for easy reference. The following is an illustration of such an entry:

3360   Mukherjee, R.
Urbanization and Social
Transformation in India
Int.J.Comp.Sociol.,1963,
4,2,Sep.,178-210,
SA,XII,8,B3652

The entries of completed doctoral dissertations (India) indicate name of the university, year doctorate degree was awarded and name of the supervisor in parentheses, as in the following:

3663   Singh (Miss), B.Q.
The Communication of Ideas
Through Adult Education in
India

INTRODUCTION

Doct., Bombay U., 1957
(Prof. G.S. Ghurye)

The entries of completed doctoral dissertations (America) generally appear in the following way:

> 4049 Aird, J.S.
> *Fertility Levels and Differentials*
> *In Two Bengali Villages*
> American Doctoral Dissertations
> (1956-1957)
> University of Michigan (Sociology)

Almost all relevant doctoral dissertations in progress in Indian universities during 1969 are included in this bibliography. The following entry is an example:

> 3947 Bishwas, D.K.
> *Social Barriers to Family*
> *Planning in India*
> Doct.st., Bhagalpur U., 1969
> (Prof. I. Prasad)

Papers presented at conferences are entered differently. Information relating to name of the conference, year in which conference was held and place of conference have been recorded in that order:

> 3539 Das, Man Singh, Donald E. Allen
> & F. Gene Acuff
> *Brain Drain and Students from Less*
> *Developed and Developing Countries*
> Paper presented at 7th World Congress
> of Sociology, 1970, Varna, Bulgaria

Studies in foreign languages include the title of the work in the original language followed by its English translation in parentheses. The citation also includes reference to *Sociological Abstracts* for locating a summary of the article in

INTRODUCTION

English. The following entry is a sample of citation of foreign language studies:

> 3323 Joshi, P.
>   *Tradition, Vie Urbane et Vie*
>   *Rurale dans L'Inde Dunord—*
>   *Etude Comparative de Quelques*
>   *Attitudes dans L'Uttar Pradesh*
>   *(Life in North India. Comparative*
>   *Study of Attitudes in Uttar Pradesh)*
>   (Fr.) R.Franc.Sociol., 1966,7,4,
>   Oct-Dec,485-490
>   SA,XV,5,C6706

Unpublished reports are entered in the following format:

> 144 Sociological Research Unit,
>   Indian Statistical Institute,
>   Calcutta
>   *Some Characteristics of*
>   *Sociological Studies in India*
>   1967, pp. 10 (mimeographed)

For purposes of sociological analysis a major portion of this bibliography was completed by the end of June 1973. Later additions include an asterisk beside the author's name as in the following citation:

> 2793 *Beals, A.R.
>   *Village Life in South India*
>   Chicago, Aldine, 1974

VI

The bibliography completed by the end of June 1973 consisted of 5,226 citations. After classification by subject area the data contained in these citations were then coded and keypunched on IBM cards and later transferred to magnetic tape for computer analysis. A detailed sociological analysis based on this bibliography will appear in a forthcoming publication.[8] The following is an overview of some of the major trends in Indian sociological research during 1947-1972:

In order to ascertain major trends in Indian sociological research, frequency counts were obtained for each variable for each five-year time period.

Table I

Number of Studies and Percentage Distribution
by Five-Year Time periods

Date of Publication	Number of Studies	Relative Frequency
1968-1972	1.911	36.6%
1963-1967	1.501	28.6%
1958-1962	944	18.1%
1953-1957	527	10.1%
1947-1952	323	6.2%
not known	20	0.4%
1947-1972	5.226	100.0%

The most obvious trend that has emerged is the greatly increased productivity of Indian sociological research. From Table I it is evident that the number of studies has increased by almost 600% since the first five-year time period (1947-1952) until the last (1968-1972). Over one third of the sociological research for twenty-five years has been published in the last five years. This tremendous increase in research output is perhaps partially due to better bibliographic coverage for later years. However, the magnitude of the

xxi

INTRODUCTION

increase in research cannot be totally accounted for by these possible biases. In fact, Indian sociological research has increased dramatically over the last few years.

Some reasons for the increase in research productivity can be stated. Since Independence (1947), Indian universities generally have expanded in enrollment and in teaching and research facilities. In Indian universities sociology has come to be recognized as an independent discipline instead of a branch of other social sciences. Sociology has attracted many students who have been engaged in research. In an effort to assess the impact of programs of economic development the Government of India through the Research Committee of the Planning Commission has in the past financed several research projects. The University Grants Commission has also provided funds to several scholars to undertake research. Various other national and international agencies have aided sociological research in India. The number of foreign sociologists conducting research in India has also tended to increase. In recent years the Indian Council of Social Science Research has been encouraging and financing research on a large scale. Research centers and universities have given impetus to research by academics through incentives such as salary increases and promotion. These forces have led to increased sociological research productivity in India.

The six most highly researched subject areas according to our bibliography, in terms of productivity, are 0500 – Culture and Social Structure-12.9 per cent; 1000 – Social Differentiation-8.6 per cent; 1100 – Rural Sociology-8.4 per cent; 1900 – the Family and Socialization – 7.5 per cent; 0700 – Social Change and Economic Development-6.3 per cent; 1800 – Demography and Human Biology-6.0 per cent. Although subject category 0500, culture and social structure, has declined sharply since the first time period, it still holds the dominant position. The least researched subject areas, with less than one per cent productivity, include 2400 – Planning, Forecasting and Spec-ulation; 2200 – Sociology of Knowledge; 1700 – Sociology of Science; 2700 – Studies in Poverty; 2600 – Environmental Interactions; 2800 – Studies in Violence. Other subject areas in terms of productivity range from a low of 1.3 per cent to a high of 5.8 per cent.

A total of 5,226 studies were classified by type of publication, such as book, journal article, dissertation, etc.

Table II
Percentage Distribution and Number of
Studies by Type of Publication

Type of Publ.	1947-52	1953-57	1958-62	1963-67	1968-72	1947-72
Journal Article	37.5% (121)	65.1% (343)	55.6% (525)	57.6% (864)	36.7% (701)	48.9% (2.555)
Book	31.9% (103)	13.7% (72)	11.7% (110)	11.8% (177)	18.4% (351)	15.8% (824)
Dissertation In Progress	11.1% (36)	10.6% (56)	17.8% (168)	18.7% (280)	14.3% (273)	15.6% (814)
Book Chapter	12.7% (41)	5.1% (27)	9.7% (92)	4.9% (73)	9.8% (188)	5.1% (423)
In Progress	– –	– –	– –	– –	14.1% (270)	5.2% (170)
Other	3.4% (11)	3.0% (16)	3.6% (34)	5.1% (76)	5.7% (109)	4.7% (246)
Gov't Report	2.5% (8)	2.1% (11)	1.1% (10)	1.1% (16)	0.5% (9)	1.0% (54)
Not Known	0.9% (3)	0.4% (2)	0.5% (5)	1.0% (15)	0.5% (10)	0.8% (40)
TOTAL	100% (323)	100% (527)	100% (944)	100% (1.501)	100% (1.911)	100% (5.226)

INTRODUCTION

From Table II it is evident that the most common form of publication for sociological research has been journal articles. During 1953-57 there appears to be a peak in the number of research findings published in journals. Following this peak, the relative frequency for journal articles has declined to approximately the same level of the first time period. One of the causes of this decline may be attributed to the growing importance of other types of publication as well as increase in the number of doctoral dissertations, some of which may be eventually published.

Books constitute 15.8 per cent of sociological research publication during the past twenty-five years. In the last ten years studies published in book form have been gaining in relative and absolute frequencies. Dissertations have increased greatly in absolute number and to a lesser extent in relative number. From Table II it appears that in the past five years the number of dissertations have decreased from previous levels. These figures, however, are soemwhat misleading because dissertations for 1969-72 from Indian universities were not available for inclusion in this bibliography. In 1969 there were 270 doctoral dissertations, or 14 per cent of total research still in progress. It is highly probable that the number of dissertations being completed each year is increasing relative to other types of publication.

Book chapters have fluctuated widely in relative frequency but in absolute numbers they are generally increasing. The category "other" contains studies such as research reports from universities and institutes and papers presented at conferences. During the past twenty-five years this category has increased, reflecting in part the important role played by conferences as an outlet for research findings. Government reports have declined in importance, probably because government departments have in recent years transferred most of their research responsibilities to research institutes and universities.

INTRODUCTION

As mentioned earlier journals have been the dominant channel for researchers to publish their findings. All major Indian sociological journals have increased in absolute number of articles published. *The Indian Journal of Social Work* has experienced the greatest increase during the period under review. This journal is followed by others, in terms of absolute and relative frequency of total research published, such as *Man in India, Sociological Bulletin, Eastern Anthropologist, Indian Journal of Social Research, Indian Sociological Bulletin, Journal of Social Research, Economic and Political Weekly, Controbutions to Indian Sociology.*

The data on place of publication showed a distinct trend toward more publication of research findings in India (68.3%) and to a lesser extent more publication (21.6%) in North America. This greater increase in amount of publication in India and North America has been at the expense of publication in the United Kingdom (3.1%). Of the research output 4.9% was published in Europe. Other places of publication and "not known" categories formed 2.1% of the total number of studies.

Since 1947 Indian sociological research has been dominated by scholars working alone and this trend is continuing. Of the total 5,226 studies 88.2% had single authorship, 7.3% studies were done by a team of two persons and 2.2% were by a team of three or more researchers. Government reports, not known and other categories formed 2.3 per cent. Time series data revealed that studies undertaken by two and three or more scholars have increased during the last quarter of a century.

Indian sociological research has been dominated by men. Analysis of sex of authors showed that 77.6% of the studies were made by men and 6% were by women. And 15.7% of the studies belonged to the not known or not applicable category. Studies undertaken by a husband-wife team from North America constituted .7 per cent. During the last

INTRODUCTION

twenty-five years the number of male authors has increased over six times, but the number of female authors has increased over nine times. The number and proportion of female authors is thus growing at a faster rate than male authors, especially in recent years.

The findings from frequency counts of authors' nationality indicated an increase in the proportion of total research output by Indian authors. In fact, 74.5% of the studies were the result of Indian researchers. Studies conducted by North Americans formed 11.9% of our total sample. Authors from the United Kingdom and Europe were 1.8% and 1.5% respectively. Of the studies with two or more authors in 1.4% of the cases we could identify at least one Indian as a collaborative author. In case of .2% of the studies we could observe the collaborative efforts of authors from the United Kingdom and Europe. The remaining .2% of authors belonged to other nationalities.

Out of the 5,226 entries approximately one third of them could be classified according to regional variables. Studies that did not have an areal basis, for example, those on theory and methodology, and also studies that did not clearly indicate a particular region as the basis of study were excluded from analysis. Of the total number of studies 32% belonged to the category of regional studies.

Time-series data on regional studies showed that research in almost every region has increased in number. Relative frequency changes indicated that broadly speaking northern regions of India have replaced southern regions of India as the major focus of research. Central and Eastern Indian regions have been the most poorly researched areas. However, these regions are not declining in importance as areas of research. On the other hand, the regions in western India and north-east India have been moderately researched.

I hope that this reference work might act as a catalyst in inducing Indian sociology to enter into the "diagnostic stage." In the past, Indian sociology has been exposed to diverse schools of thought and historical processes.[9] Presently, as M.N. Srinivas and Panini observe, "The danger of conformism in research is real, the double conformism to fashions in Western coutries as well as to local ones, but there are also signs of independence, earnestness and intelligence in the choice of themes and methods. A new dawn in Indian sociology may not be long in coming."[10]

VII

In an effort to overcome cultural and national limitations of sociological theories, in recent years sociologists have shown great interest in cross-cultural and international comparative reserach. In the task of universalizing sociological theory and in developing comparative macro sociology sociologists seem to have recognized the importance of utilizing micro sociological studies from different nations. Researchers interested in cross-cultural verification and validation of propositions, in the absence of codified empirical data[11] from various countries are at a loss in making the best use of available, though scattered, empirical research. Furthermore, the rapid growth of comparative studies[12] has in turn given rise to a need for preparing an inventory of empirical findings that are diffuse.

The present bibliography, it is hoped, will aid researchers in avoiding duplication of work and in concentrating on otherwise neglected though important problems and areas of research. More importantly, this bibliography can not only serve as an important reference volume for social scientists all over the world interested in cross-national research but also such a work would aid them in expanding the horizons of sociological theory and sophistication of research methodology.

INTRODUCTION

REFERENCES AND NOTES

1. For a general introduction to India's cultural heritage and social system refer:

    Basham A.L., *The Wonder That Was India*, New York, Grove Press, 1954.

    Lamb, Beatrice P., *India: A World In Transition*, New York, Praeger, 3rd Ed. Revised & Expanded, 1968.

2. Parsons, Talcott (ed.), *Knowledge and Society: American Sociology*, New York, Basic Books, 1968, pp. 345.

3. An admirable clarification of these fundamental concepts can be found in:

    Kroeber, A.L. & Parsons, T., "The Concepts of Culture and Social System," *American Sociological Review,* Vol. 23, No. 5, Oct. 1958, pp. 582-583.

4. Parsons, Talcott, *Op. cit,* 1968, p. vi.

5. Tibbits, Helen G., "Research In the Development of Sociology: A Pilot Study In Methodology," *American Sociological Review* 27, p. 892.

6. Barnsley, John H., "On the Sociology of Values: Patterns of Research," *The Sociological Review,* 20,2,1972, p. 230.

7. Tibbits, Helen G., *Op. cit,* p. 893.

8. Chekki, Danesh A., *The Sociology of Contemporary India* (Forthcoming)

9. For an understanding of historical developments and present problems of Indian sociology and social anthropology refer:

Mukherjee, Ramkrishna, "Indian Sociology: Historical Development and Present Problems," *Sociological Bulletin* 22, 1, March 1973, pp. 29-58.

Also:

Srinivas, M.N. & Panini, "The Development of Sociology and Social Anthropology In India," *Sociological Bulletin,* 22, 2, September 1973, pp. 179-215.

10. Srinivas, M.N. & Panini, *Ibid.,* 1973, pp. 211-12.

11. Marsh, Robert M., *Comparative Sociology,* New York, Harcoutt, Brace & World, 1967, pp. 5-20, 313-327.

12. During the last few years there has been a burgeoning of cross-national comparative research encouraged by various national and international research councils, foundations, and several reserach committees of the International Sociological Association.

Acknowledgments

The "knowledge explosion" in recent decades makes it almost impossible for any one person to undertake the arduous task of preparing a bibliography of this nature and magnitude. I wish to express my sincere thanks to Donna Krawetz, who worked as research assistant under my direction. She took considerable interest and worked diligently in scrutinizing numerous studies and verifying the authenticity of several references.

Many scholars from India, the United States, Canada, and other countries have contributed their share by sending their bibliographies. I owe a special debt to them.

I take this opportunity to express my gratitude to Dr. H.E. Duckworth, President of the University of Winnipeg, Dr. B.G. Hogg, Dean of Research, and Dr. J. Clake, Dean of Arts and Science, who have encouraged this project through an award of a research grant. Grateful acknowledgments are due to Professors John R. Hofley, Boris Raymond, and William A. Morrison for their valuable comments on this reference volume.

The University of Winnipeg library staff were extremely helpful in obtaining many books and periodicals through the inter-library loan system. Heartfelt thanks should go to Raymond Wright, John Wilde, Sandra Zuk, Shirley Payment and Louise Sloane, among others, who met my rather unusual requests to secure original sources, often within a short time. The computer analysis portion of this bibliography was directed by Gerry Miller of the University Computer Centre.

For hundreds of days I had to devote long hours to the preparation of this volume. During this time I was somewhat

ACKNOWLEDGMENTS

delinquent in my roles as husband and father. My wife Sheela's understanding and patience have made it possible to complete this work. Without her encouragement the publication of this book would have been further delayed. It is for her inimitable qualities of love and sacrifice that this book is dedicated.

I should like to extend my thanks to Mavis Reimer, Mary Berchard, Donna Taylor, and Elizabeth Crozier who, at various stages, have provided efficient secretarial services. Many thanks to Renate Liebig who, with her excellent skills at the typewriter, was responsible for producing this entire volume ready for the press.

To Peter Kemeny, Editor-In-Chief of Garland Publishing, Inc., I owe special thanks for his interest in this venture.

University of Winnipeg,   DANESH A. CHEKKI
Manitoba, Canada,
August 15, 1974

ABBREVIATIONS
==============

A:

Admin.Sci.Quart.	= Administrative Science Quarterly
A. Amer.Acad.Pol.Soc.Sc.	= Annals of the American Academy of Political and Social Science
Amer. Anthrop.	= American Anthropologist
Amer.Doct.Dissert.	= American Doctoral Dissertations
Amer.J.Econ.& Sociol.	= American Journal of Economics and Sociology
Amer.J.Sociol.	= American Journal of Sociology
Amer. Sociol.	= American Sociologist
Ant. Rev.	= Antioch Review
Anthrop.Quart.	= Anthropological Quarterly
Asian Sur.	= Asian Survey
Austr.J.of Polit.Hist.	= Australian Journal of Politics and History

B:

Behavioural Scis. & C.D.	= Behavioural Sciences and Community Development
Brit.J. Psychol.	= British Journal of Psychology
British J.Sociol.	= British Journal of Sociology
B.Anthrop.Sur.Ind.	= Bulletin of the Anthropological Survey of India
Bul.Cult.Res.Inst.	= Bulletin of the Cultural Research Institute

C:

C.D.Jour.	= Community Development Journal
Cdn.Sociol. & Anthrop. Assoc.	= Canadian Sociology & Anthropology Association
Comp. Edu.Rev.	= Comparative Education Review
Comp.Pol.Stud.	= Comparative Political Studies
Comp.Stud.Soc.Hist.	= Comparative Studies in Society and History
Contemp. R.	= Contemporary Review
Contrib. Asian Stud.	= Contributions to Asian Studies
Cont.Ind.Soc.	= Contributions to Indian Sociology
Cont. to Stats.	= Contributions to Statistics
Current Soc.	= Current Sociology

D:

Doct.	= Doctorate
Doct. st.	= Doctoral student
Du.	= Dutch

E:

East Anthrop.	= Eastern Anthropoligist
Eco.Dev.Cult.Change	= Economic Development and Cultural Change

E:

Eco.Wkly	= Economic Weekly
Eco. & Polit. Wkly	= Economic and Political Weekly
Edu. & Psy.	= Education and Psychology
Ethnol.	= Ethnology
Eug.Quart.	= Eugenics Quarterly
Eur.J.Sociol.	= European Journal of Sociology

F:

Fam.Process	= Family Process
Fin.	= Finnish
Fr.	= French

G:

Ger.	= German
Geogr.R.	= Geographical Review

H: .

Hum.Biol.	= Human Biology
Hum.Org.	= Human Organization
Hung.	= Hungarian

I:

Impact Sci.Soc.	= Impact of Science on Society
Ind.Agr.Res.Inst.	= Indian Agricultural Research Institute
Ind.Coop.R.	= Indian Cooperative Review
Ind.Eco.J.	= Indian Economic Journal
Ind.Eco. & Social Hist.R.	= Indian Economic and Social History Review
Ind.J.Agr.Eco.	= Indian Journal of Agricultural Economics
Ind.J.Agron.	= Ind.Journal of Agronomics
Ind.J.Ext.Edu.	= Indian Journal of Extension Education
Ind.J.Med.Edu.	= Indian Journal of Medical Education
Ind.J.Polit.Sci.	= Indian Journal of Political Science
Ind.J.Pub.Admin.	= Indian Journal of Public Administration
Ind.J.of Psy.	= Indian Journal of Psychology
Ind.J.Soc.Res.	= Indian Journal of Social Research
Ind.J.Social Wrk	= Indian Journal of Social Work
Ind.Soc.B.	= Indian Sociological Bulletin
Int.R.Com.Dev.	= International Review of Community Development
Int.Jour.of Comp.Sociol.	= International Journal of Comparative Sociology
Int.J. of Soc. of the Family	= International Journal of Sociology of the Family
Int.J. of Legal Res.	= International Journal of Legal Research

I:

Int.J. Soc.Psychiat.	= International Journal of Social Psychiatry
Int.Labour Rev.	= International Labour Review
Int.R.Commu.Develop.	= International Review of Community Development
Int.R.Hist.Polit.Sci.	= International Review of History and Political Science
Int.R.Mod.Soc.	= International Review of Modern Sociology
Int.Soc.Sc.J.	= International Social Science Journal
It.	= Italian

J:

Jap.Sociol.R.	= Japan Sociological Review
(Jap.)	= Japanese
J. of Amer.Stat.Assoc.	= Journal of American Statistical Association
J. Appl. Behav. Sci.	= Journal of Applied Behavioral Science
J.of As.& Af.Stud.	= Journal of Asian and African Studies
J.Consti. Parl.Stud.	= Journal of Constitutional and Parliamentary Studies
J.of Comm.Polit.Stud.	= Journal of Commonwealth Political Studies
J.Educ.Sociol.	= Journal of Educational Sociology
J. of Gujarat Res.Soc.	= Journal of Gujarat Research Society
J.Hum.Rel.	= Journal of Human Relations
J.Indu.Rel.	= Journal of Industrial Studies
J.Int.Affairs	= Journal of International Affairs
J.Loc.Adm.Overseas	= Journal of Local Administration Overseas
J.Psych.Res.	= Journal of Psychological Research
Jour.Quart.	= Journalism Quarterly
J.Soc.Issues	= Journal of Social Issues
J. of Soc.Psy.	= Journal of Social Psychology
J.Soc.-Sc.	= Journal of Social Science
J.Univ.Edu.	= Journal of University Education

K:

Koelner Z.Soziol.Soz.-Psychol.	= Koelner Zeitschrift Soziologie und Sozial-Psychologie

M:

Mil.Mem.Fd.Quart.	= Milbank Memorial Fund Quarterly

M:

Mod.Rev.	= Modern Review
Mthly.Publ.Opin.Sur.	= Monthly Public Opinion Survey
Mysore Eco.R.	= Mysore Economic Review

N:

Nor.	= Norwegian

P:

Pacific Aff.	= Pacific Affairs
Pol.	= Polish
Pol.Sci.R.	= Political Science Review
Pop.Stud.	= Population studies
Practic.Anthrop.	= Practical Anthropology
Publ.Opinion Quart.	= Public Opinion Quarterly

Q:

Quart.J.stud.Alcohol	= Quarterly Journal of Studies in Alcoholism

R:

Rev.of Rel.Res.	= Review of Religious Research
Rur.Soc.	= Rural Sociology
Ru.	= Russian

S:

SA	= Sociological Abstracts
Ser.	= Serbian
Soc.Comp.	= Social Compass
Soc.Forces	= Social Forces
Sociol.B.	= Sociological Bulletin
Soc.Prob.	= Social Problems
Soc.Sci.Info.	= Social Science Information
Social Sci.Quart.	= Social Science Quarterly
Society & Cult.	= Society and Culture
Sociol.Soc.Res.	= Sociology and Social Research
Southw.J.Anthrop.	= Southwestern Journal of Anthropology
Sp.	= Spanish

U:

Urban Res.Plan - Thought	= Urban Research Planning and Thought

W:

Wrld.Polit.	= World Politics

* * * * * * * * *

0103   methodology   (social science and behavioral)

1   Bopegamage, A.

       A METHODOLOGICAL PROBLEM IN INDIAN URBAN
       SOCIOLOGICAL RESEARCH
       Sociol. Soc. Res. 1966, 50, 2, Jan., 236-240.
       SA, XIV, 5, C1397

2   Chapple, Elliot D.

       THE INTERACTION MONOGRAPHS: ITS EVOLUTION AND
       RECENT APPLICATION
       Personnel, 1949, 80, 4, 295-307

3   Chattopadhyaya, K. and S. Bandopadhyaya

       NOTES ON A METHOD OF STUDYING RURAL SOCIETY
       Man In India, 1962, 42, 3, 206-16

4   Dasgupta, S. (ed.)

       METHODOLOGY OF SOCIAL SCIENCE RESEARCH
       Intl. Pubns. Serv.   1967

5   Dube, Leela

       TRAINING IN METHODS OF SOCIAL RESEARCH
       in Sociology in India, Agra, Inst. of Soc. Sci.,
       1965, 104-13

6   Dube, S.C.

       METHODOLOGICAL PROBLEMS IN GROUP RESEARCH
       Lucknow, Convention of Social Anthropologists, 1960

7   Krishnarao, B.

       THE DESCRIPTIVE METHOD IN SOCIAL RESEARCH
       Sociol. B., 1961, 10, 2, 46-52

0103   methodology   (social science and behavioral)

8   Mahapatra, L.K.

        THE VALUES AND LIMITATIONS OF HOLISTIC SMALL SCALE
        STUDIES
        Proceedings and Papers of the Seminar on Research
        Methodology in the Social Sciences
        Indian Inst. Eco., 1967

9   Mandelbaum, D.G.

        CONCEPTS AND METHODS IN THE STUDY OF CASTE
        Eco. Wkly., 1959, 11, 145-48

10   Naik, T.B.

        ACTION, ANTHROPOLOGY AND CULTURE CHANGE
        Seminar on Research Methodology Ranchi, 1968

11   Rastogi, P.N.

        STRUCTURE, FUNCTION AND PROCESS: CYBERNETIC APPROACH
        TO SOCIAL PHENOMENA
        4th Annual Int'l Symposium of the Amer. Society for
        Cybernetics
        Washington, D.C. 1970   1-12

12   Research Programmes Committee of the Planning Commission
        Gov't of India

        SEMINAR ON RESEARCH METHODOLOGY IN THE SOCIAL
        SCIENCES: A REPORT
        Osmania '   + ' - works, 1968

13   Sahay, A

        SOCIOLOGICAL ANALYSIS
        London, Routledge and Kegan Paul, 1972

14   Saksena, R.N.

        INTERDISCIPLINARY APPROACH IN SOCIAL RESEARCH
        Regional Sem. on Techniques of Research, UNESCO Res.
        Center New Delhi, 1959, 141-43

- 2 -

15   Sarana, G.

        COMPARATIVE METHODS (APPROACHES) IN SOCIAL-
        CULTURAL ANTHROPOLOGY: A METHODOLOGICAL ANALYSIS
        Typescript, Ph.d Dissertation Harvard Univ., 1966

16   Sinha, S.

        TRIBAL CULTURES OF PENINSULAR INDIA AS A DIMENSION
        OF LITTLE TRADITION IN THE STUDY OF INDIAN
        CIVILIZATION: A PRELIMINARY STUDY
        Man In India; 1957, 37, 2, Apr-June 93-118
        S.A., VIII, 1, 6937

17   Sirsikar, W.M.

        NICKTORE PROBLEMY METHODOLOGIEZNE BADAN NAD
        WARTOSCIAMI W POLITYCE I ICH TLO W INDII
        (Some Methodological Problmes of the Research Scheme
        on Political Values and Its Indian Background)
        Studia Socjologiczno Polityczne, 1967, 23,
        107-113 (pol)
        S.A., XVII, 3, D6946

18   Srivastava, H.C.

        RADHAKAMAL MUKERJEE'S INTERDISCIPLINARY METHOD
        AND FRAME OF REFERENCE IN SOCIAL SCIENCE
        Ind. J Soc. Res., 1967, 8, 1, Apr., 33-38.
        SA, XVII, 5, D8165

19   The National Sample Survey: General Report No;
        1, Sankhya, 1953, 13, Parts 1 and 2, 47-218

        REPORT OF THE NATIONAL SAMPLE SURVEY OF INDIA
        COVERING THE PERIOD 10/1950 - 3/1951
        SA, vol. III, #3, 1445

20   Thoothi, N.A.

        METHODS OF SOCIAL RESEARCH
        Int'l Pubns Serv., 1966

0103   methodology   (social science and behavioral)

21   Uberoi, J.P.A.

       SCIENCE AND SWARAJ
       Cont. to Ind. Soc. 1968, 2, 119-23

22   Varma, H.S.

       SOME THOUGHTS REGARDING RESEARCH IN ROLE TAKING
       Interdiscipline, 1967, 4, 2, 1-7

0104   research technology

23   Balkrishna, R.

       URBAN AND RURAL SURVEYS
       Regional Seminar on Techniques of Social Research,
       Delhi, UNESCO, Res Center,1959, p. 59-62

24   Basu, M.N.

       FIELD METHODS IN ANTHROPOLOGY AND OTHER SOCIAL
       SCIENCES
       Calcutta, Bookland, 1961

25   Carvoll, C.M. and F. Carroll

       METHODS OF SOCIOLOGICAL RESEARCH
       Meerut, 1971

26   Chapple, Elliot D.

       FIELD METHODS AND TECHNIQUES
       Hum. Org., 1949, 8,2, 22-28

27   Dandapani, S.

       FUNDAMENTALS OF SOCIAL SURVEY AND RESEARCH METHODOLOGY
       Delhi, (post 1968)

28   Dandekar, K.B.V.

        METHODOLOGY OF FAMILY PLANNING SURVEYS
        Artha Vijnan, 11 (4)   Dec. 1969, 651-661

29   Dube, Leela

        SOME FIELD TECHNIQUES IN THE STUDY OF RURAL
        LEADERSHIP: AN ANTHROPOLOGICAL APPROACH
        in Emerging Patterns of Rural Leadership in
        Southern Asia
        Hyderabad,   N.I.C.D., 1965, 191-8

30   Epstein, T.S.

        THE DATA OF ECONOMICS IN ANTHROPOLOGICAL ANALYSIS
        M.A.L. Epstein (ed.)
        The Craft of Social Anthropolgoy   London, 1967, p. 153-80

31   Gil, P.

        A COMPARATIVE STUDY IN THE PROJECTIVE AND SOCIOMETRIC
        APPROACH TO PERSONALITY   (Ph.d.)
        Doct, Gujarat U, 1963
        (Prof. P.H. Prabhu)

32   Gopal, M.H.

        SOME PROBLEMS OF RESEARCH IN SOCIAL SCIENCES AND
        HUMANITIES IN INDIA
        Ind. Eco. J.   14, 3, Oct-Dec, 1966, 327-337

33   Gopal, M.H.

        INTRODUCTION TO RESEARCH PROCEDURE IN SOCIAL
        SCIENCES, (2nd ed)
        Bombay, Asia, 1970   1st ed. 1964

34   Gopal, M.H.

        AN APPROACH TO RESEARCH PROBLEMS IN DEVELOPING
        SOCIETIES
        Ind. J. Soc. Res. 13, 1, April, 1972, 61-64

35   Hallen, G.C.

       TECHNIQUES OF SOCIAL RESEARCH
       Ind. J. Soc. Res.   1961, 2, 1, Jan, 29-36
       SA, XI, 6, A6286

36   Hasan, K.A.

       ON COLLECTING ANTHROPOLOGICAL DATA IN A NORTH INDIAN
       VILLAGE
       East. Anthrop. 1966, 19, 1, 55-68

37   Mahar, Pauline M.

       A MULTIPLE SCALING TECHNIQUE FOR CASTE RANKING
       Man In India, 1959, 39, 2, 127-47

38   Misra, H.

       USE OF PSYCHOLOGICAL TECHNIQUES IN SOCIAL SURVEYS
       OF INDIA
       Ind. J. Social Wrk., 1961, 22, 3, Dec, 189-192
       SA. XI, 7, A7111

39   Murthy, M.N. and A.S. Roy

       A PROBLEM IN INTEGRATION OF SURVEYS--A CASE STUDY
       J. of Amer. Stat. Assoc., 1970, 65, 329, Mar, 123-135
       SA, XIX, 6, F1296

40   Neale, Walker C.

       THE LIMITATIONS OF INDIAN VILLAGE SURVEY DATA
       J. of Asian Studies, 1958, 17, 383-402

41   Ogburn, W.I.

       A DESIGN FOR SOME EXPERIMENTS IN THE LIMITATION OF
       POPULATION GROWTH IN INDIA
       Chicago, 1952, 14p. mimeo.

42   Oommen, T.K.

        DATA COLLECTION TECHNIQUES: THE CASE OF SOCIOLOGY
        AND SOCIAL ANTHROPOLOGY
        Eco. and Polit. Weekly, 1969, 4, 19, 809-15

43   Ralis, M. Suchman, E.A., Goldsen, R.K.

        APPLICABILITY OF SURVEY TECHNIQUES IN NORTHERN
        INDIA
        Publ. Opinion Quart., 1958, 22, 3, Fall, 245-250
        SA, VIII, 4, 8200

44   Robinson, M.S. and L.E. Jornir

        AN EXPERIMENT IN THE STRUCTURE STUDY OF MYTH
        Cont. to Ind. Soc., 1968, 2, 1-37

45   Rudolph, L. and S.H. Rudolph

        SURVEYS IN INDIA: FIELD EXPERIENCE IN MADRAS
        STATE
        Pub. Opin. Quart., 1958, 22, 3, Fall, 235-244.
        SA VIII, 4, 8201

46   Shankar, Prem

        STEREOTYPE SCALE: A MULTICOMPONENTIAL APPROACH
        in Sociology in India, Agra, Inst. Soc. Sci., 1955,
        p. 137-41

47   Siryh, (Miss) K.K.

        AN ANALYSIS OF SOCIAL ATTITUDES AND CONSTRUCTION AND
        STANDARDISATION OF FIVE SOCIAL ATTITUDE SCALES
        (Ph.d.)
        Doct., Gujarat U., 1964   (Prof. P.H. Prabhu)

48   Srivastava, S.S.

        SURVEY RESEARCH TECHNIQUE
        Chaitanya pub. house, 1971

0104   research technology

49   UNESCO Research Center

        REGIONAL SEMINAR ON TECHNIQUES OF SOCIAL RESEARCH
        Proceedings and Papers, New Delhi, 1959

50   Westphal-Hellbusch, S.

        METHODEN UND PRAKTISCHE PROBLEME DER HEUTIGEN
        FELDFORSCHUNG. AUFGEZEIGT AN BEISPIELEN AUS
        INDIEN   (Methods and Practical Problems of Contemporary
        Field Research as Illustrated by Examples from
        India)
        Sociologus, 1970, 20, 1, 3-16 (Ger)
        SA, XIX, 31E8167

51   Wilson, E.C. and L. Armstrong

        INTERVIEWERS AND INTERVIEWING IN INDIA
        Int. Soc. Sci., J. 1963, 15, 1, 48-58
        SA, XII, 3, A9347

0105   statistical methods

52   Chattopadhyay, K.D.

        SOME POINTS ABOUT COLLECTING STATISTICAL DATA
        FOR SOCIAL RESEARCH
        New Delhi, UNESCO Res. Center, 1959, 80-2

53   Gupta, K.P.

        SOME OBSERVATIONS ON THE USE OF STATISTICS IN
        SOCIAL SCIENCES: THE CASE OF MODERNIZATION STUDIES
        in K.D. Sharma (ed.) Basic Issues in Social
        Sciences, Bombay, Academic journals of India, 1968,
        125-42

54   Lokanathan, P.S.

        METHODS AND PROBLEMS IN SAMPLE SURVEYS
        Regional Seminar on Techniques of Social Research
        New Delhi, UNESCO Res. Center, 1959, 124-26

0105 statistical methods

55   Mukherjee, R. and S. Bandyopadhyay

      SOCIAL RESEARCH AND MOHALANOBIS' D^2
      Calcutta, Contributions to Stats., 1963

56   Solomon, M.J.

      THE POLICYMAKER, THE ADMINISTRATOR AND THE
      STATISTICIAN
      Ind. J. Publ. Admin. 1960, 6, 4 Oct-Dec., 398-405
      SA, XII, 6, B1536

57   Srinivasan, K.

      A PROBABILITY MODEL APPLICABLE TO THE STUDY OF
      INTER-LIVE BIRTH INTERVALS AND RANDOM SEGMENTS
      OF THE SAME
      Pop. Studies, 1967, 21, 1, Jul., 63-70
      SA, XVI, 6, D3000

0200 Sociology: History and Theory

0202 of professional interest

58   Anderson, R.S.

      THE LANDSCAPE OF SOME INDIAN SCIENTISTS
      paper presented at South Asia Symposium, Canadian
      Sociology and Anthropology Annual Meetings, 1970

59   Bondurant, J.V. and M.W. Fisher

      ETHICS IN ACTION: CONTRASTING APPROACHES TO
      SOCIAL AND POLITICAL PROBLEMS IN MODERN INDIA
      Australian J. of Polit. History, 1966, 12, 1, Aug.,
      177-193.
      SA, XVI, 1, C8790

61   Chaudhuri, N.C.

       THE AUTOBIOGRAPHY OF AN UNKNOWN INDIAN
       London; Macmillan, 1951, 515 pp.

62   Clinard, M.B.

       THE SOCIOLOGIST AND SOCIAL CHANGE IN UNDERDEVELOPED
       COUNTRIES
       Soc. Prob., 1963, 10, 3, Wn, 207-219
       SA, XI, 7, A7082

63   Desai, D.

       RECENT CONCEPT OF SOCIAL SCIENCES
       Verry, 1962

64   Desai, N. and S. Gogate

       TEACHING OF SOCIOLOGY THROUGH THE REGIONAL LANGUAGE
       Sociol. B. 1970, 19, 1, Mar., 51-61
       SA, XIX, 4, E9400

65   Gopal, M.H.

       SOME PROBLEMS OF RESEARCH IN SOCIAL SCIENCES AND
       HUMANITIES IN INDIA
       Ind. Eco. J., 1966, 14, 3, Oct.-Dec., 327-337
       SA, XVII, 4, D7513

66   Guha, B.S.

       THE ROLE OF SOCIAL SCIENCES IN NATION BUILDING
       Sociol. B. 1958, 7, 2, Sep. 148-151
       SA, XI, 6, A7045

67   Jagathambika, R.

       A CASE STUDY OF MULTIPLE PERSONALITY   (Ph.d.)
       Doct., Kerala U, 1970   (Dr. V.K. Alexander)

68   Kaufman, H.F.

      A RESEARCH FOCUS FOR RURAL SOCIOLOGY
      Sociol. B. 1962, 11, 1, 2, Mar.-Sep., 199-207
      SA, XI, 7, A7085

69   Kumar, K.

      EXCELLENCE AND ANARCHY
      Ind. J. Soc. Res., 13, 3, Dec. 1971, 225-228

70   Kumar, V.K. and V. Pareek

      RESPONSE BEHAVIOR OF BEHAVIORAL SCIENTISTS
      Interdiscipline, 1966, 3, 7, Apr., 75-80
      SA, XVII, 1, D4769

71   *Madan, T.N.

      POLITICAL PRESSURES AND ETHICAL CONSTRAINTS UPON
      INDIAN SOCIOLOGISTS,in ETHICS, POLITICS, AND SOCIAL
      RESEARCH, ed. by Gideon Sjoberg
      New York, Schenkman, 1967

72   Madhavananda, S. (ed.)

      GREAT WOMEN OF INDIA
      Mayavati, Almora: Advaita Ashrama, 1953, 551 p.

73   Mazumdar, H.T.

      GRAMMAR OF SOCIOLOGY: MAN IN SOCIETY
      Bombay, Asia, 1966

74   Mukherji, M.

      ROLE OF SOCIOLOGISTS IN DEVELOPMENT
      Kurukshetra, 1969, 17, 11, Aug., 29.
      SA, XIX, 4, E9409

75   Mukerjee, R.

        "SOCIOLOGY IN A NEW KEY"
        XVth International Congress of Sociology Istanbul,
        11-17, Sept., 1952, Istanbul 53; 31-42
        Current Soc. 54-55 p. 96

76   Mukherjee, R.

        SOCIOLOGISTS AND SOCIAL CHANGE IN INDIA TODAY
        Sociol. B. 1962, 11, 1-2, Mar.-Sep., 4-13
        SA, XI, 7, A7087

77   Mukherjee, R.

        EMPIRICAL SOCIAL RESEARCH ON CONTEMPORARY INDIA
        Social Science Information, 1969, 8, 6, Dec., 69-83
        SA, XIX, 3, E8199

78   Ramachandran, P.

        TRAINING FOR SOCIAL RESEARCH
        Ind. J. Soc. Wrk., 1967, 28, 1, Apr., 109-114
        SA, XVI, 6, D3007

79   Naik, T.B.

        SOME NOVELS THAT SHOULD INTEREST THE SOCIAL SCIENTIST
        Lecutre delivered before the Anthrop. Seminar, Utkal U
        1970

80   Saberwal, S.

        COMMUNICATION CHANNELS FOR SOCIOLOGY: AN ASSESSMENT
        Sociol. B. 1969, 18, 1, Mar., 74-78
        SA, SVIIII, 1-2, E6836

81   Sanval, R.D.

        SEMINAR ON THE TRIBAL SITUATION IN INDIA, SIMLA
        Sociol. B. 1969, 18, 2, Sep., 175-180.
        SA, XIX, 3, E8201

82   Sanwal, R.D.

       NINTH ALL-INDIAN SOCIOLOGICAL CONFERENCE
       Sociol. B. 1970, 19, 1, Mar., 65-73
       SA, XIX, 4, E9412

83   Saran, A.K.

       SOME ASPECTS OF POSITIVISM IN SOCIOLOGY
       Transactions of the Fifth World Congress of
       Sociology, 1962
       p. 199-233   Int'l Soc. Assoc.

84   Saran, A.K.

       WITTGENSTEINIAN SOCIOLOGY?
       Ethics, 1965, 75, 3, 195-200

85   Saran, A.K.

       THE FAITH OF A MODERN INTELLECTUAL
       in T.K. Unnithan, I. Deva and Y. Singh (eds.)
       Towards a Sociology of Culture in India
       New Delhi; Prentice-Hall, 1965

86   Sarkar, R.M.

       S.C. ROY'S CONTRIBUTION IN BENGALI
       Man In India, 52, 4, 1972, 354-359

87   *Srinivas, M.N.

       ITINERARIES OF AN INDIAN SOCIAL ANTHROPOLOGIST
       International Social Science Journal, 25, 1-2, 1973

88   Subramanian, S.

       THE PRESENT STATE OF GOVERNMENT STATISTICS IN INDIA
       Amer. Statistician, 1963, 17, 3, Jun., 31-32
       SA, XII, 4, B0119

0202 of professional interest

89   Theodorson, G.A.

      THE FEASIBILITY OF INTERNATIONAL COOPERATION IN
      CONDUCTING CROSS-CULTURAL RESEARCH
      J. Hum. Rel. 1964, 12, 2, 309-311
      SA, XIII, 1, B3970

90   Uberoi, J.P.S.

      NATIONALISM AND INTERNATIONALISM IN SOCIAL SCIENCE
      Paper presented at 7th World Congress Int. Soc.
      Assoc., Varna, Bulgaria, 1970
      SA, SVIII, 5, Supp. 9, E4119

0206 history and present state of sociology

91   Agarwal, P.D.

      SOCIOLOGY IN INDIA--A CRITICAL STUDY OF SOME MAIN
      TRENDS (Ph.d.)
      Doct., Lucknow U, 1969, (Dr. S.R. Sharma)

92   Ahmad, I.

      NOTE ON SOCIOLOGY IN INDIA
      Amer. Sociol. 1966, 1, 5, Nov., 244-247
      SA, XV, 6, C7101

93   Aiyappan, A. and L.K. Bala Rutnam (eds.)

      ALL-INDIA CONFERENCE OF ANTHROPOLOGISTS AND SOCIOLOGISTS
      (1ST), MADRAS, 1955 SOCIETY IN INDIA
      Madras: Social Sciences Association, 1956, 252 pp.

94   Allardt, E.

      SOCIOLOGIEN OCH DE SMA GRUPPERNA (Sociology and
      Small Groups)
      Nya Argus, 1958, 8, Apr., 123-125
      SA, VIII, 2, 7288

95   Anonymous

       THE FIRST INDIAN SOCIOLOGICAL CONFERENCE
       East. Anthrop., 1955, 9, 1, Sep.-Nov., 53-55
       SA, V, #2   3081

96   Bailey, F.G.

       FOR A SOCIOLOGY OF INDIA?
       Contrib. Indian Sociol., 1959, 3, Jul., 88-101
       SA, XIV, 2-3, B9092

97   Bottomore, T.B.

       SOCIOLOGY IN INDIA
       British J. Sociol. 1962, 13, 2, Jun., 98-106
       SA, XI, 7, A7121

98   Chakrabarti, P.

       QUANTIFICATION AND SOCIAL RESEARCH: A TREND ANALYSIS
       Eco. Wkly., 1970, 5, 38, 1571-75

99   Chambard, Jean-Luc (Paris)

       TOWARD A PHENOMENOLOGICAL SOCIOLOGY OF INDIA
       Cah. Internat. Soc. 1958, Jul.-Dec. 152-176
       SA, VII, 3, 5968

100   Cohn, B.S.

       NOTES ON THE HISTORY OF THE STUDY OF INDIAN SOCIETY
       AND CULTURE
       in Structure and Change In Indian Society 1968
       Chicago: Aldine, eds., B.S. Cohn and M.B. Singer,
       pp. 3-29

101   Damle, Y.B.

       FOR A THEORY OF INDIAN SOCIOLOGY
       in Sociology in India, Agra, Inst. of Soc. Sci.,
       1965, 32-52

102   Dubey, D.C.

        INDIAN SOCIOLOGY AND THE POPULATION PROBLEM
        Indian Soc. B. 1968, 5, 4, Jul., 209-214
        SA, XVII, 7, E0020

103   Dubey, S.N.

        SOCIAL THOUGHT OF P.A. SOROKIN
        Doct., Bihar U, 1968   (Dr. V.B. Verma)

104   Dumont, L. and D. Pocock

        FOR A SOCIOLOGY OF INDIA
        Contrib. Indian Sociol. 1957, 1, Apr., 7-22.
        SA, XIV, 2-3, B9095

105   Dumont, L. and D. Pocock

        FOR A SOCIOLOGY OF INDIA: A REJOINDER TO DR.
        BAILEY
        Contrib. Ind. Sociol., 1960, 4, Apr., 82-89
        SA, XIV, 4, B9953

106   Ghurye, G.S.

        PROLOGUE
        Sociol. B. 1957, 6, 2, Sep., 1-16
        SA, VIII, 1, 6896

107   Geddes, A.

        GEOGRAPHY, SOCIOLOGY, AND PSYCHOLOGY: A PLEA
        FOR COORDINATION, WITH AN EXAMPLE FROM INDIA
        Geographical Review,   (Bibliographic footnotes),
        38, 590-7, October, 1948

108   Gopal, M.H.

        SOCIAL SCIENCE RESEARCH IN INDIA: PROBLEMS OF
        INCENTIVES AND ORGANIZATION
        Artha Vijnan, 8,4, Dec., 1966, 411-430

109   Hallen, G.C.

       THE PROPER ANTECEDENTS OF SOCIOLOGY IN INDIA
       Ind. Soc. B. 1968, 5, 2, Jan., 12H26.
       SA, XVII, 4, D7537

110   Hallen, G.C. and L. Prasad (eds.)

       TOWARDS GLOBAL SOCIOLOGY
       Agra: Shatish Book Enterprise, 1970, pp. 404

111   Hallen, G.C.

       SOCIOLOGIE V INDII   (Sociology in India)
       Socol. Cas. 4 (6) novder 68: 696-704

112   India University Grants Commission

       SOCIOLOGY IN INDIAN UNIVERSITIES; REPORT OF THE
       UNIVERSITY GRANTS COMMISSION REVIEW COMMITTEE
       New Delhi, iii-72 p.

113   Krishna, Daya

       ON THE DISTINCTIONS BETWEEN THE NATURAL SCIENCES,
       THE SOCIAL SCIENCES AND THE HUMANITIES
       Int'l Soc. Sci. J. 1964, 16, 4, 513-23

114   Madan, T.N.

       FOR A SOCIOLOGY OF INDIA
       Contrib. to Ind. Soc. 1965, 9, 9-16

115   Madan, T.N.

       FOR A SOCIOLOGY OF INDIA: SOME CLARIFICATIONS
       Contrib. to Ind. Soc., 1967, 1, 90-93

116   Madan, T.N.

       POLITICAL PRESSURES AND ETHICAL CONSTRAINTS UPON
       INDIAN SOCIOLOGISTS
       in G. Sjoberg (ed.) Ethics, Politics and Social
       Research New York, Schenkman, 1967, 162-79

117   Majumdar, D.N.

        WHAT THE SOCIOLOGISTS CAN DO, WHAT THEY MUST DO,
        HOW THEY CAN DO AND HOW THEY SHOULD DO IT
        Easter. Anthropo. 1957, 10, 2

118   *Mohan, Raj P. and G.C. Hallen

        CONTEMPORARY SOCIOLOGY IN INDIA
        International Journal of Contemporary Sociology,
        1971, 8, 3&4, Jul.-Oct., 247-255
        SA, 21, 73G1444

119   Motwani, Kewal

        SOCIOLOGICAL PAPERS AND ESSAYS
        Madras: Ganesh and Co., 1957, 212 pp.
        SA, VI, 3, 4578

120   Motwani, K.

        STUDY OF SOCIOLOGY IN INDIA: WHICH SYSTEM?
        Ind. J. Soc. Res. 1964, 5, 3, Dec., 225-235
        SA, XIV, V, C0882

121   Motwani, K.

        TOWARDS INDIAN SOCIOLOGY
        Agra: Satish Book Enterprise, 1971, xvi, 138 pp.

122   Mukerjee, R.

        THE PHILOSOPHY OF SOCIAL SCIENCE
        London: Macmillan, 1966

123   Mukherjee, R.

        SOME CONSIDERATIONS ON SOCIAL RESEARCH
        East. Anthrop., XIII, 3, 1960, 121-131

124   Mukherjee, R.

         INDIAN SOCIETY AND EMPIRICAL SOCIAL RESEARCH
         New Approaches in Humanities and Social Sciences,
         Simla, Indian Inst. of Advanced Study, 1969

125   Mukherjee, R.

         SOME OBERVATIONS ON THE DEVELOPMENT OF SOCIOLOGY
         IN "DEVELOPING SOCIETIES" (WITH SPECIAL REFERENCE
         TO INDIA)
         Paper present at the 7th World Congress of the
         Int. Soc. Assoc., 1970
         SA, XVIII, 5, Sup. 9, E3993

126   Mukherjee, R. et. al.

         DATA INVENTORY ON SOCIAL SCIENCES--INDIA (first
         phase 1967-68)
         Calcutta, 1971

127   Mukherjee, R.   (translated by A. Guaraldo)

         LO SVILUPPO DELLA SOCIOLOGIA NELLE "SOCIETA IN VIA
         DI SUILUPPO. "ALCUNE OSSERRAZIONI CON PARTICOLARE
         RIFERIMENTO ALL' INDIA (The Development of Sciology
         in the "Developing Societites" Some Observations
         With Special Reference to India)
         Quaderni di Sociologia, 1972, 20, 3-4, Jul. - Dec.,
         295-314, (Italian)
         SA, XX, 7, F9042

128   Mukerji, D.P.

         SOCIOLOGY IN INDEPENDENT INDIA
         Sociol. B. 1, 1, 1952, 13-27

129   Nandy, S.K.

         A NOTE ON SOCIOLOGY IN INDIA VIS-A-VIS SOCIOLOGY
         IN THE WEST
         Ind. Sociol. B. 1966, 3, 2, Jan., 171-175
         SA, XV, 4, C5471

130   Pieris, R.

        THE IMPLANTATION OF SOCIOLOGY IN ASIA
        Int. Soc. Sci. J., 1969, 21, 3, 433-44

131   Rao, C.R.

        QUANTITATIVE STUDIES IN SOCIOLOGY: NEED FOR INCREASED
        USE IN INDIA
        East. Anthrop. 1959, 12, 3, Mar.-May, 143-170.
        SA, X, 6, A3775

132   Roucek, J.S.   (ed.)

        CONTEMPORARY SOCIOLOGY   (includes a chapter on
        "India" by A.K. Saran)
        Philosophical Library. 1958, xii and 1, 209 pp.
        SA, VIII, 2, 7308

133   Saberwal, S.

        ACADEMIC COLONIALISM: THE PROBLEMS
        Seminar, 1968, 112, 10-13

134   Saksena, R.N.

        SOCIOLOGY IN INDIA
        Ind. Sociol. 1960, 2, 3, Mar., 20-23
        SA, XII, 7, B2319

135   Saksena, R.N.

        TRENDS IN THE TEACHING OF SOCIOLOGY AND SOCIAL
        RESEARCH IN INDIA
        J. Soc. Sci., 1958, 1, 1, Jan. 1-8.
        SA, VIII, 2, 7285

136   Saran, A.K.

        INDIA
        in Contemporary Sociology   (ed. J.S. Roucek)
        New York: Greenwood Press, 1958 (Reprint)

137   Saran, A.K.

        FOR A SOCIOLOGY OF INDIA
        East. Anthrop., 1962, 15, 1, 53-68

138   Saran, A.K.

        A CRITIQUE OF THE DEVELOPMENT OF SOCIOLOGY IN
        INDIA
        Paper presented at the 7th World Congress Int.
        Soc. Assoc.,
        SA, XVIII, 5, Sup. 9, E4064

139   Sen, L.K.

        CURRENT ISSUES IN RURAL SOCIOLOGY: A NON-AMERICAN
        VIEWPOINT
        Rural Soc., 1969, 34, 2, Jun., 246-249
        SA, XVIII, 3, E1692

140   Sharma, K.D.

        BASIC ISSUES IN SOCIAL SCIENCES
        Delhi, Academic J. of India, 1968

141   Sharma, R.N.

        PRINCIPLES OF SOCIOLOGY
        Bombay, Asia Pub. House, 1970

142   Sharma, S.R.

        BASIC CONCEPTS OF HINDU SOCIOLOGY (Ph.d.)
        Doct.,Lucknow U, 1967   (Prof. S.P. Nagendra)

143   Shukla, S.

        SOCIOLOGISTS ADRIFT
        Ind. J. Soc. Res., 12, 2, Aug. 1971, 143-145

144   Sociological Research Unit, Indian Statistical
        Institute Calcutta

        SOME CHARACTERISTICS OF SOCIOLOGICAL STUDIES IN
        INDIA
        1967, pp. 10   (mimeographed)

145   Srinivas, M.N.

        SOCIAL ANTHROPOLOGY AND THE STUDY OF RURAL AND
        URBAN SOCIETIES
        in M.N. Srinivas Caste in Modern India and Other
        Essays, Bombay: Asia Pub. House, 1962, p. 136-47

146   Srinivas, M.N.

        SOCIOLOGY AND SOCIOLOGISTS IN INDIA TODAY
        Sociol. B., 1970, 19, 1, Mar., 1-10
        SA, XIX, 4, E9451

147   Srivastava, R.N.

        SOCIOLOGY FOR INDIA: SOME CONSIDERATIONS
        Ind. J. of Social Res., 1966, 7, 3, Dec., 198-205
        SA, XVII, 3, D6743

148   Suda, J.P.

        THE TEACHING OF SOCIOLOGY IN INDIA
        Ind. J. Soc. Res., 1967, 8, 1, Apr., 25-30
        SA, XVII, 5, 5, D8210

149   The Fifth All-Indian Sociological Conference

        East. Anthrop. 1960, 13, 2, Mar.-May, 61-63
        SA, XI, 4, A5041

150   Transactions of the Fourth World Congress of
        Sociology

        I--SOCIOLOGY IN ITS SOCIAL CONTEXT
        London, G.B.: Internat'l Sociol'al Ass'n 1959, ix
        and 204 pp.
        SA, X, 4, A2709

151   Unnithan, T.K.N.

       DAS LEHREN DER SOZIOLOGIE IN INDIEN   (Teaching
       Sociology In India)
       Koelner Z. Soziol. Soz-Psychol. 1966, 18, 4, Dec.,
       724-752 (Ger.)
       SA, XV, 4, C5484

152   Unnithan, T.K., I. Deva, Y. Singh (eds.)

       TOWARDS A SOCIOLOGY OF CULTURE IN INDIA
       New Delhi, Prentice-Hall, 1965

153   Unnithan, T.K.N. et. al.

       SOCIOLOGY FOR INDIA   (All Indian Seminar on "Sociology
       for India: Teaching and Research", Mount Abu, 1964)
       New Delhi, Prentice-Hall of India, 1967, 2, ii,
       219 p.

154   Valien, Preston

       THE STATUS OF SOCIOLOGY IN INDEPENDENT INDIA
       Soc. Forces, 1954, 32, 3, Mar., 222-225
       SA, Vol. II, #3, 384

155   Verma, B.N.

       GENERAL COMMENTS CONCERNING RESEARCH IN INDIA
       in B.N. Verma (ed.), Contemporary India, Bombay:
       Asia P. House, 1964; 342-52

156   Vidyarthi, L.P.

       RESEARCHES IN SOCIAL SCIENCE IN INDIA: SOME
       PRELIMINARY OBSERVATIONS
       Soc. Sci. Info. 1966, 5, 1

157   Vidyarthi, L.P.

       RISE OF SOCIAL SCIENCE IN INDIA: AN ANTHROPOLOGICAL
       ORIENTATION
       Bombay: Asia Pub. House, 1970

0206   history and present state of sociology

   158   Wadia, A.R.

         SOCIOLOGY IN RELATION TO OTHER SOCIAL SCIENCES
         AND ITS DEVELOPMENT IN INDIA
         Agra Univ. J. Res. (LeH.) 1955, 3, Dec., 18-27
         SA, VI, 3, 4586

   159   ----------

         SUPPLEMENT--IN MEMORIAM: PITIRIM ALEXANDEROVICH
         SOROKIN
         Ind. J. Soc. Res., 1968, 9, 1, Apr., i-xvi
         SA, XVIII, 6, E4497

   160   ----------

         OBITUARY: KNANIYALAL MOTILAI KAPADIA
         Ind. J. Soc. Res., 1968, 9, 1, Apr., 54-56
         SA, SVIII, 6, E4496

   161   ----------

         KEY THEME IN MAX WEBER THESIS ON INDIA REFUTED BY
         DR. SANTOSH ĸUMAR NANDY AT CONGRESS OF ORIENTALISTS
         HELD IN AMERICA
         Ind. Soc. Bull. 1968, 5, 2, Jan., 119-120.
         SA, XVII, 4, D7562

0207   theories, ideas and systems

   162   Bendix, R.

         MAX WEBER: AN INTELLECTUAL PORTRAIT (includes a
         chapter on Religion of India)
         Garden City, N.Y.:   Doubleday and Co., 1960, 480 pp.
         SA, VIII, 2, 7316

   163   Chattarji, B.N.

         SOCIAL CONCEPTS AND VALUES IN HINDU SOCIAL SYSTEM
         (Ph.d.)
         Doct., 1969, Agra Ü.   (R.N. Saksena)

164   Chauhan, J.S.

       BELIEF-SYSTEM: A DEPENDENT VARIABLE
       J. Soc. Res. 1968, 11, 2, Sep., 103-108
       SA, XV111, 6, E4501

165   Dalton, D.G.

       M.N. ROY AND RADICAL HUMANISM: THE IDEOLOGY
       OF AN INDIAN INTELLECTUAL ELITE
       in: ELITES IN SOUTH ASIA, eds., E.Leach
       and S.N. Mukerjee, London: Cambridge U.
       Press, 1970, p. 152-172

166   Deshpande, V.N.

       MODELS IN SCIENCE
       Hubli, Book Center, 1966

167   Gopalan, S.

       THE HINDU PHILOSOPHY OF SOCIAL RECONSTRUCTION
       U of Madras, center of advanced study in
       philosophy, Madras, India

168   Habib, I.

       USURY IN MEDIEVAL INDIA
       Comp. Stud. Soc.Hist. 1964, 6, 4, Jul., 393-419
       SA, X111, 1, B4008

169   Hanif, S.

       SOCIAL PHILOSOPHY OF SHRI JAWAJARLAL NEHRU (Ph.D.)
       Doct. Patna U, 1968, Dr. Z. Ahmad (Dept.of Soc.)

170   Heiman, B.

       OUTSIDER IN SOCIETY: A STUDY IN THE SOCIAL
       PSYCHOLOGY OF ANCIENT INDIA AND THE WEST
       Hibbert, J. 49, 73-7, Oct., 1950

171   Khan, N.A.

        THE PLACE OF THEORY IN SOCIAL SCIENCE
        East. Anthrop., 1961, 14, 2, 136-41

172   Biswas, S.C. (ed.)

        GANDHI: THEORY AND PRACTICE, SOCIAL IMPACT AND
        CONTEMPORARY RELEVANCE
        Simla, Indian Instit, of Advanced Study, Transactions
        #11, 1969

173   Khanna, D.P.S.

        INDIAN SOCIAL SYSTEM AND DR. BHAGAVAN DAS
        Doct., Agra U., 1969 (R.N. Saksena)

174   Long, James

        FIVE HUNDRED QUESTIONS ON THE SUBJECTS REQUIRING
        INVESTIGATION IN THE SOCIAL CONDITION OF THE
        PEOPLE OF INDIA
        Calcutta, Indian Publications, 1966, 72 p.

175   *Mudiraj, G.N.R.

        SOCIOLOGY OF ABUSES--AN EXPLORATORY ANALYSIS
        Indian Journal of Sociology, 1971, 2, 2, Sep.,
        194-204
        SA, 21, 73G1478

176   Mukerji, K.P.

        IMPLICATIONS OF THE IDEOLOGY CONCEPT
        Bombay, Popular Book Depot, "Bombay U. Political
        Series, 1", 1955, xvi and 222 p.

177   Mukherjee, R.

        A GENERAL THEORY OF SOCIETY
        in Baljit Singh (ed.) The Frontiers of Social Science
        Bombay; Macmillan, 1955, 21-74

178   Nagendra, S.P.

         THE CONCEPT OF RITUAL IN MODERN SOCIOLOGICAL THEORY
         (Ph.d.)
         Doct., Agra U., 1968

179   Namboodiri, N.K.

         ANOTHER LOOK AT STRUCTURAL-FUNCTIONAL ANALYSIS
         Sociol. B. 1966, 15, 1, Mar., 75-89.
         SA, XIV, 6, C1820

180   Oommen, T.K.

         THE RURAL-URBAN CONTINUIM REEXAMINED IN THE INDIAN
         CONTEXT
         Sociologia Ruralis, 1967, 7, 1, 30-48
         SA, XVI, 1, C8861

181   Panchanadikar, K.C.

         CAUSATION IN HUMAN SOCIETY (Ph.d.)
         Doct., Bombay U., 1956 (Prof. G.S. Ghurye)

182   Pangborn, C.R.

         ANALYSIS OF A CLICHE: EASTERN SPIRITUALISM AND
         WESTERN MATERIALISM
         Contrib. to Asian Studies, vol. 3, 1973, 109-120

183   Prakash, B.

         THE SOCIAL THOUGHT OF PT. JAWAHASLAL NEHRU
         1969 Doct. S., Agra U., (Dr. B.R. Chauhan)

184   Pye, L.W.

         ADMINISTRATORS, AGITATORS, AND BROKERS
         Pub. Opin. Quart. 1958, 22, 3, Fall, 342-348
         SA, VIII, 4, 8179

185   Rastoji, P.N.

         A CYBERNETIC MODEL OF TOTAL INDIAN SOCIETY: AN
         INTRODUCTORY FRAMEWORK
         M.I.T. (mimeographed), 1967, 40

186   Saran, A.K.

         THE MARXIAN THEORY OF SOCIAL CHANGE
         Inquiry, 1963, 6, 70-128

187   Saran, A.K.

         THE CONCEPT OF SOCIAL SCIENCE
         in K.D. Sharma (ed.) Basic Issues in Social Sciences,
         Bombay, Acad, J. of India, 1968

188   Savita

         GANDHI AND SOCIAL POLICY IN INDIA: A SOCIOLOGICAL
         ANALYSIS
         Lat. Pub. House, 1970

189   Shah, M.V.

         SOCIAL PHILOSOPHY OF GANDHIJI (Ph.d.)
         Doct., Bombay U., 1954   (Prof. K.M. Kapadia)

190   Sharma, K.D.

         MAX WEBER'S IDEAL TYPES AND CONCEPT OF SALVATION
         (Ph.d.)
         Doct., Agra U., 1968   (Dr. R.N. Saxena)

191   Shujaat, (Mrs.) F.

         SOCIAL THOUGHT OF HALI   (Ph.d.)
         Doct., Osmania U., 1957   (Dr. J. Hasan)

192   Siddiqui, M.

         SOCIAL THOUGHT OF SIR SYED AHMED KHAN   (Ph.d.)
         Doct., Osmania U., 1960   (Dr. I. Topa)

0207   theories, ideas and systems

  193   Sinha, S.

        TRIBE-CASTE AND TRIBE-PEASANT CONTINUA IN CENTRAL INDIA
        Man In India, 1965, 45, 1, Jan.-Mar., 57-83
        SA, XIV, 2-3, B9142

  194   Varma, B.N.

        THE ROLE OF CONCEPTS AND MODELS IN SOCIAL SCIENCE
        in B.N. Varma (ed.) A New Survey of the Social Sciences
        Bombay: Asia Pub. House, 1962, p. 170-190

  195   Welty, Paul Thomas (Amer.)

        THE IDEOLOGY OF INDIA
        in The Asians; Their Heritage and Destiny, Philadelphia,
        J.B. Lippincott, 1962, pp. 58-61

0300   Social Psychology (general)

  196   Adinarayan, Samuel P.

        SOCIAL PSYCHOLOGY WITH SPECIAL REFERENCE TO INDIAN
        CONDITIONS
        Bombay and N.Y.: Allied Pub., 1964

0308   attitudes, sentiments, motives

  197   Adinarayan, S.P.

        "BEFORE AND AFTER INDEPENDENCE: A STUDY OF RACIAL
        AND COMMUNAL ATTITUDES IN INDIA"
        Brit. J. Psychol. 44, 2, May, 1953, 108-115

  198   Agrawala, V.S.

        GROUP PREJUDICES IN INDIA: SOCIAL AND RELIGIOUS
        in Group Prejudices in India, ed. M.B. Nanavati
        and C.N. Vakil, p. 135-144
        Bombay, Vora, 1951

199   Anant, S.S.

        CASTE PREJUDICE AND ITS PERCEPTION BY HARIJANS
        J. of Soc. Psy. 1970, 82, 165-172, p. 165-172

200   Akhtar, S.S., C.M. Pestonjee and F. Farooqi

        ATTITUDES TOWARDS WORKING WOMEN
        Ind. J. Soc. Wrk. 1969, 30, 1, Apr., 93-98
        SA, XVIII, 7, E5637

201   Bhatia, H.S.

        INTERCASTE RELATIONS AND ASPIRATIONAL LEVELS:
        AN ATTITUDINAL STUDY
        Ind. J. Soc. Wrk., 1970, 31, 1, Apr., 43-48
        SA, XX, 1-2, F3453

202   Bopegamage, A.

        STATUS IMAGES IN CHANGING INDIA
        Paragon, 1967

203   . Chavan, Y.B.

        TRAINING AND REORIENTATION OF CIVIL SERVICE ATTITUDES
        Ind J.of Publ. Adm., 1969, Jan.-Mar., 15, 1, 1-4

204   Cohelho, George

        CHANGING IMAGES OF AMERICA: A STUDY OF INDIAN
        STUDENT'S PERCEPTIONS
        Glencoe; The Free Press, 1958

205   Das, M.S.

        EFFECT OF FOREIGN STUDENTS' ATTITUDES TOWARD RETURNING
        TO THE COUNTRY OF ORIGIN:ON THE NATIONAL LOSS OF
        PROFESSIONAL SKILLS
        Oklahoma State U., 69-70

206   Deo, (Mrs.) K.

       TRADITIONALISM TO NON-TRADITIONALISM: A SOCIO-
       CULTURAL STUDY OF THE CHANGING NORMS AND VALUES
       OF U. STUDENTS OF UJJAIN CITY
       1969, Doct. St., Indore, (Pothen)

207   Desai, R.

       A COMPARISON OF THE IMAGES OF GANDHI AND NEHRU
       IN INDIA AND AMERICA: A STUDY IN CONTENT ANALYSIS
       American Doctoral Dissertations, (Michigan State U.)
       (1960-61)

208   Giri, V.V.

       GROUP PREJUDICES IN INDIA
       in Group Prejudices In India, ed. M.B. Nanavati and
       C.N. Vakil, p. 213-219, Bombay, Vora, 1951

209   Gorevaney, (Miss) N.

       ROLES STRUCTURE, SELF-IMAGE AND SOCIAL CHANGE--A
       STUDY OF SELECTED CATEGORIES OF FEMALES
       Doct. St., Rajasthan, 1969

210   John, Melathathil J.

       SOCIAL PSYCHOLOGICAL VARIABLES RELATED TO THE
       ROLE PERFORMANCE OF THE GRAM SEVAKS
       (Ph.d.), U.S., 1966

211   Kamala, (Miss) M.N.

       THE MEASUREMENT OF ATTITUDES TOWARDS SOME SOCIAL AND
       ECONOMIC PROBLEMS   (Ph.d.)
       Doct. Mysore U., 1961, (Dr. B. Kuppuswamy)

212   Mandelbaum, D.G.

       THE WORLD AND THE WORLD VIEW OF THE KOTA   (Madras)
       in Village India, ed. M. Marriott, Chicago, U. of
       Chicago Press, 1956, p. 223-255

213   Kidder, L.M.H.

        FOREIGN VISITORS: A STUDY OF CHANGES IN SELVES, SKILLS,
        AND ATTITUDES OF WESTERNERS IN INDIA
        (Ph.d.--Soc. Psy.), Northwestern U., 1971

214   Mehta, Ashoka

        GROUP PREJUDICES AND POLITICAL PARTIES
        in Group Prejudices in India, ed. M.B. Nanavati and
        C.N. Vakil, p. 167-173, Bombay, Vora, 1951

215   Mehta, B.H.

        THE SOCIOLOGICAL BACKGROUND OF PREJUDICE
        in Group Prejudices in India, ed. M.B. Nanavati and
        C.N. Vakil, p. 34-45, Bombay, Vora, 1951

216   Mehta, Hansa

        WOMEN AND GROUP PREJUDICES IN INDIA
        in Group Prejudices in India, Ed. M.B. Nanavati and
        C.N. Vakil, p. 144-147, Bombay, Vora, 1951

217   Mishra, Lakshmipati

        GROUP PREJUDICES IN INDIA
        in Group Prejudices in India, ed. M.B. Nanavati and
        C.N. Vakil, p. 209-213, Bombay, Vora, 1951

218   Nanavati, M.B.

        GROUP PREJUDICES IN RURAL INDIA
        in Group Prejudices in India, ed. M.B. Nanavati and
        C.N. Vakil, p. 147-157, Bombay, Vora, 1951

219   Nanavati, M.B. (ed.)

        GROUP PREJUDICES IN INDIA: A SYMPOSIUM
        Bombay, Vora, 1951, 223 pp.

220   Nat'l Instit. C.D.

       PERCEPTION OF NATIONAL EMERGENCY IN VILLAGE INDIA
       Missourie, N.I.C.D., 1963

221   Nigam, (Miss) M.

       WORKING WOMEN IN INDIAN CITIES--A SOCIOLOGICAL
       STUDY OF THEIR ATTITUDES AND THEIR WAY OF LIFE
       Doct. St., Agra U., 1969, (A.N. Saksena)

222   Ojha, A.B.

       ATTITUDES OF INDIAN STUDENTS TO THE FIVE YEAR
       PLANS OF INDIA
       Ind. J. of S. Work, 1965, 26, 3, Oct., 281-286
       SA, XVI, 4, D1591

223   Parry, Benita

       DELUSIONS AND DISCOVERIES: STUDIES ON INDIA IN
       THE BRITISH IMAGINATION 1880-1930
       Berkeley, U. of Calif. Press, 1972

224   Pool, I. and Prasad, K.

       INDIAN STUDENTS IMAGES OF FOREIGN PEOPLE
       Pub. Opin. Quart. 1958, 22, 3, Fall, 292-304
       SA, VIII, 4, 8416

225   Rao, P. Kodanda and Mary C.

       CRITIQUE OF GROUP PREJUDICE (with special ref. to
       Harijans)
       in Group Prejudices in India, eds. M.B. Nanavati and
       C.N. Vakil, p. 45-56, Bombay, Vora, 1951

226   Ramamurthi, S.V.

       GROUP PREJUDICES IN ADMINISTRATION
       in Group Prejudices in India, eds. M.B. Nanavati and C.N.
       Vakil, p. 163-167, Bombay, Vora, 1951

227   Roy, T.

        INDIVIDUAL AND GROUP PREJUDICES AND UNITY
        in Group Prejudices in India, eds. M.B. Nanavati and
        C.N. Vakil, p. 64-71, Bombay, Vora, 1951

228   Sabnis, G.K.

        CONCERNING SENTIMENTS--AN ESSAY IN THE PSYCHOLOGY OF
        SOCIETY   (Ph.d.)
        Doct., Bombay U., 1947, (Prof. G.S. Ghurye)

229   Saiyed, A.R.

        EDUCATION AND MODERNIZATION OF ATTITUDES IN INDIA:
        A GROUP-MEDIATED ANALYSIS
        Amer. Doct. Dissert., (68-69), U. of Kentucky

230   Saiyidain, K.G.

        THE CONFLICT BETWEEN CULTURE AND PREJUDICE
        in Group Prejudices in India, eds. M.B. Nanavati and
        C.N. Vakil, p. 25-34, Bombay, Vora, 1951

231   Saxena, A.P.

        CONJUNCTIVE EFFECTS OF INDIVIDUAL AND SYSTEM
        VARIABLES ON INNOVATIVENESS
        Int. R. Modern Sociology, 2, 2, Sept/72, 210-218

232   Shah, P.G.

        SUBLIMATION OF GROUP FEELINGS
        in Group Prejudices in India, eds. M.B. Nanavati and
        C.N. Vakil, p. 56-64, Bombay, Vora, 1951

233   Sinjhai, (Miss) S.

        SOCIAL INTERESTS AND ATTITUDES OF ADOLESCENT
        COLLEGE-GOING GIRLS IN INDORE CITY
        Doct. St., Indore, 1969

0308   attitudes, sentiments, motives

234   Sitaramaiyya, B.P.

        GROUP PREJUDICES IN INDIA
        in Group Prejudices In India, eds. M.B. Nanavati and
        C.N. Vakil, p. 157-163, Bombay, Vora, 1951

235   Unnithan, T.K.N., and Y. Singh

        SOCIOLOGY OF NON-VIOLENCE AND PEACE: SOME
        BEHAVIORAL AND ATTITUDINAL DIMENSIONS
        Munshi Ram, 1969

236   Van Groenou, W.B.

        WORLD VIEWS OF TEXTILE WORKERS IN INDIA
        Ph.d. Soc., University of Illinois, (69-70),
        (Urbana-Champaign)

0309   interaction within small groups

237   Bhatia, H.S.

        INTERCASTE RELATIONS AND ASPIRATIONAL LEVELS--
        AN ATTITUDINAL STUDY
        Ind.J.of Soc. Wrk., 1970, 31, 1, Apr., 43-48
        SA, XX, 1-2, F3453

238   Basu, (Mrs.)M.

        A SURVEY OF SOME FACTORS RESPONSIBLE FOR GROUP
        PRODUCTIVITY--A QUESTION OF GROUP DYNAMICS (D.Phil.)
        Doct., Calcutta U., 1968

239   Bose, S.P.

        SOCIAL INTERACTION IN AN INDIAN VILLAGE
        Sociologia Ruralis, 1967

240   Farooqi, M.A.

        COOPERATION AND COMPETITION IN GROUP STRUCTURE
        (Ph.d.)
        Doct., Madras U., 1961, (Dr. G.D. Boaz)

0309 interaction within small groups

241   Malhotra, (Miss) S.

       AN EXPERIMENTAL STUDY OF THE SOCIOLOGICAL AND
       PSYCHOLOGICAL FACTORS UNDERLYING INTERPERSONAL
       RELATIONSHIPS AMONG PUPILS DURING LATER ADOLESCENT
       PERIOD (D.Phil.)
       Doct., Allahabad U., 1963, (Dr. S.B. Adaval)

242   *Mittal, A.

       PATTERNS OF INTERACTION AND GROUP FORMATION IN A
       GOVERNMENT EMPLOYEES' COLONY IN DELHI
       Sociological Bulletin, 1971, 20, 1, Mar., 39-53
       SA, 21, 73G5649

243   Rosenthal, D.B.

       DEFERENCE AND FRIENDSHIP PATTERNS IN TWO INDIAN
       MUNICIPAL COUNCILS
       Soc. Forces, 1966, 45, 2, Dec., 178-191
       SA, XV, 3, C4807

244   Pareek, U. and T.K. Moulik

       SOCIOMETRIC STUDY OF A NORTH INDIAN VILLAGE
       Int. J. Sociom. Sociat., 1963, 3, 1-2, Mar.-Jun.,
       6-16
       SA, XII, 6, B1634

245   Siegel, B.J. and A.R. Beals

       PERVASIVE FACTIONALISM
       Amer. Anthrop., 1960, 62, 3, Jun., 394-417
       SA, X, 5, A3248

0312 personality and culture

246   Anant, S.S.

       SELF AND MUTUAL PERCEPTION OF SALIENT PERSONALITY
       TRAITS OF DIFFERENT CASTE GROUPS
       J. of Cross-Cultural Psy., 1, 1, 1970, pp. 41-52

247   Anant, S.S.

        INTER-CASTE DIFFERENCES IN PERSONALITY PATTERNS AS
        A FUNCTION OF SOCIALIZATION
        Phylon, 1966, 27, 2, Sum., 145-154
        SA, XVI, 3, D0570

248   Baral, B.

        A PROBE INTO A FEW FACTORS CAUSING BREAKDOWN OF
        SOCIAL ADAPTABILITY AMONGST SCHOOL-GOING POPULATION
        (BETWEEN 9TH AND 11TH GRADE) OF WEST BENGAL (D.Phil.)
        Doct., Calcutta U., 1969

249   Beg, M.A.

        A STUDY OF THE DESIRABLE AND UNDESIRABLE CONCEPTION
        OF INDIAN AND AMERICAN STUDENTS   (Ph.d.)
        Doctorate, Aligarh Muslim U., 1962, (Late) Prof.
        M. Umaruddin

250   Bhajwatwar, P.A.

        A COMPARATIVE PSYCHOSOCIAL STUDY OF THE IMPACT OF
        COMMUNITY DEVELOPMENT PROGRAMME ON PERSONALITY
        DYNAMICS, ATTITUDES AND SOCIAL CHANGE IN RURAL
        COMMUNITY IN MAHARASHTRA WITH SPECIAL REFERENCE
        TO MULSHI AND PURANDHAR TALUKA   (Ph.d.)
        Doct., Poona U., 1969, (Prof. W.K. Kothurkar)

251   Bohlke, R.H.

        AUTHORITARIANISM AND ATTITUDES OF COLLEGE STUDENTS
        TOWARD INDIA
        J. Educ. Sociol., 1960, 34, 4, Dec., 145-159
        SA, X, 5, A3285

252   Chatterjee, R.G. and S. Banerjee

        INTEREST IN AMUSEMENTS AND ITS RELATION TO PERSONALITY
        TYPES
        Ind. J. Soc. Wrk., 1958, 19, 3, Dec., 217-224
        SA, VIII, 2, 7400

253   Deo, P. and S. Sharma

         SELF-IDEAL DISCREPANCY AND SCHOOL ACHIEVEMENT
         Adolescence, 1970, 5, 19, Fall, 353-360
         SA, XIX, 7, F2192

254   Devi, G.

         CORRELATION BETWEEN TENSION AND CONTACT IN A STUDY
         OF PROVINCIAL STEREOTYPES
         Ind. J. Soc. Wrk., 1968, 29, 2, Jul., 123-134
         SA, XVIII, 4, E2870

255   Driver, E.D.

         SELF-CONCEPTIONS IN INDIA AND THE UNITED STATES:
         A CROSS-CULTURAL VALIDATION OF THE TWENTY STATEMENT
         TEST
         Sociological Quart., 1969, 10, 3, Sum., 341-354
         SA, XVIII, 3, E1738

256   Dubey, S.N.

         POWERLESSNESS AND ORIENTATIONS TOWARDS FAMILY AND
         CHILDREN: A STUDY IN DEVIANCE
         Ind. J. Soc. Wrk., 1971, 32, 1, Apr., 35-43
         SA, XX, 7, F9096

257   Gist, N.P.

         CULTURAL VERSUS SOCIAL MARGINALITY: THE ANGLO-INDIAN CASE
         Phylon, 1967, 28, 4,   in., 361-375
         SA, XVII, 1, D4837

258   Gorjh, H.G. and H.S. Sandhu

         VALIDATION OF THE CPI SOCIALIZATION SCALE IN INDIA
         J. Abnormal and Soc. Psychol., 1964, 68, 5, 544-547
         SA, XIII, 6-7, B7568

259   Hallen, G.C.

      ALIENATION IN INDIAN SOCIETY
      Ind. J. of Soc. Res., 1966, 7, 3, Dec., ii-iv
      SA, XVII, 3, D6791

260   Guha, U.

      EFFECT OF SOCIAL CATACLYSM ON PERSONALITY
      Bulletine of the Anthrop. Survey of India, 1956, 5,
      1, 1-10

261   Hardgrave, R.L. Jr.

      POLITICAL CULTURE AND PROJECTIVE TECHNIQUES
      Comp. Political Studies, 1969, 2, 2, Jul., 149-
      255.
      SA, XVIII, 7, E5654

262   Lahiri, Mrs. A.

      PERSONALITY TYPES AMONG THE TRIBES OF BIHAR--STUDIES
      IN CULTURE PERSONALITY
      Ranchi, 1969

263   Mahayan, A.

      WOMEN'S TWO ROLES: A STUDY OF ROLE CONFLICT
      Ind. J. of Soc. Wrk., 1966, 26, 4, Jan., 377-380
      SA, XVI, 5, D2309

264   *Mandelbaum, D.G.

      THE STUDY OF LIFE HISTORY: GANDHI
      Current Anthropology, 14, 3, June, 1973

265   Master, R.S., S.C.S. Master

      A COMPARISON OF INTELLIGENCE TESTS IN INDIAN
      CONDITIONS
      Ind. J. of Soc. Wrk., 1959, 20, 2, Sep., 125-128
      SA, XI, V, A5748

266   Mehta, (Mrs.) V.M.

         PROBLEMS OF WOMEN IN GUJARAT--A PSYCHOLOGICAL
         STUDY OF THE NATURE AND FACTORS OF STRESS AND
         CONFLICT   (Ph.d.)
         Doct., M.S. U. of Baroda, 1969, (Prof. A.S. Patel),
         Faculty of Education and Psy.

267   Moulik, T.K. and A.R. Kahn

         FACTOR ANALYSIS OF FARMER'S SELF-IMAGE OF PERSONALITY
         TRAITS
         Man In India, 1967, 47, 4, Oct.-Dec., 295-308
         SA, XVII, 3, D6801

268   Nandy, A.

         VALUES AND PERSONALITY
         Journal of Social Research, 1967, 10, 1, Mar., 7-13
         SA, XVI, 5, D2312

269   Narain, D.

         HINDU CHARACTER
         Bombay: U. of Bombay Press, 1957

270   Narain, D.

         INDIAN NATIONAL CHARACTER IN THE TWENTIETH CENTURY
         A. Amer. Acad. Soc. Sci., 1967, 370, Mar., 124-132
         SA, XV, 5, C6357

271   Ogburn, W.F.

         THE WOLF BOY OF AGRA
         Amer. J. Sociol., 1959, 64, 5, Mar., 449-454
         SA, VII, 4, 6442

272   Ojha, R.S.

         ATTITUDE OF COLLEGE STUDENTS TOWARDS CERTAIN SOCIAL
         PROBLEMS   (Ph.d.)
         Doct., Bihar U., 1968, (Dr. A. Hazan)

273   Paranjpe, A.C.

        CASTE, PREJUDICE AND THE INDIVIDUAL
        Bombay, Lalvani Pub. House, 1970, xvi and 236 pp.

274   Ray, P.C.

        THE EFFECT OF CULTURE-CONTACT ON THE PERSONALITY
        STRUCTURE OF TWO INDIAN TRIBES--THE RIANG OF
        TRIPURA AND BAIGA OF M.P.
        B. of Anthrop. Sur. India, 6, 2, 1-84, 1957

275   Roy, M.

        STUDY ON SOME PSYCHOLOGICAL CHARACTERISTICS OF
        VILLAGE LEVEL WORKERS   (Ph.d.)
        Doct., Kalyani U., 1969, (Dr. A. Kr. Majumdar)

276   Roy, M. and A.K. Majumder

        STUDY IN SOME PERSONALITY ADJUSTMENT VARIABLES OF
        VILLAGE LEVEL WORKERS
        Society and Cult., 1970, 1, 1, Jul., 17-24
        SA, XX, 7, F918

277   Roy, M. and A.K. Muzumdar

        STUDY ON SOME PERSONALITY VARIABLES OF VILLAGE
        LEVEL WORKERS
        Ind. J. Soc. Res., 13, 3, Dec. 1972, 218-223

278   Savur, (Mrs.) M.G.M.

        FREUD--ON MAN AND SOCIETY   (Ph.d.)
        Doct., Bombay U., 1963, (Dr. A.R. Desai)

279   Schulze, R.

        AN EXPLORATION OF ALIENATION AND COMMITTMENT
        AMONG INDIAN COLLEGE STUDENTS
        Int. J. of Contemporary Sociol., 1971, 8, 2, Apr.,
        143-159
        SA, XX, 6, F8091

280   Singh, R.N.

        A STUDY OF THE SCORES ON CALTELL'S CULTURE FAIRE
        TEST OF INTELLIGENCE (SCALE TWO) IN THE INDIAN
        BACKGROUND: A SPECIAL REFERENCE TO SOCIO-ECONOMIC
        VARIABLES   (Ph.d.)
        Doct., Gorakhupur U., 1968, (Dr. S. Jalota)

281   Sinha, G.S. and S.P. Sinha

        A STUDY OF NATIONAL STEREOTYPES
        Ind. J. Soc. Wrk., 1966, 27, 2, Jul., 163-174
        SA, XVI, 5, D2315

282   Sinha, N.K.

        THE ADOPTION PROCESS AS RELATED TO SOME SOCIO-PERSONAL
        FACTORS   (Ph.d.)
        Doct., Indian Agricultural Research Inst., 1963,
        (Prof. K.N. Singh)

283   Sinha, R.R.P.

        A COMPARATIVE STUDY OF TRIBAL AND NON-TRIBAL
        INTELLIGENCE   (Ph.d.)
        Doct., Ranchi U., 1966, (Dr. A.K.D. Sinha)

284   Spratt, P.

        HINDU CULTURE AND PERSONALITY: A PSYCHOANALYTIC
        STUDY
        Bombay, Manaktalas, 1966, ix-400 pp.

285   Srivastava, A.L.

        MODERN VALUE-ORIENTATION AND STYLES OF LIFE
        J. of Social Res., 1969, 12, 1, Mar., 47-55
        SA, XIX, 6, F1427

286   Srivastava, (Mrs.) P.

        THE CULTURAL BACKGROUND OF THE DEVELOPMENT OF
        PERSONALITY IN THE HINDU MIDDLE CLASS SOCIETY   (Ph.d.)
        Doct., Agra U., 1969, (Dr. R.N. Saksena)

287   Steed, G.P.

       NOTES ON AN APPROACH TO A STUDY OF PERSONALITY
       FORMATION IN A HINDU VILLAGE IN GUJARAT
       in Village India, (ed. M. Merriott), Chicago,
       U. of Chicago Press, 1958, 102-144

288   Straus, M.A.

       ANAL AND ORAL FRUSTRATION IN RELATION TO SINHALESE
       PERSONALITY
       Sociometry, 1957, 20, 1, Mar., 21-31
       SA, VIII, 3, 7828

289   Subbannachar, N.V.

       THE SOCIAL PSYCHOLOGY OF SRI AUROBINDO   (Ph.d.)
       Doct., Mysore U., 1959, (Dr. K.C. Varadachar)

290   Suman, B.N. and S.L. Jones

       A STUDY OF THE RELATIONSHIP BETWEEN EMOTIONAL
       MATURITY AND ANXIETY
       Ind. J. Soc. Wrk., 1966, 27, 3, 287-289
       SA, XVI, V, D2317

291   Taylor, W.S.

       BASIC PERSONALITY IN THE ORTHODOX HINDU CULTURE
       PATTERNS
       J. of Abnormal and Social Psychology, 43, 3-12, Jan.,
       1948

292   Veeraraghavan, P.V.

       THE MIGRATED RURAL WORKER IN INDUSTRY--A STUDY
       OF PERSONALITY AND SOCIO-CULTURAL CHANGE   (Ph.d.)
       Doct., Madras U., 1968, Human Relations Dept., South
       India Textile Research Assoc., Coimbatore

0312   personality and culture

   293   Wenger, M.A. and B.K. Bagchi

         STUDIES OF AUTONOMIC FUNCTIONS IN PRACTITIONERS
         OF YOGA IN INDIA
         Behavioral Sci., 1961, 6, 4, Oct., 312-323
         SA, XI, 1and 2, A4650

   294   ------------

         A NOTE ON CULTURAL DETERMINATION OF REALITY-
         FANTASY PREFERENCE
         Character and Personality, V. 15, 1946-7, p. 208-14

0322   leadership

   295   Abraham, M.F.

         THE DYNAMICS OF LEADERSHIP IN VILLAGE INDIA   (Ph.d. Soc.)
         Michigan State U., 1970-71

   296   Bachenheimer, R.

         ELEMENTS OF LEADERSHIP IN AN ANDHRA VILLAGE
         in Leadership and Political Inst. in India, (eds.
         R. ParK and I. Tinker), Oxford U. Press, 1960, 445-452

   297   Balakrishna, S. and B.P. Iyer

         SACRED-SECULAR DISPOSITION OF LEADERS: AN APPLICATION
         OF LATENT DICHOTOMY ANALYSIS
         Behav. Scis. and C.D., 1970, 4, 1, Mar., 41-51
         SA, XIX, 6, F1439

   298   Barnabas, A.P.

         WHO ARE THE VILLAGE LEADERS
         Kurukshetra, 1957

   299   Barnabas, A.P.

         CHARACTERISTICS OF "LAY LEADERS" IN EXTENSION WORK
         J. of the M.S.U. of Baroda, 1958

300   Beals, A.R.

       CHANGE IN THE LEADERSHIP OF A MYSORE VILLAGE
       India's Villages, (ed. M.N. Srinivas), Dev.Depart.,
       West Bengal Govt., 1955, 132-143

301   Beals, A.R.

       LEADERSHIP IN A MYSORE VILLAGE
       in Leadership and Political Inst. in India, (eds.
       A. Park and I. Tinker), Oxford U. Press, 1960, 427-437

302   Bhatnagar, G.S.

       MONOMORPHIC AND POLYMORPHIC LEADERSHIP IN SOME
       NORTH INDIAN VILLAGES
       East. Anthrop., XXv, 3, Sept.-Dec., 1972, 235-241

303   Bhouraskar, K.M.

       LEADERSHIP IN A TRIBAL VILLAGE
       Man In India, 1964, 44, 4, Oct.-Dec., 329-340
       SA, XIV, 1, B8353

304   Bhushan, L.I.

       LEADERSHIP-PREFERENCE AS RELATED TO AGE, EDUCATION,
       RESIDENCE, AND SEX
       Ind. J. Soc. Wrk., 1968, 29, 2, Jul., 193-196
       SA, XVIII, 4, E2912

305   Bhushan, L.J.

       PERSONALITY FACTORS AND LEADERSHIP PREFERENCE (Ph.d.)
       Doct., Bhagalpur U., 1968, (Dr. B. De)

306   Bondurant, Joan V.

       THE NON CONVENTIONAL POLITICAL LEADER IN INDIA
       in Leadership and Political Inst. in India, (eds.
       R.L. Park and I. Tinker), N.Y.: Greenwood, 1969
       (Reprint), p. 279-299

307   Bose, A.B. and P.C. Saxena

        OPINION LEADERS IN A VILLAGE IN WESTERN RAJASTHAN
        Man In India, 1966, 46, 2, Apr.-Jun., 121-130
        SA, XVI, 6, D3447

308   Brecher, M.

        POLITICAL LEADERSHIP IN INDIA: AN ANALYSIS OF
        ELITE ATTITUDES
        Amer. Polit. Sci. Re., 64(1), Mar., 7970, 197-198

309   Brown, D. Mackenzie

        TRADITIONAL CONCEPTS OF INDIAN LEADERSHIP
        in Leadership and Political Inst. in India, (eds. R.L.
        Park and I. Tinker), N.Y.:   Greenwood Press, 1969
        (Reprint), p. 3-18

310   Chandra, P.

        RURAL LEADERSHIP IN INDIA
        East. Anthrop., 1959, 13, 1, Sep.-Nov., 41-48
        SA, X, 6, A3912

311   Chopra, S.L. and D.N.S. Chauhan

        EMERGING PATTERN OF POLITICAL LEADERSHIP IN INDIA
        J. Constit. Parl. Stud., 4, 1, Jan.-Mar., 1970,
        119-129

312   Crane, Robert I.

        THE LEADERSHIP OF THE CONGRESS PARTY
        in Leadership and Political Inst. in India, (eds.
        R.L. Park and I. Tinker), N.Y.:   Greenwood Press,
        1969 (Reprint), p. 169-188

313   Dube, Leela

        SOME FIELD TECHNIQUES IN THE STUDY OF RURAL LEADERSHIP:
        AN ANTHROPOLOGICAL APPROACH
        in Emerging Patterns of Rural Leadership in Southern
        Asia, Hyderabad, N.I.C.D., 1965, 191-8

314   Dube, S.C.

        A FRAMEWORK FOR THE STUDY OF RURAL LEADERSHIP IN
        TRANSITIONAL SOCIETIES
        in Emerging Patterns of Rural Leadership in Southern
        Asia, Hyderabad, N.I.C.D., 1965

315   Erikson, E.H.

        ON THE NATURE OF PSYCHO-HISTORICAL EVIDENCE: IN
        SEARCH OF GHANDI
        Daedalus, 1968, 97, 3, Sum., 695-730
        SA, SVII, 7, E0113

316   Fisher, Margaret W.

        NEHRU: THE HERO AS RESPONSIBLE LEADER
        in Leadership and Political Inst. in India, eds. R.L.
        Park and I. Tinker, N.Y.: Greenwood Press, 1969
        (Reprint), p. 41-66

317   Gaikwad, V.R. and G.L. Verma

        ELECTED LEADERS AS KEY COMMUNICATIORS OF AGRICULTURAL
        PRACTICES
        Behav. Scis. and C.D., 1970, 4, 1, Mar., 52-62
        SA, XIX, 6, F1441

318   Gangrade, K.C.S.

        A COMPARATIVE STUDY OF LEADERSHIP AND SOCIAL STRUCTURE
        IN A DELHI VILLAGE
        Doct., Delhi U., 1969, (M.S.A. Rao)

319   Goodall, Merrill R.

        ORGANIZATION OF ADMINISTRATIVE LEADERSHIP IN THE
        FIVE YEAR PLANS
        in Leadership and Political Inst. in India, (eds.
        R.L. Park and I. Tinker), N.Y.: Greenwood, 1969
        Reprint, p. 314-329

320   Government of India

LEADERSHIP AND GROUPS IN A SOUTH INDIAN VILLAGE
New Delhi, Programme Evaluation Organization Planning
Commission, 19, 1955, 134 pp.

321   Gupta, L.C.

CHANGING PATTERN OF RURAL LEADERSHIP: A CASE STUDY
Sociol. B., 1966, 15, 2, Sep., 27-36
SA, XV, 6, C7536

322   Guruswamy, P.A.

LEADERSHIP AND SOCIAL STRUCTURE IN KERALA
Doct. St., Rajasthan U., 1969

323   Harjindar, S.

VILLAGE LEADERSHIP; A CASE STUDY OF VILLAGE MOHALI
IN PUNJAB
Delhi, Sterling Publishers, 1968, 82 p.

324   Harjinder, S.

GENERALITY AND SPECIFICITY OF INFLUENCE: A STUDY
OF LEADERSHIP IN TWO PUNJABI VILLAGES IN INDIA
Paper present. at the 1972 Annual Meeting of the
Rural Sociol. Society
SA, XX, 5, Sup., 25, F7856

325   Harrison, S.S.

LEADERSHIP AND LANGUAGE POLICY IN INDIA
in Leadership and Political Inst. In India, (eds.
R.L. Park and I. Tinker), N.Y.: Greenwood Press, 1969
Reprint, p. 151-167

326   Hitchcock, J.T.

LEADERSHIP IN A NORTH INDIAN VILLAGE: TWO CASTE
STUDIES
in Leadership and Political Inst. In India, (eds.
R.L. Park and I. Tinker), Oxford U. Press, 1960,
395-414

327   Jagamohan, Rao

        STUDY OF THE TYPES, FUNCTIONS AND FACTORS OF A
        TESTING RURAL LEADERSHIP IN THE SELECTED VILLAGES
        OF REWA BLOCK
        M.Sc. Thesis, India, 1966 (unpublished)

328   Jain, S.P.

        LEADERSHIP IN A NORTH INDIAN COMMUNITY
        Sociology and Social Research, 1971, 55, 2, Jan.,
        170-180
        SA, XIX, 4, E9558

329   Jassal, H.S.

        LEADERS AND LEADERSHIP STRUCTURE IN TWO VILLAGES
        IN PUNJAB, INDIA (Ph.d.--Soc.)
        Cornell U.-N.Y. State Coll. of Agriculture and
        Life Sciences, 70-71

330   Jha, S.S.

        POLITICAL LEADERSHIP IN BIHAR--A SOCIOLOGICAL
        ANALYSIS (Ph.d.)
        Doct., Bombay U., 1967, (Dr. A.R. Desai)

331   John, P.V.

        CHANGING PATTERN OF LEADERSHIP IN A VILLAGE IN
        MADHYA PRADESH
        Sociol. B., 1963, 12, 1, Mar., 32-38
        SA, XI, 7, A7324

332   Kochanek, S.A.

        THE RELATION BETWEEN SOCIAL BACKGROUND AND ATTITUDES
        OF INDIAN LEGISLATORS
        J. of Commonwealth Political Studies, 1968, 6, 1,
        Mar., 34-53
        SA, XX, 1-2, F3465

333   Lamb, Helen B.

        BUSINESS ORGANIZATION AND LEADERSHIP IN INDIA
        TODAY
        in Leadership and Political Inst. in India, (eds.
        R.L. Park and I. Tinker), N.Y.: Greenwood Press,
        1969, p. 251-268

334   Mathur, S.M.

        A SOCIAL STUDY OF TRADE UNION LEADERSHIP IN RAJASTHAN
        Doct. St., Rajasthan U., 1969

335   Orenstein, H.

        LEADERSHIP AND CASTE IN A BOMBAY VILLAGE
        in Leadership and Political Inst. in India, (eds.
        R.L. Park and I. Tinker), Oxford U. Press, 1960,
        415-426

336   Overstreet, Gene D.

        LEADERSHIP IN THE INDIAN COMMUNIST PARTY
        in Leadership and Political Inst. in India, (eds.
        R.L. Park and I. Tinker), N.Y.: Greenwood Press,
        1969, pp. 225-249

337   Pareek, V. (ed.)

        STUDIES IN RURAL LEADERSHIP
        Delhi, Behaviour Sciences Center, 1966, 116 pp.

338   Punit, A.E.

        STRUCTURAL DETERMINENTS IN RURAL LEADERSHIP   (Ph.d.)
        Doct. St., Karnatak U., 1969, (Dr. K.C. Sekhariah)

339   Perinbanayagam, R.S.

        THE DIALECTICS OF CHARISMA
        Sociological Quart., 1971, 12, 3, Sum., 387-402
        SA, XX, 3, F4695

340   Rangnath

        THE CHANGING PATTERN OF RURAL LEADERSHIP IN UTTAR
        PRADESH--A SURVEY IN THE COMMUNITY DEVELOPMENT
        AREAS (Ph.d.)
        Doct., Lucknow U., 1965, (Dr. R.K. Muherjee)

341   Redlich, F.

        BUSINESS LEADERSHIP: DIVERSE ORIGINS AND VARIANT
        FORMS
        Econ. Dev. Cult. Change, 1958, 6, 3, Apr., 177-190
        SA, X, 6, A3798

342   Rout, B.C.

        RURAL LEADERSHIP PROBLEMS
        Kurukshetra, 1967, 15, 5, Feb., 15-16
        SA, XVIII, 6, E4986

343   Rusch, Thomas A.

        DYNAMICS OF SOCIALIST LEADERSHIP IN INDIA
        Leadership and Political Inst. in India, (eds.
        R.L. Park and I. Tinker), N.Y.: Greenwood Press,
        1969, pp. 188-211

344   Sahay, B.N.

        CHANGES IN THE LEADERSHIP PATTERN AMONG THE
        MALER AND THE SANTHAL OF SANTHAL PARGANAS (BIHAR) (Ph.d.)
        Doct., Ranchi U., 1967, (Prof. L.P. Vidyarthi)

345   Sahay, B.N.

        DYNAMICS OF LEADERSHIP
        New Delhi, Book Hive, 1968

346   Sahay, B.N.

        LEADERSHIP CONFLICT AND DEVELOPMENT PROGRAMME IN A
        NORTH INDIAN VILLAGE
        in Vidyarthi (ed.), Conflict, Tension and Cultural
        Trend in India, India, 1969

0322   leadership

347   Saika, P.D.

         VILLAGE LEADERSHIP IN NORTH-EAST INDIA
         Man In India, 1963, 43, 1, Apr.-Jun., 92-99
         SA, XII, 7, B2573

348   Saraswati, B.

         A NOTE ON RABBARI CASTE PANCHAYAT
         Man In India, 1962, 42, 3, Jul.-Sep., 195-205
         SA, XII, 5, B0861

349   Sen, L.K.

         OPINION LEADERSHIP IN INDIA
         Mich. State U., Res. Report, 1969

350   Sengupta, T.

         OPINION LEADERS IN RURAL COMMUNITIES
         Man In India, 1969, 48, 2, Apr.-Jun., 159-166
         SA, XVIII, 1-2, E1210

351   Sharma, K.N.

         PANCHAYAT LEADERSHIP AND RESOURCE GROUPS
         Sociol. B., 1963, 12, 1, Mar., 42-52
         SA, XI, 7, A7333

352   Sharma, O.P.

         EMERGING PATTERN OF RURAL LEADERSHIP IN INDIA
         Amer. Doctoral Dissertations, Indiana U., 1966-67

353   Sherif, M. (ed.)

         INTERGROUP RELATIONS AND LEADERSHIP: APPROACHES
         AND RESEARCH IN INDUSTRIAL, ETHNIC, CULTURAL, AND
         POLITICAL AREAS
         New York, John Wiley and Sons, Inc., 1962, xiv and 284
         pp.
         SA, XIII, 6-7, B7605

354   Singh, A.

       REPUTATIONAL MEASURE OF LEADERSHIP: A STUDY OF
       TWO INDIAN VILLAGES
       State College: Mississippi State U., 1964

355   Singh, A.

       ACTION MEASURE OF LEADERSHIP: A STUDY OF TWO
       INDIAN VILLAGES
       paper presented at the Rural Soc. Society, San
       Francisco, 1967

356   Singh, A.

       LEADERSHIP PATTERNS AND VILLAGE STRUCTURE: A
       STUDY OF SIX INDIAN VILLAGES
       Amer. Doctoral Dissertations, Mississippi State U.,
       1967-68

357   Singh, B.N.

       THE IMPACT OF THE COMMUNITY DEVELOPMENT PROGRAMME
       IN RURAL LEADERSHIP
       in Leadership and Political Inst. In India, (eds.
       R.L. Park and I. Tinker), Oxford U. Press, 1960,
       358-371

358   Singh, H.

       BASES OF VILLAGE LEADERSHIP--AN ANALYSIS
       J. of Soc. Res., 1967, 10, 1, Mar., 22-25
       SA, XVI, 5, D2973

359   Singh, H.

       VILLAGE LEADERSHIP A CASE STUDY OF VILLAGE MOBALI
       IN PUNJAB
       Delhi: Sterling Pub., 1968, 82 pp.

360   Singh, R.N.

        PERSONAL ORIENTATIONS OF VOLUNTARY ACTORS RELATED
        TO THEIR INVOLVEMENT IN PROGRAM LEADERSHIP ROLES
        (Ph.d. Soc.), Mississippi State U., 1970-71

361   Singh, S.

        EMERGING PATTERNS OF LEADERSHIP AMONG INDUSTRIAL
        WORKERS IN UTTAR PRADESH--A STUDY OF LEADERSHIP
        AMONG THE WORKERS IN FACTORIES OF LUCKNOW AND KANPUR
        (Ph.d.)
        Doct., Lucknow U., 1969, (Dr. S. Chandra)

362   Singh, Y.P. and U. Pareek

        SOCIO-ECONOMIC CHARACTERISTICS OF KEY-COMMUNICATIONS
        Sociol. B., 1966, 15, 1, Mar., 52-60
        SA, XIV, 6, C1897

363   Sinha, A.C.

        LEADERSHIP IN A TRIBAL SOCIETY
        Man In India, 1967, 47, 3, Jul.-Sep., 222-227
        SA, XVII, 2, D5798

364   Sirsikar, V.M.

        LEADERSHIP PATTERNS IN RURAL MAHARASHTRA
        Asian Sur., 1964, 4, 6, Jul., 929-939
        SA, XIV, 2-3, B9580

365   Srivastava, (Mrs.) S.

        THE PATTERN OF POLITICAL LEADERSHIP IN EMERGING
        AREAS--A CASE STUDY OF U.P. (Ph.d.)
        Doct., Banaras Hindu U., 1970, (Dr. K.V. Rao)

0322 leadership

366   Tandon, I.B.

       EMERGING PATTERNS OF LEADERSHIP AMONG STUDENTS IN
       ROHILKHAND DIVISION IN U.P. (A SOCIO-PSYCHOLOGICAL
       STUDY)
       1969, Doct., Agra U., (Dr. R.N. Mukerjee)

367   Trivedi, D.N.

       OPINION LEADERSHIP AND ADOPTION OF AGRICULTURAL
       INNOVATIONS IN EIGHT INDIAN VILLAGES
       Amer. Doct. Dissert., 1968-69, Pennsylvania State U.

368   Trivedi, D.N.

       MODERNIZATION, OPINION LEADERS AND THEIR INSTRUMENTAL
       INFORMATION-SEEKING BEHAVIOR
       Man In India, 52, 4, 1972, 359-371

369   UNESCO Res. Center and N.I.C.D.

       EMERGING PATTERNS OF RURAL LEADERSHIP IN SOUTHERN
       ASIA
       Rept. of the Mussori Confer., 1965

370   Vepa, R.K.

       TRAINING VILLAGE LEADERS
       Kurukshetra, 1966, 14, 6, Mar., 9-11
       SA, XVII, 2, D6182

371   Vidyarthi, L.P.

       THE HISTORIC MARCH OF JHARKHAND PARTY: A STUDY OF
       ADIVASI LEADERSHIP IN TRIBAL BIHAR
       Ind. Sociol. B., 1964, 1, 2, Jan., 5-10
       SA, XIII, 3-4, B6036

0322 leadership

372   Vidyarthi, L.P.

       LEADERSHIP IN INDIA
       New York, Asia, 1967

373   Weiner, Myron

       POLITICAL LEADERSHIP IN WEST BENGAL: THE IMPLICATIONS
       OF ITS CHANGING PATTERNS FOR ECONOMIC PLANNING
       in Rural Sociology in India, ed. A.R. Desai,
       Bombay, Popular Prakashan, 1969, p. 724-736

374   Yadav, G.S.

       A STUDY OF EMERGING PATTERN OF RURAL LEADERSHIP AND
       PACHAYATI RAJ IN UTTAR PRADESH (Ph.d.)
       Doct. St., 1969, Agra U., (P.N. Tandon)

375   Yadav, K.S.

       LEADERSHIP IN THE TRIBAL VILLAGES OF MADHYA PRADESH
       Kurukshetra, 1969, 17, 5, Feb., 8-9
       SA, XIX, 4, E9565

0400 Group Interactions

0410 interaction between large groups (race relations, group
      relations etc.)

376   Acharya, J.C.

       STUDY OF AN INTERSTITIAL AREA IN A DOUBLE TOWN,
       BHUBANESWAR (Ph.d.)
       Doct., Utkal U., 1967, (Dr. A. Aiyappan)

377   Agarwalla, N.

       THE HINDU-MUSLIM QUESTION
       Calcutta: A Chakrabarti, 1951, 80 p.

0410 interaction between large groups   (race relations, group
      relations etc.)

378   Asimi, A.A.D.

       CHRISTIAN MINORITY IN WEST PUNJAB
       American Doctoral Dissertations, New York U., 1963-64

379   Aurora, G.S.

       THE NEW FRONTIERSMEN: A SOCIOLOGICAL STUDY OF THE
       INDIAN IMMIGRANTS IN THE UNITED KINGDOM
       N.Y.: Humanities, 1968

380   Aurora, G.S.

       SOME ASPECTS OF RURAL-URBAN RELATIONS IN ALIRAJPUR
       (WEST-CENTRAL TRIBAL ZONE)
       Doct. St., Delhi, 1969, (Dr. M.S.A. Rao)

381   Barpujari, S.K.

       ANGLO-NAGA RELATIONS   (D.Phil.)
       Doct., Gauhati U., 1970, (Dr. A.C. Banerjee)

382   Benedict, Buston

       INDIANS IN A PLURAL SOCIETY, A REPORT ON MAURITIES
       London, H.M. Stationery Office, 1961, 167 p.

383   Beteille, A.

       RACE, CASTE, AND ETHNIC IDENTITY
       International Soc. Sci. J., 1971, 23, 4, 519-535
       SA, XX, 7, F9145

384   Bhandarkar, D.R.

       FOREIGN ELEMENTS IN THE HINDU POPULATION
       Calcutta, 1968

0410   interaction between large groups   (race relations, group
       relations etc.)

385   Bharati, A.

       PROBLEMS OF THE ASIAN MINORITIES IN EAST AFRICA
       Pakistan Horizon, 1964, 17, 4, 342-349
       SA, XIV, 6, C1899

386   Yogi Shri Shuddhananda Bhartiar

       INDIA'S UNION
       in Group Prejudices In India, (eds. M.B. Nanavati
       and C.N. Vakil), pp. 108-115, Bombay, Vora, 1951

387   Bhattacharya, D.K.

       THE ANGLO-INDIANS IN BOMBAY: AN INTRODUCTION TO
       THEIR SOCIO-ECONOMIC AND CULTURAL LIFE
       Race, 1968, 10, 2, Oct., 163-172
       SA, XVIII, 3, E1792

388   Bose, N.K.

       PROBLEMS OF NATIONAL INTEGRATION
       Simla, 1967

389   Bose, N.K.

       UNITY IN INDIAN DIVERSITY
       in Rural Sociology in India, ed. by A.R. Desai,
       Part II--Readings in Rural Soc., Bombay; Popular
       Prakashan, 1969, pp. 134-137

390   Burman, B.K. Roy

       STRUCTURE OF BRIDGE AND BUFFER COMMUNITIES IN THE
       BORDER AREAS
       Man In India, 1966, 46, 2, Apr.-Jun., 103-107
       SA, XVI, 6, D3801

0410   interactions between large groups   (race relations, group
        relations etc.)

    391   Chakravarti, N.R.

           THE INDIAN MINORITY IN BURMA; THE RISE AND DECLINE
           OF AN IMMIGRANT COMMUNITY; WITH A FORWARD BY
           H. TINKER (pub.) FOR THE INST. OF RACE RELATIONS
           Oxford, 1971

    392   Chatterji, A.K.

           A STUDY OF THE ROLE OF REGIONALISM IN NATIONAL
           INTEGRATION (Ph.d.)
           Doct., Agra U., 1968, (Dr. K.K. Gangadharan)

    393   Chauhan, I.S.

           RACE IN FIJI POLITICS. A NOTE ON THE INDIAN COMMUNITY
           Economic and Political Weekly, 1970, 5, 42, Oct., 1739-1741
           SA, XX, 5, F6965

    394   Cohn, B.S. and M. Marriot

           NETWORKS AND CENTERS IN THE INTEGRATION OF INDIAN
           CIVILIZATION
           J. of Soc. Res., 1958, 1, 1, 1-9

    395   *Cottrell, Ann Baker

           CONTRIBUTIONS OF MIXED MARRIAGE TO INTERGROUP RELATIONS:
           INDIAN-WESTERN COUPLES IN INDIA
           SA, 21, 73G0589

    396   Das, N.

           TRIBAL INTERACTION OF THE SAORAST PAROS OF GANJAM
           AGENCY
           Adivsi, 1967-68, 12-13

    397   Das, T.C.

           ASSIMILATION: INTEGRATION: ACCULTURATIONS
           J. of Soc. Res., 3, 2, 6-10, 1960

0410   interaction between large groups   (race relations, group
       relations etc.)

398   Desai, R.

         INDIAN IMMIGRANTS IN BRITAIN
         New York, Oxford Press, 1963

399   Eapen, P.C.

         A STUDY FOR IMPROVED INTERGROUP RELATIONS IN THE
         KERALA STATE INDIA
         American Doctoral Dissertations, New York U., 1962-63

400   Firth, R.

         FACTIONS IN INDIAN AND OVERSEAS INDIAN SOCIETIES:
         I--INTRODUCTION
         Brit. J. Sociol., 1957, 8, 4, Dec., 291-295
         SA, IX, 1, 8960

401   Gathani, (Miss) H.B.

         INDIAN SETTLEMENT IN NAIROBI: SOCIO-CULTURAL STUDY
         Doct. St., Bombay U., 1969, (Dr. J.V. Ferriera)

402   Gaikwrad, U.S.R.

         THE ANGLO INDIANS--A STUDY IN THE PROBLEMS AND PROCESS
         INVOLVED IN EMOTIONAL AND CULTURAL INTEGRATION (Ph.d.)
         Doct., Sargar U., 1963, (Dr. (Mrs.) L. Dube)

403   Ghurye, G.S.

         INDIAN UNITY: A RETROSPECT AND PROSPECT
         in Group Prejudices in India, eds. M.B. Nanavati and
         C.N. Vakil, pp. 115-124, Bombay, Vora, 1951

404   Gist, N.P.

         CONDITIONS OF INTER-GROUP RELATIONS: THE ANGLO-INDIANS
         Int. Jour. of Comp. Sociol., 1967, 8, 2, Sep., 199-208
         SA, XVII, 1, D4878

0410   interaction between large groups   (race relations, group
        relations etc.)

    405   Grimshaw, A.D.

            THE ANGLO-INDIAN COMMUNITY: THE INTEGRATION OF A
            MARGINAL GROUP
            J. Asian Studies, 1959, 18, 2, Feb., 227-240
            SA, IX, 2, 9386

    406   Gupta, A.

            INDIANS ABOARD: ASIA AND AFRICA
            New Delhi, 1971

    407   Gupta, R.

            HINDU-MUSLIM RELATIONS IN THE CITY OF DEHRA DUN   (Ph.d.)
            Doct., Lucknow U., 1960, (Prof. D.K. Sen)

    408   Gulati, R.K.

            AN ANALYSIS OF THE INTER-GROUP DIFFERENCES IN AN
            ARTISAN CASTE OF MAHARASHTRA   (Ph.d.)
            Doct., Poona U., 1069, (Dr. (Mrs.) I. Karve)

    409   Henderson, W.

            THE REFUGEES IN INDIA AND PAKISTAN
            J. of Int. Affairs, v.7, 1953, p. 57-65

    410   Kapoor, S.N.

            SOCIAL INTEGRATION OF INTER-STATE MIGRANTS IN KANPUR
            (Ph.d.)
            Doct., Agra U., 1969, (Dr. N.G. Pandey)

    411   *Khan, R.

            MUSLIM LEADERSHIP AND ELECTORAL POLITICS IN HYDERABAD.
            A PATTERN OF MINORITY ARTICULATION
            Economic and Political Weekly, 1971, 6, 15, Apr., 783-
            794 and 1971, 6, 16, Apr., 833-840
            SA, 21, 73G4046

0410   interaction between large groups (race relations, group
       relations etc.)

    412   Khosla, G.D.

          HINDU-SIKH RELATIONS
          in Group Prejudices In India, eds. M.B. Nanavati and
          C.N. Vakil, pp. 196-203, Bombay, Vora, 1951

    413   Kulkarni, J.R.

          PATTERNS OF INTER-TRIBAL RELATIONSHIPS
          Doct. St., Saugar U., 1969

    414   Labecka, B.

          INDUSI W AFRYEE WSCHODNIEJ (The Indians in East Africa)
          Przeglad Socjologiczny, 1969, 23, 41-56, (Pol.)
          SA, XVIII, 7, E5698

    415   Lambert, R.D.

          RELIGION, ECONOMICS, AND VIOLENCE IN BENGAL; BACKGROUND
          OF THE MINORITIES AGREEMENT
          Middle East J., 4, 307-28, Jul., 1950

    416   Lambert, R.D.

          SOME MINOR PATHOLOGIES IN THE AMERICAN PRESENCE
          IN INDIA
          A. Amer. Acad. Pol. Soc. Sci., 1966, 368, Nov.,
          157-170
          SA, XV, C4817

    417   Lewis, O.

          GROUP DYNAMICS IN A NORTH INDIAN VILLAGE
          Programme Evaluation Organization, Planning Commission,
          Government of India, 1954, 48 p.

    418   Mandelbaum, D.G.

          HINDU-MOSLEM CONFLICT IN INDIA
          Middle East J., v. 1, 1947, p.369-85

0410 interactions between large groups (race relations, group
     relations etc.)

   419   Mason, Philip (ed.)

         INDIA AND CEYLON: UNITY AND DIVERSITY
         New York, Oxford University Press, 1967

   420   Mayer, Adrian C.

         INDIANS IN FIJI
         New York, Oxford University Press, 1963, 152 pp.

   421   Mekhari, S.M.

         SOCIAL BACKGROUND OF HINDU-MUSLIM RELATIONSHIPS (Ph.d.)
         Doct, Bombay U., 1947, (Prof. G.S. Ghurye)

   422   Mills, J.P.

         SOME RECENT CONTACT PROBLEMS IN KHASI HILLS
         in J.P. Mills (ed.) Essays in Anthropology: Presented
         to S.C. Roy,
         Lucknow, 1948

   423   Morris, H.S.

         COMMUNAL RIVALRY AMONG INDIANS IN UGANDA
         Brit. J. Sociol., 1957, 8, 4, Dec. 306-317
         SA IX, 1, 8964

   424   Morris H.S.

         THE INDIANS IN UGANDA
         Chicago, U. of Chicago Press, 1968

   425   Mukherjee, R.

         A MINORITY-MARGINAL GROUP IN CALCUTTA
         Transactions of the 5th World Congress of Sociology,
         Belgium, 1964

0410   interactions between large groups (race relations, group
        relations etc.)

    426   Mukherjee, R.

          A MINORITY REFUGEE GROUP IN CALCUTTA
          in Minority Problems, ed. A.N. Rose and C.B. Rose
          New York, 1965

    427   Narain, R. and T.R. Venkatasubrahmanyan

          JUDGMENT OF GROUP PREJUDICES BEFORE AND AFTER ANTI-HINDI
          AGITATION IN MADRAS STATE
          in Vidyarthi, L.P. (ed.), Conflict, Tension and Cultural
          Trend in India, Calcutta, Punthi Pustak, 1969

    428   Pakrasi, K.

          A STUDY OF THE REFUGEES (DISPLACED PERSONS) OF WEST
          BENGAL (1947-48) WITH SPECIAL REFERENCE TO THE RURAL
          PEOPLE OF UNDIVIDED BENGAL (1946-47) (D.PHIL.)
          Doct, Calcutta U, 1968

    429   Pakrasi, K.B.

          THE UPROOTED: A SOCIOLOGICAL STUDY OF REFUGEES OF
          WEST BENGAL, INDIA
          Calcutta, South Asia Books, 1972

    430   Panchbhaim, S.C.

          INTERCOMMUNAL STEREOTYPES IN A PLURAL SOCIETY
          Man In India, 1966, 46, 4, Oct - Dec. 331-344
          SA, XVI, D4118

    431   Pithani, T.D.

          SOCIO-ECONOMIC SURVEY OF DISPLACED PERSONS IN
          RAJASTHAN (Ph.d.)
          Doct, Rajasthan U, 1962 (Dr. M.P. Mathur)

0410   interactions between large groups (race relations, group
       relations etc.)

      432   Prasad, S.

            WHERE THE THREE TRIBES MEET: A STUDY IN TRIBAL
            INTERACTION (Ph.d.)
            Doct, Ranchi U, 1967 (Prof. L.P. Vidyarthi)

      433   Punekar, V.

            NEIGHBORHOOD RELATIONS AMONG REGIONAL GROUPS IN INDIA,
            Sociology and Soc. Res., 1969,5,4,1, Oct, 42-55
            SA, XVIII,6,E5454

      434   Qureshi, I.H.

            RELATIONS BETWEEN THE HINDUS AND THE MUSLIMS IN THE
            SUBCONTINENT OF INDIA AND PAKISTAN
            Civilisations, 1955,5,1, 43-51
            S.A. Vol. III, #4, 1854

      435   Ram, P.

            RECENT INVESTIGATIONS OF HINDU-MUSLIM RELATIONS IN INDIA
            Hum. Org., V.II, n.2, 1952, pp.13-16

      436   Ray, P.C.

            THE TENSIONAL FEELINGS AMONG THE ABOSS AND GALLONG
            AS INDICATED BY RORSCHACH TECHNIQUE
            Ind. J. of Psy., 1955,30, 95-103

      437   Roy Burman, B.K.

            MEANING AND PROCESS OF TRIBAL INTEGRATION IN A
            DEMOCRATIC SOCIETY
            Sociol. B., 1961, 10,1,27-41

      438   Sandwar, A.N.

            IMPACT OF HINDUZATION ON BIKORS AND HOS IN CHHOTANNAGPUR
            Doct, st. Ranchi, U, 1969

0410   interactions between large groups (race relations, group
        relations etc.)

    439   Sarkar, R.M.

           STUDY OF SOCIAL INTERACTION IN A MULTI-ETHNIC COMMUNITY
           (Ph.d.)
           Doct, Patna U, 1969 (Dr. Sachdhidanand)

    440   Sarma, M.A.

           GROUP DOMINATION IN VILLAGE PANCHAYATS
           Rur. India, 1960, Mar. 83-88
           SA, XII,6,B1905

    441   Schermerhorn R.A.

           A TENTATIVE THEORETICAL APPROACH TO THE STUDY OF
           MINORITIES IN INDIA
           East. Anthrop, 1961,14,1, Jan-Apr, 59-69
           SA XI,5,A5720

    442   Schermerhorn R.A.

           WHERE CHRISTIANS ARE A MINORITY?
           Antioch R. 1961-62,21,4,497-509
           SA, XII,4,B0524

    443   Seminar on Indians Abroad

           INDIANS ABROAD; ASIA, AND AFRICA; REPORT OF AN
           INTERNATIONAL SEMINAR
           New Delhi, 1971

    444   Seth, S.C.

           THE GROWTH OF COMMUNALISM IN INDIA AND THE PROBLEM OF
           HINDU-MUSLIM RELATIONS (Ph.d.)
           Doct, Agra U, 1959

    445   Shelvankar, K.S.

           THE UNITY OF INDIA
           in Rural Sociology in India Part II - Readings in Rural
           Sociology, ed. A.R. Desai
           Bombay: Popular Prakashan, 1969, pp.145-148

0410   interactions between large groups (race relations, group
       relations etc.)

   446   Singer, P. and E. Araneta, Jr.

         HINDUIZATION AND CREOLIZATION IN GUYANA: THE PLURAL
         SOCIETY AND BASIC PERSONALITY
         Social and Economic Studies, 1967,16,3, Dep,221-236
         SA, XVII,3,D6828

   447   Singh, J.J.

         HINDU-MUSLIM RELATIONS
         Interdiscipline, 1966,3,4, Oct-Dec, 205-200
         SA, XVII,1,D5806

   448   Singh, T.

         TOWARDS AN INTEGRATED SOCIETY
         Delhi, Orient Longmans, 1969

   449   Sinha, G.S. and M.N. Karna

         STUDYING STEREOTYPES CROSS-CULTURALLY
         Man in India, 1967,47,2, Apr-Jun, 92-102
         SA, XVII,1,D4885

   450   M.R. Sinha (ed.)

         INTEGRATION IN INDIA
         All India Scholar's Conference on National Integration,
         Bombay, 1969
         Bombay, 1971

   451   Sinha, S.

         THE MEDIA AND NATURE OF HINDU BHUMIJ INTERACTION
         Asiatic Society, 1957, 23,1,23-27

   452   Smoker, P.

         A TIME SERIES ANALYSIS OF SINO-INDIAN RELATIONS
         Journal of Conflict Resolution 1969,13,2, Jun, 172-191
         SA, XVIII,7,E5918

0410 interactions between large groups (race relations, group
      relations etc.)

    453 Soma Sundaram, A.M.

         SEGREGATION OR ASSIMILATION
         Man in India, 1947, 27,1,66-73

    454 Spate, O.H.K.

         DIVERSITY AND UNITY IN THE SUB-CONTINENT
         in Rural Sociology in India
         Part II - Readings in Rural Sociology, ed. A.R. Desai
         Bombay; Popular Prakashan, 1969, pp.131-134

    455 Srivastava, L.R.N.

         SOME ASPECTS OF INTEGRATION OF THE TRIBAL PEOPLE
         Report of the Symposium on Problems of Education of
         the Tribal People of India, New Delhi, N.C.E.R.T., 1966

    456 Srivastava, L.R.N.

         THE PROBLEMS OF INTEGRATION OF THE TRIBAL PEOPLE
         Ind. J. Soc. Wrk., 1966,27,1,51-57

    457 Tinker, H.

         INDIANS IN ISRAEL: THE ACCEPTANCE MODEL AND ITS LIMITATIONS
         Race, 1971, 13,1,81-84
         SA, XX,5,F6989

    458 Thorner, P.

         HINDU-MOSLEM CONFLICT IN INDIA
         Far Eastern Survey 17,77-80, April 7,1948

    459 Uberoi, N.

         SIKH WOMEN IN SOUTHDALE
         Race, 1964,6,1, Jul, 34-40
         SA, XIII, 6-7,B7946

0410 interactions between large groups (race relations, group
     relations etc.)

   460   Venkatasubramanian, T.R.

         EXPERIMENTS IN THE REDUCTION OF GROUP PREJUDICES OF
         STUDENTS IN MADRAS STATE (Ph.d.)
         Doct, Lucknow U, (Dr. R. Narain), 1968

   461   Vidyarthi, L.P.

         SOME PRELIMINARY OBSERVATIONS ON INTER-GROUP CONFLICTS
         IN INDIA: TRIBAL, RURAL AND INDUSTRIAL

         J. of Social Research, 1967,10,2, Sep,1-10
         SA,XVII,2,D5807

   462   Wright, R.D.

         A STUDY OF THE ANGLO-INDIAN COMMUNITY OF INDIA
         (Ph.d. Soc)
         U. of Missouri, (69-70)

   463   Ziegler, G.H.

         SOCIAL FARNESS BETWEEN HINDUS AND MOSLEMS
         Sociology and Social Res. 33,194-5, Jan. 1949

0500 CULTURE AND SOCIAL STRUCTURE

0508   social organisation

    464   Aalok, S.W.

          THE MORANG ORGANISATION AMONG THE NOKTE NAGAS
          Vanyajati, 1956, 4, 2, 73-78

    465   Ahluwalia, H.

          INTER-CASTE RELATIONS IN A KULU VILLAGE
          Ind. J. S. Wrk. 1966, 27, 2, Jul, 187-195
          SA, XVI, 5, D2344

    466   Ahmad, I.

          THE ASHRAF-AJLAF DICHOTOMY IN MUSLIM SOCIAL STRUCTURE
          IN INDIA
          Indian Economic and Social History Review, 1966, 3, 3,
          Sep. 268-278
          SA, XVII, 1, D4892

    467   Ahmad, I.

          SOCIAL STRUCTURE OF A MULTI-CASTE VILLAGE IN U.P.
          Doct. St., Delhi U, 1969
          (M.N. Srinivas) (M.S.A. Rao)

    468   Appadorai, A.

          TOWARDS A JUST SOCIAL ORDER
          New Delhi, 1970

    469   Banerjee, S.

          PHAR KINSHIP SYSTEM
          B. of the Anthrop. Sur. of India, 1964, 13, 1-2

    470   Bareau, A.

          INDIAN AND ANCIENT CHINESE BUDDHISM: INSTITUTIONS
          ANALOGOUS TO THE JISA
          Comp. Stud. Soc. Hist. 1961, 3, 4, Jul, 443-451

471   Barnouw, V.

      THE SOCIAL STRUCTURE OF A SINDHI REFUGEE COMMUNITY
      Soc. Forces, 1954, 33, 2, Dec, 142-52
      S.A. vol. III, #2, 1228

472   Beech, M.H.

      SEX ROLE DEVELOPMENT AND AGE GROUP PARTICIPATION IN
      CALCUTTA
      Paper presented at the 67th Annual Meeting of the
      Amer. Sociol. Assoc.
      SA, XX, 7, Sup. 28, G0008

473   Beidelman, Thomas O.

      A COMPARATIVE ANALYSIS OF THE JAJMANI SYSTEM
      Locust Valley, N.Y.:   J.I. Augustin, 1959

474   Berreman, G.D.

      SIB AND CLAN AMONG THE PAHARI OF NORTH INDIA
      Ethnol. 1962, 1, 4, Oct, 524-528
      SA, XII, 1, A7980

475   Bose, A.B. and P.C. Saxena

      SOME CHARACTERISTICS OF NUCLEAR HOUSEHOLDS
      Man in India, 1965, 45, 3, Jul - Sep, 195-200
      SA, XVI, 5, D2347

476   Buradhar, M.P.

      SOCIAL ORGANISATION OF GONDS IN THE CENTRAL PROVINCES
      AND BERAR (Ph.d.)
      Doct, Nagpur U, 1951

477   Chaube, Ganesh

      AN UNIQUE ORGANIZATION OF SHIVA PILGRIMS
      Indian Folklore, 1958, 1

478   Chekki, D.A.

      THE STUDY OF KINSHIP IN ANTHROPOLOGY
      J. of the Karnatak U., Humanities and Social Sciences, 1962

479   Chekki, D.A.

      MODERNIZATION AND KIN NETWORK IN A DEVELOPING SOCIETY: INDIA
      Paper presented at the 7th World Congress of the
      International Sociological Association, Varna, Bulgaria, 1970
      SA, XVIII, 5, Supp. 9, E3792

480   Chekki, D.A.

      PREFERENTIAL KIN MARRIAGE IN INDIA
      J. of Asian and African Studies, 1968, 3, 3-4, Jul-Oct,287-291
      SA, XVIII, 6, E4592

481   Chekki, D.A.

      INTERKIN MARRIAGE: A THEORETICAL FRAMEWORK
      Man in India, 1968, 4, Oct-Dec, 337-344
      SA, XVIII, 4, E2926

482   Chekki, D.A.

      NAMING PATTERNS AND KINSHIP COHESIVENESS
      Ind. Soc. B. 1968, 5, 4, Jul, 233-237
      SA, XVII, 7, E0136

483   Chekki, D.A.

      MODERNIZATION AND KINSHIP IN URBAN INDIA
      J. of Karnatak University - Soc. Sciences
      Vol. V - April, 1969

484   Chekki, D.A.

      KALYAN AND GOKUL: KINSHIP AND MODERNIZATION IN
      NORTHERN MYSORE
      Contributions to Asian Studies, Leiden, E.J. Brill, 1971

485   Chekki, D.A.

      MEASURING KINSHIP ORIENTATION
      Ind. J. Soc. Res. XI, 1970, 1, pp.47-50

486   Cohn, B.S.

      THE BRITISH IN BENARES: A NINETEENTH CENTURY
      COLONIAL SOCIETY
      Comp. Stud. Soc. Hist., 1962, 4, 2, Jan, 169-199
      SA, XII, 1, A7982

487   Das, T.C.

      SOCIAL ORGANIZATION OF THE TRIBAL PEOPLES
      Ind. J. Soc. Wrk, 1953, 14, 3, Dec. 245-262
      S.A. vol. II, #4, 702

488   Das Gupta, S.

      SOCIAL STRUCTURE OF DULE BAGDI COMMUNITY OF JAINAGAR
      (24 Parganas) (D. Phil.)
      Doct, Calcutta U, 1963 (Prof. M. Basu)

489   Delfendahl, B.

      PARENTE, FONCTION ET TERRITOIRE DANS LES CULTES CHAMPETRES
      D'UN VILLAGE DE L'INDE (KINSHIP, FUNCTION AND TERRITORY
      IN THE CULTS IN THE FIELDS OF A VILLAGE IN INDIA)
      L'Homme, 1971, 11, 1, Jan-Mar, 52-67 (French)
      SA, XX, 7, F9163

490   Desai, A.R.

      A SOCIOLOGICAL ANALYSIS OF INDIA
      L. Ges. Staatswiss, 1957, 113, 1, 116-127
      S.A. VI, 4, 4996

491   D'Souza, V.S.

      MOTHER-RIGHT IN TRANSITION
      Sociol. Bull., 1953, 2, Sep, 135-142
      S.A. vol. II, #1, 47

492   Dube, S.C.

      SOCIAL STRUCTURE AND CHANGE IN INDIAN PEASANT COMMUNITIES
      in Rural Sociology in India, ed. A.R. Desai
      Bombay: Popular Prakashan, 1969, pp.201-206

493   D'Souza, V.S.

      CHANGES IN SOCIAL STRUCTURE AND CHANGING ROLES OF
      OLDER PEOPLE IN INDIA
      Sociol. and Soc. Res. 1971, 55, 3, Apr, 297-304
      SA, XX, 3, F4713

494   Dumont, L.

      THE CONCEPTION OF KINGSHIP IN ANCIENT INDIA
      Contrib. Ind. Sociol., 1962, 6, Dec, 48-77
      SA, XIV, 5, C0992

495   Dumont, L.

      THE FUNCTIONAL EQUIVALENTS OF THE INDIVIDUAL IN CASTE SOCIETY
      Contrib. Ind. Sociol. 1965, 8, Oct, 85-99
      SA, XIV, 6, C1921a

496   Dumont, L. and D. Pocock

      KINSHIP
      Contrib. Ind. Sociol. 1957, 1, Apr, 43-64
      SA, XIV, 2-3, B9218

497   Ehrenfels, V.R.

      TOWARDS UNDERSTANDING SOUTH INDIAN SOCIAL STRUCTURE
      in B. Ratnam (ed.) Anthropology on the March
      Madras, Social Science Assoc., 1963, 155-164

498   Epstein, S.

      SOCIAL STRUCTURE AND ENTREPRENEURSHIP
      Int. J. Comp. Sociol, 1964, 5, 2, Sep, 162-165
      SA, XIV, 1, B8607

0508   social organisation

499   Ferreira, J.V.

      THE PROBLEM OF MARATHA TOTEMISM
      Ind. J. Soc. Wrk, 1964, 25, 2, Jul, 135-152
      SA, XIII, 3-4, B5913

500   Ferreira, J.V.

      TOTEMISM IN INDIA
      Bombay, Oxford U. Press, 1965

501   Fik, Richard

      THE SOCIAL ORGANIZATION IN THE NORTH EAST INDIA IN
      BUDDHAS TIME
      Delhi, (1968?)

502   Fox, R.G.

      AVATARS OF INDIAN RESEARCH
      Comp. Studies in Society and Hist. 1970, 12, 1, Jan,59-72
      SA, XIX, 6, F1460

503   Freed, S.A.

      CASTE RANKING AND THE EXCHANGE OF FOOD AND WATER IN A
      NORTH INDIAN VILLAGE
      Anthropological Quart. 1970, 43, 7, Jan, 1-13
      SA, XX, 6, F8153

504   Frykenberg, R.E.

      BRITISH SOCIETY IN GUNTUR DURING THE EARLY NINETEENTH
      CENTURY
      Comp. Stud. Soc. Hist, 1962, 4, 2, Jan, 200-208
      SA, XII, 1, A7987

505   Fuchs, S.

      CLAN ORGANIZATION AMONG THE KORKUS
      J. of As. and Af. Studies, 1966, 1, 3, Jul, 213-219
      SA, XVI, 3, D0642

506   Gandhi, M.K.

      COMMUNAL UNITY
      Ahmedabad: Navajivan pub. house, 1949, 1006 pp.

507   Gangadharan, K.K.

      ASPECTS OF A REGIONAL SOCIOLOGY
      Sociologist, 1956-57, 1, 1, 76-83
      S.A. VIII, 1, 6949

508   Ghosh, D.

      DESCENT AND CLAN AMONG THE DIMASA
      Man in India, 1965, 45, 3, Jul-Sep, 185-194
      S.A. XVI, 5, D2350

509   Goswami, B.B.

      KINSHIP SYSTEM OF THE LUSHAI (ASSAM)
      B. Dept. of Anthropol. 9, 2, 1960

510   Goswami, M.C. and D.N. Majumdar

      CLAN ORGANIZATION AMONG THE GARO OF ASSAM
      Man in India, 1967, 47, 4, Oct-Dec, 249-262
      S.A. XVII, 3, D6835

511   Gough, K.

      CHANGING KINSHIP USAGES IN THE SETTING OF POLITICAL-
      ECONOMIC CHANGE AMONG THE NAYARS OF MALABAR
      J. of Royal Anthrop. Instit. 1952, 82, 71-88

512   Gough, E. Kathleen

      THE SOCIAL STRUCTURE OF A TANJORE VILLAGE
      in Village India, M. Marriott (ed.)
      Chicago, The U. of Chicago Press, 1955, 36-52

513   Gould, Harold A.

      TIME-DIMENSION AND STRUCTURAL CHANGE IN AN INDIAN
      KINSHIP SYSTEM: A PROBLEM OF CONCEPTUAL REFINEMENT
      in Structure and Change in Indian Society
      eds. M.B. Singer and B.S. Cohn, Chicago: Aldine, 1968,
      pp.413-423

514   Gout am, P.

      CIVILISATION ET ECONOMIE PASTORALE (CIVILIZATION AND
      PASTORAL ECONOMY)
      L'Homme 1963, 3, 2, May-Aug, 123-129 (Fr)
      S.A. XII, 5, B0887

515   Haekel, J.

      SOME ASPECTS OF THE SOCIAL LIFE OF THE BHILALA IN
      CENTRAL INDIA
      Ethnol, 1963, 2, 2, Apr, 190-206
      S.A. XII, 3, A9470

516   Hanssen, B.

      FIELDS OF SOCIAL ACTIVITY AND THEIR DYNAMICS
      Transactions of Westermark Society
      1953, 2, 92-133

517   Hartwig, W.

      SOME PROBLEMS PERTAINING TO THE SOCIAL STRUCTURE OF THE
      NAGA IN THE LATE XIX AND EARLY XX CENTURIES
      Sovetshaya Ethnografiya, 1971, 46, 1, Jan-Feb, 54-66 (Russian)
      S.A. XX, 4, F6057

518   Ishwaran, K.

      KINSHIP AND DISTANCE IN RURAL INDIA
      Int. J. Comp. Sociol. 1965, 6, 1, Mar, 81-94
      S.A., XIV, 5, C1001

519   Ishwaran, K.

LINGAYAT KINSHIP
J. of Af. and As. Studies, 1966, 1, 2, Apr, 147-160
S.A., XVI, 3, D0643

520   Jain, S.P.

SOCIAL STRUCTURE OF A HINDU MUSLIM COMMUNITY IN
UTTAR PRADESH
Doct, Panjab U, 1968 (Dr. V.S. D'Souza) (Dept. of Soc.)

521   Jay, E.J.

STRUCTURAL OBSTACLES TO TRIBAL ACCULTURATION: THE
CASE OF REGIONAL CEREMONIAL INTEGRATION IN BASTAR (M.P.)
East. Anthrop, 1965, 18, 3, 159-163
S.A. XIV, 6, B1956

522   Jinwar Das Jain

THE CHANGING PATTERN OF JAIN SOCIAL INSTITUTIONS IN
UTTAR PRADESH (Ph.d.)
Doct, Lucknow U, 1966 (Prof. S.R. Sharma)

523   Joseph, T.

SOCIAL STRUCTURE OF THE HILL TRIBES IN ASSAM
Doct, St., Delhi U., 1969 (R.D. Sanwal)

524   Kapadia, K.M.

HINDU KINSHIP
Bombay: Popular Book Depot, 1947, 320 pp.

525   Kapoor, S.

FAMILY AND KINSHIP GROUPS AMONG THE KHATRIS IN DELHI
Sociol. B. 1965, 14, 21, Sep, 54-63
S.A. XIV, 5, C1002

526 Karve, I.

KINSHIP ORGANIZATION IN INDIA
Poona: Deccan College, 1953, 304 pp.

527 Karve, Irawati

KINSHIP ORGANIZATION IN INDIA (3RD ED.)
Bombay, Asia, 1965

528 Kochar, V.K.

NUCLEAR UNITS IN THE DOMESTIC GROUPS OF A SANTAL VILLAGE
East. Anthrop. 1965, 18, 1, Jan-Apr, 12-21
SA, XIV, 5, C1003

529 Kochar, V.

SOCIAL ORGANIZATION AMONG THE SANTAL
Calcutta, (1968?)

530 Kochar, V.K.

SOCIO-CULTURAL DENOMINATORS OF DOMESTIC LIFE IN
A SANTAL VILLAGE
East. Anthrop. 1963, 16, 3, Sep - Dec, 167-180
S.A. XII, 3-4, B5915

531 Koyano, S.

SOCIAL CHANGE IN PRESENT-DAY INDIA AND ITS CORRESPONDING
PROBLEMS OF SOCIAL STRUCTURE IN MODERN INDIA
Jap. Sociol. R. 1961, 12, 2, 2, Sep, 61-66
S.A., XI, 6, A6346

532 Madan, T.N.

KINSHIP TERMS USED BY THE PANDITS OF KASHMIR, A
PRELIMINARY ANALYSIS
East. Anthrop. 1953, 7, 1, Sep - Nov, 37-46
S.A. vol. II, #4, 715

533   Madan, T.N.

IS THE BRAHMANIC GOTRA A GROUPING OF KIN?
Southw. J. Anthrop. 1962, 18, 1, Apr. 59-75
S.A. XI, 2and 3, A4591

534   Mandelbaum, D.G.

FAMILY,JATI , VILLAGE
in Structure and Change in Indian Society, Chicago: Aldine
ed. B.S. Cohn and M.B. Singer, Chicago, Aldine, 1968, pp.29-51

535   Mandelbaum, D.G.

SOCIAL ORGANIZATION AND PLANNED CULTURE CHANGE IN INDIA
in Rural Sociology in India, ed. A.R. Desai, Bombay,
pp. 693-697

536   Mashruwalla, K.G.

THE HINDU SOCIAL ORDER
in Group Prejudices in India, eds. M.B. Nanavati and
C.N. Vakil, pp. 124-130, Bombay, Vora, 1951

537   Mathur, K.S.

SOME ASPECTS OF SOCIAL ORGANIZATION IN A   MALWA VILLAGE
Agra U. J. of Res. 3, 1955, 100-108

538   McDougal, C.

THE SOCIAL STRUCTURE OF THE HILL JUANG: A PRECIS
Man in India, 1963, 43, 3, Jul-Sep, 183-190
S.A., XII, 7, B2453

539   McDougal, C.

JUANG CATEJONES AND JOKING RELATIONS
Southw. J. Anthropol. 1964, 20, 4, W.N. 319-345
S.A., XIII, 6-7, B7629

0508   social organisation

540   Mehra, J.D.

       SOME ASPECTS OF SOCIAL STRUCTURE IN A GROUP IN TRANSITION
       in Biswas. and Singh (eds.) Aspects of Indian Anthropology
       Delhi, 1966

541   Mencher, J.P.

       KERALA AND MADRAS: A COMPARATIVE STUDY OF ECOLOGY AND
       SOCIAL STRUCTURE
       Ethnol. 1966, 5, 2, April 135-171
       S.A. XV, 1, C3760

542   Misra, J.K.

       THE SOCIO-ECONOMIC CONDITIONS OF SADHUS AND THEIR
       ORGANISATION IN PILGRIMAGE CENTERS IN U.P.
       Doct. St., Agra U, 1969 (R.N. Saksena)

543   Misra, P.K.

       THE NOMADIC GADULIA LOHARS: THEIR REGION OF MOVEMENT
       AND THE COMPOSITION OF A BAND
       East. Anthrop. 1965, 18, 3, Sep-Dec, 165-171
       XIV, 6, C1960

544   Mukherjee, B.

       COMPARATIVE STUDY OF THE KINSHIP SYSTEM OF SIX
       MATRILINEAL TRIBES
       East. Anthrop. 1961, 14 (3), 216-228

545   Mukherjee, B.B.

       DUAL ORGANIZATION AMONG THE URALIS OF TRAVANCORE
       Vanyajati, 1954, 2,4,

546   Mukherjee, P.

       SOME NOTES ON THE STUDY OF THE "WOMAN QUESTION" IN
       ANCIENT INDIA
       Man in India, 1964, 44, 3, Jul-Sep, 264-274
       SA, XIII, 3-4, B5922

0508   social organisation

547   Mukherjee, R.

A NOTE ON THE MEASUREMENT OF KINSHIP DISTANCE
Ind. J. Soc. Res. IV, 1, 12-14
Meerut, India, 1963

548   Nakene, Chie

ECONOMIC AND SOCIAL STRUCTURE OF LEPCHA, BHUTIA OF
CENTRAL SIKKIM
Plural Society - in Sikkim - A Study of the Interrelations
of Lepchas, Bhotias and Nepalis in Caste and Kin in Nepal,
India and Ceylon
ed. C. von Furer-Hoemendorf, Bombay, 1966

549   Narain, V.A.

SOCIAL HISTORY OF MODERN INDIA, 19TH CENTURY
Meerut, 1972

550   Nataraj, P. and S. Murthy

STUDY OF SOCIAL DISTANCE OF COLLEGE GIRLS
Ind. J. Soc. Wrk. 1963, 24, 2, Jul, 103-105
SA. XII, 5, B0893

551   Newell, W.H.

THE SUBMERGED DESCENT LIFE AMONG THE GADDI PEOPLE
OF NORTH INDIA
J. Roy, Anthrop. Inst. G.B. Irel. 1962, 92, 1, Jan-Jun, 13-22
SA, XIV, 6, C1932

552   Norang, G.

HINDU SOCIAL ORGANIZATION
in Group Prejudices in India: eds. M.B. Nanavati and
C.N. Vakil, pp. 130-135, Bombay, Vora, 1951

0508   social organisation

553   Panchanadikar, K.C.

DETERMINANTS OF SOCIAL STRUCTURE AND SOCIAL CHANGE IN INDIA
Sociol. B. 1962, 11, 1-2, Mar-Sep, 14-35
SA, XI, 7, A7182

554   Pandey, S.M.

INTER-UNION RIVALRY IN INDIA: AN ANALYSIS
Jour. of Indust. Rel. 1967, 9, 2, Jul. 140-154
SA, XVI, 5, D2351

555   Prabhu, P.

HINDU SOCIAL ORGANIZATION; A STUDY IN SOCIAL-PSYCHOLOGICAL
AND IDEOLOGICAL FOUNDATIONS (new rev. ed.)
Bombay: Popular Book Depot, 1954, xvii and 393 p.

556   Prabhu, P.H.

HINDU SOCIAL ORGANIZATION
Bombay, 1972

557   Raghuvanshi, V.P.S.

INDIAN SOCIETY IN THE EIGHTEENTH CENTURY
New Delhi, 1969

558   Raha, M.K.

SOCIAL ORGANIZATION OF THE RABHA OF JALPAIGURI,
WEST BENGAL (Ph.d.)
Doct, Calcutta U, 1970 (Dr. M.N. Bose)

559   Ramachandra, Rao, S.K.

SOCIAL INSTITUTIONS AMONG THE HINDUS
Mysore, Rao and Raghavan, 1969, 85 and 1p.

560   Rao, D.V.R.

DOMB KINSHIP TERMS
Man in India, 1968, 48, 2, Apr-Jun, 115-123
SA, XVIII, 1-2, E0928

561   Rao, V.V.

SOCIALISTIC PATTERNS OF SOCIETY
Indian J. Soc. Wrk. 1955, 16, 3, Dec,   163-175
SA VI, 1, 3935

562   Raol, V.K.

SOCIAL ORGANIZATION OF RAJPUTS IN SAURASHTRA (Ph.d.)
Doct, Bombay U., 1969   (Dr. A.R. Desai)

563   Redfield, R.

THE SOCIAL ORGANIZATION OF TRADITION
Far East. Quarterly, 1955, 15, 20-21

564   Rout, S.P.

SOCIAL ORGANIZATION OF THE BHUIYAS OF KOLAHANDI
Adivasi, 1967-68, 91, pp.50-58

565   Roy Burman, B.K.

A NOTE ON THE SCHEDULED CASTES AND SCHEDULED TRIBES
OF WEST BENGAL
Vanyajati, 1956, 4, 2, Apr, 60-72
SA VIII, 1, 6955

566   Sangave, V.A.

CHANGING PATTERNS OF CASTE ORGANIZATION IN KOLHAPUR
Sociol. B. 1962, 11, 1-2, Mar-Sep, 36-61
SA XI, 7, A7184

567   Saraswati, B.

THE INSTITUTION OF PANJI AMONG MAITHIL BRAHMANS
Man in India, 1962, 42, 4, Oct-Dec, 263-276
SA, XII, 6, B1670

0508   social organisation

568   Sarkar, S.S.

      TWO PEDIGREES OF INBREEDING FROM NORTH INDIA
      Man in India, 1967, 47,3, Jul-Sep, 238-243
      SA, XVII, 2, D5815

569   Schneider, D.M. and E.K. Gough (eds.)

      MATRILINEAL KINSHIP
      Berkeley, U. of Calif. Press, 1961

570   Sharma, M.T.

      SOCIAL ORGANIZATION IN A REFUGEE POPULATION (PUNJAB)   (Ph.d.)
      Doct, Bombay U, 1957 (Prof. K.M. Kapadia)

571   Shukla, N.K.

      THE SOCIAL STRUCTURE OF A VILLAGE IN BIHAR (Ph.d.)
      Doct, Ranchi U, 1968, (Dr. L.P. Vidyarthi)

572   Singer, M.

      THE SOCIAL ORGANIZATION OF INDIAN CIVILIZATION
      Diogenes, 1964, 45, 84-119

573 * Singh, Roop

      THE ROLE OF BHAGAT MOVEMENT IN THE INCEPTION OF CASTE
      FEATURES IN THE BHIL TRIBE
      Eastern Anthropologist, 1970, 23, 2, May-Aug, 163-170
      SA, 21, 3, G4065

574   Singh, Y.

      SOCIAL STRUCTURE AND VILLAGE PANCHAYATS
      in Rural Sociology in India, ed. A.R. Desai, Bombay,
      Popular Prakashan, 1969, pp. 570-580

575   Sinha, A.P.

      SOCIAL STRUCTURE OF A PINAR VILLAGE
      Man in India, 1967, 47, 3, Jul-Sep, 189-199
      SA, XVII, 2, D6177

576   Sinha, R.R.

      SOCIAL STRUCTURE OF TRIBAL VILLAGE - A COMPARATIVE
      STUDY OF MUNDA AND ORAON VILLAGES
      Doct. St., Ranchi U, 1969

577   Sircar, D.C.

      STUDIES IN THE SOCIETY AND ADMINISTRATION OF ANCIENT AND
      MEDIEVAL INDIA
      Calcutta, (1968?)

578   Sircar, D.C. (ed.)

      SOCIAL LIFE IN ANCIENT INDIA
      Calcutta, 1971

579   Smith, M.W.

      SOCIAL STRUCTURE IN THE PUNJAB
      in India's Village (M.N. Srimvas, ed)
      Dev. Dept. W. Bengal, 1955, 144-160,

580   Srinivas, M.N.

      THE SOCIAL STRUCTURE OF A MYSORE VILLAGE
      in Srinivas (Ed.) India's Villages
      Bombay: Asia Pub. House, 1956
      also in Village India, ed. M. Marriott, U. of Chicago Press,
      1956, p. 136

581   Srinivas, M.N.

      THE NATURE OF THE PROBLEM OF INDIAN UNITY
      Econ. Wkly, 1958, 10, 17, 26 Apr., 571-577
      SA, VIII, 2, 7375

582   Surendranath, Y.V.

SOCIAL STRUCTURE OF THE BHILS OF RATANMAL (Ph.d.)
Doct, M.S., U. of Baroda, 1956, (Prof. M.N. Srinivas)

583   Sushil Chandra

SOCIOLOGY OF WORK PLANT (ASPECTS OF SOCIAL ORGANIZATION
AND STRUCTURE) (Ph.d.)
Doct, Agra U, 1963

584   Tulja Ram Singh

THE MADIYAS OF TELANGANA - A STUDY OF THEIR STRUCTURE
AND CHANGES (Ph.d.)
Doct, Saugar U, 1963 (Prof. S.C. Dube)

585   Tyler, Stephen A.

KOYA SOCIAL ORGANIZATION: CHANGE AND PERSISTENCE IN
ANDHRA PRADESH
in Change and Continuity in India's Villages
ed. K. Ishwaran, New York, Columbia U. Press, 1970,
pp. 271-291

586   Ulken, H.Z.

LA FEODALITE EST-ELLE UNE CATEGORIE HISTORIQUE OU BIEN
UNE FORME SOCIALE? (IS FEUDALISM A HISTORICAL CATEGORY
OR A SOCIAL FORM?)
Sosyol. Derg. 1955-56, 10/11, 155-162
SA, X, 3, A2204

587   Valunjakar, T.N.

SOCIAL ORGANIZATION AND THE MIGRATION PATTERNS OF
A VILLAGE COMMUNITY (Ph.d.)
Doct, Poona U., 1960 (Dr. Mrs. I. Karve)

588   *Vatuk, Sylvia J.

TRENDS IN NORTH INDIAN URBAN KINSHIP: "THE MATRILINEAL
ASYMMETRY" HYPOTHESIS
South Western Journal of Anthropology, 1971, 27, 3,
Ant. 287-307
SA, 21, 73 G5673

589   Varma, (Miss) P.

         SOCIAL ORGANIZATION OF A NON-TRIBAL
         VILLAGE
         Doct. st, Ranchi U, 1969

590   Vatuk, S.

         REFERENCE, ADDRESS, AND FICTIVE KINSHIP
         IN URBAN NORTH INDIA
         Ethnology, 1969, 8, 3, Jul, 255-272
         SA, XX, 1-2, E7038

591   Wakil, P.A.

         EXPLORATIONS INTO THE KIN-NETWORKS OF THE
         PUNJABI SOCIETY: A PRELIMINARY STATEMENT
         J. of Marriage and the Family, 1970, 32,
         4, Nov. 700-707,
         SA, XX, 1-2, F3523

592   Wakil, P.A.

         ZAT AND QOUM: CONTINUITIES IN THE ANALYSIS
         OF THE PUNJABI SOCIAL STRUCTURE
         Paper presented at the 1971 Annual Meeting
         of the Cdn Sociol. and Anthrop. Association
         SA, X1X, 3, Sup.16, E9337

593   Welty, Paul T.

         SOCIAL LIFE IN INDIA
         in: THE ASIANS: THEIR HERITAGE AND DESTINY,
         P.T.Welty Philadelphia, J.B. Lippincott Co.,
         1962, p.78-81

594   Wiser, W.H.

         THE HINDU JAJMANI SYSTEM (new ed.)
         Ludknow: Lucknow Publishing House 1959

595   -----

         THE DOMS AND THEIR RELATIONS,
         Mysore: Wesley Press, 1953, 680 p.

0500   CULTURE AND SOCIAL STRUCTURE

0513   culture (evolution)

   596   Agrawal, V.S.

         VEDIC FOLKLORE
         Folklore (India), 4, 1-3, 1965

   597   Aiyappan, A.

         IRAVAS AND CULTURAL CHANGE
         Amer. Anthropologist 49, 294-6, April 1947

   598   Aiyappan, A.

         THEORIES OF CULTURE CHANGE AND CULTURE CONTACT
         in J.P. Mills et. al. (ed.) Essays in Anthropology:
         Presented to S.C. Roy
         Lucknow: Maswell and Co., 1948

   599   Avalaskar, S.V.

         SOME NOTES ON SOCIAL LIFE IN NAJAON IN THE EARLY
         NINETEENTH CENTURY
         Ind. Eco. and Social Hist. Review, 1966, 3, 2, Jun, 169-173
         SA, XVII, 1, D5214

   600   Bareh, Hamlet

         THE HISTORY AND CULTURE OF THE KHASI PEOPLE
         Calcutta, (1968?)

   601 *Basham, A.L.

         INDIAN SOCIETY AND THE LEGACY OF THE PAST
         Australian Journal of Politics and History, 1966,
         12, 1, Apr. 131-145
         SA, 21, 73 G2351

   602   Berreman, G.D.

         CULTURAL VARIABILITY AND DRIFT IN THE HIMALAYAN HILLS
         Amer. Anthrop. 1960, 62, 5, Oct, 774-794
         SA, X, 5, A3312

0513   culture (evolution)

603   Bhagwat, Durga

AN OUTLINE OF INDIAN FOLKLORE
Bombay, Popular Book Depot, 1958

604   Bhanu, B.V.

POPULATION DISTANCES - BIOLOGICAL, CULTURAL AND
GEOGRAPHICAL - A STUDY OF EZHAVAS, PULAYAS AND PARAYAS
OF KERALA
Doct. St., Poona U, 1969

605   Bhatnagar, (Miss) M.

ORAL TRADITION AND SOCIETY IN RAJASTHAN - A SOCIOL.
STUDY OF FOLK SONGS IN SELECTED REGIONS
Doct. St., Rajasthan U, 1969

606   Bhattacharya, Asutosh

THE CULTS OF THE DEIFIED DEAD IN BENGAL
Indian Folklore, 1956, 2, 26, 46

607   Bhattacharya, A.

STUDY OF FOLKLORE IN BENGAL
1959, 293-97

608   Bhattacharya, A.

BASIS OF BENGALI FOLK CULTURE
Folklore (India), 1960, 1, 26-46

609   Biswas, K.

FOLK LIFE AND CULTURE OF RANGPUR (BASED ON THE LOCAL
DIALECT) (D. Phil)
Doct, Calcutta U, 1956

0513   culture (evolution)

610   Bogue, P.

      THE WORLD DIRECTIONS IN GREECE, INDIA, AND MESO-AMERICA
      Wisconsin Sociologist, 1966-67, 1&2, Win, 1-10
      SA, XVI, 3, D0649

611   *Bose, Nirmal Kumar

      SOME ASPECTS OF INDIAN CIVILIZATION
      Man in India, 1971, 51, 1, Jan-Mar, 1-14
      SA, 21, 73 G3208

612   Bose, N.K.

      INTEGRATION OF TRIBES IN ANDHRA PRADESH
      Man in India, 1964, 44, 2, Apr-Jun, 98-104
      SA, XIII, 1, B4111

613   Bose, N.K.

      CULTURAL RELATIVISM
      Man in India, 1969, 49, 1, Jan-Mar, 1-90
      SA, XVIII, 6, E4599

614   Bose, N.K.

      EXPERIENCES IN CULTURAL ENQUIRIES
      Man in India, 52, 3, 1972, 201-212

615   Bose, N.K.

      CULTURAL ZONES OF INDIA
      Geo. Rev. of India, 17, 4, 1956

616   Bose, N.K.

      CULTURE AND SOCIETY IN INDIA
      Bombay, Asia Pub. House, 1967

617   Brown, W.N.

      CLASS AND CULTURAL TRADITIONS IN INDIA
      Traditional India: Structure and Change
      Journal of American Folklore, 71, 281, 1958, 241-245

0513   culture (evolution)

618   Capener, H.R.

TRADITIONALISM AND THE DEVELOPMENT OF HUMAN RESOURCES
Civilisations, 1968, 18, 4, 544-550
SA, XVIII, 6, E4601

619   Carstairs, G.M.

ATTITUDES TO DEATH AND SUICIDE IN AN INDIAN
CULTURE SETTING
Int. J. Soc. Psychiat. 1955, 1, 3, Win, 33-42
SA, XV, 4, C5621

620   Chakrabarti, D.K.

ORIGIN OF AHAR CULTURE
Man in India, 1968, 48, 2, Apr-Jun, 97-105
SA, XVIII, 1-2, E0929

621   Chandewarkar, Puskar

FOLKLORE A UNIFYING FORCE
Folklore (India), 1962, 3, 229-232

622   Chatterji, S.K.

THE INDIAN SYNTHESIS, AND RACIAL AND CULTURE INTERMIXTURE
IN INDIA. PRESIDENTIAL ADDRESS, ALL INDIAN ORIENTAL
CONFERENCE, 17TH SESSION, 1953
Ahmedabad: R.C. Parikh, 1953,
also in: Indo-Asian Cult, 3 (1,2) 56pp.,

623   Chatterji, S.K., B.L. Atreya, A. Danielow

INDIAN CULTURE
Delhi, Universal Book and Stationery Co., 1966,
viii - 110-1p.

624   Chattopadhyaya, G.

SOME RECENT CHANGES IN TRIBAL AND RURAL CULTURE IN
MIDDLE EASTERN INDIA (D. Phil.)
Doct., Calcutta U, 1960 (Prof. T.C. Das)

0513   culture (evolution)

625   Chattopadhyaya, K.P.

CULTURE CONTACT AND CHANGES IN THE VEDIC AGE
Proceedings of the 4th International Congress of
Anthropological and Ethnological Sciences, Vienna, 1952

626   Chattopadhyaya, Sudhalar

TRADITIONAL VALUES IN INDIAN LIFE
New Delhi: India International Center, 1961, iii, 46 pp.

627   Chaube, Ramngrile

SCOPE OF HINDU FOLKLORE
J. of the Royal Asiatic Society of Bengal, 1969, 178-80

628   Chaudhari, H.N.

FOLKLORE RESEARCH IN INDIA: SOME IDEAS AND ATTITUDES
Folklore (India), 1964, 5, 178-80

629   Choudhury, N.C.

CULTURAL TYPES AND LEVELS OF INDIAN TRIBAL SOCIETIES:
THE TRIBES OF CHOTANAGPUR
Proceedings of Summer School in Anthropology,
Darjeeling; Anthrop. Survey of India, Calcutta, 1966

630   Cohn, B.

THE PASTS OF AN INDIAN VILLAGE
Comp. Stud. Soc. Hist. 1961, 3, 3, 241-249
SA. XI, 7, A7262

631   Coulborn, R.

THE ORIGIN OF CIVILIZED SOCIETIES
Princeton, N.J.:   Princeton U. Press, 1959, x and 200 pp.
SA. VII, 4, 6366

0513 culture (evolution)

632 Das, Kunj Behari

     A STUDY OF ORRISAN FOLKLORE
     Vishwa Bharati, 1953

633 Das, K.B.

     A GLIMPSE OF ONYA FOLKLORE
     Indian Folklore, 1959, 38-46

634 Datta, K.K.

     A SURVEY OF INDIA'S SOCIAL LIFE AND ECONOMIC CONDITIONS
     IN THE 18TH CENTURY
     Calcutta, (1968?)

635 Datta, K.

     SOCIO-CULTURAL BACKGROUND OF MODERN INDIA
     Meeru t, 1972

636 Datta-Majumdar, N.

     ONGE CULTURE IN TRANSITION
     B. of the Inst. of Traditional Culture
     Madras, 1957

637 Desai, B.L.

     FOLKLORE FROM SOUTH GUJARAT
     Folklore (India), 1961, 49-55

638 Desai, N.Y.

     ANCIENT INDIAN SOCIETY, RELIGION AND MYTHOLOGY AS
     DEPICTED IN THE MARKANDEYA-PURANA
     Baroda, Faculty of Arts, 1968

639 Dhar, J.

     THE ESSENCE OF INDIAN CULTURE
     Careers and Courses 4, 9, Sept. 1952, 804-806 and 811

0513   culture (evolution)

640   Dole, E.G. and B.L. Carneiro

      ESSAYS IN THE SCIENCE OF CULTURE
      New York, Thomas Y. Crowell Co., 1960, viii and 509 pp.
      SA, XII, 7, B2456

641   Doshi, J.K.

      SOCIAL STRUCTURE AND CULTURAL CHANGE IN A BHIL VILLAGE (Ph.d.)
      Doct, Saugar U, 1970, (Dr. Mrs) L. Dube)

642   Doshi, S.P.

      BHILS: BETWEEN SOCIETAL SELF AWARENESS AND CULTURAL
      SYNTHESIS
      New Delhi; Sterling Publishers, 1971, pp. vii and 248

643   Doshi, S.L.

      CHANGING PATTERN OF BHIL LIFE IN CULTURE CHANGE (Ph.d.)
      Doct, Rajasthan U, 1963 (Dr. R.N. Saxena)

644   D'Souza, L. (ed.)

      KONKANI LOVE
      Bombay, Konkani Life, 1955, 1-2

645   Dua, Shiva

      SOCIAL CONDITIONS IN NORTHERN INDIA IN THE SECOND HALF
      OF THE 19TH CENTURY, WITH SPECIAL REFERENCE TO THE
      POSITION OF WOMEN (Ph.d.)
      Doct, Delhi U., 1966 (Dr. B. Prasad)

646 *Dubey, K.C.

      ON THE BISON-HORN MARIA PHRATRIES, CLANS, AND TOTEMS
      Eastern Anthropologist, 1969, 22, 3, Sept-Dec, 371-376
      SA, 21, 73 G0640

0513   culture (evolution)

647   Dutta, Bhupendranath

AN INTRODUCTION TO INDIAN FOLK CULTURE
Indian Folklore, 1958, 277-286
(Presidential Address at Caife Allahabad)

648   Dyer, D.T.

HUMAN PROBLEMS IN AN INDIAN CULTURE
Family Coordinator 18, 4, Oct., 1969, 322-325

649 *Elder, J.W. (ed.)

CHAPTERS IN INDIAN CIVILIZATION
Dubuque, Kendall/Hunt, 1970, 1974

650 *Elder, J.W. (ed.)

LECTURES IN INDIAN CIVILIZATION
Dubuque, Kendall/Hunt, 1970, 1974

651   Epstein, Scarlett

A SOCIOLOGICAL ANALYSIS OF WITCH BELIEFS IN A
MYSORE VILLAGE
East. Anthrop., 1959, 234-457

652   Fernandes, (Miss) B.V.

THE FISHERFOLK OF KERALA: A SOCIAL CULTURAL STUDY
Doct. St., Bombay U, 1969 (Dr. J.V. Ferriera)

653   Foster, G.M.

WHAT IS FOLK CULTURE
Amer. Anthrop., 1953, 55, 2, 152-173

654   Fuimoli, P.M.

CHAMAR COMMUNITY OF MAHARASHTRA: A SOCIAL AND
CULTURAL STUDY
Doct. St., Poona, 1969

0513   culture (evolution)

655   Ganapathy, B.D.

KODAVAS (COORGS), THEIR CUSTOMS AND CULTURE
Mercara, Kodag, 1967, xii and 224 - 1 p.

656   Gautam, V.S.

ASPECTS OF INDIAN SOCIETY AND ECONOMY IN THE 19TH CENTURY
Delhi, 1972

657   Ghosh, A.K.

STUDIES IN THE PALEOTITHIE CULTURE OF SINGBHUM (D.Phil.)
Doct, Calcutta U, 1965 (Prof. D. Sen)

658   Ghosh, K.L.

THE INDIAN WAY
New Delhi, (1968?)

659   Gopal Krishnan, M.S.

HINDU CULTURAL PATTERN
J. of Madras U., 1957, 29, 1

660   Goswami, Prafulladatta

WOMEN IN ASSAMI FOLKLORE
Folklore (India), 1963, 9, 2

661   Gough, E. Kathleen

CULTS OF THE DEAD AMONG THE NAYARS
in Traditional India: Structure and Change
eds. M.B. Singer, 1959, p. 240-273
Phil: Amer. Folklore Society

662   Ginsburg, N.S. (ed.)

THE PATTERN OF ASIA
Englewood Cliffs, N.J.: Prentice-Hall, 1958, 929 pp.

0513   culture (evolution)

663   Goyal, R.N.

CULTURAL AND ECONOMIC BACKGROUND OF PILGRIMAGE IN
VRAJ BHUMI (Ph.d.)
Doct, Agra U, 1968 (Dr. R.N. Saxena)

664   Gumperz, J.J.

SPEECH VARIATION AND THE STUDY OF INDIAN CIVILIZATION
Amer. Anthrop. 1961, 63, 5, Oct. 976-988
SA. XI, 4, A5195

665   Gupta, D.K.

SOCIETY AND CULTURE IN THE TIME OF DANDIN
Delhi, 1972

666   Gupta, (Mrs.) R.

CULTURE OF A SACRED TOWN: A SOCIOLOGICAL STUDY
OF NOTHDWARA
Doct. St., Rajasthan U, 1969

667   Guttal, Chandrika

FOLKLORE OF KARNATAK
Man in India, 1957, 27-30

668   Ikram, S.M.

MUSLIM CIVILIZATION IN INDIA
New York, Columbia U. Press, 1964

669   Ingalls, D.

THE BRAHMIN TRADITION
Traditional India: Structure and Change, Journal of
Amer. Folklore, 71, 281, 1958, 209-215

0513 culture (evolution)

670 Jha, M.

THE SACRED COMPLEX IN JANAHPUR - AN APPROACH TO THE
STUDY OF HINDU CIVILIZATION (Ph.d.)
Doct, Ranchi U, 1969 (Dr. L.P. Vidyarthi)

671 *Jha, Makhan

SPIRIT POSSESSION AMONG THE MAITHIL BRAHMINS
Eastern Anthropologist, 1969, 22, 3, Sept-Dec., 361-368
SA, 21, 73 G0641

672 Jha, Y.

SOCIAL HISTORY OF MITHILA FROM 14TH TO THE 16TH
CENTURY (Ph.d.)
Doct, Patna U, 1970, (Dr. J.C. Jha)

673 Jindal, (Mrs.) R.

CULTURE OF A SACRED TOWN - A SOCIOLOGICAL STUDY OF
NATHDWARA (Ph.d.)
Doct, Rajasthan U, 1970 (Dr. R.N. Saxena)

674 Kabiraj, Sib Narayan

FERTILITY CULT AND TREES
Folklore (India), 1965, 6

675 Kant, R.

THE MATRIX OF BHOKSA CULTURE (A STUDY IN CULTURAL
DYNAMICS OF THE BHOKSAS OF BHABHAR, DISTRICT NARNITAL)
Doct. St. Lucknow U, 1969

676 Kanwar, H.I.S.

FOLKLORE OF KHASIS OF ASSAM
Indian Folklore, 1959, 206-12

0513   culture (evolution)

677   Karve, Iravati

SOME STUDIES IN THE MAKING OF A CULTURE PATTERN
in J.P. Mills (ed.) Essays in Anthropology Presented
to S.C. Roy, Lucknow, 1948, p.206-214

678   Karve, I.

THE CULTURAL PROCESS IN INDIA
Society in India, 1956, 29-48 (ed. A. Aiyappan and
L.K. Balartnam)

679   Karve, I.

INDIA AS A CULTURAL REGION
in T. Madan and   G. Sarana (eds.) Indian Anthropology,
Bombay; Asia Pub. House, 1962

680   King, Arden, A.

A NOTE ON EMERGENT FOLK CULTURES AND WORLD CULTURAL
CHANGE
Social Forces, 31, 1953, 234-237

681   Koppar, D.H.

SOCIAL AND ECONOMIC CONDITIONS UNDER HOYSALAS (Ph.d.)
Doct, Karnatak U, 1958 (Prof. R.S. Panchamukhi)

682   Kroeber, A.L.

CULTURE GROUPINGS IN ASIA
Southwestern J. of Anthrop. V.3, 1947, p.322-330

683   Kurup, C.P.D.

THE EVOLUTION OF SOVIET SOCIETY (Ph.d.)
Doct, Bombay U, 1956 (Prof. K.M. Kapadia)

684   Lal, B.B.

A DELUGE? WHICH DELUGE? YET ANOTHER FACET OF THE PROBLEM
OF THE COPPER HOARD CULTURE.
Amer. Anthropologist, 1968, 70, 5, Oct, 857-863
SA, XVII, 6, D9316

0513   culture (evolution)

685   Lal, B.

CULTURE CONFIGURATION OF THE BHARS OF EASTERN U.P.
Doct. St., Agra U, 1969 (R.N. Saksena)

686   Lannoy, R.

THE SPEAKING TREE: A STUDY OF INDIAN CULTURE AND SOCIETY
New York: Oxford U. Press, 1971, xxvi, 466 pp.

687   Lesser, A.

SOCIAL FIELDS AND THE EVOLUTION OF SOCIETY
S.W. J. of Anthrop., 1961, 17, 1, 40-48

688   Lewis, O.

PEASANT CULTURE IN INDIA AND MEXICO: A STUDY
IN CONTRASTS
Transact. New York Acad. Sci. Series II, 16, 4, 1954, 219-223

689   Luschinsky, M.S.

PROBLEMS OF CULTURE CHANGE IN THE INDIAN VILLAGE
Hum. Org. 1963, 22, 1, Spr, 66-74
SA, XII, 5, B0907

690   Madigan, F.C.

STRUCTURAL CHANGE AND CULTURE CONFLICTS IN INDIA
Phillippine Sociol. R. 1958, 6, 2, Apr, 1-9
SA, XIII, 1, B4114

691   Mahadevan, I.

BELIEF SYSTEMS IN FOOD OF THE TELUGU-SPEAKING PEOPLE
OF THE TELENGANA REGION
Ind. J. Soc. W., 1961, 21, 4, Mar, 387-396
SA. XI, 7, A7269

0513   culture (evolution)

692   Maity, P.K.

A NOTE ON THE SNAKE CULTURE IN ANCIENT INDIA
Folklore (India), 1963, 120-129

693   Majumdar, D.N.

MATRIX OF INDIAN CULTURE
Lucknow: Universal Publishers, 1947

694   Majumdar, D.N.

ACCULTURATION AMONG THE HAJONG OF MEGHALAYA
Man in India, 52, 1, 1972, 46-64

695   Majumdar, D.N.

A STUDY OF CULTURE - CHANGE AMONG THE GAROS OF
MATCHAKOLGIRI AND WAJADAGIN VILLAGES (Ph.d.)
Doct, Gauhati U, 1968 (Prof. M.C. Goswami)

696   Majumdar, Satyendra Narayan

FOLKLORE OF THE LAPCHAS
Folklore (India), 1961, 294-97

697   Malik, S.C.

INDIAN CIVILIZATION: THE FORMATIVE PERIOD
Simla, Ind. Inst. Advanced Studies, 1969

698   Malinowski, B.

A SCIENTIFIC THEORY OF CULTURE AND OTHER ESSAYS
London, Oxford U. Press, 1960

699   Marriot, M. (ed.)

CULTURAL POLICY IN THE NEW STATES
in Old Societies and New States, (ed.) Geertz -
Glencoe, The Free Press, 1963

0513   culture (evolution)

700   Masani, R.P.

     FOLK CULTURE REFLECTED IN NAMES
     Bombay, Popular Prakashan, 1966

701   Mayor, A.C.

     LAND AND SOCIETY IN MALABAR
     New York; Oxford University Press, 1952, 158p.

702 *Mies, Maria

     KULTURANOMIE ALS FOLGE DER WESTLICHEN BILDUNG -
     DARGESTELLT AM BEISPIEL DES INDISCHEN ERZIEHUNGSSYSTEMS
     (ANOMIE OF CULTURE AS A RESULT OF WESTERN EDUCATION
     AS EXEMPLIFIED BY INDIA'S SYSTEM OF EDUCATION)
     Dritte Welt, 1972, 1, 1, 23-38 (Ger)
     SA, 21, 73 G0624

703 *Misra, P.K.

     REHABILITATION OF NOMADS: A REVIEW
     Eastern Anthropologist, 1969, 22, 3, Sept-Dec 307-315
     SA, 21, 73 G0646

704 *Misra, V.D.

     CHALCOLITHIC CULTURES IN EASTERN INDIA
     Eastern Anthropologist, 1970, 23, 3, Sept-Dec. 243-259
     SA, 21, 73 G4077

705   Mitra, Ashok

     A SURVEY OF FAIRS AND FESTIVALS OF WEST BENGAL
     Indian Folklore, 1959, 121-128

706   Moore, C.A.

     PHILOSOPHY AND CULTURE EAST AND WEST: EAST-WEST
     PHILOSOPHY IN PRACTICAL PERSPECTIVE
     Honolulu, Hawaii: U. of Hawaii Press, 1962, viii and 832 pp.
     SA, XIII, V, B6824

0513   culture (evolution)

707   Motwani, K.

        INDIA: A CONFLICT OF CULTURES
        Bombay; Thacker, 1947, 99 pp.

708   Mukerjee, R.

        VALUES IN SOCIAL SCIENCE - CHAPTER IN A NEW SURVEY OF
        SOCIAL SCIENCES
        B.M. Varma (ed.)
        London: Asia Publishing, 1962, 248 pp.
        SA, XIII, 5, B6825

709   Mukerjee, Radhakamal

        THE CULTURE AND ART OF INDIA
        New York: Frederick A. Praeger, 1959, 447 pp.
        SA, VII, 4, 6576

710   Mukerjee, R.

        SOCIOLOGY AND FOLKLORE
        Souvenir of All India Conference, Calcutta, 1964, 15-17

711   Muherji, D.P.

        DIVERSITIES
        New Delhi - People's Pub. House, 1958

712   Nandi, R.N.

        SOCIAL AND RELIGIOUS DEVELOPMENTS IN DECCAR (AD 600-1000)
        (Ph.d.)
         Doct, Patna U, 1970 (Prof. R.S. Sharma)

713   Navlakha, S.K.

        THE SOCIETY AND CULTURE OF THE BHILS OF NORTH EASTERN
        BANSWARA
        (Rajasthan) (D. Phil)
        Doct., Calcutta U., 1961 (Late) Prof. K.P. Chattopadhyaya

0513   culture (evolution)

714   Nitsure, K.G.

      CRITICAL STUDY OF THE PROVISION FOR WELFARE ACTIVITIES
      IN THE MARATHA EMPIRE (Ph.d.)
      Doct, Poona U., 1964 (Dr. D.R. Garde)

715   Noble, Marg. G.

      THE WEB OF INDIAN LIFE
      Mayavati, Almora, Advaita Ashrama, 1950, pp. 324, xii

716   Opler, M.E.

      PARTICULARIZATION AND GENERALIZATION AS PROCESSES
      IN RITUAL AND CULTURE
      in Religion in South Asia, ed. E.B. Harper
      Seattle: U. of Washington, 1966, p. 83-89

717   Opler, M.K.

      CULTURE AND MENTAL HEALTH
      New York, MacMillan Co, 1959, xxi and 533 pp.
      SA X, 6, A3828

718   Orans, Martin

      A TRIBAL PEOPLE IN AN INDUSTRIAL SETTING
      in Traditional India: Structure and Change
      eds. M.B. Singer, Philadelphia, Amer. Folklore Society,
      1959, pp. 216-240

719   Pandey, R.B.

      STRUCTURAL **EVOLUTION** OF THE INDIAN SOCIETY
      J. Banaras Hindu U, 2, 1, 952-53, p. 53-66

720   Pantalu, G.R.

      FOLKLORE OF THE TELUGUS
      Madras,1965

0513 culture (evolution)

721 Patnaik, N.

A COMPARATIVE ANALYSIS OF THE ECONOMIC ASPECT OF
MUNDA CULTURE
Geographical Review of India, V. 15, 1953, p. 29-43

722 Prasad, R., G.C. Hallen and K. Paihah (eds.)

CONSPECTUS OF INDIAN SOCIETY
Satish Book Enterprise, 1971, xvi, 608 pp.

723 Rajhanathan, N.

REASON AND INTUITION IN INDIAN CULTURE
Madras, U. of Madras, 1969, 86 pp.

724 Raghuvanshi, V.P.

INDIAN SOCIETY IN THE EIGHTEENTH CENTURY
Verry, 1969

725 Rao, D.L.P.

PROBLEMS OF CULTURAL CONTACT AMONG THE SAMANTHOS
Doct. St. Andhra U, 1969, (Prof. N.S. Reddy) (Dept. of Anthrop)

726 Rao, D.V.R.

CULTURAL CHANGE AMONG KONDA DORAS
Doct. St. Andhra U, 1969 (Prof. N.S. Reddy) (Dept. of Anthrop)

727 Rao, M.S.A.

CHANGING PATTERN OF CULTURE IN MALAYALAM REGION (Ph.d.)
Doct, Bombay U, 1953 (Prof. G.S. Ghurye)

728 Rao, S.

CULTURE AND MENTAL DISORDER: A STUDY IN AN INDIAN MENTAL
HOSPITAL
Int. J. Soc. Psychiat. 1966, 12, 2, Spr, 139-148
SA, XV, 7, C8105

0513 culture (evolution)

729 Rashid, A.

SOCIETY AND CULTURE IN MEDIEVAL INDIA
Verry, 1969

730 Ray, N.R.

SOME OUTSIDE ELEMENTS IN INDIAN CULTURE
Indo-Asian Cult, 4, 2, Oct, 1955, p.167-174

731 Ray, P.C.

THE LODHA AND THEIR SPIRIT POSSESSED MEN: A
PSYCHOSOCIO-CULTURAL STUDY
Anthrop. Survey of India, Calcutta, 1965

732 Redfield, R.

THE NATURAL HISTORY OF FOLK SOCIETY
Soc. Forces, 1953, 31, 224

733 Redfield, R.

PEASANT SOCIETY AND CULTURE
Chicago, U. of Chicago Press, 1956

734 Redfield, Marg. P. (ed.)

HUMAN NATURE AND THE STUDY OF SOCIETY: THE PAPERS
OF R. REDFIELD
Chicago, The University of Chicago Press, 1962

735 REGIONAL MEETING OF EXPERTS ON TRADITIONAL CULTURES IN
SOUTH-EAST ASIA
Madras, 1958. International Seminar on Traditional
Cultures in South-East Asia
Bombay; Orient Longmans, 1960, 202 pp.

736 Roy, S.

ASPECTS OF PADAM - MINYONG CULTURES
Shillong, The Adviser, NEFA, 1960

0513   culture (evolution)

737   Sachchidananda

      CULTURE CHANGE IN TRIBAL BIHAR
      Calcutta: Bookland Private Ltd, 1964

738   Sachachidananda

      PROFILES OF TRIBAL CULTURE IN BIHAR
      Calcutta, (1968?)

739   Sahu, L.N.

      THE FOLKLORE OF ORISSA AND NILGIRI HILLS
      Folklore (India), 1960, pp. 158-159

740   Saika, Padma Dhar

      STUDIES IN DELFA CULTURE AND RELIGIOUS LIFE
      Gauhati Dept. of Tribal Culture and Folklore Res.
      Gauhati U, 1964

741   Saiyidain, K.G.

      THE CONFLICT BETWEEN CULTURE AND PREJUDICE
      in Group Prejudices in India
      eds. M.B. Nanavati and C.N. Vakil, p. 25-34
      Bombay, Vora, 1951

742   Saran, (Mrs.) S.D.

      SOCIAL HISTORY OF BIHAR IN THE FIRST HALF OF THE
      11TH CENTURY (Ph.d.)
      Doct, Patna U, 1970 (Dr. V.A. Narain)

743   Saraswati, B.N.

      CULTURAL RE-INTEGRATION OF LADAKH
      Presented in a Seminar on Tribal Situation in India
      Simla, I.I.A.S., 1969

0513   culture (evolution)

744   Sareen, (Mrs.) S.

      SOME ASPECTS OF SOCIAL AND CULTURAL LIFE OF THE
      PEOPLE OF NORTHERN INDIA IN THE SECOND HALF OF THE
      16TH CENTURY (D. Phil.)
      Doct, Allahabad U, 1970 (Prof. L. Shankar)

745   Sarkar, S.S.

      SOME CULTURAL PARALLELS AMONG AUSTRALOIDS
      Man in India, 1958, 38, 4, Oct.-Dec. 296-300
      SA, VIII, 2, 7643

746   Sastug, V.N.V.K.

      KOYAS - A STUDY IN CULTURAL TRANSITION
      Doct. St., Andhra U, 1969 (Prof. N.S. Reddy)
      (Dept. of Anthrop.)

747   Sen, B.

      THE KHAMPTIS: AN OUTLINE OF THEIR CULTURE
      Man in India, 1965, 45, 3, Jul-Sep, 237-243
      SA, XVI, 5, D2362

748   Sen, Gopinath

      FOLKLORE MOVEMENT AROUND THE WORLD
      Indian Folklore, 1956-57, 57

749   Sen, Indra

      TRADITIONAL CULTURE AND INDUSTRIALIZATION IN SOUTH INDIA
      Bombay, Orient Longman, 1958

750   Sengupta, K.N.

      SOME ASPECTS OF ASSIMILATION OF CULTURAL TRAITS BY
      THE MOHALIS OF MIDNAPUR
      J. of Soc. Res. 1966, 9, 2, 91-103

0513   culture (evolution)

751   Sengupta, S.

TRAIN IN INDIAN LIFE AND LOVE
Calcutta, 1963

752   Sengupta, S.

A SURVEY OF FOLKLORE STUDY IN BENGAL
Calcutta, 1967

753   Shaikh, (Miss) A.M.H.

MUSLIM WOMEN IN POONA: A CULTURAL STUDY
Doct. St., Poona U, 1969

754   Sharma, B.N.

SOCIAL LIFE IN NORTHERN INDIA, 600 A.D. TO 1000 A.D. (Ph.d.)
Doct, Delhi U, 1962

755   Sharma, L.L.

STRUCTURAL CONTINUITY IN THE FACE OF CULTURAL CHANGE
East Anthrop 1969, 22, 2, May-Aug, 177-186
SA, XX, 3, F4741

756   Sharma, R.S.

LIGHT ON EARLY INDIAN SOCIETY AND ECONOMY
Paragon, 1966

757   Sharma, T.C.

THE CONTRIBUTION OF THE INDO-MONGOLOIDS IN THE
FORMATION OF ASSAMESE CULTURE
Abstract of Papers, 28th Int'l. Congress of Orientalists
Canberra, 1971

758   Shashtri, I.C.

TWO PHASES OF INDIAN CULTURE
Int. R. Hist. Polit. Sci, 1966, 3, 1, Jun, 41-48
SA, XV, 4, C5649

759 Shreevastava, M.P.

CULTURE AND ECONOMY
Sociol. B. 1963, 12, 1, Mar, 66-71
SA, XI, 7, A7271

760 Shrivastava, R.P.

THE CULTURAL PATTERN AMONG THE BHOTIA (Ph.d.)
Doct., Saugar U, 1958 (Prof. S.C. Dube)

761 Singer, M.

THE CULTURAL PATTERN OF INDIAN CIVILIZATION: A
PRELIMINARY REPORT OF THE METHODOLOGICAL FIELD STUDY
Far East. Quart., 1955, 15, 1

762 Singh, B.P.

A VIEW ON THE KOLS OF MIRZAPUR
Ind. Sociol. B. 1965, 7, 2, Jan. 92-97
SA, XIV, 4, C0128

763 *Singh, Banvir

POLITICAL ORGANISATION OF A NORTH INDIAN TRIBE
Eastern Anthropologist, 1969, 22, 3, Sept-Dec. 317-325
SA, 21, 73 G0651

764 Singh, T.P.

SOME IMPRESSIONS ON INDIAN AND FILIPINO VALUE SYSTEMS
Phillippine Sociological Review, 1965, 13, 4, Oct, 210-214
SA, XVII, 2, D5826

765 Singh, Yogendra

A NOTE ON CULTURAL INTEGRATION ON TRIBAL SOCIETY IN INDIA
Tribe, 1968, 2, 1-3, 13-16

0513   culture (evolution)

766   Singh, Yogendra

CHANUKHERA: CULTURAL CHANGE IN EASTERN UTTAR PRADESH
in Change and Continuity in India's Villages
ed. K. Ishwaran, New York, Columbia U. Press, 1970
pp. 241-271

767   Sinha, (Mrs.) A.

SANTHAL OF SANIBAL PARGANAS (BIHAR):   A STUDY IN
CULTURAL CHANGES
Doct. St. Bhagalpur U. (Prof. I. Prasad)

768   Sinha, D.P.

THE ROLE OF PHARIYA IN TRIBAL ACCULTURATION IN A
CENTRAL INDIAN MARKET
Ethnol. 1963, 2, 2, Apr, 170-180
SA, XII, 3, A9497

769   Sinha, D.P.

CULTURE CHANGE IN AN INTER-TRIBAL MARKET
Bombay, Asia Pub. House, 1968

770   Sinha, S.

EVOLUTIONISM RECONSIDERED
Man in India, 1955, 35, 1, 1-18

771   Sinha, Surajit

TRIBAL CULTURES OF PENINSULAR INDIA AS A DIMENSION
OF THE LITTLE TRADITION: A PRELIMINARY STÀTEMENT
ed. M.B. Singer, in Traditional India: Structure and
Change, Philadelphia, American Folklore Society, 1959
pp. 298-313

772   Sivaramamurti, C.

SOME ASPECTS OF INDIAN CULTURE
Delhi, 1969

0513   culture (evolution)

773   Spear, Thomas G.P.

THE NABALS: A STUDY OF THE SOCIAL LIFE OF THE
ENGLISH IN 18TH CENTURY INDIA
London: Oxford U. Press, 1963, 213 p.

774   Srivastava, S.K.

SOME PROBLEMS OF CULTURE CONTACTS AMONG THE THARUS
East. Anthrop., 1949, 3, 1, 36-39

775   Srivastava, S.K.

THARUS: A STUDY OF CULTURAL DYNAMICS
Agra U. Press, 1958

776   Srivastava, S.L.

FOLK CULTURE AND ORAL TRADITION - A COMPARATIVE STUDY
OF REGIONS IN RAJASTHAN AND EASTERN U.P. (Ph.d.)
Doct, Rajasthan U, 1969 (Dr. D. Deva)

777   Suri, (Mrs.) Pushpa

THE SOCIAL CONDITIONS IN NORTHERN INDIA DURING THE FIRST
HALF OF THE EIGHTEENTH CENTURY (Ph.d.)
Doct, Delhi U., 1968 (Dr. F. Singh)

778   Tamil Culture

TUTICORIN, SOUTH INDIA: THE TAMIL SOCIETY,
V.1 - 1952 - A Quarterly Review dedicated to the Study
of Tamiliana

779   Tandon, (Mrs.) S.D.

CHANGING ATTITUDES AND CULTURE PATTERNS AMONG EDUCATED
EARNING WOMEN IN UTTAR PRADESH (Ph.d.)
Doct. Agra U, 1959

0513   culture (evolution)

780   Thakur, V.T.

SINDHI CULTURE
Bombay: U. of Bombay Press, 1959

781   Tod, James

ANNALS AND ANTIQUITIES OF RAJASTHAN OR THE CENTRAL
AND THE WESTERN RAJPUT STATES IN INDIA
(2 vols.)
London, Routledge and Kegan Paul, 1950

782   Tod, James

ANNALS AND ANTIQUITIES OF RAJASTHAN
London; Routledge and Kegan Paul, 1960

783   Unnithan, T.K.N., Deva, Indra, and Singh. Yogendra

TOWARDS A SOCIOLOGY OF CULTURE FOR INDIA
New Delhi, Prentice-Hall of India, 1965

784   Vibhawati, (Miss)

SOME ASPECTS OF CULTURAL LIFE AS DEPICTED IN VISHNUDHA-
RMOTTARA PURANA, ESPECIALLY II AND III KHANDAS (Ph.d.)
Doct., Banaras Hindu U, 1970 (Dr. A.K. Narain)

785   Vidyarthi, L.P.

CULTURAL CHANGE IN THE TRIBES OF MODERN INDIA
J. of Social Res. 1968, II, 1, Mar, 1-36
SA, XVIII, 3, E1834

786   Vidyarthi, L.P.

CULTURAL CONTOURS OF TRIBAL BIHAR
Calcutta, Punthi Pustak, 1964

787   Vyas, K.C.

RENASCENT INDIA (Ph.d.)
Doct., Bombay U, 1948, (Prof. G.S. Ghurye)

0513　culture (evolution)

788　Vyas, R.P.

ROLE OF NOBILITY IN MARWAR 1800 - 1873 A.D.
New Delhi, Jain Bros, 1969 XV and 266 p.

789　Wagle, N.

SOCIETY AT THE TIME OF THE BUDDHA
Bombay: Popular Prakashan, 1966, viii and 314 p.

790　Wiser, W.H. and C.M.

BEHIND MUD WALLS, 1930 - 1960
Berkeley, Calif. U. Press, 1963

791　Yash, Pal

A CULTURAL STUDY OF THE EARLY PALI TRIPIT HAKAS(Ph.d.)
Doct, Delhi U, 1967

792

INDIA: A SYNTHESIS OF CULTURES
Bombay: Thacker, 1947, 319 pp.

0500 <u>CULTURE AND SOCIAL STRUCTURE</u>

0514 social anthropology (& ethnology)

    793   Abbi, B.L. and S. Saberwal (eds.)

           URGENT RESEARCH IN SOCIAL ANTHROPOLOGY
           Simla, Indian Instit. of Advanced Studies, 1969
           Transactions #10

    794   Agrawal, B.C.

           DIKSHA CEREMONY IN JAINISM: AN ANALYSIS OF ITS SOCIO-
           POLITICAL RAMIFICATIONS
           East. Anthrop. 25, 1, Jan-Apr. 1972, 13-21

    795   Ahuja, R.

           THE SOCIAL STUDY OF BHILS OF RAJASTHAN (Ph.d.)
           Doct., Agra U, 1962

    796   Aiyappan, A.

           URGENT ANTHROPOLOGY FOR SOUTHERN INDIA
           in B. Abbi and S. Sabarwal (eds.) Urgent Research in
           Social Anthropology
           Simla, Indian Inst. of Advanced Study, 1969, pp. 34-40

    797   *Alexander, C. Alex and M.K. Shivaswamy

           TRADITIONAL HEALERS IN A REGION OF MYSORE
           Social Science and Medicine,1971, 5, 6, Dec. 595-601
           SA, 21, 73 G2361

    798   Amir, Hasan

           THE KOLS OF PATHA
           Allahabad, 1972

    799   Anantha Krishna, I, and R. Krishna

           THE COORG TRIBES AND CASTES
           Madras; Gordon Press, 1948, 74 pp.

0514   social anthropology (& ethnology)

800   Arga, S.P.

       A SOCIOLOGICAL STUDY OF FOLK-LORE IN WESTERN UTTAR
       PRADESH (LINGUISTIC REGION - KURU PRADESH) (Ph.d.)
       Doct., Agra U, 1969 (Dr. Rajeshwar)

801   Ashraf, K.M.

       LIFE AND CONDITION OF THE PEOPLE OF HINDUSTAN
       New Delhi; Munashiram Manoharlal, 1970

802   Baghel, B.S.

       THE KORWAS - A STUDY IN SOCIAL DYNAMICS (Ph.d.)
       Doct, Jabalpur University, 1970 (Dr. D. Chandra)

803   Bailey, F.G.

       TRIBE, CASTE AND NATION
       Bombay, Oxford U. Press, 1960

804   Bailey, F.G.

       THE SCOPE OF SOCIAL ANTHROPOLOGY IN THE STUDY OF
       INDIAN SOCIETY
       in T.N. Madan and G. Sarana(eds.) Indian Anthropology:
       Essays in Memory of D.N. Majumbar
       Bombay; Asia Pub. House, 1962

805   Balaratnam, L.K.

       SOCIETY IN INDIA
       Madras, Soc. Sci. Assoc., 1958

806   Balaratnam, L.K.

       ANTHROPOLOGY ON THE MARCH
       Madras; The Book Center, 1963

807   Barkaraki, S.

       TRIBES OF ASSAM
       New Delhi, 1969

0514   social anthropology (& ethnology)

808   Barnouw, Victor

      THE CHANGING CHARACTER OF A HINDU FESTIVAL
      Amer. Anthrop., 1954, 56, 1, Feb., 74-85
      SA, Vol. II, #3, 561

809   Bandhopadhyay, B.N.

      CEREMONIAL FRIENDSHIP AMONG THE BHUMJI OF MANBHUM
      Man in India, 1955, 35, 4, Oct.-Dec. 274-286
      SA VI, 1, 144

810   Beals, A.R.

      CONFLICT AND INTERLOCAL FESTIVALS IN A SOUTH
      INDIAN REGION
      in Religion in South Asia, ed. E.B. Harper
      Seattle; U. of Washington,1964, pp. 99-115

811   Bernatzih, H.A.A. and Miao

      PROBLEMS OF APPLIED ETHNOGRAPHY IN NORTHERN INDIA
      Behaviour Science Translations Ser., HRAFP, 1971

812   Berreman, G.D.

      BEHIND MANY MASKS: ETHNOGRAPHY AND IMPRESSION
      MANAGEMENT IN A HIMALYAN VILLAGE
      Ithaca, N.Y.: Society for Applied Anthrop. Monograph
      No. 4, 1962, 24 pp.
      SA XV, 3, C4846

813   Berreman, G.D.

      URGENT ANTHROPOLOGY IN INDIA
      in B. Abbi and S. Sabarwal (ed.) Urgent Researches in
      Social Anthropology
      Simla, Ind. Inst. of Advanced Study, 1969

814   Berreman, G.D.

    HINDUS OF THE HIMALAYAS: ETHNOGRAPHY AND CHANGE
    (rev. ed.)
    Berkeley and Los Angeles: U. of Calif. Press
    1972, lvii and 440 pp.

815   Bhaduri, T.C.

    CHAMBAL; THE VALLEY OF TERROR
    Delhi, 1972

816   Bhagbati, Ananda

    ANTHROPOLOGICAL RESEARCHES IN ASSAM REGION
    in B. Abbi and S. Sabarwal (eds.) Urgent Researches in
    Social Anthropology,
    Simla, Ind. Inst. Adv. Stud., 1969

817   Bhagbati, Ananda and P.K. Bhowmick

    THE LODHAS OF WEST BENGAL: A SOCIO-ECONOMIC STUDY
    Calcutta; Punthi Pusak, 1963

818   Bhatt, B.J.

    RAJ-KHEDRAL BRAHMINS OF GUJARAT   (Ph.d.)
    Doct, Bombay U. 1949 (Dr. N.A. Thoothi)

819   Bhatt, G.S.

    SOCIOLOGY AND ANTHROPOLOGY IN INDIA AND THE WEST
    J. of Soc. Res. 7(1-2) Mar.-Sept. 64, 143-152

820   Bhatt, S.K.

    THE BHILS OF PIPLIPADA VILLAGE
    Ind. Sociol. 1961, 3, 4, Mar, 30-32
    SA, XIII, 1, B4119

0514   social anthropology (& ethnology)

821   Bhowmik, P.K.

      THE LODHAS OF MIDNAPUR (D. Phil.)
      Doct, Calcutta U, 1959 (Prof. N.K. Bose)

822   Bhowmik, P.K.

      THE LODHAS OF WEST BENGAL
      Varanasi, 1963

823   Bigaria, (Miss) S.D.

      GUJARS OF KASHMIR (Ph.d.)
      Doct, St, Agra U, 1969 (Dr. R.N. Saxena)

824   Biswas, P.C.

      THE SANTAL
      Delhi, Bhartiya Adimjati Sevak Sangh, 1956

825   Biswas, P.C.

      THE SANTAL
      Delhi, Bharatiya Adim Jati Sevak Sangh, 1966

826   Bose, A.B.

      PASTORAL NOMADISM IN INDIA: NATURE, PROBLEMS
      AND PROSPECTS
      Ind. J. Soc. Wrk. 1968, 28, 4, Jan, 399-410
      SA, XVII, 5, D8304

827   Bose, A.B. and N.S. Jodha

      SOME OBSERVATIONS ON FACTORS INFLUENCING SETTLEMENT
      OF HOUSEHOLDS
      Man in India, 1967, 47, 4, Oct-Dec, 272-278
      SA, XVII, 3, D6852

828 *Bose, N.K.

    LAND-MAN RATIO IN TRIBAL AREAS
    Man in India, 1971, 51, 4, Oct-Dec. 267-273
    SA, 21, 73 G3223

829 *Bose, N.K.

    BIJAY CHANDRA MAZUMDAR LECTURES 1969 SCHEDULED CASTES
    AND TRIBES: THEIR PRESENT CONDITION
    Man in India, 1970, 50, 4, Oct-Dec. 319-349
    SA, 21, 73 G3222

830   Bose, N.K.

    CULTURAL ANTHROPOLOGY AND OTHER ESSAYS
    Calcutta; Indian Associated Publishing, 1953, 289 pp.

831   Bose, N.K.

    THE HINDU METHOD OF TRIBAL ABSORPTION
    in Bose, N.K., Cultural Anthropology and Other Essays
    Calcutta; 1953, pp. 45-64

832   Bose, N.K.

    RESEARCHES IN INDIAN ANTHROPOLOGY
    Man in India, 1962, 42, 3, Jul-Sep. 175-180
    SA XII, 5, B0915

833   Bose, N.K.

    THE TRIBAL SITUATION
    Man in India, 1969, 49, 3, Jul-Sep, 217-223
    SA, XIX, 4, E9618

834   Bose, N.K.

    TRIBAL LIFE IN INDIA
    Verry, 1972

835   Bose, S.

    LAND AND PEOPLE OF THE DHAULIGANGA VALLEY
    Man in India, 1962, 42, 4, Oct-Dec, 292-304
    SA, XII, 6, B1685

836   Bose, S.

    THE BHOT OF NORTHERN SIKKIM
    Man in India, 966, 46, 2, Apr-Jun, 164-171
    SA, XVI, 6, D3154

837   Bower, U.G.

    NAGA PATH
    London: Murray, 1950, 260 pp.

838   Bower, U.G.

    THE HIDDEN LAND; MISSION TO A FAR CORNER OF INDIA
    London; Murray, 1953, 244 pp.

839   Bunker, M.L.

    A SOCIOLOGICAL STUDY OF KORKU TRIBES IN MADHYA PRADESH (Ph.d.
    Doct. St., Agra U, 1969 (Dr. R.N. Saxena)

840   Burling, Robbins

    RENGANG IRI (A GARO VILLAGE)
    Philadelphia, U. of Pennsylvania Press, 1963

841   Carstairs, G.M.

    DARU AND BHANG CULTURAL FACTORS IN THE CHOICE OF INTOXICANT
    Quart. J. Stud. Alcohol, 1954, 15, 2, Jun, 220-237
    SA, II, #4, 853

842   Carstairs, M.

    THE BHILS OF KOTRA BHOMET
    East. Anthrop., 1954, 7, 3/4, Mar-Aug. 169-181
    SA, III, #3, 1657

843   Census of India

ONAM FESTIVAL
Census of India, Kerala; 1961

844   Census of India

THE SIDDIS, A NEGROID TRIBE OF GUJARAT
Census of India; 1961, 1968, 5

845   Census of India

THE SCHEDULED TRIBES OF MAHARASHTRA
Census of India, 1961, 1970, 8 (Part V)

846   Chambard, J.

LA POTHI DU JAGA OU LE REGISTRE SECRET D'UN GENEALOGISTE
DE VILLAGE EN INDE CENTRALE (THE POTHI OF JAGA, OR THE
SECRET REGISTER OF A VILLAGE GENEOLOGIST IN CENTRAL INDIA)
L'Homme, 1963, 3, 1, Jan-Apr. 5-85 (Fr.)
SA, XII, 5, B0917

847   Chanda, R.P.

INDO-ARYAN RACES
Calcutta, (1968?)

848   Chapekar, L.N.

THAKURS: AN ETHNIC STUDY (Ph.d.)
Doct, Bombay U, 1949 (Prof. G.S. Ghurye)

849   Chapekar, L.N.

THE THAKURS OF SAHADRI
Bombay, Oxford U. Press, 1960

850   Chattopadhyaya, S.

SOCIAL LIFE IN ANCIENT INDIA
Longman, 1972

0514 social anthropology (& ethnology)

851 Chauhan, B.R.

     TRIBALISATION
     Tribe, 1966, 2, 1-2

852 Chekki, D.A.

     THE STUDY OF KINSHIP IN ANTHROPOLOGY
     J. of the Karnatak U., Humanities and Social Sciences, 1962

853 Chopra, P.N.

     SOME ASPECTS OF SOCIAL LIFE DURING THE MUGHAL AGE
     1526 - 1707
     Verry, 1963

854 Chowdhury, J.N.

     HILL MIRIS OF SUBANSIRI
     Shillong, 1971

855 Chowdhury, P.C. Roy and K.D. Prasad

     THE RAHARIAS
     Man in India, 1964, 44, 2, Apr-Jun, 132-145
     SA, XIII, 1, B4120

856 Cohn, B.C.

     INDIA: THE SOCIAL ANTHROPOLOGY OF A CIVILIZATION
     Englewood Cliffs, Prentice-Hall, 1971
     C.B.I. 75, 3

857 Culshaw, W.J.

     THE SANTALS OF WEST BENGAL
     Man, 1947, 47, 103

858 Culshaw, W.J.

     TRIBAL HERITAGE: A STUDY OF THE SANTALS
     London; Butterworth Press, 1949, 211 pp.

0514   social anthropology (& ethnology)

859   Dalal, F.M.

      THE SOCIAL LIFE AND MANNERS OF THE PARSIS IN IRAN
      AND IN INDIA (Ph.d.)
      Doct, Bombay U, 1949 (Dr. N.A. Thoothi)

860 *Danda, S.N.

      ECONOMY AND SOCIETY AMONG THE FISHERMEN OF COASTAL ORISSA
      Man in India, 1971, 51, 2, Apr-Jun, 121-129
      SA, 21, 73 G3225

861   Das, A.K.

      THE KORAS AND SOME LITTLE KNOWN COMMUNITY OF WEST BENGAL
      Calcutta, Cultural Res. Inst., Gov't of West Bengal, 1964

862   Das, A.K.

      THE TOTOS
      Calcutta, Cultural Res. Inst., Gov't. of West Bengal, 1969

863   Das, A.K. and S.K. Banerjee

      THE LEPCHAS OF DARJEELING DISTRICT
      Calcutta, Cultural Res. Inst., Gov't. of W. Bengal, 1962

864   Das, A.K. and M.K. Raha

      THE ORAONS OF SUNDERBAN
      Calcutta, Cult. Res. Inst. Gov't of W. Bengal, 1963

865   Das, A.K., M.K. Raha and B.K. Roy Choudhary

      THE MALAPAHARIAS OF WEST BENGAL
      Calcutta, Cult, Res. Inst., Gov't of W. Bengal, 1966

866   Das, A.K., M.K. Raha, and B.K. Roy Choudhary

      HANDBOOK ON SCHEDULED CASTES AND TRIBES OF WEST BENGAL
      Calcutta, Cult. Res. Inst., Gov't of W. Bengal, 1966

867   Das, D.

      THE VANISHING MAHARAJAS
      Intl. Pubns. Serv.

868   Datta-Majumdar, N.

      REPLY TO "VILLAGE NOTES FROM BENGAL; BASED ON A COURSE
      IN ETHNOLOGICAL FIELD TECHNIQUES"
      by M.W. Smith in Amer. Anthropologist 4, 574-92, Oct.'46
      Amer. Anthrop. 49, 334-7, April 1947

869   Dave, P.C.

      THE GRASIAS
      Delhi, Bhartiya Adimiak Sevak Sangh, 1960

870   Dhir, D.N.

      TRIBES OF THE NORTH WESTERN BORDER OF INDIA
      Read in the Seminar on Tribal Situation in India
      Simla, Ind. Inst. of Advanced Study, 1969

871   Dua, V.

      SOCIAL ORGANIZATION OF THE ARYA SAMAJ; A STUDY OF
      TWO LOCAL ARYA CENTERS IN JULLUNDUR
      Sociol. B. 1970, 19, 1, Mar, 32-50
      SA, XIX, 4, E9622

872   Dube, B.K. and F. Bahadur

      A STUDY OF THE TRIBAL PEOPLE AND TRIBAL ARCAS OF
      MADHYA PRADESH
      Indore; Gov't. Reg. Press (M.P.), 1967

873   Dube, S.C.

      THE KAMAR
      Lucknow: Universal Publishers, 1951, 216 pp.

0514   social anthropology (& ethnology)

874   Dube, S.C.

SOCIAL ANTHROPOLOGY IN INDIA
in T.N. Madan & G. Sarna (eds.) Indian Anthropology,
Essays in Memory of D.N. Majumdar
Bombay; Asia Pub. House, 1962

875   Dube, S.C.

THE URGENT TASK OF ANTHROPOLOGY IN INDIA
Proceedings of the IVth Int'l. Congress of Anthrop.
and Ethnological Congress, Vienna, 1952, 1956, pp.273-275

876   Ehrenfels, V.R.

ABORIGINAL WOMANHOOD AND CULTURE CONTACT
East. Anthrop. 3, 1, 48-54, 1949

877   Ehrenfels, V.R.

ANTHROPOLOGY AND TRADITIONAL CULTURE
Ind. J. Soc. Wrk. 1958-59, 19, 4, 323-324

878   Ehrenfels, O.R.L.W.

KADAR OF COCHIN
Madras; University of Madras, 1952, 319 pp.

879   Elwin, V.

BONDO HIGHLANDER
Bombay, Oxford University Press, 1950, 290 pp.

880   Elwin, Verrier

THE BEAUTY OF TRIBAL ASSAM
Folklore (India), 1961

881   Elwin, V.

THE MURIA AND THEIR GHOTUL
Bombay, Oxford University Press, 1947, 730 p.

882 Finni, P.P.M.

A STUDY OF THE PALLIYOR OF KALTAYAM DISTRICT
Doct. St., Indore, (Abraham)

883 Fox, R.G.

'PROFESSIONAL PRIMITIVES': HUNTERS AND GATHERERS OF
NUCLEAR SOUTH ASIA
Man in India, 1969, 48, 2, Apr-Jun, 139-160
SA, XIX, 3, E8441

884 Fox, R.G.

KIN, CLAN, RAJA AND RULE
Berkeley, Univ. of Calif. Press, 1971

885 Freed, S.A.

FICTIVE KINSHIP IN A NORTH INDIAN VILLAGE
Ethnol. 1963, 2, 1, Jan, 86-103
SA, XII, 2, A8792

886 Freed, R.S. and S.A. Freed

UTILITARIAN POTTERY MANUFACTURE IN A NORTH INDIAN VILLAGE
Anthrop. Quart. 1963, 36, 1, Jan, 34-42
SA, XII, 6, B1689

887 Freed, R.S. and S.A. Freed

CALENDARS, CEREMONIES AND FESTIVALS IN A NORTH INDIAN
VILLAGE: NECESSARY CALENDRIC INFORMATION FOR FIELDWORK
Southw. J. Anthrop. 1964, 20, 1, Spr. 67-90
SA, XII, 6, B1690

888 Freed, R.S. and S.A. Freed

UNITY IN DIVERSITY IN THE CELEBRATION OF CATTLE: CURING
RITES IN A NORTH INDIAN VILLAGE: A STUDY IN THE RESOLUTION
OF CONFLICT
Amer. Anthrop. 1966, 68, 3, Jun, 673-692
SA, XV, 3, C4849

0514   social anthropology (& ethnology)

   889   Frykenberg, R.E. (ed.)

         LAND CONTROL AND SOCIAL STRUCTURE IN INDIAN HISTORY
         Madison , U. of Wisconsin Press, 1969

   890   Fuchs, S.

         THE CHILDREN OF HARI; A STUDY OF THE NIMAR BALAHIS
         Vienna: V. Herold, 1950, 463 pp. (Wiener Beitrage zur
         Kultur Geschichte und Linguistik, v.8)

   891   Fuchs, S.

         THE SCAVENGERS OF THE NIMAR DISTRICT IN MADHYA PRADESH
         Journal of the Bombay Branch of the Royal Asiatic
         Society, 27, 1, 1951, 86-98

   892   Fuchs, S.

         ANTHROPOLOGICAL RESEARCH PROBLEMS IN INDIA
         Int. Soc. Sci, Bull, 1957, 9, 3, 341-351
         SA, VIII, 2, 7636

   893   Fuchs, S.

         THE GOND AND BHUMIA OF EASTERN MANDLA
         Bombay, Asia Pub. House, 1960

   894   Furer - Haimendorf, Von C.

         EXPLORATION IN THE EASTERN HIMALAYAS
         Shillong; Assam Gov't Press, 1947

   895   Furer - Haimendorf, Von C.

         THE RAJ GONDS OF ADILABAD: A PEASANT CULTURE OF DECCAN
         London; MacMillan and Co., 1948

   896   Furer - Haimendorf, Von C.

         THE PARDHANS: THE BARDS OF THE RAJ GONDS
         Eastern Anthrop. V. 4, 1951, pp.172-84

897   Furer - Haimendorf, Von C.

THE CULT OF AYAK AMONG THE KOLAMS OF HYDERABAD
Wenner Beitrazur Kulturgeschichte und Linguistic,
1952, 9, p. 108-123

898   Furer - Haimendorf, Von C.

HIMALAYAN BARBARY
London; John Murray, 1955

899   Furer - Haimendorf, Von C.

PROBLEMS AND PROSPECTS OF INDIAN ANTHROPOLOGY
Man in India, 1958, 29, 147-168

890   Furer - Haimendorf, Von C.

THE APA TANIS AND THEIR NEIGHBOURS: A PRIMITIVE
CIVILIZATION OF THE EASTERN HIMALAYA
London; Routledge and Kegan Paul, 1962

891   Gamini, Paul

ANTHROPOLOGY AND TRIBAL ADMINISTRATION
Vanyajati, 1957, 5, 1

892   Ghosh, D.

POST-FUNERAL RITUAL IN A DIMASA KACHARI VILLAGE
Man in India, 1964, 44, 3, Jul-Sep, 247-251
SA, XIII, 3-4, B5939

893   Ghurye, G.S.

THE TEACHING OF SOCIOLOGY, SOCIAL PSYCHOLOGY AND
SOCIAL ANTHROPOLOGY
Delhi, Unesco Pub.; Universal Publishers, 1956

0514 social anthropology (& ethnology)

894 Ghurye, G.S.

THE MAHADEO KOLIS
Bombay, Popular Book Depot, 1957, pp.267

895 Ghurye, G.S.

MAHADEO KOLIS
Bombay: Popular Book Depot, 1959

896 Ghurye, G.S.

ANTHROPO-SOCIOLOGICAL PAPERS
New York, Humanities, 1963

897 Ghurye, G.S.

ANTHROPO-SOCIOLOGICAL PAPERS
Varansi, (1968?)

898 Gnanamble, K.

THE MAGICAL RITES OF URALIS (AGRICULTURE, PUBERTY,
PREGNANCY AND CURING OF DISEASES)
B. of the Dept. of Anthrop., 1955, 4, 2

899 Gnanamble, K.

FUNERAL CUSTOMS OF URALI
B. of the Dept. of Anthrop., 1955, 4, 2

900 Goheen, J.

A COMMENT ON PROFESSOR SINGER'S "CULTURAL VALUES ON
INDIA'S ECONOMIC DEVELOPMENT"
Econ. Dev. Cult. Change, 1958, 7, 1, Oct, 1-12
SA, XI, 5, A5776

0514   social anthropology (& ethnology)

901   Gondal, R.P.

      CHANGES IN CUSTOMS AND PRACTICES AMONG SOME LOWER
      AGRICULTURAL CASTES OF KOTAH STATE
      East. Anthrop, 1948, 1, 4, 21-28

902   Gopala - Krishna, M.S.

      THE CULT OF MOTHER GODDESS
      in Balaratnam (ed.) Anthropology on the March
      Madras, Soc. Sci. Assoc., 1963, pp. 334-351

903   Gopalkrishnan, M.S.

      THE NAMBUDIRIES (THE SOCIO-RELIGIOUS ARISTOCRACY OF
      THE MALABAR COAST (Ph.d.)
      Doct, Madras U, 1967 (Dr. A. Aiyappar)

904   Gorer, Geoffrey

      HIMALAYAN VILLAGE; AN ACCOUNT OF THE LEPCHAS OF SIKKIM
      (2nd ed.)
      New York, Basic, 1967

905   Goswami, B.B.

      THE TRIBES OF ASSAM: A FEW COMMENTS ON THEIR SOCIAL
      AND CULTURAL TIES WITH THE NON-TRIBES
      (Read in the Seminar on Tribal Situation in India, Inst.
      of Advanced Study, Simla), 1969

906   Goswami, M.C.

      TRIBE - PEASANT RELATIONSHIP
      in Rathimmitra and B.D. Gupta (eds.) Assam - A Common
      Perspective for North-East India
      Pannalal Das Gupta, 1967

907   Gov't. of India

      SCHEDULED AREAS AND SCHEDULED TRIBES
      New Delhi, 1963

0514   social anthropology (& ethnology)

908   Gov't. of India

HILL AREAS COMMISSION
New Delhi, 1966

909   Grigson, W.V.

THE MARIA GONDS OF BASTAR
London; Oxford University Press, 1949, 427 pp.

910   Guha, B.S. (ed.)

TRIBES IN INDIA
New Delhi, Bharatiya Adimjati Sevak Sangh, 1950

911   Guha, B.S.

INDIAN ABORIGINES AND WHO THEY ARE
Adivasis, 1955

912   Guha, U.

THE FOREST DWELLERS
Man in India, 1965, 45, 3, Jul-Sep, 228-232
SA, XVI, 5, D2372

913   Gulati, R.K.

PONGAL: A DEEPLY TRADITION-ORIENTED FESTIVAL OF THE SOUTH
J. Soc. Res. 1968, 11, 2, Sep, 150-154
SA, XVIII, 6, E4615

914   Gupta, (Mrs.) L.S.

A SOCIO-GEOGRAPHICAL STUDY OF A HILL RESORT, WITH
SPECIAL REFERENCE TO NAINI TAL (Ph.d.)
Doct, Agra U, 1962

915   Harper, E.B.

FEAR AND THE STATUS OF WOMEN
Southwestern J. of Anthrop. 1969, 25; 1, Spr, 81-95
SA, XVIII, 6, E4616

0514   social anthropology (& ethnology)

916   Hasan, K.A. and B.G. Prasad

      A NOTE ON THE CONTRIBUTION OF ANTHROPOLOGY TO
      MEDICAL SCIENCES
      Ind. J. of Medical Assoc. 1959   33, 182-190

917   Hermanns, M.

      STUDY OF MAGIC: BHARWA SYSTEM
      1952

918   Herzfeld, Regina Flannery

      SOME RECENT ANTHROPOLOGICAL PUBLICATIONS ON INDIA
      AND AFRICA
      Anthrop. Quart, 1963, 36, 2, Apr, 71-73
      SA, XII, 6, B1693

919   Hitrec, J.G.

      SON OF THE MOON
      New York: Harper Brothers, 1948, 383 pp.

920   Hockings, P.

      ON GIVING SALT TO BUFFALOES: RITUAL AS COMMUNICATION
      Ethnology, 1968, 7, 4, Oct, 417-426
      SA, XVII, 6, D9327

921   Hodgson, B.H.

      THE ABORIGINES OF THE EASTERN FRONTIER
      J. of the Royal Asiatic Society of Bengal, 1948,
      18, Part II, 967-975

922   Hoffman, J.

      ENCYCLOPAEDIA MUNDARICA
      Gov't. Printing Press, Patna, 1950

0514   social anthropology (& ethnology)

923   Hussain, S.K.M.

KOYAS
Man in India, 1951,31, 1, 33-39

924   Iyer, L.A. Krishna

KERALA AND HER PEOPLE
Palghat, The Education Supplies Depot, 1961

925   Iyer, L.A.K. and L.K. Balaratnam

THE COORG TRIBES AND CASTES
Madras, Gordon Press, Madras, 1948

926   Jaiswal, L.H.

STUDY OF THE ECONOMY OF ORAON TRIBES IN MADHYA PRADESH (Ph.d.)
Doct, Vikram U,1968 (Dr.A.C. Minocha)

927   Jay, E.J.

STRUCTURAL OBSTACLES TO TRIBAL ACCULTURATION: THE
CASE OF REGIONAL CEREMONIAL INTEGRATION IN BASTAR (M.P.)
East. Anthrop, 1965, 18, 3, 159-163
SA, XIV, 6, B1956

928   Jay, E.J.

A CASE OF ABSENCE OF CONFLICT.   THE HILL MARIA GONDS
OF BASTAR
Man in India, 1965, 45, 4, Oct-Dec, 275-283
SA, XVI, 5, D2376

929   Jay, E.J.

RELIGIOUS AND CONVIVIAL USES OF ALCOHOL IN A GOND
VILLAGE OF MIDDLE INDIA
Quart. J. Stud. Alcoh. 1966, 27, 1, Mar, 88-96
SA, XIV, 7, C2842

930   Jay, Ed. J.

THE ANTHROPOLOGISTS AND TRIBAL WELFARE
HILL MARIAS - A CASE STUDY (M.P.)
in Vidyarthi (ed.) Anthropology and Tribal Welfare
in India, 1968

931   Jha, M.

DEATH - RITES AMONG MAITHIL BRAHMANS
Man in India, 1966, 46, 3, Jul-Sep, 241-247
SA, XVI, 6, D3161

932   Jha, U.

PANJI AND PANJIKARS OF MITHILA (Ph.d.)
Doct, Bihar U, 1965 (Dr. S. Nand)

933   Johari, P.C.

TRIBAL ECONOMY OF KUMAON (Ph.d.)
Doct, Agra U., 1965

934   Kapadia, K.M. (ed.)

PROFESSOR GHURYE FELICITATION VOLUME,
Bombay; Popular Book Depot, 1954

935   Kapfo, Weprenyi

CHAIRMAN'S ADDRESS IN THE 3RD SUMMER SCHOOL ON SOCIOLOGY
ON NEFA, KOHIMA, APRIL 7-14, 1970
Sociology of North Eastern Areas, Proceedings of the
Third Summer School; U. of Delhi, 1970

936   Kapoor, D.

THE PEOPLE OF KINNAUR - AN ESSAY IN THE PROBLEM OF TRIBES
(Presented in the Seminar on Tribal Situation in India,
Ind. Inst. Advance. Stud.), Simla, 1969

937   Kapoor, D. and S.R.K. Chopra

ETHNIC AND CULTURAL UNITS OF LAHAUL
(presented in the Seminar on Tribal Situation in India,
Ind. Inst. of Advanc. Study), Simla, 1969

938   Karan, P.K. and W.M. Jenkins

THE HIMALAYAN KINGDOMS: BHUTAN SIKKIM AND NEPAL
New York, D. Van Norstand and Co., 1963

939   Karve, D.G.

INDIA'S CULTURAL VALUES AND ECONOMIC DEVELOPMENT:
A DISCUSSION, COMMENTS
Econ. Dev. Cult. Change, 1958, 7, 1, Oct, 7-9
SA, XI, 5, A5779

940   Karve, Irawati

BHILS OF WESTERN KHANDESH
J. of Anthrop. Soc. of Bombay, 1958

941   Karve, Irawati

THE TRIBALS OF MAHARASHTRA
in B. Abbi and S. Sabarwal (eds.) Urgent Research in
Social Anthrop. in India, Inst. of Advanced Study, Simla, 1959

942   Karve, I.

HINDU SOCIETY; AN INTERPRETATION
Poona, Deccan College, 1961, 171 pp.

943   Khan, P.M. and V.K.R. Manchirajlu

THE BAIDS OF ANDHRA PRADESH
Man in India, 1966, 46, 7, Jan-Mar, 14-32
SA, XVI, 6, D3811

944   Khare, R.S.

RITUAL PURITY AND POLLUTIONS RELATING TO DOMESTIC
SITUATION
East. Anthrop, 1962, 15, 2, 125-139
SA, XIII, 1, B4743

945   Khare, R.S.

DOMESTIC SANITATION IN A NORTH INDIAN VILLAGE - AN
ANTHROPOLOGICAL STUDY (Ph.d.)
Doct, Lucknow U, 1962 (Dr. T.N. Madan)

946   Kochar, V.K.

OBJECTIFICATION OF RESEARCH PROCESS IN SOCIAL ANTHROPOLOGY
Ind. J. of Social Wrk, 1967, 27, 4, Jan, 387-392
SA, XVI, 6, D3164

947   Kochar, V.K.

THE GREAT ANDAMESE TODAY
Man in India, 1969, 49, 3, Jul-Sep, 247-252
SA, XIX, 4, E9631

948   Koppar, D.H.

PARJAN AMONG THE DHODIAS
East. Anthrop., 1956, 9, 3&4, Mar-Aug, 191-195
SA, VI, 1, 4148

949   Koppers, W.

DIE BHIL IN ZENTRALINDIEN (THE BHILS OF CENTRAL INDIA)
Horn: F. Berger, 1948, 353 pp.

950   Kumar, G.

THE ETHNIC AFFINITIES OF THE RAJBANSIS OF NORTH BENGAL
(D.Phil.) Doct, Calcutta U, 1969

0514   social anthropology (& ethnology)

951   Leuva, K.K.

      THE ASUR: A STUDY OF PRIMITIVE IRON SMELTERS
      New Delhi, Bharatiya Adimjati Sevak Sangh, 1963

952   Luiz, A.A.D.

      TRIBES OF KERALA
      New Delhi, Bharatiya Adimjati Sevak Sangh, 1962

953   Lyall, Sir Charles

      THE MIKIRS
      Gauhati, (1968?)

954   Madan, T.N.

      URGENT RESEARCH IN SOCIAL ANTHROPOLOGY IN KASHMIR
      in B. Abbi and S. Sabarwal (eds.) Urgent Research in
      Social Anthrop., Simla, Indian Inst. Advanced Stud., 1959

955   MacNaughton, A.

      FOREIGN MISSIONS AND THEIR WORK AMONG TRIBAL PEOPLES
      Indian J. Soc. Wrk., 1953, 14, 3, Dec. 276-281
      SA, Vol. II, #4, 855

956   Madan, T.N.; Sarana, G. (eds.)

      INDIAN ANTHROPOLOGY
      Bombay, Asia, 1965

957   Mahapatra, L.K.

      THE DAPHALA AND MIJI SOCIETY: A PRELIMINARY ECOLOGICAL
      ANALYSIS
      Sociologus, 1962, 12, 2, 58-167

958   Majumdar, D.N.

      ANTHROPOLOGY UNDER CLASS
      J. of Anthrop. Society of Bombay, 1950

959   Majumdar, D.N.

      THE AFFAIRS OF A TRIBE
      Lucknow; Ethnographic and Folk-Culture Society, U.P.,
      Universal Publishers, 1950, 367 pp.

960   Majumdar, D.N.

      RACE REALITIES IN CULTURAL GUJARAT; REPORT ON THE
      ANTHROPOMENTRIC, SEREOLOGICAL AND HEALTH SURVEY OF
      MAHA GUJARAT
      Bombay; Gujarat Research Society, 1950, 87 pp.

961   Majumdar, D.N.

      TRIBAL ECONOMY OF THE CIS-HIMALAYAS
      Ind. J. Soc. Wrk, 1953, 14, 3, Dec, 263-275
      SA, II, #4, 856

962   Majumdar, D.N.

      SPECIAL REPORT ON THE TEACHING OF SOCIAL ANTHROPOLOGY
      in The Teaching of Social Sciences in India,
      Delhi, UNESCO, 1956

963   Majumdar, D.N.

      LINEAGE STRUCTURE IN A HIMALAYAN SOCIETY, HIMALAYAN
      DISTRICT
      Int. J. Compar. Sociol. 1960, 1, 1, Mar, 17-42
      SA, XI, 7, A7282

964   Majumdar, D.N. and T.N. Madan

      AN INTRODUCTION TO SOCIAL ANTHROPOLOGY,
      New York, Asia Publishing House, 1960, 304 pp.
      SA, IX, 2, 9811

965   Mandelbaum, D.G.

      SOCIAL USES OF FUNERAL RITES
      East. Anthrop., 1958-59, 12

966   Mandelbaum, D.G.

      SOCIETY IN INDIA (2 vols.)
      Berkeley, Univ. of Calif. Press, 1970

967   Mann, R.S.

      SOCIAL PROBLEMS IN TRIBAL INTEGRATION
      Khadi Gramodyog, 1966, 12, 4, 304-307
      SA, XVII, 2, D5838

968   Mann, R.S.

      'SOCIAL CHANGE AND CONTINUITY' AMONG THE GAMITS
      OF PANCHOL
      Ind. J. Soc. Wrk. 1971, 32, 1, Apr, 87-94
      SA, XX, 7, F9203

969   Mann, R.S.

      SOME PROBLEMS OF INDIAN TRIBES
      Kurukshetra, 1966, 14, 11, Aug, 22-25
      SA, XVIII, 1-2, E0947

970   Mathur, S.

      MARRIAGE AMONG THARUS OF CHANDANCHOWGKI
      East. Anthrop, 1967, 20, 1, Jan-Apr, 33-46
      SA, XVI, 2, C9821

971   Mathur, K.S.

      SOCIO-ECONOMIC SURVEY OF PRIMITIVE TRIBES OF
      MADHYA PRADESH
      Delhi, Nat'l. Council of Applied Economic Res., 1963

972   Mathur, K.S.

      TRIBAL IDENTITY
      East. Anthrop., 1969, 22, 2, May-Aug, 135-140
      SA, XX, 3, F4756

973   Mayer, A.C.

      LAND AND SOCIETY IN MALABAR
      Bombay, Oxford University, 1952, 158 pp.

974   Mayer, A.C.

      THE HOLI FESTIVAL AMONG THE INDIANS OF FIJI
      East. Anthrop., V. 6, 1952, Sept. p.3-17
      SA, I, 4, 543

975   Mayer, A.C.

      THE SIGNIFICANCE OF QUASI-GROUPS IN THE STUDY OF
      COMPLEX SOCIETIES
      in M. Banton (ed.) The Social Anthropology of Complex
      Societies, London, 1966

976   Mehra, J.D.

      ETHNOLOGICAL STUDY OF THE SHOKAOS WITH SPECIAL EMPHASIS
      ON SOCIAL STRUCTURE AND CULTURE CHANGE (Ph.d.)
      Doct, Delhi U., 1960 (Prof. P.C. Biswas)

977   Mehta, B.H.

      GONDS AND THE GONDWANA LAND
      The Report Submitted to the Planning Commission,
      (unpublished), 1968

978   Metzger, D. and G. Williams

      TENEJAPA MEDICINE: THE CURER
      Southw. J. Anthrop, 1963, 19, 2, Sum, 216-234
      SA, XII, 2, A8796

979   Minturn, L. and J.T. Hitchcock

      RAJPUTS OF KHALAPUR, INDIA
      Wiley, (?)

980 Misra, P.K.

THE ECONOMY OF A NOMADIC ARTISAN COMMUNITY: A STUDY
OF THE ECONOMY AND SOCIETY AMONG THE NOMADIC GADULIA
LOHARS OF EASTERN RAJASTHAN (Ph.d.)
Doct, Lucknow U, 1967, (Dr. K.S. Mathur)

981 Misra, R.C.R.

MULLUKURUMBAS OF KAPPALA
Calcutta, 1971

982 Mitra, A.

THE TRIBES AND CASTES OF WEST BENGAL
West Bengal Gov't. Press, 1953, 413 p.

983 Mittal, (Mrs.) M.

MOTHER AND HER OFFSPRING - A SOCIO-ANTHROPOMETRIC STUDY
(Ph.d.) Doct, Lucknow U, 1970 (Dr. K.S. Mathur)

984 *Mookherjee, H.N. and Dasgupta, S.

CASTE STATUS AND RITUAL OBSERVANCES IN A WEST BENGAL VILLAGE
Man in India, 1970, 50, 4, Oct-Dec, 390-402
SA, 21, 73 G3228

985 Mukherjee, B.B.

MACHONG AMONG THE GOROS OF ASSAM
East. Anthrop., 1955-56, 9, 2, 112-116

986 Mukherjee, K.L.

THE BIRTH OF A CULT: CHANDI IN BARBANDHA
Man in India, 52, 1, 1972, 82-87

987 Mukherjee, P.N.

GRAMDAN IN BIHAR - A SOCIOLOGICAL ANALYSIS (Ph.d.)
Doct, Patna U., 1968 (Dr. N. Prasad)

988 Mukherjee, R.

SOCIOLOGY AND FOLKLORE
Proceedings of the All India Folklore Conference
Calcutta, 15-17, 1964

989 Mukhopadhyay, T.

A NOTE ON THE PALIYAS OF WEST DINAJPUR
Man in India, 1965, 45, 3, Jul-Sep, 233-236
SA, XVI, 5, D2378

990 Mukhopadhyay, T.

ECONOMIC LIFE OF THE DULE BEHARS OF MIDNAPUR
Man in India, 1968, 49, 1, Jan-Mar, 40-45
SA, XVII, 76, E0159

991 Murthy, K.R.K.

FOLKLORE IN ANDHRA PRADESH
Doct, St, Andhra U, 1969 (Prof. M.V. Murthy)

992 Murty, A.R.

A STUDY OF TRIBAL ECONOMY IN THE ANDHRA AGENCY (Ph.d.)
Doct, Osmania U, 1968 (Dr. K.T. Ramakrishna)

993 Nag, D.S.

TRIBAL ECONOMY: AN ECONOMIC STUDY OF THE BAIGA
Delhi, 1958

994 Naik, T.B.

THE BHILS: A STUDY
Delhi, Bhartiya Adimjati Sevak Sangh, 1956

0514   social anthropology (& ethnology)

995   Naik, T.B.

      THE ABHUJH MARIAS
      Chhindwara, Tribal Res. Inst., 1963

996   Naik, T.B.

      THE TURBULENT BHILS OF ALIRAJPUR
      B. of the Anthrop. Society of Bombay, 1968

997   Naik, T.B.

      URGENT RESEARCH IN SOCIAL ANTHROPOLOGY
      (with ref. to Madhya Pradesh)
      in B. Abbi and J. Babarwal (ed.) Urgent Research in
      Social Anthropology,
      Simla, Ind. Inst. Advan. Study, 1969

998   Naik. T.B. and K.K. Bhouraskar

      CHANGING TRIBES
      Chhindwara, Tribal Res. Inst., 1961

999   Nath, D.

      A HISTORY OF INDIANS IN BRITISH GUIANA
      London; Nelson, 1950, 251 pp.

1000 Nath, Y.V.S.

      BHILS OF RATNAMAL (M.P.)
      Baroda, U. of Baroda, 1960

1001 Neiggemeier, H.

      KUTTIA KHOND OF ORISSA
      Frankfurt, Frobenius Institute, 1964

1002 Nepali, Gopal S.

      AN ETHNO-SOCIOLOGICAL STUDY OF A HIMALAYAN COMMUNITY
      Bombay; United Asia Pub., 1965

0514 social anthropology (& ethnology)

1003 Newell, W.H.

GOSHEN: A GADDI VILLAGE IN THE HIMALAYAS
in M.M. Srinivas (ed.) India's Villages
Bombay, Asia Pub. House, 1960, 56-57,

1004 Orans, M.

THE SANTHAL: A TRIBE IN SEARCH OF A GREAT TRADITION
Detroit, Wayne State U. Press, 1965

1005 Pagdi, S.M.R.

AMONG THE GONDS OF ADILABAD
Bombay; Popular Book Depot, 1952, 122 pp.

1006 Pande, Trilochan

A RACIAL OUTLINE OF KUMARJAN HILL
Folklore (India), 1961, 161-165

1007 Patnaik, N.

RESETTLEMENT SCHEMES AMONG THE PAURIS BHUIYAS,
1952-57

1008 Patnaik, N.

CASTE AND SOCIAL CHANGE: AN ANTHROPOLOGICAL STUDY OF
THREE ORISSA VILLAGES
Hyderabad: National Instit. of C.D., 1969, ii-76-1p

1009 Peter, P.

THE PROBLEM OF TODA SURVIVAL
Vanyajati, 1953, 1,3,59-68

1010 Peter, P.

POSSIBLE SURVIVALS OF TODA RITUALS
B. of Madras Gov't. Museum, 1953, 6, 1

0514   social anthropology (& ethnology)

1011   Peter, P.

THE TODAS, SOME ADDITIONS AND CORRECTIONS TO W.H.R. RIVERS
BOOK OBSERVED IN THE FIELD
Man, 1955, 4

1012   Pocock, D.F.

KANBI AND PATIDOR; A STUDY OF THE PATIDOR COMMUNITY
OF GUJARAT
Oxford, 1972, 190 pp.

1013   Prasad, N.

GAYAWALS OF BIHAR
Am. Anthrop., 54, 2, pt. 1, 279-83, April, 1952

1014   Prasad, N.

LAND AND PEOPLE OF TRIBAL BIHAR
Ranchi, Tribal Welf. Res. Inst., 1964

1015   Prasad, S.D.

JOJOHATU;   A MUNDA VILLAGE
Census of India, 1961
Delhi, Manager of Publications, 1963

1016   Punekar, V.B. (Mrs.)

THE SONKOLIS OF BOMBAY
Bombay; Popular Book Depot, 1959

1017   Raj, H.

THE MATERNAL UNCLE IN SOUTH INDIA
East. Anthrop., 1953, 6, 3-4, Mar-Aug, 164-171
SA, II, #4, 857

- 147 -

0514   social anthropology (& ethnology)

1018   Rao, A.V.S.

       SOCIAL AND ECONOMIC LIFE OF THE GADABAS
       Doct. St. Andhra U, 1969 (Prof. N.S. Reddy)

1019   Rao, K.P.

       ETHNOGRAPHIC STUDY WITH SPECIAL REFERENCE TO SOCIAL
       ORGANIZATION, MYTHS AND RITUAL AND CULTURAL CHANGE,
       1952-53

1020   Rao, M.S.A.

       SOCIOLOGY OF NORTH EASTERN HILL AREAS
       Proceedings of the Third Summer School, Kohima,
       April 7-14, Delhi, 1970

1021   Rao, R.P.

       VILLAGE ORGANIZATION AND AUTHORITY AMONG THE LAMBADAS
       OF THE DECCAN
       East. Anthrop. 1954, 8, 1, Sep - Nov. 3-12
       SA, Vol. IV, #2, 2391

1022   Ray, S.N.

       ADIS OF THE NORTH-EAST FRONTIER AGENCY (Ph.d.)
       Doct, Delhi U, 1966 (Prof. P.C. Biswas)

1023   Ray Chaudhari, M.L.

       TRIBAL LIFE AND SOCIETY: GATHERED FROM RAMAYANA
       Ind. Folklore, 1959, 2, 1-8

1024   Raza, M.

       THE MAZAR WORSHIP IN BUDAUN
       J. of Social Res. 1967, 10, 2, Sep, 26-36
       SA, XVII, 2, D5843

0514   social anthropology (& ethnology)

1025   Reddy, A.M.

BAJATHOS IN THE MULTI-TRIBAL SOCIETY OF VISAKHAPATNAM
AGENCY
Doct. St., Andhra U, 1969 (Prof. N.S. Reddy)

1026   Risley, Sir. H.H.

THE PEOPLE OF INDIA (2nd ed.)
Delhi, Oriental Books Reprint Corp., 1969

1027   Rose, H.A.

A GLOSSARY OF THE TRIBES AND CASTES OF THE PUNJAB
AND N.W.F.P. (3 vols.)
Patiala, (1968?)

1028   Rout, S.P.

SOCIO-ECONOMIC IMPLICATIONS OF PUS PUNI RITUALS OF
THE HILL JUANG OF KEONJHAR
Adivasi, 1966-67, 8

1029   Roy, Prodipto

THE SACRED COW IN INDIA
Rural Sociol. 1955, 20, 1, Mar. 8-15,
SA, Vol. IV, #3, 2651

1030   Roy, P.C.

THE SOCIO-CULTURAL INFLUENCE ON THE PERSONALITY
FORMATION OF THE LODHA AND THEIR SPIRIT-POSSESSED MEN
Doct. St., Ranchi, 1969

1031   Roy, S.C.

SOME INTERESTING ASPECTS OF ORISSA ETHNOLOGY
J. of the Bihar & Orissa Res. Soc., 1963

1032   Roy Burman, B.K.

WARMOUNG, AN AO-NAGA VILLAGE
Census of India, 1961
Office of the Registrar General, New Delhi, 1961
Monograph Series, (Part VI)

1033   Roy Burman, B.K.

THE MAHALIS
B. of Cult. Res. Inst. 1963, 1, 3, 31-32

1034   Roy Burman, B.K.

THE BIRHORS
B. of Cult. Res. Inst., 1964,3,1,19-30

1035   Roy Burman, B.K.

FORESTS AND TRIBALS IN INDIA
in L.P. Vidyarthi (ed.) Applied Anthrop. in India
Allahabad, Kitab Mahal, 1968

1036   Ruhela, S.

THE GADOLIA LOHARS OF RAJASTHAN - A STUDY OF NOMADIC TRIBE
Doct, Rajasthan U, 1966 (Dr. R.N. Saxena)

1037   Ruhela, S.

GODULIYA LOHAR
Tribe, 1967, 3, 2, 1-14

1038   Ruhela, S.P.

THE GADULIYA LOHARS OF RAJASTHAN; A STUDY IN THE
SOCIOLOGY OF NOMADISM
New Delhi, Impex India, 1968, 296 pp.

0514 social anthropology (& ethnology)

1039 Saksena, R.N.

SOCIAL ECONOMY OF A POLYANDROUS PEOPLE
Bombay; Asia Pub. House, 1962

1040 Saksena, R.

TRIBAL ECONOMY IN CENTRAL INDIA
Calcutta, K.L. Mukhopadhyaya, 1964

1041 Sachchidananda

BITLAHA
East. Anthrop. 1955, 9, 4, Sep-Nov, 42-48
SA, V, 2, 3318

1042 Sandwar, A.N.

KORWA SOCIETY AND ECONOMY IN PALAMAU DISTRICT -
MONOGRAPHIC STUDY
Doct. St., Ranchi U., 1969

1043 Sangave, V.A.

PHANSE-PARADHIS OF KOLHAPUR: A TRIBE IN TRANSITION
Sociol., 1967, 16, 1, Mar 81-88
SA, XVII, 2, D5845

1044 Sankalia, H.D.

STUDIES IN THE HISTORICAL AND CULTURAL GEOGRAPHY
AND ETHNOGRAPHY OF GUJARAT
Poona, Deccan College,post-graduate and research institute,
1949, 245 pp.

1045 Saraf, S.

THE HINDU RITUAL PURITY-POLLUTION COMPLEX
East. Anthrop, 1969, 22, 2, May-Aug, 161-176
SA, XX, 3, F4761

0514   social anthropology (& ethnology)

1046   Sarana, Gopala

       COMPARATIVE METHODS (APPROACHES) IN SOCIAL ANTHROPOLOGY:
       A METHODOLOGICAL ANALYSIS
       Doct, Harvard University, 1966

1047   Sarana, G. and T. Madan

       INDIAN ANTHROPOLOGY: ESSAYS IN MEMORY OF D.N. MAJUMDAR
       Bombay; Asia Pub. House, 1962

1048   Saraswati, B.

       THE LADAKHI CUSTOM OF CREMATION
       Man in India, 1967, 47, 4, Oct-Dec, 263-271
       SA, XVII, 3, D6869

1049   Saraswati, B.N.

       THE PEASANT POTTERS OF NORTH INDIA
       Doct. Ranchi U, 1968 (Dr. Sachidananda)

1050   Saraswat, A.P.

       SOCIAL ECONOMY OF NOMADIC TRIBES OF RAJASTHAN
       Doct, Agra U., 1965

1051   Sasaki, G.H.

       SOCIAL AND HUMANISTIC LIFE IN INDIA
       Verry, 1972

1052   Saxena, R.N.

       ANTHROPOLOGISTS AND UNDERDEVELOPED TERRITORIES
       in Balarathnam (ed.) Anthropology on the March, 1963

1053   Saxena, R.P.

       TRIBAL ECONOMY IN MADHYA BHARAT
       Doct, Agra U, 1957

0514   social anthropology (& ethnology)

1054   Sen, S.C., H. Sen and S. Panchbhai

       THE CONCEPT OF DIKU AMONG THE TRIBES
       Man in India, 1969, 49, 2, Apr-Jun, 121-138
       SA, XIX, 3, E8449

1055   Sengupta, S.

       SOCIETY AND ECONOMY OF THE MAHALIS OF MIDNAPUR,
       WEST BENGAL (D. Phil.)
       Doct, Calcutta U., 1968

1056   Sengupta, S.K.

       THE PORTRAIT OF MAHALI ECONOMY IN MIDNAPUR, THE EARNING
       PATTERN OF TRIBAL BASKET MAKERS
       Calcutta, 1969

1057   Sethi, A.S.

       STUDY IN A POLYANDROUS TRIBE
       Doct, Agra U., 1967

1058

       NOTES ON THE JUANG
       Man in India, V. 28, 1948, p. 1-146

1059   Shah, A.M.

       CASTE, ECONOMY AND TERRITORY OF THE CENTRAL PANCHMAHALS
       J. of the M.S.U. of Baroda, 4, 1, 1955, 65-95

1060   Shah, A.M.

       SOCIAL ANTHROPOLOGY AND THE STUDY OF HISTORICAL SOCIETIES
       Eco. Wkly, 1959, 11, (28, 29&30), 953-62

1061   Shah, P.G.

       DABLA
       Bombay, Gujarat Res. Society, 1958

0514   social anthropology (& ethnology)

1062   Shah, P.G.

       NAIKAS - NAIKDAS: A GUJARAT TRIBE
       Bombay, Gujarat Res. Soc., 1959

1063   Shah, P.G.

       TRIBAL LIFE IN GUJARAT
       Bombay, Gujarat Res. Society, 1964

1064   Sharma, B.N.

       SOCIAL LIFE IN NORTHERN INDIA A.D. 600 - 1000
       Verry, 1966

1065   Sharma, D.S.

       TRIBAL ECONOMY OF BAIGA
       Doct, Agra U, 1954

1066   Sharma, R.R.P.

       THE PEOPLE OF NEFA: THE SHERDUKPENS
       Shillong, NEFA Admin, 1961

1067   Sharma, U.M.

       THE IMMORTAL COWHERD AND THE SAINTLY CARRIER: AN
       ESSAY IN THE STYLE OF CULTS
       Sociol. B. 1970, 19, 2, Sep, 137-152
       SA, XX, 3, F4762

1068   Shukla, B.K.

       THE DAFLAS OF SUBANSIRI REGION
       Shillong, The People of NEFA Sines, 1959

0514   social anthropology (& ethnology)

1069 *Shukla, B.R.K.

      ON DRINKS AND DRUGS IN HISTORICAL PERSPECTIVE
      Eastern Anthropol., 1970, 23, 3, Sept-Dec, 299-306
      SA, 21, 73 G4096

1070   Shull, E.M.

      WORSHIP OF THE TIGER-GOD AND RELIGIOUS RITUALS
      ASSOCIATED WITH TIGERS AMONG THE DANGI HILL TRIBES
      OF THE DANGS DISTRICT, GUJARAT STATE WESTERN INDIA
      East. Anthrop. 1968, 21, 2, May-Aug, 201-207
      SA, XVIII, 6, E4626

1071   Singh, K.

      THE SIKHS
      London, George Allen and Unwin, 1953, 215 pp.

1072   Singh, K.B.

      THE METEIS OF MANIPUR
      Doct, Bombay U, 1963, (Prof. G.S. Ghurye)

1073   Singh, K.S. (ed.)

      TRIBAL SITUATION IN INDIA
      Simla, 1971

1074   Singh, R.B.

      GANGAPUTRA PANDAS OF VARANASI: A STUDY OF THEIR
      SOCIAL AND ECONOMIC CONDITIONS
      Doct, Gorakhpur U, 1967, (Dr. S.P. Nagendra)

1075   Singh, S.

      A SOCIOLOGICAL STUDY OF THE GADDI TRIBE IN
      HIMACHAL PRADESH
      Doct, Agra U, 1968 (Dr. R.N. Saxena)

0514   social anthropology (& ethnology)

1076   Singh, S.K.

       DUST-STORM AND HANGING MIST - STUDY OF BIRSA MUNDA
       AND HIS MOVEMENT
       Calcutta, K.L. Mukhopadhyaya, 1966

1077   Sinha, A.P.

       THE MATRELIAL PANAR - THE CHANGING PATTERN IN
       MATRELIAL TRIBE IN ASSAM
       Doct., Lucknow U, 1968 (Dr. K.S. Mathur)

1078   Sinha, B.K.

       THE PINDARIS
       Calcutta, (1968?)

1079   Sinha, R.

       THE AKAS OF SHILLONG
       Adviser's Secretariat, NEFA, 1963

1080   Sinha, S.

       TRAINING OF A BHUMIJ MEDICINE MAN
       Man in India, 1958, 38, 2, Apr-Jun, 111-128
       SA, VIII, 2, 7645

1081   Sinha, S.

       URGENT PROBLEMS FOR RESEARCH IN SOCIAL AND CULTURAL
       ANTHROPOLOGY IN INDIA: PERSPECTIVE AND SUGGESTIONS
       Sociol. B., 1968, 17, 2, Sep, 123-132
       SA, XVIII, 7, E5746

1082   Sinha, S.

       THE ACCULTURATION OF THE BHUMIJ OF MANBHUM: A STUDY
       IN SOCIAL CLASS FORMATION AND ETHNIC INTEGRATION
       Ph.d., U.S.A., 1956

1083   Sinha, S.

       CHANGE IN THE CYCLES OF FESTIVALS IN BHUMIJ VILLAGE
       J. of Soc. Res., 1958, 1, 24-49

1084   Sinha, S.

       BHUMIJ KSHATRIYA MOVEMENT IN SOUTH MANBHUM
       Bu. of Anthrop. Survey of India, 1959, 8, 2, 9-32

1085   Sinha, S.

       STATE FORMATION AND RAJPUT MYTH IN TRIBAL CENTRAL INDIA
       Man in India, 1962, 42, 1, Jan-Mar, 35-80
       SA, XII, 5, B0927

1086   Sinha, Surajit

       TRIBE-CASTE AND TRIBE-PEASANT CONTINUUM IN CENTRAL INDIA
       Man in India, 1965, 45, 1, 58-83

1087   Sinha, S.

       IS THERE AN INDIAN TRADITION IN SOCIAL CULTURAL
       ANTHROPOLOGY?   RETROSPECT AND PROSPECT.
       Presented in the Conference The Nature and Function of
       Anthropological Tradition, Wenner Grenn Foundation for
       Anthrop. Res. New York, 1968

1088   Sinha, T.C.

       THE PSYCHE OF THE GAROS
       Anthrop. Survey of India, 1966

1089   Sinhasarma, T.C.

       THE PSYCHE OF THE GAROS (D.Sc.)
       Doct, Calcutta U., 1954

0514   social anthropology (& ethnology)

1090   Smith, M.W.

       SYNTHESIS AND OTHER PROCESSES OF SIKHISM
       Amer. Anthrop., 1948, 50, 3, 457-62

1091   Solanky, A.N.

       DHODIAS OF SOUTH GUJARAT
       (M.A. thesis)
       1955, (India)

1092   Srivasta, L.R.N.

       THE GALLONG
       Res. Dept., Adviser's Secretariat, Shillong, 1962

1093   Srivastava, S.K.

       PATTERNS OF RITUAL FRIENSHIP IN TRIBAL INDIA
       Int. J. Compar. Sociol., 1960, 1, 2, Sep, 239-247
       SA, XI, 7, A7287

1094   Stack, Ed.

       THE MIKIRAS
       Gauhati, 1972

1095   Stack, G.J.

       NIETZSCHE AND THE LAWS OF MANU
       Sociol. Soc. Res., 1966, 51, 1, Oct, 94-106
       SA, XV, 1, C3531

1096   Stanton, W.A.

       THE AWAKENING OF INDIA; FORTY YEARS AMONG THE TELUGUS
       Portland, Maine: Falmouth Publishing House, 1950, 213 pp.

0514   social anthropology (& ethnology)

1097   Strizower, S.

       THE JEWS IN INDIA
       New Society, 1964, 2, 67, Jan,16-17
       SA, XIII, 6-7, B7663

1098   Subba Rao, B.

       THE PERSONALITY OF INDIA
       Archaeological Series, #3, M.S. U of Baroda, 1958

1099   Thomas, P.T.

       A TRAVANCORE TRIBE AND ITS PROBLEMS, VIZ THE MATHURANS
       OF TRAVANCORE
       Doct, M.S. U. of Baroda, 1958 (Prof. M.N. Srinivas)

1100   Thusu, K.N.

       THE DHURWA OF BASTOR
       Anthropological Survey of India, Calcutta, 1965
       (Memoir #16)

1101   Tiemann, G.

       BEGRIFF UND WEST DER BRUDERSCHAFT BEI DEN JAT VON
       HARYANA IN NORDINDIEN (THE CONCEPT AND VALUE OF
       BROTHERHOOD AMONG THE JAT OF HARYANA IN NORTHERN INDIA)
       Sociologus, 1968, 18, 1, 35-45 (Ger.)
       SA, XVII, 5, D8313

1102   Tiwari, S.C.

       ETHNOLOGICAL STUDY OF THE RAJIS
       Doct, Delhi U, 1959

1103   Trivedi, H.R.

       A STUDY OF MEHERS OF SAURASHTRA
       Doct, M.S. U. of Baroda, 1956 (Prof. M.N. Srinivas)

0514   social anthropology (& ethnology)

1104   Venkataraman, S.R.

VILLIARS OF CHINGLEPUT DISTRICT
Indian J. Soc. Work, 1955, 16, 1, Jun. 27-32
SA, E, 2, 3319

1105   Verman, Manikulal

REPORT OF THE ALL INDIA GADODIA LOHOR CONVENTION
All India Gadodia Lohar Seva Singh, Chittorgarh, 1955

1106   Vidyarthi, L.P.

SOCIAL ANTHROPOLOGICAL RESEARCHES IN INDIA: SOME
PRELIMINARY OBSERVATIONS
J. of Soc. Res. 1966', 9, 1, Mar, 1-74

1107   Vidyarthi, L.P.

ANTHROPOLOGY AND ADMINISTRATION IN INDIA

1108   Vidyarthi, L.P.

AN ANTHROPOLOGIST LOOKS AT FOLKLORE·
Ind. Folklore, 1959, 2, 3, 182-95

1109   Vidyarthi, L.P.

URGENT ANTHROPOLOGY FOR TRIBAL BIHAR
J. of Soc. Res. 1968, 11, 2, Sep, 121-140
SA, XVIII, 6, E4628

1110   Vidyarthi, L.P.

ANTHROPOLOGY VS. ADMINISTRATORS CASE ANALYSIS
in Vidyar thi (ed.) Anthropology and Tribal Welfare
in India, 1959

514 social anthropology (& ethnology)

1111 Vidyarthi, L.P.

ANTHROPOLOGY AND ADMINISTRATION IN INDIA
J. of Soc. Res., 1959, 2, 1-2

1112 Vidyarthi, L.P. (ed.)

INDIAN ANTHROPOLOGY IN ACTION
Ranchi U, 1960

1113 Vidyarthi, L.P.

THE SACRED COMPLEX IN HINDU GAYA
Bombay, Asia Pub. House, 1961

1114 Vidyarthi, L.P.

SOCIAL SCIENCE IN INDIA: A SOCIAL ANTHROPOLOGICAL
APPROACH
Soc. Sci. Information, 1966, 5, 1, Mar, 90-109
SA, XVI, 1, C8941

1115 Vidyarthi, L.P.

APPLIED ANTHROPOLOGY IN INDIA
Kitab Mahal, 1968

1116 Virendra Kumar Singh

SOCIOLOGICAL STUDY OF BUNDELKHAND FOLKLORE - A STUDY
BASED ON FIELD INVESTIGATIONS IN THE DISTRICTS OF
JALAUN, JHANSI, HAMIRPUR AND BANDA IN U.P.
Doct, Lucknow U, 1967 (Dr. G.R. Madan)

1117 Vyas, N.N.

BANJARAS: THE MERCHANTILE NOMADS OF RAJASTHAN
Tribe, 1967, 3, 2

0514   social anthropology (& ethnology)

1118   Vyas, N.N.

THE BHILS ON THE BORDER OF RAJASTHAN - AN EMERGING
SITUATION
Read in the Seminar on Tribal Situation in India
I.I.A.S., Simla, 1969

1119   Wagh, M.C.

RIGVEDI DESASTHA BRAHMINS OF MAHARASHTRA
Doct, Bombay U, 1948 (Prof. (Mrs.) I, Karve)

1120   Yazdani, G. (ed.)

A HISTORY OF THE DECCAN
London; Oxford U. Press, 1952, v.1

1121

SUPERSTITION IN THE DAILY LIFE OF KASHMIRI PANDITS
Eastern Anthropo. V.6, 1952, pp.37-41

1122

THE NAGAS
Civilisations, 1953, 3, 3, 355-359
SA, II, #1, 146

1123

THE RAJ GONDS OF ADILABAD.   THE ABORIGINAL TRIBES
OF HYDERABAD
London; Macmillan, 1948, v.1

- 162 -

0600 COMPLEX ORGANIZATIONS (MANAGEMENT)

0621 industrial sociology and labour

1124 Acharya, T.L.

PHILOSOPHIES OF LABOUR WELFARE
Indian J. Soc. Wrk., 1953, 14, 1, Jun 41-44
SA, II, #2, 325

1125 Agarwal, B.L.

ORGANISATION OF MANPOWER IN INDIA (D. Phil)
Doct, Allahabad U., 1963 (Dr. A.N. Agarwala)

1126 Agarwal, G.K.

INDUSTRIAL RELATIONS IN THE GLASS INDUSTRY OF U.P.
Doct. St., Agra U, 1969 (Dr. A.S. Mathur)

1127 Agarwal, K.M.

CONFLICT IN INDUSTRY (A SOCIAL WORK STUDY IN THE
CAUSES OF INDUSTRIAL CONFLICT AND OF THE POSSIBILITIES
OF ITS PREVENTION AND CURE IN THE TEXTILE INDUSTRY
AT KANPUR
Doct. St., Lucknow U, 1969

1128 Akhauri, R.K.

LABOUR IN COAL INDUSTRIES IN INDIA
Doct., Patna U, 1966 (Dr. G. Prasad)

1129 Ahluwalia, G.S.

PHILOSOPHIES OF LABOUR WELFARE
Indian J. Soc. Wrk., 1953, 14, 1, Jun 50-54
SA, II, #2, 326

1130 Anand, M.M.

SOCIO-ECONOMIC AND MANAGERIAL ASPECTS OF TOURIST INDUSTRY
Doct, Calcutta U, 1970 (Prof. A. Dasgupta)

1131   Athavale, (Mrs.) M.V.

EMPLOYEE COMMUNICATION AND CONSULTATION IN PRIVATE
SECTOR INDUSTRY (WITH SPECIAL REFERENCE TO INDUSTRIAL
UNITS IN POONA)
Doct, Poona U., 1968 (Dr. M.R. Dhekney)

1132   Badhwar, M.

THE WORKMEN'S COMPENSATION ACT OF 1923 AS APPLIED
TO THE INDIAN COAL-MINING INDUSTRY
Doct, Patna U, 1964 (Dr. G. Prasad)

1133   Badganjan, S.D.

A SOCIOLOGICAL STUDY OF THE EFFECTS OF THE
INDUSTRIALIZATION OF BHILAI TOWN ON SURROUNDING VILLAGES
Doct. St., Delhi U, 1969 (M.S.A. Rao)

1134   Bahl, (Miss) S.

CONDITIONS OF LABOUR OF WORKING WOMEN IN THE ORGANIZED
INDUSTRIES OF MADHYA PRADESH
Doct. Jabalpur U, 1966 (Prof. K.C. Varma)

1135   Bajpai, R.K.

LABOUR MANAGEMENT AND TRADE UNIONS IN RAILWAY TRANSPORT
IN INDIA
Doct, Agra U, 1969
(Dr. R.N. Saksena)

1136   Banerji, P.C.

LABOUR AND INDUSTRIAL HOUSING IN KANPUR (D. Phil.)
Doct., Allahabad U., 1948 (Prof. S.K. Rudra)

1137   Baviskar, B.S.

A SOCIOLOGICAL STUDY OF COOPERATIVE SUGAR FACTORY IN
RURAL MAHARSHTRA
Doct, Delhi U, 1970 (Prof. M.S.A. Rao)

1138   Basu, K.S.

       PHILOSOPHIES OF LABOUR WELFARE
       Indian J. Soc. Wrk., 1953, 14, 1, Jun 58-59
       SA, II, #2, 328

1139   Berceerieux, K.C.

       SOCIO-ECONOMIC EFFECTS OF THE NATIONALISATION OF
       MOTOR TRANSPORT IN UTTAR PRADESH
       Doct, Agra U., 1959

1140   Berna, J.J.

       INDUSTRIAL ENTREPRENEURSHIP IN MADRAS
       New York: Asia Publishing Company, 1960, 239 pp.
       SA, X, 3, A2359

1141   Bhar, B.K.

       PERSONNEL MANAGEMENT, TRADE UNIONS AND INDUSTRIAL
       ADJUDICATION IN INDIA
       Calcutta, Academic Publishers, 1969, xi and 195 p.

1142   Bharatiya, L.N.

       THE SOCIOLOGICAL STUDY OF VILLAGE AND KHADJ
       GRAMODYOG INDUSTRIES IN INDIA
       Doct, Agra U, 1970 (Dr. R.K. Saksena)

1143   Bhardwaj, R.C.

       EMPLOYMENT AND UNEMPLOYMENT IN INDIA
       New York, Humanities Press, 1969, 140 pp.

1144   Bhattacharya, B.C.

       LABOUR-MANAGEMENT RELATIONS IN SUGAR FACTORIES OF
       EAST U.P. WITH SPECIAL REFERENCE TO THREE SUGAR
       FACTORIES OF BASTI DISTRICT
       Doct. St, Gorakhpur U, 1969 (D.P. Saxena)

1145   Biraj, A.M.

TEXTILE LABOUR IN BOMBAY CITY
Ind. J. Soc. Wrk., V. 14, Sept., 1953, p.168-177

1146   Birjay, R.M.

TEXTILE LABOR IN BOMBAY CITY: ITS EVOLUTION AND
COMPOSITION 1934-1949
Ind. J. Soc. Wrk., 1953, 14,2,Sep, 168-177
SA, II, #3, 590

1147   Brown, Irving

TRADE UNIONISM IN INDIA
Ind. J. Soc. Wrk., 10, 1949, p.205-17

1148   Bose, A.

PERSONNEL MANAGEMENT DURING NATIONAL EMERGENCY
Industr. Relat. (Calcutta) 1963, 15, 2, 57-60
SA, XIV, 7, C2850

1149   Bredo, Wm.

INDUSTRIAL DECENTRALIZATION IN INDIA
in India's Urban Future, (ed.) R. Turner
Berkeley; U. of Calif. Press, 1962, pp.240-261

1150   Cartwright, B.C.

THE INDIAN INDUSTRIAL TRIBUNALS: A CASE STUDY OF
NORMATIVE RATIONALIZATION
Northwestern U, ('69-'70)
(Ph.d. - Soc.)

1151   Chansarkar, M.A.

SOCIAL INSURANCE FOR INDUSTRIAL WORKERS IN INDIA
Doct, Nagpur U, 1959

1152   Chander, H.

SOCIAL SECURITY OF INDUSTRIAL WORKERS IN INDIA
Ind. J. Soc. Wrk. 1968, 29, 3, Oct, 225-232
SA, XVIII, 4, E2983

1153   Chandrashekar, B.K.

LABOUR RELATIONS IN INDIA
Int. J. Industr. Relat. 8, 3, Nov., 1970, 369-388

1154   Chapple, Elliot D.

APPLIED ANTHROPOLOGY IN INDUSTRY
in A.L. Kroeber (ed.), Anthropology Today,
Chicago U. Press, 1953

1155   Chatterjee, S.C.

A SOCIO-ECONOMIC STUDY OF ABORIGINAL LABOUR WORKING
IN MINING INDUSTRY IN MADHYA PRADESH
Doct, Jabalpur U, 1961, (Dr. D.S. Nag)

1156   Chellaswami, T.

POPULATION TRENDS AND LABOUR FORCE IN INDIA: 1951-66
Popul. R. 1958, 2, 2, Jul, 42-48
SA, XII, 5, B0940

1157   Chirde, S.B.

INDUSTRIAL LABOUR IN BOMBAY: A SOCIO-ECONOMIC ANALYSIS,
WITH SPECIAL REFERENCE TO INDUSTRIAL WORKERS RESIDING
IN BOMBAY DEVELOPMENT DEPARTMENT CHAWLS, BOMBAY
Doct, Bombay U, 1949 (Prof. G.S. Ghurye)

1158   Chowdhry, K.

RELATION OF ORGANIZATION AND SOCIAL STRUCTURE - A
CASE STUDY OF TWO TEXTILE MILLS
Reg'l. Sem. on Techniques of Soc. Res.,
New Delhi, 1959, 85-7

1159   Chowdhry, K. and A.K. Pal

PRODUCTION PLANNING AND ORGANIZATIONAL MORALE
Hum. Org. 1957, 15, 4, Win, 11-16
SA, VIII, 3, 7929

1160   Dabholhar, V.A.

LIFE AND LABOUR OF EMPLOYED WOMEN IN POONA
Doct, Poona U, 1960 (Dr. T.M. Joshi)

1161   Desai, N.D.

INDUSTRIAL MORALE: A COMPARATIVE STUDY OF TWO
INDUSTRIAL ORGANISATIONS
Doct, Gujarat U, 1965 (Prof. P.H. Prabhu)

1162   Das, A.K.

SPECIAL PROBLEMS OF TRIBAL TRANSFORMATION INDUSTRIALIZATIOI
AS A MEANS OF SUCH TRANSFORMATION
B. of the Cult. Res. Inst., Calcutta, 1966, 5, 1-2

1163   Das, A.K. and S.K. Banerjee

IMPACT OF INDUSTRIALIZATION IN AN INTER TRIBAL MARKET
AMONG THE HILL PEOPLE OF CHOTANAGPUR
Calcutta; Asia Pub. House, 1962

1164   Das, A.K. and S.K. Banerjee

IMPACT OF INDUSTRIALIZATION ON THE LIFE OF THE TRIBALS
OF WEST BENGAL
Calcutta, Cult. Res. Inst.; Gov't of West Bengal, 1962

1165   Das, A.K. and Banerjee, H.N.

THE IMPACT OF THE TEA INDUSTRY ON THE LIFE OF THE
TRIBALS OF WEST BENGAL
Calcutta, Cult. Res. Inst., Gov't of W. Bengal, 1964

1166   Das, A.M.

IMPACT OF TEA INDUSTRY ON THE LIFE OF TRIBES OF
WEST BENGAL
Calcutta, Gov't. of W. Bengal, 1949

1167   Devaki, (Miss) K.

CONDITIONS OF WOMEN LABOUR IN TEXTILE INDUSTRIES
IN MADHYA PRADESH
Doct, Saugar U, 1960 (Prof. J.N. Mishra)

1168   Dhanuka, K.C.

INDUSTRIAL LABOUR MOVEMENT IN MADHYA PRADESH
Doct, Vikram U, 1966, (Dr. G.P. Gupta)

1169   Dixit, L.M.

EMPLOYEE MOTIVATION AND BEHAVIOUR: A REVIEW
Ind. J. Soc. Wrk. 1971, 32, 1, Apr, 17-24
SA, XX, 7, F9222

1170   Dubey, B.

A SOCIOLOGICAL STUDY OF MIGRANTS FROM EASTERN U.P.
SERVING AS FACTORY WORKERS IN KANPUR CITY
Doct, Gorakhpur U, 1965, (Dr. I. Deo)

1171   Dufty, N.F.

THE EVOLUTION OF THE INDIAN INDUSTRIAL RELATIONS SYSTEM
J. of Indust. Rel. 1965, 7, 1, Mar, 40-49
SA, XVI, 2, C9842

1172   Dufty, N.F.

INDIAN WORKERS' OPINIONS ON TRADE UNION LEADERSHIP
J. Ind. Rel. 1968, 10, 2, Jul, 146-153
SA, XVIII, 6, E4640

1173   Edwards, S.T.

       PHILOSOPHIES OF LABOUR WELFARE
       Indian J. Soc. Wrk., 1953, 14, 1, Jun, 44-50
       SA, II, #2, 332

1174   Jaiswal, V.R. and Tripathy, R.N.

       SOCIO-PSYCHOLOGICAL FACTORS INFLUENCING INDUSTRIAL
       ENTREPRENEURSHIP IN RURAL AREAS
       Hyderabad, Nat'l. Instit. of C.D., 1970

1175   Gangrade, K.D.

       EMPLOYEE MORALE
       Indian J. Soc. Wrk., 1954, 15, 3, Dec., 175-183
       SA, IV, #2, 2398

1176   Ganguli, H.C.

       AN ENQUIRY INTO INCENTIVES FOR WORKERS IN AN
       ENGINEERING FACTORY
       Ind. J. Soc. Wrk, 1954, 15, 1, Jun. 30-40
       SA, III, #3, 1663

1177   Ganguli, H.C.

       EFFECTS OF UNION MEMBERSHIP ON ATTITUDE OF INDUSTRIAL
       WORKERS
       Ind. J. Soc. Wrk, 1954, 15, 3, Dec, 189-199
       SA, Vol. IV, #2, 2399

1178   Ganguli, H.C.

       INDUSTRIAL COOPERATION
       Indian J. Soc. Wrk. 1955, 16, 2, Sep. 83-89
       SA, VI, 1, 4156

1179   Ganguli,H.C.

       DISTRIBUTION OF I.Q. IN COTTON TEXTILE WORKERS
       Ind. J. of Soc. Wrk, 1970, 30, 4, Jan, 261-276
       SA, XIX, 6, F1492

0621 industrial sociology and labour

1180 Ganguli, T.

      WORK PSYCHOLOGY - VOCATIONAL SELECTION, TRAINING
      AND INTEGRATION OF WORKERS IN INDUSTRY
      Industr. Relat. 1963, 15, 4, 127-133
      SA, XIV, 7, C2857

1181 Gangwal, V.K.

      A STUDY OF HUMAN RELATIONS IN ORGANIZED INDUSTRIES
      OF MADHYA PRADESH
      Doct, Vikram U, 1964 (Dr. G.P. Gupta)

1182 Garza, J.M. and N. Rao

      ATTITUDES TOWARD EMPLOYMENT AND EMPLOYMENT STATUS
      OF MOTHERS IN HYDERABAD, INDIA
      J. of Marriage and the Family, 1972, 34, 1, Feb, 153-155
      SA, XX, 6, F8207

1183 *Ghosh, Arabinda and Sarkar, A.K.

      SIZE STRUCTURE OF INDIAN ENGINEERING INDUSTRIES
      Indian Economic Journal, 1969, 16, 3, Jan-Mar, 375-381
      SA, 21, 73 G2387

1184 Gisbert, P.

      FUNDAMENTALS OF INDUSTRIAL SOCIOLOGY
      Bombay, 1972

1185 Goil, R.M.

      LABOUR RELATIONS IN ORGANIZED INDUSTRIAL PRODUCTION
      IN MADHYA PRADESH
      Doct, Vikram U, 1962 (Prof. P.C. Malhotra)

1186 Gokhale, R.G.

      STUDY OF PREVAILING PRACTICES
      Indian J. Soc. Wrk, 1953, 14, 1, June 6-63
      SA, II, #2, 333

1187   Gupta, A.K.

A STUDY OF HUMAN RELATIONS IN SUGAR FACTORIES
OF BASTI, U.P., WITH SPECIAL REFERENCE TO SARIYA,
RAMHOLA AND CAPTAINGARIJ SUGAR FACTORIES
Doct. St., Gorakhpur U, 1969 (D.P. Saxena)

1188   Gupta, K.N.

SOCIO-ECONOMIC CONDITIONS OF THE WORKERS IN THE
LOCO WORKSHOP OF AJMER
Doct, Agra U., 1966

1189   Gupta, (Mrs.) V.

A SOCIO-ECONOMIC SURVEY OF THE WORKING AND LIVING.
CONDITIONS OF WOMEN WORKERS AT TEA GARDENS IN UTTAR PRADESH
Doct, Agra U, 1968, (Dr. R.N. Saxena)

1190   Haldar, A.K.

THE COAL AND IRON MINES' LABOURERS IN CHHOTANAGPUR: A
STUDY IN MODERNITY OF TRIBAL LABOURERS
Doct. St., Ranchi U, 1969

1191   Hudder, A.K.

LABOUR WELFARE ACTIVITIES IN COTTON TEXTILE
MILLS IN VIDARBHA REGION
Doct, Indore U, 1970 (Prof. S.D. Wishard)

1192   India. Labour Bureau

REPORT ON A SURVEY OF LABOUR CONDITIONS IN METAL
ROLLING FACTORIES IN INDIA
Simla, 1966, ix - 54 pp.

1193   India. Labour Bureau

REPORT ON A SURVEY OF LABOUR CONDITIONS IN COFFEE
PLANTATIONS IN INDIA, 1961-62
Simla, 1967, IV - 62 p.

1194 India. Labour Bureau

      FAMILY LIVING SURVEY AMONG INDUSTRIAL WORKERS; 1958-59
      GENERAL REPORT
      Simla, 1971

1195 Inder Mohan Lal

      LARGE SCALE FACTORIES IN THE PUNJAB - A STUDY OF
      SOCIAL RELATIONS
      Doct, Punjab U, 1970 (Dr. M.L. Sharma)

1196 International Sociological Association

      TRANSACTIONS OF THE THIRD WORLD CONGRESS OF SOCIOLOGY
      London, 1956, ix and 352 pp.
      SA, VIII, 2, 7507

1197 Ismail, Smt. F.

      THE HANDICAPPED IN THE NATION'S ECONOMY
      Ind. J. Soc. Wrk. 1960, 20, 4, Mar, 102-103
      SA, XI, 7, A6639

1198 Jagadeesh, T.K.

      INDUSTRIAL ADJUDICATION AND ARBITRATION PROCEDURE
      Indust. Relat. 1963, 15, 1, 15-24
      SA, XIV, 7, C2861

1199 Jain, K.K.

      LABOUR PROBLEMS IN JUTE MILL INDUSTRIES IN WEST BENGAL
      Doct, Agra U, 1968 (Dr. T.R. Sharma)

1200 Jain, P.C.

      INDUSTRIAL RELATIONS IN INDIA
      Commerce, 1955, Annual, Dec, 102
      SA, VI, 1, 4159

1201   Jetley, K.K.

SOCIAL AND ECONOMIC CONDITIONS OF POSTS AND TELEGRAPH
WORKERS (CLASS III AND CLASS IV) IN INDIA
Doct, Agra U, 1965

1202   Jha, (Mrs.) S.V.

SOCIO-ECONOMIC CONDITIONS OF WOMEN WORKERS IN
ORGANIZED INDUSTRIES OF UTTAR PRADESH
Doct, Agra U., 1961

1203   Johri, S.P.

INDUSTRIAL COOPERATIVES IN UTTAR PRADESH
Doct, Vikram U, 1965 (Dr. K.C. Bhandari)

1204   Joshi, L.G.

TRADE UNION SITUATION IN INDIA
In. J. Soc. Wrk, 1964, 24, 4, Jan, 271-280
SA, XIII, 1, B4146

1205   Joshi, V.P.

STRIKES IN THE BOMBAY COTTON TEXTILE INDUSTRY
Artha Vijnana, 11, 3, Sept, 1969, 431-491

1206   Kakade, R.G.

A SOCIO-ECONOMIC SURVEY OF WEAVING COMMUNITIES IN
SHOLAPUR (BEING A PART OF "SHOLAPUR" A SOCIO-ECONOMIC
SURVEY)
Poona; Gokhale Instit. of Politics and Economics,
(Publication no. 14), 1947

1207   Kannappan, S.

REVIEW ARTICLE: UNLIMITED LABOR SUPPLY AND THE
PROBLEMS OF SHAPING AN INDUSTRIAL LABOR FORCE IN INDIA
Eco. Dev. and Cult. Change, 1968, 16, 3, Apr, 451-469
SA, XVII, 3, D6889

1208   Kapadia, K.M. and Pillai, S.D.

        INDUSTRIALIZATION AND RURAL SOCIETY - A STUDY OF
        ATUL-BULSAR REGION
        Bombay, 1972

1209   Kapoor, S.D.

        EMPLOYEE JOB SATISFACTION: BASIC IMPERATIVES AND
        MEASUREMENT
        Ind. Sociological B., 1967, 4, 4, Jul, 263-268
        SA, XVII, 2, D5871

1210   Kapoor, S.K.

        SOCIAL SECURITY FOR INDUSTRIAL WORKERS IN MADHYA
        PRADESH
        Doct, Vikram U, 1964 (Dr. V.K. Nagar)

1211   Kapoor, T.N.

        PERSONNEL MANAGEMENT AND INDUSTRIAL RELATIONS IN INDIA
        Bombay: N.M. Tripathi, 1968, x-287 p.

1212   Kaut, (Miss) D.

        SUBJECTIVE FACTORS IN INDUSTRIAL UNREST
        Doct, Agra U, 1964

1213   Kennedy, Van D.

        THE SOURCES AND EVOLUTION OF INDIAN LABOUR RELATIONS
        POLICY
        (South Asia Series); Berkeley: U. of California, 1965

1214   Kennedy, V.D.

        UNIONS, EMPLOYERS, AND GOVERNMENT; ESSAYS ON INDIAN
        LABOUR QUESTIONS
        Bombay, Manaktalas, 1966, xi - 227 p.

1215   Keshari, J.P.

THE SYSTEM OF WORKERS' PARTICIPATION IN MANAGEMENT
IN INDIA
Ind. J. Soc. Wrk. 1961, 21, 4, Mar, 351-359
SA, XI, 7, A7447

1216   Khanna, L.C.

LABOUR WELFARE PRACTICES IN THE DELHI CLOTH AND
GENERAL MILLS CO. LTD.
Indian J. Soc. Wrk, 1953, 14, 1, Jun, 69-75
SA, II, #2, 339

1217   Khatri, S.K.

STUDY OF ENTREPRENEURS IN TWO INDUSTRIAL AREAS IN
DELHI AND PUNJAB REGIONS
Doct. St. Delhi U, 1969 (M.S.A. Rao)

1218   Krishnamurty, J.

CHANGES IN THE COMPOSITION OF THE WORKING FORCE IN
MANUFACTURING, 1901-51: A THEORETICAL AND EMPIRICAL
ANALYSIS
Ind. Eco. and Social Hist. Rev. 1967, 4, 1, Mar, 1-16
SA, XVII, 5, D8325

1219   Kuthiala, S.K.

INDUSTRIAL WORKERS IN INDIA
(Ph.d. Soc.)
University of Georgia (1969-'70)

1220   Lahalle, D. and C. Newman

AHMEDABAD TEXTILES INDUSTRY'S RESEARCH ASSOCIATION
R. Franc. Sociol. 1961, 2, 3, p.202
SA, XI, 6, A6643

0621   industrial sociology and labour

1221   Lambert, R.D.

       WORKERS, FACTORIES AND SOCIAL CHANGE IN INDIA
       Princeton, Princeton University Press, 1963

1222   Mahajan, Y.S.

       INDUSTRIALISATION OF KARNATAK; REPORT OF THE INDUSTRIAL
       SURVEY OF KARNATAK CONDUCTED BY THE KARNATAK CHAMBER OF
       COMMERCE, HUBLI
       Hubli; R.V. Sirur, 1950, 240 p.

1223   Makharia, M.P.

       SOCIAL CONDITIONS OF TEXTILE LABOUR IN BOMBAY, WITH
       SPECIAL REFERENCE TO PRODUCTIVITY
       Doct., Bombay U, 1959 (Prof. G.S. Ghurye)

1224   Masanori, K.

       TRADITIONAL AND MODERN INDUSTRIES IN INDIA
       The Developing Economies, 1968, 6, 3, Sep, 300-323
       SA, XVIII, 4, E2998

1225   Masani, M.R.

       PHILOSOPHIES OF LABOUR WELFARE
       Indian J. Soc. Wrk, 1953, 14, 1, Jun, 32-37
       SA, Vol. II, #2, 342

1226   Mathur, A.S.

       LABOUR POLICY AND INDUSTRIAL RELATIONS IN INDIA
       Doct, Agra U, 1967

1227   Mathur, J.S.

       INDIA'S LABOUR POLICY
       J. of Ind. Rel. 1966, 8, 3, Nov, 283-297
       SA, XVI, 3, D0708

1228   Mehra, D.S. and J.D. Kundra

A STUDY OF THE SCHEDULED CASTES AND SCHEDULED TRIBES
WORKING FORCES IN INDIA
AICC Economic Review, 1966, 18, 8, 31-36 and 39 and 41

1229   Mehrotra, B.N.

LABOUR PARTICIPATION IN MANAGEMENT IN INDIAN INDUSTRY
Doct, Panjab U, 1965 (Dr. P. Chandra)

1230   Mehrotra, G.H.

COLLECTIVE BARGAINING IN INDIA - A SOCIOLOGICAL ANALYSIS
Doct, Lucknow U, 1965, (Dr. S. Chandra)

1231   Mhetras, V.G.

LABOUR PARTICIPATION IN MANAGEMENT
Doct, U. of Bombay, 1963 (Dr. (Miss) A.J. Dastur)

1232   Misra, D.C.

PROBLEMS OF U.P. TEXTILE INDUSTRY
Doct. St., Lucknow U, 1969

1233   Misra, K.K.

LABOUR WELFARE IN SUGAR FACTORIES OF GORAKHPUR DIVISION
Doct., Gorakhpur U, 1966, (Prof. R.P.S. Gour)

1234   Morris, D.

THE RECRUITMENT OF AN INDUSTRIAL LABOUR FORCE IN INDIA,
WITH BRITISH AND AMERICAN COMPARISONS
Comp. Stud. Soc. Hist. 1960, 2, 3, Apr, 305-328
SA, XI, 6, A6647

1235   Morris, Morris D.

EMERGENCE OF AN INDUSTRIAL LABOUR FORCE IN INDIA:
A STUDY OF THE BOMBAY COTTON MILLS 1854 - 1947
Berkeley, U. of Calif Press, 1965

1236   Morris, Morris David

TRADE UNIONS AND THE STATE
in Leadership and Political Institutions in India
ed. R.L. Park and I. Tinker, New York; Greenwood, 1969
pp. 268-279

1237   Moses, Dorothy

TRAINING OF LABOUR AND WELFARE PERSONNEL
Indian J. Soc. Wrk, 1953, 14, 1, Jun 87-93
SA, Vol. II, #2, 343

1238   Muniratnam Naidu, E.

LABOUR PROBLEMS OF INDUSTRIAL EMPLOYMENT - A STUDY
IN INDISTRIAL RELATIONS
Doct, Sri Venkateswara U, 1967 (Dr. D.L. Narayana)

1239   Murty, P.S.K.

A SOCIOLOGICAL STUDY OF WORKER'S PARTICIPATION IN THE
JOINT CONSULTATION SCHEME OF INDIAN INDUSTRIES
(American Doctoral Dissertations), (1959-60)
Duke University, (Sociol.)

1240   Muthuchidambaram, S.P.

DETERMINANTS OF INCOME IN MADRAS LABOR MARKET
Amer. Doct. Dissert. ('68-'69)
U. of Wisconsin (Soc.)

1241   Naik, T.B.

LABOUR PROBLEMS OF TRIBAL GUJARAT
Adkhadananda, Dec., 1950

0621   industrial sociology and labour

1242   Narain, I.

       THE MANAGEMENT OF PUBLIC ENTERPRISES: A STUDY OF
       SOME ASPECTS IN THE CONTEXT OF THE "SOCIALISTIC PATTERN"
       Ind. J. Pub. Admin., 1958, 4, 3, Jul-Sep, 302-318
       SA, VIII, No. 2, 7511

1243   Narasimhan, P.S.

       LABOUR REFORMS IN CONTEMPORARY INDIA
       Pacific Affairs, 26, 44-58, March 1953

1244   Niehoff, A.

       FACTORY WORKERS IN INDIA
       Milwaukee, Public Museum, 1959

1245   Nigam, R.G.

       INDUSTRIAL COOPERATIVES IN UTTAR PRADESH
       Doct, Agra U., 1963

1246   Omar, (Mrs.) S.S.

       A SOCIOMETRIC STUDY OF INDUSTRIAL WORKS GROUPS
       Doct, Delhi U, 1968, (Prof. H.C. Ganguli)

1247   Ornati, O.C.

       JOBS AND WORKERS IN INDIA
       Ithaca, N.Y.: Cornell U., 1955, xix & 215 pp.
       SA, XI, 7, A7462

1248   Palakshappa, T.C.

       THE INDUSTRIAL WORKER IN THE WEST COAST PAPER MILLS -
       A STUDY IN CAREER MOBILITY
       Ind. J. Soc. Research, 1963, 4, 2, Jul, 69-74
       SA, XIV, 2-3, B9292

1249   Pandey, R.N.S.

       THE ROLE OF WAGE BOARDS IN THE DETERMINATION OF WAGES,
       WITH SPECIAL REFERENCE TO INDIA
       Doct., Patna U, 1967 (Dr. G.P. Sinha)

1250   Paniker, N.G.A.

       FACTORY LABOUR: A STUDY IN COMMITTMENT
       Doct. St, Poona U, 1969

1251   Pant, S.C. (ed.)

       INDIAN LABOUR PROBLEMS
       Chaitanya pub.

1252   Papola, T.S.

       THE PLACE OF COLLECTIVE BARGAINING IN INDUSTRIAL
       RELATIONS POLICY IN INDIA
       J. of Industrial Relations, 1968, 10, 1, Mar, 25-33
       SA, XVII, 5, D8330

1253   Parthasarathy, V.S.

       CASTE IN A SOUTH INDIAN TEXTILE MILL
       Econ. Wkly 1958, 10, 11, 15 Mar, 384-389
       SA, VIII, 2, 7512

1254   Pestonjee, D.M.

       A STUDY OF EMPLOYEES' MORALE AND JOB SATISFACTION AS
       RELATED TO VARIOUS TYPES OR ORGANIZATIONAL STRUCTURE
       Doct, Aligarh Muslim U, 1967 (Dr. A. Jamil Qadri)

1255   Pherwani, J.S.

       MANAGEMENT AND MEN IN AN INDUSTRIAL ORGANIZATION
       Ind. J. Soc. Wrk, 1960, 21, 1, Jun, 55-62
       SA, XI, 6, A6652

1256   Pillai, P.P.

LABOUR IN SOUTHEAST ASIA
New Delhi; Indian Council of World Affairs, 1947, 277 pp

1257   Pillai, S.D.

ASPECTS OF HUMAN ORGANIZATION OF FACTORIES
Doct., Bombay U, 1964 (Prof. K.M. Kapadia)

1258   Prabhu, P.

SOCIAL EFFECTS OF URBANIZATION ON INDUSTRIAL WORKERS
IN BOMBAY
Sociol. B., Part I, 1956, 5, 1, Mar, 29-50 and
Part I, 5, 2, Sep. 127-143
SA, V, #4, 3849

1259   Prasad, L.

PERSONNEL MANAGEMENT AND INDUSTRIAL RELATIONS IN THE
PUBLIC SECTOR WITH SPECIAL REFERENCE TO HINDUSTAN STEEL
LIMITED
Doct, Panjab U, 1969, (Dr. T.N. Kapoor)

1260   Punekar, S.D.

SOCIAL INSURANCE TO INDIAN INDUSTRIAL WORKERS
Doct., Bombay U, 1949 (Prof. C.N. Vakil)

1261   Punekar, S.D.

TRADE UNIONISM IN INDIA
Bombay; New Book Co., 1948, 407 p.

1262   Punekar, S.D.

CONFERENCE OF LABOUR ECONOMISTS
Ind. J. Soc. Res. 1961, 2, 1, Jan, 78-80
SA, XI, 6, A6654

1263   Punekar, S.D.

CASE STUDIES IN INDUSTRIAL RELATIONS
Ind. J. Soc. Res. 1962, 3, 2, Jul, 1-6
SA, XI, 6, A6653

1264   Ram, M.R.

REPORT OF THE ATTITUDES OF WIVES OF WORKERS FROM
UTTAR PRADESH, BENGAL AND BIHAR
Sociologus, 1961, 11, 1, 79-86
SA, XI, 6, A6655

1265   Ram, E.J.S.

STUDY OF PREVAILING PRACTICES
Indian J. Soc. Wrk, 1953, 14, 1, Jun, 63-69
SA, Vol. II, #2, 344

1266   Raman, R.A.V.

EVOLUTION OF INDUSTRIAL LAW IN INDIA
Ind. J. Soc. Wrk, 1959, 20, 1, Jun. 39-56
SA, XI, 6, A6656

1267   Raman, E.J.

NEUROSIS IN INDUSTRY - A STUDY OF FACTORS AFFECTING
PERSONAL ADJUSTMENTS AMONG INDUSTRIAL WORKERS
Doct, Ind. Inst. of Science, Bangalore (Prof. A. Hafeez)

1268   Ramaswami, E.A.

A SOCIOLOGICAL STUDY OF TRADE UNIONS IN A TOWN IN
TAMILNAD
Doct, Delhi U., 1969 (Prof. M.N. Srinivas)

1269   Ramesh Chandra Singh

TRADE UNION MOVEMENT AND COLLECTIVE BARGAINING IN THE
INDIAN POST AND TELEGRAPHS DEPARTMENT
Doct, Patna U, 1966 (Dr. G. Prasad)

1270   Rao, B.S.S.

       BONDED LABOUR IN ORISSA
       Man in India, 52,1, 1972, 64-73

1271   Rastogi, J.L.

       COST OF INDUSTRIAL ABSENTEEISM IN UTTAR PRADESH
       AICC Econ. R., 1959, 11, 10, 15, Sept. 29-31
       SA, XII, 5, B0960

1272   Ravindra, Mohan

       LABOUR PARTICIPATION IN MANAGEMENT WITH SPECIAL
       REFERENCE TO INDIA (Ph.d.)
       Doct, Agra U., 1958

1273   Report of the Team for the Study of Community Projects
       and N.E.S.

       RURAL INDUSTRIES
       in Rural Sociology in India (ed.) A.R. Desai,
       Bombay, Popular Prakashan,1969, pp. 518-20

1274   Rice, A.K.

       PRODUCTIVITY AND SOCIAL ORGANIZATION IN AN INDIAN
       WEAVING SHED
       Hum. Relat., 1953, 6, 4, 297-330
       SA, II, #2, 345

1275   Rice, A.K.

       THE EXPERIMENTAL REORGANIZATION OF NON-AUTOMATIC
       WEAVING IN AN INDIAN MILL
       Hum. Relat., 1955, 8, 3, 199-249
       SA, V, #2, 3329

0621   industrial sociology and labour

1276   Rice, A.K.

       PRODUCTIVITY AND SOCIAL ORGANIZATION IN AN INDIAN
       WEAVING MILL
       Hum. Rel. 1955, 8, 4, 399-428
       SA, V, 2, 3330

1277   Rizui, S.S.A.

       INTER-RELATIONSHIP BETWEEN LABOUR AND INDUSTRIAL
       PRODUCTIVITY IN SUGAR MILLS OF WESTERN U.P.
       Doct, Meerut U, 1970 (Dr. K.K. Bhatnagar)

1278   Sarkar, J.K.

       UPROOTED FAMILIES IN BOKARO INDUSTRIAL COMPLEX -
       A STUDY OF IMPACT OF INDUSTRIALIZATION
       Doct, Ranchi U, 1970 (Dr. L.P. Vidyarathi)

1279   Saksena, S.K.

       A SOCIOLOGICAL STUDY OF INDUSTRIAL RELATIONS IN A TEXTILE
       INDUSTRY IN KANPUR
       Doct. St., Agra U, 1969 (Dr. R.N. Saxena)

1280   Sanyal, D.K.

       TRAINING OF LABOUR AND WELFARE PERSONNEL
       Indian J. Soc. Wrk., 1953, 14, 1, Jun, 83-87
       SA, Vol. II, #2, 349

1281   Saxena, R.N.

       LABOUR TENSIONS IN INDIA
       Ind. J. Soc. Wrk. 1954, 15, 1, Jun. 12-21
       SA, III, #3, 1670

1282   Sen, Indra

       TRADITIONAL CULTURE AND INDUSTRIALIZATION IN SOUTH INDIA
       Bombay, Orient Longman, 1958

1283 Sen, S.N.

INDUSTRIAL RELATIONS IN THE JUTE INDUSTRY IN WEST
BENGAL - A CASE STUDY
Calcutta, Bookland Private, 1964, viii - 242p.

1284 Sengupta, A.K.

SOME FEATURES OF MALFUNCTIONING OF AN INDUSTRIAL
ORGANIZATION
Sociol. B., 1969, 18, 2, Sep, 122-137
SA, XIX, 3, E8495

1285 Sengupta, P.

THE PROBLEMS OF WOMEN IN INDIAN INDUSTRIES
Soc. Welfare, 1958, 4, 12, Mar, 2-4
SA, VIII, 2, 7513

1286 Sengupta, P.

PROTECTION FOR THE WOMEN WORKERS
Soc. Welfare, 1958, 5, 2, May, 6-8
SA, VIII, 2, 7514

1287 Shanmugham, N.

THE SOCIO-ECONOMIC SURVEY OF THE PERIANAICHEN -
PALAYAM PANCHAYAT UNION
Ind. J. of Soc. Wrk, 1967, 28, 3, Oct, 303-316
SA, XVII, 4, D7687a

1288 Sharma, B.D.

LABOUR PROBLEMS IN COTTON TEXTILE INDUSTRY IN INDIA
Doct, Nagpur U, 1958

1289 *Sharma, Baldev, R.

ALIENATION IN INDIAN WORKERS
Indian Journal of Sociology, 1971, 2, 2, Sep, 175-194
SA, 21, 73 G1620

0621   industrial sociology and labour

1290   Sharma, B.R.

       THE INDIAN INDUSTRIAL WORKER
       Int. J. Comparative Sociology, 1969, 10, 1-2,
       Mar-Jun, 161-177
       SA, XVIII, 4, E3008

1291   Sharma, G.R.

       LIVING CONDITIONS OF COLLIERY WORKERS IN JHARIA COAL
       FIELD
       Doct. St., Ranchi U, 1969

1292   Sharma, H.S.

       A CRITICAL STUDY OF BENEFITS TO WORKERS IN SUGAR INDUSTRY
       IN WESTERN U.P.
       Doct, Agra U, 1968 (Dr. R.C. Saxena)

1293   Sheth, N.R.

       TRADE UNIONS IN INDIA - A SOCIOLOGICAL APPROACH
       Sociol. B., 1968, 17, 1, Mar, 5-18
       SA, XVII, 5, D8333

1294   Sheth, N.R.

       THE SOCIAL FRAMEWORK OF AN INDIAN FACTORY
       New York; Hamanities, 1968

1295   Sheth, N.R.L.

       THE SOCIAL BACKGROUND OF SOME INDUSTRIAL WORKERS
       IN BARODA CITY
       Doct, M.S., U. of Baroda, 1962 (Dr. I.P. Desai)

1296   Sheth, N.R.

       SOCIETY AND INDUSTRIAL WORK IN INDIA: A CASE STUDY
       Hum. Org. 1967, 26, 1-2, Spr-Sum, 77-89   ·
       SA, XVI, 2, C9863

1297   Shetty, M.C.

       ENTREPRENEURSHIP IN SMALL INDUSTRY (PAPERS FROM THE
       CALCUTTA REGIONAL CONFERENCE: EVALUATION OF PLANNED
       DEVELOPMENT IN THE UNDERDEVELOPED COUNTRIES)
       Int. Dev. R. 6, 2, Jun, 13, 1962
       SA, XIII, 5, B6871

1298   Shintre, V.P.

       A STUDY OF COMMUNICATION BETWEEN MANAGEMENT AND
       EMPLOYEES
       Ind. J. of Soc. Wrk, 1967, 28, 3, Oct, 329-334
       Sa, XVII, 4, D7688

1299   Shrivastava, P.C.

       SOCIAL INSURANCE FOR THE INDUSTRIAL WORKERS IN INDIA
       Doct, Saugar U, 1961 (Prof. J.N. Mishra)

1300   Shukla, A.C.

       WORKER'S PARTICIPATION AND INDUSTRIAL DEMOCRACY
       Doct. St., Lucknow U., 1969

1301   Siddiqui, M.R.

       LABOUR IN FRUIT-PRESERVATION INDUSTRY IN UTTAR
       PRADESH - A STUDY OF SOCIO-ECONOMIC CONDITIONS OF WORKERS
       Doct, Lucknow U, 1968 (Dr. S.J. Hasan)

1302   Siddiqui, M.R.

       PERSONNEL MANAGEMENT IN FRUIT PRESERVATION INDUSTRY
       IN INDIA (A SOCIOLOGICAL STUDY)
       Doct. St., Lucknow U., 1969

1303   Singh, J.N.

       WORKER'S EDUCATION AND INDUSTRIAL PRODUCTIVITY IN INDIA
       Doct, Agra U., 1968 (Dr. S.N. Srivastava)

1304   Singh, P.

INDUSTRIAL MORALE IN A TEXTILE MILL
Ind. J. Soc. Wrk. 1971, 32, 2, Jul, 163-168
SA, XX, 7, F9228

1305   Singh, R.

IMPACT OF INDUSTRIALIZATION ON PATRAHI AND FOUR
OTHER VILLAGES
Doct, Ranchi U., 1967, (Prof. L.P. Vidyarathi)

1306   Singh, R.K.

JOB SATISFACTION AMONG INDUSTRIAL WORKERS (A SOCIAL
WORK STUDY OF 500 WORKERS IN COTTON TEXTILE FACTORIES
OF KANPUR)
Doct. St., Lucknow U., 1969

1307   Sinha, D.

SOCIAL AND BEHAVIOURAL PROBLEMS IN INDUSTRY
Ind. J. Soc. Wrk. 1960, 21, 3, Dec, 235-45
SA, XI, 7, A7472

1308   Sinha, G.S. and N.P. Singh

A STUDY OF JOB SATISFACTION AMONG SKILLED WORKERS
Ind. J. S. Wrk, 1965, 26, 1, Apr, 19-30
SA, XVI, 4, D1662

1309   Som, Ranjan K.

STATISTICAL STUDIES:LABOUR PROBLEMS - A REVIEW
Ind. J. Soc. Wrk. 1954, 15, 2, Sep, 110-116
SA, Vol. III, #3, 1672

1310   Som, R.K.

SEASONABILITY IN THE INCIDENCE OF STRIKES IN THE
BOMBAY TEXTILE INDUSTRY
Sankhya, 1954, 13, 423-428
SA, IV, #1, 2151

1311   Srivastava, K.C.

WOMEN LABOUR IN GLASS INDUSTRY OF U.P.
Doct. St. Agra U, 1969 (A.S. Mathur)

1312   Srivastava, R.K.

CONCILIATION AND ARBITRATION IN UTTAR PRADESH
Doct, Agra U., 1966

1313   Srivastava, R.M.L.

THE PROBLEM OF INDUSTRIAL HOUSING IN UTTAR PRADESH
Doct, Agra U., 1960

1314   Srivastava, V.L.

THE SOCIO-ECONOMIC SURVEY OF WORKERS IN THE COAL
MINES OF BIHAR
Doct, Agra U., 1963

1315   Subba, R.A.V.

COLLECTIVE BARGAINING IN INDIAN INDUSTRIES
Ind. J. Soc. Wrk, 1961, 22, 2, Sep, 81-87
SA, XI, 7, A7475

1316   Subbash Chandra

THE ROLE OF TRADE UNIONS IN DEVELOPING COUNTRIES
Doct, Patna U, 1967 (Dr. G.P. Sinha)

1317   Sundaram, V.S.

MANAGEMENT DEVELOPMENT, PART I
Indust. Relat. (Calcutta) 1963, 15, 6, Nov-Dec, 212-215
SA, XIV, 7, C2874

0621   industrial sociology and labour

1318   Tata, N.H.

       PHILOSOPHIES OF LABOUR WELFARE
       Indian J. Soc. Wrk. 1953, 14, 1, 37-41
       SA, Vol. II, #2, 354

1319   Thakkar, G.K.

       A STUDY OF THE LABOUR PROBLEMS OF THE COTTON MILL
       INDUSTRY IN BOMBAY
       Doct, Bombay U. 1960 (Prof. G.L. Maini)

1320   Thakur, C.P.

       ROLE OF THE STATE IN INDUSTRIAL RELATIONS IN INDIA
       Doct, Patna U, 1965 (Dr. G. Prasad)

1321   Thorner, D.

       CASUAL EMPLOYMENT OF A FACTORY LABOUR FORCE. THE CASE
       STUDY OF INDIA 1939 - 1950
       Economic Wkly, Jan. 1957

1322   Tinberg, T.A.

       A STUDY OF A GREAT MARAVADI FIRM: 1860 - 1914
       Ind. Eco. and Soc. Hist. Rev., 1971, (8)

1323   Tandon, J.S.

       SOCIAL PROCESS IN THE INDUSTRIALIZATION OF ROURKELA
       Census of India, 1961, 1, Part XIE, 1970

1324   Unwalla, D.B.

       HUMAN RELATIONS IN FACTORIES
       Doct, Bombay U, 1957, (Prof. G.S. Ghurye)

1325   Unwalla, D.B.

       DELEGATION OF DUTIES: AN ASPECT OF THE FACTORY SYSTEM
       Sociol. B. 1958, 7, 1, Mar, 1-22
       SA, XI, 6, A6666

1326   Vaid, K.N.

       POLITICAL UNIONISM AND INDUSTRIAL RELATIONS IN INDIA
       Ind. J. Social Wrk. 1968, 29, 2, Jul, 157-166
       SA, XVIII, 4, E3014

1327   Vanden Bogaert, M.J.

       THE BONUS QUESTION IN INDIA: FROM EX CRATIA
       PAYMENT TO INDUSTRIAL CLAIM
       Eco. Dev. and Cult. Change, 1968, 17, 1, Oct, 50-64
       SA, XVIII, 1-2, E0968

1328   Van Groenow, W.B.

       WORLD VIEWS OF TEXTILE WORKERS IN INDIA
       (Ph.d. Soc.)
       University of Illinois ('69-'70)

1329   Ved, G.K.

       PHILOSOPHIES OF LABOUR WELFARE
       Indian J. Soc. Wrk., 1953, 14, 1, Jun 54-58
       SA, II, #2, 355

1330   Verma, O.P.

       LABOUR WELFARE AND INDUSTRIAL PEACE IN INDIA
       Doct, Agra U., 1965

1331   Verma, R.B.S.

       THE SUPERVISION OF INDUSTRIAL WORKERS
       Doct. St., Lucknow U., 1969

1332   Vidyarthi, L.P.

STUDY OF TRIBAL LABOURERS OF BOTH INDUSTRIAL AND
AGRICULTURAL AREAS IN AND AROUND RANCHI
Delhi, Nat'l. Commission on Labour Management
Publications, 1968

1333   Vidyarthi, L.P.

ASPECTS OF TRIBAL LABOUR FORCE IN CHHATTISGARH
Tribe, 1969, 6, 3

1334   Vidyarthi, L.P.

SOCIO-CULTURAL IMPLICATIONS OF INDUSTRIALIZATION IN
INDIA: A CASE STUDY OF TRIBAL BIHAR
Dept. of Anthrop; Ranchi U, 1970, xxiii - 552 pp.

1335   Whyte, W.B.

INCENTIVES FOR PRODUCTIVITY: BUNDY TUBING COMPANY CASE
Applied Anthrop., 1948, 7, 2

1336

SOME COMMENTS ON THE SUPPLY OF LABOUR TO THE BOMBAY
COTTON TEXTILE INDUSTRY, 1854-1951

0623 military sociology

1337 Bopegamage, A.

THE MILITARY AS A MODERNIZING AGENT IN INDIA
Eco. Dev. and Cult. Change, 1971, 2, 1, Oct, 71-79
SA, XX, 5, F7076

1338 Choudhary, L.S.

ROLE OF CASTE SYSTEM IN THE ORGANIZATION OF INDIAN ARMY
Doct. St., 1969, Agra U. (R.N. Saxena)

1339 Cohen, S.P.

THE UNTOUCHABLE SOLDIER: CASTE, POLITICS, AND THE
INDIAN ARMY
J. of Asian Studies, 1969, 28, 3, May, 453-468
SA, XIX, 7, F2312

1340 Cohn, Stephen P.

INDIAN ARMY: ITS CONTRIBUTION TO THE DEVELOPMENT
OF A NATION
Berkeley, U. of Calif. Press, 1971

1341 Kapoor, (Mrs.) A.

PROBLEMS OF ROLE - RESTRUCTURING AND ADJUSTMENT IN
THE 'SEPARATED' FAMILIES OF ARMY OFFICERS
Doct. St., Lucknow U, 1969

1342 Mehrotra, (Mrs.) M.

A STUDY OF ATTITUDES OF THE WOMEN STUDENTS OF AGRA
UNIVERSITY TOWARDS COMPULSORY MILITARY TRAINING
Doct, Agra U, 1969 (Dr. L. Singh)

1343 Singh, R.M.P.

ATTITUDE OF UNIVERSITY STUDENTS TOWARDS COMPULSORY
MILITARY TRAINING
Doct, Patna U, 1969 (Dr. A.K.P. Sinha)

0600 COMPLEX ORGANIZATIONS (MANAGEMENT)

0624 bureaucratic structures

1344 Bathija, A.H.

HUMAN RELATIONS IN MANAGEMENT (WITH REFERENCE TO
PUBLIC AND PRIVATE SECTORS)
Doct, Bombay U, 1969 (Prof. G.S. Ghurye)

1345 Chaturvedi, H.R.

THE STUDY OF DISTRICT BUREAUCRACY: A SOCIOLOGICAL
ANALYSIS
Doct. St., Poona U., 1969

1346 Dixit, L.M.

MANAGEMENT OF ORGANIZATIONAL CHANGE
Ind. J. of Soc. Wrk. 1970, 30, 4, Jan, 311-314
SA, XIX, 6, F1515

1347 Gaikwad, V.R.

PANCHAYATI RAJ AND BUREAUCRACY
Hyderabad, India: Nat'l. Instit. of CD, 1969, 76 pp.
SA, XIX, 6, F1516

1348 Gandhi, R.S.

BUREAUCRACY AND BUSINESS ELITE IN INDIA
Int. R. of Modern Sociology 2, 2, Sept, 1972, 167-271

1349 *Ghildyal, U.C.

BEHIND DECENTRALISED DEMOCRACY: SOME REFLECTIONS ON
ADMINISTRATIVE BEHAVIOUR
Behavioral Sciences and Community Development, 1970,
4, 2, Sep, 128-145
SA, 21, 73 G0680

1350   Gorwala, A.D.

REPORT ON PUBLIC ADMINISTRATION
New Delhi, Planning Commission, 1953, 74 pp.

1351   Goswami, V.L.

THE STRUCTURE OF DEVELOPMENT ADMINISTRATION
Ind. J. Publ. Admin., 1, April-June, 1955, 110-118

1352   Goyal, S.K.

BUREAUCRACY: A SOCIOLOGICAL STUDY OF LEVELS OF
ORIENTATION OF CLERKS TOWARDS THE NORMS OF BUREAUCRACY
Ind. Soc. B., 1968, 5, 4, Jul, 248-257
SA, XVII, 7, E0202

1353   Jain, B.C.

JOINT CONSULTATION IN MAJOR PUBLIC ENTERPRISES IN INDIA
Doct, Agra U., 1966

1354   Kahar, S.

AUTHORITY PATTERNS AND SUBORDINATE BEHAVIOUR IN
INDIAN ORGANIZATIONS
Administrative Sci. Quart. 1971, 16, 3, Sep, 298-307
SA, XX, 6, F8253

1355   Khanna, R.L.

SOCIAL ADMINISTRATION IN INDIA
Chandigarh, Mohindra Capital Publishers, 1970, ii & 191pp.

1356   Kulkarni,V.M.

ESSAYS ON SOCIAL ADMINISTRATION
New Delhi, 1972

1357   Mathur, J.S.

TRIBAL DEVELOPMENT IN ADMINISTRATION IN INDIA
in Vidyarthi (ed.) Applied Anthropology in India,
Allahabad, Kitab Mahal, 1968

1358   Nandy, M.

THE ROLE OF MANAGEMENT IN A DEVELOPING COUNTRY
Ind. J. Soc. Wrk. 1970, 31, 2, Jul, 115-124
SA, XX, 6, F8266

1359   Nayar, P.K.B.

BUREAUCRACY AND SOCIO-ECONOMIC DEVELOPMENT: A CASE
STUDY OF PLANNING DEPARTMENTS IN TWO INDIAN STATES
(Amer. Doct. Dissertations) ('67-'68)
U. of Pittsburgh (Soc.)

1360   Prasad, G.K.

SOCIOLOGY OF BUREAUCRACY IN INDIA (D. Litt.)
Doct, Patna U, 1967

1361   Rieger, H.C.

BUREAUCRACY AND THE IMPLEMENTATION OF ECONOMIC PLANS
IN INDIA
Ind. J. of Public Admin. 1967, 13, 1, Jan-Mar, 32-42
SA, XIX, 6, F1521

1362   Saxena, R.P.

SOCIAL ADMINISTRATION IN UTTAR PRADESH
Doct, Agra U, 1969

1363   Sinhi, N.K.

BUREAUCRACY - A SOCIOLOGICAL ANALYSIS
Doct. St., Rajasthan U, 1969

0624   bureaucratic structures

1364   Taub, Richd. P.

       BUREAUCRATS UNDER STRESS: ADMINISTRATORS AND
       ADMINISTRATION IN AN INDIAN STATE
       Berkeley, U. of Calif. Press, 1969

1365   Tungar, S.D.

       THE STUDY OF BUREAUCRACY IN HOSPITAL ORGANIZATION
       Doct. St., Poona U, 1969

1366   Venkatarangaiya

       THE PATTERN OF PUBLIC ADMINISTRATION IN THE
       FIVE-YEAR PLAN
       Ind. J. Polit. Sci. 14, 3, July-Sept, 1953, 210-229

1367   Vidyarthi, L.P.

       ANTHROPOLOGY AND ADMINISTRATION IN INDIA

1368   Vidyarthi, L.P.

       ANTHROPOLOGY VS. ADMINISTORS CASE ANALYSIS
       in Vidyarthi (ed.) Anthropology and Tribal Welfare
       in India, 1959

0700 SOCIAL CHANGE AND ECONOMIC DEVELOPMENT

0715 social change and economic development

1369 Acharya, (Mrs.) H.N.

NASIK THROUGH A CENTURY: A STUDY IN SOCIAL CHANGE (Ph.d.)
Doct, Poona U., 1966

1370 Agarwal, B.C.

FROM COMMERCE TO CONQUEST: A HISTORICAL STUDY OF
ACCULTURATION IN INDIA
East. Anthrop. 1968, 21, 1, Jan-Apr, 45-58
SA, XVIII, 4, E3040

1371 Aiyappan, A.

SOCIAL REVOLUTION IN A KERALA VILLAGE
Bombay, Asia Pub. House, 1965

1372 Aiyappan, A.

THEORIES OF CULTURE CHANGE AND CULTURE CONTACT
in J.P. Mills et. al. (ed.) Essays in Anthropology:
Presented to S.C. Roy, Lucknow: Maxwell and Co.,1948

1373 Akhauri, N.

SOCIO-CULTURAL BARRIERS TO RURAL CHANGE IN AN EAST
BIHAR COMMUNITY
East. Anthrop. 1958, 11, 3-4, p. 212-19
SA, VIII, 2, 7427

1374 Alatas, Syed H.

THE CAPTIVE MIND IN DEVELOPMENT PLANNING
11th World Conference of the Society for Int'l.
Development, New Delhi, 1969

1375 Ambirajan, S.

ECONOMIC IDEAS AND ECONOMIC POLICY IN BRITISH INDIA
Ind. Eco. J. 1967, 15, 2, Oct-Dec, 188-208
SA, XVII, 7, E0213

1376   Anand, V.K.

       NAGALAND IN TRANSITION
       New Delhi, 1968

1377   Asirvatham, E.

       SOCIAL CHANGES IN INDIA
       Ind. J. Soc. Wrk., 1960, 21, 2, Sep. 123-130
       SA, XI, 6, A6462

1378   Ayyangar, M.A.

       ECONOMIC DEVELOPMENT AND MORAL VALUES IN INDIA:
       AN HISTORICAL APPROACH
       J. Soc. Res. 1965, 8, 1, Mar, 1-6
       SA, XIV, 5, C1371

1379   Balakrisna, R.

       UNDERDEVELOPMENT, A WORLD LIABILITY
       Indian Yearbook of International Affairs
       Madras, 1952, 65-77

1380   Ballhatchet, Kenneth

       SOCIAL POLICY AND SOCIAL CHANGE IN WESTERN INDIA
       1817 - 1830
       London, Oxford U. Press, 1957

1381   Bandopadhyaya, S.

       ECONOMIC DEVELOPMENT AND LABOUR SUPPLY: A NOTE
       Ind. Eco. J. 1966, 14, 1, Jul-Sep, 106-109
       SA, XVII, 4, D7699

1382   Barlinge, S.S.

       THE PROBLEMS OF CHANGE (Ph.d.)
       Doct, Nagpur U., 1957

0715   social change and economic development

1383   Barnabas, A.P.

       SOCIAL CHANGE IN A NORTH INDIAN VILLAGE
       New Delhi, Indian Inst. of Public Admin. 1969, xviii - 17 pp.

1384   Beals, A.R.

       INTERPLAY AMONG FACTORS OF CHANGE IN A MYSORE VILLAGE
       in Village India, ed. M. Marriott
       Chicago, U. of Chicago Press, 1956, pp. 78-102

1385   Beals, Alan R.

       NAMAHALLI, 1953 - 1966: URBAN INFLUENCE AND CHANGE
       IN SOUTHERN MYSORE
       in Change and Continuity in India's Villages
       ed. K. Ishwaran, New York, Columbia U. Press, 1970
       pp. 57-73

1386   Beech, R.P. and M.J. Beech

       BENGAL: CHANGE AND CONTINUITY
       East Lansing, Mich: Asian Studies Center, Michigan
       State U, 1969, May, 270 pp.
       SA, XX, 6, F8266

1387   Benedict, B.

       FAMILY FIRMS AND ECONOMIC DEVELOPMENT
       Southwest. J. of Anthrop, 24, 1968

1388   Berreman, Gerald D.

       PAHARI CULTURE: DIVERSITY AND CHANGE IN THE
       LOWER HIMALAYAS
       in Change and Continuity in India's Villages,
       ed. K. Ishwaran, New York, Columbia U. Press,
       1970, pp. 73-105

1389   Berreman, G.D.

       CASTE AND ECONOMY IN THE HIMALAYAS
       Eco. Dev. Cult. Change, 1962, 10, 4, Jul, 386-394
       SA, XIII, 1, B4186

1390   Bhatnagar, C.P.

THE CRISIS IN INDIAN SOCIETY
Int'l. Pubrs. Serv., 1972

1391   Bhatnagar, S.R.

SOCIETAL CHANGE IN THE FAR EAST: DILEMMAS OF
EDUCATION, ECONOMICS, AND POLITICS: INDIA AND JAPAN
Annual Meeting of the Rural Sociological Society,
Session 49, 1970
SA, XVIII, 5, Supp. 10, E4181

1392   Bhatt, V.V.

SOME NOTES ON TWO RECENT THEORIES OF STAGES OF
ECONOMIC GROWTH
Ind. Eco. Soc. Hist. R. 1964, 1, 4, Apr-Jun, 183-191
SA, XV, 3, C4906

1393   Bhatt, V.V.

SOME ASPECTS OF DEVELOPMENT STRATEGY
Ind. Eco. J. 1967, 14, 5, Apr-Jun, 562-575
SA, XVII, 6, D9365

1394   Bhowmick, P.K.

DEVELOPMENT SCHEMES AS FACTORS OF SOCIAL AND ECONOMIC
CHANGES.
J. of Social Res, 1968, 11, 1, Mar, 95-101
SA, XVIII, 3, E1899

1395   Blackett, P.M.S.

THE EVER WIDENING GAP
Bucknell Review, 1967, 15, 2, May, 96-111
SA, XVIII, 3, E1900

1396   Boel, J.

SANSKRITIZATION AND WESTERNIZATION: AN ANALYSIS OF
SOCIAL CHANGE IN INDIA
Social Action, 1967, 17, 6, 411-419
SA, XVIII, 6, E4690

1397   Bondurant, J.

TRADITIONAL POLITY AND THE DYNAMICS OF CHANGE IN INDIA
Hum. Org. 1963, 22, 1, Spring, 5-10
SA, XII, 5, B0986

1398   Bopegamage

THE MILITARY AS A MODERNIZING AGENT IN INDIA
Eco. Dev. and Cult. Change, 1971, 2, 1, Oct, 71-79
SA, XX, 5, F7076

1399   Bose, A.B.

DIRECTED SOCIAL CHANGE IN INDIA
Ind. J. Soc. Wrk., 1969, 29, 4, Jan, 353-360
SA, XVIII, 6, E4691

1400   Bose, N.

MAN MANAGEMENT IN A CHANGING SOCIETY
Interdiscipline, 1967, 4, 2, Su, 137-141
SA, XVII, 4, D7701

1401   Bose, N.K.

COMPETING PRODUCTIVE SYSTEMS IN INDIA
Man in India, 1968, 48, 1, Jan-Mar, 1-17
SA, XVII, 7, E0221

1402   Bose, N.K.

THE USE OF PROCEEDINGS OF CASTE PANCHAYATS
J. Soc. Res. (India), 1960, 1, 1, Jul, 98-100
also; Regional Seminar on Techniques of Social Research,
UNESCO Research Center, Calcutta, 1958, 65-67
SA, XI, 2&3, A4670

1403   Bose N.K.

       SOME METHODS OF STUDYING SOCIAL CHANGE
       Man in India, 1967, 47, 3, Jul-Sep, 169-177
       SA, XVII, 2, D5921

1404   Bose, N.K.

       OUR ECONOMISTS AND GANDHI
       Man in India, 52, 4, Oct-Dec, 1972, 297-303

1405   Bose, S.

       IMPACT OF CHANGING CONDITIONS ON THE ECONOMY OF THE
       HIGH ATTITUDE PEOPLE
       Read in a Seminar on Tribal Situation in India, Ind·.
       Inst. of Advanced Study, Simla, 1969

1406   Bottomore, T.B.

       THE CHANGING SHAPE OF CASTE
       New Society, 1963, 2, 40, Jly 4, 10-12
       SA, XIII, 1, B4188

1407   Bulsara, J.F.

       NATURE AND EXTENT OF SOCIAL CHANGE IN RURAL SOCIETY
       Sociol. B. 1962, 11, 1, 2, Sep, 166-172
       SA, XI, 7, A7295

1408   Burman, B.K. Roy

       HILLMEN OF NORTH EAST INDIA AND TENSIONS OF SOCIO-
       ECONOMIC DEVELOPMENT
       J. of Soc. Research, 1967, 10, 2, Sep, 37-50
       SA, XVII, 2, D5924

1409   Burman, B.K. Roy

       SOME DIMENSIONS OF TRANSFORMATION OF TRIBAL SOCIETIES
       IN INDIA
       J. of Social Res., 1968, 11, 1, March, 88-94
       SA, XVIII, 3, E1842

1410 Cabinetmaker, P.H.

      INDUSTRIALIZATION AND URBANIZATION
      Ind. Sociol., 1959, 1, 1, Mar, 3o-32
      SA. XII, 5, B0884

1411 Carstairs, G.M.

      A VILLAGE IN RAJASTHAN: A STUDY IN RAPID SOCIAL CHANGE
      Economic Weekly, 1952,75-77

1412 Carstairs, G.M.

      BHIL VILLAGES OF WESTERN UDAIPUR: A STUDY IN
      RESISTANCE TO SOCIAL CHANGE
      Eco. Weekly, 1952, 231-233, 4

1413 Chacko, V.M.

      ECONOMIC PLANNING IN INDIA AND SOCIAL CHANGE
      Ind. Sociol. 1959, 1, 1, Mar. 39-42
      SA, XII, 5, B0991

1414 Chandra, N.

      LITERACY IN TRADITIONAL SOCIETIES
      East. Anthrop. 25, 2, May-Aug, 1972, 169-183

1415 Chandrasekhar, S.

      POPULATION GROWTH AND ECONOMIC DEVELOPMENT IN INDIA:
      1951-61
      Pop. R. 1961, 5, 2, Jul, 58-73
      SA, XII, 8, B3349

1416 Chandrasekhar, S.

      THE POPULATION FACTOR IN ECONOMIC DEVELOPMENT
      Pop R. 1964, 8, 2, Jul, 54-57
      SA, XIV, 1, B8483

1417   Chatterjee, B.B.

IMPACT OF SOCIAL LEGISLATION ON SOCIAL CHANGE
Calcutta, 1971

1418   Chattopadhyaya, K.P.

SOME APPROACHES TO THE STUDY OF SOCIAL CHANGE
Kale Memorial Lecture, Poona, 1959

1419   Chattopadhyaya, K.P.

CHANGING VALUES AND SOCIAL PATTERNS IN CASTE SOCIETIES
IN WEST BENGAL VILLAGES
in A. Dutta (ed.) An Int'l. Seminar on Paths to Eco.
Growth, Poona, Allied Publishers, 1962

1420   Chandrasekhar, M.

SOCIAL CHANGE IN INDIA (PLANNING PERIOD) (Ph.d.)
Doct, Poona U, 1964 (Dr. Y.B. Damle)

1421   Choudhuri, M.K. (ed.)

TRENDS OF SOCIO-ECONOMIC CHANGE IN INDIA, 1871-1961
Indian Instit. of Advanced Study Transactions,
No. 7, 1969

1422 *Chekki, Danesh A.

MODERNIZATION AND KIN NETWORK
Leiden, E.J. Brill, 1974

1423   Chekki, D.A.

KALYAN AND GOKUL: KINSHIP AND MODERNIZATION IN
NORTHERN MYSORE
Contributions to Asian Studies, Leiden, E.J. Brill, 1971

1424   Chekki, D.A.

MODERNIZATION AND KINSHIP IN URBAN INDIA
J. of Karnatak University - Soc. Sciences, Vol. V -
April, 1969

1425   Cohn, B.S.

CHANGING TRADITIONS OF A LOW CASTE
Traditional India: Structure and Change, Journal
of American Folklore, 71, 281, 1958, 413-421

1426   Dalton, D.

EXPERIMENTS WITH TRADITION: AN INTERPRETATION OF
MODERN INDIAN IDEAS ON THE NATURE OF SOCIAL AND
POLITICAL CHANGE
J. Dev. Stud. 1965, 1, 2, Jan. 195-216
SA, XV, 1, C3577

1427   Danda, A.K. and D.G. Danda

DEVELOPMENT AND CHANGE IN A BENGAL VILLAGE
India: Nat'l. Inst. C.D., 1961

1428   Darling, M.L.

AT FREEDOM'S DOOR
London: Oxford University Press, 1949, 369 pp.

1429   Darling, M.

PROBLEMES PEDAGOGIQUES DE L'EXPANSION COOPERATIVE.
L'EXPERIENCE DE L'INDE (PEDAGOGIC PROBLEMS OF COOPERATIVE
EXPANSION.   THE INDIAN EXPERIMENT)
Archiv. Int. Sociol. Coop. 1960, 7, Jan-Jun, 95-111 (Fr.)
SA, XIII, 6-7, B7717

1430   Das, T.C.

NATURE AND EXTENT OF SOCIAL CHANGE IN TRIBAL SOCIETY
OF EASTERN INDIA
Sociol. B. 1962, 11, 1, 2, Mar-Sep, 221-238
SA, XI, 7, A7298

1431   Das, T.C.

ASPECTS OF TRIBAL CULTURE UNDER MODERN IMPACT IN
EASTERN INDIA

L.K. Balaratnam (ed.) Anthropology on the March
Madras Social Science Assoc., 1963, pp. 137-154

1432   Dasgupta, S.

HINDU ETHOS AND THE CHALLENGE OF CHANGE
Calcutta, 1972

1433   Dasgupta, A.

INDIA'S CULTURAL VALUES AND ECONOMIC DEVELOPMENT:
A COMMENT
Econ. Dev. Cult. Change, 1964, 13, 1, Part I,
Oct, 100-102
SA, XIV, 6, C2044

1434   Dasgupta, P.K.

CULTURE FACTORS IN INDUSTRIALIZATION: A CASE STUDY
AT CHITTARANJAN, WEST BENGAL
J. Soc. Res. 1965, 8, 1, Mar, 76-81
SA. XIV, 5, C1127

1435   Dasgupta, S.

SOCIAL WORK AND SOCIAL CHANGE
US: Extending Horizons Books, 1968, pp. 222

1436   Datta-Majumdar, N.

THE SANTHAL: A STUDY IN CULTURAL CHANGE
Anthrop Survey of India, Calcutta, 1955

1437   Desai, A.R.

TRIBES IN TRANSITION
Rural Sociology in India ed. A.R. Desai, 1969
Bombay, Popular Prakashan, pp. 221-232

1438   Desai, A.R.

SOCIOLOGICAL PROBLEMS OF ECONOMIC DEVELOPMENT
Rural Sociology in India, ed. A.R. Desai
Bombay: Popular Prakashan, 1969, pp. 117-125

1439   Desai, A.R. (ed)

ESSAYS ON MODERNIZATION OF UNDERDEVELOPED SOCIETIES,
2 vols.
Bombay, Thacker, 1971

1440   Desai, (Mrs.), N.A.

GUJARATI SOCIETY IN NINETEENTH CENTURY: AN ANALYSIS
OF SOCIAL CHANGE (Ph.D.)
Doct, Maharaja Sayajarao, U.Baroda, 1965
(Dr. I.P. Desai)

1441   Deva, Indra

SOCIAL CHANGE IN ASIA AND ITS IMPACT ON FOLKLORE
AND FOLK CULTURE
First Asian Folklore Conference, Bloomington, India.
U.S.A.   also in: Conspectus of Indian Society,
ed. R. Prasad et. al. Agra, 1966, pp 350-364

1442   Deva, Indra

THE COURSE OF SOCIAL CHANGE: A HYPOTHESIS
Diogenes, 1966, 56

1443   Dhäwan, C.L.

DEVELOPMENT OF INDIA, M.I.
Chandigarh, 1971

1444   D'Souza, B.G.

GOAN SOCIETY IN TRANSITION (A STUDY IN SOCIAL CHANGE)
(PH.d.)
Doct, Bombay N., 1969, (Dr. A.R. Desai)

1445   Dube, S.C.

SOCIAL STRUCTURE AND CHANGE IN INDIAN PEASANT
COMMUNITIES
Rural Sociology in India ed. A.R. Desai
Bombay Popular Prakashan, 1969, pp.201-206

1446   Dumont, L. and D. Pocock

INTRODUCTORY NOTE: CHANGE, INTERACTION AND COMPARISON
Contrib. Ind. Sociol 1964, 7, Mar, 7-17,
SA, XIV, 6, C2646

1447   Dube, S.C.

INDIA'S CHANGING VILLAGES
London; Routledge and Kegan Paul, 1955, pp.230

1448   Dutta, R.

VALUES IN MODELS IN MODERNIZATION
Delki, 1971

1449   Eames, E.J.

SOCIAL CHANGE IN NEW VILLAGES OF UTTAR PRADESH, INDIA
Americal Doctoral Dissertations, (65-66)
Cornell U. (Soc. Psy)

1450   Ehrenfels, U.R.

EXAMPLE AND RESPONSIBILITY - TWO ACCULTRURATION PROBLEMS
Ind. J. Soc. Work, 1958, 19, 2, Sep, 143-149
S.A. VIII, 2, 7650

1451   Eisenstadt, S.N.

REVIEW ARTICLES: SOME NEW LOOKS AT THE PROBLEM OF
RELATIONS BETWEEN TRADITIONAL SOCIETIES AND MODERNIZATIO
Eco. Dev. and Cult. Change, 1968, 16, 3, Apr. 436-450
SA XVII, 3, D6930

1452   Eisenstadt, S.N.

       PROLOGUE: SOME REMARKS ON PATTERNS OF CHANGE IN
       TRADITIONAL AND MODERN INDIA
       Change & Continuity in India's Villages
       ed. K. Ishwaran New York Columbia U. Press 1970,
       pp. 21-37

1453   Elder, J.W.

       INDUSTRIALISM IN HINDU SOCIETY: A CASE STUDY IN
       SOCIAL CHANGE
       Americal Doctoral Dessirtations (1958-59)
       Harvard U. (Sociology)

1454   Elder, Joseph W.

       RAJPUR: CHANGE IN THE JAJMANI SYSTEM OF AN UTTAR
       PRADESH VILLAGE
       Change and Continuity in India's Villages ed. K. Ishwaran
       New York Columbia U. Press, 1970 pp. 105-129

1455   Epstein, T.S.

       ECONOMIC DEVELOPMENT AND SOCIAL CHANGE IN SOUTH
       INDIA
       Manchester; Manchester U. Press, 1962

1456   Fraser, T.M., Jr.

       SOCIO-CULTURAL PARAMETERS IN DIRECTED CHANGE
       Hum. Org. 1963, 22, 1, Spring, 95-104
       SA, XII, S, B0999

1457   Fraser, T.M. Jr.

       CULTURE AND CHANGE IN INDIA: THE BARPALI EXPERIMENT
       U. of Mass. Press, 1969

1458   Gadgil, D.R.

       NOTES ON THE GOVERNMENT OF INDIA'S FIRST FIVE-YEAR
       PLAN: JULY '51
       Eco. Dev. and Cult. Change, v.1, n.1, March, 1952,
       p. 57-72

1459 Gadgil, D.R.

ECONOMIC DEVELOPMENT IN INDIA
India Quarterly, 8, 2, April-June 1952, 171-205

1460 Gandhi, I.

MOVING ASIA FORWARD
Impact of Science on Society, 1969, 19, 1, Jan-Mar,
7-12
SA, XVIII, 6, E4698

1461 Gautam, V.

SOME ASPECTS OF SOCIAL CHANGE IN THE BHOJPURI
SPEAKING AREA (1858-1920)
Abstract of Papers, 28th International Congress of
orientalists.
Canberra, 1971

1462 Ghurye, G.S.

SOCIAL CHANGE IN MAHARASHTRA
Sociol.B. v.1, 1952, p. 71-86
           v.3, 1954, p. 42-60
SA, III, 2, 1374

1463 Ghurye, K.G.

PRESERVATION OF LEARNED TRADITION IN INDIA
Bombay: Popular Book Depot, 1950, 70 pp.

1463 Ghurye, G.S.

APPRAISAL
Rural Sociology in India ed. A.R. Desai, 1969,
Bombay, Popular Prakashan, pp. 253-269

1464 Godchot, Z.

ASPECTS DES PROBLEMES SOCIO-ECONOMIQUES DE L'INDE
CONTEMPORAIRE (ASPECTS OF CONTEMPORARY INDIA'S
SOCIO-ECONOMIC PROBLEMS.)
Cahiers de Sociologive Economique, 1971, 1,
Second Series, Jun, 35-49 (Fr.)
SA, XX, 3, F4849

1465 Gorevaney, (Miss) N.

ROLES STRUCTURE , SELF-IMAGE AND SOCIAL CHANGES-
A STUDY OF SELECTED CATEGORIES OF FEMALES
Doct. St., Rajasthan, 1969

1466 Goswami, M.C. and D.N. Majumdar

A STUDY OF SOCIAL ATTRIBUTES AMONG THE GARO
Man In India, 1068, 40. 1, Jan-Mar, 55-70
Sa, XVII, 7, E0152

1467 Gough, Kathleen

PALAKKARA: SOCIAL AND RELIGIOUS CHANGE IN CENTRAL
KERALA
Change and Continuity in India's Villages
ed. K. Ishwaran, New York Columbia U. Press, 1970
pp. 129-165

1468 Gough, K.

CHANGING KINSHIP USAGES IN THE SETTING OF POLITICAL-
ECONOMIC CHANGE AMONG THE NAYARS OF MALABAR
J. of Royal Anthrop Instit., 1952, 82, 71-88

1469 Gupta, K.P.

A THEORETICAL APPROACH TO HINDUISM AND MODERNIZATION
OF INDIA
Ind. J. of Soc. Res., 1971, 2, 1, Mar, 59-91
SA, XX, 3, F4851

1470 Gupta, (Miss) S.

SOCIAL CHANGE IN THE MIDDLE CLASS HINDU FAMILIES (PH.d.)
Doc., Agra U, 1962

1471 Gusfield, J.R.

TRADITION AND MODERNITY: CONFUSED POLARITIES IN THE
STUDY OF SOCIAL CHANGE
Microfiche, 65-15, available from CFSL, U of Wisconsin-
Milwaukee, Amer. J. Soc.
SA, XIV, 6, C2056

1472   Harrison, S.S.

       INDIA;   THE MOST DANGEROUS DECADES
       Princeton U., Press, 1960

1473   Hause, E.M.

       INDIA UNDER THE IMPACT OF WESTERN POLITICAL IDEAS
       AND INSTITUTIONS
       West Polit. Quart. 1967, 14, 4, Dec, 879-895
       SA, XII, 1, A8104

1474   India Planning Commission

       THE FIRST FIVE YEAR PLAN
       New Delhi; 1953(?), 671 pp.

1475   Indian Institute of Agricultural Economics Publication

       CHANGES IN SOCIAL LIFE IN A GUJARAT VILLAGES: A
       COMPARATIVE STUDY (1914-1955)
       Rural Sociology in India ed. A.R. Desai, 1969
       Bombay: Popular Prakashan, pp. 364-372

1476 *Inkeles, Alex

       THE MODERNITY OF THE FACTORY AS A DETERMINANT OF
       INDIVIDUAL MODERNITY
       Paper presented at the ASA Annual Meeting, New York,
       27-30, 1973

1477   Ishwaran, K. (ed.)

       POLITICS AND SOCIAL CHANGE
       New York Humanities, 1966

1478   Ishwaran, K. (ed.)

       CHANGE AND CONTINUITY IN INDIA'S VILLAGES
       New York, Columbia U.P. 1970, 296 pp.

1479   Ishwaran, K.

MALLU R: INTERNAL DYNAMICS OF CHANGE IN A MYSORE
VILLAGE
Change and Continuity in India's Villages ed. K. Ishwaran,
New York, Columbia U. Press 1970, pp. 165-197

1480   Izmirlian, H., Jr.

THE IMPLICATIONS OF POLITICAL STRUCTURE FOR ECONOMIC
BEHAVIOR-A STUDY IN THE COMMUNICATION OF IDEAS
Asian Survey, 1968, 8, 11, Nov, 911-920
SA,XIX, 7, F2340

1481   Jain, P.N.

SOCIAL CHANGE AND PANCHAYAT RAJ
Kurukshetra, 1967, 15, 7, Apr, 2-3
SA XVIII, &, E6058

1482   *Javillona'r Gloria, V, and Peters, G.R.

SOCIOLOGICAL AND SOCIAL PSYCHOLOGICAL ASPECTS OF INDIAN
ENTERPRENEURSHIP
British Journal of Sociology, 24, 3, Sept, 1973

1483   Jayaprakash, W.

TOWARDS A NEW SOCIETY
New Delhi, Congress for Cultural Freedom, 1958
170 pp.

1484   Jayawardena, C.

MIGRA ITON AND SOCIAL CHANGE: A SURVEY OF INDIAN
COMMUNITIES OVERSEAS
Geogr. R. 58,3, Jul, 1968, 476-449

1485   Jena, K.

THE BROJAS OF KORAPUT
Ind. J. Soc. Work, 1961, 22, 2, Sep, 107-111
SA. XI, 7, AD03

1486   Jethey (Mrs.) S.

       PLANNED SOCIAL CHANGE AND MODERNIZATION AMONG INDIAN
       PEASANTS - A STUDY OF SIX VILLAGES IN UTTAR PRADESH
       (Ph d)
       Doct, Banaras, Hindu U, 1970 (Dr. S.K. Srivastava)

1487   Joshi, P.C.

       THE RELEVANCE OF GANDHI FOR INDIAN DEVELOPMENT
       Ind. J. of Sociol, 1970, 1, 2, Sep, 139-152
       SA, XIX, 5, Fo572

1488   Joshi, V.H.

       ECONOMIC DEVELOPMENT AND SOCIAL CHANGE IN A SOUTH
       GUJARIAT VILLAGE, SOCIAL CONSEQUENCES OF INDUSTRIALIZATION
       AND URBANIZATION IN A VILLAGE IN SOUTH GUJARAT WITH SPECIAL
       REFERENCE TO TENSIONS BETWEEN GROUPS AND CLASSES
       Barado, Moharaja Sayajirao, U of Bareda 1966

1489   Kapadia, K.M.

       A PERSPECTIVE NECESSARY FOR THE STUDY OF SOCIAL CHANGE
       IN INDIA
       Sociol B. 1957, 6, 1, Mar 43-60
       SA, VIII, 1, 7223

1490   Kapp, K.W.

       RIVER VALLEY PROJECTS IN INDIA: THEIR DIRECT EFFECTS
       Eco, Dev. Cult. Change 1959 8,1, Oct 24-27
       Sa, XI, 7, A7304

1491   Karunatilake, H.D.B.

       THE IMPACT OF SOME TRADITIONAL SOCIAL INSTITUTIONS--
       AN ECONOMIC DEVELOPMENTAL MOTIVATION IN INDIA -
       HYPOTHETICAL TYPICAL DISCUSSION OF SOME CURRENT ASSUM-
       PTIONS (Ph d)
       Doct., Bombay U., 1965, (Dr. A.R. Desai)

1492 Karve, D.G.

INDIA'S CULTURAL VALUES AND ECONOMIC DEVELOPMENT:
A DISCUSSION, COMMENTS
Econ. Dev. Cult. Change, 1958, 7, 1, Oct, 7-9
SA, XI, 5, A5779

1493* Katano, Hikoji

OPTIMAL STRATEGIES FOR DEVELOPMENT: THE CASE OF INDIA
DEVELOPING ECONOMIES, 1970, 8, 1, Mar, 3-23
SA, 21, 73 G2419

1494 *Kessinger, T.G.

VILAYATPUR 184801968: SOCIAL AND ECONOMIC CHANGE IN A
NORTH INDIAN VILLAGE
Berkeley, University of California Press, 1974

1495 Khan, I.Y.

THE ECONOMIC DEVELOPMENT OF BHILAI-A SOCIAL-ECONOMIC
STUDY (Ph d)
Doct., Agra U., 1967

1496 Khan, N.A.

RESOURCE MOBILIZATION FROM AGRICULTURE AND ECONOMIC
DEVELOPMENT IN INDIA
Econ. Dev. Cult. Change 1963, 12, 1, Oct, 42-54,
SA, XIV, 5, BC1138

1497 Khare, P.C.

THE TRANSFORMATION OF A CLASS: THE SOCIOLOGICAL STUDY
OF FORMER'ILAKEDARS' of REVA STATE
Doct. St., Saugar U. 1969

1498 Khare, R.S.

THE CHANGING BRAHMANS
U. of Chicago Press, 1970

1499   Khare, R.S.

HOME AND OFFICE: SOME TRENDS OF MODERNIZATION AMONG THE
KANYA-KUBJA BRAHMANS
Comparative Studies in Society Hist., 1971, 13, 2, April
196-216,
SA, XX, 7, F9726

1500   Klein, L.R.

WHAT KIND OF MACROECONOMETRIC MODEL FOR DEVELOPING
ECONOMIES?
Ecometric Annual of the Indian Eco. J.,
1965, 13, 3, 313-324, SA, XV11, 2, D5937

1501   Krishna, Daya

CONSIDERATIONS TOWARDS A THEORY OF SOCIAL CHANGE
Bombay, Manaktalas, 1965

1502   Krishnamurti, Jiddu

LIFE AHEAD
ed. by D. Rajagopal,
New York, Harper Row, 1963, 191 pp.

1503   Kulkarni, M.G.

PROBLEMS OF TRIBAL DEVELOPMENT, A CASE STUDY
- HARSUL BLECK, NASIK DISTRICT (MAHARASHTRA)
Poona, Gokhale Instit. of Politics Economics,
1968, X1, 234p.

1504   Kuppaswamy, B.

SOCIAL CHANGE IN INDIA
Dehli, Vikas, 1972

1505   Kuppaswamy, B. & Mehta, P.

SOME ASPECTS OF SOCIAL CHANGE IN INDIA
Verry, 1968, BIP 1972

1506   Kuthiala, S.K.

     IMPACT OF FACTORY PRODUCTION ON TRADITIONAL SOCIETIES:
     MODERNIZATION, SOME ALTERNATIVE VIEWS ON INDIA
     Brit. J. of Sociol.   1971, 22, 2, Jun, 149-159
     SA, XX, 3, F4858

1507   Lokanathan, P.S.

     REGIONAL COOPERATION AND DEVELOPMENT
     Ind. Eco. J., 1968, 15, 3, Jan-Mar, 396-402,
     Comment, 403-409,
     SA, XVIII, 3, E1920

1508   Lall, G.G.

     SOCIAL FACTORS IN ECONOMIC CHANGE-- A FIELD STUDY OF
     TWO VILLAGES IN THE DELHI REGION.
     Doct.St. Delhi U. 1969, (M. N. Srinivas)

1509   Lambert, R.D.

     SOME CONSEQUENCES OF SEGMENTATIONS IN INDIA
     Eco. Dev. Cult. Change, 1964, 12, 4, Jul, 416-424
     SA, XIV, 6, C2062

1510   Lambert, R.D.

     WORKERS, FACTORIES, AND SOCIAL CHANGE   IN INDIA
     Princeton University Press, 1963

1511   La Palombara, J.

     LA CIENCIA SOCIAL EN HOS PAISES EN DESASSOLIO:
     PROBLEMS DE CULTURIZACION (THE SOCIAL SC IENCES IN THE
     DEVELOPING COUNTRIES: A PROBLEM OF ACCULTURATION.)
     Revista Espanola de la opinion Publcia, 1967, 9,
     Jul-Sept, 8-43 (Sp.)
     SA, XVII, ii, D5075

1512   Loomis, C.P.

     SOCIAL ORGANIZATION AND SOCIAL CHANGE
     XXII Congress of the Insitute International de Sociologies
     SA, XVII, 56, Supp. 6,   D9930

1513   Loomis, C.P. & Abraham, F.

SOCIAL AND CULTURAL CHANGE IN MODERN INDIA: A SYSTEM
ANALYSIS AS MANIFEST IN THE WORKS OF M.N. SRINIVAS
Int. R. of Modern Sociology 2, 2, Sep, 1972, 197-210

1514   Madan, G.R.

SOCIAL CHANGE AND PROBLEMS OF DEVELOPMENT IN INDIA
Bombay, Allied Pubs, 1971

1515   Mahapatra, L.K.

SOCIO-CULTURAL CHANGES IN RURAL AND TRIBAL INDIA
Int.J. Comp. Sociol. 1962, 3, 2, Dec, 254-261,
SA, X11, 5, B1010

1516   Mahapatra, L.K.

TECHNOLOGICAL DEVELOPMENT AND CULTURAL RESISTANCE
Balssler Archiv Neve Folge, 1965, 12, 103-114

1517   Mahto, S.N.

TRADING COM. IN CHHOTANAGPUR: A STUDY IN SOCIO-
ECONOMIC CHANGE
Doct, st., Ranchi U, 1969

1518   Majumdar, D.N.

THE DYNAMICS OF SOCIAL CHANGE
Agra Univ. J. Res. (Ph.D.), 1955, 3, Dec, 28-40,
SA, Vol. V1, 1, 4113

1519   Mandelbaum, D.G.

PLANNING AND SOCIAL CHANGE IN INDIA
Human Organ. 12, 3, 4-12, 1953

1520   Mandelbaum, D.G.

SOCIAL ORGANIZATION AND PLANNED CULTURE CHANGE IN
INDIA
Rural Sociology in India ed. A.R. Desai, Bombay,
Popular Prakashan, pp. 693-697

1521   Mann, R.S.

STATIC GRASIAS OF SOUTH RAJASTHAN IN AN ERA OF
PLANNED CHANGE
Ind. Soc. Bull., 1968, 5, 4, Jul, 221-232
SA, XVII,7, EO229

1522 Manndorf, H.

SOCIO-ECONOMIC STRUCTURE AND CULTURAL CHANGE IN
SOUTH INDIAN VILLAGES
Sociologus, 1955, 5, 2, 156-175
SA, V, 4, 3802

1523   Manndorf H.

ZUM STAND DER FORSCHENGEN UBER, AKKULTASATION UND
UNTEGRATION DER BORENENSTAMME INDIENS (THE PRESENT
SITUATION OF ACCULTURATION AND INTERGRATION - RESEARCH
ON THE ABORIGINAL TRIBES OF INDIA)
Sociologus, 1961, 11, 2o-33
Sa XI, 6, A6483

1524   Mathur, V.K.

A SOCIOLOGICAL APPROACH TO ECONOMIC DEV: STUDY IN TWO
VILLAGES AS INDICATORS
Doct. St., Ranchi U., 1969

1525   McDonald, E.E.

STRUCTURAL ANALYSIS OF SOCIETAL CHANGE: THE CASE OF
ELITE FORMATION IN 19th CENTURY WESTERN INDIA
Annual Meeting of the Rural Sociological Society
(1970), Session 44.
Sa, XVlll, 5, Supp. 10, E4210

1526   McRobie, G.

INTERMEDIATE TECHNOLOGY
Com. Dev. J. 1968, 3, 4, Oct, 186-190
Sa, XVIII, 1-2, E 1001

1527   Meagher, R.F.

INDIA'S FIVE YEAR PLAN: THE FINAL DRAFT
Far Eastern Survey, 22, 42-3, March 25, 1953

1528   Mehta, G.H.

DEVELOPMENT AND FOREIGN COLLABORATION
Ind. Eco. J. 1968, 15, 3, Jan-Mar, 343-358,
Comment, 359-376,
SA, XVIII, 3, E1921

1529   *Morris, M.D.

VALUES AS AN OBSTACLE TO ECONOMIC GROWTH IN SOUTH
ASIA: AN HISTORICAL SURVEY
Journal of Economic History, 27, 4, Dec., 1967

1530   Mukerji, D.P.

DIVERSITIES
New Delhi, People"s Pub House, 1958

1531   Mencher, Joan P.

A TAMIL VILLAGE: CHANGING SOCIO-ECONOMIC STRUCTURE
IN MADRAS STATE,
Change and Continuity in India"s Villages.
ed. K. Ishwaran, New York, Columbia U. Press, 1970
pp. 197-219

1532   Mies, M.

DAS INDISCHE DILEMMA NEO-HINDUISMUS, MODERNISMUS AND
DIE PROBLEME DER WIRTSCHAFTLICHEN ENTWICHLUNG (THE
INDIAN DILEMMA.   NEO-HINDUISM, MODERNISM AND THE
PROBLEMS OF ECONOMIC DEVELOPMENT.)

Koelner Zeitschirf and fuer Sociologie and Sozial
psychologie, 1969, Supplement 13, 163-181, (Ger.)
SA, XVIIII, 1-2, E7159

1533 Mishra, S.

      SOCIAL STRUCTURE AND CHANGE AMONG THE KORHUS
      Doct. St., Saugar U., 1969

1534 Moddie, A.

      THE BRAHMANICAL CULTURE AND MODERNITY
      London; Asia Pub. House 1968, vii, 143p.

1535 Mohan, R.P.

      RELIGION AND ECONMIC DEVELOPMENT IN INDIA
      Negro Educational Review, 1964, 15, 3-4, Jul-Oct,
      104-110. SA, XVI, 4, D1587

1536 Mohan, R.P.

      A PRELIMINARY MODEL FOR ORGANIZATION RENEWAL, CHANGE
      AND DEVELOPMENT
      Ind. J. Soc. Res., 13, 3, Dec. 1972, pp. 179-193

1537 Moore, C.D. and D. Eldredge

      INDIA: YESTERDAY AND TODAY
      New York, Bantam Books, 1970

1538 Kewal Motwani

      SAVE INDIA
      Ind. J. Soc. Res, 13,2, Aug, 1972, 85-97

1539 Mukherjee, M.

      NATIONAL INCOME OF INDIA: TRENDS AND STRUCTURE
      Calcutta: Statistical Publishing Society, 1969,
      pp. XXIXT, 521.

1540 Mukherjee, R.

      THE SOCIOLOGIST AND SOCIAL CHANGE IN INDIA TODAY
      Delhi, Prentice Hall of India, 1965, XX229pp.

1541   Mukherjee, R.

STUDY OF SOCIAL CHANGE AND SOCIAL DEVELOPMENT
IN THE DEVELOPING SOCIETIES
Eco. and Pol. Weekly, Bombay, 1970

1542   Mukherjee, R.

SOME OBSERVATIONS ON THE DIACHRONIC AND SYNCHRONIC
ASPECTS OF SOCIAL CHANGE
Social Sci. Information, 1968, 7, 1, Feb. 31-53,
Comment, 54-55
SA, XVll, 2, D5949

1543   Mukherjee, D.P.

INDIAN TRADITION AND SOCIAL CHANGE
Econ. Weekly, 1955, 30, 7, 23, Jul, 877-882,
also in D.P. Mukerji: DIVERSITIES,
New Delhi, People's Pub. House, 1955, pp. 228-241
SA, Vl, 1, 4115

1544   Mukherji, P.N.

A SURVEY IN INDUCED SOCIAL CHANGE: AN INDIAN
EXPERIMENT
Human Organization 1970, 29, 3, Fall, 169-177,
SA, XX, 5, F7088

1545   Muthuswamy, V.R.

COMPARATIVE STUDY OF SOCIAL STRUCTURE AND CHANGE
AMONG HILL AND PLAIN MALYALEES IN SALEM DISTRICT
OF MADRAS STATE
Doct. st, Agra U, 1969 (Dr.B.R.Chauchan)

1546   Nagpaul, H.

TOWARDS MODERNIZATION IN INDIA: SOCIOLOGICAL SURVEY
OF DOMINANT TRENDS
Int. Review of Community Development
n.s. 27-28, Summer 1972

1547   Nandy S.K.

A NOTE ON THE MAJOR DIMENSIONS IN THE STUDY OF POLITICS
AND SOCIAL CHANGE IN DEVELOPING COUNTRIES
Int. J. Comp. Soc., 1966, 7, 1-2, Mar, 143-59
SA, XVI, 7, D4214

1548   Nair, B.N.

SYSTEMATIC APPROACHES TO INDIAN SOCIO-ECONOMIC
DEVELOPMENT
Associated Pub., 1971

1549   Nandy S.k.

THE TRADITIONAL AND THE MODERN IN THE IDEA OF SOCIAL
CHANGE IN POST-INDEPENDENCE INDIA
American Doctoral Dissertations ('62-'63)
(U of Minnesota) (Soc.)

1550   Narain, I.

DECENTRALISATION, DEVELOPMENT, AND DEMOCRACY
Pol. Sci. Review, 1966, 5, 2, Oct, 230-250
SA,XVI, 5, D1588

1551   Nayer, Sushilla

OUR CHANGING LIFE IN INDIA
Woman In the New Asia, ed. B.G. Ward,
Unesco, Paris, 1965, pp. 204-216
pp. 204-216

1552   Nayudamma, Y.

PROMOTING THE INDUSTRIAL APPLICATION OF RESEARCH IN
THE UNDERDEVELOPED COUNTRY
Minerva, 1967, 5, 3, Spr, 323-339
SA, XVIII, $, E3068

1553   Neurath, P.M.

RADIO FARM FORUM AS A TOOL OF CHANGE IN INDIAN
VILLAGES
Eco. Dev. Cult. Change 1962, 10, 3, Apr, 275-283.
SA,XIII, 1, B4220   pp. 37-57

1554   Newell, W.H.

AN UPPER RAVI VILLAGE: THE PROCESS OF SOCIAL CHANGE IN
HIMACHAL PRADESH
Change and Continuity in India's Villages
ed. K. Ishwaran   New York, Columbia U. P, 1970
pp. 37-57

1555   Oommen, T.K.

CHARISMA, SOCIAL STRUCTURE AND SOCIAL CHANGE
Comp. Studies in Society and Hist., 1967, 10, 1,
Oct, 85-99
SA, XVII, 3, D6942

1556   Opler, M.E.

ECONOMIC, POLITICAL AND SOCIAL CHANGE IN A VILLAGE
OF NORTH CENTRAL INDIA
Hum. Org., 11, 2, 1952, p. 5-12

1557   Opler, M.E.

POLITICAL ORGANIZATION AND ECONOMIC GROWTH-
THE CASE OF VILLAGE INDIA
Int. R. Com. Dev. 1960, 5, 187-197
SA, XII, 6, B1753

1558   Orenstein, H.

VILLAGE, CASTE AND THE SOCIAL WELFARE STATE
Hum. Org. 1963, 22, 1, Spr. 83-89
SA, XII, 5, B1017

1559   Pakrasi, K.B.

THE UPROOTED;   A SOCIOLOGICAL STUDY OF WEST BENGAL,
INDIA
Calcutta, 1968

1560   Panchanadikar, K.C. and J.M. Panchandikar

PROCESS OF SOCIAL CHANGE IN INDIA UNDER THE COLONIAL
AND DECOLONIAL ERA - AN ANALYSIS OF CHANGING RURAL-
URBAN COMPLEX
Sociol B. 1965, 14, 2, Sep, 9-26
SA, XIV, 5, C1149

1561   Panchanadikar, K.C.   and J. Panchanadikar

DETERMINANTS OF SOCIAL STRUCTURE AND SOCIAL CHANGE
IN INDIA AND OTHER PAPERS
Bombay, Popular Prakashan, 1970

1562   Pandey, R.S.

SOCIALIZATION AND SOCIAL POLICY IN A MODERNIZING
SOCIETY (BASED ON FIELD STUDY IN INDIA)
(Ph d - Social Work)
Brandeis U., 1971

1563   Pandey, R.S.

IMPACT OF INDUSTRIALIZATION ON RURAL COM.: A STUDY
IN SOCIAL CHANGES IN DEORIA DISTRICT
Doct. St. Gorakhpur U., 1969 (S.P. Nag ndra)

1564   Panikkar, K.M.

HINDU SOCIETY AT CROSS ROADS (3rd ed.)
New York, Asia Pub. House, 1961, 139 pp.

1565   Mukhopadhyaya, T.

ECOLOGY AND MARKETS IN EASTERN MIDNAPUR
Man in India, 1967, 47, 1, Jan-Mar, 61173
SA, XVI, 7, D4231

1566   Pareek, U.

A MOTIVATIONAL PARADIGM OF DEVELOPMENT
J. of Social Issues, 1968, 24, 2, Apr, 115-122
SA, XVII, 2, D5951

1567   Pareek, U.

MOTIVATIONAL PATTERNS AND PLANNED SOCIAL CHANGE
Int. Soc. Sci. J. 1968, 20, 3, 464-473
SA, XVII, 7, E0232

1568   Prasad, N.

CHANGE STRATEGY IN A DEVELOPING SOCIETY: INDIA
Minakshi Prakashan, 1970

1569   Prasad, R.K.

ECONOMIC AND SOCIAL CHANGE AMONG THE PARAHAIRGA
OF PALAMAN - A STUDY IN TRIBAL DYNAMICS (Ph d)
Doct, Ranchi U., 1968 (Dr. L.P. Vidyarthi)

1570   Punekar, S.D.

HUMAN RIGHTS, SOCIAL WELFARE AND LEVEL OF SOCIO-
ECONOMIC DEVELOPMENT
Ind. J. Soc. Work., 1968, 29, 1, Apr, 13-18
SA, XVIII, 1-2, E1009

1571   Raghunandan,Swarup

THE HIMALAYAN REGION OF U.P. - A SOCIO ECONOMIC
SURVEY OF RESOURCES, POSSIBILITIES AND DEVELOPMENT (Ph d)
Doct. Agrau , 1964

1572   Rajagopalan, C.

Social Change: AN ANALYSIS OF ROLE CONFLICT AND
DEVIATION
Ind. J. Soc. work, 1963, 24, 1, Jan 11-18
SA, XII, 4, B0310

1573   Ranadive, K.R.

CONCEPT OF PERSONAL INCOME IN UNDER-DEVELOPED COUNTRIES
Ind. Eco. J. 1966, 12, 5, Apr-Jun, 667-681
SA, XVII, 3, D6945

1574   Ranganathananda

ETERNAL VALUES OF A CHANGING SOCIETY (3ed ed.)
Bharatiya Vidya, 1971

0715   social change and economic development

1575   Rao, G.R.S.

       PROCESS OF INDUSTRIALIZATION AND DIRECTION OF
       SOCIAL CHANGE IN TRIBAL SOCIETY
       J. of Soc. Res. 1966, 9, 2, Sept, 65-69
       SA XVI, 4, D1595

1576   Rao, G.R.S.

       SOCIAL CHANGE AND CONFLICTS IN TRIBAL COMMUNITIES
       Vidyarthi (ed.) Conflict, Tension and Cultural
       Trend in India   India 1969

1577   Rao, L.J.

       STATUS INCONSISTENCY AND MODERNIZATION: THE
       INDIAN CASE
       Paper presented at the 3rd World Congress for rural
       soc.
       SA, XX, V, Sep 24, F7793

1578   Rao, M.S.A.

       SOCIAL CHANGE IN KERALA
       Sociol. Bull. 1953, 2, Sep., 124-134
       SA, vol II, #1, 78

1579   Rao, M.S.A.

       SOCIAL CHANGE IN MALABAR
       Bombay, Popular Book Depot, 1957, vit 228 p.

1580   Rao, M.S.A.

       TRADITION, RATIONALITY AND CHANGE
       Bombay, 1968

1581   Rao, V.K.R.V.

       INDIA'S FIRST FIVE-YEAR-PLAN - A DESCRIPTIVE ANALYSIS
       Pacific Affairs, 25, March 1952, 3-23

                        - 229 -

1582   Rao, V.K.R.V.

SOCIAL CHANGE AND THE TRIBAL CULTURE
also in: Conflict, Tension and Cultural Trend in
India (ed.) L.P. Vidyarthi, India, 1969
J. of Social Res., 1966, 9, 2, Sep, 1-9

1583   Reddy, G.G.

SOCIAL CHANGE AND ARAKU DEVELOPMENT BLOCK
Doct. St., Andhra U., 1969
(Prof. N.S.Reddy) , (Dept. of Anthrop)

1584   Reddy S.K.

ECONOMIC AND SOCIAL DEVELOPMENT
Kurukshetra, 1964, 13, 3, Dec, 21-22, 34.
SA, XIV, 4, C0236

1585   Repetto, R.C.

TIME IN INDIA'S DEVELOPMENT PROGRAMMES
Harvard U. Press, 1971

1586   Rogers, Everett M.

MODERNIZATION AMONG PEASANTS
New York, Holt, Rinehart and Winston, Inc., 1969

1587   Rolnick, P.J.

CHARITY,TRUSTEESHIP, AND SOCIAL CHANGE IN INDIA:
A STUDY OF POLITICAL IDEOLOGY
World Politics 1962, 14, 3, Apr, 439-460
SA, XII, V, B1021

1588   Rose, A.M.

SOCIOLOGICAL FACTORS AFFECTING ECONOMIC DEVELOPMENT
IN INDIA
Studies in Comparative International Dev, 1967-68, 3, 9,
169-183
SA, XVIII, 4, E3070

1589   Rosen, G.

INDUSTRIAL CHANGE IN INDIA: INDUSTRIAL GROWTH,
CAPITAL REQUIREMENTS AND TECHNOLOGICAL CHANGE,
1937-1955
Glencoe   Ill: The Free Press, 1958, 243 pp.
SA, X, 4, A2808

1590   Rosen G.

DEMOCRACY AND ECONOMIC CHANGE, IN INDIA
Berkeley;   U of Calif Press, 1966, 326 pp.

1591   Roy-Burman, B.K.

DYNAMICS OF PERSISTENCE AND CHANGE OF A SMALL
COMMUNITY - THE TOTO (D. Phil.)
Doct., Calcutta U, 1960
(Prof. T.C. Das)

1592   Roy Burman, B.K.

MODERNIZATION PROCESS IN THE BHILS OF NORTH EAST INDIA
J. of the Inst. of Defence Strategy, 1970

1593   Roy Burman, B.K.

MEANING AND PROCESS OF TRIBAL INTEGRATION IN A
DEMOCRATIC SOCIETY
Sociol. B. 1961, 10, 2, Mar 27-40
SA, XI, 6, A6467

1594   Russett, B.

CAMBIO SOCIAL Y ACTITUDES EN RELACION AL DESAROLLO
Y EL SISTEMA POLITICO EN LA INDIA (SOCIAL CHANGE
AND ATTITUDES TOWARDS ECONOMIC DEVELOPMENT AND POLITICAL
SYSTEM IN INDIA
Revista Mexicana de Sociologia, 1968, 30, 2, Apr-Jun,
331-352 (sp.)
SA, XVIII, 1-2, 1178

1595   Sachchidananda

LEADERSHIP AND CULTURE CHANGE IN KULLU
Man in India, 1964, 44, 2, Apr-Jun, 116-131
SA, XIII, 1, B4228

1596 Sachchidananda

DIRECTED CHANGE AMONG THE BIRHOR
East. Anthrop. 1965, 28, 3, Sep-Dec. 172-176
SA, XIV, 6, C2075

1597 Sahay, B.N.

SOCIO-CULTURAL DEVELOPMENT
Pragmatism in Development
Delhi, Bookhouse, 1969

1598 Sahay, K.N.

CHRISIANITY AS A SOURCE OF ECONOMIC DEVELOPMENT
AMONG THE URAON CONVERTS OF CHAINPUR
Ind. J. of Soc. Work, 1967, 28, 2, Jul, 185-194
SA, XVII, 2, D5955

1599 Sahear, (Miss) G.H.

SOCIAL CHANGE, WITH PARTICULAR REFERENCE TO THE
PARSEE COMMUNITY (Ph.d.)
Doct, Bombay U., 1955, (Prof. K.M. Ka padia)

1600 *Saksena, R.N.

MODERNIZATION AND DEVELOPMENT: TRENDS IN INDIA
Sociological Bulletin, 21, 2, Sept, 1972

1601 *Saksena, R.N.

SOCIOLOGY OF DEVELOPMENT AND PLANNING IN INDIA
Sociological Bulletin, 1971, 20, 1, Mar, 1-11
Sa, 21, 73, G5706

1602 Sandwar, A.N.

IMPACT OF HINDUIZATION IN BIHORS & HOS IN CHHOTANNAGPUR
Doct. St. Ranchi, U., 1969

1603 Saran, A.B.

HINDUISM AND ECONOMIC DEVELOPMENT IN INDIA
Archiv. Sociol. Relig. 1963, 8, 15, Jan-Jun, 87-94
SA, XII, 8, B3386

1604   Sarma J.

SOCIAL CHANGE IN BENGAL IN THE LATTER HALF OF THE
NINETEENTH CENTURY
Man In India. 33. 1953, p. 104-26

1605   Sekhar, M.

SOCIAL CHANGE IN INDIA: FIRST DECADE OF PLANNING:
A THEORETICAL ANALYSIS
Poona; Deecan College Post-graduate and research Insti.,
1968

1606   Sen, J.

PROBLEMS IN TRIBAL TRANSFORMATION
Man In India, 1966, 46, 4, Oct-Dec, 319-330
SA XVI, 7, D4225

1607   Sen, L.K.

SOCIAL DIMENSIONS OF MODERNIZATION IN FOUR INDIAN
VILLAGES
American Doctoral Dessertations (1962-63)
(The U. Of Wisconsin), (Soc.)

1608   Shah, A.M.

SOCIAL STRUCTURE AND CHANGE IN GUJARAT VILLAGE (Ph d)
Doct, Maharaja Sayajirao, 1964
U of Baroda   (Dr. I.P. Desai)

1609   Shah, C.H.

CO-OPERATION, DEVELOPMENT AND SOCIO-ECONOMIC FORCE:
A CASE STUDY OF KODNAR TALUKA
Sociol,B. 1966, 15, 2, Sep, 38-44
SA, XV, 6, C7355

1610   Sharma, M.

ROLE OF DEVELOPMENT BANKS
Ind. Finance, 1964, 73, 9, Feb 29, 311-313
SA, XIV, 2-3, B9364

1611   Sharma, M.

AGRICULTURAL DEVELOPMENT IN INDIA
Ind. Coop. R., 1,1, Oct, 41-48
SA, XIV, 2-3, B9363

1612   Sharma, (Miss) S.

ROLE AND RESPONSE OF WOMAN IN DIRECTED CHANGE (Ph d)
Doct, Saugar U, 1966 (dr. (Mrs.) L. Dube)

1613   Sheth, N.R.

MODERNIZATION AND THE URBAN-RURAL GAP IN INDIA: AN ANALYSJ
Sociol B., 1969, 18, 1, Mar, 16-34
SA XIX, 1-2, E7176

1614   Sheth, T.N.

A NOTE ON THE UNITY OF INDIA
Social, B. 1960, 9, 1, Mar, 39-45
SA XI, 6, A6492

1615   Shils, E.

THE INTELLECTUAL BETWEEN TRADITION AND MODERNITY:
THE INDIAN SITUATION
Comp. Stud. Soc. Hist. 1961, Supplement I, 120 pp.
SA, XIIIm 3-4, B6192

1616   Shils E.

TRADITION
Comp. Stud. Soc. Hist., 13, 2, 1971, pp. 122-159

1617   *Singer, M. (ed.)

ENTERPRENEURSHIP AND MODERNIZATION OF OCCUPATIONAL
CULTURES IN SOUTH ASIA
Durham, Duke Univeristy, (south Asia Program), 1973)

1618   Singh, A.K.

        THE IMPACT OF FOREIGN STUDIES: THE INDIAN EXPERIENCE
        Minerva, 1962, 1, 1, Aug, 43-53

1619   Singh, B.K.

        MODERNIZATION AND DIFFUSION OF INNOVATIONS:
        AN INCLUSIVE THEORETICAL MODEL
        Paper presented at the 3rd World Congress
        for Rural Soc.
        SA, XX, 5, Sup, 24, F7804

1620   Singh, R.

        SOCIAL STRUCTURE AND VALUES OF INDUSTRIAL
        WORKERS - A STUDY OF INDUSTRIALISATIONAL
        SOCIAL CHANGE IN SELECTED FACTORIES IN THE
        STATE OF RAJASTHAN
        Doct. st, Rajasthan U, 1969

1621   Singh, R.S.

        LEADERSHIP, INNOVATION AND ECONOMIC DEVELOPMENT
        (EASTERN U.P.)
        Doct, St., Rajasthan U, 1969

1622   Singh, S.

        DEVELOPMENT SCHEMES AS A FACTOR OF CHANGE
        IN TRIBAL AREAS
        Jour. of Soc. Res. 1966, 9, 2, Sep, 52-64,
        SA, XV1, 4, D1601

1623   Singh, T.

        POVERTY AND SOCIAL CHANGE, WITH A REAPPRAISAL (2nd ed.)
        Bombay, Orient Longmans, 1969

1624   Singh, V.B.

        SOCIAL AND ECONOMIC CHANGE IN INDIA
        Paragon, 1967

0715   social change and economic development

1625   Singh, Yogendra

CHANUKHERA: CULTURAL CHANGE IN EASTERN UTTAR PRADESH
Change and Continuity in India's Villages, New York,
Columbia U Press, 1970, pp. 241, 171

1626   Sinha, D.P.

PRINCIPLES AND PROBLEMS OF PLANNED CULTURAL CHANGE
L.P. Vidyarthi (ed.)
Applied Anthropology in India, Allahabad,
Kitab Mahab, 1968, pp. 72-83

1627   Sinha, D.P.

CULTURE CHANGE IN AN INTERTRIBAL MARKET
London, Asia Publishing House, 1968

1628   Sinha, N.

LAND REFORM AND SOCIAL CHANGE AMONG MUNDAS
Doct. st., Ranchi U, 1969

1629   Sinha, R.

SURVIVAL OF THE RICHEST
New Statesman, 47, 398, March 27, 1954

1630   Singer, H.W.

INDIA'S FIVE YEAR PLAN: A MODEST PROPOSAL
Far Eastern Survey, 21, 97-101, June 18, 1952

1631   Singer, M. (ed.)

TRADITIONAL INDIA: STRUCTURE
AND CHANGE
Philadelphia, American Folklore
Society, 1959

1632   Singer, M.

BEYOND TRADITION AND MODERNITY
IN MADRAS
Comp. Studies in Society and Hi., 1971,
13, 2, Apr, 160-195,
SA, XX, 7, F9273

1633   Singer, M. & Cohn, B.S. (eds.)

STRUCTURE AND CHANGE IN INDIAN SOCIETY
(Publications in Anthropology, No. 47)
Chicago, Aldine, 1968, B1D1972

1634   Singer, M.B.

WHEN A GREAT TRADITION MODERNIZES
New York, Praeger, 1972

1635   Singhania, P.

POPULATION GROWTH AND INDIAN ECONOMY
Popul. P. 1957, 1, 2, Jul, 17-20,
SA, Xll, V, B1025

1636   Sovani, N.V.

INDIA'S RECENT ECONOMIC AND SOCIAL DEVELOPMENT WITH
SPECIAL REFERENCE TO POSSIBILITIES OF INTERNATIONAL
COOPERATION
New Delhi, Indian Council of World Affairs, 1950,
63 pp.

1637   Spindler, L. & Spindler, S.

MALE AND FEMALE ADOPTION IN CULTURE CHANGE
Amer. Anthrop., 1958, 56

1638   Srinivas, M.N.

A NOTE ON SANSKRITISATION AND WESTERNIZATION
Far East. Quart, 1956, 15, 4, 481-96

1639   Srinivas, M.N.

SANSKRITISATION
Social Change in Modern India, M.N. Srinivas,
Bombay, 1966, pp. 1-45

1640   Srinivas, M.N.

WESTERNIZATION
M.N. Srinivas Social Change in Modern India
Bombay 1966, p.46-88

1641   Srinivas, M.N.

      SOCIAL CHANGE IN MODERN INDIA
      (Rabindranath Tagore Memorial Lectures)
      Berkeley, U. of Calif. Press, 1966
      1972-BID

1642   Srivastava, L.R.N.

      DEVELOPMENTAL NEEDS OF THE TRIBAL PEOPLE
      New Delhi, 1971

1643   Srivastava, R.P.

      RANG-BANG IN THE CHANGING BHOTIA LIFE
      East. Anthrop., 1953, 6, 3-4, Mar-Aug. 190-203
      SA., vot II, #4, 751

1644   Srivastava, S.K.

      DIRECTED CULTURAL CHANGE AMONG THE THARUS
      Agra U. Jo. of Res., 1956, 4.

1645   Srivastava, S.S.

      A NOTE ON THE QUESTION OF DRESS FOR THE TRIBALS

      Sociol. B., 1961, 10, 2, Sep. 42-45
      SA, XI, 6, A 6494

1646   SubrahmnyamY.S.

      SOME ASPECTS OF SOCIAL CHANGE IN A FRINGE VILLAGE
      IN ANDHRA PRADESH   (Ph d)
      Doct. Delhi, U. 1970   (Dr. J.D. Mehra)

1647   Subudhi, P.C.

      FATALISM AND THE CASTE SYSTEM OF INDIA: A CASE
      STUDY OF THE EFFECTS OF PLANNED SOCIAL CHANGE
      Americal Doctoral Desseratations ('66-67),
      Wayne State U., (soc.)

1648   Subudhi, P.C.

FATALISM AND THE CASTE SYSTEM OF INDIA: A CASE
STUDY OF THE EFFECTS OF PLANNED SOCIAL CHANGE
American Doctoral Dissertations (1966-67)
Wayne State U, (Soc.)

1649   Tandon, P.

PANJABI CENTURY
Berkeley, U of Calif. Press, 1968

1650   Tandon, P.

BEYOND PUNJAB: A SEQUEL TO PUNJABI CENTURY
Berkeley, U of Calif. Press, 1971

1651   Thorner, D.

THE VILLAGE PUNCHAYAT AS A VEHICLE OF CHANGE
Eco. Dev. and Cult. Change, V. 2, Oct, 1953,
p. 209-215

1652   Trent, S.

IRRIGATION AND SOCIO-ECONOMIC CHANGE IN A
MYSORE VILLAGE
Econ. Weekly, 1955, 37, 7, 19, Sep. 1091-1094
SA, V1, 1, 4117

1653   Tripathi, G.

TRIBAL SOCIETY IN A FLUX
Social Welfare, 19, 9, Dec. 1972, B-15

1654   Tripathi, S.

SOCIAL CHANGE AND ANOMIE IN A RURAL URBAN SETTING
SOCIOLOGICAL STUDY OF A SELECTED REGION IN RAJASTHAN
(Ph.D.), Doct, Rajasthan U, 1968
Dr. T.K.N. Unnithan, Dept. of Soc.

1655   Trivedi, D.N.

        MODERNIZATION, OPINION LEADERS AND THEIR INSTRUMENTAL
        INFORMATION-SEEKING BEHAVIOUR
        Man in India, 52, 4,1972, 359-371

1656   Upreti, H.C.

        INDIAN TRIBALS IN TRANSITION
        2nd Sociol. 1963, 5, 6, Mar, 4-5,
        SA, Xlll,3-4, B6035

1657   Useem, J. & Useem, R.H.

        AMERICAN EDUCATED INDIANS AND AMERICANS IN INDIA:
        A COMPARISON OF TWO MODERNIZING ROLES
        Jour. of Social Issues, 1968, 24, 2, Oct, 143-158
        SA, XVll, 5, D8510

1658   Vakil, C.N.

        DEVELOPMENT WITH STABILITY
        Ind. Eco. J. Jan-Mar, 295-315, Comment, 315-319,
        SA, XVlll, 3, E1933

1659   Vakil, C.N. & Brahmananda, P.R.

        REFLECTIONS ON INDIA'S FIVE YEAR PLAN
        Pacific Affairs, 25, 248-62, Sep, 1952

1660   Varma, Baidya, N.

        COMMUNICATION AND SOCIAL CHANGE IN RURAL INDIA
        American Doctoral Dissertations, (1958-59)
        Columbia U. (Soc.)

1661   Vatuk, V.P.

        THESES IN MY HOUSE: FOUR STUDIES IN INDIAN FOLKLORE
        OF PROTEST AND CHANGE
        Varanasi, Viswyidyalaya Prakashan, 1969

1662   Vepa, R.K.

        PROBLEMS OF RURAL INDUSTRIALIZATION
        Kurukshetra, 1964, 12, 10, Jul, 19-21
        SA, XlV, 2-3, B9369

1663   Vishwa Nath

        CHANGES IN KINSHIP AND SOCIETY IN TWO SELECTED AREAS
        IN INDIA
        Doct. st, Delhi U, 1969

1664   von Vorys, K.

        SOME ASPECTS OF THE ECONOMIC DEVELOPMENT IN INDIA:
        THE PROBLEM OF ACCELERATED REACTION
        Politics, 1961, 13, 4, Jul, 504-599
        SA, Xll, 1, A8117

1665   Vyas, N.N.

        TRENDS OF CHANGE AMONG THE BHILS OF RAJASTHAN
        Tribe, 1966, 3, 1, 1-3

1666   Vyas, N.N. & Choudhury, N.D.

        FOREST CO-OPERATIVES AND CHANGE AMONG THE
        TRIBES
        Tribe, 1969, 5, 4

1667   Weiner, M.

        POLITICAL LEADERSHIP IN WEST BENGAL: THE IMPLICATIONS
        OF ITS CHANGING PATTERNS FOR ECONOMIC PLANNING
        Rural Sociology in India ed. A.R. Desai,
        Bombay, Popular Prakashan, 1969

1668   Wertheim, W.F.

        A SOCIOLOGICAL APPROACH TO THE PROBLEMS OF
        UNDERDEVELOPMENT

1669   Wertheim, W.F.

A SOCIOLOGICAL APPROACH TO THE PROBLEMS OF
UNDERDEVELOPMENT
Rural Soc. in India, 1969, ed. A.R. Desai,
Bombay, pp. 950-963

1670   Wiebe, P.D.

CHRISTIANITY AND SOCIAL CHANGE IN SOUTH INDIA
Practic. Anthrop., 17, 3, May-Jun 1970, 128-136

1671   Wilcox, W.

POLITICIANS, BUREAUCRATS, AND DEVELOPMENT
IN INDIA
A. Amer. Acad. Polit. Soc. Sci. 1965, 358,
Mar, 114-122
SA, Z1V, 1, B8510

1672   Winter, D.G. & McClelland, D.C.

MOTIVATING ECONOMIC ACHIEVEMENT
New York Free Press, 1969, pp. xiii-409

1673   Wood, E.

RURAL DEVELOPMENT: LESSONS FROM EUROPE
Int. R. Community Develop. 196, 6, 95, 106
SA, X11, 6, D1759

1674   Vidyarthi, L.P.

STUDIES ON SOCIAL CHANGE IN TRIBAL INDIA:
A METHODOLOGICAL REVIEW
Vidyarthi (ed.) Conflict, Tension and
Cultural Trend in India, India 1969

1675   Zachariah, M.

WHITHER KERALA? SOCIAL CHANGE IN TWENTIETH
CENTURY KERALA
Amer. Doct. Dissert. (1968-69)
U of Minnesota (Soc.)

1676   Zagorski, K.

OPERACJONALIZACJA POJEC "ROZWOJU EKONOMICZNEGO"
I "INTEGRACJI SPOLECZNEJ" W. INDII (OPERATIONALIZATION
ON THE CONCEPTS OF "ECONOMIC DEVELOPMENT" AND
"SOCIAL INTEGRATION" IN INDIA) (Pol.)
Studia Socjologiczno polityczne, 1967, 23, 219-229,
SA, XVll, 3, D6955

1677   -----

INDIA:PROGRESS OR POVERTY
Transatlantic, 1972

1678   -----

SOCIAL REFORM IN INDIA: THE HINDU CODE BILL
World Today, 8, 123-32, March, 1952

1679   Agarwal, N.C.

THE REHABILITATION OF COOPERATIVE SOCIETIES IN
UTTAR PRADESH (Ph.D.
Agra U., 1962

1680   Baichwal, P.R.

WORKING OF THE MULTI-PURPOSE CO-OPERATIVE IN
MYSORE, WITH SPECIAL REFERENCE TO THE WORKING
OF THE MULTI-PURPOSE CO-OPERATIVES IN DHARWAR
DISTRICT (Ph.D.)
Doct. Bombay U, 1963
Dr. M.B. Desai

1681   Basu, B.

ACCOUNTING OF GOODWILL AND ITS EFFECT ON SOCIAL
AND ENTERPRISE ECONOMY (D.Phil.)
Doct, Calcutta U, 1968)

1682   Bhattacharya, N. & Mahalanobis, B.

REGIONAL DISPARITIES IN HOUSEHOLD CONSUMPTION
IN INDIA
J. Amer. Statist. Assoc. 1967, 62, 317, Mar,
143, 161,
SA, XV, 6, C7366

1683   *Bose, Saradindu, R. Jagannadha Rao

MARKETING OF CASTOR SEEDS IN DERARKONDA, TALUKA
Behaviorial sciences and community development
1972, 6, 1, Mar, 98-107
SA, 21, 73, G2432

1684   Dandapani, S.

CONSUMPTION PATTERN OF CLASS III CLERICAL STAFF
OF N.E. RAILWAY HEADQUARTERS AT GORAKHPUR: A
SOCIOLOGICAL SURVEY AND ANALYSIS (Ph.D.)
Doct. Gorakhpur U, 1967
(Dr. S.P. Nagendra)

0749   market structures and consumer behaviour

1685   Devi Prasad

THE WORKING OF CONSUMER COOPERATIVES OF MADHYA
PRADESH (Ph.D.)
Doct. Agra U, 1970
(Dr. R.P. Mittal)

1686   Ghosal, S.N. & Sharma, M.D.

MASS MARKETING MODEL FOR A DEVELOPING ECONOMY
Ind.J.Commerce, 1964, 15, 51
(Part iv) Dec, 293-300,
SA, XlV, 2-3, B9374

1687   Goyal, S.K.

CONSUMER'S COOPERATION IN INDIA WITH
SPECIAL REFERENCE TO U.P. (Ph.D.)
Doct. Agra U, 1966

1688   Iyengar, N.S., Jain, C.R. & Srinivasan, T.N.

ECONOMIES OF SCALE IN HOUSE-HOLD CONSUMPTION:
A CASE STUDY
Econometric Annual of the Ind.Eco.J. 1968,
15,4, 465-477

1689   *Kochanek, S.A.

BUSINESS AND POLITICS IN INDIA
Berkeley, University of California Press, 1974

1690   Krishnamurty, K.

CONSUMPTION FUNDTION FOR INDIA: A MICRO-TIME
SERIES STUDY
Ind.Eco. J. 1965, 13, 2, Oct-Dec. 217-231,
SA, XVll, 2, D5967

1691   Kpde, M.B.

        COOPERATIVE MARKETING IN PALI DISTRICT
        Kurukshetra, 1967, 15, 6, Mar, 21-22,
        SA, XV111, 7, E5834

1692   Mathur, M.P.

        CO-OPERATIVE MARKETING IN U.P. (Ph.D.)
        Doct. Agra U, 1949

1693   Mehta, S.C.

        CONSUMER CO-OPERATION IN INDIA (Ph.D.)
        Doct. Rajasthan U, 1959 (Prof.B.D.Bhargava)

1694   Mohanti, K.K.

        A WEEKLY MARKET IN RURAL ORISSA
        J. of Soc. Res. 1968, 11, 1, Mar, 108-115,
        SA, XV111, 3, E2139

1695   Neale, W.C., Singh, J. & Singh, J.P.

        KURALI MARKET: A REPORT ON THE ECONOMIC
        GEOGRAPHY OF MARKETING IN NORTHERN PANJAB
        Eco. Dev. Cult. Change 1965, 13, 2, Jan, 129-168,
        SA, X1V, 6, C2091

1696   Shekhawat, G.S.

        TRAINED MANPOWER AND CADRES FOR COOPS-RAJASTHAN'S
        PROBLEM
        Kurukshetra, 1967, 15, 4, Jan, 10-12,
        SA, XV111, 6, E5456

1697   Singh, A.P.

        COOPERATIVE BANKS (D.Phil.)
        Doct. Allahabad U, 1951 (Prof. S.K.Rudra)

0749 market structures and consumer behaviour

1698   Thakur   , B.K.G.

       CONSUMER BEHAVIOUR IN THE STATE OF WEST BENGAL WITH
       SPECIAL REFERENCE TO RATIONING (Ph d)
       Doct., Jadavpur U., 1969
       (Dr. A. Jhosh)

1699   The General Report of the Committee of Direction of the
       All India Rural Credit Survey

       VILLAGE COOPERATIVES - AN ANALYSIS OF THEIR FAILURE
       Rural Sociol in India, ed. A.R. Desai.
       pp. 484-489 Bombay; Popular Prakashan, 1969

1700   *Varma, G.L.

       AN ANALYSIS OF FUNCTIONS OF RETAIL KIRANA STORES IN
       SURYAPET TALUKA
       Behavioral Sciences and Community Development
       1972, 6, 1, Mar, 121-126
       SA, 21, 73G2441

1701   Venugopal, C.N.

       ANALYSIS OF A WEEKLY MARKET
       Ind. J. of Soc. Work. 1967, 28, 3, Oct, 335, 337.
       SA, XVII, 4, D7891

1702   Verma, B.B.

       CONSUMERS COOPERATIVE IN BIHAR (Ph d)
       Doct, Lucknow U., 1969
       (Dr. K.C. Sarkar)

1703   Vyas, N.N. and N.D. Choudhury

       FOREST CO-OPERATIVES AND CHANGE AMONG THE TRIBES
       Tribe, 1969, 5,4,

0880   MASS PHENOMENA

0826   social movements

1704   Bhatt, R.N.

THE COOPERATIVE MOVEMENT IN SURAT DISTRICT (Ph d)
Doct., Gujaratand U., 1959
Prof. D.R. Samant

1705   Bhave, A.V.

BHOODANYAGNA

Rural Sociology in India,   ed. A.R. Desai,
Bombay, Popular, 1969, pp. 629-633

1706   Chandra B.

TWO ROLES ON THE AGRARIAN POLICY OF INDIAN NATIONALISTS,
1880 - 1905
Ind. Eco. Soc. Hist. R.   1964, 1, 4, Apr-Jun, 143-174
SA XV, 3, C4956

1707   Choudhuri, M.

THE GRAMDAN MOVEMENT
Rural Sociology in India ed. A.R. Desai,   Bombay
Polular, 1969, pp. 642-553

1708   Choudhury S.

PEASANT'S AND WORKERS'MOVEMENTS IN INDIA,
1905-1929
New Delhi, 1971

1709   Desai, A.R.

INDIAN KISAN: THEIR PRINCIPLE MOVEMENTS BEFORE
INDEPENDENCE
Rural Sociology in India, ed. A.R. Desai,
Bombay, Popular 1969, pp. 390-395

1710   Desai, A.R.

SOCIAL BACKGROUND OF INDIAN NATIONALISM
New York, Humanities, 1966

0825   social movements

1711   Dua, R.P.

       SOCIAL FACTORS IN THE BIRTH AND GROWTH OF INDIAN
       NATIONAL CONGRESS MOVEMENT, WITH REF. TO THE PERIOD
       LEADING TO 1885 UNTIL 1935
       Delhi, S. Chand, 1967, xii-163 p.

1712   Ekka, W.

       REFORM MOVEMENTS AMONG THE NAGESIA
       Man In India, 52, 2, 1972, 174-182

1713   Ghosh, S.K.

       PEASANT REVOLUTION IN BENGAL
       (ed. by J. C. Bagal)
       Calcutta, Bharati Library, 1953, 50 pp.

1714   Gupta, K.C.

       COOPERATIVE MOVEMENT IN MADHYA, BHARAT AND
       BHOPAL (Ph d)
       Doct., Agra U., 1959

1715   Hardgrave, Robt. L.

       THE DRAVIDIAN MOVEMENT
       Bombay: popular Prakashan; New York, The Humanities Press,
       1968.

1716   Hough, E.M.

       THE COOPERATIVE MOVEMENT IN INDIA
       London: Oxford Universitiy, Press 1953, 435 pp.

1717   Hunashal, S.M.

       THE LINGAYAT MOVEMENT: A SOCIAL REVOLUTION IN KARNATAK
       Dharwar; Karnatak. Sahitya Mandira, 1947, 268 pp.

1718   Indra, Deva

       MODERN SOCIAL FORCES IN INDIAN FOLK SONGS
       AGRA u. J. Res. (LeH.) 1955, 3, Dec, 134-147
       SA. VI, 1, 3965

1719   Kotdawala, M.R.

     CO-OPERATIVE MOVEMENT IN INDIA (Ph d)
     Doct, Maharaja Sayajirao   U of Baroda, 1954
     (Dr. S. Chandrashekharan)

1720   Lamba, S.C.S.

     SOCIAL REFORM IN THE PUNJAB (1850-1914)
     Doct. St., Delhi, U., 1969   (S.N. Ranade)

1721   Leonard J.G,

     POLITICS AND SOCIAL CHANGE IN SOUTH INDIA:
     A STUDY OF THE ANDHRA MOVEMENT
     J. of Commonwealth Polit. Studies, 1967, 5, 1, Mar,
     60-77
     SA, XVI, 2, C9963

1722   Mahapatra, L.K.

     SOCIAL MOVEMENTS AMONG TRIBES IN EASTERN INDIA WITH SPECIAL
     REFERENCE TO ORISSA - A PRELIMINARY ANALYSIS
     SOciologus, 1968, 18, 1, 46-62
     SA, XVII, 5, D8386

1723   Mathur, J.S.

     INDIAN WORKING CLASS MOVEMENT (D.L.H.)
     Doct., Allahabad U., 1965, (Prof. J.K. Mehta)

1724   Mehta, B.S.

     COOPERATIVE MOVEMENT IN THE STATE OF RAJASTHAN (Ph d)
     Doct. Rajasthan U., 1964   (Dr. R.N. Baghi)

1725   Motwani K.

     INDIA AND THE WEST: THE ROMANTIC MOVEMENT
     Ind. J. Sol. Res. 13, 1, April, 1972, 1-26

1726   Muzumdar, H.T.

        A COMPARISON OF THE CIVIL DISOBEDIENCE MOVEMENT
        IN INDIA LED BY MAHATMA GANDHI AND THE CIVIL
        DISOBEDIENCE MOVEMENT LED BY REV. MARTIN LUTHER
        KING, JR. AND HIS FOLLOWERS
        Proceedings of the southwestern Sociological Assoc.
        1969, 19, Apr, 9-13, SA, XVlll, 6, E4747

1727   Naik, K.N.

        THE COOPERATIVE MOVEMENT IN BOMBAY STATE
        Bombay: Popular Book Depot
        1953, 282pp.

1728   Oommen, T.K.

        CHARISMATIC MOVEMENTS AND SOCIAL CHANGE (ANALYSIS
        OF BHOODAN-GRAMDAR MOVEMENT IN INDIA) (Ph.D.)
        Doct, Poona U, 1969 (Dr. Y.B.Damle)

1729   Oommen, T.K.

        CHARISMA, STABILITY AND CHANGE: AN ANALYSIS OF
        BHOODAN-GRAMDAN MOVEMENT IN INDIA
        Verry, 1972

1730   Ostergaard, G.N. & Currell, M.

        THE GENTLE ANARCHISTS: A STUDY OF THE LEADERS OF
        THE SARVODAYA MOVEMENT FOR NON-VIOLENT REVOLUTION
        IN INDIA
        1971, Oxford, Clarendon Press, 1971, 421 pp.

1731   Park, R.L.

        THE RISE OF MILITANT NATIONALISM IN BENGAL:
        A REGIONAL STUDY OF INDIAN NATIONALISM (Ph.D.)
        Combridge, Mass., 1950, 298 pp. on micro-film
        (negative), Harvard University

1732   Pillay, T.S.

AN OUTLINE OF THE COOPERATIVE MOVEMENT IN INDIA
Madras: The little Flower
1951, viii and 252 p.

1733   Rao, C.V.H.

COOPERATIVE MOVEMENT IN ANDHRA PRADESH
Kurukshetra, 1964, 12, 7, Apr. 26-28
SA XIV, 1, B8691

1734   Rathra, (Miss) N.

COOPERATIVE MOVEMENT IN HYDERABAD STATE (Ph d)
Doct, Mysore U., 1961,   (Prof. S.K. Iyengar)

1735   Sahajanandan, V.M.

SOCIAL REFORM MOVEMENT IN KERALA 1805-1947
Doct. St., Delhi, U., 1969 (S.N. Rarade)

1736   Saksena, P.S.

THE COOPERATIVE MOVEMENT IN UTTAR PRADESH, (Ph d)
Doct. Agra U., 1962

1737   Sehgal, V.

A SOCIOLOGICAL STUDY OF ARYA SAMAJ
Doct., St., Delhi U., 1969   (A.M. Shah)

1738   *Schnitt, Erika

"SONAT SANTAL SAMAJ" - A SOCIOLOGICAL MOVEMENT AMONG
THE SANTALS IN DHANBAD DISTRICT, BIHAR INDIA
Sociologus, 23, 2, 1973

1739   Shah, C.G.

SAMPATTIDAN AND BHOODON MOVEMENT
Rural Sociology in India, ed. A.R. Desai
Bombay, Popular, 1969, pp. 636-642

1740   Sharma, G.K.

LABOUR MOVEMENT IN INDIA: ITS PAST AND PRESENT
(1885-1960) (Ph.D.)
Doct., Rajasthan U., 1962,   (Dr. R.P. Singh)

1741   Sharma, H.D.

NON-COOPERATIVE MOVEMENT 1919-1922, (Ph d)
Doct, Delhi U., 1970   (Prof. B. Prasad)

1742   Shirodkar, S.L.
COOPERATIVE MOVEMENT IN KOLHAPUR DISTRICT - A STUDY (Ph d)
Doct, Poona U., 1968
(Dr. D.L. Gadgil)

1743   Shukla S.

SOCIOLOGY OF SOCIALIST REVOLUTION
10th All Indian Sociological Conference
Hyderabad, 1970   (Mimeographed)

1744   Stokes, E.

TRADITIONAL RESISTANCE MOVEMENTS AND AFRO-ASIAN
NATIONALISM: THE CONTEXT OF THE 1857 MUTINY REBELLION IN
INDIA
Past and Present 1970, 48, Aug, 100-118
SA, XX, 7, F9302

1745   Thomas, J.K.

THE RISE OF THE INDIAN LABOUR MOVEMENT   (thesis)
Chicago, University of Chicago, 1950, 46 pp.

1746   Thorner, D.

RURAL SOCIOLOGY IN INDIA
ed. A.R. Desai   Bombay Popular, 1969, pp. 633-636

0825   social movements

  1747   Wallbank, T.N.

          INDIA: A SURVEY OF THE HERITAGE AND GROWTH OF
          INDIAN NATIONALISM
          New York, Holt, 1949, 118 pp.

  1748   Winthrop H.

          THE QUIET REVOLUTIONS AND THE PERMANENT ONE
          J.of Human Relations, 1969, 17, 3, 359-473
          SA, XlX, 3, E8549

  1749   -----

          SATYAGRAHA: NON-VIOLENT RESISTANCE
          Ahmedabad: Navajivan, 1951, 406pp.

0827   public opinion

  1750   Agarwal, (Miss) S.

          THE INFLUENCE OF THE PRESS ON THE GOVERNMENT AND
          PUBLIC OPINION IN INDIA FROM 1900 TO 1935 (D.Phil.)
          Doct. Allabad U, 1956, Capt.A.B.Lal.

  1751   Brainthal, G.

          AN ATTITUDE SURVEY IN INDIA
          Public Opinion Quart. 1969, 33, 1, Apr, 69-82,
          SA, XVlll, 1-2, E1029

  1752   Cantril, A.H.Jr.

          THE INDIAN PERCEPTION OF THESINO-INDIAN BORDER CLASH
          Publ. Opin.Quart. 1964, 28,2, Sum, 233-242,
          SA, Xll, 8, B34,8

  1753   Goel, M.L.

          DISTRIBUTION OF CIVIC COMPETENCE FEELING IN INDIA
          Social Sci. Quart, 1970, 51, 3, Dec, 755-768,
          SA, XX, 3, F4895

1754 Karna, M.N.

INDIAN STATES ON SOCIAL DISTANCE SCALE
Man In India, 1967, 47, 3, Jul-Sep, 228,237
SA XVII. 2. D5983

1755 Kogekar, S.V.

THE STUDY OF PUBLIC OPINION IN INDIA
Ind. J. Polit. Sci., 1957, 18, 1, Jan- Mar, 1-4
SA VII 2, 5802

1756 Lal Goel J.
THE RELEVANCY OF SEX DIFFERENCES FOR POLITICAL
PARTICIPATION IN INDIA
Political Scientist, 1969, 6, 1-2, Jul-Dec, 1-1970
Jan-jun, 49-56
SA, XX, 4, F6188

1757 Mukerji, K.P.

MORPHOLOGY OF PUBLIC OPINION
Ind. J. Polit. Sci. 1957, 18, 3-4, Jul-Dec 217-223
SA VII, 4, 6546

1758 **Murty,** V.L.

PUBLIC OPINION AND PARLIAMENTARY GOVERNMENT IN INDIA
Ind. J. Polit. Sci., 1956, 17, 4, Oct-Dec 378-384
SA, VII, 1, 5394

1759 Palmier, L.

INDIAN ATTITUDES
New Society, 1966, 7, 174, 12-15
SA XIV 6, C2120

1760 Ramachandran, P.

PUBLIC OPINION ON EDUCATION
Ind. J. Soc. Work, 1971, 31, 4, Jan, 355-356
SA, XX 6, F8307

0827   public opinion

    1761   Ramachandran, P.

           PUBLIC OPINION ON EDUCATION
           Ind. J. Soc. Work. 1971, 31, 4, Jan, 355-365
           SA, XX, 6, F8307

0828   communication; adoption of innovations

    1762   Ahluwalia, (Miss) V.

           A STUDY IN COMMUNICATION AND CHANGE
           Doct. St., Saugar U., 1969

    1763   Alam, S.S.F., N.K. Jaiswal, D.K. Singh, and A.K. Singh

           ATTITUDE OF TRIBALS AND NON-TRIBALS OF RANCHI TOWARD
           FERTILIZERS
           Man in India, 52, 4, 1972, Oct-Dec 328-335

    1764   Allababad   Agricultural Institute

           EXTENSION EVOLUTION
           Allababad, India, 1957

    1765   Anand, A.

           A STUDY OF SELECTED VALUE-ORIENTATIONS OF RURAL
           WOMEN AS RELATED TO ADOPTION OF RECOMMENDED
           HEALTH PRACTICES   (Msc. Thesis)
           U. of Delhi, 1966

    1766   Basu, S.K.

           ADOPTION OF TWO IMPROVED PRACTICES BY FARMERS IN
           WEST BENGAL
           Society and Cult. 1970, 1, 1, Jul, 37-40
           SA, XX, 7, F9496

    1767   Bahvara, (Miss) R.K.

           COMMUNICATION AND SOCIAL CHANGE
           Rajasthan U., 1969

0828   communication; adoption of innovations

1768   Bhowmik, K.L., Das, P., & Chatterjee, S.

         ADOPTION OF A HEALTH VARIABLE AND SOCIO-CULTURAL
         CHARACTERISTICS OF A MUSLIM POPULATION IN A RURAL
         REGION OF WEST BENGAL
         Society and Cult, 1970, 1, Special number, 23-32,
         SA, XX, 7, F9500

1769   Bhasin, H.S.

         AN INVESTIGATION INTO SOME FACTORS INFLUENCING
         HOW ADOPTION OF SELECTED FARM PRACTICES IN SAMANA
         BLOCK, PATIALA, PUNJAB
         Summaries of Extension by Post-graduate students
         Punjab Agri U, 1966

1770   Bhatia, R.

         A STUDY OF SOME FACTORS AFFECTING ADOPTION OF
         POULTRY FARMING IN HESSIAN DISTRICT, PUNJAB
         Summaries of Extension by Post-graduate students
         India, Punjab Agri U, 1966

1771   Bhosale, R.J.

         RELATIVE EFFECTIVENESS OF EXTENSION TECHNIQUES FOR
         POPULARIZING IMPROVED VEGETABLE GROWING IN THE
         I.C. SCHEME AREA, NANGLOI
         (MS Thesis)
         Indian, Agri. Res.Inst., 1960

1772   Bhowmik, K.L., Gupta, S. & Das, P.

         RELATION OF TENURE STATUS AND FARM EFFICIENCY TO
         ADOPTION BEHAVIOUR OF FARMERS IN A WEST BENGAL VILLAGE
         Society and Culture, 1970, 1, 1, Ju, 1-15,
         SA, XX, 7, F9499

1773   Bose, A.B.

         MASSCOMMUNICATION: THE CINEMA IN INDIA
         Ind. J. Soc. Res. 1963, 4, 80-82,
         SA, XlV, 2-3, B9397

1774   Bose, A.B.

THE NEWSPAPER READER IN INDIA
Ind. J. Soc. Res. 1964, 5, 1, Apr, 34-40
SA, XIV, 2-3, B9396

1775   Bose, A.B.

THE PROCESS OF ADOPTION OF AGRICULTURAL INNOVATIONS IN
W. RAJASTHAN
Ind. Jour. of S.W. 1966, 27, 3, Oct, 263-268
SA, XIV, 5, D2594

1776   Bose, A.B.

THE STRUCTURE OF COMMUNICATION IN DIFFERENT SOCIAL
STRATA IN RURAL U.P.   (Ph d)
Doct. Lucknow U., 1969
(Dr. R.K. Mukerji)

1777   Bose, S.P.

RELATIVE INFLUENCE OF SOCIO-ECONOMIC FACTORS ON THE
ACCEPTANCE OF THE COW-DUNG GAS PLANT BY THE FARMERS
WHEN EXPOSED TO EXTENSION TEACHING   (M.S. Thesis)
Ind. Agr. Res. Inst., 1960

1778   Bose, S.P.

CHARA CTERISTICS OF FARMERS WHO ADOPT AGRICULTURAL
PRACTICES IN INDIAN VILLAGES
Rural Sociol. 1961 26, 2, Jun, 138-145
SA, IX, 3, 9968

1779   Bose, S.P.

PEASANT VALUES AND INNOVATION IN INDIA
Amer. J. Sociol, 1962, 2, Mar, 552-560
SA, X, 3, A2276

1780   Bose, S.P.

THE DIFFUSION OF A FARM PRACTICE IN INDIAN VILLAGES
Rur. Soc. 1964, 29, 1, Mar, 53-66
SA, XII, 6, B1893

0828   communication; adoption of innovations

1781   Bose, S.P.

THE DIFFUSION OF A FARM PRACTICE IN INDIAN VILLAGES
Rur. Soc. 1964, 29, 1, Mar, 53-66

1782   Bose, S.P:

AIMS AND METHODS OF AGRI.EXTENSION AND THEIR ADAPTION
TO THE HUMAN FACTORS IN DEVELOPING COUNTRIES.
Paper presented at Rehovoth Convention on
comprehensive Planning of Agri. in Developing
Countries, Isreal, 1963

1783   Bose, S.P.

THE ADOPTERS
Calcutta;   West Bengal Dept of Agri, Ext. Bulletin, 1964

1784   Bose, S.P. and S.K. Basu

INFLUENCE OF REFERENCE GROUPS ON ADOPTION
BEHAVIOUR OF FARMERS
Cultural Res. Inst., 1963

1785   Bose, S.P. and S. Dasgupta

THE ADOPTION PROCESS
Calcutta;   Socio-Agro-Economic Res. Org.
Ext. Bulletin, 1962

1786   Chakrabarti, A.K.

A DISSONANCE THEORY APPROACH TO COMMUNICATION
CHANNEL USAGE
Ind. J. Soc. Res. 13, 2, Aug,/72, 98-110

1787   Chandra P.

COMMUNICATION OF SOME NEW IDEAS IN A MADHYA PRADESH
VILLAGE, A SOCIOLOGICAL STUDY CONDUCTED IN A MIXED VILLAGE
East. Anthrop. 1964, 17, 3, Sep-Dec, 183-214
SA, XIV, 4, C0433

0828   communication; adoption of innovations

1788   Chattopadhyaya,S.

A STUDY OF SOME PSYCHOLOGICAL CORRELATES OF
ADOPTION OF INNOVATIONS IN FARMING, (ph d)
Doct. of Indian Agri. Res. Inst., 1965
(Dr. V. Pareek)

1789   Chattopadhyaya, S.N.

PSYCHOLOGICAL CORRELATES AND ADOPTION OF INNOVATIONS
Selected Readings in Community Development
T.P.S. chowdhari
India: Nat'l Instit. of C.D.   1967

1790   Chattopadhyaya, S.N. and U. Pareek

PREDICTION OF MULTI-PRACTICE ADOPTION BEHAVIOUR FROM
SOME PSYCHOLOGICAL VARIABLES
Rural Sociology, 1967

1791   Choudhary, K.M.

FACTORS AFFECTING ACCEPTANCE OF IMPROVED AGRICULTURAL
PRACTICES
India; Agro-Eco Res. Center, 1965

1792   Choudhary K.M. and M. Maharaja

ACCEPTANCE OF IMPROVED PRACTICES AND THEIR
DIFFUSION AMONG WHEAT GROWERS IN THE PALI DISTRICT
OF RAJASTHAN
Ind. J. Agr.   Eco., 1966

1793   Damle, Y.B.

THE PROBLEM OF CULTURAL COMMUNICATION OF MODERN
IDEAS IN INDIAN VILLAGES
Agra U., J. Res. (Lett.) 1955, 3, Dec, 109-114
SA VI, 3, 4768

1794   Damle, Y.B.

COMMUNICATION OF MODERN IDEAS AND KNOWLEDGE IN
INDIAN VILLAGES
Pub. Opin. Quart. 1956, 20, 1, Apring, 257-270
SA, VI, 3, 4769

1795   Damle, Y,B.

COMMUNICATION OF MODERN IDEAS AND KNOWLEDGE IN
INDIAN VILLAGES
Rural Sociology in India   ed. A.R. Desai
Bombay: Popular Prakashan, 1969   pp. 378-389

1796   Danda, A.K.

A NOTE ON ADOPTION OF INNOVATIONS
The Proceedings of 57th Session of the IndianScience
congress, 1970.

1797   Danda, A.K. and D.G.

ADOPTION OF AGRICULTURAL INNOVATION IN A WEST BENGAL VILLAGE
Man in India   52, 4, Oct-Dec, 1972   303-320

1798   Dantre, M.P.

Adoption of Improved Farm Practices and Related Factors
(M.S. thesis)   India, 1963

1799   Das. K.K.

ADOPTION OF IMPROVED FARM PRACTICES IN A WEST BENGAL VILLAGE
Society and Cult. 1970, 1, 1, Jul, 81-93
SA, XX, 7, F9505

1800   Das, K.K. and A.K. Majumdar

STUDY ON SOME ASPECTS OF ADOPTION OF HEALTH INNOVATION
BY MIGRATED AND MON-MIGRATED FARMERS
Society and Cult. 1970 1, Special number, 57-64
SA, XX, 7, F9504

1801   Dasgupta, S.

SOCIOLOGY OF INNOVATION
Bul. of the Cult. Res. Inst., 1962

1802   Dasgupta, S.

THE INNOVATORS
Calcutta; Dept. of Agri,   West Bengal, 1963

1803   Dasgupta, S.

INNOVATION AND INNOVATORS IN INDIAN VILLAGES
Man In India, 1963, 43, 1, Jan, Mar   27-34
SA, XII, 6, B1894

1804   Dasgupta, S.

COMMUNICATION AND INNOVATION IN INDIAN VILLAGES
Soc. Forces, 1965, 43, 3, Mar 330-337
SA, XIII, 6-7, B7918

1805   Dasgupta, S.

USE OF TRACELINE ANALYSIS IN THE CONSTRUCTION OF AN
ADOPTION SCALE OF RECOMMENDED FARM PRACTICES
Man in India 1967, 47, 4, Oct-Dec, 279-294
SA, XVII, 3, D7101

1806   Dasgupta, S.

VILLAGE (OR COMMUNITY) FACTORS RELATED TO THE LEVEL OF
AGRICULTURAL PRACTICE
paper presented at South Soc. Society, New Orleans, 1966

1807   Deb, P.C.

DIFFERENTIAL CHARACTERISTICS OF ADOPTERS AND
NON-ADOPTERS OF AN IMPROVED PRACTICE
Ind. Soc. B. 1960, 5, 4, Jul, 243-247
SA, XVII, 7, E0400

0828   communication; adoption of innovations

1808   Deb, P.C., H. Singh, and M.L. Sharma

        SOURCES OF INFORMATION USED IN THE ADOPTION OF
        IMPROVED PRACTICES
        Man in India, 1968, 48, 2, Apr-Jun, 167-173
        SA, XVIII, 1-2, E1184

1809   Desai, D.K., and B.M. Sharma

        TECHNOLOGICAL CHANGE AND RATE OF DIFFUSION
        Ind. J. Agri. Eco., 1966

1810   Deshpande, W.R.

        SOCIO-ECONOMIC ASPECTS OF INTRODUCING COWDUNG GAS PLANT
        (unpublished) New Delhi, IARI, 1962

1811   Dey, P.K.

        RELATIVE EFFECTIVENESS OF RADIO AND TELEVISION AS
        MASS COMMUNICATION MEDIA IN DESSIMINATION OF
        AGRICULTURAL INFORMATION(Ph d)
        Doct., Indian Agricultural Research Inst., 1968
        (Dr. S.K. Sharma)

1812   Dhaliwal, A.J. Singh

        A STUDY OF SOME IMPORTANT FACTORS AFFECTING THE
        ADOPTION OF A FEW SELECTED AGRICULTURAL PRACTICES BY
        THE CULTIVATORS OF LUDHANA C.D. BLOCK
        Summaries of Extension Research by post-graduate
        students India: punjab, Agri, U., 1963

1813   Dhaliwal, A.J., Singh, and T.S. Sohal

        EXTENSION CONTACTS IN RELATION TO ADOPTION OF AGRICULTURAL
        PRACTICES AND SOCIO-ECONOMIC STATUS OF FARMERS
        Ind. J. Ext. Edu., 1965

1814   Dhillen, H.S. and Mukerji

        BELIEFS, CUSTOMS, AND HABITS THAT AFFECT THE USE OF
        LABORERS AND ITS MAIN FINANCE
        Ind. Sociol. Confer.; Calcutta, 1959

1815   Dobbs, T. and P. Foster

INCENTIVES TO INVEST IN NEW AGRICULTURAL INPUTS IN
NORTH INDIA
Eco. Dev. and Cult. Change, 21, 1, Oct. 1972,   101-118

1816   Dube, S.C.

COMMUNICATION, INNOVATION AND PLANNED CHANGE IN INDIA
Communication and Change in Developing Countries
ed. D. Lerñr, and W. Schramm Honolulu, 1967

1817   Dubey, S.C.

ADOPTION OF A NEW CONTRACEPTIVE IN URBAN INDIA: ANALYSIS
OF COMMUNICATION AND FAMILY DECISION-MAKING PROCESS
Americal Doctoral Dessertations   (1966-'67)
Michigan State U., (Soc. family)

1818   Dubey, D. C.

ADOPTION OF A NEW CONTRACEPTIVE IN URBAN INDIA
New Delhi, Central Family Planning Insit; 1969, 132 pp.

1819   Dubey, D.N.

STUDY OF FACTORS INFLUENCING COMMUNITY ADOPTION PROCESS
IN RELATION TO IMPROVED FARM PRACTICES IN ANAND TALUKA OF
GUJARAT STATE
M.S. Thesis , India, 1966

1820   *Dunn, Max, Gilbert

THE ROLE OF THE MEDIA IN INDIAN POPULATION CONTROL
Human Mosaic, 1972, 5, 2, Spr., 15-25
SA, 21, 73 G1680

1821   Durgadas

INDIAN PRESS AND ITS INFLUENCE
Group Prejudices in India
ed. M.B. Nanavti and C.N. Vakil
Bombay, Vora, 1951 pp. 2-3-209

0828 communication; adoption of innovations

1822 Eapen, K.E.

DAILY NEWSPAPERS IN INDIA: THEIR STATUS AND PROBLEMS
Journalism Quest, 1967, 44, 3,
Act, 520-532
SA, XVII, 1, D5044

1823 Eldersveld, S.J.

BUREAUCRATIC CONTACT WITH THE PUBLIC IN INDIA:
SOME PRELIMINARY FINDINGS IN DELHI STATE
Ind. J. Pub., Admin. 1965,1, 2, Apr-Jun 216,235
SA, XV, 1, C3623

1824 Fliegel, F.C.

INNOVATION IN INDIA: THE SUCCESS OR FAILURE OF AGRICULTURAL
DEVELOPMENT PROGRAMS IN 108 INDIAN VILLAGES
India; Nat'l Inst. C.D. 1967

1825 Fliegel, F.C.

MESSAGE DISTORTION AND THE DIFFUSION OF INNOVATIONS IN
NORTHERN INDIA
Sociologia Ruralis , 1971, 11, 2, 178-192
SA, XX, 3, F5083

1826 Fliegel, F.C., J.E. Kivlin and G.S. Sekhon

A CROSS-NATIONAL COMPARISON OF FARMERS' PERCEPTIONS
OF INNOVATIONS AS RELATED TO ADOPTION BEHAVIOUR

Rural Sociology, 1968, 33, 4, Dec, 437-449
SA, XVII, 6, D9552

1827 Fliegel, F.C. and G.S. Sekhon

BALANCE THEORY AND THE DIFFUSION OF INNOVATIONS
AN EMPICAL TEST
1969 Meeting of the Rural Sociological Society, Session 42
SA, XVII, 5, Supp. 4. D8820

1828   Gaikwad, V.R.

LOCATION OF CONTRIBUTION OF VARIABLES IN ADOPTION PROCESS
Behav. Sci. and C.D., 1969, 3, 1, Mar, 23-37
SA, XIX, 4, F287
Also - an unpublished report   Nat'l Inst. of C.D.
Hyderabad, 1968

1829   Gaikwad,V.R.

REVIEW OF RESEARCHES CONDUCTED IN N.I.C.D. ON DIFFUSION AND
ADOPTION OF AGRICULTURAL INNOVATIONS
2nd All India Seminar on Research in Extension, May 14-17, 19

1830   Grewal, I.S.

DIFFENTIAL CHARACTERISTICS OF FARMERS OF PREDOMINANTLY
REFUGEE, A NATIVE AND A MIXED VILLAGE, AFFECTING THE
ADOPTION OF IMPROVED AGRICULTURE PRACTISES IN A
BLOCK IN LUDHIANA DISTRICT OF PUNJAB STATE
Summaries of Extension by Post-graduate students, India,
1965

1831   Gupta, P.K.

A STUDY OF SOME FACTORS AFFECTING ADOPTION OF POULTRY
FARMING IN MOGA TEH SIL, PUNJAB
Summaries of Extension Research by Post-graduate Students, In
1966

1832   Hodgdon, LL. and H. Singh

THE ADOPTION OF AGRICULTURAL PRACTICES IN TWO VILLAGES
OF MADHYA PRADESH
Delhi, Ford Foundation Report, 1963

1833   Honingmann, J. and M. van Doorslayer

SOME THEMES IN INDIAN FILM REVIEWS
East. Anthrop. 1956-57, 10, 2, Dec. Feb; 87-97
SA, VIII, 1, 7108

1834   Husain, Asad

THE FUTURE OF ENGLISH-LANGUAGE NEWSPAPERS IN INDIA
Jour. Quart., 1956, 33, 2, spring 213-219
SA. VI, 1, 4038

1835   Jain, N.C.

A STUDY OF RELATIVE EFFECTIVENESS OF EXTENSION METHODS
IN ADOPTION OF IMPROVED AGRICULTURAL PRACTICES IN
DEV. BLOCK AMRAUDHA,   DISTRICT KANPUR
(M.S. thesis)   India, 1963

1836   Jain, N.C.

AN EXPERIMENTAL INVESTIGATION OF THE EFFECTIVENESS OF
GROUP LISTENING, DISCUSSION, DECISION COMMITMENTS,
AND CONSENSUS IN INDIAN RADIO FORUMS
Amer. Doc. Dissertations, ('68-'69)
Michigan State U., (Soc. Psy.)

1837   Jaiswal, N.K.

A STUDY OF FACTORS ASSOCIATED WITH LOW LEVEL OF ADOPTION OF
IMPROVED AGRICULTURAL PRACTICES (Ph d)
Doct, Indian Agricultural Research Instit, 1965.
(Prof. A.R. Khan)

1838   Jha, P.N.

A CRITICAL ANALYSIS OF FACTORS ASSOCIATED WITH COMMUNICATION
FIDELITY WITH REFERECE TO HIGH YIELDING VARIETIES PROGRAMME.
(Ph d Thesis)   New Delhi, IARI, 1968.

1839   Jha, P.N. and B.N. Singh

UTILIZATION OF SOURCES OF FARM INFORMATION AS RELATED
TO CHARACTERISTICS OF FARMERS
Ind. J. Ext. Educ.   1966.

1840   Junghare, Y.N.

FACTORS INFLUENCING THE ADOPTION OF FARM PRACTICES
Ind. J. Soc. work, 1962, 23, 2, Oct., 292-296
SA, XII, 2, A9043

0828 communication; adoption of innovations

1841 Junghare, Y.N. and W.B. Lahudkar

THE INFLUENCE OF FAMILY MEMBERS ON DECISION-
MAKING IN FARM OPERATIONS
Nagpur Agri. Coll. Mag, 1962

1842 Kahon, A.S. and M.P. Kaushal

ADOPTION OF IMPROVED AGRICULTURAL PRACTICES IN THE
PLAINS OF THE PUNJAB

Punjab Agri. U., India, 1967

1843 *Kaminski, Edward

PRASA W. INDIACH (THE PRESS IN INDIA)
Zeszyty Prasoznawcze, 1971, 12,3, 86-98 (Polish)
SA, 21, 73g4221

1844 Kapoor, J.M. an Roy P.

ROLE OF MASS MEDIA AND INTERPERSONAL COMMUNICATION IN
THE DIFFUSION OF A NEWS EVENT IN INDIA
(unpublished paper)
Mich. State U., 1969

1845 Kapoor, R.P.

RELATIVE EFFECTIVENESS OF INFORMATIVE SOURCES IN THE
ADOPTION PROCESS OF SOME IMPROVED FARM PRACTICES
Summaries of Extension by Post-graduate Students, 1966

1846 Kar, L.N.

DIFFUSION AND ADOPTION OF INNOVATION AND SOCIAL CHANGE IN
AGRICULTURE WITH SPECIAL REFERENCE TO THE PROBLEMS OF
SMALL FARMERS
I.A.R.I. (unpublished)
New Delhi, 1959

0828 communication; adoption of innovations

1847 Kar, Mati Lal

THE ADOPTION PROCESS AND THE ADOPTER CATEGORIES OF
SOME IMPROVED PRACTISES IN PADDY CULTIVATION IN A
WEST BENGAL VILLAGE
Research Studies in Ext. Educ. India, 1967

1848 Kerr, G.B. and J.M. Kapoor

FIELD EXPERIMENTS ON THE DIFFUSION OF INNOVATIONS
IN BRAZIL, INDIA AND NIGERIA

1969 Annual Meeting of the Rural Sociological Society
Session 3
SA, XVII, 5, Sup 4, D8847

1849 Kivlin, J.E.

COMMUNICATION AND DEVELOPMENT SUCCESSS-FAILURE
IN INDIAN VILLAGES
(Ph d) U.S. 1967

1850 Kivlin, J., Fliegel, F., Sen L and P. Ray.

COMMUNICATION IN INDIA: EXPERIMENTS IN INTRODUCING CHANGE
Nt'l Inst. of C.D., Hyderabad, 1968

1851 Kuswaha, B.S.

EFFECTIVEMESS OF THE RESULT DEMONSTRATION IN THE
ADOPTION OF THE IMPROVED FARM PRACTICES
(M.S.), India, 1963

1852 Lakshmanna, C. and M. Satyanarayana

PERSONAL CORRELATES AND THE DEPENDENCE UPON THE
SOURCES OF INFORMATION IN THE ADOPTION PROCESS.
Ind. Sociol B., 1969, 6, 4, Jul, 267-274
SA XIX, 1-2, E7434

1853 Lakshminarayana

DIFFERENTIAL COMMUNICATIONS AND PROCESS OF ADOPTION
OF FARM INNOVATIONS IN LADP VILLAGES
Ind. J. Soc. Res, 13, 3, Dec, 1972, 208-211

1854   Lakshninarayana, H.D.

       DIFFERENTIAL CHARACTERISTICS OF ADOPTERS AND NON-
       ADOPTERS OF FARM PRACTISES
       Beh, Scis.& C.D., 1970, 4, 1, Mar, 16-22
       SA, XIX, 6, F1700

1855   Mahajan, B.S.

       RELATIVE EFFECTIVENESS OF SELECTED EXTENSION METHODS IN
       ACCEPTANCE OF AGROSAN G.N. SEED TREATMENT TO COTTON
       A.P. Agri. U., 1966

1856   Mann, R.S.

       ATTITUDE OF MINAS TOWARDS IMPROVED AGRICULTURAL PRACTICES
       Man In India, 1966, 46, 2, Apr-Jun, 131, 134
       SA, XVI, 6, D3467

1857   Marriot, M.

       CHANGING CHANNELS OF CULTURAL TRANSMISSION IN INDIAN
       CIVILISATION
       Intermediate Societies, Social Mobility and
       Communication
       ed. V.F. Ray, Seattle, 1959, pp. 66-74

1858   Mayfield, R.C.

       FOOD HABIT CHANGES ACCOMPANYING AN AGRICULTURAL DIFFUSION
       IN SOUTH EAST MYSORE
       Abstract of Papers, 28th International Congress of
       Orientalists, Canberra, 1971

1859   Mishra, V.M.

       MASS MEDIA U SE AND MODERNIZATION IN GREATER DELHI BASTIES
       Journalism Quart. 1970, 47, 2, Sum, 331-339
       SA, XIX, 6, F 1568

1860   Mishra V.M.

       MASS MEDIA USE PATTERN IN THE INDIAN SLUMS: A STUDY OF
       OF FOUR VASTIES IN GREATER DELHI
       Gazette, 15, 1, 1970, 27-38

1861   Mishra, V.M.

        FACTORS AFFECTING THE ADOPTION OF IMPROVED
        AGRICULTURAL PRACTICES AND ITS IMPACT ON
        AGRICULTURAL PRODUCTIVITY IN DINA BLOCK OF
        SHAHABAD DISTRICT, BIHAR (Ph.D.)
        Doct, Banaras Hindu U, 1969

1862   Mohanti, B.B.

        IMPACT OF AUDIO-VISUAL AIDS
        Kurukshetra, 1967, 15, 5, Feb, 20-22,
        SA, XVlll, 6, E4768

1863   Mookherjee, D.K. & Singh, H.

        UTILIZATION OF TUBEWELL
        IRRIGATION IN WEST BENGAL: AN ANALYSIS
        West Bengal, Dept. of C.D. 1966

1864   Moulik, T.K.

        A STUDY OF THE PREDICTIVE VALUES OF SOME FACTORS
        OF NITRO-GENEOUS FERTILIZERS AND THE INFLUENCE
        OF SOURCES OF INFORMATION ON ADOPTION BEHAVIOUR (Ph.D.)
        Doct, Indian Agr.Res.Inst., 1965
        (Dr. C.S.S.Rao)

1865   Moulik, T.K., Hrabovszky, J.P. & Rao, C.S.S.

        PREDICTIVE VALUES OF SOME FACTORS OF ADOPTION
        OF NITROGENEOUS FERTILIZERS BY NORTH INDIAN FARMERS
        Rur. Sociol. 1966, 21, 4, Dec, 467-478
        SA, XV, 3, C5154

1866   Moulik, T.K. & Lokhande, M.R.

        VALUE ORIENTATION OF NORTH INDIAN FARMERS AND ITS
        RELATION TO ADOPTION OF FARM PRACTICES
        Rur. Soc., 1969, 34, 3, Sep, 375-382
        SA, XVlll, 4, E3267

1867 Mulay, S. and G.L. Ray

CASTE AND ADOPTION OF IMPROVED FARM PRACTICES
Ind. J. Ext. Edu., 1965

1868 Murty, A.S.

SOCIAL AND PSYCHOLOGICAL CORRELATES IN PREDICTING
COMMUNICATION BEHAVIOUR OF FARMERS (Ph d)
Doct. Indian Agri. Res. Inst., 1969
(Dr. S.N. Singh)

1869 Nagoke, J.S.

RELATIVE EFFECTIVENESS OF EXTENSION METHODS ON THE
ADOPTION OF APPROVED AGRICULTURAL PRACTICES IN
SELECTED N.E.S. BLOCK, DISTRICT AMRITSAR
Summaries of Extension by Post-Graduate Students, India
1964

1871 Nair, G.T.

A MULTIVARIABLE STUDY IN ADOPTION OF HIGH YIELDING
PADDY VARIETIES BY THE FARMERS OF KERALA STATE (Ph d)
Doct. Indian Agri. Res., Inst., 1970
(Dr. S.K. Sharma)

1871 Narasimhan, V.K.

SHAPING OF EDITORIAL POLICY IN THE INDIAN PRESS
Journ. Quart. 1956, 33, 2, Spring, 208-213
SA. VI, 1, 4042

1872 Narayan, J.P.

FARMERS' ATTITUDES AND BELIEFS IN RELATION TO ADOPTION
OF IMPROVED AGRICULTURAL PRACTICES
(M.S. Thesis) India, 1963

1873 Natarajan, S.

THE PRESS AND SOCIAL REFORM
Ind. J. Soc. Wk. 1965, 25, 4, Jan, 327-332
SA XV, 5, C6529

0828   communication; adoption of innovations

1874   Neurath, Paul

       RADIO FARM FORUM IN INDIA
       Delhi; Gov't India Press, 1960

1875   Neurath, P.M.

       RADIO FARM FORUM AS A TOOL OF CHANGE IN INDIAN VILLAGES
       Eco. Dev. Cult. Change 1962, 10, 3, Apr, 275-283
       SA, XIII, 1, B4220

1876   Neurath, Paul

       RADIO FARM FORUM AS A TOOL OF CHANGE IN INDIAN VILLAGES
       Eco. Dev. and Cult. Change 1962

1877   Pande, B.M.

       PADDY CULTIVATION PRACTICES: DIFFUSION OF INNOVATIONS
       (A CASE STUDY OF EXTENSION WORK IN COMMUNITY DEVELOPMENT
       BLOCK IN INDIA)
       Com. Dev. J., 1968, 3, 2, Apr, 82, 85
       SA, XVIII, 5, D8529

1878   Pareek, U. and S.N. Chattopadhyay

       ADOPTION QUOTIENT: A MEASURE OF MULTI-PRACTICE ADOPTION
       BEHAVIOUR
       J. Appl. Behav. Sci, 1966, 2, 1, Jan-Mar, 95-108
       SA, XIV, 6, C2071

1879   Pareek, U. and Y.P. Singh

       SOCIOMETRY AND COMMUNICATION NETWORK IN AN INDIAN VILLAGE
       Inter, J. of Psychology, 1968, 3, 3, 157-165
       SA, XVIII, 1-2, E1203

1880   Parikh, R.D.

       PRESS AND SOCIETY - A SOCIOLOGICAL STUDY WITH SPECIAL
       REFERENCE TO THE NATURE AND GROWTH OF GUJARATI PRESS
       (Ph d)
       Doct, Maharaja Sayagirao, 1961
       (Dr. I.P. Desai)

1881   Patel, I.C.

COMMUNICATION BEHAVIOUR OF VILLAGE LEVEL WORKERS IN
SURAT AND MEHSANA DISTRICTS, GUJARAT, STATE, INDIA
Amer. Doctoral Dessertations (1966-1967)
Cornell U., (Soc)

1882   Patel, N.B.

STATUS DETERMINANTS OF INTERPERSONAL COMMUNICATION:
A DYADIC ANALYSIS
(Ph d)   U.S., 1966

1883   Patel, P.M.

DIFFERENTIAL CHARACTERISTICS OF ADOPTORS AND NON-
ADOPTORS OF FARM-PLANNING
New Delhi, IARI,   (Unpublished), 1967

1884   Potti, V.S.S.

A STUDY OF DIFFERENT ADOPTION OF IMPROVED FARM PRACTICES
IN RELATION TO REFERENCE GROUP INFLUENCE AND COMMUNITY
NORMS (Ph d)
Doct, Indian Agri. Res. Instit,. 1966
Dr. S.K. Sharma)

1885   Prasada, R.

A STUDY OF THE PROCESS OF ACCEPTANCE OF AN IMPROVED
HOME PRACTICE IN ONE VILLAGE OF DELHI STATE
(M.S. Thesis)   India, 1968

1886   Rahudkar, W.B.

IMPACT OF FERTILIZER EXTENSION PROGRAMME ON THE MINDS
OF THE FARMERS AND THEIR REACTIONS TO DIF. EXTENSION METHOD
Ind. J. of Agron., 1958

1887   Rahudkar, W.B.

LOCAL LEADERS AND THE ADOPTION OF FARM PRACTICES
Nagpur Agri. Coll. Mag., 1060

0828 communication; adoption of innovations

1888 Rahudkar, W.B.

      TESTING A CULTURALLY BOUND MODEL FOR ACCEPTANCE OF
      AGRICULTURAL PRACTICES
      (M.A. thesis) U.S. 1961

1889 Rahudkar, W.B.

      COMMUNICATION OF FARM INFORMATION IN AN INDIAN COMMUNITY
      Ind. J. Soc. Work, 1962, 23, 1, Apr., 99-103
      SA, XII, 7, B2779

1890 Rahudkar, W.B.

      COMMUNICATION PATTERNS IN THE ACCEPTANCE OF AGRICULTURAL
      PRACTICES
      T.P.S. Chaudhary (ed.) Selected Readings in C.D.
      India, 1967

1891 Rai, B.D.

      CHANNELS OF COMMUNICATION FOR IMPROVED FARM PRACTICES IN
      BARELA BLOCK, M.P.
      (M.S. thesis) India, 1967

1892 Rajendra, C.

      ADOPTION OF IMPROVED FARM PRACTICES AND CASTE SYSTEM
      J. of Ext. Educ. 1966

1893 Rangarao, K.

      INFLUENCE OF EXTENSION METHODS ON INDIVIDUAL ADOPTION
      PROCESS IN RELATION TO SELECTED AGRICULTURAL PRACTICES AROUND
      ANAND.
      (M.S. Thesis) India 1966

1894 Rangarao, K. and A.V. Patel

      INFLUENCE OF EXTENSION METHODS ON INDIVIDUAL ADOPTION
      PROCESS IN RELATION TO SELECTED AGRICULTURAL PRACTISES
      AROUND ANAND, GUJARAT STATE.
      Ind. J. of Ext. Educ., 1966

- 275 -

0828   communication; adoption of innovations

1895   Rao, C.R.P.

RELATIVE INFLUENCE OF SOCIO-ECONOMIC FACTORS ON THE
ACCEPTANCE OF COW-DUNG GAS PLANT BY THE FARMER WHEN
EXPOSED TO EXTENSION TEACHING
(M.S. Thesis) India, 1961

1896   Rao, G.N.

A STUDY ON EXTENT OF KNOWLEDGE AND ADOPTION OF HYBRID
MAIZE CULTIVATION IN HUZURABAD PANCHAYAT SAMITHI OF
KARIMNAGAR DISTRICT
Research Studies in Extension Education, India, 1966

1897   Rao, L.J.

CHANNELS OF COMMUNICATION IN THE INNOVATION-DECISION
PROCESS: A REVEIW AND A RECONSEPTUALIZATION
Paper presented at the 3rd World Congress for Rural Soc.,
SA, XX, 5, Sup, 24, F7792

1898   Rao, (Miss) M.U.

THE ROLE OF TELEVISION AS A MEDIUM OF MASS
COMMUNICATION
Doct. st, Poona U, 1969

1899   Rao, V.M. and Shetty, N.S.

A PRINCIPAL COMPONENT STUDY OF TECHNOLOGICAL
PROGRESSIVENESS OF FARMERS - ILLUSTRATION OF AN
APPROACH TO EVALUATION
Ecometric Annual of the Indian Eco. J. 1961, 15, 4,
478-495
SA, XlX, 4, E9921

1900   Reddy, S.K.

A STUDY OF ADOPTION OF IMPROVED AGRICULTURAL PRACTICES
AS A FUNCTION OF SOME SOCIO-ECONOMIC FACTORS AND
SOURCES OF INFORMATION
(M.S.Thesis) 1962

0828 communication; adoption of innovations

1901 Reddy, S.K.

A STUDY OF LEADERSHIP PATTERN AND RATES IN THE ADOPTION OF
IMPROVED FARM PRACTICES
(Ph d) New Delhi, I.A.R.I. 1966

1902 Reddy, S.K. and J.E. Kivlin

ADOPTION OF HIGH-YIELDING VARIETIES: A STUDY IN THREE
INDIAN VILLAGES
Behavioural Scis, and C.D. 1968, 2, 2, Sep, 121-142
SA, XIX, 3, E8776

1903 Reddy, S.V.

A STUDY OF LEADERSHIP PATTERN IN THE ADOPTION OF SOME
AGRICULTURAL INNOVATIONS IN RURAL A.P.
(MSc Thesis) Hyderabad, A.P.M.V. College
1961.

1904 REPORT

AGRO-INFROMATION FLOW AT VILLAGE LEVEL
Indian Inst. of Mass Communication, 1966

1905 Rogers, E.M.

CROSS-CULTURAL GENERALIZATIONS ABOUT THE DIFFUSION OF
INNOVATIONS: RESEARCH IN BRAZIL, NIGERIA, AND INDIA
Paper presented, 7th World Congress Int. Soc. Assoc.
SA, XVIII, 5, Sup. 9, E4044

1906 Rogers, E.M. and F.F. Shoemaker

COMMUNICATION OF INNOVATIONS (2nd ed.)
New York, The Free Press, 1971

1907 Roy, P.

THE IMPACT OF COMMUNICATIONS ON RURAL DEVELOPMENT IN INDIA
Mimeo. report.   Nat'l Inst. of C.D. India, 1967

0828   communication; adoption of innovations

1908   Roy, P. et.al.

       PATTERNS OF AGRICULTURAL DIFFUSION IN RURAL INDIA
       Nat'l Inst. of C.D. India, 1968

1909   Roy, P. et al.

       THE IMPACT OF COMMUNICATION ON RURAL DEVELOPMENT: AN
       INVESTIGATION IN INDIA AND COSTA RICA
       Nat'l Instit. of C.D., India 1968

1910   Roy, P., F. Fliegel,, J.E. Kivlin and L.K. Sen

       AGRICULTURAL INNOVATION AMONG INDIAN FARMERS
       Nat'l Inst. of C.D., India, 1968

1911   Roy, P., F. C. Fliegal, J. E. Kivlin, and L.K. Sen.

       COMMUNICATION IN INDIA: EXPERIMENTS IN INTRODUCING CHANGE
       Nat'l Inst. of C.D. India, 1969

1912   Roy, R.N.

       STUDY OF THE CAUSES OF SUCCESS AND FAILURE OF IMPROVED FARM
       PRACTICES IN AN EAST BIHAR VILLAGE
       (M.S. Thesis)   India, 1959

1913   Roy, R.N.

       A STUDY OF CHARACTERISTICS OF IMPROVED FARM PRACTICES
       AS RELATED TO ADOPTION
       (unpublished)   New Delhi, IARI, 1966

1914   Saha, N.K.

       RELATION OF TENURE STATUS TO ADOPTION OF RECOMMENDED
       PRACTICES IN INDIAN VILLAGES
       Ind. J. Soc. Res. 13, 2, Aug/72   131-135

1915   Saksena, R.N.

       FILMS ET HEROS DE FILMS EN INDE   (FILMS AND FILM HEROES
       IN INDIA)
       Communications, 1961, 1, 60-69 (Fr.)
       SA, XIV, 6, C2161

0828   communication; adoption of innovations

1916   Saigaonkar, P.B.

        RELATIONSHIP OF CERTAIN FACTORS WITH THE SUCCESS OF
        GRAMSEVAKS IN KAIRA DISTRICT OF GUJARAT STATE
        Anand, India, Sardar Patel U, 1967

1917   Saikia, P.D.

        FARMER'S RESPONSE TO IMPROVED AGRICULTURAL PRACTICES
        IN CACHAR DISTRICT (ASSAM)
        Man in India 1968, 48, 1, Jan-Mar, 86-96
        SA, XVll, 7, E0414

1918   Sanath Kumar Reddy, M.

        A STUDY OF LEADERSHIP PATTERNS AND ROLES IN THE
        ADOPTION OF IMPROVED FARM PRACTICES (Ph.D.)
        Doct. Indian Agriculture Research Inst. 1965,
        (Dr.(Mrs.)S.Mulay)

1919   Sa, hu, A.S.

        CHARACTERISTICS, LISTENING BEHAVIOUR AND
        PROGRAMMES PREFERENCES OF THE RADIO OWNING
        FARMERS IN PUNJAB (Ph.D.)
        Doct, Ind. Agr. Re. Inst. 1970, (Dr. K.N.Singh)

1920   Sandria, Y.P.

        FACTORS AFFECTING ADOPTION OF IMPROVED PRACTICES
        IN M.P. STATE
        (M.S.Thesis) India, 1962

1921   Sangle, G.K.
        KNOWLEDGE AND ACCEPTANCE OF RECOMMENDED FARM
        PRACTICES AMONG SMALL CULTIVATORS
        (M.S.Thesis) India, 1962

1922   Sarkar, D.R. & Sen, D.

        VALUE ORIENTATION AND ADOPTION BEHAVIOUR
        Society and Culture, 1970, 1, Special numbers, 11-21,
        SA, XX, 7, F9525

0828   communication; adoption of innovations

1923   Satyanarayana, C.

A STUDY OF THE SOURCES OF INFORMATION IN THE DIFFERENT
STAGES OF ADOPTION OF IMPROVED ANIMAL HUSBANDRY PRACTICES IN
KEY VILLAGE BLOCK KARMNAGAR, A.P.
In: Research Studies in Ext. Educ.,India 1967.

1924   Satyanarayana, M.

AN ANALYSIS OF CHANNELS OF COMMUNICATION IN THE ADOPTION
OF SOME IMPROVED AGRICULTURAL PRACTICES IN AN A.P. VILLAGE
in: Research Itudies, in Ext. Educ. India   1966

1925   Sawhney, M.M.

DIFFUSION AND ACCEPTANCE OF INNOVATIONS IN AGRICULTURE
WITH SPECIAL EMPHASIS ON THE ROLE OF RURAL LEADERS AND RURAL
YOUTH
(Ph d Thesis)   India   1962

1926   Sawhney, M.M.

FARM PRACTISE ADOPTION AND THE USE OF INFORMATION SOURCES
AND MEDIA IN A RURAL COMMUNITY IN INDIA
Rur. Soc., 1967, 32, 3, Sep, 310-323
SA, XVI, 2, D0142

1927   Saxena, A.P.

COMMUNICATION OF AGRICULTURAL INFORMATION IN MIRAR BLOCK
(M.S. Thesis)   India 1963

1928 ‹Saxena, A.P.

SYSTEM EFFECTS ON INNOVATIVENESS AMONG INDIAN FARMERS
Amer. Doct. Dissertations   ('68-'69)
Michigan State U. (Soc. Psy.)

1929   Sen, L.K.

Social Psychological Correlates of Adoption of
Agricultural Innovations
Behavioural Sciences and Com Dev., 1968, 2, 1, Mar, 45-57
SA, XVIII, 6, E4989

0828   communication; adoption of innovations

1930   *Sen, M.L.A.

        MASS COMMUNICATION IN A DESERT VILLAGE
        Annals of the Arid Zone, 1970, 8, 1, Mar, 135-142
        SA, 21, 73G3308

1931   Sengupta, A.K.

        INNOVATIONS IN AGRICULTURE
        Kurukshetra, 1966, 14, 10, Ju, 8-10,
        SA, XVll, 4, D7887

1932   Shah, (Miss) P.

        A SOCIAL STUDY OF THE CINEMA IN BOMBAY (Ph.D.)
        Doct, Bombay U, 1949 (Prof. G.S.Ghurye)

1933   Shankariah,C.

        A STUDY OF DIFFENTIAL CHARACTERISTICS OF VEGETABLES
        GROWERS AND NON-GROWERS
        New Delhi, IARI, (unpublished), 1965

1934   Shankariah, C.

        A STUDY OF DIFFERENTIAL COMMUNICATION PATTERNS IN A
        PROGRESSIVE AND NON-PROGRESSIVE VILLAGE (Ph.D.)
        Doct, Indian, Agricultural Res. Inst. 1969
        (Dr. K.N.Singh)

1935   Sharma, S.K. & Potti, V.S.S.

        DIFFERENTIAL ADOPTION OF IMPROVED FARM PRACTICES
        IN RELATION TO REFERENCE GROUP INFLUENCE
        J.of Ext. Educ. 1966

1936   Shaw, E.F.

        AN INTRA-INDIA ANALYSIS OF SELECTED COMMUNICATION
        DEVELOPMENT VARIABLES
        American Doctoral Dissertations (1966-67)
        Stanford U (Soc.)

0828   communication; adoption of innovations

1937   Sheth, N.S.

FORMAL AND INFORMAL SOCIAL PARTICIPATION AS RELATED TO
DIFFUSION OF INFORMATION AND ADOPTION OF FARM PRACTICES
IN A VILLAGE IN INDIA
Americal Doctoral Disseratations ('65-'66)
U. of Missouri (soc.)

1938   Singh, Brahmajit

ACCEPTANCE OF PUSA GRAIRT NAPIER GRAIN
(unpublished)   New Delhi, IARI   1964

1939   Singh, B.N. and P.N. Jha

UTILIZATION OF SOURCES OF FARM INFORMATION IN RELATION
TO ADOPTION OF IMPROVED AGRICULTURAL PRACTICES
Ind. J. Ext. Edu., 1965

1940   Singh, G.B.

DIFFERENTIAL CHARACTERISTICS OF EARLY AND LATE ADOPTERS OF
NEW FARM PRACTICES, PUNJAB,STATE, INDIA
American Doctoral Disseratations ('65-'66)
Cornell U., (soc. Psy.)

1941   Singh, H.

ECONOMIC INNOVATION IN A NORTH INDIAN VILLAGE: A CASE STUDY
J. Pakistan Acad. Ru. Dev. 1964, 5, 1, Jul, 19-28
SA, XIII, 6-7, B7945

1942   Singh, I.B. & Sahay, B.N.

Communication Behaviour and Social Change
New Delhi, 1972

1943   Singh, K.N. & Akhouri, M.M.P.

RELATIONSHIP BETWEEN FARMERS' BACKGROUND KNOWLEDGE
GAINED THROUGH DIFFERENT EXTENSION TEACHING METHODS;
AN EXPERIMENTAL EVIDENCE
J. of Ext. Educ. 1966

1945   Singh, K.N. & Jha, P.N.

A CONCEPT OF COMMUNICATIONS SENSITIVITY AND ITS
MEASUREMENT WITH REFERENCE TO HIGH-YIELDING
VARIETIES PROGRAMME
Ind.J.Soc.Res., pp. 16-122, 12, 2, Aug. 1971

1946   Singh, K.N. & Shankariah, C.

FACTORS RELATED WITH THE ADOPTION OF IMPROVED
PRACTICES OF VEGETABLE CULTIVATION
Interdiscipline, 1967, 4, 3, Aut, 207-218
SA, XVlll, 3, E2150

1947   Singh, L.R., Bhati, J.P. & Jain, S.L.

SOCIO-ECONOMIC FACTORS AND THE ADOPTION OF IMPROVED
FARM PRACTICES
Man in India, 52, 4, Oct-Dec, 1972, 320-328

1948   Singh, N.P.

RISK-TAKING AND ANXIETY AMONG SUCCESSFUL AND
UNSUCCESSFUL TRADITIONAL AND PROGRESSIVE AGRICULTURAL
ENTREPRENEURS OF DELHI
Int.J.Soc.Clin.Psychol. 9, 4, Dec,1970, 301-308

1949   Singh, R.

CORRELATIONAL STUDY OF THE LEVELS OF ASPIRATION WITH
THE ACCEPTANCE OF CROP PRODUCTION PLANS BY THE CULTIVATORS
in: SUMMARIES OF EXTENSION by Post-Graduate Students
India, 1966

1950   Singh, R.

ADOPTION OF NITROGENEOUS FERTILIZERS AS RELATED TO
SELECTED FACTORS AND USE OF INFORMATION SOURCES IN
ADOPTION PROCESS (Ph.D. Thesis)
US. Cornell U, 1967

1951   Singh, R.D.

THE VILLAGE LEVEL: AN INTRODUCTION OF GREEN
MANURING IN RURAL INDIA
in: HUMAN PROBLEMS AND TECHNOLOGICAL CHANGE
ed. E.H.Spicer, New York, 1952

1952   Singh, L.N.

CHARACTERISTICS OF FARM INNOVATIONS ASSOCIATED
WITH THE RATE OF ADOPTION
Guelph, Ont. Agr. Ext. Edu. Report, 1966

1953   Singh, S.N.

A STUDY ON ADOPTION OF HIGH YIELDING VARIETIES AND
INVESTMENT PATTERN OF ADDITIONAL INCOME BY THE
FARMERS OF DELHI TERRITORY (Ph.D.)
Doct. Ind. Agr. Res.Inst. 1970 (Dr.K.N.Singh)

1954   Singh, S.K.

COMMUNICATION AND DIFFUSION PROCESS CONTRIBUTING TO
THE ADOPTION OF IMPROVED FARM PRACTICES
(M.S.Thesis) India, 1962

1955   Singh, S.N.

VALUE ORIENTATIONS AND ADOPTION BEHAVIOUR
OF INDIAN CULTIVATORS
Amer. Doctoral Dissertations (1966-67)
Iowa State U, of Science and Technology (Soc.)

0828   communication; adoption of innovations

1956   Singh, S.N. and S.K. Reddy

        ADOPTION OF IMPROVED AGRICULTURAL PRACTICES OF
        FARMERS
        Ind. J. Soc. Work, 1956, 26, Oct, 263-269
        SA, XVI, 4 D1791

1957   Singh, S.N. and George M. Beal

        VALUE ORIENTATIONS AND ADOPTION BEHAVIOUR OF INDIAN
        CULTIVATORS
        paper present. at Rural So. Society, San Francisco,
        1967

1958   Singh, S.B. and S.K. Reddy

        ADOPTION OF IMPROVED FARM PRACTICES AS RELATED TO
        SOURCES OF INFORMATION
        Ind. J. Agron., 1965

1959   Singh, Y.P.

        A STUDY OF COMMUNICATION NETWORKS IN SEQUENTIAL
        ADOPTION AND KEY COMMUNICATORS
        Doct, Indian Agri. Res. Inst., (Dr. V. Pareek), 1965

1960   Singh, Y.P.

        STUDY IN AGRICULTURAL COMMUNICATION IN INDIA
        2nd all Indian Seminar on Researches in Extension
        Bangalore, 1969

1961   Singh, Y.P.

        A SOCIOLOGICAL STUDY OF THE CHARACTERISTICS OF KEY
        COMMUNICATORS , WITH SPECIAL REFERENCE TO THEIR ROLE
        IN THE CHRONOLOGICAL CHANGE IN AGRICULTURE
        (Ph.d.) Doct. Agra U, 1970 (Dr. R.N. Saksena)

0828   communications; adoption of innovations

1962   Singh, Y.P. and U. Pareek

        CHANGE AGENT LINKAGE AS A CHARACTERISTIC OF KEY-
        COMMUNICATIONS
        Interdiscipline, 1966, 3, 3, Jul, 129-134
        SA, XVII, 1, D 5053

1963   Singh, Y. P. and U. Pareek

        SOURCES OF COMMUNICATION AT DIFFERENT STAGES OF
        ADOPTION OF FARM PRACTICES
        Ind. Jour. Soc. Work 1966, 21, 4, Jan, 385-391
        SA, SVI, 5, D2621

1964   Singh, Y. P. and U. Pareek

        INTERPERSONAL COMMUNICATION AT DIFFERENT STAGES OF
        ADOPTION
        Ind. J. Soc. Work 1967, 27, 4, Jan. 343-352
        SA, SVI, 6, D3477

1965   Singh, Y. P. and U. Pareek

        A PARADIGM OF SEQUENTIAL ADOPTION
        Ind. Educ. Rev. 1968

1966   Singhal, P.

        DIFFUSION OF TECHNOLOGY FROM JAPAN TO INDIA
        (MA Thesis) U.S., 1966

1967   Sinha, B. P.

        A STUDY OF SOME MOTIVATIONAL FACTORS IN DIFFUSION
        OF FARM INFORMATION THROUGH TELEVISION
        (Ph. d.) Doct, Ind., Agri. Res. Inst., 1970
        (Dr. S.K. Sharma)

1968   Sinha, B. P. and P. Mehta

        FARMERS' NEED FOR ACHIEVEMENT AND CHANGE -- PRONENESS
        IN ACQUISTION OF INFORMATION FROM A FARM-TELECAST
        Rural Sociology, 37,, 2, Sept. 1972 417-428

1969   Sinha, M. P.

A STUDY OF THE VILLAGE LEVEL WORKERS' UNDERSTANDING
OF CONCEPT, PURPOSE AND PROCESS OF FARM PLANNING
AND RESPONSE OF THE PARTICIPATING FARMERS TO FARM
PLANNING EFFECT IN THE I.A.D.P. (Ph. d.)
Doct, Indian Agricultural Research Instit. 1966
(Dr. K. N. Singh)

1970   Sinha, N.K.

THE ADOPTION PROCESS AS RELATED TO SOME SOCIO-
PERSONAL FACTORS
(Unpublished) New Delhi, IARI, 1963

1971   Sinha, N.K. and D.P. Yadav

EVALUATION STUDY SHOWING UTILIZATION OF MEDIUM TERM
TACCAVI LOANS FOR MINOR IRRIGATION TO CULTIVATORS IN
LUDHIANA DISTRICT, (Oper. Res. Rept.)
India; State Gov't. of Punjab, 1964

1972   Sinha, N.K. and D.P. Yadav

A STUDY TO DETERMINE CULTIVATOR'S AWARENESS AND
KNOWLEDGE OF PACKAGE PROGRAMME AND THE NATURE OF
CONTACTS WITH THE EXTENSION STAFF, LUDHIANA DISTRICT
(Oper. Res. Rept.)
India; State Gov't. of Punjab, 1964

1973   Sinha, N. K. and D. P. Yadav

CULTIVATOR'S ATTITUDES TOWARDS ADOPTION OF CHEMICAL
FERTILIZERS, PACKAGE PROGRAMME, LUDHIANA, (oper. Res.
Report)
India; State Gov't. of Punjab, 1964

1974   Sinha, N. K. and D. P. Yadav

ATTITUDES OF FARMERS TOWARDS THE ADOPTION OF
INSECTICIDES AND PESTICIDES IN I.A.D.P. LUDHIANA
(Oper. Res. Rept.)
India; State Gov't. of Punjab, 1964

0828   communication; adoption of innovations

   1975   Sinha, P.R.R.

           A STUDY OF FARMER'S DECISION-MAKING PROCESS WITH
           RESPECT TO USE OF ARTIFICAL FERTILIZERS AND
           VEGETABLE CULTIVATION (PH.D.)
           Doct, Indian Agricultural Research Instit., 1966
           (Dr. K.N. Singh)

   1976   Sinha, P.R.R. and R. Parshad

           SOURCES OF INFORMATION AS RELATED TO ADOPTION
           PROCESS OF SOME IMPROVED FARM PRACTICES
           J. of Educ., 1966

   1977   Sohoni, A.W.

           CHARACTERISTICS OF FARM PRACTICES ASSOCIATED WITH THE
           RATE OF ADOPTION
           (M.S. Thesis), India, 1963

   1978   Sohoni, A.W.

           IMPACT OF FARM MECHANIZATION OF SOME ASPECTS OF
           FARMING IN KANJHAWALA BLOCK (DELHI TERRITORY) (PH.D.)
           Doct, Indian Agricultural Research Institute, 1968
           (Prof. A.R. Khan)

   1979   Supe, S.V.

           FACTORS RELATED TO DIFFERENT DEGREES OF RATIONALITY
           IN DECISION-MAKING AMONG FARMERS (PH.D.)
           Doct, Indian Agricultural Research Inst., 1969
           (Dr. S. N. Singh)

   1980   Supe, S.V. and N.V. Kolle

           VALUES AND ADOPTION OF FARM INNOVATIONS
           Ind. J. Soc. Work, 1971, 32, 1, Apr, 9-16
           SA. XX, 7, F9528

   1981   Subramaniam, R.

           RURAL BROADCASTING
           Kurukshetra, 1966, 14, 5, Feb, 12-13
           SA, XVII, 2, D6010

0828   communication; adoption of innovations

1982   Thorat, S.S.

CERTAIN SOCIAL FACTORS ASSOCIATED WITH THE ADOPTION OF
RECOMMENDED AGRICULTURAL PRACTICES BY RURAL LOCAL LEADERS
AND ORDINARY FARMERS IN INDIA
American Doctoral Dissertations (65-66) Michigan State U.
(Soc.)

1983   Thorat, S.S.

SOME SALIENT CHARACTERISTICS OF SARPANCHAS AND THE
SUCCESS OR FAILURE OF AGRICULTURAL INNOVATIONS IN
INDIA'S VILLAGES
Behavioral Scis. and CD 1968, 2, 1, Mar, 26-37
SA, XIX, i-2, E7448

1984   Thorat, S.S.

THE PROPAGANDA BATTLE IN INDIA AND BURMA
    Amer. Acd. Pol. Soc. Sci. 1959, 324, Jul, 56-63
SA VIII, 3, 7548

1985   Verma, H. S.

MASS MEDIA CONSUMPTION IN EIGHT NORTH INDIAN VILLAGES
Behavioral Sciences and Community Development
1971, 5, 1, Mar, 38-50
SA, 21, 73 G9754

1986   Varma, O. S.

SOCIAL-PSYCHOLOGICAL AND CORRELATES OF INTERPERSONAL
COMMUNICATION AND INFLUENCE IN FARMING COMMUNITIES
(PH.D.)
Doct, Ind. Agri. Res. Inst., 1970,
(Dr. S. N. Singh)

1987   Wood, Evelyn

PATTERNS OF INFLUENCE WITHIN RURAL INDIA
in. Leader.and Political Institutions In India
ed. R. L. Park and I. Tinker
New York: Greenwood Press, 1969
pp. 372-391

0828   communication; adoption of innovations

   1988   Yadav, D.P.

           COMMUNICATION STRUCTURE AND INNOVATION DIFFUSION IN
           TWO INDIAN VILLAGES
           Mic. State U., Technical Rept., 1967

0829   collective behaviour

   1989   Bayley, D.H.

           THE PEDAGOGY OF DEMOCRACY: COERCIVE PUBLIC PROTEST IN
           INDIA
           Amer. Polit. Sci. R. 1962, 56, 3, Sep, 663-672
           SA, XII, 8, B3471

   1990   Pundalik,V. G. and S. Patwardhan

           A NOTE ON THE BEHAVIOR OF THE CASTE IN A CRISIS-
           SITUATION
           Social. B., 1962, 11, 1-2, Mar-Sep, 68-72
           SA, XI, 7, A7584

0842   sociology of leisure

   1991   Bose, N.K.

           THE EFFECT OF URBANIZATION ON WORK AND LEISURE
           Man in India, 1957, 37, 1, Jan-Mar. 1-9
           SA, VIII, 1, 7133

   1992   Brewster, P. G.

           "LONG BREATH" AND "TAKING FIRE"
           CULTURE SURVIVALS IN GAMES OF CHASE
           East. Anthrop. 1958, 12, 1, Sep-Nov. 41-46
           SA, VIII, 2, 7563

1993   Gupta, D.

       A STUDY OF SPAN (LEISURE TIME) INTERESTS OF HINDI-
       SPEAKING VILLAGES (PH.D.)
       Doct, Lucknow U., 1968
       (Dr. R. Narain)

1994   Mistry, D.K.

       THE INDIAN CHILD AND HIS PLAY
       Sociol. B. 1958, 7, 2, Sept, 137-147
       SA, VIII, 2, 7565

1995   Modi, I.P.

       LEISURE AND SOCIAL STRUCTURE (STUDY OF PATTERNS OF
       LEISURE AND RECREATION IN THE CITY OF JAIPUR IN
       COMPARISON TO A FEW SELECTED VILLAGES IN RAJASTHAN
       Doct. St., Rajasthan U., 1969

1996   Nakhooda, (Mrs.) Z.Y.

       LEISURE AND RECREATION IN SOCIETY (PH.D.)
       Doct., Bombay U., 1958
       (Prof. G. S. Ghurye)

1997   Puri, B.

       RECREATION AND SOCIAL EDUCATION
       Verry, 1963

0900   Political Interactions

0911   interactions between societies, nations and states

    1998   Basi, R.S.

            COMMUNIST CHINA AND INDIA'S NON-ALIGNMENT
            Soc. Sci., 1964, 29, 4, Oct, 226-233
            SA, XIII, 3-4, B6105

    1999   Cottrell, A.B.

            CROSS-CULTURAL MARRIAGES AS LINKAGES BETWEEN SOCIETIES
            --INDIAN-WESTERN MARIAGES IN INDIA
            1969 Annual Meeting of the American Sociological
            Association, Session, 93
            SA, XVII, 5, Supp 5, D8954

    2000   Buchanan, K. and N. Hurwitz

            ASIATIC IMMIGRANT COMMUNITY IN THE UNION OF SOUTH AFRICA
            Geog. Rev. 39, 440-9, Jul, 1949

    2001   Dutta, Amita

            AN ECONOMETRIC STUDY OF INDO-CEYLON LABOR MIGRATION,
            1920-1938: A CRITIQUE
            Eco. Dev. and Cult, Change
            21, 1, Oct 1972, 142-157

    2002   Fersh, S.H.

            INDIA AND SOUTH ASIA
            New York, Macmillan 1964, VIII and 152 pp.

    2003   Gosavami, V. L.

            WORK OF THE FORD FOUNDATION IN INDIA
            Int. Labour Rev. 70, 323-33, Sept/Oct, 1954

0911   interactions between societies, nations and states

2004   Rosinger, L.K. et all

        INDIAN-AMERICAN RELATIONS, FAR EASTERN SURVEY
        19, 9-19 Jan 25, 1950

2005   Lynch, M.D. and A. Effendi

        EDITORIAL TREATMENT OF INDIA IN THE NEW YORK TIMES
        J-ism Quart. 1964, 41-3, Sum, 430-432
        SA, XIII, 3, B5185

2006   Mason, P. (ed.)

        INDIA AND CYLON, UNITY AND DIVERSITY, A SYMPOSIUM
        London, Oxford U. Press, 1967

2007   Maurarka, D.

        INDIA-PAKISTAN ANTAGONISM
        New Society, 1964, 86, 21, May   11-12
        SA, XIV, 1, B8568

2008   Mehrotra, S.R.

        THE DEVOLOPMENT OF THE INDIAN OUTLOOK ON WORLD
        AFFAIRS BEFORE 1947
        J. Dev. Stud. 1965, 1, 3, Apr. 269- 94

2009   Meyer, M. W.

        INDIA, PAKISTAN AND THE BORDERLAND
        U.S., 1968

2010   shankar Pal Singh

        UNESCO, WITH SPECIAL REFERENCE TO INDIA (PH.D.)
        Doct, Saugar U, 1967
        (Dr. S. C. Singh)

0911   interactions between societies, nations and states

2011   Wilkinson, T.S.

        THE IMPACT OF EURO-AMERICAN CULTURE ON INDIA FROM
        1498 ONWARD WITH SPECIAL REFERENCE TO CULTURAL LAG
        American Doctoral Dissertations (1955-56)
        Duke University (Sociology)

2012   Wint, G.

        AFTERMATH OF IMPERIALISM (THE IMPACT OF BRITISH
        CIVILISATION UPON INDIA)
        Pacific Affairs, 22, 64-5, March '49

2013

        CHANGING STRUCTURE OF INDIAN INTERNATIONAL IMAGES--
        A FOUR YEAR TREND STUDY: JAN. 1965 to JULY 1969
        Monthly Publ. Opin. Surv. 14 (9-10), Jun-Jue, 1969 3-62

0925   political sociology

2014   *Agrawal, B.C.

        CULTURAL FACTORS IN POLITICAL DECISION-MAKING.
        A SMALL TOWN ELECTION IN INDIA
        Economic and Political Weekly, 1971, 6, 8, Feb,
        495-502
        SA, 21, 79 G0774

2015   Agrawal, B.C.

        DIKSHA CEREMONY IN JAINISM: AN ANALYSIS OF ITS SOCIO_
        POLITICAL RAMIFICATIONS
        East. Anthrop. 25, 1, Jan-Apr. 1974, 13-21

2016   Agrawal, R.L.

        THE POLITICS OF AN INDIAN VILLAGE
        Doct. St.Saugar U., 1969

0925   political sociology

2017a   Ahmad, M.

         TAXATION AND THE CHANGES IN INCOME DISTRIBUTION
         Indian Economic J. 1965, 7, 4, Apr-Jun, 379-396
         SA, XVII, 1, D5139

2017b   Ahmad, M.

         THE CONCEPT OF WELFARE STATE, WITH SPECIAL REFERENCE
         TO ITS IMPLEMENTATION IN INDIA (PH.D.)
         Doct. Lucknow U. 1966
         (Prof. A.K. Saran)

2018   Ahmed, B.

         POLITICAL STRATIFICATION AND THE INDIAN ELECTORATE
         Economic and Political Weekly, 1971, 6, 3-5,
         Jan, 251-258
         SA, 21, 73 G0775

2019   Alexander, H. G., et al

         SOCIAL AND POLITICAL IDEAS OF MAHATMA GANDHI
         New Delhi: Indian Council of World Affairs, 1949, 84 pp

2020   Apter, D. E.

         THE POLITICS OF MODERNIZATION
         U of Chicago Press, 1965

2021   Arora, S.K.

         POLITICIZATION IN PEASANT SOCIETY
         Behavioural Sciences and Community Development,
         1967, 1, 1, Mar, 28-46
         SA, XVIII, 6, E4946

2022   Arora, S.K.

         THE POLITICAL RELEVANCE OF SOCIAL VALUES: A CROSS-
         NATIONAL COMPARISON
         Behavioral Scis and C.D. 1969, 3, 1, Mar, s 1-65

0925   political sociology

2023   Arora, S.K.

        EXPLORING POLITICAL PREDISPOSITION: EFFICACY AND
        CYNICISM IN RURAL ANDHRA PRADESH
        Beh. Scis. and C.D. 1969, 3, 2, Sep, 126-128
        SA, XIX, 5, F066

2024   Arora, V.K.

        SOCIAL AND POLITICAL PHILOSOPHY OF SWAMI VIVEKANANDA
        Verry, 1968

2025   Aryamane, R.V.

        BACKWARD CLASSES IN THE INDIAN CONSTITUTION
        Polit. Scientis, 1966, 2, 1, Jul-Dec, 27-36

2026   Atal, Y.

        LOCAL COMMUNITIES AND NATIONAL POLITICS: A STUDY
        IN COMMUNICATION LINKS AND POLITICAL INVOLVEMENT
        Intl. Pubns. Serv. 1972

2027   Avasthi, R.K.

        SOCIAL AND POLITICAL IDEAS OF M. N. ROY (PH.D.)
        Doct., Agra U., 1960

2028   Awasthi, A.P.

        RURAL LOCAL SELF-GOVERNMENT IN MADHYA PRADESH UNDER
        THE JANPADA SCHEME (PH.D.)
        Doct. Saugar U., 1961
        (prof. M.P. Sharma)

2029   Bailey, F. G.

        TRADITIONAL SOCIETY AND REPRESENTATION: A CASE STUDY
        IN ORISSA
        Eur. J. Social. 1960, 1, 1, 121-141

        SA XI, 6, A6691

2030   Bailey, F. G.

POLITICS AND SOCIAL CHANGE: ORISSA IN 1959
U. of Calif. Press, 1963

2031   Bailey, F. G.

TRIBE, CASTE, AND NATION
Bombay, Oxford U. Press, 1960

2032   Bailey, S. D.

PARILIAMENTARY GOVERNMENTS IN SOUTHERN ASIA: SURVEY
OF DEVELOPMENTS IN BURMA, CEYLON, INDIA ' AND PAKISTAN,
1947-1952
New York, Institute of Pacific Relations 1953, 100 pp

2033   Bandyopadhyay, J.

THE SOCIAL AND POLITICAL THOUGHT OF GANDHI (D. Litt.)
Doct., Jadavpur U., 1968

2034   Bari, S.A.

GANDHI'S DOCTRINE OF CIVIL RESISTANCE (PH.D.)
Doct., Marathwada U., 1967
(Dr. G. N. Sarma)

2035   *Baviskar, B.S.

FACTIONS AND PARTY POLITICS: GENERAL ELECTIONS IN AN
ASSEMBLY CONSTITUENCY IN MAHARASHTRA
Sociological Bulletin, 1971, 20, 1, Mar, 54-77
SA 21, 73G5731

2036   Baxter, C.

DISTRICT VOTING TRENDS IN INDIA: A RESEARCH TOOL
New York; Columbia U. Press
1969, xxii-278 pp

2037   Bendix, Richard

        PUBLIC AUTHORITY IN A DEVELOPING POLITICAL COMMUNITY:
        THE CASE OF INDIA
        Eur. J. Sociol., 1963, 4, 1, 39-85
        SA, XII, 7, B2663

2038   Bernstorff, Dajnar (jr.)

        CANDIDATES FOR THE 1969 GENERAL ELECTIONS IN HYDERABAD,
        S.P.
        in. E. Leach and S. M. Mukherjee (ed.)
        Elites in South Asia 1970

2039   Bhalerao, C.M.
        SOME SOCIAL, POLITICAL AND ADMINISTRATIVE
        CONSEQUENCES OF PANCHAYATI RAJ
        Asian Surv. 1964, 4, 4, Apr, 804 -811
        SA, XIV, 1, B8674

2040   Bharil, (Mis) C.

        SOCIAL AND POLITICAL IDEAS OF DR. B. R. AMBEDKAR--
        A STUDY OF HIS LIFE, SERVICES, AND SOCIAL AND POLITICAL
        IDEAS (PH.D.)

        Doct., Rajasthan U., 1970
        (Dr. C. P. Bhambhari)

2041   Bhaskaran, R.

        ASOCIOLOGY OF POLITICS: TRADITION POLITICS IN INDIA
        Bombay: Asia Pub. House, 1967

2042   Bhatnagar, S.V.

        PANCHAYATI RAJ IN KANGRA DISTRICT (PH.D.)
        Doct., Panjab U., 1968
        (Dr. B. S. Khanna)
        Dept. of Public Admin.

2043   Bhatt, R.S., Chinwalla, R.J., Shah, F.M.,
       Bhuwalka, S.K., Dalvi, G.R., Parikh, G.D., Ghurye,G.S.

       OUR PRESENT DISCONTENT AND FRUSTRATION
       Sociol. Bull. 1953, 2, Sep, 81-102
       SA vol II #1   164

2044   *Bondurant, Joan and Margaret W. Fisher

       ETHICS IN ACTION: CONTRASTING APPROACHES TO SOCIAL
       AND POLITICAL PROBLEMS IN MODERN INDIA
       Australian Journal of Politics and History, 1966,
       12, 3, Aug. 177-193
       SA 21, 73G2513

2045   Bose, A. B. and S.P. Malhotra

       STUDIES IN GROUP DYNAMICS (I): FACTIONALISM IN A
       DESERT VILLAGE
       Man in India, 1964, 44, 4, Oct-Dec, 311-328
       SA XIV, 1, B 8675

2046   Brass, Paul R.

       FACTIONAL POLITICS IN AN INDIAN STATE: THE CONGRESS
       PARTY IN UTTAR PRADESH
       U. of California Press, 1965

2047   Brecher, Michael

       SUCCESSION IN INDIA 1967: THE ROUTINIZATION OF
       POLITICAL CHANGE
       Asian Survey, 1967, VII, 7, pp 423-444

2048   Brown, D. MacKenzie

       NATIONALIST MOVEMENT: INDIAN POLITICAL THOUGHT FROM
       RANADE TO BHAVE
       U. Of Calif. Press, 1961

2049   Brown, D. MacKenzie

WHITE UMBRELLA: INDIAN POLITICAL THOUGHT FROM
MANU TO GANDHI
U. of Calif Press, 1953

2050   Burnham, J.

PARAKEETS AND PARCHESI: AN INDIAN MEMORANDUM
Partisan Rev., 12, 337-68, Sept. 1951

2051   *Carras, Mary C.

THE ECONOMIC DETERMINANTS OF POLITICAL FACTIONALISM:
A CASE STUDY OF AN INDIAN RURAL DISTRICT
Economic Development and Cultrual Change, 1972, 21, 1,
Oct, 118-141
SA 21 73G5100

2052   Chaturvedi, (Miss)C.

THE SOCIAL AND POLITICAL IDEAS OF THE HINDI POETS OF
BHAKTI KAL (D.PHIL.)
Doct., Allahabad U., 1967
(Prof. A. D. Pant)

2053   Chaturvedi, D.C.

CONCEPTS OF RIGHTS IN THE LIBERAL TRADITION
Ind. J. Soc. Res. 1962, 2, 2, Jul, 11-21
SA XI, 6, A6701

2054   Chekki, D. A. and R. T. Jangam

HOW FAIR ARE THE ELECTIONS?
AICC Economic Rev., Dec, 15, 1968, 20, 11, pp 7-25

2055   Chauhan, S. K.

PARTY PREFERENCES: A STUDY OF POLITICAL ATTITUDES IN
UPPER ASSAM
Man In India, 53, 4, 1972, 371-379

2056   Chaudhari, P.K.

        PANCHAYTI RAJ IN ACTION: A STUDY OF RAJASTHAN
        in. Rural Sociology In India
        ed. A. R. Desai, Bombay, Popular Prakashan, 1969
        pp 540-553

2057   Chopra, S.L.

        VILLAGE ELECTIONS
        Kurukshetra, 1966, 14, 7, April, 23-24
        SA XVII, 3, Dm099

2058   Curran, J.A., Jr.
        MILITANT HINDIUSIM IN INDIAN POLITICS: A STUDY OF THE
        R.S.S.
        New York; Institute for Pacific Relations, 1951, 94 pp

2059   Das, T.

        STATUS OF HYDERABAD DURING AND AFTER BRITISH RULE IN
        INDIA
        Amer. J. of International Law, 43, 57-72, Jan, 1949

2060   Davar,S.R.

        THE HISTORY OF THE PARSI PUNCHAYET   OF BOMBAY
        Bombay: New Book Co. 1949, 80 pp

2061   De, (Miss) N.
        THE TANA BHAGATS OF CHHOTANAGPUR: STUDIES IN THEIR
        SOCIO POLITICAL MOVEMENT AND PERSONALITY STRUCTURE (PH.D.)
        DOCT., PATNA U.,1964
        (Dr. N. Prasad)

2062   Desai, A.R.

        RECENT TRENDS IN INDIAN NATIONALISM: SUPPLEMENT TO
        SOCIAL BACKGROUND OF INDIAN NATIONALISM
        Bombay: Popular Book Depot, 1960
        xii 149 pp.

2063   Desai, A.R.

        SOCIAL BACKGROUND OF INDIAN NATIONALISM
        Bombay: Oxford U. Press, 1948
        XVI 416 pp

2064   Desai, A.R.

        SOCIAL BACKGROUND OF INDIAN NATIONALSIM (4TH ED.)
        Bombay: Popular Prahashan, 1966
        xix 461 p

2065   Devanandan, P.D. and M.M. Thomas

        CULTURAL FOUNDATIONS OF INDIAN DEMOCRACY
        Calcutta: YMCA Publishing House, 1955, iv 110 p

2066   Dhar, M.N.

        PANCHAYATS IN JAMMU AND KASHMIR
        Kurakshetra, 1964, 12, 8, May, 19-30
        SA, XIV, 1, B8678

2067   Eldersveld, S.J.

        THE POLITICAL BEHAVIOUR OF THE INDIAN PUBLIC
        Monthly P.O. Survey, 1964, 9, 4, Jan, 3-9
        SA, XIII, 6-7, B7831

2077   Erdman, H.L.

        THE SWATANTRA PARTY AND INDIAN CONSERVATISM
        London: Cambridge U. Press, 1967, xii 356 p

2078   Fellman, G. A.

        INDIAN SOCIALISTS AND JAYAPRAKASH NARAYAN:
        A STUDY IN POLITICAL SOCIOLOGY AND BIOGRAPHY
        American Doctoral Dissertation (63-64)
        Harvard U. (Soc.)

2079   Fic, M.V.

        PEACEFUL TRANSFORMATION TO COMMUNISM IN INDIA--1954-57:
        A COMPARATIVE CASE STUDY OF KERALA (PH.D.)
        Doct, Indian School of International Studies, 1964
        (Dr. Tara Chand)

2080   Fox, Richard S.

        FROM ZAMINDAR TO BALLOT BOX
        Cornell U. Press, 1969

2081   Frykenberg, R.E.

        TRADITIONAL PROCESSES OF POWER IN SOUTH INDIA: AN
        HISTORICAL ANALYSIS OF LOCAL INFLUENCES
        Ind. Eco Soc. Hist R. 1963, 1, 3, Oct-Dec, 122-142
        SA XV 3, C5038

2082   Galanter, Marc

        SECULARISM, EAST AND WEST
        Comp. Stud. Soc. Hist, VII, 2, 1965
        (4) p. 133-159

2083   Gandhi, I.

        INDIA AND THE WORLD
        Foreign Affairs, 51, 1, 1972

2084   Gandhi, M.K.
        SELECTED WRITINGS (ED. BY RONALD DUNCAN)
        Boston; Beacon Press, 1951, 253 p.

2085   Gandhi, M.K.

        TOWARDS NON-VIOLENT SOCIALISM (ED. BY B. KUMARAPPA)
        Ahmedabad; Navajivan publ, 1951, 165 p.

2086   Ganguli, H.C. and P.R. Chatterjee

        SOCIAL ATTITUDES AND VOTING BEHAVIOUR IN SMALL
        INDUSTRIAL SAMPLES
        Ind. J. Soc. W. 1959, 20, 3, Dec, 192-199
        SA XI, 5, A5978

2087   Ganguly, S.k.

CASTE PANCHAYAT OF THE KURMI MAHATOS OF SINGHBHUM
Man In India, 1965, 45, 2, Apr-Jun, 159-166
SA XVI, 5, D2603

2088   Garde, D. K.

SOCIAL AND POLITICAL THOUGHTS OF SAINTS OF MAHARASHTRA
FROM JANESHWARA TO RAMDASA, WITH SPECIAL REFERENCE TO
RAMDASA (D. LITT)
Doct. Allababad U. 1958

2089   Gautam. M.L.

STUDENT POLITICS AND HIGHER EDUCATION (SOCIOL STUDY
OF POLITICAL BEHAVIOUR OF UNIVERSITY STUDENTS)
Doct. St., Rajasthan U., 1969

2090   Geevarghese,P.K.

A SOCIOLOGICAL PERSPECTIVE OF KERALA COMMUNISM
Paper presented at the 46th Annual Meeting of The
Southwestern Sociological Association
SA XIX, 102, Sup. 14, E8931

2091   Ghurye, G. S.

INDIAN SADHUS
Bombay, (1968)

2092   Gokhale, Balkrishna Govind
SARDAR VALLABHBHAI PATEL: THE PARTY ORGANIZER AS
POLITICAL LEADER
in. Leadership and Political Instutions in India
ed. R. L. Park and I. Tinker
New York, Greenwood Press, 1969   p 87-101

2093   Gokte, V.K.

THE ROLE OF CASTE IN OUTER DELHI PARLIAMENTARY ELECTIONS
Ind. Political Sci. Rev. 1967, 1, 3-4, Apr-Sept, 225-238
SA XX, 1-2, F3790

2094   Gorwala, A.D.

THE PUBLIC SERVICES AND DEOMCRACY
in. Leadership and Political Institutions In India
New York: Greenwood Press, 1969, p. 329-337

2095   Gouraha, N.K.

INDIAN VILLAGE AND THE POLITICAL NETWORK
Doct. St., Saugar U., 1969

2096   Gough, E.K.

VILLAGE POLITICS IN KERALA
Rural Sociology in India
ed. A. R. Desai, Bombay, 1969, p. 736-768

2097   Gough, K.

COMMUNIST RURAL COUNCILLORS IN KERALA
J. of Asian and African Studies, 1968, 3, 3-4, Jul-Oct,
181-202
SA XVIII, 6, E4966

2098   Gould, H.A.

TOWARD A "JATI MODEL" FOR INDIAN POLITICS
Eco. and Pol. Weekly IV, 5, 1969, p. 1-5

2099   Goyal, O.P.

CASTE-SPLIT IN VOTING BEHAVIOR
Political Scientist 1966, 3, 3, Jan-Jun, 27-35
SA, XVI, 3, D0038

2100   Goyal, O.P.

POLITICS, CASTE AND VOTING BEHAVIOUR
Poli. Sci. Rev. 1969, 8, 2, Apr-jun, 237-244
SA XX, 5, F7194

2101   Gray, Hugh

THE PROBLEM
Rural Sociology in India
ed. A. R. Desai
Bombay Popular Prakashan, 1969, p. 535-540

2102   Guha, (Miss) L.

THE GROWTH OF SOCIALISM IN INDIA   (D. PHIL)
Doct., Allahabad U., 1954, (Capt. A. B. Lal)

2103   Gupta, B. B.

THE THEORY AND PRACTICE OF WELFARE STATE IN INDIA
(PH.D.)
Doct., Agra U., 1962

2104   Gupta, K. A.

SOCIOLOGY OF POLITICS IN A SMALL TOWN
Doct. St., Delhi U., 1969 (N. R. Sethi)

2105   Gupta, S.K.

ELECTIONS AND THE SCHOOL CHILDREN
Political Science Rev. 1969, 8, 3-4, Jul-Dec,361-378
SA XX 5, F7200

2106   Gupta, S.K.

SOCIALIZATION FOR CITIZENSHIP ROLE IN A DEMOCRATIC
SOCIETY
Doct. St. Agra U., 1969
(Dr. Y. Atal)

2107   Hardgrave, Robert. L.

NADARS OF TAMILNAD: THE POLITICAL CULTURE OF A
COMMUNITY IN CHANGE
U. of Calif. Press, 1969

2108   Harpal Singh

PANCHAYATI RAJ IN MERUT DISTRICT
Doct, Agra U., 1970
(Dr. R.K. Awasthi)

2109   Harper, Ed. B. and Louise S.

POLITICAL ORGANIZATION   AND LEADERSHIP IN A KARNATAKA
VILLAGE
in. Leadership and Political Institutions In India
ed. R. L. Park and I. Tinker
New York, Greenwood Press, 1969, p. 453-471

2110   Harrison, S. S.

CASTE AND THE ANDHRA COMMUNISTS
Amer. Polit. Sci. Rev. 1956, 50, e, Jun, 378-404
SA VI, 1, 4019

2111   Hess, R.

THE VILLAGE PANCHAYAT IN INDIA
Ind. Sociol. 1963, 5, 6, Mar, 1-3, and 6-8
SA XIII, 3-4, B6249

2112   India Planning Commission

THE NEW INDIA: PROGRESS THRU DEMOCRACY
New York, MacMillan, 1958, 412 p.

2113   Irschick, E.F.

POLITICS AND SOCIAL CONFLICT IN SOUTH INDIA: THE
NON-BRAHMAN MOVEMENT AND TAMIL SEPARATION, 1916-1929
U. of Calif Press, 1969

2114   Ishwaran, K. (ed.)

        POLITICS AND SOCIAL CHANGE
        New York, Humanities, 1966

2115   Iyer, H.R.S.

        PANCHAYATRAJ AND POLITICAL PARTIES
        Kurukshetra, 1965, 13, 5, Feb, 14-15
        SA XIV, 6, C2382

2116   Iyer, H.R.S.

        PANCHAYATI RAJ: CONCEPT AND SIGNIFICANCE
        Kurkshetra, 1966, 14, 7, Apr, 18-21
        SA XVII, 3, D7042

2117   *Iyer, Pashupati, N.

        POLITICS OF COALITION IN INDIA: A THEORETICAL
        ANALYSIS
        Indian Journal of Sociology, 1971, 2, 2, Sep,
        127-166
        SA 21, 73G1744

2118   Jain, H.C.

        THE ORGANIZATION AND WORKING OF THE PANCHAYATS
        IN CERTAIN TRIBAL SOCIETIES OF MADHYA PRADESH (PH.D.)
        Doct, Vikram U, 1970
        (Dr. P.N. Mathur)

2119   Jain, P.N.

        SOCIAL CHANGE AND PANCHAYAT RAJ
        Kurukshetra, 1967, 15, 7, Apr 2-3
        SA, XVIII, 7, E6058

2120   Jayaraman, K.

        A STUDY OF PANCHAYATS IN MADRAS
        Bombay, Indian Society of Agricultural Economics
        1947, 157 p

2121   Jayaraman, K.

A STUDY OF PANCHAYATS IN MADRAS
Bombay; Indian Society of Agricultural Economics, 1947
157 p.

2122   Jeevaratnam, A.G.

POLITICAL IMPLICATIONS OF UNTOUCHABILITY (PH.D.)
Doct, Bombay U., 1969
(Dr. (Miss) U. H. Metha)

2123   Joshi, T.D.

SOCIAL AND POLITICAL THOUGHT OF RAMDAS(PH.D.)
Doct, Bombay U., 1968
(Dr. (Miss) U.H. Mehta)

2124   Kapur, Ashok

STRATEGIC CHOICES IN INDIAN FOREIGN POLICY
Int'l J. 27, 39, 1972

2125   Kate, D.B.

SOCIAL AND POLITICAL THOUGHT IN THE DHARMA SHASTRA
WITH SPECIAL REFERENCE TO BRIHASPATHI(PH.D.)
Doct, Poona U., 1969
(Dr. D.K.Garde)

2126   Khan, A.M.

LIFE AND SPEECHES OF SARDAR PATEL: A STUDY OF THE
CAREER AND CHARACTER OF SARDAR PATEL, AS WELL AS HIS
IDEAS AND IDEALS, INCLUDING ALL HIS IMPORTANT SPEECHES
UNTIL HIS DEATH
New Delhi; Indian Printing Works, 1951, 276 p.

2127   Khan, I.H.

WELFARE PROGRAMME UNDER PANCHAYATI RAJ
Doct. St., Delhi U., 1969
(S.N. Ranade)

2128   Khan, I.H.

         GOVERNMENT IN RURAL INDIA
         Bombay, Asia, 1971

2129   Khan, I. Y.

         LIFE AND LABOUR AT BHILAI--A SOCIO-POLITICAL STUDY
         (PH.D.)
         Doct, Saugar U., 1963
         (Prof. M.P. Sharma)

2130   Kahn, R.

         CHARMINAR: COMMUNAL POLITICS AND ELECTORAL BEHAVIOUR
         IN HYDERABAD CITY
         Political Sci. Rev., 1969, 8, 1, Jan-Mar. 58-90
         SA, XX, 1-2, F3801

2131   Khanna, S.

         SOCIAL BACKGROUND, VALUES AND ATTITUDES OF POLITICAL
         LEADERS
         Doct. St.. Saugar U., 1969

2132   Kamal, T.

         TOWARDS A SECULAR STATE IN INDIA
         Interdiscipline,1966, 3, 4, Oct-Dec, 248-264
         SA, XVII, 2, D6058

2133   Kantowsky, D.

         INDIEN--AM VORABEND DER REVOLUTION?
         (INDIA--AT THE EVE OF A REVOLUTION?)
         Korlner Zeitscherftfuer Soziologie und Sozial--
         Psychologie, 1969, Supp. 13, 219-236 (Ger.)
         SA, XIX, 1-2, E7293

2134   Kautsky, J.H.

         COMMUNISM AND THE POLITICS OF DEVELOPMENT
         New York, John Wiley and Sons, Inc., 1968, vii and 216
         SA, XVII, 1, D5013

2135   Khare, R.S.

GROUPS AND PROCESSES OF POLITICAL CHANGE IN NORTH
INDIAN GOPALPUR
Man In India, 1969, 49, 2, Apr-Jun, 188-210
SA, XIX, 3, E8639

2136   Kini, N.G.S.

MODERNIZATION IN INDIA, WOMEN VOTING BEHAVIOUR
AS INDEX
Political Sci. Rev. 1969, 8, 1, Jan-Mar, 12-22
SA, XX, 1-2, F3805

2137   Kodanda, R.P.

PLAN QUINQUENNAL (INDIA FIVE YEAR PLAN)
Civilizations, 1953, 3, 3, 411-17
SA, Vol. II, #1, 166

2138   Kothari, R. (ed.)

CASTE IN INDIAN POLITICS
Fernhill, 1972

2139   Kothari, R. et. al.

PARTY SYSTEM AND ELECTION STUDIES
Bombay, Allied Publishers, 1967, ix-294 p.

2140   Kothari, R. and J.J. Wiatr

SYSTEMY PARTYJNE A PLUALIZM POLITYCZNY POROWNANIA
MIEDZY INDA I POLSKA (PARTY SYSTEMS AND POLITICAL
PLURALISM: COMPARISONS BETWEEN INDIA AND POLAND)
Studia Socjologuzno Polityezne, 1968, 25, 177-188
(Pol)
(SA XVII, 7, E0325

2141   Krishnamachari, V.T.

INDIAN STATES AND THEIR FUTURE
in. Group Prejudices in India
ed. M.B. Nanavati and C.N. Vakil p. 173-176
Bombay, Vora, 1951

2142   Krishna Murthy, K.G.: Rao, G.L.

POLITICAL PREFERENCES IN KERALA: AN ELECTORAL
ANALYSIS OF THE KERALA GENERAL ELECTIONS 1957,
1960, 1965, and 1967
Delhi, Radha Krishna, 1968, xii-99 p.

2143   Krishna Murthy, K.G. and G.L. Rao

SOCIO-ECONOMIC AND DEMOGRAPHIC FACTORS AND VOTING
BEHAVIOR.   THE CASE OF KERALA
Poli. Sci. Rev. 1969, 8, 2, Apr-Jun, 193-212
SA, XX, 5, F7213

2144   Kuber, W.N.

A CRITICAL STUDY OF THE SOCIAL AND POLITICAL THOUGHT
OF DR. B.R. AMBEDKAR (PH.D.)
Doct., Poona U., 1968
(Dr. D.K. Gardi)

2145   Kumar, R.

CLASS, COMMUNITY OR NATION?   GANDHI'S QUEST FOR A
POPULAR CONSENSUS IN INDIA
Modern Asian Studies, 1969, 3, 4, Oct, 357-376
SA, XX, 1-2., F3809

2146   Lakshman, P.P.

CONGRESS AND THE LABOUR MOVEMENT IN INDIA
Allahabad; All India Congress Committee, 1947, 174 p.

0925   political sociology

2147   Lakshminarayana, H.D.

       LEADERSHIP AND POLITICAL DEVELOPMENT IN A MYSORE
       VILLAGE: A CASE STUDY
       J. of Soc. Res., 1969, 12, 1, Mar, 17-26,
       SA, XIX, 6, F1605

2148   Lambert,Richard D.

       HINDU COMMUNAL GROUPS IN INDIAN POLITICS
       in. Leadership and Political Institutions in India
       ed., R. L. Park and I. Tinker
       New York: Greenwood Press, 1969

2149   Leigh, M.

       MARTYED MAHATMA
       Church Quart. Rev. 146, 1-14, April, 1948

2150   Lichtheim, G.

       THE FUTURE OF SOCIALISM
       Partisan R., 1963, 30, 1, Spr, 83-98
       SA, XV, 3, C5058

2151   Lloyd, G.P.

       LOCAL SELF-GOVERNMENT IN INDIA
       J. Afr. Adm. 4, 2, Apr. 1951, 51-57

2152   Loomis, C.P. and J. Rytina

       MARXIST THEORY AND INDIAN COMMUNISM: A SOCIOLOGICAL
       INTERPRETATION
       East Lansing Michigan State U, 1970, vi & 148 p.

2153   Mahendra Kamar

       THE SOCIAL AND POLITICAL PHILOSOPHY OF QUAKERS (PH.D.)
       Doct., Lucknow U., 1963
       IDr. P.N. Masaldan)

2154   Malaviya, H.D.

        PANCHAYATS AND VILLAGE CONFLICTS
        in. Rural Sociology in India
        ed. A. R. Desai
        Bombay Popular Prakashan, 1969, p. 403-410

2155   Malhotra, S. L.

        SOCIAL AND POLITICAL ORIENTATIONS OF NEO-VEDANTISM
        Chand, 1969

2156   Malik, Y.K.

        AGENCIES OF POLITICAL SOCIALIZATION AND EAST INDIAN
        ETHORIC INDENTIFICATION IN TRINIDAD
        Sociol. B. 1969, 18, 2, Sup, 101-121
        SA, XIX, 3, E8644

2157   Malik, Y.K.

        SOCIO-POLITICAL PERCEPTIONS AND ATTITUDES OF EAST
        INDIAN ELITES IN TRINIDAD
        Western Political Quart, 1960, 23, 3, Sep, 552-563
        SA XX 4, F6285

2158   Mastin, Briton Jr.

        NEW INDIA, 1885: BRITISH OFFICAL POLICY AND THE
        EMERGENCE OF THE INDIAN NATIONAL CONGRESS
        U of Calif Press, 1969

2159   Mathur, M.V. and Narain, I. (ed.)

        PANCHAYATI RAJ PLANNING AND DEMOCRACY
        Asia,

2160   Maxwell, N.

        INDIA AND THE POLITICS OF LOCALITY

        New Society, 1971, 17, 440, Mar 4, 344-346
        SA XX, 3, F4978

2161   Mayer, A.C.

SYSTEM AND NETWORK: AN APPROACH TO THE STUDY OF
POLITICAL PROCESS IN DEWAS
M.T.C. Madan and S. Sarana (ed.)
Indian Anthropology
Bombay: Asia Pub. House, 1962, p. 266-78

2162   McComack, Wm.

FACTIONALISM IN A MYSORE VILLAGE
in. Leadership and Political Institutions in India
(R. Park, I. Tinker,ed.)Oxford U. Press, 1960, 438-444

2163   McDonough, P.

PARTICIPATION ELECTORALE ET CONCURRENCE ENTRE LES
PARTIS LE CAS DE L'INDE--1952-1967 (THE ANATOMY OF
PARTY COMPETITION AND ELECTORAL PARTICIPATION IN INDIA,
1952-1967)
Revue Franciase de Sociologie, 1970, 11, 4, Oct-Dec,
488-515, (Fr)
SA, XIX, 7, F2442

2164   Mehta, Ashoka

GROUP PREJUDICES AND POLITICAL PARTIES
in. Group Prejudices in India
ed. M.B. Nanavati and C.N. Vakil
Bombay, Vora, 1951, pp. 167-173

2165   Mehta, A.

SOCIALISM AND PEASANTRY
Bombay; Socialist Party, 1953, 88 p.

2166   Mehta, (Miss) U.H.

SOCIAL AND POLITICAL THOUGHT OF MAHATMA GANDHI (PH.D.)
Doct., Bombay U. 1951
(Dr. N. A. Thoothi)

2167   Mehta, Uday

THE IMPACT OF THE PANCHAYATI RAJ ON RURAL INDIA
in Rural Sociology in India
ed. A. R. Desai
Bombay, 1969, p. 580-599

2168   Menon, V.K.N.

CASTE, POLITICS AND LEADERSHIP IN INDIA: NOTES
TOWARD A DEFINITION OF THE SUBJECT
Contribution to the Bombay Round Table
Jan. 4-10, 1964
Paris: Intl Polit. Sci. Assoc. 1964, 8 p.

2169   Milton, I.

THE INDIAN PARTY SYSTEM AND THE 1974 PARLIAMENTARY
ELECTIONS
Int'l. J. 27, 3, 1972

2170   Misra, R. N.

VILLAGE   SELF-GOVERNMENT IN UTTAR PRADESH (PH.D.)
Doct. Agra U. 1958

2171   Mohan, R.P.

NATIONAL INTEGRATION
Interdiscipline, 1966, 3, 4, Oct-Dec, 211-215
SA, XVII, 2, D6070

2172   Morris, Morris David

TRADE UNIONS AND THE STATE
in. Leadership and Political Institutions in India
ed. R. L. Park and I. Tinker
New York: Greenwood, 1969, pp. 268-279

2173   Morrison, W.A.

KNOWLEDGE OF POLITICAL PERSONAGES HELD BY THE MALE
VILLAGERS OF BADALPUR: AN INTRODUCTORY DELINEATION
Sociol. B. 1961, 10, 2, Sep. 1-26
SA, XL, 6, A6715

2174   Morrison, Jones, W.H.

INDIAN ELECTIONS
Political Quart. V. 23, 1952, P. 235-49

2175   Mrozek, B.

SYSTEM PARTYING W INDIACH
(PARTY SYSTEM IN INDIA)
Kultura i Spoleczenshov, 1961, 5, 1, Jan-Mar,
131-144 (Pol.)   SA XVII, 5, D8441

2176   Mudaliar, C.

STATE AND RELIGION IN INDIA: A STUDY OF "SECULAR STATE"
IN INDIA
Social Compass 1966, 13, 5-6, 391-399
SA XVIII, 6, E4842

2177   Mukherji, P.

GRAMDAN IN VILLAGE BERAIN: SOCIOLOGICAL ANALYSIS
Hum. Org. 1966, 25, 1, Spr, 33-41
SA, XIV, 5, C1358

2178   Mukhopadhyay, S.

SOCIAL AND POLITICAL IDEAS OF SWAMI VIVEKANANDA (D.Phil)
Doct., Calcutta U., 1968

2179   Muley, D.S.

WORKING OF VILLAGE PANCHAYATS IN BHANDORA DISTRICT
(PH.D.)
Doct., Nagpur U., 1966   (Dr. N. Desppande}

2180   Muthamma, I.M.

A TINY MODEL STATE OF SOUTH INDIA
Coorg, Isted, Pollibetta, Cooyg: "Tiny Spot",
1953, 362 P.

2181   *Muthayya, B. C.

ELECTED VILLAGE LEADERS OF INDIA: A PSYCHOLOGICAL
ANALYSIS
Behavioral Sciences and Community Development,
1971, 5, 1, Mar, 14-20
SA, 21, 73G0816

2182   Rudolph, L.I. and S.H. Rudolph

THE POLITICAL MODERNIZATION OF AN INDIAN FEUDAL ORDER:
AN ANALYSIS OF RAJPUT ADAPTION IN RAJASTHAN
J. of Social Issues, 1968, 24, 4, Oc, 93-128
Sa, XVII, 5, D8453

2183   Nagarajan,V.

SOCIETY UNDER AN IMPERIAL STATE   (PH.D.)
Doct., Nagpur U., 1967
(Dr. T. S. Wilkinson)

2184   *Nandy, Ashis

THE MAKING AND UNMAKING OF POLITICAL CULTURES IN
INDIA
Daedalus, 1973, 102, 1, Win, 115-137
SA 21, 73G5123

2185   Narain, I.

THE CONCEPT OF PANCHAYATI RAJ AND ITS INSTITUTIONAL
IMPLICATIONS IN INDIA
Asian Surv. 1965, 5, 9, Sept, 456-466
SA, XV, 1, C3747

2186   Narayan, S.

SOCIALISM IN INDIAN PLANNING
Bombay, Asia, 1964

2187   Nicholas, R. W.

STRUCTURES OF POLITICS IN THE VILLAGES OF SOUTHERN
ASIA
in. Structure and Change In Indian Society
ed. M.B. Singer and B. S. Cohn
Chicago; Aldine, 1968, p 243-284

2188   Nicholas, R.W.

VILLAGE FACTIONS AND POLITICAL PARTIES IN RURAL WEST
BENGAL
J. Commonwealth Polit. Stud. 1963, 2, 1, Nov. 17-32
Sa XIII, 5, B7141

2189   Nicholson, N.K.

INDIA'S MODERNIZING FACTION AND THE MOBILIZATION OF
POWER
Int. J. of Comparative Sociology, 1968, 9, 3-4,
Sep-Dec, 302-317
SA, XVIII, 1-2-, E1111

2190   Nigam, M.

PANCHAYATI RAJ IN MADHYA PRADESH AND ITS IMPLEMENTATION
(IN HINDI) (PH.D.)
Doct, Vikram U., 1968
(Dr. P.K. Bhattacharya)

2191   Opter, M. E.

FACTORS OF TRADITION AND CHANGE IN A LOCAL ELECTION
IN RURAL INDIA
in. Leadership and Political Institutions in India
(Park and Tinker (ed.))
Oxford U. Press, 1960, 137-150

2192   Opler, M.E. and W.L. Rowe, and M.L. Stroop

        INDIAN STATE AND NATIONAL ELECTIONS IN A VILLAGE
        CONTEXT
        Hum. Org. 1959, 16, 1, Spr, 30-35
        SA, X, 2, A1896

2193   Orenstein, H.

        GAON: THE CHANGING POLITICAL SYSTEM OF A MAHARASHTRIAN
        VILLAGE
        in   Change and Continuity in India's villages
        ed. K. Ishwaran
        New York: Columbia U. Press, 1970, p. 219-241

2194   Palmer, N.D.

        LOKALRE SYSTEMY POLITCZNE W POLUDNIOWEJ ASJI:
        EHSPERYMENTY W "DEOMKRATYCZNEJ DECENTRALIZACJI"
        (LOCAL POLITICAL SYSTEMS IN SOUTH ASIA: EXPERIMENTS
        IN DEMOCRATIC "DECENTRALIZATION)
        Studia Socjologiczno Polityczne, 1967, 23, 125-141
        (pol)   SA, XVII, 3, D7027

2195   Palmer, Norman D. and Irene Tinker

        DECISION MAKING IN THE INDIAN PARLIAMENT
        in. Leadership and Political Institutions in India
        ed. R.L. Park and I. Tinker
        New York: Greenwood Press, 1969   p 115--137

2196   *Panini, M.N.

        GENERAL ELECTIONS OF 1967 IN RAMPURA
        Sociological Bulletin, 21, 1, Mar. 1972

2197   Randey, V. C.

        COMMUNAL POLITICS AND SOCIAL AND POLITICAL REVIVALISM
        IN INDIA--A SOCIOLOGICAL ANALYSIS OF REPERCUSSIONS
        OF COMMUNALISM ON THE SOCIO-POLITICAL CHANGES IN INDIA
        DURING THE 20TH CENTURY (PH.D.)
        Doct. St. Agra U., 1969   (B.S. Haikerwal)

0925   political sociology

2198   Panikkar, K.M.

        STATE AND THE CITIZEN
        Asia

2199   Park, R. L.

        LABOR AND POLITICS IN INDIA
        Far Eastern Survey, v. 18, 1949, p. 181-7

2200   Park, R.L.

        INDIAN ELECTION RESULTS
        Far Eastern Survey, V. 21, 1952, p. 61-70

2201   Park. R.L.

        INDIAN DEMOCRACY AND THE GENERAL ELECTION
        Pacific Affairs, V. 25, 1952, p. 130-39

2202   Park, Richd. L.

        DISTRICT ADMINISTRATION AND LOCAL SELF-GOVERNMENT
        in. Leadership and Political Institutions In India
        ed. R.L. Park and I. Tinker
        New York: Greenwood, 1969, p. 337-345

2203   Park, R.L. and I. Tinker (ed.)

        LEADERSHIP AND POLITICAL INSTITUTIONS IN INDIA
        Princeton U. Press, 1969

2204   Park, R.L.

        INDIA'S GENERAL ELECTION
        Far Eastern Survey, V. 21, 1952, p. 1-8

2205   Patil, A.P.

        SOCIAL AND POLITICAL IDEAS OF MAHATMA PHULE (PH.D.)
        Doct., Poona U., 1969
        (Dr. D. K. Garde)

2206   Patnaik, N. and H.D. Lakshminarayana

FACTIONAL POLITICS IN VILLAGE INDIA
Man In India, 1969, 49, 2, Apr.-Jun., 161-187

2207   Phadnis, (Mrs.) U.

TOWARDS THE INTEGRATION OF INDIAN STATES (PH.D.)
Doc., Banaras Hindu U., 1961

2208   Prasad, K.P.

GROWTH AND WORKING OF MUNICIPAL SELF-GOVERNMENT IN
BIHAR (PH.D.)
Doct., Bihar U., 1965
(Dr. V.P. Varma)

2209   Prasad, R.

STUDY OF LOCAL SELF-GOVERNMENT IN VINDHYA PRADESH (PH.D.)
Doct., Saugar U., 1959

2210   A Study of Panchayats' Programme Evaluation
Organization: Planning Commission

STRUCTURE OF PANCHAYATS

in. Rural Sociology in India
ed. A.R. Desai, Bombay, 1969
p. 553-570

2211   Puri, M.M

SARVODAYA: MIRAGE OR REALITY?

Revue du Sud-Est Asiatique, 1965, 2, 101-110
SA, XVI, 7, D4307

2212   Purwar, (Miss) V.L.

THE PANCHAYAT SYSTEM IN U.P. (D.PHIL.)
Doc., Allaharad U., 1957 (Prof. A. D. Pant)

2213   Rajkumar, N.V.

        INDIAN POLITICAL PARTIES
        New Delhi: All Indian Congress Committee, 1948, 139 p

2214   Ramaswamy, E.A.

        TRADE UNIONS AND POLITICS
        Sociol. B. 1969, 18, 2, Sep, 138-147
        SA, XLX, 3, E8654

2215   Rao, C.V.H.

        POLITICS AND PANCHAYATI RAJ
        Kurukshetra, 1966, 15, 2, Nov, 22-25
        SA, XVIII, 6, E4857

2216   *Rao, M.S.A.

        THE MID-TERM POLL IN A VILLAGE IN OUTER DELHI
        CONSTITUENCY
        Sociological Bulletin, 21, 1, Mar, 1972

2217   Ram Reddy, S.

        PANCHAYATI RAJ IN ANDRA PRADESH: A CASE STUDY OF
        BLOCK ADMINISTRATION   (PH.D.)
        Doct., Olmania U., 1967   (Dr. A. Avasthy)

2218   Rao, G.R.S.

        CONCEPTUAL AND OPERATIONAL DIMENSIONS OF NATIONAL
        INTEGRATION
        Interdiscipline, 1966, 3, 4, Oct-Dec., 220-232
        SA, XVII, 2, D6077

2219   Rastogi, P.N.

        FACTION SITUATION AT BRAHMINPURA
        Man In India, 1963, 43, 4, Oct-Dec, 328-336

2220   Rastogi, P.N.

FACTIONALISM, POLITICS AND CRIME IN A UTTAR PRADESH
VILLAGE
East. Anthrop. 1964, 17, 3, Sep-Dec, 168-182
SA, XIV, IV, C0630

2221   Rastogi, P.N.

VECTORS OF FACTIONALISM
Ind. J. Soc. Res. 1966, 7. 3, Dec, 186-193
SA, XVII, 3, D7029

2222   Reddy, G. N.

AN EVALUATIVE STUDY OF THE AWARD WINNING VILLAGE
PANCHAYATS OF ANDHRA PRADESH
Doct. St. Agra U., 1969, (B.R.Chauhan)

2223   *Reinhardt, W.W.

THE LEGISLATIVE COUNCIL OF THE PUNJAB
Durham, Duke University

2224   Rittenberg, S.

CASTE'S ROLE IN INDIAN POLITICS: A STUDY OF
COALITION FORMATION
Columb. Essays. int. Aff. 4, 1968, 150-167

2225 . Robson, W.A.

INDIA AS A WELFARE STATE
Political Quarterly 25, 116-31, April'54

2226   Rosenthal, D.B.

FACTIONS AND ALLIANCES IN INDIAN CITY POLITICS
Midwest J. of Pol. Sci., 1966, 10, 3, Aug., 320-349
SA, XVI, 2, D0171

2227   Rosenthal, D.B.

        DEURBANIZATION, ELITE DESPLACEMENT AND POLITICAL
        CHANGE IN INDIA
        Comparative Politics, 1970, 2, 2, Jan, 169-201
        SA, XX, 1-2, F3831

2228   Rosser, C.

        AN ASPECT OF THE POLITICAL ORGANIZATION OF MALANA
        Eastern Anthrop, V6, 1952, p. 68-82

2229   Rothermund, D.

        BEWEGUNG UND VERFASSUNG
        (MOVEMENT AND CONSTITUTION)
        Vjh. Zeitgesch 1962, 10, 2, Apr, 126-148, (Gr.)
        SA, XII, 6, B1837

2230   Roy Burman, B.K.

        MEANING AND PROCESS OF TRIBAL INTEGRATION IN A
        DEMOCRATIC SOCIETY
        Sociol. B., 1961, 10, 1, 27-41

2231   Rudolph, L.I. and S.H. Rudolph

        THE POLITICAL ROLE OF INDIA'S CASTE ASSOCIATIONS
        Pacific Aff. 1960, 33, 1, Mar, 5-22
        SA, IX, 4, A0517

2232   Rudolph, L.I. and S.H.Rudolph

        THE MODERNITY OF TRADITION: POLITICAL DEV. IN INDIA
        U. of Chicago Press, 1967

2233   Saberwal, S.

        INTERNATIONAL SOCIAL SCIENCE: SOME POLITICAL ASPECTS
        Eco. and Pol. Weekly, 1970, 5, 27, 1044-52

2234   Sahni, P.R.

        WELFARE STATE IN UTTAR PRADESH   (PH.D.)
        Doc, Agra U., 1959

2235   Samant, S.V.

        VILLAGE SELF-GOVERNMENT IN BOMBAY STATE (PH.D.)
        Doct., Bombay U., 1957
        (Dr. (Miss) A.J. Dastur)

2236   Samra, Chaffar Singh

        SUBHAS CHANDRA BOSE: AN INDIAN NATIONAL HERO
        in. Leadership and Political Institutions in India
        ed.   R.L. Park and I. Tinker
        New York: Greenwood Press. 1969   p. 66-87

2237   *Sanwal, R.D. and Sushila Sanwal

        THE ELECTORAL PROCESS IN AN ASSEMBLY CONSTITUENCY IN
        KUMAON
        Sociological Bulletin, 1971, 20,2, Sep. 178,-201
        SA, 21, 73G5744

2238   Sarswathi, (Miss) S.

        MINORITIES IN MADRAS STATE: A STUDY OF GROUP'S INTERESTS
        AND THEIR ORGANIZATION IN MADRAS POLITICS SINCE 1890
        (PH.D.)
        Doct., Madras U., 1965   (Prof. R. Bhaskaran)

2239   Sarup, A.

        NOTES AND QUERIES ON DECISION-MAKING IN GOVERNMENT
        Interdiscipline, 1966, 3, 3, Jul, 157-161
        SA, XVII, 1, D5132

2240   Saxena, P.K.

        PROGRESSIVE DEMOCRATIZATION IN RAJASTHAN (PH.D.)
        Doc., Agra U., 1967

2241   Shah, A.M.

       POLITICAL SYSTEM IN EIGHTEENTH CENTURY GUJARAT
       Enquiry, 1964, 1, 1, 83-95

2242   Shah, P.J.

       CASTE AND POLITICAL PROCESS
       Asian Survey, 1966, 6, 9, Sep, 516-522
       SA, XVI, 1, C9166

2243   Shankarnarayan Bhat, K.

       PANCHAYATI RAJ IN MYSORE (PH.D.)
       Doct. Bombay U., 1966
       (Dr. (Miss) A.G. Dastur)

2244   Sharma, H.P.

       FACTIONAL POLITICS IN A NORTH INDIAN VILLAGE
       Amer. Doct. Dissertations (1968-69)
       Cornell U. (Soc)

2245   Sharma, K. L.

       SOCIAL STRUCTURE AND POLITICAL CHANGE
       Poli. Sci. Rev. 1969, 8, 1, Jan-Mar, 91-102
       SA, XX, 1-2, F3837

2246   Sharma, K.N.

       PANCHAYAT   LEADERSHIP AND RESOURCE GROUPS
       Sociol. B. 1963, 12, 1, Mar 47-52
       SA, XI. 7, A7333

2247   Sharma, M.P.

       LOCAL SELF-GOVERNMENT IN INDIA
       Bombay: Hind Kitabs, 1951, 129 p.

2248   Shrivastava, K.K.

A STUDY OF POLITICS AND VOTING BEHAVIOUR IN A RURAL
CONSTITUENCY: A CASE STUDY
Doct., Saugar U., 1969
(Prof. S.C. Dube)

2249   Shrivastava, P.K.

ELITE VALUES AND SOCIAL POLICIES (PH.D.)
Doct., Saugar U., 1970
(Prof. H. S. Asthana)

2250   Singh, K.K., A. Ashraf and H. Teune

PEWNE WYMIARY SOIJO--PSYCHOLOGICZNE ODPOWIEDZIALNOSCI
POLITZCYNEJ (SOME SOCIO-PSYCHOLOGICAL DIMENSIONS OF
POLITICAL RESPONSIBILITY)
Studia Socjolojiczno Politczne, 1967, 23, 207-218 (Pol.)
SA XVII, 3, Dm031

2251   Singh, Y.

THE SOCIO-CULTURAL BASES AND FUNCTIONING OF POLITICAL
PARTIES IN U.P.
Doct. St. Lucknow U., 1969

2252   Singh, Y.

SOCIAL STRUCTURE AND VILLAGE PANCHAYATS
in. Rural Sociology in India
Ed., A. R. Desai, Bombay, Popular Prakashan, 1969,
p.p. 570-580

2253   Sinha, (Mrs.) A.

SOCIAL AND POLITICAL PHILOSOPHY OF SARVODAYA
Doct. St. Bhagalpur U., 1969   (Dr. P. S. Muhar)

2254   Sirsikar, W.M.

NICHTORE PROBLEMY METHODOLOGICZNE BADAN NAD WARTOSCIAMI
W POLITYCE I ICH TLO W INDII (SOME METHODOLOGICAL
PROBLEMS OF THE RESEARCH SCHEME ON POLITICAL VALUES AND
ITS INDIAN BACKGROUND)
Studia Socjologiczno Polityczne, 1967, 23, 107-113 (Pol.)
SA XVII, 3, D6946

0925   political sociology

2255   Sirsikar, V.M.

THE RURAL ELITE IN A DEVELOPING SOCIETY: A STUDY IN
POLITICAL   SOCIOLOGY
New Delhi: Orient Longmans, 1970, IX, 227 pp

2256   Sisson, Richd.

CONGRESS PARTY IN RAJASTHAN: POLITICAL INTEGRATION AND
INSTITUTION--BUILDING IN AN INDIAN STATE
U of Calif. Press, 1972

2257   Smith, D.E.

INDIA AS A SECULAR STATE
Princeton: Universtiy Press, 1963

2258   Somjee, A.H.

FORMS AND LEVELS OF POLITICAL ACTIVITY IN INDIAN VILLAGES
Polit. Stud. (Oxford) 1963, 11, 1, Feb, 1-10
SA, XIII, 2, B5299

2259   Srinivasan, N.

VILLAGE GOVERNMENT IN INDIA
Far East. Quart. 1956, 15, 2, Feb, 201-213
SA, VI, 2, 4336

2260   Srivastva, H.C.

ROLE FAILURE OF INDIAN POLITICAL ELITE
Ind. Sociol. B. 1966, 3, 4, Jul, 286-288
SA, XV, 7, C8318

2261   Suda, J.P.

THE CHOICE BEFORE US
Ind. J. Soc. Res. 1968, 9, 2, Aug., 123-129
SA, XX, 1-2, F3843

2262   Surendra Bahadpur Singh

SOCIAL AND POLITICAL IDEAS OF JAWAHAR LAL NEHRU (PH.D.)
Doct., Lucknow U., 1967
(Prof. R. Singh)

2263   Suri, S.

ZUR SOZIOLOGIE DER INDISCHEN PARTEIEN (ON THE SOCIOLOGY
OF INDIAN PARTIES)
Z. Soziol. Soz. Psychol. 1963, 15, 4, 643-663 (Ger.)
SA, XII, 8, B3510

2264   Suri, S.

POLITICAL ASSASSINATIONS IN INDIA
Sociol   Quart. 1971, 12, 3, Fall, 403-406
SA, XX, 3, F4993

2265   Sutaria, D.H.

WELFARE STATE (PH.D.)
Doct., Gujarat U. 1957

2266   Swaroop, B.B.

TRIBE AND JUDICAL FRONTIER: A STUDY OF NYAYA
PANCHAYATIN DUNGARPUR DISTRICT OF RAJASTHAN
Doct. St. Agra U., 1969
(Dr. B. R. Chauhan)

2267   Tak, B.L.

SOCIOLOGICAL DIMENSIONS OF GRAMRAJ (A CASE STUDY IN
RAJASTHAN) (PH.D.)
Doct. Agra U., 1968
(Dr. R.N. Saxena)

2268   Tandon, V.N.

THE SOCIAL AND POLITICAL PHILOSOPHY OF SARVODAYA
AFTER GANDHIJI (PH.D.)
Doct., Agra U., 1964

2269   Taylor, C.C. et al

INDIA'S ROOTS OF DEMOCRACY
Bombay, Orient Longmans, 1965

2270   Thomas, P.T.

THE MUTHUVANS OF TRAVANCORE AND THE GENERAL ELECTIONS
(SOCIAL ANALYSIS)
J. of the M.S.U. of Baroda,
1952, 1, **2**

2271   Thorner, D.

THE VILLAGE PANCHAYAT AS A VEHICLE OF CHANGE
Eco. Dev. and Cult. Change, V.2, Oct, 1953, p. 209-215

2272   Thusu, K.N.

THE PANCHAYAT SYSTEM OF THE DHURWAS OF BASTAR (M.P.)
Man In India, 1965, 45, 2, Apr-Jun, 134-151
SA, XVI, V, D2628

2273   Trivikram, T.K.N.

STATE AND CULTURE (PH.D.)
Doct., Bombay U., 1955
(Prof. B.P. Mukerji)

2274   Venktarao, V.

LOCAL SELF-GOVERNMENT IN ASSAM (D.LITT.)
Doct., Allahabad U., 1965
(Prof. A. B. Lal)

2275   Verma, D.P.

WORKING OF PANEHAYATS IN THREE MADHYA BHARAT VILLAGES
Doct. St., Saugar U, 1969

2276   Verma, R.K.

VILLAGE PANCHAYATS IN THE STATES OF MADHYA PRADESH
AND RAJASTHAN (PH.D.)
Doct., Vikram U., 1967
(Dr. R.P. Pandey)

2277   Wadia, A.R.

NATIONAL INTEGRATION
Interdiscipline, 1966, 3, 4, Oct.-Dec., 207-210
SA, XVII, 2, D6087

2278   *Wehr, P.

THE GHANDIAN MODEL OF SELF-LIMITING CONFLICT
Paper presented at the ASA Annual Meetings,
Montreal, August 25-29, 1974

2279   Weiner, Myron

SOME HYPOTHESES ON THE POLITICS OF MODERNIZATION
IN INDIA
in. Leadership and Political Institutions In India
ed. R. L. Park and I. Tinker
New York; Greenwood Press, 1969   p. 18-39

2280   Welty, Paul t.

POLITICS IN INDIA
in. The Asians: Their Heritage and Destiny
Philadelphia, J.P. Lippincoot Co., p. 108-120

2281   Wiebe, P.

ELECTIONS IN PEDDUR: DEMOCRACY AT WORK IN AN INDIAN
TOWN
Hum. Org. 1969, 28, 2, Sum, 140-147
SA, XVIII, 4, E3177

2282   Yadava, J.S.

       GROUP DYNAMICS AND PANCHAYAT ELECTIONS IN A PUNJAB
       VILLAGE
       J. of Social Res., 1968, 11, 2, Sep, 58-72
       SA, XVIII, 6, E 4876

2283   Yadava, J.S.

       FACTIONALISM IN A HARYANA VILLAGE
       Amer. Anthrop. 1968, 70, 5, oct, 898-910
       SA, XVLL, 6, D9575

2284   Yadav, G.S.

       A STUDY OF EMERGING PATTERN OF RURAL LEADERSHIP AND
       PACHAYATI RAJ IN UTTAR PRADESH   (PH.D.)
       Doct. St. Agra U., 1969 (P.N. Tandon)

2285   Zamora, M.D.

       POLITICAL INNOVATION AND RESPONSE IN AN INDIAN
       VILLAGE
       Philippine Soc. Sci. Human R. 29, 2, Jun 1964, 105-150

2286

       ANALYSIS OF INDIAN POLITICAL BEHAVIOUR
       Monthly Publ. Opinion Surv. 12 (7-8-9) Apr-May-June
       1967, 3-110

2287

       CONVEGNI SULL 'EGITTO, SULLO DI ISRAELE, SULL NON
       VIOLENZA E L'ABIEZIONE DI COSCIENZA IN RELAZIONE ALL
       INDIA (MEETINGS ON EGYPT, THE STATE OF ISRAEL AND
       CONSCIENTIOUS OBJECTORS WITH REGARD TO INDIA)
       Annal. Social., 1965, 2, 61-71 (It.)
       SA, XV, 6, C7454

0925   political sociology

2288

          INDIA AND THE PROTEIN PROBLEM
          Kurukshetra, 1969, 17, 8, May, 5-9
          SA, XIX, 4, E9833

2289

          INDIAN POLITICAL BEHAVIOUR
          Mthly Publ. Opin. Surv. 14 (4-5-6) Jan-Feb-Mar
          1969, 3-94

2290

          THE LIFE OF MAHATMA GANDHI
          New York: Harper, 1950, 558 p.

1000   Social Differentiation

1019   Social Stratification

   2291   Abraham, C.M.

          CASTE SYSTEM
          Ind. Sociol. 1961, 3, 4, Mar,43-56
          SA XIII, 1, B4369

   2292   Acharya, H.

          SYMPOSIUM ON CASTE AND JOINT FAMILY: IN AN IMMIGRANT
          ARTISAN COMMUNITY
          Sociol. B. 1955, 4, 2, Sep. 129-138
          SA, V, 1, 2960

   2293   Agarwala, B.R.

          SYMPOSIUM ON CASTE AND JOINT FAMILY: IN A MOBILE
          COMMERCIAL COMMUNITY
          Sociol B. 1955, 4, 2, Sep, 138-146
          SA, V, 1, 2905

2294   Agarwal, (Miss) P.

        SOME CHANGING ASPECTS OF CASTE IN AN URBAN COMMUNITY
        (PH.D.)
        Doct. St., Agra U., 1969
        (Dr. S. Chandra)

2295   Agarwal, (Mrs.) S.P.

        STATUS AND ROLE PERCEPTION OF EDUCATED MIDDLE-CLASS
        MARRIED HINDU WOMEN (PH.D.)
        Doct. St., Agra U., 1969
        (Dr. R.N. Saxena)

2296   Agarwal, P.C.

        CASTE, RELIGION, AND POWER: AN INDIAN CASE STUDY
        New Delhi: Shri Ram Center for Industrial Relations
        1971, xiv, 270 pp

2297   Ahmad, I.

        SOCIAL STRUCTURE OF A MULTI-CASTE VILLAGE IN U.P.
        Doct. St., Delhi U., 1969
        (M.N. Srinivas)   (M.S.A. Rao)

2298   Ahmed, L.N. and A. Hajura

        THE POLITICS   OF SOCIAL MOBILITY IN INDIA: A
        HYPOTHESIS
        Ind. J. Soc. Res. 1964, 5, 3, Dec, 246-44
        SA, XIV, 5, C1256

2299   Ahmad, Z.

        A STUDY OF CHANGING PATTERN OF STRATIFICATION IN A
        VILLAGE IN U.P.
        Doct. St., Delhi U., 1969
        (Dr. M.N. Srinivas)

2300   Aiyappan, A.

SYMPOSIUM ON CASTE AND JOINT FAMILY: IN TAMILAND
Social B. 1955, 4, 2, Sep, 117-122
SA. V . 1. 2961

2301   Ames, Michael

INDIAN CASTES OLD AND NEW
Pacific Affairs, XLIV, 1, 1971, p. 81-91

2302   Ansari, G.

MUSLIM CASTE IN INDIA
East. Anthrop. 1955-1956, 9, 2, Dec-Feb. 104-111
SA, V, 4, 3700

2303   Ansari, G.

MUSLIM CASTE IN UTTAR PRADESH: A STUDY OF CULTURAL
CONTACT
East. Anthrop. 1959-1960, 13-2, Dec-Feb, 1-83
SA, XI, 4, A5293

2304   Arokiaswami, M.

CASTES IN SOUTH INDIA
Tamil Culture, 3, 3-4, Oct, 1954, 326-330

2305   Aryamane, R.V.

BACKWARD CLASSES IN THE INDIAN CONSTITUTION
Polit. Scientist, 1966, 2, 1, Jul-Dec, 27-36
SA, XV, 5, C6567

2306   Atal, Y.C.

THE CHANGING FRONTIERS OF CASTE (PH.D.)
Doct., Saugar U., 1966
(Prof. S.C. Dube)

2307   **Aurora**, G.S.

CASTE AND THE BACKWARD CLASSES
Man In India, 1968, 48, 4, Oct-Dec, 297-306

2308   Bailey, F.G.

CASTE AND ECONOMIC FRONTIERS
New York, Humanities, 1957

2309   Bailey, F.**G**.

TRIBE AND CASTE IN INDIA
Contrib. Ind. Sociol. 1961, 5, Oct., 7-19
SA, XIV, 5, C1260

2310   Bailey, F.G.

CLOSED SOCIAL STRATIFICATION IN INDIA
Eur. J. Sociol. 1963, 4, 1, 107-124
SA, XII, 7, B2710

2311   Bailey, F.G.

TRIBE, CASTE, AND NATION
Bombay, Oxford U. Press, 1960

2312   Barno**uw** , V.

SOCIAL STRUCTURE OF A SINDHI REFUGEE COMMUNITY: CASTE
Social Forces, 33; 144-6, Dec. 1954

2313   **Baviskar**, B.S.

CO-OPERATIVES AND CASTES IN MAHARASHTRA: A CASE STUDY
Sociol. B. 1969, 18, 2, Sep, 148-166
SA, XIX, 3, E8676

2314   *Berreman, G.D.

CASTE IN THE MODERN WORLD
Morristown, General Learning Press, 1973

2315   Berreman, G. D.

CASTE IN INDIA AND THE UNITED STATES
Amer. J. Sociol. 1960, 66 2, Sep. 120-127
SA, VII, 4, 8658

2316   Berreman, G.D. and L. Dumont

CASTE, RACISM AND "STRATIFICATION"
Contrib. Ind. Sociol. 1962, 6, Dec, 122-125
SA, XIV,5, C1262

2317   Berreman, G.D.

THE STUDY OF CASTE RANKING IN INDIA
Southw J Anthrop. 1965, 32, 2, Sum, 115-129
SA, XIV, 2-3, B9480

2318   Berreman, G.D.

CASTE AS SOCIAL PROCESS
Southwestern J. of Anthrop., 1967, 23, 4,
Win. 351-370
SA, XVII, 1, D5142

2319   Beteille, A.

A NOTE ON THE REFERANTS OF CASTE
Eur. J. Sociol. 1964, 5, 1, 130-134
SA, XIII, 1, B4371

2320   Beteille, A.M.

A STUDY OF A MULTI-CASTE VILLAGE IN MADRAS (PH.D.)
Doct., Delhi U., 1964
(Dr. M.N. Sririvas)

2321   Beteille, A.

CLOSED AND OPEN SOCIAL STRATIFICATION IN INDIA
Archives Europeennes de Sociologie 1966, 7, 2, 224-248
SA, XVI, 1, C9181

2322   Beteille,A.

IDEAS AND INTEREST: SOME CONCEPTUAL PROBLEMS IN
THE STUDY OF SOCIAL STRATIFICATION IN RURAL INDIA
Int. Soc. Sci. J. 1969, 21, 2, 219-234
SA, XVIII, 6, E4881

2323   Beteille, A.

CASTES: OLD AND NEW: ESSAYS IN SOCIAL STRATIFICATION
Bombay, New York, Asia Publ. House, 1969, vii and 254 p.

2324   Beteille, A.

CASTE, CLASS AND POWER: CHANGING PATTERNS OF
STRATIFICATION IN A TANJORE VILLAGE
Berkeley and Los Angles: U. of Calif Press, 1971
iii, 238 pp.   SA, XX, 5F7244

2325   Bhargava, B.C.

THE CRIMINAL TRIBES, A SOCIO-ECONOMIC STUDY OF THE
PRINCIPAL CRIMINAL TRIBES AND CASTES IN NORTHERN INDIA
Lucknow Universal Publishers, 1957-8

2326   Bhat, C.S.

SOCIAL MOBILITY AMONG THE WADDARS OF SOUTH INDIA
Doct. St. Delhi U., 1969
(M.S.A. Rao)

2327   Bhatia, B.M.

GROWTH AND COMPOSITION OF MIDDLE CLASS IN SOUTH INDIA
IN NINETEENTH CENTURY
Ind. Econ. Soc. Hist. R. 1965, 2, 4, Oct., 341-356
SA XV, 3, C5169

2328   Bhatia, M.S.

CASTE SYSTEM AND THE FIVE-YEAR PLAN
Careers and Courses, 7, 2, Feb, 1955
p. 120-122

2329   Bhatnagar, R.C.

        CASTE DYNAMICS IN RURAL UTTAR PRADESH (PH.D.)
        Doct., Lucknow U., 1958
        (Dr. S. J. Hasan)

2330   Bhatt, G.S.

        THE CHAMAR OF LUCKNOW
        East. Anthrop. 1954, 8, 1, Sep-Nov, 27-41
        SA, vol IV, #2, 2266

2331   Bhattacharjee, J.N.

        HINDU CASTES AND SECTS
        Calcutta, 1968

2332   Blunt, E.A.H.
        CASTE SYSTEM OF NORTHERN INDIA
        New Delhi, 1969

2333   *Bopegamage, A.
        CASTE AND POVERTY
        Sociology and Social Research, 57, 1, Oct., 1972

2334   Bopegamage, A. and R.N. Kulahalli

        CASTE AND OCCUPATION IN RURAL INDIA: A REGIONAL
        STUDY IN URBANIZATION AND SOCIAL CHANGE
        Rural Sociology, Sept, 1972, 37, 3, 352-389

2335   Borale, P.T.

        SEGREGATION AND DESEGRATION IN INDIA
        Paragon, 1968

2336   Bose, N.K.

        SOME OBSERVATIONS ON NOMADIC CASTES IN INDIA
        Man In India, 1956, 36, 1, Jan-Mar, 1-6
        SA, VIII, 1, 7033

2337   Bose, N.K.

NATIONAL INTEGRATION AND THE SCHEDULED CASTES AND
SCHEDULED TRIBES
Man In India, 1968, 48, 4, Oct-Dec, 289-296
SA, XVIII, 4, E3187

2338   Bose, N.K.

SOME ASPECTS OF CASTE IN BENGAL
in. Traditional India: Structure and Change
ed. M.B. Singer
Philadelphia, Amer. Folklore Society, 1959, pp 191-207

2339   Bose, N.K.

CLASS AND CASTE
Man In India, 1965, 45, 4,Oct-Dec., 265-274
SA, XVI, 5, D2545

2340   Bose,N.K.

SOME ASPECTS OF CASTE IN WEST BENGAL
in. Rural Sociology In India
ed. A. R. Desai
Bombay Popular Prakashan, 1969, p. 328-331

2341   Bose, N.K.

THE USE OF PROCEEDINGS OF CASTE PANCHAYATS
J. Soc. Res. (India), 1960, 1, 1, Jul, 98-100
also: Regional Seminar on Techniques of Social
Research, UNESCO Research Center, Calcutta, 1958, 65-67
SA, XI, 2&3, A4670

2342   Bottomore, T.B .

THE CHANGING SHAPE OF CASTE
New Society, 1963, 2, 40, Jul 4, 10-12
SA, XIII, 1, B4188

2343   Bougle, C.

THE ESSENCE AND REALITY OF THE CASTE SYSTEM
Contrib. Ind. Sociol. 1958, 2, Apr, 7-30
Sa, XIV, 2-3, B9482

2344   Bougle, C.

ESSAYS ON THE CASTE SYSTEM
New York, Cambridge U. Press, 1971, XV and 228 pp
SA, XX, 3, F4596

2345   Brown, W. Norman

CLASS AND CULTURAL TRADITIONS IN INDIA
in. Traditonal India: Structure and Change
ed. M.B. Singer
Philadelphia: Amer. Folklore Society
1959, p. 35-40

2346   Carstairs, G.M.

THE TWICE-BORN: A STUDY OF A COMMUNITY OF HIGH-
CASTE HINDUS
Peter Smith

2347   Chakravarty, U.

CONDITIONS OF BENGALI WOMEN AROUND THE 2ND HALF OF
THE 19TH CENTURY
Calcutta, 1968

2348   Chanana, S. R.

STUDIES ON THE PROBLEM OF SLAVERY SINCE THE 17TH
CENTURY
Ind. J. Soc. Wrk.,1958, 19, 3, Dec, 203-209
SA, VII, 2, 7462

2349   Chandy A.R.

STUDY OF THE CHANGING PATTERN OF BEHAVIOUR OF AN
UNTOUCHABLE CASTE: THE PULAYAS OF KERALA (PH.D.)
Doct., Poona U, 1966
(Dr. Y. B. Damle)

2350   Chattopadhyaya, B.

CASTE IN THE VEDAS
Calcutta R, 145, 3, Dec- 1957, 237-242

2351   Chattopadhyay, G.

CASTE DOMINANCE AND DISPUTES IN A VILLAGE IN
WEST BENGAL
Man In India, 1966, 46, 4, Oct-Dec, 287-318
SA, XVI, 7, D4323

2352   CHAUHAN, B.R.

RECENT TRENDS AMONG DEPRESSED CLASSES IN RAJASTHAN
Agra U. J. of Res., 3, 3, 1955, 158-161

2353   Chauhan, B.R.

THE NATURE OF CASTE AND SUB-CASTE IN INDIA
Sociol B., 1966, 15, 1, 40-51
SA, XIV, 6, C2261

2354   Chauhan, S.K.

CASTE, CLASS AND POWER: AN ANALYSIS OF THE
STRATIFICATION SYSTEM IN RURAL UPPER ASSAM.
East. Anthrop. 25,2, May-august, 1972, 149-161

2355   Chauhan, S.K.

CASTE HEIRARCHY IN THREE VILLAGES OF UPPER ASSAM
Man In India, 52, 1, 1972, 39-46

2356   Chekki, D.A.

SOCIAL STRATIFICATION AND TRENDS OF SOCIAL MOBILITY
IN MODERN INDIA
Ind. J. Soc. Wrk, 1971, 31, 4, Jan, 367-380
SA, XX, 6, F8386

2357   Chekki, D.A.

CHANGING FEMININE ROLES: CROSS-CULTURAL PERPECTIVES
J. of the Karnatak U., 1964
(Humanities and Social Sciences)

2358   Choudari, R.K.

A SURVEY OF SOCIAL STRATIFICATION IN INDIA
J. of the Oriental Instit. M.S.U. of Baroda
6, 1, 1956, 140-155

2359   Chhibbar, Y.P.

FROM CASTE TO CLASS--A STUDY OF THE INDIAN MIDDLE
CLASSES
Verry, 1968

2360   Cohn, B.S.

CHANGING TRADITIONS OF A LOW CASTE
in. Traditional India: Structure and Change
ed.   M.B. Singer   p. 207-216
Philadelphia, Amer. Folklore Society, 1959, p 207-216

2361   Cormack, M.L.

THE HINDU WOMAN
New York; Bureau of Publications, Teachers College,
Columbia University, 1953, 207p.

2362   *Cove, John, V.

A MULTI-DIMENSIONAL MODEL OF CASTE RANKING
Eastern Anthropologist, 26, 2, Apr-Jun, 1973

2363   Damle, Y.B.

REFERENCE GROUP THEORY WITH REGARD TO MOBILITY IN CASTE
Soc. Action, 13 (4), April 1963,19-199

2364   Damle, Y.B.

CASTE IN MAHARASHTRA
J. of the U. of Poona
Humanities Section, 9, 1758, 87-98

2365   Danda, A.K. and D.G. Danda

FUNCTIONS OF CASTE IN MODERN INDIA
Man In India, 1968, 48, 1, Jan-Mar, 29-39
SA, XVII, 7, E0354

2366   Das, M.S.

AN EXPLORATORY STUDY OF TOUCHABLE-UNTOUCHABLE
INTERCASTE MARRIAGE IN INDIA
Ind. J. of Sociol.   1970, 1, 2, Sep, 130-138,
SA, XIX, 5, F1010

2367   Das, M.S.

MAINTENANCE OF CASTE HICRARCHY IN INDIA AND THE
UNITED STATES
Ind. Soc. B.,1970, 7, 3-4, Apr-Jul, 159-166
SA, XX, 5, F7249

2368   Das, M.S. and F.G. Acuff

THE CASTE CONTROVERSY IN COMPARATIVE PERSPECTIVE:
INDIA AND THE UNITED STATES
Int. J. of Comparative Sociology, 1970, 11, 1,
Mar, 48-53
SA, XIX, B, E8679

2369   Das, V.

A SOCIOLOGICAL APPROACH TO THE CASTE PURANAS:
A CASE STUDY
Sociological B., 1968,17, 2, Sep, 141-164
SA, XVIII, E5975

2370   Das, V.M.V.

A SOCIOLOGICAL INVESTIGATION OF THE CASTE PURANAS IN
GUJARAT
Doct. St., Delhi U., 1969, (M.N. Srinivas)

2371   Datta, N.K.

        ORIGIN AND GROWTH OF CASTE IN INDIA
        (2 vols)   Calcutta, 1968

2372   Desai, I.P. and Y.B. Damle

        A NOTE ON THE CHANGE IN THE CASTE
        in. Professor Ghurye Feliciation Volume
        ed. K.M. Kapadia
        Bomba; Popular Book Depot, 1954, 266-276

2373   Dhammaratana, B.

        BUDDHA AND CASTE SYSTEM
        Maha Bodhi 60, 7, July 1952, 240-246

2374   Dhindsa, Rajwinder K.

        CHANGING STATUS OF WOMEN IN RURAL INDIA
        American Doct. Dissertation ('68-'69)
        University of Illinois (Soc)

2375   Driver, E.D.

        FERTILITY DIFFERENTIALS AMONG ECONOMIC STRATA IN
        CENTRAL INDIA
        Eugenics Quart. 1960, 7, 2, Jun 77-85
        SA, XI, 5, A5875

2376   D'Souza, V.S.

        CASTE IN INDIA
        J. of the U. of Poona
        Humanities Section, 7, 1957, p 80-88

2377   D'Souza, V.S.

        MEASUREMENT OF RIGIDITY--FLUIDITY DIMENSIONS OF
        SOCIAL STRATIFICATION IN SIX INDIAN VILLAGES
        Sociol. B. 1969, 18, 1, Mar, 35-49
        SA, XIX, 1-2, E7340

2378   D'Souza, V.S.

CASTE AND CLASS: A REINTERPRETATION
J. of Asian and African Studies, 1967, 2, 3-4
Jul-Oct, 192-211
SA, XVII, 2, D6100

2379   D'Souza, V.S.

CASTE STRUCTURE IN INDIA IN THE LIGHT OF SET THEORY
Current Anthrop., 13, 1, 1972, p. 5-22

2380   Dube, L.

CASTE, CLASS AND POWER
Eastern Anthrop. 1967, 20, 2, May-Aug, 215-226
SA, XVII, 6, D9496

2381   Dube, S.C.

MEN'S AND WOMEN'S ROLES IN INDIA: A SOCIOLOGICAL
REVIEW
in. Women In The New Asia
ed. B. E. Ward
UNESCO, Paris, 1965, p. 174-204

2382   Dube, S.C.

RANKING OF CASTES IN TELAGANA VILLAGES
East. Anthrop., 1955, 8, 3-4, Mar-Aug, 182-190
SA, Vol IV #2, 2269

2383   Dube, S.C.

DOMINANT CASTE AND LEADERSHIP IN A CENTRAL INDIAN
VILLAGE
India, 1964, p. 1-20

2384   Dube, S.M.

DISPLACEMENT, SOCIAL MOBILITY AND CONFORMITY WITH THE
OUT-GROUP
Interdiscipline, 1967, 4, 2, Sum, 124-136
SA, XVII, r, D7825

2385   Dumont, L.

        CASTE, RACISME ET "STRATIFICATION"
        (CASTE, RACISM AND "STRATIFICATION")
        Cah, Internat. Soc., 1960, 29, Jul-Dec, 91-112 (Fr.)
        SA, X, 1, A1298

2386   Dumont, L.

        "TRIBE" AND "CASTE" IN INDIA
        Contrib. Ind. Sociol. 1962, 6, dec, 120-122
        SA, XIV, 5, C1308

2387   Dumont, L.

        A FUNDAMENTAL PROBLEM IN THE SOCIOLOGY OF CASTE
        Contribution to Indian Soc. 1966, 9, Dec. 17-32
        SA, XVI, 5 D2547

2388   Dumont, L.

        CASTE: A PHENOMENON OF SOCIAL STRUCTURE OF AN
        ASPECT OF INDIAN CULTURE
        in. A.V.S. de Reuch and J. Knight (ed.)
        Ciba Foundation Symposium on Caste and Race:
        Comparative Approaches
        London, J. & A. Churchill Ltd., 1967, 38-38

2389   Dumont, L.

        HOMO HIERARCHICUS: AN ESSAY ON THE CASTE SYSTEM
        Chicago: University of Chicago Press, 1970, pp 385

2390   Elder, Joseph W.

        CASTE AND WORLD VIEW: THE APPLICATION OF SURVEY
        RESEARCH METHODS
        in. Structure and Change in Indian Society
        eds. M.B. Singer and B. S. Cohn
        Chicago; Aldine Publ, 1968, pp 173-189

2391   Fraser-Tytler, K.

FAREWELL TO BEARERS: THE SERVANT CLASS OF INDIAN
SOCIETY
Blackwood's Magazine, 264, 387-92, Nov '48

2392   Freed, S.A.

AN OBJECTIVE METHOD FOR DETERMINING THE COLLECTIVE
CASTE HIERARCHY OF AN INDIAN VILLAGE
Amer. Anthrop., 1963, 65, 4, Aug, 879-891
SA, XII, 3, A9727

2393   Freed, S.A.

CASTE RANKING AND THE EXCHANGE OF FOOD AND WATER
IN A NORTH INDIAN VILLAGE
Anthropological Quart, 1970, 43, 1, Jan, 1-13
SA, XX, 6, F8153

2394   Fox, R. G.

VARNA SCHEMES AND IDEOLOGICAL INTEGRATION IN INDIAN
SOCIETY
Comparative Studies in Society and History
1969, 11, 1, Jan, 27-45
SA, XVIII, 3, E2057

2395   Fuerer--Haimendorf, C. Von

CULTURE STRATA IN THE DECCAN
Man, 1948, 47, 87-90

2396   Gadgil, D.R.

TWO POWERFUL CLASSES IN AGRA**RIAN** AREAS
In.   Rural Sociology in India
ed. A. R. Desai
Bombay Popular Prakashan, 1969, pp 333-336

2397   Galanter, M.

LAW AND CASTE IN MODERN INDIA
Asian Surv. 1963, 3, 11, Nov,544-559
SA, XIII, 5, B7067

2398   Galantet, Marc

CHANGING LEGAL CONCEPTIONS OF CASTE
In. Structure and Change in Indian Society
ed. B.S. Cohn and M.B. Singer
Chicago, Aldine, 1968, pp 299-339

2399   Galanter, Marc

UNTOUCHABILITY AND THE LAW
Paper presented at conference on "The Untouchable in
Contemporary India"
U. of Arizona, Nov. 1967
also: Eco. and Polit. Weekly, Annual, Jan, 1969

2400   Gangrade, K. D.

GENERATIONAL MOBILITY: A STUDY
Social Welfare, 19, 6, 1972,1-3

2401   Ganguli, B.N.

THE INDIAN MIDDLE CLASS
Econ. Wkly., 1955, 42, 7, 15 Oct., 1226-230
SA, VI, 1, 4004

2402   Gardner, P.M.

TOWARD A COMPONENTIAL MODEL OF INDIAN CASTE
J. of Social Res., 1968, 11, 1, Mar, 37-48
SA,XVIII, 3, E2060

2403   Garg, B.M.

STATUS OF WOMEN IN TRIBAL COMMUNITIES IN INDIA
Ind. J. Soc. W. 1960, 21, 2, 191-197
SA, XL, 6, A6573

2404   Ghurye, G.S.

SCHEDULED TRIBES
(3rd ed.) New York; Humanities, 1963
Bombay; Popular Book Dept., 1959

2405   Ghurye, G. S.

CASTE, CLASS AND OCCUPATION
Bombay, Popular Book Dept., 1961

2406   Ghurye, G. S.

CASTE AND CLASS IN INDIA
Bombay, Popular Book Depot, 1960

2407   Ghurye, G. S.

CASTE AND RACE IN INDIA (5th ed.)
New York, Humanities, 1969

2408   Ghurye, G. S.

CASTE AND CLASS IN INDIA
Bombay: Popular Book Depot., 1950, 240 p.

2409   Gist, N.P.
CASTE IN TRANSITION: SOUTH INDIA
Phylon, 15, 155-64, June, 1954

2410   Gist, Noel P.

CASTE DIFFERENTIALS IN SOUTH INDIA
Amer. Sociol. Rev., 1954, 19, 2, April 126-137
S.A. vol II #4, 707

2411   Gorndi, S.

BACKWARD CLASSES IN U.P. (D.PHIL.)
Doct., Allahbad U., 1958
(Prof. M.G. Gupta)

2412   Goldstein R. L.

INDIAN WOMEN IN TRANSITION: A BANGALORE CASE STUDY
Metuchen M.J., Scarerow Press, 1972

2413   Gordon, L.A. and L.A. Firdman

OSOHENNOSTI SOSTAWA I STRAKTINY RABOCEGO KLASSA
B EKONOMICHESKI SLALORAZVITYKH STRANNAKH AZII
AFRIKII (NA PRMEIRE INDII I OAR) NARODY AZII I
AFRIKI, (DISTINCTIVE ASPECTS OF THE COMPOSITION
AND STRUCTURE OF THE WORKING CLASS IN THE
ECONOMICALLY UNDERVELOPED COUNTRIES OF ASIA AND
AFRICA (BASED ON DATA FOR INDIA AND THE UAR))
People of Africa and Asia, 1963, 2, 3-22
Tr of article in Sov. Sociol. 1963-64, 2, 3, 46-63
SA XIV, 5, C1131

2414   Goswami, M.C. and S.N. Ratha and F. Nesha

CASTE AND OCCUPATION IN AN ASSAMESE VILLAGE
Man In India, 1966, 46, 3, Jul-Sep, 191-197
SA, XVI, 6, D3396

2415   Gough, E.K.

BRAHMAN KINSHIP IN A TAMIL VILLAGE
Amer. Anthrop, 1956, 58, 5, Oct., 826-853
SA, vol VII, #1, 5349

2416   Gould, H.A.

CASTES, OUTCASTES AND THE SOCIOLOGY OF STRATIFICATION
Int. J. Compar. Sociol., 1960, 1, 2, Sep, 220-238
SA, XI, 7, A7375

2417   Gould, H.A.

CASTE AND CLASS: A COMPARATIVE VIEW
Reading, Mass. Addison-Wesley, 1971

2418   Goyal, O.P.

CASTE AND POLITICS--A CONCEPTUAL FRAMEWORK
Asian Surv., 1965, 5, 10, Oct, 522-525
SA, XV, 1, C3700

2419   Goyal, P.P.

UNTOUCHABILITY IN A DEMOCRATIC SOCIETY (PH.D.)
Doct., Agra U., 1968
(Dr. R.N. Saxena)

2420   Gracias, V.

THE POSITION OF CHRISTIANS IN A SECULAR STATE
in. Group Prejudices in India
ed. M. B. Nanavati and C. N. Vakil
Bombay, Vora, 1951, pp 183-188

2421   Gray, Hugh

THE LANDED GENTRY OF THE TELENGANA, A.P.
in. Elites in South Asia
ed. E. Leach and S.N. Mukerjce
London; Cambridge U. Press, 1970, pp 119-136

2422   Grant, Swadesh S.

SPATIAL BEHAVIOUR AND CASTE MEMBERSHIP IN SOME
NORTHERN INDIAN VILLAGES
(Ph. D.--Soc. Psy.)
The City University of New York, 1971

2423   Guha, A.

LAND RIGHTS AND SOCIAL CLASSES IN MEDIEVAL ASSAM
Indian Economic and Social History Review
1966, 3, 3, Sep, 217-239
SA, XVII, 1, D5151

2424   Guha, U.

CASTE AMONG RURAL BENGALI MUSLIMS
Man In India, 1965, 45, 2, Apr-Jun, 1967-1969
SA, XVI, D2548

2425   Guha, U, Kaul, M.N.

A GROUP DISTANCE STUDY OF THE CASTES OF U.P.
Bu. of the Dept. Of Anthrop. Govt. of India
Calcutta, 2, 2,1953, 11-32

2426   Gupta, Anima Sen

THE ROLE OF WOMEN IN INDIAN PUBLIC LIFE IN MODERN
TIMES
American doctorla dissertations 91957-58)
The American University (Sociology)

2427   Gupta, A.

OUR INTELLIGENTSIA AS SUBSERVIENT
Ind. J. Soc. Res. 1968 9, 2, Aug, 114-118
SA, XX, 1-2 , F3860

2428   Gupta, B.K.D.

CASTE--MOBILITY AMONG THE MAHATO OF SOUTH MANBHUM
Man In India, 1962, 42-3, July-Sep, 228-236
SA, XII, 5, B1103

2429   Gupta, G. R.

MULTIPLE REFERENCE MODELS AND SOCIAL MOBILITY IN
RURAL INDIA
Intern's Rev. of Modern Sociology 2, 1, Mar, 1972
83-91

2430   Gupta, M.

STATUS AND ROLE OF HINDU WIDOWS--A SOCIOLOGICAL
STUDY OF 400 WIDOWS IN THE CITY OF LUCKNOW
Doct. St. Lucknow U., 1969

2431   Gupta, (Miss) N.

CHANGING STATUS OF WOMEN IN HINDU MIDDDLE CLASS
SOCIETY
Doct. St., Agra U., 1969
(R. N. Saksena)

2432   Gupta, S. K.

ON CASTE STRATIFICATION IN A VILLAGE OF UTTAR PRADESH
East Anthrop., 1968, 21, 1, Jan-Apr, 87-94
SA, XVIII, 4, E2194

2433   Hames, C.

LA SOCIETE MAUSE OU LE SYSTEME DE CASTES HORS DE
L'INDE (THE MAUR SOCIETY OR SYSTEM OF CASTE OUTSIDE
INDIA)
Chiers Internationaux de Sociologie, 1969, 46,
Jan-Jun, 163-174 (Fr.)

2434   Harper, E. B.

RITUAL POLLUTION AS AN INTEGRATOR OF CASTE AND RELIGION
in. Religions in South Asia
ed. E. B. Harper
Seattle; U. of Washington, 1964, pp 151-199

2435   Harper, E. B.

FEAR AND THE SATUS OF WOMEN
Southwestern J. of Anthrop. 1969, 25, Spr. 81-95
SA, XVIII, 6, E4616

2436   Harper, Ed. E.

A COMPARATIVE ANALYSIS OF CASTE: THE UNITED STATES
AND INDIA
in. Structure and Change In Indian Society
ed. M. B. Singer and B. S. Cohn
Chicago: Aldine, 1968, pp 51-81

2437   Hasan, S.N.

THE POSITION OF THE ZAMINDARS IN THE MUGHAL EMPIRE
Ind. Eco. Soc. Hist. R. 1964, 1, 4, Apr-Jun,
107-119
SA, XV, 3, C5097

2438   Hate, (Mrs.) C.A.

        SOCIAL POSITION OF HINDU WOMEN (PH.D.)
        Doct., Bombay U., 1947
        (Prof. G.S. Ghurye)

2439   Hate, C.A. (Mrs.)

        CHANGING STATUS OF WOMEN IN POST-INDEPENDENCE INDIA
        Delhi, 1967

2440   Hazari

        UNTOUCHABLE: THE AUTOBIOGRAPHY OF AN INDIAN OUTCASTE
        New York; Praeger, 1969

2441   Hazlehurst, L.W.

        CASTE AND MERCHANT COMMUNITIES
        in. Structure and Change in Indian Society
        ed. B.S. Cohn and M.B. Singer
        Chicago; Aldine Pub., 1968, pp 285-299

2442   Hertel, B.R.

        RURAL PATTERNS OF UPWARD MOBILITY IN EASTERN UTTAR
        PRADESH (INDIA)
        PH.D.--SOC)
        U. of Wisconsin ('69-'70)

2443   Hiebert, P.G.

        CASTE AND PERSONAL RANK IN AN INDIAN VILLAGE:
        AN EXTENSION IN TECHNIQUES
        Amer. Anthropologist, 1969, 71, 2, Jun, 424-453
        SA, XVIII, 3, E2128

1019   social stratification

2444   Hocart, A.M.

        CASTE: A COMPARATIVE STUDY
        London; Meutten & Co., 1950, 157 pp

2445   Holstrom, M.

        CASTE AND STATUS IN AN INDIAN CITY
        Eco. and Pol. Wkly, 7, 15, April 8, 1972

2446   Hopkins, E.W.

        THE STATUS OF WOMEN
        Calcutta, 1968

2447   Hutton, J.H.

        CASTE IN INDIA: ITS NATURE, FUNCTION AND ORIGINS
        Review of Religion, 12, 409-15, May, 1948

2448   Hutton, J. H.

        CASTE IN INDIA: ITS NATURE, FUNCTION AND ORIGINS
        (2ND. ED.)
        Bombay, London and New York, Oxford U. Press, 1952
        X and 315 p.

2449   India (Repbulic) Commissioner for Scheduled Castes
        and Scheduled Tribes
        REPORT 1951
        New Delhi: Manger, Government of India Press, 1951-V

2450   *Jain, S.P.

        RELIGION & CASTE RANKING IN A NORTH INDIAN TOWN
        Sociological Bulletin, 1971, 20, 2, Sep. 134-144
        SA, 21, 73G5748

2451   Jain, S.P.

RELIGION, CASTE, CLASS AND EDUCATION IN A NORTH
INDIAN COMMUNITY
Sociology and Social Research, 53, 4, Jul., 1969

2452   Jamal, (Mrs.) K.

THE CHANGING STATUS OF MUSLIM WOMEN BASED ON A
STUDY OF MIDDLE CLASS M.W. IN THE CITY OF GORAKHPUR
Doct. St. Gorakhpur U., 1969   (S.P. Nagendra)

2453   James, P.V.

MALAVETANS OF KERALA: A STUDY ON TRIBE CASTE
Doct., St. Saugar U., 1969

2454   Jaulair, B.B.

INTER-CASTE RELATIONS IN URBA HINDU SOCIETY (PH.D.)
Doct., Agra U., 1960

2455   Jauhari, (Miss) P.

STATUS OF WORKING WOMEN (PH.D.)
Doct., Lucknow U., 1970
(Dr. K.S. Jaulair)

2456   Jha, M.L.

A STUDY OF ATTITUDES TOWARDS UNTOUCHABILITY (PH.D.)
Doct., Agra U., 1967

2457   Jha, U.

THE ORIGIN OF PANJI SYSTEM
East Anthrop 1966, 19, 3, Sep-Dec 190-204
SA, XV, 6, C7497

2458   Johnson, Sipya Bose and M.G. Johnson

INDIA AND THE UNITED STATES: DIVERGENT ATTACKS ON
DISCRIMINATION
Man In India, 52, 2, 1972, 113-123

2459   Jones, K.W.

THE BENGALI ELITE IN POST-ANNEXATION PUNJAB
Ind. Eco. and Social Hist. Review. 1966, 3, 4,
Dec, 376-395
SA, XVII, 1, D5155

2460   Joseph, B.

A COMPARATIVE STUDY OF THE CASTE SYSTEM IN TWO LINGUSTIC
AREAS: ONE IN AN INDO-ARYAN REGION, THE OTHER IN A
DRAVIDIAN REGION
Doct. St., Delhi U., 1969
(A. Beteille)

2461   Kadetotad, N.K.

CASTE HEIRARCHY AMONG THE UNTOUCHABLES OF DHARWAR
East. Anthrop. 1966, 19, 3, Sep-Dec, 205-214
SA, XV, 6, C7498

2462   Kannan, C.T.

INTER-CASTE MARRIAGE IN BOMBAY STATE (PH.D.)
Doct., Bombay U., 1961
(Prof. K.M. Kapadia)

2463   Kapadia, K.M.

CASTE IN TRANSITION
Sociol B., 1962 11, 1-2, Mar-Sep 73-90
SA, XI, 7, A7377

2464   Karve, I.

CASTE IN MODERN TIMES AND SOME MEASURES TO COMBAT
ITS EVILS
Report of the Seminar on Casteism and Removal of
Untouchability
Bombay, 1955, 54-59

2465   Kausalyayana, B.A.

        HOW TO GET RID OF UNTOUCHABILITY
        Mahabodhi, 63, 5, May 1955, 173-179

2466   Kemp, T.

        LEADERS AND CLASSES IN THE INDIAN NATIONAL CONGRESS
        1918-1939
        Sci. and Soc. 1964, 28, 1, Win, 1-19
        SA, XIV, 1, B8612

2467   *Khare, R. S.

        HIERARCHY AND HYPERGAMY: · SOME INTERRELATED ASPECTS
        AMONG THE KANYAKUBJA BRAHMANS
        American Anthropologist, 1972, 74, 3, June, 644-628
        SA, 21, 73G0855

2468   *Kidder, R.L.

        LITIGATION AS A STRATEGY FOR PERSONAL MOBILITY: THE
        CASE OF URBAN CASTE ASSOCIATION LEADERS
        Journal of Asian Studies, 33, 2, Feb, 1974

2469   Kiratkudave, U.S.

        THE ORIGIN AND DEVELOPMENT OF UNTOUCHABILITY IN INDIA
        Doct. St. Bombay U., 1969
        (Dr. G. M. Moraes)

2470   Kumar, D.

        CASTE AND LANDLESSNESS IN SOUTH INDIA
        Comp. Stud. Soc. Hist. 1962, 4, 3, Apr 337-363
        SA, XII, 2, A9004

2471   Kuppuswamy, B. & B. Singh

        SOCIO-ECONOMIC STATUS STRATIFICATION IN WESTERN UTTAR
        PRADESH
        Sociol. B. 1967, 16, 1, Mar, 62-68
        SA, XVII, 2, D6105

2472   Lakshmana, C.M.

        INTER-CASTE RELATIONS IN RURAL ANDHRA WITH PARTICULAR
        REFERENCE TO ROYAL ASEEMA AND NORTHERN CIRCARS (PH.D)
        Doct., Lucknow U., 1967
        (Prof. S.R. Nagendra)

2473   Lakshmanna, C.

        CASTEISM--AN ANALYSIS OF THE SOCIAL PROCESS
        Ind. Soc. B., 1968, 5, 4, Jul, 238-242
        SA, XVII, 7 E0360

2474   Lakshminarayana, H.D.

        DOMINANT CASTE AND POWER STRUCTURE
        Behavioral Sciences and Community Development,1970
        4,2, Sep, 146-160   SA, 21, 73G0856

2475   Leach, E.R.

        INTRODUCTION: WHAT SHOULD WE MEAN BY CASTE?
        from Aspects of Caste in South India, Ceylon and
        North-West Pakistan
        (Leach, E.R. ed.) Cambridge Papers in Social
        Antrhop, Cambridge U. Press, 2, 60, 1-10

2476   Leach,E.R.

        INTRODUCTION: WHAT SHOULD WE MEAN BY CASTE?
        from Aspects of Caste in South India, Ceylon and
        North-West Pakistan
        (Leach, E.R. ed.) Cambridge Papers in Social Anthrop.
        Cambridge U. Press, 2, 60, 1-10

2477   Leach, E. and S.N. Mukherjee (eds.)

        ELITES IN SOUTH ASIA
        Cambridge, Eng.: Cambridge U. Press, 1970
        xiv and 266 pp

2478   Lewis, O. and V. Barnouw

        CASTE AND THE JAJMANI SYSTEM IN A NORTH INDIAN VILLAGE
        The Scientific Monthly 83, 2, 1955, 66-81

2479   Luchinsky, Mildred S.

        THE LIFE OF WOMEN IN A VILLAGE OF NORTH INDIA: A
        STUDY OF ROLE AND STATUS
        American Doctoral Dissertations (61-62)
        Cornel U. (Soc)

2480   Lynch, Owen M.

        THE POLITICS OF UNTOUCHABILITY--A CASE FROM AGRA, INDIA
        in. Structrue and Change in Indian Society
        eds. B.S. Cohn and M.B. Singer
        Chicago; Aldine, 1968, pp 209-243

2481   Lynch, Owen M.

        THE POLITICS OF UNTOUCHABILITY: SOCIAL MOBILITY AND
        SOCIAL CHANGE IN A CITY OF INDIA
        New York: Columbia U. Press 1970

2482   Maddison, Angus

        CLASS STRUCTURE AND ECONOMIC GROWTH: INDIA AND
        PAKISTAN SINCE THE MOGHULS
        New York, Norton 1972, 181 p.

2483   Mahar, P.M.

        CHANGING CASTE IDEOLOGY IN A NORTH INDIAN VILLAGE
        J. Soc. Issues, 1958, 14, 4, 51-65
        SA, X, 2, A1821

2484   Mahar, P.M.

        A RITUAL POLLUTION SCALE FOR RANKING HINDU CASTES
        Sociometry, 1960, 23, 3, Sep, 292-306
        SA, X, IV, A3845

2485   Majumdar, D.N.

        FLUIDITY OF STATUS STRUCTURE IN INDIA
        ed. A/R. Decai
        in. Rural Sociology in India
        Bombay, Popular, 1969, pp 697-700

2486   Majumdar, D.N.

        CASTE AND COMMUNICATION IN AN INDIAN VILLAGE
        Bombay; Asia Publishing House, 1958

2487   Majumdar, D.N.; Pradhan, M.C.; Misra, C.S.

        INTER-CASTE RELATIONS IN GOHANAKALLAN, A VILLAGE NEAR
        LUCKNOW
        East. Anthrop., 1955, 8,   3-4, mar-Aug., 191-224
        SA, Vol. IV #2, 2274

2488   Malhotra, S.P. and L.P. Bharara

        SOCIO-ECONOMIC CHARACTERISTICS OF DIFFERENT CASTES
        Ind Soc. B. 1965, 2, 3, Apr,1 14-123
        SA, XIV, 4, C0367

2489   Maloney, C.

        THE PARATAVAR: 2000 YEARS OF CULTURE DYNAMICS OF A
        TAMIL CASTE
        Man In India, 1969, 49, 3, Jul-Sep, 224-240
        SA, XIX, 47E9853

2490   Mandelbaum, D.

STATUS-SEEKING IN INDIAN VILLAGES
South Asia Series; U. of Calif, 1968

2491   Mann, R.S.

STATUS OF WOMEN IN A DELHI VILLAGE
Social Welfare, 19, 2, 1972, 7-9

2492   Marriott, M.

CASTE RANKING AND COMMUNITY STRUCTURE IN FIVE
REGIONS OF INDIA AND PAKISTAN
Bulletin of the Deccan Coll. Res. Inst.
19, 162, 1958, 31-105

2493   Marriot, M.

CASTE RANKING AND FOOD TRANSACTIONS: A MATRIX ANALYSIS
in. Structure and Change in India Society
eds. B. S. Cohn and M.B. Singer, Chicago, Aldine, 1978
pp 133-173

2494   Martin M.E.R.

WOMEN IN ANCIENT INDIA
Varanasi, 1968

2495   Marulasiddaiah, H.M.

CASTE CONSOLIDATION, SOCIAL MOBILITY AND AMBIVALENCE:
A CASE STUDY OF CASTE HOSTELS IN MYSORE STATE
Ind. J. Soc. Wrk., 1971, 31, 4, Jan, 391-399
SA, XX, 6, F8397

2496   Masani, R.P.

in. Group Prejudices In India
eds. M.B. Nanavati and C.N. Vakil
Bombay, Vora, 1951, pp 188-196

2497   Masani, R.P.

PARSEES IN INDIA
in. Group Prejudices In India
eds. M.B. Nanavati and C.N. Vakil
Bombay, Vora, 1951, pp 188-196

2498   Mathur, K.S.

CASTE AND OCCUPATION IN A MATUA VILLAGE
in. Rural Profiles 1960, 19-83
ed. D.N. Majamdar, Ethorographic and Folk Culture
Society, Lucknow

2499   Mathur, K.S.

CASTE AND RITUAL IN A MALWA VILLAGE
Bombay, Asia Pub. House, 1964

2500   Mathur, P.R.G.

CASTE COUNCIL AMONG THE NAMPUTINI BRAHMANS OF KERALA
East. Anthrop. 1969, 22, 2, May-Aug, 297-224
SA, XX, 3, F5015

2501   Mayer, A.

SOME HIERARCHICAL ASPECTS OF CASTE
South W. J. Anthrop. 1956, 12, 2, Summer, 117-144
SA, VI, 3, 4736

2502   Mayer, A.C.

THE DOMINANT CASTE IN A REGION OF CENTRAL INDIA
Southw. J. Anthrop., 1958, 14, 4, Win., 407-427
SA, IX, 3, A0011

2503   Mencher, Joan. P.

PAST AND PRESENT IN AN EX-UNTOUCHABLE COMMUNITY OF
CHINGLEPUT DISTRICT, MADRAS
paper presented at Wenner-Gren Conference on "The
Untouchable in Contempory India", Tucson, Arizona
April 21-23, 1967

2504   Miller, S.M.

        COMPARATIVE SOCIAL MOBILITY
        Curr. Sociol., 1960, 9, 1, 1-89
        SA, XI, 2 & 3, A4741

2505   Mines, M.

        CASTE DOMINANCE AND SOCIAL MOBILITY IN INDIA:
        A MATRIX THEORY
        Cornell J. Soc. Relat. 1966,1, 2, Oct., 51-63
        SA, XV, 5, C6629

2506   Misra, B.B.

        THE INDIAN MIDDLE CLASSES: THE GROWTH IN MODERN
        TIMES
        New York, Oxford U. Press, 1961 viii 438 pp
        SA, XII, 3, A 9737

2507   Mohan, R.P.

        TRADITIONALISM AND CHANGE IN INDIAN CASTE SYSTEM:
        AN OVERVIEW
        Ind. Soc. B., 1970, 7, 3-4, Apr=Jun, 202-209
        SA, XX, 5, F7260

2508   Mookherjee, H.N. and S. Dasgupta

        CASTE STATUS AND RITUAL OBSERVANCES IN A WEST BENGAL
        VILLAGE
        32nd Annual Meeting of the Southern Sociological
        Society, Session 9
        SA, XVII, 2, Suppl., D6618

2509   Morab, S.G.

        THE BHANDARI CASTE COUNCIL
        Man In India, 1965, 45, 2, Apr-June 152-158
        SA, XVI, 5, D2554

2510   Morab, S.G.

        CASTE COUNCIL OF THE BHANDARI OF DAPOLI
        Man In India, 1966, 46, 2, Apr-Jun, 154-163
        SA, XVI, 6, D3403

2511   Moray, V.E.

        THE PATTERNS OF CASTE AND FAMILY IN WAI TUⅡKA (PH.D.)
        Doct., Bombay U., 1959
        (Prof. S.S. Ghurye)

2512   Morrison, D.E.; K. Kumart and E. Rogers

        STRATIFICATION, MODERNIZATION AND INNOVATION:
        EVIDENCE FROM INDIA AND NOTES TOWARD REFORMULATED
        THEORY
        Paper presented at the 3rd World Congress for Rural
        Sociology
        SA, XX, 5, Sup. 24, F7778

2513   Muir, J.

        THE ORIGIN OF CASTES IN THE VEDIC AGE
        Delhi, 1972

2514   Mukherjee, B.

        INTERCASTE TENSIONS
        Lucknow: U. of Lucknow, 1956, 108 pp

2515   Mukherjee, R.

        THE INDIAN WORKING CLASS
        Bombay, Hind Kitabs, 1951, 407 pp

2516   Mukherjee, B.B.

        SANTAL IN RELATION TO INDIAN CASTES
        Man In India, 1960, 40, 4, 300-306

2517   Mukherjee, Ila

SOCIAL STATUS OF NORTH INDIAN WOMEN,
1526-1707 A.D.

2518   Mukherjee, R.

TAGORE AND CLASS FORCES IN INDIA
Science and Society 14, 2, 97-114, 1950

2519   Mukherjee, R.

CASTE IN BENGAL
Wissenschafthiche
Zeitschinft der humboldt Universitat zu Berlin 1953
II, 1, 13-23

2520   Mukherjee, R.

CASTE AND ECONOMIC STRUCTURE IN WEST BENGAL IN
PRESENT TIMES
in. Sociology, Social Research and Social Problems
in India
ed. R.N. Saksena, Bombay, 1961

2521   Mukherjee, R.

RURAL CLASS STRUCTURE IN WEST BENGAL
In. Rural Sociology in INdia
ed. A.R. Desai
Bombay, Popular, 1969, pp 281-287

2522   Mukherjee, R.; S. Bandyophyay and K. Chattopadhyay

A NOTE ON THE USE OF SOCIETAL FACTORS FOR
STRATIFICATION IN SOCIAL SURVEYS
B. of the Cultural Res Inst.
Calcutta, 11, 2, 41-44, 1963

2523   Mukerji, D.P.

        THE STATUS OF INDIAN WOMEN
        Int. Soc. Sci. J. V. 3, 1951, p. 793-801

2524   Murthy, B.S.

        DEPRESSED AND OPPRESSED
        Delhi, 1968

2525   Nair, B.N.

        THE DYNAMIC BRAHMINS
        Bombay, Popular Book Depot, 1959, 251 pp

2526   Nanavatty, M.C.

        SEMINAR ON CASTEISM AND REMOVAL OF UNTOUCHABILITY:
        A REVIEW
        Ind. J. Adult Educ., 16, 4, Dec., 1955, 41-50

2527   Nandi, P.K.

        A STUDY OF CASTE ORGANIZATIONS IN KANPUR
        Man In India, 1965, 45, 1, Jan-Mar, 84-99
        SA, XIV, 2-3, B9500

2528   Narain, D.

        HINDU SOCIAL TYPES (PH.D.)
        Doct., Bombay U., 1957
        (Prof. G. S. Ghurye)

2529   Narasimhan, (Mrs.) U.

        CASTE AND SOCIAL MOBILITY
        Doct. St., Bagalore U., 1969
        (Dr. C. Rajagopalan)

2530   Navalakh, S.K.

AUTHORITY STRUCTURE AMONG THE BHUMIJ AND BHILS:
STUDY OF HISTORICAL CAUSATION
East. Anthrop. 1959, 12, 1

2531   Newell, W.H.

THE BRAHMIN AND CASTE ISOGAMY IN NORTH INDIA
The Journal of the Royal Anthropological Instit.
of Gr. Britain and Ireland 85, (1,2,), A55, pp 101-110

2532   Newell, W.H.

REPORT ON SCHEDULED CASTES AND SCHEDULED TRIBES
(A STUDY OF GADDI SCHEDULED TRIBES AND AFFILITATED
CASTES)
Census of India, 1961, 20 (Part V b)
Himachal Pradesh, Simla, 1967

2533   Niehoff, A.

CASTE AND INDUSTRIAL ORGANIZATION IN NORTH INDIA
Admin. Sci. Quart. 1959, 3, 4, Mar 494-508
SA, X, 2, A1823

2534   Opler, (M.) and R.P. Singh

"THE DIVISION OF LABOUR IN AN INDIAN VILLAGE"
in. A Reader In General Anthropology
Carleton S. Coon (ed.)
New York, Henry Holt, 1948, 464-456

2535   Orans, M.

MAXIMIZING IN JAJMANILAND: A MODEL OF CASTE
RELATIONS
Amer. Anthrop, 1968, 70,50, Oct, 875-897
SA, XVII, 6, D9505

2536   Orenstein, H.

LEADERSHIP AND CASTE IN A BOMBAY VILLAGE
in. Leadership and Political Institutions in India
eds. R. Park and I. Tinker
Oxford U. Press, 1960, 415-426

2537   Orenstein, H.

EXPLOITATION OF FUNCTION IN THE INTERPRETATION
OF JAJMANI
South W. J. Anthrop, 1962, 18, 4, Win., 302-316
SA, XII, 1, A8287

2538   Orenstein, H.

CASTE AND THE CONCEPT "MORATHA" IN MAHARASHTRA
East. Anthrop. XVI, 1, 1963, 1-10
SA, XIII, 2, B5242

2539   Orenstein, H.

THE STRUCTURE OF HINDU CASTE VALUES: A PRELIMINARY
STUDY OF HEIRARCHY AND RITUAL DEFILEMENT
Ethnol. 1965, 4, 1, Jan, 1-15
SA, XIV, 2-3-, B9502

2540   Patnaik, N.

FROM TRIBE TO CASTE: THE JUANJS OF ORISSA
Eco. Wkly., 1963

2541   Phillips, W.S.K.

SOCIAL DISTANCE (A STUDY OF THE ATTITUDES OF THE
UPPER CASTES TOWARDS THE LOWER CASTES
Eastern Anthrop., 1967, 30, 2, May-Aug, 177-196
SA, XVII, 6, D9507

2542   Philips, B.S.K.

THE CHANGING PATTERNS OF INTER-CASTE RELATIONS IN
VILLAGES OF RAJASTHAN (PH.D.)
Doct., Vikram U., 1968,
(Dr. C.M. Abrahama)

2543   Paranjape, A.C.

A PSYCHO-SOCIAL STUDY OF CASTE (PH.D.)
Doct., Poona U., 1966
(Prof. V.K. Kothurkar)

2544   Pareek, V. & G. Trivedi

RELAIBILITY AND VALIDITY OF A RURAL SOCIO-ECONOMIC
STATUS SCALE
Ind. J. Appl. Psy. 1964, 1, 1, Jan, 34-40
SA, XIV, C0374

2545   Pareek, V, and G. Trivedi

FACTOR ANALYSIS OF SOCIOECONOMIC STATUS OF FARMERS
IN INDIA
Rur. Sociol. 1965, 30, 39, Sep, 312-321
SA, XIV, 4, C0373

2546   Patterson, Maureen L.

CASTE AND POLITICAL LEADERSHIP IN MAHARASHTRA:
A REVIEW AND CURRENT APPRAISAL
The economic Weekly, Sept 25, 1954, p. 1065-1067

2547   Patterson, Maureen L.

INTERCASTE MARRIAGE IN MAHARASHATRA
The Eco. Weekly Annual, Jan., 1958, pp 139-142

2548   Patwardhan, S.P.

STUDY OF THE SCHEDULED CASTES IN AN URBAN SETTING
(PH.D)
Doct., Poona U., 1965
(Dr. (Mrs.)I. Karve)

2549   Patwardhan, S.

SOCIAL MOBILITY AND CONVERSION OF THE MAHARS
Sociol. B. 1968, 17, 2, Sep, 187-202
SA, XVIII, 7, E5996

2550   Paulus, C. R.

A STUDY OF THE SOCIAL STRATIFICATION IN BANGALORE
CITY
Pacific Sociological Review, 1968, 11, 1, Fall 49-56
SA, XVII, 2, D6107

2551   Pillai, G.K.

ORIGIN AND DEVELOPMENT OF CASTE
Bombay; Kitab Mahal, 1959, 271 pp

2552   Pocock, D.F.

"DIFFERENCE" IN EAST AFRICA: A STUDY OF CASTE AND
RELIGION IN INDIAN SOCIETY
Southw. j. Anthrop. 1957, 13, 4, Win., 289-300
SA, VIII, 3, 7908

2553   Pohlman, E.W.

EVIDENCES OF DISPARITY BETWEEN THE HINDU PRACTISE
OF CASTE AND THE IDEAL TYPE
Amer. Sociol. R. 16, 375-9, June, 1951

2554   Prakash, J. and B.G. Reddy

A STUDY OF SOCIAL DISTANCE AND ORDER OF PREFERENCES
AMONG SOME SOCIAL AND CASTE GROUPS
Ind. J. Soc. Wrk., 1967, 28, 2, Jue, 221-228
SA, XVII, 2, D6108

2555   Prasad, K.

SOCIAL POSITION OF WOMEN IN INDIA IN RECENT TIMES
Doct. St., Bhagalpur U., 1969
(Prof. I. Prasad)

2556   Prasad, N.

THE MYTH OF THE CASTE SYSTEM
Patna; Samjna Prakashan, 1957, 319 pp

2557   Prasad, N.

THE MYTH OF THE CASTE SYSTEM
(D.LITT.)
Doct. Patna U., 1959

2558   Raj, Hilda

PERSISTENCE OF CASTE IN SOUTH INDIA--AN ANALYTICAL
STUDY OF THE HINDU AND CHRISTIAN NADARS
The American University (Sociology), 1957-58

2559   Ramamurthy

ROLE OF THE MIDDLE CLASSES IN INDIA
Commerce, 85, 3186, Dec., 1952, 16-17

2560   Raman Unni, K.

CASTE IN MALABAR (PH.D.)
Doct., M.S. u. of Baroda, 1961
(Dr. i.P. Desai)

2561   Ramana, V.K.

CASTE AND SOCIETY IN AN ANDHRA TOWN
(PH.D. SOC.)
University of Illinois
Urbana--Champaign

2562   Ramanamma, (Mrs.) A.

POSITION OF WOMEN IN INDIA (WITH SPECIAL REFERENCE TO
POONA) (PH.D.)
Doct., Poona U., 1969
(Dr. Y. B. Damle)

2563   Ramanujan, A.A.

THE STRUCTURE OF VARIATION: A STUDY IN CASTE
DIALECTS
in.   Structure and Change in Indian Society
eds. M. B. Singer and B. S. Cohn
Chicago: Aldine, 1968, pp 461-475

2564   *Ramu, G. N. and Wiebe, P.D.

OCCUPATIONAL AND EDUCATIONAL MOBILITY IN REALTION TO
CASTE IN URBAN INDIA
Sociology and Social Research, 58, 1, Oct, 1973

2565   Ramu, G. N.

CASTE SERVICE IN RURAL MARRIAGES: A CASE STUDY FROM
MYSORE
East. Anthrop. 1968, 21, 1, Jan-Apr., 1-10
SA, XVIII, 4, E3270

2566   Ramu, G.N.

UNTOUCHABILITY IN RURAL AREAS
Ind. J. Soc. Wrk. 1968, 29, 2, Jul, 147-156
SA, XVIII, 4, E3271

2567   Ramu, G.N.

MIGRATION, ACCULTURATION AND SOCIAL MOBILITY AMONG
THE UNTOUCHABLE GOLD MINERS IN SOUTH INDIA: A CASE
STUDY
Hum. Org., 30, 2, 1971, pp 171-178

2568   Randev, (Miss) M.

OCCUPATION, EDUCATION AND FAMILY STATUS AMONG TWO
LOWER CLASS GROUPS IN AN URBAN CENTER
Doct. St., Agra U., 1969

2569   Rao, K. R.

CASTE, SECULARISM AND DEMOCRACY IN INDIA
Int. J. of Comp. Soc., 1966, 7, 1-2, Mar, 197-208
SA, SVI, 7, D4333

2570   Rao, M.S.A.

SYMPOSIUM ON CASTE AND JOINT FAMILY: IN KERALA
Sociol. B. 1955, 4, 2, Sep. 123-129
SA, V, 1, 2966

2571   Rao, M.S.A.

EDUCAITON, SOCIAL STRATIFICATION AND MOBILITY
M.S. Gore, I.P. Desai and S Chitnis (eds.)
Papers on Sociology of Education in India
Delhi, N.C.E.R.F., 1967, p. 126-146

2572   Rao, N.V.K.

CASTE AND KINSHIP IN COASTAL ANDHRA PRADESH
Doct. St. Andhra U., 1969
(Dept. of Anthrop)

2573   Rastogi, P.N.

DOMINANT CASTE AND FACTION SITUATION AT BRAHMINPURA
J. Pakistan Acad. Rur. Develop. 1963, 4, 1 Jul 18-25
SA, XII, 8, B3534

2574   Ratha, S.N.

CASTE IN A SOUTH ORISSAN VILLAGE
Man In India, 1968, v8, 2, Apr-Jun, 149-158
SA, XVIII, 1-2-, E1208

2575   Report of the Agricultural Labour Enquiry

AGRARIAN STRATIFICATION IN INDIA
in Rural Sociology in INDIA
ed. A. R. Desai
Bombay, Popular Prakashan 1969, pp 271-281

2576   Rocher L. and R. Rocher

LA SACRALITE DU POURVOIR DANS L'IND ANCIENNE D'APRES
LES TEXTES DE DHARMA (SACREDNESS OF POWER IN ANCIENT
INDIA ACCORDING TO THE TEXTS OF DHARMA: LE POUVOIS
ET LE SACRE POWER AND THE SACRED)
A Cent. Et. Relig. 1961, 1, 123-139
SA, XI, 5, A5896

2577   Rosenblum, A.L.

ONE CASTE AND CLASS IN INDIA: A THEORETICAL APPROACH
OF SOCIAL CHANGE
Ind. Sociological B., 1969, 6, 2, Jan, 87-96
SA, XVIII, 4, E3205

2578   Rowe, Wm. L.

SOCIAL AND ECONOMIC MOBILITY IN A LOW-CASTE NORTH
INDIAN COMMUNITY
American Doctoral Dissertations   196-61
Cornell U. (Soc.)

2579   Rowe, Wm. L.

MOBILITY IN THE NINETEEN-CENTURY CASTE SYSTEM
in. Structure and Change in Indian Society
eds. B. S. Cohn and M.B. Singer
Chicago: Aldine, 1968, pp 201-209

2580   Roy Burman, B.K.

A NOTE ON THE SCHEDULED CASTES AND SCHEDULED TRIBES
OF WEST BENGAL
SA, VII, 1, 6955

2581   Rudolph, L. I. and S.H. Rudolph

THE POLITICAL ROLE OF INDIA'S CASTE ASSOCIATIONS
Pacific Aff. 1960, 33, 1, Mar, 5-22
SA, IX, 4, A0517

2582   Sachidanandar

CLASS AND CASTE IN TRIBAL BIHLAR
Man In India, 1955, 35, 3, Jul-Sep
Also in Agra U. J. Res. (LeH.) 1955, 3, Dec 82-87
SA VI, 1, 4013

2583   Sachidanada, A.N.

CASTE AND CONFLICT IN A BIHAR VILLAGE
East. Anthrop, 1967, 20, 2, May-Aug. 143-150
SA, XVII, 6, D9508

2584   *Sachchidanada, A.N,, Sinha, K., Gopal Iyer

CASTE TENSION IN PATNA
Eastern Anthropologist
1969, 22, 3, Sept-Dec 327-348
SA, 21, 73G0863

2585   *Sahay, Arun

SOCIOLOGY OF CASTE AND SECT: ANALYSIS OR DESCRIPTION?
Sociological Analysis (Sheffield), 1970, 1, 1, Oct
51-60
SA, 21, 73G0864

2586   Sahay, K.N.

A STUDY IN THE PROCESS OF TRANSFORMATION FROM A
TRIBE TO CASTE: PARAHIYAS OF TOLKI--A CASE STUDY
Jour. of Soc. Res. 1967, 10, 1, Mar 64-89
SA, XVI, 5, D2558

2587   Sahay, K.N.

CASTE AND OCCUPATION IN A VILLAGE IN BIHAR
Man In India, 1967, 47,3, Jul-Sep, 178-188
SA, XVII, 2, D6170

2588   Saksena, H.P.

THE PROBLEMS AND ADMINISTRATION OF SCHEDULED TRIBES
AREAS IN MADHYA PRADESH (PH.D.)
Doct., Vikram U., 1964
(Porf. R.P. Pandey)

2589   Sanghvi, L.D.

CHANGING PATTERNS OF CASTE IN INDIA
Social. Biology 1970, 17, 4, Dec. 299-301
SA, XX, 6, F8402

2590   Sarwal, R.P.

CHANGES IN CASTE IN RURAL KUMAON
PH.D. Thesis, U. of London, 1966

2591   Sanwal, R.D.

STUDY ON SOCIAL STRATIFICATION IN THE HILL REGIONS
OF UTTAR PRADESH
in. B. Abbi and S. Sebarwal (eds.)
Urgent Research in Social Anthropology
Simla IIAS, 1969

2592   Sanjal, H.

CONTINUITIES OF SOCIAL MOBILITY IN TRADITIONAL AND
MODERN SOCIETY IN INDIA: TWO CASE STUDIES OF CASTE
MOBILITY IN BENGAL
J. of Asian Studies, XXX, 2, 1971, pp 315-339

2593   Sarkar, R.M.

THE BAHUBIR SAMMELAN--A CASE OF SOCIAL MOBILITY
MOVEMENT
East. Anthrop 1966, 19,3, Sep-Dec., 225-230
SA, XV, 6, C7504

2594   Sarma, J.

THE SECULAR STATUS OF CASTES
East. Anthrop, 1958-1959, 12, 2, Dec, Feb 87-106
also in Rural Profiles (ed.) D.N. Majumdar
SA, X, 6, A3887
Ethnic and Folklore Society, Lucknow, 1960

2595   Schwartzberg, J.E.

CASTE REGIONS OF THE NORTH INDIAN PLAIN
in. Structure and Change In Indian Society
eds. M.B. Singer and B.S. Cohn
Chicago; Aldine, 1968   pp 81-115

2596   *Sebring, James M.

THE FORMATION OF NEW CASTES: A PROBABLE CASE FROM
NORTH INDIA
American Anthropologist, 1972, 74,3, Jun, 587-600
SA, 21, 73G0865

2597   Sebring, J.M.

CASTE INDICATORS AND CASTE INDETIFICATION OF STRANGERS
Hum. Org. 1969, 28, 3, Fall, 199-207
SA,XVII, 6, E4899

2598   Sen, B.

CASTE, CLASS AND LEADERSHIP IN A HIMALAYA DISTRICT
presented in a seminar on Tribal Situation in India
Simla, IIAS, 1969

2599   Sengupta, S.

A STUDY OF THE WOMEN OF BENGAL
Calcutta, 1968

2600   Shah, A.M. & R.G. Shroff

THE VAHIVANCA BAROTS OF GUJARAT: A CASTE OF
GENEALOGIST AND MYTHOGRAPHERS
in. Traditional India: Structure and Change
ed. M.B. Singer
Pheladelphia; Amer. Folklore Society, 1959 p40-73

2601   Shah, S.A.

THE CLASS STRUCTURE OF CONTEMPORARY INDIA
Sci. and Soc. 1964, 28, 3, Sum, 275-285
SA, XIV, 1, B8618

2602   Shah, S.M.

RURAL CLASS STRUCTURE IN INDIA WITH SPECIAL
REFERENCE TO GUJARAT (PH.D.)
Doct., Bombay U., 1952
(Prof. M.L. Dantwala)

2603   Shah, S.M.

RURAL CLASS STRUCTURE IN GUJARAT
in. Rural Sociology in India
ed. A.R. Desai
Bombay, Popular Prakashan, 1969, pp 287-291

2604   *Shah, Vimal, P. and Tara Patel and William H. Sewell

SOCIAL CLASS AND EDUCATIONAL ASPIRATIONS IN AN INDIAN
METROPOLIS
Sociological Bulletin, 1971, 20, 2, Sep, 113-133
SA, 21, 73G5752

2605   * Sharma, K.L.

CASTE AND CLASS CONSCIOUSNESS IN RURAL RAJASTHAN: SOME
SOCIAL AND PSYCHOLOGICAL EXPRESSIONS
Sociology and Social Research, 54, 3, Apr, 1970

2606   *Sharma, K.L.

CHANGING CLASS STRATIFICATION IN RURAL RAJASTHAN
Man InIndia, 1970, 50, 3, Jul-Sep 257-268
SA, 21, 73G3380

2607   Sharma, K.L.

THE CHANGING RURAL STRATIFICATION SYSTEM (A

COMPARATIVE STUDY OF SIX VILLAGES IN RAJASTHAN) (PH.D.)
Doct. Rajasthan U., 1969
(Dr. Y. Singh)

2608   Sharma, M.L.

GANDHI AN THE CURSE OF CASTE
Amer. J. Of Economics and Sociology 1971, 30-3,
Jul, 242
SA,XX, 7, F9458

2609   Sharma, R.S.

"POLITICO-LEGAL ASPECT OF THE CASTE SYSTEM"
J. Bihar Res. Soc. 39, 3, Sept 1953, 306-330

2610   Sharma, R.S.

CASTE AND MARRIAGE IN ANCIENT INDIA
(c 600 BC--AD 500)
J. of Bihar Res. Soc. 40, 1, 1954, 39-54

2611   Siaram, G.R.U.

A SOCIOLOGICAL STUDY OF THE BACKWARD CLASSES MOVEMENT
IN SOUTH INDIA, WITH SPECIAL REF TO ANDHRA PRADESH
Doct. St. Delhi, U., 1969
(M.N. Srinivas)

2612   Silverberg, J. (ed.)

       SOCIAL MOBILITY IN THE CASTE SYSTEM IN INDIA: AN
       INTERDISCIPLINARY SYMPOSIUM
       Humanities, 1968

2613   Singh, B.B.

       CHANGING PATTERN OF STRATIFICATION IN THE RURAL
       COMMUNITY
       Doct. St., Gorakhpur U., 1969
       (S.P. Nagéndra)

2614   Singh, J.

       TRADE UNION LEADERS: A STUDY IN CLASS BACKGROUND
       AND SOCIAL MOBILITY
       Ind. J. Soc. Wrk, 1971, 32, 1, Apr, 63-75
       SA, XX, 7, F9459

2615   Singh, M.

       THE DEPRESSED CLASSES, THEIR ECONOMIC AND SOCIAL
       CONDITION
       Bombay; Hind Kitabs, 1947, 312p

2616   Singh, S.

       THE CHANGING SOCIO-ECONOMIC CONDITIONS OF SCHEDULED
       CASTES IN JAUNPUR DISTRICT
       Doct. St. Gorakhpur U., 1969
       (S.P. NAJENDRA)

2617   Singh, V.P.

       EMERGING PATTERNS OF SOCIAL STRATIFICATION
       IN THREE INDIAN COMMUNITIES: 1930-65
       Paper present. at the 66th Annual Meeting of the
       Amer. Sociol. Assoc.
       SA, XLX, &, F3174

2618   Singh, V.P.

THE EVOLUTION OF A RURAL STRATIFICATION SYSTEM IN
INDIA (1930-1965)   (PH.D.)
U. of Wisconsin (69-70)

2619   Sinha, G.S. and R.C. Sinha

EXPLORATION IN CASTE STEROTYPES
Social Forces, 1967, 46, 1, Sep, 42-47
SA, XVI, 2, D0085

2620   Singh, K.K.

INTER-CASTE TENSION IN TWO VILLAGES IN NORTH INDIA
American Doctoral Dissertations (1956-57)
Cornell U. (Soc. Psy.)

2621   Sinha, S.

INTELLIGENTSIA NEEDS INVOLVEMENT IN SOCIETY
Ind. J. Soc. Res., 1968, 9, 2, Aug, 119-122
SA, XX, 1-2, F3876

2622   Sinha, S.

THE ACCULTURATION OF THE BHUMIJ OF MANBHUM:
A STUDY IN SOCIAL CLASS FORMATION AND ETHNIC INTEGRATION

PH.D., U.S.A, 1956

2623   Sivertsen, D.

WHEN CASTE BARRIERS FALL: A STUDY OF SOCIAL AND
ECONOMIC CHANGE IN A SOUTH INDIAN VILLAGE
New York Humanities Press; oslo, Univeriitets for laget,
1963, 141p.

2624   Smythe, H.H. and T. Gershuny

JEWISH CASTES OF COCHIN, INDIA
Sociol. Soc. Res., 1956, 41, 2, Nov-Dec. 108-114
SA, VII, 2, 5756

2625   Solanki, R.M.

UNTOUCHABILITY IN TRANSITION IN RURAL AREAS (PH.D.)
Doct., Vikram U., 1964
(Prof. C.M. Abraham)

2626   Spear, Percival

THE MUGHAL MANSABDARI SYSTEM
in. Elites in South Asia
eds. E. Leach and S.N. Mukherjee
London, Cambridge U. Press, 1970, pp 1-16

2627   Srinivas, M.N.

A CASTE DISPUTE AMONG WASHERMEN OF MYSORE
East. Anthrop, 1954, 7, 3/4, Mar-Aug 148-168
SA, vol, III, #3, 1543

2628   Srinivas M.N.

CASTE IN MODERN INDIA
Sci. & Cult. 1957, 22, 8, Feb, 412-426
SA, VII, 1, 7045

2629   Srinivas, M.N.

THE DOMINANT CASTE IN RAMPURA
Amer. Anthrop. 1959, 61, 1, Feb 1-16
SA, X, 2, A 1828

2630   Srinivas, M.N.

CASTES: CAN THEY EXIST IN INDIA OF TOMORROW?
Econ. Wkly, 1955, 42, 7, 15, Nov, 1230-1232
SA, VI, 3, 4740

2631   Srinivas, M.N.

CASTE IN MODERN INDIA AND OTHER ESSAYS
Bombay; Asia PUb House, 1962

2632   Srinivas, M.N.

MOBILITY IN THE CASTE SYSTEM
in. Structure and Change in Indian Society
eds. B.S. Cohn and M.B. Singer
Chicago: Aldine 1968, pp 189-201

2633   Srinivas, M.N.

CASTE IN MODERN INDIA AND OTHER ESSAYS
Bombay, Asia, 1970

2634   Srinivas, M.N.; Y.B. Damle, S. Shahani and A. Beteille

CASTE: A TREND REPORT AND BIBLIOGRAPHY
Curr. Sociol, 1959, 8, 3, 135-183
SA, XI, 2 &3, A47479

2635   Stevenson, H.N.C.

STATUS EVALUATION IN THE HINDU CASTE SYSTEM
Royal Anthropological Institute of Gt. Brit. and
Ireland, Journal, V. 84, 1954, pp 45-65

2636   Strizower, S.

JEWS AS AN INDIAN CASTE
Jew. J. Sociol., 1959, 1, 1, Apr., 43-57
SA, X, 4, A2854

2637   Subrahmanyam, Y.S.

A NOTE ON CROSS COUSIN MARRIAGE AMONG ANDHRA BRAHMINS
J. of Asian and African Studies, 1967, 2, 3-4,
Jul-Oct, 266-272
SA, XVII, 2, D612

2638   Subudhi, P.C.

FATALISM AND THE CASTE SYSTEM OF INDIA: A CASE
STUDY OF THE EFFECTS OF PLANNED SOCIAL CHANGE
American Doctoral Dissertations ('66-'67)
Wayne State U. (Soc.)

2639   Suryav anshi, G.S.

INTRA-STRUCTURE OF MARATHA CASTE
Doct. S., Poona U., 1969

2640   Thakkar, K.K.

THE PROBLEM OF CASTEEISM AND UNTOUCHABILITY
Ind. J. Soc. Wrk., 1956, 17, 2, Jun 44-48
SA, VIII, 1, 7046

2641   Tharpar, Romila

THE HISTORY OF FEMALE EMANCIPATION IN SOUTHERN ASIA
in. Women in the New Asia
Ed. B. E. Ward.
UNESCO, Paris, 1965, p 473-500

2642   Thorner, Daniel

MALIKS AND MONEY LENDERS--THEIR ROLE
in Rural Sociology in India
Part II Readings in Rural Sociology
ed. A.R. Desai
Bombay: Popular Prakashan, 1969, pp 331-333

2643   Thurston, Edgar and K. Rangachari

CASTES & TRIBES OF SOUTHERN INDIA
Madras, Governement Press, 1965 (first reprinting)

2644   Tripathi, B.D.

ON MINIMIZING SOCIAL DISTANCE EXISTING BETWEEN THE
UPPER CASTES AND HARIJANS
Interdiscipline, 1967, 4, 4, Win, 316-321
SA, XVIII, 6, E4901

2645   Upreti, H.C.

STATUS DETERMINANTS IN CASTE HIERARCHY
Ind. Journal of S.Wrk., 1967, 28, 2 Jul, 195-205
SA, XVII, 2, D6507

2646   Venkatarayappa, K.N.

FEMININE ROLES
Bombay, Popular, 1967

2647   Verba, S.; B. Ahmed and A. Bhatt

CASTE, RACE, AND POLITICS: A COMPARATIVE STUDY OF
INDIA AND THE UNITED STATES
Beverly Hills, Calif: Sage, 1971

2648   Verma, A.K.

THE PROBLEM OF MINORITIES IN INDIA (1900-1950)
(D.PHIL.)
Doct., Allahabad U., 1954   (Capt. A.B. Lal)

2649   Vidyarthi, L.P.

THE CHANGING LIFE OF AN INDIAN PRIESTLY CASTE:
A CASE OF DE-SANSKRITIZATION
Ind. Sociol. B. 1965, 3, 4, Jul, 183-195
SA, XIV, 5, C1307

2650   Vreede-de Stuers, Cora

PARDA: A STUDY OF MUSLIM WOMEN'S LIFE IN NORTHERN INDIA
New York, Humanities, 1968

2651   Vyas, S.N.

      THE CASTE SYSTEM IN THE RAMAYANA AGE
      J. of the Oriental Inst., M.S. u. of Baroda
      3, 2, 1953-54, 111-133

2652   Wadia, P.A.

      PARIS **ESE** THE SHADOWS THICKEN
      By P.A. Wadia, with the collaboration of four ex-
      members of the Central Investigation Bureau,
      Sheroo Mehta, and others, Bombay, 1949, 170 p.

2653   Ward, Barbara E.

      MEN, WOMEN AND CHANGE: AN   ESSAY IN UNDERSTANDING
      SOCIAL ROLES IN SOUTH AND SOUTH-EAST ASIA
      in. Women in the New Asia
      ed., B. E. Ward
      UNESCO, Paris, 1965, pp 25-104

2654   Welty, Paul T.

      THE WOMEN OF INDIA
      in   The Aisans: Their Heritage and Destiny
      ed. p. T. Welty
      Philadelphia, J.P. Lippincott Co. 1962, pp 99-108

2655   Welty, Paul T.

      CASTE IN INDIA
      in.   The Asians: Their Heritage and Destiny
      ed. y.T. Welty
      Philadelphia, J.B. Lippincott Co., 1962, pp 81-93

2656   Yamin, (Miss) S.

      STATUS AND ROLE OF WOMEN IN ISLAM (A SOCIAL STUDY OF
      THE STATUS AND ROLE OF WOMEN IN ISLAMIC SCRIPTURES
      IN COMPARISON WITH THE ACTUAL PRACTISE IN THE INDIAN
      SOCIAL SETTING
      Doct. St., Lucknow U., 1969

1019   social stratification

2657   Y.M.C.A, India

        THE EDUCATED WOMAN IN INDIAN SOCIETY TODAY
        Bombay, 1971

2658   Zinkin, T.

        CASTE TODAY
        London; oxford U. Press, 1965, 19 pp

2659   INDIAN WORKING WOMAN'S NEW HORIZONS
        Monthly Publ. Opin. Surv., 13, (11-12) Aug-Sep.
        1968, 61 pp

1020   sociology of occupations and professions

2660   Adiseshiah, M.S.

        UNEMPLOYMENT OF ENGINEERS IN INDIA
        Impact of Science on Society, 1969, 19, 1,
        Jan-Mar, 63-74
        SA, XVIII, 6, E4906

2661   Adyanthaya, N.K.

        WOMEN'S EMPLOYMENT IN INDIA
        Int. Labour R., 70, 44-66, July, 1954

2662   Ambastha, C.K. and Jaiswal, N.K.

        CASTE AND OCCUPATIONAL MOBILITY IN EAST BIHAR
        VILLAGES
        Ind. J. Soc. Res., 13, 3, Dec., 1972, 202-207

2663   Atal, Y.

        PROFESSIONALISATION OF SOCIOLOGISTS
        Ind. J. Soc. Res., 12, 2, Aug, 1971, 137-142

2664   *Banerjee, B.

AGRICULTURE AS A CASTE PROFESSION
Man in India, 1970, 50, 3, Jul-Sep, 240-247
SA 21 73G3386

2665   Banerjee, G.R.

SOME THOUGHTS ON PROFESSIONAL SELF IN SOCIAL WORK
Ind. J. Soc. Wrk., 1972, 32, 2, Jul, 105-113
SA, XX, 7, F9461

2666   Behura, N.K.

THE POTTER SERVANTS OF JAGANNATH AT PURI
Man In India, 1965, 45, 2, Apr-Jun, 127-133
SA, XVI, 5, D2590

2667   Bhatia, O.P.

THE PERSONIFIED IMAGE OF PERSONNEL OFFICIERS IN INDIA
Ind. J. Soc. Wrk, 1969, 30, 2, Jul, 157-164
SA, XIX, 1-2, E7367

2668   Bhattacharya, S.S.

THE SHOE-SHINERS OF Pat Patna
Sociol. B. 1969, 18, 2, Sep, 167-174
SA, XIX, 3, E8713

2669   Bhowmick, P.K.

OCCUPATIONAL CHANGES IN TWO VILLAGES IN BENGAL
Man in India, 1968, 48, 1, Jan-Mar, 46-54
SA, XVII, 7, E0397

2670   Bhowmick, P.K.

OCCUPATIONAL MIBILITY AND CASTE STRUCTURE IN BENGAL:
STUDY OF RURAL MARKETS
Calcutta; Indian Publications, 1969, viii 98 pp

2671   Chibbar, Y.P.

CHANGES IN THE OCCUPATIONAL STRUCTURE OF MIDDLE
CLASS PEOPLE BETWEEN 1945 AND 1955 (PH.D.)
Doct., Agra U., 1962

2672   Calkins, P.B.

A NOTE ON LAWYERS IN MUSLIM INDIA
Law and Society Rev., 1968-69, 3, 2-3, Nov-Feb,
403-406
SA, XVIII, 4, E3211

2673   Das, A.K.

TRENDS OR OCCUPATIONAL PATTERN THROUGH GENERATIONS
IN RURAL AREAS OF WEST BENGAL
Calcutta, Cultural Res. Inst., Gov't. of
w. Bengal, 1968

2674   Desai, K.G.

A COMPARATIVE STUDY OF MOTIVATION OF BLUE COLLAR
AND WHITE COLLAR WORKERS
Ind. J. Soc. Wrk. 1968, 38, 4, Jan, 379-388
SA, XVII, 5, D8487

2675   *D'Souza, V.S. and Sethi RajMohini

SOCIAL CLASS AND OCCUPATIONAL PRESTIGE IN INDIA:
A CASE STUDY
Sociological Bulletin, 21, 1, Mar, 1972

2676   D'Souza, V.D.

SOCIAL GRADINGS OF OCCUPATIONS IN INDIA
Sociol. R. 1962, 10, 2, Jul, 145-159
SA, XI, 6, A6571

2677   Driver, E.D.

CASTE AND OCCUPATIONAL STRUCTURE IN CENTRAL INDIA
Soc. Forces, 1962, 41, 1, Oct., 26-31
SA, XI, 7, A7403

2678   Dubey, S.M.

WHITE-COLLAR WORKERS IN GORAKKPUR U.P.
Man in INdia, 1965, 45, 3, Jul-Sep, 244-246
SA, XVI, 5, D2571

2679   Emeneau, M.B.

ORAL POETS OF SOUTH INDIA: THE TODAS
in Traditional India: Structure and Change
ed. M.B. Singer
Philadelphia, American Folklore Society, 1959,
pp 106-119

2680   Farooqui, J.

ACADEMIC ELITE AND SOCIAL STRUCTURE: A STUDY IN THE
SOCIOLOGY OF PROFESSIONS (PH.D.)
Doct. St., Agra U., 1969
(Dr. Y. Atal)

2681   Gadbois, G.H. Jr.

INDIAN SUPREME COURT JUDGES: A PORTRAIT
Law and Society Rev., 1968-69, 3, 2-3, Nov-Feb,
317-331
SA, SVIII, 4, E3217

2682   Galanter, M.

INTRODUCTION: THE STUDY OF THE INDIAN LEGAL
PROFESSION
Law and Society Rev., 1968-69, 3, 2-3, Nov-Feb,
201-208
SA, XVIII, 4, E3218

2683   Gandhi, R.S.

THE PROFESSIONAL AND SOCIOL ORIENTATIONS OF THE
POTENTIAL INTELLECTUALS OF INDIA
Sociologus , 22, 1972

2684   Gilbert, Irene A.

THE INDIAN ACADEMIC PROFESSION: THE ORIGINS OF A
TRADITION OF SUBORDINATION
Minerva, X, 3, July, 1972, 384-412

2685   Gist, N.P.

OCCUPATIONAL DIFFERENTIATION IN SOUTH INDIA
Soc. Forces, 1954, 33, 2, Dec., 129-138
SA, Vol III, #2, 1284

2686   Gharpurey, (Miss) P.M.

LIFE AND LABOUR OF THE FULL-TIME DOMESTIC SERVANTS
IN POONA CITY (PH.D.)
Doct., Poona U., 1959
(Prof. N.V. Sovani)

2687   Goldstein, R. L.

WORK--AN EMERGING VALUE FOR THE DAUGHTERS OF THE
INDIAN MIDDLE CLASS
Int. J. of Sociol. of the Family 1971, 1, 2, Sep,
186-196
SA, XX, 4, F6353

2688   *Goswami, B.B. and S.G. Morab

OCCUPATIONAL CHANGES IN A PRIESTLY CASTE OF MYSORE
Man In India, 1970, 50, 1, Jan-Mar, 98-102
SA, 21, 73G3399

2689   Gould, H.A.

LUCKNOW RICKSHAWALLAS: THE SOCIAL ORGANIZATION OF
AN OCCUPATIONAL GATEGORY
Int. J. Comp. Sociol, 1961, 6, 1, Mar, 24-47
SA, XIV, 5, C1317

2690   Government Printing Office

THE BRAIN DRAIN OF SCIENTISTS, ENGINEERS AND
PHYSICIANS FROM THE DEVELOPING COUNTRIES INTO THE
UNITED STATES
Washington, D.C., 1968

2691   Hardwar Rai

THE DISTRICT OFFICER IN BIHAR: A STUDY OF HIS
OFFICE AND FUNCTIONS (PH.D.)
Doct., Patna U., 1965

2692   Institute of Applied Manpower Research, New Delhi

MIGRATION OF INDIAN ENGINEERS, SCIENTISTS AND
PHYSICIANS TO THE UNITED STATES
New Delhi, 1968

2693   Ishwaran, K.

GOLDSMITH IN A MYSORE VILLAGE
J. of Asian and African Studies, 1966, 1, 1, Jan, 50-84
SA, XVI, 2, D0098

2694   Jain, S.C.

INDIAN MANAGER: HIS SOCIAL ORIGIN AND CAREER
Bombay: Somaiya Publications 1971, XIV, 263 PP

2695   Javillonar, G.V. and G. Peters

SOCIOLOGICAL AND SOCIAL PSYCHOLOGICAL ASPECTS OF
INDIAN ENTREPRENEURSHIP
1969 Annual Meeting of the Rural Sociological Society
Session 15   SA, XVII, V, Supp. 4, D8842

2696   Jorapur, P.S.

        INTERGENERATIONAL OCCUPATIONAL MOBILITY
        Ind. J. Soc. Wrk, 1971, 31, 4, Jan, 461-467
        SA, XX, 6, F8434

2697   Kaushal, M.P.

        OCCUPATIONAL EVALUATION AND PRESTIGE: A STUDY OF
        SUBURBAN INHABITANTS
        Ind. J. Soc. Wrk, 1970, 30, 4, Jan, 285-290
        SA, XIX, 6, F1668

2698   Kapoor, S.D.

        SOME DETERMINANTS OF JOB SATISFACTION
        Ind. J. Soc. Res., 1967, 8, 1, Apr, 51-54
        SA, XVII, 5, D8491

2699   Kassem, M.S.

        BUSINESS EXECUTIVES IN EGYPT, INDIA AND THE US
        Int. J. of Comp. Sociol . 1971, 12, 2, Jun, 101-113
        SA, XX, 7, F9476

2700   Khan, A.G.

        ENTREPRENEURIAL BEHAVIOUR AND THE ANALYSIS OF
        GROWTH WITH REFERENCE TO UNDERDEVELOPED SOCIETIES
        Ind. Eco. J. 1955 (Conference #), Dec. 44-50
        SA, VI, 3, 4718

2701   Khurana, B.K.

        A SOCIO-ECONOMIC STUDY OF CLERKS
        Sociol. B. 1957, 6, 1, Mar, 72-79
        1958, 7, 2, Sep, 134-136
        SA, VIII, 1, 7054

2702   Kidder, R.

REPORT OF THE CONFERENCE ON THE COMPARATIVE STUDY
OF THE LEGAL PROFESSION WITH SPECIAL REFERENCE TO
INDIA
Law and Society Rev. 1968-69, 3, 2-3, Nov-Feb,414-444
SA, XVIII, 4, E3228

2703   Kothari, V.N.

LEVEL AND STRUCTURE OF EMPLOYMENT IN A DEVELOPING
ECONOMY (PH.D.)
Doct., Bombay U.- 1962
(Prof. C.N. Lakdawala)

2704   Kramrisch, Stella

TRADITIONS OF THE INDIAN CRAFTSMAN
Traditional India; Structure and Change
J. Of American Folklore 71, 281, 1958, 224-230

2705   Kuthiala, S.K.

INDUSTRIAL WORKERS IN INDIA (PH.D. SOC.)
University of Georgia, 1969-70

2706   Lamb, Helen

THE INDIAN MERCHANT
Traditional India: Structure and Change.
J. of American Folk-lore, 71, 281, 1958, 231-240

2707   Levy, H.L.

LAYERS-- SCHOLARS, LAWYERS--POLITICIANS AND THE
HINDU CODE BILL, 192-1956
Law and Society Rev., 1968-69, 3, 2-3, Nov-Feb. 303-316
SA, XVIII, 4, E3231

2708   *Malik, Y.K. and Marquetté, J.F.

        OCCUPATIONAL PREFERENCES OF COLLEGE STUDENTS IN
        NORTH INDIA
        Journal of Asian and African Studies, 8, 1-2
        Jan-Apr, 1973

2709   Mandal, B.B.

        OCCUPATIONAL MOBILITY
        Ind. J. Soc. Res. 13, 3, Dec. 1972, 194-201

2710   Mathur, K.S.

        CASTE AND OCCUPATION IN A MAYWA VILLAGE
        in Rural Profiles 1960, 69-83
        ed. D. N. Majumdar, Ethrographic and Folk Culture
        Society, Lucknow

2711   McCormack, Wm.

        OCCUPATION AND RESIDENCE IN RELATION TO DHARWAR DISTRICT
        in Structure and Change In Indian Society
        eds. M.B. Singer and B.S. Cohn
        Chicago; Aldine, 1968, pp 475-487

2712   Mehta, (Miss) A.B.

        A SOCIO-ECONOMIC SURVEY OF THE DOMESTIC SERVANT CLASS
        In BOMBAY U., 1960
        (Prof. G.S. Ghurye)

2713   *Merriam, Marshall F.

        REVERSING THE BRAIN DRAIN: A CASE STUDY FROM INDIA
        International Development Review, 1970, 12, 3, 16-22
        SA, 21, 73G2595

2714   Misra, J.P.

        INTELLIGENTSIA OF A METROPOLIS: THE WAY OF LIFE AND
        OUTLOOK OF EDUCATED WORKERS IN THE CITY OF LUCKNOW
        Doct. St. Lucknow U., 1969

2715   Morrison, Charles

KINSHIP IN PROFESSIONAL RELATIONS: A STUDY OF NORTH
INDIAN DISTRICT LAWYERS
Comp. Stud. Soc. Hist. 14, 1,1972, pp 100-125

2716   Mukhopadhyay, T.

A NOTE ON THE DEBASARMAS OF WEST DINAPUR
Man in India, 1964, 44, 3, Jul-Sep., 233-246
SA, XIII, 3-4, B6230

2717   *Nagarajan, K.V.

brain drain; a preliminary survey
Indian Economic Journal, 1970, 17, 3, Jan-Mar,
324-342
SA, 21, 73G2596

2718   Nagpaul, H.

THE NATURE AND CHARACTERISTICS OF PROFESSIONS:
A REVIEW OF LITERATURE
Ind. J. Soc. Res. Aug., 1971, 12, 2, 99-110

2719   Nambudripad, K.N.S.

A SURVEY OF THE OCCUPATIONAL AND EMPLOYMENT STRUCTURE
IN SOME VILLAGES OF MALBAR (PH.D.)
Doct., Bombay U., 1949
(Dr. D.R. Gadgil)

2720   Nanavatty, M.C.

GROWTH AND PROBLEMS OF THE PROFESSION OF SOCIAL
WORK IN INDIA
Ind. Jour. Soc. Wrk., 1967, 28, 1, Apr. 55-62
SA, XVI, 6, D3434

2721   *Nemann, Alfred, K.; J.C. Bhatia; S. Andrews and
        A.K.S. Murphy

        ROLE OF THE INDIGENOUS MEDICINE PRACTIONER IN TWO
        AREAS OF INDIA--REPORT OF A STUDY
        Social Science and Medicine, 1971, 5, ?, Apr. 137-149
        SA, 21, 73G1809

2722   *Nijhawan, N.K.

        OCCUPATIONAL MOBILITY AND POLITICAL DEVELOPMENT:
        SOME PRELIMINARY FINDINGS
        Economic and Political Weekly, 1971, 6, 3-5
        Jan, 317-324
        SA, 21, 73G0886

2723   North, Robert C.

        THE INDIAN COUNCIL OF MINISTERS: A STUDY OF ORIGINS
        in. Leadership and Political Institutions in India
        eds. R.L. Park and I. Tinker
        New York; Greenwood Press, 1969, pp 103-115

2724   Panda, B.M.

        THE DIMENSIONS OF TRAINING: A STUDY OF THE IMPACT
        OF TRAINING OF C.D. PERSONNEL
        Doct. St. Ranchi U., 1969

2725   Pandit, D.P.

        EARNING ONE'S LIVELIHOOD IN MAHUVA
        Bombay, Asia

2726   Patil, B.K.

        A STUDY OF ROLE AND RELATIONSHIP OF PANCHAYATI
        SAMITI PERSONNEL IN DELHI TERRITORY (PH.D.)
        Doct., Indian Agricultureal Research Institute,
        New Delhi
        (Dr. S.K. Sharma)

2727   Pasthasarathi, Ashok

INDIA'S BRAIN DRAIN AND INTERNATIONAL NORMS
Int'l. Educ. and Cult. Exchange
Washington, U.S.
Advisory Commission on Intl. Educ. and Cult. Affairs
1967

2728   Patterson, M.L.P.

CHANGING PATTERNS OF OCCUPATION AMONG CHITPAVAN
BRAHMANS
The Indian Eco. and So. His. Rev., 1970, 7,3,376-96

2729   Prakash, O.

THE PROBLEM OF ENTREPRENEURSHIP IN SOCIALIST ECONOMY
Ind. J. Econ. 1958, 39, 1, Jul, 59-70
SA, VIII, 2, 7497

2730   Pushpa, (Mrs.) D.V.

SOCIAL MIBILITY AND OCCUPATIONAL CAREER PATTERNS
Doct. St. Bangalore U., 1969
(Dr. C. Rajagopalan)

2731   Randev, (Miss) M.

OCCUPATION, EDUCATION AND FAMILY STATUS AMONG TWO
LOWER CLASS GROUPS IN AN URBAN CENTER
Doct., St., Agra U., 1969

2732   *Ratha, S.N.

RELIGION AND OCCUPATIONAL DIFFERENTION
Man in India, 1970, 50,3, Jul-Sep, 248-256
SA, 21, 73G3417

2733   Ratha, S.N.

CASTE AND OCCUPATION IN TWO PERIURBAN ASSAMESE
VILLAGES
East. Anthrop. 1968, 21, 2, May-Aug, 155-166
SA, XVIII, 6, E4933

2734   Raj Rami,A.

WOMEN LEGISLATIVE ELITE IN RAJASTHAN, 1962-1965
Polit. Sci. R. 6 (1), Jan-Mar 1967, 39-57

2735   Reddy, G.P.

CASTE AND CHANGE OF OCCUPATION IN A VILLAGE IN
ANDHRA PRADESH
East. Anthrop. 1969, 21, 2, May-Aug, 167-182
SA, XVIII, 6, E4934

2736   Rocher, L.

"LAWYERS" IN CLASSICAL HINDU LAW
Law and Society Review, 1968-69, 3, 2-3, Nov-Feb, 383-40
SA, XVIII, 4, E3240

2737   Sane, G.D.

THE INDIAN WORKING CLASS--SIZE AND SHAPE
New Delhi, All India Trade Union Congress, 1966
vi-72 pp

2738   Saraswati, B.N.

THE PEASANT POTTERS OF NORTH INDIA
Doct. Ranchi U., 1968
(Dr. Sachidananda)

2739   Sarveswara   Rao, G.V.

JOB CONTENT AND CONTEXT FACTORS IN JOB SATISFACTION
OF FEMALE CLERICAL EMPLOYEES
Ind. J. Soc. WRk., 1971, 32, 1, Apr, 45-51
SA, XX 7, F9488

2740   Schmitthener, S.

A SKETCH OF THE DEVELOPMENT OF THE LEGAL PROFESSION
IN INDIA
Law and Society Rev., 1968-69, 3, 2-3, Nov-Feb,
337-382
SA, XVIII, 4, E3241

2741   Sharda, R.

LEGISLATORS AS ELITES--A SOCIOL. STUDY OF LEGISLATORS
OF UTTAR PRADESH
Doct. St., Lucknow U., 1969

2742   Sharma, B. R.

TECHNOLOGY AND WORK EXPERIENCE: A STUDY OF THE
INDIAN AUTOMOBILE WORKERS
Amer. Doctoral Dissertations ('67-'68)
Michigan State U. (Soc.).

2743   Sharma, B.R.

OCCUPATIONAL ASPIRATIONS
Ind. J. of Sociol. 1970, 1, 2, Sep, 153-172
SA, XIX, 5, F0746

2744   Sharma, K.L.

CASTE AND OCCUPATIONAL MOBILITY: A STUDY OF A
VILLAGE IN RAJASTHAN
Jour of Soc. Res., 1967, 10, 1, Mar, 26-32
SA, XVI, 5, D2581

2745   Sharma, K.L.

OCCUPATIONAL MOBILITY AND CLASS STRUCTURE
Man in India, 1968, 48, 2, Apr-June, 106-114
SA, XVIII, 1-2, E1174

2746   Sharma, K.N.

OCCUPATIONAL MOBILITY OF CASTES IN A NORTH INDIAN
VILLAGE
Southw. J. Anthrop. 1961, 17, 2, Sum 146-164
SA, X, 3, A2330

2747   Sharma, R.C.

SOCIAL MOBILITY AMONG LEATHER INDUSTRY WORKERS OF
KANPUR   (PH.D.)
Doct., Lucknow U., 1965
(Dr. S. Chandra)

2748   Sharma, S.C.

AN ASSESSMENT OF THE RELATIVE PRESTIGE VALUE OF
REPRESENTATIVE OCCUPATIONS IN INDIA WITH SPECIAL
REFERENCE TO UTTAR PRADESH (PH.D.)
Doct. Agra U., 1969
(Prof. M. A. Hakim)

2749   Shils, E.

THE ACADEMIC PROFESSION IN INDIA
Minerva, 1969, 7, 3, Spr. 345-372
SA, XIX, 4, E9898
also in Elites in South Asia
eds. E. Leach and S.N. Mirkherjee,
London; Cambridge U. Press, 1970, pp 172-201

2750   Shrimali, P.D.

PATTERN OF EMPLOYMENT AND EARNINGS AMONG UNIVERSITY
GRADUATES IN LUCKNOW, INDIA
Industrial and Labor Relations Review, 1969, 22, 2,
Jan, 249-256
SA, XVIII, 6, E4937

2751   Shukla, R.S.

OCCUPATIONAL DIFFERENTIATION AND SOCIAL MOBILITY
IN A DEVELOPING CITY: A STUDY OF GORAKHPUR,
Doct. St. Gorakhpur U., 1969
(S.P. Nagendra)

2752   Singh, H.

SOCIAL GRADING OF CASTES AND OCCUPATION IN AN
INDIAN VILLAGE
Ind. J. Soc. Work, 1967, 27, 4, Jan, 381-392
SA, XVI, 6, D3409

2753   Singh, I. J.

SOCIAL REHABILITATION AND CAREER ORIENTATION
Jour. of Soc. Res., 1967, 10, 1, Mar, 18-21
SA, XVI, 5, D2583

2754   Singh, T.N.

A STUDY OF RELATIONSHIP BETWEEN NEEDS AND JOB
BACKGROUND FACTORS AMONG FACTORY WORKERS (PH.D.)
Doct. Bihar U., 1970
(Dr. A. Hazari)

2755   Sovani, N.V. and Pradhan, K.

OCCUPATIONAL MOBILITY IN POONA CITY BETWEEN THREE
GENERATIONS
Ind. Econ. Rev., 1955, 2, 4, Aug, 23-36
SA, VI, 1, 3997

2756   Sri Chandra

A SOCIO-PSYCHOLOGICAL STUDY OF SENIOR SCIENTISTS OF
UTTAR PRADESH (PH.D.)
Doct., Agra U., 1967

2757   Tewari, A.S.

THE INDIAN DOCTOR--A STUDY OF THE STATUS, ROLE AND
VALUES OF PRACTITIONERS OF ALLOPATHY IN THE CITY
OF LUCKNOW
Doct. St. Lucknow U., 1969

2758   Tomar, (Miss) N.

THE INDIAN NURSE
Doct. St., Lucknow U., 1969

2759   Trivedi, (Miss) Kumud Prabha

THE SOCIAL AND ECONOMIC CONDITIONS OF RURAL SECONDARY
TEACHERS IN U.P.
Doct., Lucknow U., 1962,
(Dr. R.K. Mukerjee)

2760   Trivedi, V.K.

THE INDIAN LAWYER
(ref. to Lucknow)
Doct. St. Lucknwow U, 1969

2761   Useem, J.

WORK PATTERNS OF AMERICANS IN INDIA
A. Amer. Acad. Polit.Soc. Sci. 1966, 268, Nov. 146-156
SA, XV, 3, C5131

2762   Veda, B.R.

SOCIOLOGICAL STUDY OF SOME CAREER WOMEN IN BANGALORE
Doct. St. Delhi U., 1969
(A. Beteille)

2763   Verma, (Miss) M.R.

FEMALE NURSES
Doct. St. Gorakhpur U., 1969
(D.P. Saxena)

1020   sociology of occupations and professions

2764   Wilcox, W.A.

        NEW ELITES OF INDIA AND PAKISTAN
        Trans-Action,1967, 4, 9, Sep, 43-50
        SA, XVI, 2, D0119

2765

        THE ROLE OF THE ADMINISTRATOR: PAST, PRESENT
        AND FURTURE
        Poona: Gokhale Institue of Economics & Politics, 1952
               44 pp

1116   rural sociology (village, agricult.)

2766   Abraham, C.M.

RURAL SETTING IN KERALA
Ind. Sociol. 1961, 3, 4, Mar, 10-12
SA, XIII, 1, B4413

2767   Abraham, M.F.

SOCIAL CONTOURS OF A SOUTH INDIAN VILLAGE
Interdiscipline, 1966, 3, 3, Jul, 135-149
SA, XVI, 4, D1763

2768   Ahmad, E.

RURAL SETTLEMENT TYPES IN UTTAR PRADESH
Assoc. of Amer. Georgraphers, Annals
V. 42, 1952, 332-46

2769   Ahmad, I.

SOCIAL STRUCTURE OF A MULTI-CASTE VILLAGE IN U.P.
Doct. St. Delhi U., 1969
(M.N.Srinivas)
(M.S.A. Rao)

2770   Adams, J.

THE ANALYSIS OF RUAL INDIAN ECONOMY: ECONOMICS
AND ANTHROPOLOGY
Man in India, 52, 1, 1972, 1-21

2771   Adams, J. and U.J. Woltemade

VILLAGE ECONOMY IN TRADITIONAL INDIA: A SIMPLIFIED
MODEL
Hum. Org. 1970, 21, 1, Spr. 49-56
SA, XIX, 1-2-, E7421

2772   Ahmad, E.

        THE RURAL POPULATION OF BIHAR
        Geogr. Rev. 51, 2, Apr, 1961, 253-276

2773   Ahmed, L.N. and H. Ahmed

        A COMPARATIVE INQUIRY INTO RURAL-URBAN, DICHOTOMY
        VS RURAL-URBAN CONTINUUM IN THE UNITED STATES AND
        INDIA: ITS ADMINISTRATIVE CHALLENGES
        Ind. J. of Soc. Res., 1966, 7, 2, Aug, 101-109
        SA, XVII, 2, D6149

2774   Ahmed, S.

        CLASS AND POWER IN THE PANJABI VILLAGE
        American Doctoral Dissertation ('67-68)
        Michigan State U. (Soc.)

2775   Aiyappan, A.

        REPORT ON THE SOCIO-ECONOMIC CONDITIONS OF THE
        ABORGINAL TRIBES OF THE PROVINCE OF MADRAS
        By Secretary,Aboriginal Tribes Welfare Enquiry
        Committee
        Madras, Govt. press, 1948, 185 p.

2776   Aiyer, A.K.Y.N.

        COOPERATION AND INDIAN AGRICULTURE
        Bangalore; Bangalore Printing and Publishing, 1951,
        210 pp.

2777   Akhauri, N.P.S.

        STUDIES INTO THE SOCIAL BUSINESS AND RURAL DEVELOPMENT
        WORK IN BIHAR (PH.D.)
        Doct. Patna U., 1963
        (Dr. N. Prasad)

2778   Alavi, H.

PEASANTS AND REVOLUTION

IN Rural Sociology in India
ed. A.R. Desai
Bombay, Popular Prakashan, 1969, p. 410-425

2779   Ali, M.Z.

FARMER's RESPONSE TO CROP PLANNING (PH.D.)
Doct., Indian, Agricultural Research Institute, 1963
(Prof. A.R. Kahn)

2780   Anderson, S. and D. Barnerji

REPORT ON A STUDY OF MIGRATION IN FOUR TALUKS OF
BANGALORE DISTRICT
Pop. R., 1962, 6, 1, Jan, 69-77
SA, XII, 8, B3581

2781   Antrhopoligical Survey of India

PEASANT LIFE IN INDIA: A STUDY IN INDIAN UNITY AND
DIVERSITY
Calcutta, Gov't. of India, 1962

2782   Atal, Y.

RURAL STUDIES: INDIAN VILLAGE
East. Anthrop. 1961, 14, 3, 249-257
also in Rural Sociology In India
ed. A.R. Desai, Bombay Popular, 1969, pp 716-805
SA, XII, 8, B3583

2783   Badgaiyan, S.D.

RURAL ELITE IN THE CONTEXT OF PLANNED CHANGE IN
VILLAGE INDIA
Kurukshetra, 1969, 17, 5, Feb, 6-7 and 15
SA, XIX, 4, E9910

1116   rural sociology (village, agricult.)

2784   Bailey, F. G.

        TWO VILLAGES IN ORISSA
        in. M. Gluckman (ed.)
        Closed Systems and OPen Minds
        Manchester, 1964, p. 52-82

2785   Bailey, F. G.

        AN ORIYA HILL VILLAGE (Part I & II)
        in. M.N. Srinivas (ed.)
        India's Villages
        Bombay, 1955, 122- 130, 131-146

2786   Ballard, R.E.H.

        LAND, CASTE AND KIN--A STUDY OF A VILLAGE IN HIMACHAL
        PRADESH (PH.D.)
        Doct., Delhi U., 1970
        ((Late) Dr. R. D. Sanwal)

2787   Bandyopadhyay, S. and K. Chattopadhyay
        A NOTE ON DEVELOPMENT IN SOME BENGAL VILLAGES
        Man in India, 52, 4, 1972 346-354

2788   Barnabas, A.P.

        SOCIAL CHANGE IN A NORTH INDIAN VILLAGE
        New Delhi, Indian Inst. of Public Admin, 1969,
        xviii-179 pp

2789   Basu, S.K.

        LEADERSHIP IN INNOVATION
        Society and Cult. 1970, 1, Special Number, 51-56
        SA, XX, 7,F9497

2790   Basu, Tara Krishna

        THE BENGAL PEASANT FROM TIME TO TIME
        London; Asia Publishing House, 1962

2791   Bathgate, J.

CHRISTIAN PARTICIPATION IN RURAL DEVELOPMENT IN INDIA
Int. R. Missions, 1963, 52, 289-299
SA, XV, 5, C6667

2792   Bawa , B.S.

PANCHAYAT PLANTATIONS IN POROMBOKE LAND
Kurukshetra, 1966, 15, 2, Nov, 25-27
SA, XVIII, 6, E4949

2793   *Beals, A.R.

VILLAGE LIFE IN SOUTH INDIA
Chicago, Aldine, 1974

2794   *Beals, A.R.

GOPALPUR: ASOUTH INDIAN VILLAGE
New York, Holt, 1962

2795   Beidelman, T.O.

A COMPARATIVE ANALYSIS OF THE JAJMANI SYSTEM
New York; 1959, 86 pp

2796   *Beteille, A.

AGRARIAN RELATIONS IN TANJORE DISTRICT, SOUTH INDIA
Sociological Bulletin, 21, 2,Sept, 1972

2797   Bhandari, J.S.

LAND AND SOCIAL STRUCTURE: AN ECONOMIC STUDY OF
MISHING VILLAGE
East Anthrop. 1968, 21, 1, Jan-Apr, 21-36
SA,XVIII, 4, E3255

2798   Bhardwaj, K.R. and R.Bharadwaj

AN ACTIVITY ANALYSIS APPROACH TO MEASURE PRODUCTIVE
EFFICIENCY IN AGRICULTURE: A CASE STUDY OF
AHMEDNAGAR AND NASIK DISTRICTS
Indian Economic J. 1965, 12, 3, Jan-Mar, 211-231
SA, XVII, 1, D5215.

2799   Bhatnagar, K.K.

A STUDY OF THE PRESENT POSITION AND FUTURE PROSPECTS
OF CO-OPERATIVE FARMING IN UTTAR PRADESH (PH.D.)
Doct. Agra U., 1960

2800   Bhatt, G.S.

RURAL RESEARCH IN INDIA
East. Anthrop. 1963, 16, 1, Jan-Apr., 20-27
SA, XIII, 2, B5283

2801   Bhoite, (Mrs.) A.

THE PURPOSE STUDY OF EMPLOYED WOMEN IN RURAL AREAS,
WITH SPECIAL REFERENCE TO MAHARASHTRA
Doct. St. Poona U., 1969
(Y.B. Damle)

2802   Bhowmik, A.; M.K. Chowdhuri and T.N. Ghosh

ATTITUDE OF TIYARS IN LIMITING FAMILY SIZE AND THEIR
SOCIO-CULTURAL CHARACTERISTICS
Society and Culture, 1970, 1, Special number, 43-50
SA, XX, 7, F9501

2803   Bhowmilk, P.K.

KASBA NARAYANGARH: A MUSLIM VILLAGE
Man In INdia, 1965, 45, 3, Jul-Sep, 201-222
SA, XVI, 5, D2593

2804   Bhowmick, P.K.

        MIRPUR, A CHRISTIAN VILLAGE
        Man in India, 1966, 46, 3, Jul-Sep, 158-206
        SA, XVI, 6, D3446

2805   Blyn, G.

        AGRICULTURAL TRENDS IN INDIA, 1891-1947
        Philadelphia, Pa.: U. of Penn Press, 1966, 370 pp
        SA, XV, 3 C5137

2 06   Board of Economic Inquiry, Punjab (Pakistan)

        PUNJAB VILLAGE SURVEYS, v.13
        Lahore: Civil and Military Gazette Publishing, 1947

2807   Bopegamage, A.

        VILLAGE WITHIN A METROPOLITAN AURA
        Sociol. B. 1956, 5, 2, Sep, 102-110
        SA, VI, #1, 2971

2808   *Bopegamage, A and Kulahalli, R.N.

        CASTE AND OCCUPATION IN RURAL INDIA: A REGIONAL
        STUDY IN URBANIZATION AND SOCIAL CHANGE
        RURAL SOCIOLOGY, 37, 3, Sept, 1972

2809   Bose, A.B.

        SOCIETY, ECONOMY AND CHANGE IN A DESERT VILLAGE
        A. Arid Zone 1962, 1, 1, Dec, 1-15
        SA, XI, 7, A7320

2810   Bose, A.B. & L.P. Bharara
        SOME SOCIOLOGICAL CONSIDERATIONS IN FARM FORESTRY
        A. Arid Zone, 1965, 4, 1, 24-31
        SA, XIV, 6, C2337

2811   Bose, A.B. and N.S. Jodha

THE JAJMANI SYSTEM IN A DESERT VILLAGE
Man in India, 1965, 45, 2, Apr-Jun, 105-126
SA, XVI, 5, D2595

2812   Bose, A.B. and N.S. Jodha

ECOLOGICAL STUDY OF A VILLAGE ABADI IN WESTERN
RAJASTHAN
East. Anthrop. 1968, 21, 1, Jan-Apr, 27-44
SA, XVIII, 4, E3256

2813   Bose, A.B. and S.P. Malhotra

STUDIES IN AGRICULTURAL SOCIOLOGY AT THE CENTRAL
ARID ZONE: SOME CHARACTERISTICS OF LOWER, MIDDLE,
AND UPPER CLASS FARMERS
Ind. J. Soc. Res., 1964, 5, 2, Aug, 201-212
SA, XIV, 4, C0432

2814   Bose, A.B., S.P. Malhotra, and L.P. Bharara

ANIMAL HUSBANDRY IN THE ARID ZONE, (II) A SOCIO-
ECONOMIC STUDY OF HOUSEHOLDS RAISING SHEEP IN CENTRAL
AND LOWER LUNI BASIN.
A. Arid Zone, 1964, 3, 1 & 2, Sep-Dec, 44-53
SA, XIV, 6, C2336

2815   Bose, A.B.; S.P. Malhorta; L.P. Bharara and C.S.K.
Johony

SOCIO-ECONOMIC ASPECTS OF ANIMAL HUSBANDRY
A. of the Arid Zone, 1966, 5, 1, Mar, 72-80
SA, XVI, 3, D0914

2816   Bose, A.B.; S.P. Malhotra; C.S.K. Johny and
M.L. Sen

AGRICULTURE IN CENTRAL AND LOWER LUNI BASIN IN
WESTERN RAJASTHAN
A. Arid Zone 1965, 4, 2, Sep, 195-206
SA, XV, 5, C6668

2817   Bose, A.B. and Mohan L.S.

        SPATIAL ASPECTS OF RURAL LIVING
        Man in India, 1963, 43, 1, Jan-Mar, 9-26
        SA, XII, 6, B1892

2818   Bose, A.B. and P.C. Saxena

        OPINION LEADERS IN A VILLAGE IN WESTERN
        RAJASTHAN
        Man in INdia, 1966, 46, 2, Apr-Jun, 121-130
        SA, XVI, 6, D3447

2819   Bose, A.B. and M.L.A. Sen

        SOME CHARACTERISTICS OF THE WIDOWS IN RURAL SOCIETY
        Man in India, 1966, 46, 3, Jul-Sep, 226-232
        SA, XVI, 6, D3448

2820   Bose, N.k. and S. Sinha, (ed.)

        PEASANT LIFE IN INDIA
        Memoir of Anthrop. Survey of India
        Calcutta, 1961

2821   Bose, S.P.

        SOCIAL AND CULTURAL FACTORS IN FARM MANAGEMENT
        EFFICIENCY
        Calcutta; West Bengal Dept. of Agriculture, 1964
        (unpublished paper)

2822   Bose, S.

        LAND USE SURVEY IN A JUANG VILLAGE
        Man in INdia, 1961, 41, 3, 172-183

2823   Bose, S.P.

        SOCIAL INTERACTION IN AN INDIAN VILLAGE
        Sociologia Ruralis, 1967, 7, 2, 155-173
        SA, XVI, 2, D0125

2824   Bose, S.P.

        EADPUR: A WEST BENGAL VILLAGE
        Calcutta, Directorate of Agriculture
        Gov't of West Bengal, 1963, 68 pp.

2825   *Breman, J.

        PATRONAGE AND EXPLOITATION: CHANGING AGRARIAN
        RELATIONS IN SOUTH GUJARAT
        Berkeley, University of California Press, 1974

2826   Burman, B.K.R.

        CONFLICT AND TENSION IN RURAL INDIA
        J. of Soc. Res., 1966, 9, 2, Sep, 46-51
        SA, XVI, 4, D1764

2827   Catanach, I. J.

        RURAL CREDIT IN WESTERN INDIA 1875-1930: RURAL CREDIT
        AND THE CO-OPERATIVE MOVEMENT IN THE BOMBAY PRESIDENCY
        Berkeley, U. of Calif. Press,1970

2828   Centerwall, W.R.; G. Savannathan; L.R. Mohan;
        V. Booshanam and M. Zachariah

        INBREEDING PATTERNS IN RURAL SOUTH INDIA
        Social Biology,1969, 16, 2, Jun, 81-91
        SA, XVIII, 7, E6047

2829   Chakravarti, A.K.

        A SOCIOLOGICAL STUDY OF THE CHANGING PATTERN OF POWER
        AND AUTHORITY IN A VILLAGE COMMUNITY IN A HINDI-
        SPEAKING AREA   (PH.D.)
        Doct., Delhi U., 1970
        (Prof. M.N. Srinivas)

2830   Chanda, S.

        ECONOMIC STRUCTURE OF A NICOBARESE VILLAGE:
        IN CHOWRA ISLAND
        Ind. J. Soc. Wrk, 1971, 32, 1, Apr, 25-33
        SA, XX, 7, F9502

2831   Chandra Kumar

        KOTHI: A VILLAGE SURVEY
        Census of India, 1961; Himachal Pradesh
        Simla, Gov't of India Press, 1963

2832   Chatterjee, M.

        THE TOWN/VILLAGE DICHOTOMY IN INDIA
        Man in India, 1968, 48, 3, Jul-Sep, 192-300
        SA, XVIII, 3, E2121

2833   Chattopadyay, S.N.

        RANJANA: A VILLAGE IN WEST BENGAL
        Calcutta, Bookland, 1964

2834   Chattapadhyay, S.N. and V. Pareek

        VALUE ORIENTATION OF FARMERS OF A NORTH INDIAN
        VILLAGE
        J. of the Indian Academy of Applied Psy. 1965,
        2,2, May, 55-60
        SA, XVI, 6, D3449

2835   Chattopadhyaya, D.

        VILLAGE COMMUNITIES
        in. Rural Sociology in India, ed. A.R. Desai,
        Bombay, Popular Prakashan, 1969, pp 155-167

1116   rural sociology (village, agricult.)

2836   *Chattopadhyay, Kumarananda

        RITES AND RITUALS: MEDIA OF RURAL INTEGRATION
        Eastern Anthropologist, 1970, 23, 3, sep-Dec,
        217-233
        SA, 21, 73G4386

2837   Chattopadhyaya, K.P.

        KHOSI LAND OWNERSHIP AND SCALE
        East, Anthrop, 1949, 2, 115-124

2838   Chaubey, B.

        THE CHANGING PATTERN OF POWER STRUCTURE AND VILLAGE
        LIABILITIES, WITH SPECIAL REFERENCE TO CHOLAPUR BLOCK
        OF VARANASI DISTRICT
        Doct. St., Gorakhpur U., 1969
        (S.P. Nagendra)

2839   Caudhuri, B.R.

        SOME FISHING COMMUNITIES OF WEST BENGAL
        Man in India, 1969, 49, 3, Jul-Sep, 241-246
        SA, XIX, 4, F0281

2840   Chauhan, B.R.

        AN INDIAN VILLAGE: SOME QUESTIONS
        Man in India, 1960, 40, 2, Apr-Jun, 116-127
        SA, XII, 5, B1167

2841   Chauhan, Brij Raj

        A STUDY OF A SOCIAL INSTITUTION IN INDIAN VILLAGES
        Rural Sociol. 1961, 26, 2, Jun, 191-197
        SA, IX, 3, 9876

- 419 -

2842   Chauhan, B.R.

A STUDY OF A LITTLE COMMUNITY IN RAJASTHAN
(PH.D.)
Doct. Lucknow U., 1964
(Dr. S.K. Sen)

2843   Chauhan, B.R.

A RAJASTHAN VILLAGE
New. Delhi, Viv Publ. House, 1967, viii & 330 p

2844   Chauhan, J.S.

DEVELOPMENT OF AGRICULTURE IN INDIA
Kurukshetra, 1964, 12, 9, Jun, 9-10
SA, XIV, 1, B8647

2845   Chauhan, S.S.

AGRICULTURAL PRODUCTION PROGRAMMES AND SOCIAL
CHANGE IN UTTAR PRADESH   (PH.D.)
Doct. St., Agra U, 1969
(A.S. Mathur)

2846   *Chekki, Dan A.

COMMUNITY RESEARCH IN INDIA: SOME TRENDS
Paper presented at the 8th World Congress of
Sociology, Toronto, August 19-24, 1974

2847   Chitambar, J.B.Y.

A STUDY OF CONTACTS AND CHANGES AMONG DIFFERENT GROUPS
OF RURAL PEOPLE SERVED BY DIFFERENT TYPES OF EXTENSION
WORKERS IN A PROGRAM OF RURAL DEVELOPMENT IN NORTH
INDIA
American Doctoral Dissertations (1957-'58)
Cornell University (Sociology)

2848   Cohn, B.S.

        COMMENTS ON PAPERS ON LAND TENURE
        Ind. Eco. Soc. Hist. R., 1963, 1, 2, Oct-Dec,177-183
        SA, XV, 3, C5139

2849   Cohn, B.S.

        MADHOPUR REVISITED (U.P.)
        in. Rural Sociology in India
        ed. A.R. Desai, Bombay, Popular Prakashan,1969
        pp 372-378

2850   *Crane, R.I. (ed.)

        TRANSITION IN SOUTH ASIA
        Durham, Duke University

2851   Dak, T.M.

        VILLAGE COMMUNITIES AND PLANNED SOCIAL CHANGE
        Kurukshetra, 1966, 14, 8, May, 20-22
        SA, XVII, 3, D7100

2852   *Danda, A.K. and D.G. Danda

        CHANGING AUTHORITY STRUCTURE IN A BENGAL VILLAGE
        Man in India, 1970, 50, 1, Jan-Mar, 63-77
        SA, 21, 73G3431

2853   Dandekar, V.M. and G.J. Khudanpur

        EFFECT OF TENANCY ACT IN MAHATRASHTRA
        in. Rural Sociology In India
        ed. A.R. Desai
        Bombay, Popular Prakashan, 1969 pp 433-439

2854   Dasgupta   Sugata

RURAL EDUCATION THROUGH RURAL RECONSTRUCTION
Indi J. Soc. Wrk. 1954, 15, 2, Sep, 100-109
SA, vol III, #3, 1521

2855   Dasgupta, S.

CASTE STRUCTURE AND AGRICULTURAL DEVELOPMENT:
A CASE STUDY OF TWO VILLAGES IN UTTAR PRADESH,
INDIA
1968 Annual Meeting of the Rural Sociological
Society, Session 34
SA, XVI, 7, D4679

2856   Dasgupta, S.

CASTE DOMINANCE AND AGRICULTURAL DEVELOPMENT IN
VILLAGE INDIA
Paper presented at the 1972 Annual Meeting of the
Rural Sociol. Society
SA, XX, 5, Sup 25, F7841

2857   Dass, L.

A STUDY OF THE ROLE OF AGRICULTURAL EXTENSION OFFICES
IN PROGRAMME PLANNING AT BLOCK LEVEL IN PUNJAB (PH.D.)
Doct., Panjab Agricultural U., 1968
(Dr. T.S. Sohal)

2858   Datt, J.

RURAL DEVELOPMENT INDUSTRY
Kurukshetra, 1964, 12, 12, Sep, 18-19
SA, SIV, 2-3, B9552

2859   Deb, P.C.

SOCIAL LIFE OF AN INDIAN RURAL COMMUNITY (WADDHAMNA)
VILLAGE IN VIDARBHA (MAHARASHTRA)   (PH.D.)
Doct. Nagpur U., 1965
(Dr. T.S. Wilkinson)

1116   rural sociology (village, agricult.)

2860   Desai, A.R.

        INTRODUCTION TO RURAL SOCIOLOGY IN INDIA (READINGS IN
        AGRICULTURAL ECONOMICS SERIES, #4)
        Bombay: Indian Society of Agricultural Economics
        1952, 257 p.

2861   Desai, A.R.

        RURAL SOCIOLOGY: ITS NEEDS IN INDIA
        Sociol. B. 1956, 5, 1, Mar, 9-28
        SA, V, #4, 3680

2862   Desai, A.R. (ed.)

        RURAL SOCIOLOGY IN INDIA
        (4th rev. ed.)
        Bombay, Popular Prakashan, 1969

2863   Desai, A.R.

        IMPACT OF GOVERNMENTAL MEASURES ON RURAL SOCIETY
        in Rural Sociology in India
        ed. A.R. Desai
        Bombay, Popular, 1969, pp 768-777

2864   Desai, A.R.

        SOCIOLOGICAL ANALYSIS OF INDIA
        in. Rural Sociology in India
        ed. A.R. Desai
        Bombay; Popular Prakashan, 1969, p. 105-117

2865   Desai, M.B.

        IMPACT OF LAND REFORMS IN GUJARAT
        in. Rural Soc. in India
        ed. A.R. Desai
        Bombay, Popular Prakashan, 1969, pp 439-441

1116   rural sociology (village, agricult.)

2866   Desai, V.R.M.

        SOCIO-ECONOMIC SURVEY OF BHILAI (2 VOLS)
        Bombay, 1968

2867   Dhaliwal, G.S.

        AGRICULTURAL CO-OPERATION IN PUNJAB   (PH.D.)
        Doct., Banaras Hindu U., 1960

2868   Dhami, S.S.

        RURAL DEVELOPMENT IN INDIA
        Int. Labour Rev., 69, 452-73, May '54

2869   Dinesh, C.

        SOCIAL VALUES AND RURAL PLANNING
        Kurukshetra, 1966, 14, 10, Jul, 22-23
        SA, XVII, 4, D7869

2870   Doshi, H.C.

        INDUSTRIALIZATION AND NEIGHBORHOOD COMMUNITIES IN
        A WESTERN INDIAN CITY-CHALLENGE AND RESPONSE
        Sociol. B. 1968, 17, 1, Mar, 19-34
        SA, XVII, 5, D8320

2871   Doshi, J.K.

        SOCIAL STRUCTURE AND CULTURAL CHANGE IN A BHIL VILLAGE
        Doct. St., Saugar U., 1969

2872   D'Souza, S.V.

        THE SHAFFI MUSLIMS OFTHE WEST COAST OF INDIA--A SOCIAL
        SURVEY (PH.D.)
        Doct., Karnatak U., 1955

1116   rural sociology (village, agricult.)

2873   Dube, S.C.

A DECCAN VILLAGE
in India's Villages
(M.N. Srinivas, ed.)
Development Department, West Bengal, 1955, 180-191

2874   Dube, S.C.

TRADITION, SOCIAL STRUCTURE AND AGRICULTURAL
DEVELOPMENT
Kurukshetra, 1964, 13, 1, Oct, 14-19
SA, XIV, 4, C0435

2875   Dube, S.C.

INDIAN VILLAGE
New York, Harper and Row, 1967

2876   Dube, S.C.

THE STUDY OF INDIAN VILLAGE COMMUNITIES
in. Rural Sociology in India
ed. A.R. Desai, Bombay, Popular, 1969, p. 790-756

2877   Dugal, B.S.

THE VILLAGE CHIEF IN THE INDIAN CONSTRUCTION INDUSTRY
Hum. Org. 1959-60, 18, 4, Win, 174-176
SA, X, 3, A2278

2878   Dumont, L. & D. Pocock

VILLAGE STUDIES
Contrib. Ind. Sociol. 1957, 1, Apr, 23-41
SA, XIV, 2-3, B9554

2879   Dumont, L.

THE VILLAGE COMMUNITY FROM MUNRO TO MAINE
Contrib. Ind. Soc. 1966, 9, Dec, 67-89
SA, XVI, 5, D2965

2880   Eames, E.

SOME ASPECTS OF URBAN MIGRATION FROM A VILLAGE IN
NORTH CENTRAL INDIA
East. Anthrop. 1954, 8, 1, Sep-Nov., 13-26
SA, vol IV, #2, 2240

2881   Eames, E.

POPULATION AND ECONOMIC STRUCTURE OF AN INDIAN RURAL
COMMUNITY
East. Anthrop, 1955, 8, 3-4, Mar-Aug, 173-81
SA, Vol. IV, #2, 2239

2882   Eitzen, S.O.

A VILLAGE OF INDIA: AN APPLICATION OF THE THEORY OF
INCREASING SCALE OF SOCIETAL ORGANIZATION
Kansas J. of Sociol. 1968, 4,3, Sum, 91-114
SA, XX, 3, F5082

2883   Ensminger, D.

PROBLEMS OF RURAL DEVELOPMENT,TASKS BEFORE RURAL
INSTITUTES
Kurukshetra, 1967, 15, 5, Feb 2-5
SA, XVIII, 6, E4959

2884   Ensminger, D.

RURAL INDIA IN TRANSITION
New Delhi; All India Panchayat Parishad, 1972 115 pp

1116   rural sociology (village, agricult.)

2885   Fliegel, F.C.

        COMMUNITY ORGANIZATION AND ACCEPTANCE OF CHANGE IN
        RURAL INDIA

2886   *Freed, Stanley A. and Ruth S. Freed.

        CATTLE IN A NORTH INDIAN VILLAGE
        Ethnology, 1972, 11, 4, Oct. 399-408
        SA, 21, 73G4391

2887   Freed, S.A. and R.S. Freed.

        URBANIZATION AND FAMILY TYPES IN A NORTH INDIAN VILLAGE
        Southwestern J. of Anthrop. 1969, 25, 4, Win, 342-359
        SA, XIX, 3, E8763

2888   Fukutake, T. Ouchi, T. and Chie Nakane

        THE SOCIO-ECONOMIC STRUCTURE OF THE INDIAN VILLAGE
        The Institute of Asian Economic Affairs; Tokyo, 1964

2889   *Gaikwad, V.R.

        TRENDS OF CHANGE IN EIGHT INDIAN VILLAGES
        Behavioral Sciences and Community Development
        1970, 4, 2, Sep. 92-127
        SA, 21, 73G0912

2890   Gaikwad, V.R.

        EXECUTION OF AGRICULTURAL DEVELOPMENT PROGRAMMES AND
        ADMINISTRATIVE DEFICIENCIES
        Beh. Sci. & C.D. 1969, 3, 2, Sep, 101-113
        SA, XIX, 5, F0769

2891   Gandhi, I.

        FARM PERSPECTIVES
        Kurukshetra, 1969, 17, 7, Apr, 2-3
        SA, XIX, 4, E9915

- 427 -

2892   Gangrade, K.C.D.

A COMPARATIVE STUDY OF LEADERSHIP AND SOCIAL STRUCTURE
IN A DELHI VILLAGE
Doct. St. Delhi U., 1969
(M.S.A. Rao)

2893   Gangrade, K.D.

BUILDING A VILLAGE COMMUNITY THROUGH ECONOMIC AID
Ind. Jour. Soc. Wrk. 1966, 26, 4, Jan, 416-428
SA, XVI, 5, D2602

2894   Ganguli, J.

ECONOMONIC PROBLEMS OF THE JHUMIAS OF TRIPURA -
A SOCIO-ECONOMIC STUDY OF THE SYSTEM OF SHIFTING
CULTIVATION IN TRANSITION (PH.D.)
Doct., Calcutta U., 1962

2895   Geldens, M.

TWO RURAL FAMILIES IN UTTAR PRADESH
New Delhi, Directorate of Extension Ministry of Food
and Agriculture, 1960

2896   The General Report of the Committee of Direction of
the All India Rural Credit Survey

INAPPROPRIATE VILLAGE INSTITUTIONS
in. Rural Sociology in India
ed. A.R. Desai
Bombay Popular Prakashan, 1969, p 527-533

2897   Ghosal, S.

THE PERMANENT SETTLEMENT AND ITS EFFECTS ON BENGAL
London: G. Allen and Unwin 1949 52 p.

2898   Ghose, K.K.

AGRICULTURAL LABOURERS IN INDIA: A STUDY IN THE
HISTORY OF THEIR GROWTH AND ECONOMIC CONDITION
Calcutta: Indian Publications 1969, xiv-296 p

2899   Ghosh, A.

A STATISTICAL STUDY OF AGRICULTURAL ECONOMICS OF
BENGAL, WITH SPECIAL REFERENCE TO AGRARIAN CLASS
RELATIONS AND OCCUPATIONAL STRUCTURE   (D. PHIL.)
Doct., Calcutta U., 1952

2900   Ghosh, A.

CYCLICAL TRENDS IN INDIAN AGRICULTURE, 1861-1913
Ind. Eco. and Social Hist. Rev. 1967, 4, 2, Jun
177-202
SA, XVIII, 6, E4965

2901   Ghosh, B. R.

NARAINA: AN URBANIZED VILLAGE
J. of Soc. Res., 1969, 12, 1, Mar, 100-106
SA, XIX, 6, F1693

2902   Gohain, B.C.

AGRICULTURAL ORGANIZATION AMONG THE ABOR
B. of the Dept. of Anthrop., 1954, 3, 2,

2903   Gomathinayagam, V.

RURAL SOCIAL CHANGE: ITS CORRELATION TO CASTE RANKING,
ECONOMIC POSITION, AND LITERACY LEVEL
Ind. J. Soc. Res. 13, 3, Dec, 1972, 224-230

2904   Gore, F. St. J.

HILL LIFE IN INDIA
Delhi, 1972

2905   *Goswami, M.C. & C.L.B. Singh

TENURE AND ALLOCATION OF PHOOMPHAM AMONG THE THANGA
FISHERMAN OF MANIPUR
Man in India, 1970, 50, 4, Oct.-Dec., 379-389
SA, 21, 73G3437

2906   Garyl, K.E.

SOCIAL DRAMA IN A TAJORE VILLAGE
in Rural Sociology in India
ed. A.R. Desai
Bombay Popular Prakashan, 1969, p. 345-354

2907   Gough, K.

COMMUNIST RURAL COUNCILLORS IN KERALA
J. of Asian and African Studies, 1968, 3, 3-4,
Jul-Oct 181-202
SA, XVIII, 6, E4966

2908   Gould, H.A.

A JAJMANI SYSTEM OF NORTH INDIA: ITS STRUCTURE,
MAGNITUDE, AND MEANING
Ethnol. 1964, 3, 1, Jan, 12-41
SA, XII, 5, B1139

2909   Gould, H.A.

MODERN MEDICINE AND FOLK COGNITION IN RURAL INDIA
Hum. Org. 1965, 24, 3, Fal, 201-208
SA , SIV, 4, C0440

2910   *GOWDRA, G.K.

RITUAL CIRCLES IN A MYSORE VILLAGE
Sociological Bulletin, 1971, 20,1, Mar. 24-38
SA, 21, 73G5781

2911   Goyal, S.K.

SOME ASPECTS OF CO-OPERATIVE FARMING IN INDIA WITH
SPECIAL REFERENCE TO PUNJAB   (PHD)
Doct., Delhi U., 1962,
(dr. P.K. Mukherjee)

2912   Grant, Swadesh S.

SPATIAL BEHAVIOUR AND CASTE MEMBERSHIP IN SOME
NORTHERN INDIAN VILLAGES
(PH.D. - Soc. Psy.)
The City University of New York, 1971

2913   Grover, B.R.

NATURE OF DEHAT - 2 - TAALUGA (ZAMINDARI VILLAGES) AND
THE EVOLUTION OF THE TAALUQDARI SYSTEM DURING THE MUGHAL
AGE
Ind. Econ. Soc. Hist. R. 1965, 2, 2, April, 166-177
SA, XV, 3, C5144

2914   Guha, A.C.

COOPERATION AS A REMEDY
in. Rural Sociology in India
ed. A.R. Desai, Bombay, Popular Prakashan, 1969
p. 484-489

2915   Gupta, J.P.

SOCIO-ECONOMIC CONDITIONS OF AGRICULTURAL LABOURERS IN
SHRINAGAR PANCHAYAT SAMITI (AJMER)   (PH.D.)
Doct., Agra U., 1969
(Dr. B. Sahai)

2916   Gupta, L.C.

CHANGING PATTERN OF RURAL LEADERSHIP: A CASE STUDY
Sociol B. 1966, 15, 2, Sep, 27-36
SA, XV, 6, C7536

1116 rural sociology (village, agricult.)

2917   Gupta, R.

DECISION-MAKERS IN A GRAMDAN VILLAGE
Lucknow: Planning Research and Action Instiute
Publ. #342, 1971, pp 87

2918   *Gupta, R.K. & S.K. Saxena

INTEGRATED ECOLOGICAL SURVEYS FOR AGRICULTURAL
DEVELOPMENT IN THE ARID ZONES OF INDIA . I. CHOHTAN
COMMUNITY DEVELOPMENT BLOCK IN BARMER DISTRICT OF
RAJASTHAN
Annals of the Arid Zone, 1971, 10, 2-3, Jun-Sept,
85-98
SA, 21, 73G3438

2919   Gupta, S.C.

SOME ASPECTS OF INDIAN AGRICULTURE
in. Rural Sociology In India
ed. A.R. Desai, Bombay, Popular Prakashan, 1969,
p. 291-328

2920   Harper, E.B.

TWO SYSTESM OF ECONOMIC EXCHANGE IN VILLAGE INDIA
Amer. Anthrop, 1959, 61, 5, Oct., 760-778
SA, X, 3, A2284

2921   Haswell, M.R.

ECONOMICS OF DEVELOPMENT IN VILLAGE INDIA
New York, Humanities Press, Inc., 1967, xi & 105 pp
SA, XVII, 1, D5226

2922   Hiebert, P. G.

KONDURU: STRUCTURE AND INTEGRATION IN A SOUTH INDIAN
VILLAGE
Minneapolis U. of Minnesota Press, 1971

2923   Hopper, W.D.

         SEASONAL LABOUR CYCLES IN AN EASTERN UTTAR PRADESH
         VILLAGE
         East. Anthrop, 1955, 8, 3-4, Mar-Aug, 141-150
         SA, Vol. 14, #2, 2242

2924   Indian Council of Agricultural Research

         DEVELOPING VILLAGE INDIA: STUDIES IN VILLAGE PROBLEMS
         (ed. V.N. Chatterjee; planned by M.S. Randhawa;
         Rev. ed.)
         Bombay, Orient Longmans, 1951, 240 p.

2925   Ishwaran, K.

         TRADITION AND ECONOMY IN VILLAGE INDIA
         London; Routledge and Kegan Paul, 1966

2926   Ishwaran, K.

         SHIVAPUR: A SOUTH INDIAN VILLAGE
         London: Routledge and Kegan Paul 1968

2927   Ishwaran, K. (ed.)

         CHANGE AND CONTINUTIY IN INDIA'S VILLAGES
         New York, Columbia U.P. 1970, 296 pp.

2928   Iyengar, S.K.

         AGRICULTURAL TENANCY PROBLEM IN INDIA
         Commerce, 85, Dec. 1952 100-3

2929   Iyer, (Miss) I.A.

         AGENCIES OF RURAL DEVELOPMENT WITH SPECIAL REFERENCES
         TO VILLAGE PANCHAYAT, VILLAGE COOPERATIVES AND VILLAGE
         SCHOOLS IN THE KALYAN AND NAVASARI DEVELOPMENT BLOCKS
         (PH.D.)
         Doct., Bombay U., 1964
         (Prof. M.L. Dantwala)

2930   Jain, J.P.

RURAL INDUSTRIES PROJECTS IN UTTAR PRADESH
Kurukshetra, 1967, 15, 5, Feb, 13-14
SA, XVIII, 6, E4971

2931   Jain, N.P.

RUAL RECONSTRUCTION IN INDIA AND CHINA
Verry, 1971

2932   Jain, S.K.

INDIAN EXPERIMENT IN RURAL DEVELOPMENT: THE ETAWAH
PILOT PROJECT
Int. Labour Rev. V. 68, 1953, p. 393-406

2933   Jain, S.P.

RELIGION, CASTE, CLASS AND EDUCATION IN A NORTH INDIAN
COMMUNITY
Sociology and Social Res., 1969, 53, 4, Jul 482-489
SA, XVIII, 3, E2546

2934   Jaiswal, N.K. and C.K. Ambastha

RESEARCH NOTES: CASTE AND OCCUPATIONAL PREFERENCE IN
EAST BIHAR VILLAGES
Ind. J. Soc. Wrk., 1970, 31, 2, Jul, 191-296
SA, XX, 6, F8480

2935   Jaiswal, N.K. and V.C. Jha

CASTE--A DISCRIMINATOR OF SOCIO-ECONOMIC CHARACTERISTICS
OF RURAL PEOPLE
Ind. J. Soc. Wrk., 1970, 30, 4, Jan, 361-367
SA, XIX, 6, F1697

2936   Jaiswal, N.K.; A.S. Khan & J. Shanker

ATTITUDE TOWARDS AGRICULTURAL DEVELOPMENT AMONG
TRIBAL AND NON-TRIBAL PEOPLE
Man in India, 1969, 49, 3, Jul-Sep, 267-280
SA, XIX, 4, E9916

2937   Jay, E.J.

A TRIBAL VILLAGE OF MIDDLE INDIA
Calcutta, Anthrop. Surv. of India, 1970

2938   Jena, K.

MODERN IMPACT OF URBANISM ON RURAL LIFE
Ind. J. Soc. W. 1960, 21, 2, Sep. 177-179
SA, XI, 6, A6511

2939   John, P.V.

CHANGING PATTERN OF LEADERSHIP IN A VILLAGE IN
MADHYA PRADESH
Sociol. B. 1963, 12, 1, Mar. 32-38
SA, XI, 7, A7324

2940   Joshi, P.C.

LAND REFORMS IN INDIA
in Rural Sociology in India
ed. A.R. Desai
Bombay, Popular Prakashan, 1969, p. 444-476

2941   Kale, D.N.

AGRIS, A SOCIO-ECONOMIC SURVEY
Bombay; Asia Publishing House, 1952 411 p.

1116   rural sociology (village, agricult.)

    2942   Kamat, G.S.

            PANCHAYATS AND VILLAGE PRODUCTION PLAN
            Kurukshetra, 1966, 15, 1, Oct, 32-34
            SA, XVIII, **3**, E2129

    2943   Kantowsky, D.

            DIE SUKUNFT DICKTBEVOELKER TER AGRANGEBJETE
            ASIENS (THE FUTURE OF DENSELY POPULATED AGRARIAN
            AREAS IN ASIA)
            Sociologia Ruralis, 1970, 11, 3, 253-257 (Ger.)
            SA, XIX, 6, F1699

    2944   Kapil, H.K.

            PATTERNS OF SOCIAL TENSIONS IN RURAL INDIA (PH.D.)
            Doct. Agra. U., 1964

    2945   Kapuria, R.S.

            AGRICULTURAL DEVELOPMENTS IN INDIA
            Kurukshetra, 1966, 14, 8, May, 9-12
            SA, XVII, 3, D7108

    2946   Karve, I.

            THE INDIAN VILLAGE
            in. Rural Sociology in India
            ed. A. R. Desai
            Bombay Popular, Prakashan, 1969 p 186-193

2948   Katju,.N.

        LACK OF LEADERSHIP IN INDIAN VILLAGES
        Kurukshetra, 1964, 12, 9, Jun, 8-10
        SA, XIV, 1, B8659

2949   Kedar Singh

        THE IMPACT OF DEMOCRATISZTION ON THE VILLAGE
        COMMUNITY IN WESTERN U.P.   (PH.D.)
        Doct., Gorakhpur U., 1967
        (Dr. S.P. Negendra)

2950   *Kessinger, T. G.

        VILAYATPUR 1848-1968:   SOCIAL AND ECONOMIC CHANGE IN A
        NORTH INDIAN VILLAGE
        Berkeley, University of California Press, 1974

2951   *Khan, I.H.

        LOCAL GOVERNMENT IN RURAL INDIA, AUSTRALIAN JOURNAL OF
        POLITICS AND HISTORY, 1969, 15, 3, Dec. 11-25
        SA, 21, 73G3441

2952   Khan, I. H.

        GOVERNMENT IN RURAL INDIA
        Bombay, Asia, 1971

2953   Khan, M.A.

        IMPACT OF RURAL SOCIAL LEGISLATION ON A MYSORE VILLAGE
        Social Welfare, 19, 6, 1972, 9-10

2954   Khan, Z.

CASTE AND MUSLIM PEASANTRIES OF NORTH INDIA AND EAST
AND WEST PAKISTAN
Cdn. Review of Sociology and Anthropology, 1968, 5, 3,
Aug, 192-203
Also, Man in India, 1968, 48, 2, Apr-Jun, 133-148
SA, XVII, 7, E0407

2955   Khare, R.S.

AN INDIAN VILLAGE'S REACTION TO CHINESE AGGRESSION
Asian Surv. 1964, 4, 11, Nov. 1152-1160
SA, XIV, 4, C0449

2956   Khare, R.S.

A STUDY OF SOCIAL RESISTANCE TO SANITATION PROGRAMMES
IN RURAL INDIA
East. Anthrop 1964, 17, 2, May-Aug, 86-94
SA, XIV, 4, C0450

2957   Khare, R.S.

GROUP DYNAMICS IN A NORTH INDIAN VILLAGE
Hum. Org. 1962, 21, 3, Fall, 201-213
SA, XII, 3, A9774

2958   Khusro, A.M.

ECONOMIC AND SOCIAL EFFECTS OF JAGIRDARI ABOLITION AND
LAND REFORMS IN HYDERABAD
Hyderabad; Dept. of publication and university Press,
Osmania University, 1948, 240 p.

2959   Khusro, A.M.

ON LAND REFORMS
in Rural Sociology in India
ed A. R. Desai
Bombay Popular Prakashan, 1969, p 44-444

2960   Kochar, V.K.

MICRO-DEMOGRAPHY OF DOMESTIC-GROUPS IN A SANTAL
VILLAGE
Ind. J. Soc. Wrk. 1965, 26, 3, Oct, 271-279

2961   Kolhathar, V.V. and S.B. Mahabal

IMPACT OF LAND REFORMS IN BARODA DISTRICT
in Rural Sociology in India
ed A.R. Desai
Bombay, Popular Prakashan, 1969
p. 427-430

2962   Kondapalli, K.R.

THE DYNAMICS OF POWER AND CONFLICT IN VILLAGE INDIA
(PH.D. SOC.)
Michigan State U., 1970-1971

2963   Kosambi, D.D.

VICTORY OF VILLAGE
in Rural Sociology in India
ed. A.R. Desai
Bombay, Popular Prakashan, 1969, p 184-186

2964   Kosambi, D.D.

INDIAN FEUDALISM

in. Rural Sociology in India
Part II: Readings in Rural Sociology
ed. A.R. Desai
Bombay, Popular Prakashan, 1969, p. 148-150

2965   Krishnaswami, S.Y.

RURAL PROBLEMS IN MADRAS: (MONOGRAPH)
Madras: Superintendent, Gov't. Press 1947, 545 p.

2966   Kudryavtsev, M.K.

ON SOME CHARACTERISTIC FEATURES OF VILLAGE COMMUNITIES
IN NORTHERN INDIA
Sovetskayaetrografiya 1970, 45, 4, Jul-Aug, 62-73
(Russian)
SA, XIX, 7 F2529

2967   Kulkarni, A.R.

VILLAGE LIFE IN THE DEECAN IN THE 17th CENTURY
Ind. Eco. and Social Hist. Review, 1967, 4, 1, Mar
38-52
SA, XVII, 5, D8524

2968   Kulkarni, M.G.

SOCIAL AND ECOLOGICAL STUDY OF GOKAK TALUKA (PH.D.)
Doct., Bombay U., 1958
(Prof. G. S. Ghurye)

2969   Kulshrestha, G.C.

A SOCIOLOGICAL CASE STUDY OF A BHIL VILLAGE
(RATHANKARA) IN RAJASTHAN, WITH SPECIAL REFERENCE
TO THE IMPACT OF INDUSTRIALIZATIOŇ AND URBANIZATION
(PH.D.)
Doct., Agra U., 1970
(Dr. R.N. Saksena)

2970   Kumar, R.

RURAL LIFE IN WESTERN INDIA ON THE EVE OF THE
BRITISH CONQUEST
Ind. Econ. Soc. Hist. R. 1965, 2, 3, Jul, 201-220
SA, XV, 3, C5150

1116   rural sociology (village, agricult.)

2971   Kumaraswamy, M.R.

        THE ECONOMICS OF CATTLE VIS-A-VIS TRADITIONAL BELIEFS
        IN INDIA
        Interdiscipline, 1967, 4, 3, Aut, 219-223
        SA, XVIII, 3, E2131

2972   Kumari, S.

        WOMEN IN RURAL ECONOMY
        Kurukshetra, 1964, 12, 9, Jun, 15-16
        SA, XIV, 1, B662

2973   Kupuswamy, B.

        SOME RURAL PROBLEMS OF MYSORE: A STUDY OF OPINIONS
        Bombay, 1971

2974   Kushner, G.

        A SYNTHETIC MODEL OF THE HINDU JAJMANI SYSTEM
        Man in India, 1967, 47, 1, Jan-Mar, 35-60
        SA, XVI, 7, D4380

2975   Lakshminarayana, H.D.

        PRESTIGE STANDARDS AND VALUE ORIENTATION OF INDIAN
        FARMERS
        Man in India, 52, 4, 1972, 340-346

2976   Lakshmana, R.Y.V.

        COMMUNICATION AND DEVELOPMENT: A STUDY OF TWO
        INDIAN VILLAGES
        Minneapolis, The U of Min Press, 1966, 145 p.

2977   Lal, R.

        THE CASE FOR AGRICULTURAL EXTENSION
        AICC Econ. R. 1959, 11, 15, 1, Dec, 19-23
        SA, XII, 5, B1146

2978   Lambert, R. D.

THE IMPACT OF URBAN SOCIETY UPON VILLAGE LIFE

in. India's Urban Future
ed. R. Turner
Berkeley; U. of Calif Press, 1962, p. 117-141

2979   Langworthy, R.L.

SOME ECONOMIC AND SOCIOLOGICAL ISSUES OF COOPERATIVE
FARMING IN INDIA
J. of Asian & African Studies, 1966, 1, 2, Apr, 100-117
SA, XVI, 3, D0939

2980   Langworthy, R.L.

PERSPECTIVES ON THE ATOMISTIC-TYPE SOCIETY, THE
PEASANT WORLD VIEW: ITALY AND INDIA
Human Organ, 1968, 27, 3, Fall, 212-219
SA, XVII, 4, D7880

2981   Lavania, M.M.

A VILLAGE IN TRANSITION (PH.D.)
Doct., Rajasthan U., 1967
(Dr. R.N. Saxena)

2982   *Leaf, M.J.

INFORMATION AND BEHAVIOR IN A SIKH VILLAGE
New York, University of California Press, 1972

2983   Lewis, O.

PEASANT CULTURE IN INDIA AND MEXICO:
in Village India
ed. M. Marriott
U. of Chicago Press, 1956, p 145-171

1116   rural sociology (village, agricult.)

2984   Lewis, O.

ASPECTS OF LAND TENURE AND ECONOMICS IN A NORTH
INDIAN VILLAGE
Econ. Dev. & Cult. Change, 1956, 4, 3, Apr, 279-302
SA, VI, #2, 4327

2985   Lewis, O.

VILLAGE LIFE IN NORTHERN INDIA
Urbana; U. of Illinois Press, 1958, xiii & 384 pp
SA, vol II, 3, 6093

2986   Loomis, C.P.

CHANGE IN RURAL INDIA AS RELATED TO SOCIAL POWER
AND SEX
Behavioural Sciences and Com. Dev., 1967
SA, XVIII, 6, E4977

2987   Loomis, C.P.

SOCIAL ORGANIZATION AND RURAL SOCIAL CHANGE
Sociologia Ruralis, 1968, 8, 3-4, 289-304
SA, XVII, 7, E0409

2988   Luschinsky, M.S.

TRADITIONAL VILLAGE CULTURE IN MODERN INDIA
J. Hum Relat. 1961, 9, 3, 300-311
SA, XII, 3, A9777

2989   Lyngdoh, S.

THE BHOI LAND-TENURE SYSTEM
Man in India, 1966, 46, 2, Apr-Jun, 95-102
SA, XVI, 6, D3466

1116   rural sociology (village, agricult.)

2990   Mahadevan, Indira

        PATTERNS OF STRUCTURAL DIFFERENTIATION AMONG SIX
        INDIAN VILLAGES
        (PH.D. SOCIOL.)
        University of Pittsburgh, 1971

2991   Mahapatra, L.K.

        A HILL BHUIYA VILLAGE: A EMPIRICAL SOCIO-ECONOMIC
        STUDY
        D. Phil. Dissert. 1959, Hamburg, Germany

2992   Majamdar, D.N.

        RURAL PROFILES
        Lucknow, 1955

2993   Majumdar, D.N.

        A LITTLE COMMUNITY
        Sociologist, 1956-57,1 1, 1-9
        SA, VIII, 1, 7007

2994   Majumdar, D.N.

        SHRAMDAN: AN ASPECT OF ACTION ANTHROPOLOGY
        Indian Sociol. 1959 1, 1, Mar, 1-12
        SA, XII, 5, B1148

2995   Majumdar, A.K. and K.K. Das

        STUDY ON THE VALUES OF RURAL PEOPLE IN RELATION TO
        OCCUPATIONAL STRATIFICATION
        Society and Cult. 1970, 1, 1, Jul, 41-49
        SA, XX, 7, F9519

2996   Malaviya, H.D.

        AGRARIAN UNREST AFTER INDEPENDENCE
        in. Rural Sociology in India
        ed. A.R. Desai
        Bombay, Popular Prakashan,1969, p. 395-398

2997   Malaviya, H.D.

        VILLAGE COMMUNITIES IN INDIA: A HISTORICAL OUTLINE
        in. Rural Sociology in India
        ed. A. R. Desai
        Bombay, Popular Prakashan, 1969, p. 171-177

2998   Malhotra, D.K.

        SURVEY OF RURAL INDUSTRIES--STAGES OF POLICY
        Kurukshetra, 1969, 18, 7, Apr, 13-16
        SA, XIX, 4, E9917

2999   Malhotra, S.P.; L.P. Bharara & L.P. Joshi

        SOCIO-ECONOMIC CHARACTERISTICS OF INHABITANTS OF
        ANUPGARH--PUGAL REGION
        Ind. Sociol. B. 1966, 3, 2, Jan, 107-121
        SA, XV, 4, C5929

3000   Malhotra, S.P.; L.P. Bharara & P.L. Joshi

        COMPARATIVE SOCIO-ECONOMIC FACTORS OF INHABITANTS OF
        ANUPGARH PUGAL REGION AND IN LUNI BASIN OF WESTERN
        RAJASTHAN
        Annals of Arid Zone, 1967, 6, 2, Sep, 117-128
        SA, XVIII, 7, E6062

3001   Malhotra, S.P.; L.P. Bharara & P.L. Joshi

        ROLE OF ANIMAL HUSBANDRY IN ANUPGARH-PUGAL REGION
        Indian Sociological B. 1967, 5, 1, Oct, 11-20
        SA, XVII, 3, D7113

1116   rural sociology (village, agricult.)

3002   Mali, S.K.

A VILLAGE IN GOA
Doct. St. Poona U., 1969

3003   Mamoria,C.

STUDY OF AN INDIAN VILLAGE
Rural India, June, 1952 , 209-216

3004   Mandelbaum, D.G.

TECHNOLOGY, CREDIT AND CULTURE IN AN INDIAN VILLAGE
Human Organ. 11, 3, 28
also Economic Wkly., 4, 1952, p 827-828

3005   Mandelbaum, D.G.

TECHNOLOGY CREDIT AND CULTURE IN A NILGIRI VILLAGE
in. M.N. Srinivas (ed.)
India's Villages
Bombay, Asia Publishing House, 1955

3006   Mandelbaum, D.G.

STATUS SEEKING IN INDIAN VILLAGES
Trans-Action, 1968, 5, 5, Apr, 48-52
SA, XVII, 1, D5230

3007   Mann, H.

VILLAGE BETTERMENT IN THE NEW INDIA AND PAKISTAN
Asiatic Rev., 44, 154-70, April 1948

3008   Mann. R.S.

ACCULTURATION AND WOMAN'S STANDING
Ind. J. Soc. Wrk. 1961, 22, 2, Sep, 77-80
SA, XI, 7, A7327

2309   Marriott, M.

VILLAGE STRUCTURE AND THE PUNJAB GOVERNMENT: A
RESTATEMENT
Amer. Anthrop. V 55, 1953, p. 137-43

3010   Marriott, M. (ed.)

VILLAGE INDIA: STUDIES IN THE LITTLE COMMUNITY
Chicago: U. of Chicago Press, 1955, XVIII and 269 p.

3011   Marriott, M.

LITTLE COMMUNITIES IN AN INDIGENOUS CIVILIZATION
in Village India
ed. M. Marriott
U. of Chicago Press, 1956, p. 171 - 223

3012   Masters, A.

HOUSING IN AN INDIAN VILLAGE
Popul. R., 1957, 1, 2, July 52-56
SA, XII, 5, B1149

3013   Mathur, K.S.

DRAMA IN RURAL INDIA
Ind. Council for Cultural Relations
New Delhi, 1964

3014   Mayer, A.C.

CASTE AND KINSHIP IN CENTRAL INDIA: A VILLAGE AND
ITS REGIONS
Berkeley, U of Calif. Press, 1960

3015   McCormack, W.C.

MYSORE VILLAGERS' VIEW OF CHANGE
Econ. Dev. & Cult. Change 1957, 5, 3, April 257-262
SA, VII, supplement, 6787

3016   Meenakshi, S.

RURAL DEVELOPMENT IN MADRAS
Kurukshetra, 1966, 14, 17, Aug, 25-27
SA, XVIII, 1-2, E1199

3017   McLane, J.R.

PEASANTS, MONEY-LENDERS AND NATIONALISTS AT THE END
OF THE 19TH CENTURY
Ind. Econ. Soc. Hist. R., 1963, 1, 1, Jul-Sep, 67-73
SA, XV, 3, C5152

3018   Mahra, J.

A SOCIO-ECONOMIC SURVEY OF KHEDLA VILLAGE IN
RAJASTHAN
Rur. India 1960, Jul, 232-238
SA, XII, 6, B1901

3019   Mehrotra, R.

SOCIAL ACCOUNTING AND REGIONAL INCOMES IN INDIA
(PH.D.)
Doct., Poona U., 1966
(Dr. K. Mukerji)

3020   Mehta, A.

SOCIO-ECONOMIC PHILOSOPHY FOR FARMERS
Kurukshetra, 1964, 12, 10, Jul, 14-15
SA, XIV, 2-3, B9566

3021   Mehta, b.

PANCHAYATI RAJ AND AGRICULTURAL PRODUCTION
Kurukshetra, 1966, 15, 1, Oct, 29-32
SA, XVIII, 3, E2138

3022   Mehta, B.H.

RURAL COMMUNITY ORGANIZATION
Ind. J. Soc. Wrk. 1954, 15, 2, Sep 79-92
SA, vol III, #3, 1524

3023   *Mehta, S.R.

EMERGING PATTERN OF RURAL LEADERSHIP
New Delhi, Wiley Eastern, 1972

3024   Morris, M.D.

ECONOMIC CHANGE AND AGRICULTURE   IN THE NINETEENTH
CENTURY INDIA
Indian Eco. and Social Hist. Review, 1966, 3, 2,
Jun, 185-209
SA, XVII, 1, D5232

3025   Mehta, (Miss) S.

SOCIAL CONFLICTS AND FORCES OF DISINTEGRATION IN A
VILLAGE COMMUNITY (PH.D.)
Doct., Agra U., 1967

3026   Mehta, U.

THE PROBLEMS OF THE MARGINAL FARMERS IN INDIAN
AGRICULTURE
in. Rural Sociology in India
ed. A. R. Desai
Bombay, Popular Prakashan, 1969
p. 336-343

3027   Mellor, J.W. et. al.

DEVELOPING RURAL INDIA: PLANT PRACTICE
Cornell U. Press, 1968

3028   Merillat, H.C.L.

LAND AND THE CONSTITUTION IN INDIA
New York, Columbia U. Press, 1970

3029   Metcalf, T.E.

LAISSEZ-FAIRE AND TENANT RIGHT IN MID-19TH CENTURY
INDIA
Ind. Econ. Soc. Hist. R., 1963, 1, 1, Jul-Sept, 74-82
SA, XV, 3, C5153

3030   Metcalf, T.R.

LANDLORDS WITHOUT LAND: THE U.P. ZAMINDARS TODAY
South Asia Series: U. of Calif
Reprint from Pacific Affairs
XL, 1-2, 1967

3031   *Mehta, S.R.

EMERGING PATTERN OF RURAL LEADERSHIP
New Delhi, Wiley Eastern, 1972

3032   Miller, E.J.

VILLAGE STRUCTURE IN NORTH KERALA
in. India's Villages
ed. M.M. Srinivas
Dev. Dept., W. Bengal, 1955, 39-50

3033   Mishra, N.

ANJAN--A VILLAGE IN TRANSITION: STUDY OF VILLAGE
DYNAMICS
Doct. St., Rachi U., 1969

3034   Misra, D.N.

CONTINUITY AND CHANGE IN VILLAGE COM. IN INDIA WITH
SPECIAL REFERENCE TO SELECTED GROUP OF VILLAGES IN
DISTRICT GORAKHPUR OF EAST U.P.
Doct. St., Gorakhpur U., 1969
(S.P. Nagendra)

3035   *Misra, Girish K.

A METHODOLOGY FOR IDENTIFYING SERVICE CENTRES IN
RURAL AREAS: A STUDY IN MIRYALGUDA TALUKA,
Behavioral Sciences and Community Development,
1972, 6, 1, Mar, 48-63
SA, 21, 73G2625

3036   Misra, S.D.

NEW FARMING AND OUR FARMERS
Kurukshetra, 1967, 15, 5, Feb, 7-8
SA, XVII, 6, E4981

3037   Mitchell, Nora

THE INDIAN HILL--STATION: KODAIKANAL
Chicago: U. of Chicago, 1972

3038   Mohan, V.

BARGAON: A HINDUIZED GOND VILLAGE
Man in India, 1963, 43, 4, Oct-Dec, 341-348
SA, XII, 7, B2777

3039   Montemayor, J.M.

ANALYSIS OF A GOAN VILLAGE COMMUNITY
Doct. St., Delhi U., 1969
(A. Beteille)

3040   Morse, R.

AGRARIAN REFORM IN INDIA: LAND TENURE AND INDIAN
SOCIETY
FAR EASTERN SOCIETY, 79, 233-9, Dec. 20, 1950

3041   *Mudiraj, G.N.R.

CASTE-SECT DICHOTOMY IN TELANGANA VILLAGE
Man in India, 1970, 50, 3, Jul-Sep. 280-288
SA, 21, 73G3446

3042   Mukherjee, R.

THE DYNAMICS OF A RURAL SOCIETY, A STUDY OF THE
ECONOMIC STRUCTURE IN BENGAL VILLAGES
Berlin, Akademic, 1957, X, 134 p.

3043   Mukherjee, R.

SIX VILLAGES OF BENGAL: A SOCIO-ECONOMIC SURVEY
Calcutta, Asiatic Society of Bengal, 1958

3044   Mukerjee, R.

ON VILLAGE STUDIES IN INDIA
Ind. J. Soc. Res., 1963, 4, 2, Jul, 1-14
also in Rural Sociology in India
ed. A.R. Desai
Bombay, 1969, p. 805-811
SA, XIV, 2-3 B9568

3045   Mukherjee, R.

ECONOMIC STRUCTURE AND SOCIAL LIFE IN SIX VILLAGES
OF BENGAL
Amer Sociol Rev. 14, 415-25 June 1949

3046   Mukeherjee, R.

ECONOMIC STRUCTURE OF RURAL BENGAL: A SURVEY OF SIX
VILLAGES
Amer. Sociological Rev. 13, 660-72, Dec. 1948

3047   Mukherjee, R.

RECENT TRENDS OF SOCIOLOGICAL STUDIES ON RURAL
SOCIETY IN INDIA
Ajia Keizai, Tokyo, 1966 , 88-100

3048   Mukherjee, R.

THE SOCIAL ORGANISM
in Rural Sociology in India,
ed. A. R. Desai
Bombay, Popular Prakashan, 1969, p. 177-184

3049   Mukherjee, R.

SIX VILLAGES OF BENGAL
Bombay, 1970

3050   Mukherjee, V.

SRINIKETAN EXPERIMENT IN RURAL RECONSTRUCTION
Economic Weekly, V 4, 1952, p. 1007-1009

3051   Mukhopadhyay, A. and A.K. Sini

ECONOMIC EVALUATION OF IRRIGATION PROJECTS: A CASE
STUDY IN WEST BENGAL
Society and Cult., 1970, 1, 1, Jul, 63-70

3052   Mysore (State) Committee for the Revision of the Land
Revenue System

REPORT
Bangalore; 1950, 399, 83 pp

3053   Naidu, S.B.

LA COMMUNAUTE VILLAGEOISE EN INDE
(THE VILLAGE COMMUNITY IN INDIA)
Archives International de Sociologie de la Cooperation
et du Developpment 1970, 27, Jan-Jun, 139-154 (Fr)
also Commurautes 27, Jan-JUin 1970, 1390154
SA, XX, 3, F5097

3054   Naik, H.K.

LAND UTILISATION IN GUJARAT
Vidya, 1964, 7, 2, Aug, 73-93
SA, XIV, **2-3**, B9569

3055   Nainie, M.

THE HOME SCIENTIST IN RURAL AREAS
Kurukshetra, 1966, 14, 6, Mar, 15-16
SA, XVII, 2, D6164

3056   Nair, K.

LAND REFORM IN INDIA
Paper presented at the 3rd World Congress for Rural
Sociology
SA, XX, 5, Sup. 24, F7781

3057   Nair, K.

THE LONELY FURROW: FARMING IN THE UNITED STATES,
JAPAN AND INDIA
Ann Arbor, Mich;   The U. of Mich. Press,1969
pp xvi & 314

3058   Nair, S.P.

AGRICULTURAL EXTENSION
Kurukshetra, 1964, 12, 12, Sep, 12 & 22
SA, XIV, 2-3, B9570

3059   Nair, S.P.

YOUTH CLUBS AND AGRICULTURAL PRODUCTION
Kurukshetra, 1966, 15, 3, Dec, 11-12
SA, XVIII, 6, E4982

3060   Nanavati, M.B.

GROUP PREJUDICES IN RURAL INDIA
in. Group Prejedices in India
eds. M.B. Nanavati and C.N.Vakil
Bombay, Vora, 1951, p 147-157

3061   Nanavati, M.B. AND J.J. Anjana

THE INDIAN RURAL PROBLEM (7th rev. ed.)
INDIAN SOCIETY OF AGRICULTURE

3062   Nandi, S.B.

CULTURAL CHANGES IN AN ORAON VILLAGE
Vanyajati, 1960, 8, 1, Jan, 12-20
SA, XII, V, B1151

3063   Narayana, P.L.

TRADITION AND CHANGE IN THE RURAL SOCIETY OF
VISAKHAPATNAM DISTRICT
Doct. St. Andhra U., 1969
(Prof. N.S. Reddy)

3064   Narrain, I.

DEMOCRATIC DCENTRALIZATION AND RURAL LEADERSHIP IN
INDIA, THE RAJASTHAN EXPERIMENT
Asian Survey, 1964, 4, 8, Aug, 1013-1022
SA, XIV, 2-3, B9572

3065   Nath, V.

THE VILLAGE AND THE COMMUNITY
in India's Urban Future
ed R. Turner
Berkeley; U. of Calif. Press, 1962 p 141-157

3066   N.C.A.E.R.

        SURVEY OF HILLY AND BACKWARD AREAS OF PUNJAB
        New Delhi, 1956

3067   National Council of Applied Economic Research New Delhi
        SURVEY OF BACKWARD DISTRICTS IN ANDHRA PRADESH
        Intl. Prglms. Serv., 1970

3068   Neale, Walter C.

        RECIPROCITY AND REDISTRIBUTION IN THE INDIAN VILLAGE
        in. Trade and Market in the Early Empires
        Glencoe, Ill.: The Free Press, 1957, pp 218-36
        ed. Karl Dolanji

3069   Nesic, D.

        ODNOSI KASTINSKIRH GRIPA U. INDISJSKOJ SEOSKOJ
        JZJENDNICI (RELATIONSHIP OF CASTE GROUPS IN THE
        INDIAN RURAL COMMUNITY)
        Sociologija Sela, 1967, 15, Jan-Mar, 31-45 (Ser)
        SA, XVI, 7 D4388

3070   *Nesic, Dragoljug

        AGRAINE REFORME U INDIJI NJIHORI REZULTATI (LAND
        REFORMS AND THEIR RESULTS IN INDIA)
        Sociòlogija Sela, 1968, 6, 21, July-Sep, 57-77 (Ser)
        SA, 21, 73G0920

3071   Newell, W.H.

        "GOSHEN, A GADDI VILLAGE IN THE HIMALAYAS"
        in India's Villages
        ed. M.N. Srinivas,
        Dev. Dept. W. Bengal, 1955, 51-61

3072   Nicholas, R.W.

VILLAGE FACTIONS AND POLITICAL PARTIES IN RURAL WEST
BENGAL
J. Commonwealth Polit. Stud., 1963, 2, 1, Nov, 17-32
SA, XIII, 5, B7141

3073   Oommen, T.K.

MYTH AND REALITY IN INDIA'S COMMUNITARIAN VILLAGES
J. Commonwealth Polit. Stud., 1966, 4, 2,
Jul, 94-116
also in Rural Sociology in India
ed. A.R. Desai
Bombay, 1969
SA, XV, 5, C6686

3074   Oommen, T.K.

RURAL COMMUNITY POWER STRUCTURE IN INDIA
Social Forces, 1970, 49, 2, Dec, 226-238
SA, XIX, 5, F0784

3075   Opler, M.E. (ed.)

VILLAGE LIFE IN NORTH INDIA
in. Pattern of Modern Living
Cultural Patterns, Division 3,
Chicago, Delphin Society, 1950, p. 279-305

3076   Opler, M.E. and R.D. Singh

TWO VILLAGES OF EASTERN UTTAR PRADESH, INDIA: AN
ANALYSIS OF SIMILARITIES AND DIFFERENCES
Am. Anthrop. 54, 2, part 1, 179-90, April 1952

3077   Opler, M.E. and R.D. Singh

ECONOMIC, POLITICAL AND SOCIAL CHANGE IN A VILLAGE OF
NORTH CENTRAL INDIA
Hum. Org., 11, 2, 5-12, 1952

3078   Opler, M.E.

ECONOMIC, POLITICAL AND SOCIAL CHANGE IN A VILLAGE
OF NORTH CENTRAL INDIA
Hum. Org., 11, 2, 1952, p. 5-12

3079   Orenstein, H.

GAON: CONFLICT AND COHESION IN AN INDIAN VILLAGE
Princeton, N.J.: Princeton U. Press, 1965, viii
and 341 pp
SA, XV, 3, C5155

3080   Pabla, G.S. and J. R. Vashistha

TANDI: A VILLAGE IN LAHOUL AND SPITI DISTRICT OF
PUNJAB STATE
Census of India, 1961, 13, 1, Part VI, Village
Survey, Monograph #1, Manager of Publications,
Delhi, 1963

3081   *Palakshappa, T.C.

THE SIDDHIS OF NORTH KANARA (INDIA)
Hamilton, University of Waikato, (Working paper in
the Dept. of Sociology) 1973

3082   Panchanadikar,J.M.

INDIAN RURAL SOCIETY UNDER THE IMPACT OF PLANNED
DEVELOPMENT--A SOCIOLOGICAL ANALYSIS
Sociol. B. 1962, 11, 1, 2, Mar-Sept, 173-198
SA, XI, 7, A, 73330

3083   Panda, S.N.

A FISHERMAN VILLAGE OF COASTAL ORISSA--A STUDY OF
SOCIO-CULTURAL DYNAMICS IN A SPECIFIC ECONOMIC
FRAMEWORK (PH.D.)
Doct., Utkal U., 1966
(Dr. A. Aiyappan)

3084   Pandey, A.N.

THE IMPACT OF EMIGRATION OF THE RURAL FAMILY IN
EASTERN U.P.
Doct. St. Gorakhpur U., 1969
(S.P. Nagendra)

3085   Pareek, U. and Y.P. Singh

SOCIOMETRY AND COMMUNICATION NETWORK IN AN INDIAN
VILLAGE
Inter. J. of Psychology, 1968, 3, 3, 157-165
SA, XVIII, 1-2, E1203

3086   Parkash, Singh

CHANGING SOCIAL STRUCTURE OF RUAL PUNJAB (PH.D.)
Doct., Panjab U., 1970
(Dr. M.L. Sharma)

3087   Parvathamma, C.

LANDHOLDING PATTERN AND POWER-RELATIONS IN A MYSORE
VILLAGE
Sociol. B., 1968, 17, 2, Sep., 203-224
SA, SVIII, 7, E6069

3088   Patel, S.P.

INDUSTRIAL WORKERS IN RURAL INDIA
Sociol. B. 1967, 16, 1, Mar, 33-49
SA, XVII, 2, D6168

3089   Patil, S.R.V.

ALL LAND TO THE TILLER--THE PROBLEM OF LAND REFORM IN
INDIA
Eco. Dev. and Cult. Change, 1955, 3, 4, Jul, 374-380
SA, VI, 2, 4331

3090   Patnaik,   N.

RURAL DEVELOPMENT IN ORISSA--THE ROLE OF THE RURAL
LIFE ANALYST IN PLANNING, EXECUTION AND EVALUATION
(PH.D.)
Doct. Utkal U., 1963,
(Dr. A. Aiyappan)

3091   Patterson, Maureen L.

MAHARASHTRA
University of Chicago, 1964
Mimeograph, Published in encyclopedia Americana,1968
P. 1-7

3092   Paul, M.C.

THE HABITAT, ECONOMY AND SOCIETY OF CHRISTIAN VILLAGES
IN UTTAR PRADESH (PH.D.)
Doct., Agra U., 1959

3093   Patti, V.S.S.

SOCIO-PSYCHOLOGICAL ASPECTS OF AGRICULTURAL CREDIT
Kurukshetra, 1964, 13, 2, Nov., 16-18
SA, XIV, 4, C0461

3094   Prasad, B.K.

VILLAGE LIFE IN SOUTH BIHAR--A STUDY IN CASTE DOMINANCE
Doct. St. Ranchi U., 1969

3095   Prasad,S.D.

VILLAGE SURVEY MONOGRAPH ON KUMAR BHAJA, BATHBANGA
AND JAMKANALI
1061 Superintendent of Census, Bihar, 4, 2-4, Part VI
Bihar, 1961

3096   *Punit, A.E.

LEADERSHIP DIMENSIONS IN RURAL INDIA
Dharwar, Karnatak University, 1973

3097   Rahmann, R.

SHIFTING CULTIVATION AND NOTIONS ON LANDED PROPERTY
Phillipine Sociol. R. 1963, 11, 1-2, Jan-Apr 38-44
SA, XIV, 1, B8669

3098   Rahudhar, W.B.

THE RELATIONSHIP OF CERTAIN PERSONAL ATTRIBUTES TO
THE SUCCESS OF VILLAGE LEVEL WORKERS
Ind. J. Soc. Wrk, 1963, 23, 4, Jan, 319-326
SA, XII, 4, B0450

3099   Rahudhar, W.B.

THE RELATIONSHIP OF CERTAIN FACTORS TO THE SUCCESS
OF VILLAGE LEVEL WORKERS
Rur. Sociol. 1962, 27, 4, Dec. 418-427
SA, XI, 4, A5254

3100   *Ramu, G.N. & Paul D. Wiebe

PROFILES OF RURAL POLITICS IN MYSORE
Eastern Anthropologist, 1970, 23, 2, May-Aug, 131-140
SA, 21, 73G4403

3101   Ranadive, B.T.

SARVODAYA
in Rural Sociology in India
ed. A. R. Desai
Bombay Popular 1969, p. 675-689

3102   Randhawa, M.S.

DEVELOPING VILLAGE INDIA
Calcutta, Orient Longmans, 1952, 290 p.

3103   Randhawa, N.S.

RESOURCES, PRODUCTION, EMPLOYMENT AND INCOME IN
SELECTED AREAS: A STUDY OF CERTAIN BASIC TRENDS IN
THE AGRICULTURAL SECTOR
A.I.C.C. Econ. R. 1959, 11, 8, 15 Aug, 55-59
SA, XII, V, B1155

3104   Ranganathan, A.

THE AGRICULTURAL RENAISSANCE IN TANJORE
Civilisations, 1969, 19, 7, 91-97
SA, XVIII, 7, E6071

3105   *Rao, D. G. Gopal, K.N. Singh & Kumkum Pal

A STUDY OF THE MOTIVATION PATTERN OF FARMERS TOWARDS THE
ADOPTION OF HIGH-YIELDING VARIETIES OF WHEAT
Behavioral Sciences and Community Development
1971, 5, 1, Mar 64-71
SA, 21, 73G0927

3106   Rao, K.R.

THE DYNAMICS OF POWER AND CONFLICT IN VILLAGE INDIA:
A CASE STUDY
Amer. Doct. Dissert. (1968-69)
Michigan State U., (Soc.)

3107   Rao, L.J.

AN EVALUATION OF INTENSIVE AGRICULTURAL DISTRICT
PROGRAMME IN WEST GODAVARY DISTRICT A.P.
M.S. Thesis, India, 1965

1116   rural sociology (village, agricult.)

3108   Rao, M.K.

PANCHAYAT INDUSTRIES
Kurukshetra, 1964, 12, 10, Jul 22-26
SA, XIV, 2-3, B9575

3109   Rao, M.K.

A RURAL INSTITUTE COMES OF AGE: EXCITING STORY
OF GANDHIGRAM
Kurukshetra, 1967, 15, 6, Mar 4-6
SA, XVIII, 7, E6072

3110   Rao, (Miss) V.

RURAL REACTIONS TO URBANIZATION   (PH.D.)
Doct., Bombay U., 1957
(Prof. K.M. Kapadia)

3111   Rastogi, P.N.

FACTIONALISM IN INDIAN VILLAGE SOCIETY: A COMPARATIVE
SOCIOLOGICAL STUDY IN FIVE FIELD SITUATIONS IN U.P.
(PH.D.)
Agra U., 1967

3112   Rastogi, P.N.

POLARIZATION, POLITICS AND ANOMIE IN A RURAL LOCALE
IN EAST U.P.
Ind. J. Soc. Wrk. 1968, 28, 4, Jan 371-378
SA, XVII, 5, D8530

3113   Raza, M.

HABITAT, ECONOMY AND SOCIETY IN THE AGRICULTURAL
TRIBES OF THE RANCHI PLATEAU   (PH.D.)
Doct. Aligarh Muslim U. 1959
(Prof. S.M. Tahir Rizvi)

3114   Ray, G.L.

A STUDY OF SOME AGRICULTURAL AND SOCIOLOGICAL FACTORS
AS RELATED TO HIGH AND LOW LEVELS OF URBANIZATION OF
FARMERS   (PH.D.)
Doct. Indian Agricultural Research Inst. 1968
(Dr. (Mrs.) S. Mulay)

3115   Reddy, G.R.

AGRICULTURE AND PANCHAYATI RAJ
Kurukshetra, 1966, 15, 1, Oct., 36-38
SA, XVIII, 3, E2146

3116   *Reddy, S.K. and Kaufman, H.F.

COMPARATIVE STUDY OF STRUCTURE AND CHANGE IN
SELECTED SMALL COMMUNITIES IN INDIA AND THE UNITED
STATES
Papers presented at the ASA Annual Meeting
Montreal, August 25-29, 1974

3117   Reddy, V.M.

SURPLUS MANPOWR UTILIZATION IN RURAL AREAS (WITH
PARTICULAR REFERENCE TO ANDHRA PRADESH)
Pop. R. 1964, 8, 11, Jan. 90-06
SA, XIII, 3-4, B6258

3118   Rosser, C.

A "HERMIT" VILLAGE IN KULU
in India's Villages
ed. M.N. Srinivas
Dev. Dept., W. Bengal, 1955 7-81

3119   Rout, B.C.

RURAL LEADERSHIP PROBLEMS
Kurukshetra, 1967, 15, 5, Feb, 15-16
SA, SVIII, 6, E4986

3120   Rout, B.C.

RURAL LEADERSHIP PROBLEMS
Kurukshetra, 1967, 15, 5, Feb, 15-16
SA, XVIII, 6, E4986

3121   Roy, P. & R.B. Iyer

MEASURING FUNCTIONAL LITERACY IN INDIAN VILLAGES
Behavioural Sciences and C.D. 1967, 1, 2, Sep, 107-113
SA, XVIII, 7, E6073

3122   Sachchidanand

THE TRIBAL VILLAGE IN BIHAR--A STUDY IN UNITY AND
EXTENSION (D.Litt.)
Doct, Patna U., 1962

3123   Saha, N.K.

AGRICULTURE IN THE VALUE SCALE AND RURAL YOUTH
Man in India, 52, 4, Oct-Dec, 1972, 335-340

3124   Sahay, B.N.

REVIEW OF RESEARCHES DONE AT THE DIVISION OF
AGRICULTURAL EXTENSION
Seminar on Extension Research & Education
Delhi, I.A.R.I, 1969

3125   Sahay, K.N.

SOME ASPECTS OF INTERACTIONAL PATTERN AT VILLAGE
KANCHANPURA
Indian Sociological B. 1967, 5, 1, Oct. 1-10
SA, XVII, 3, D7119

3126   Sahay, R.

CO-OPERATIVE FARMING IN BIHAR (D.LITT.)
Doct., Bihar U., 1966
(Dr. S.K. Bose)

3127   Sahu, B.

LAND UTILISATION IN ORISSA: A BOOK IN FIVE PARTS
Cuttuck: Orissa Govt. Press, 1951, 309 p.

3128   Saigaonkar, P.B. & A.U. Patel

RELATIONSHIP OF CERTAIN FACTORS WITH THE SUCCESS
OF VILLAGE-LEVEL EXTENSION WORKERS IN KAIRA DISTRICT
OF GUJARAT STATE
Beh. Scis. & C.D. 1970, 4, 1, Mar 23-32
SA, XIX, 6, D1703

3129   Saikia, P.D.

SOCIO-ECONOMIC STRUCTURE OF BETGARH--A DUFLA VILLAGE
OF ASSAM   (D.PHIL.)
Doct, Gauhati U., 1970
(Dr. M.C. Goswami)

3130   Salvi, P.V. & H.S. Bhoite

ROLE OF SOME FAMILY FACTORS IN RURAL MIGRATION
Ind. J. Soc. Wrk. 1969, 29, 4, Jan, 341-346
SA, XVIII, 6 E4987

3131   Salvi, P.V. & V.M. Rade

ACTIVITIES OF RURAL YOUTH
Ind. J. Of Soc. Wrk., 1967, 28, 2, Jul, 207-212
SA, XVII, 2, D6171

3132   Samiuddin

COOPERATIVE FARMING AND ITS IMPACT ON RURAL INDUSTRIES
OF INDIA WITH REFERENCE TO UTTAR PRADESH   (PH.D.)
Doct., Aligarh U., 1968
(prof Q.H. Farooquee)

3133   Sanapiratti, S.P.

COOPERATIVES AND RURAL DEVELOPMENT--AN INDIAN CASE
Paper presented at the 3rd World Congress for Rural
Sociology
SA, XX, 5, Sup 24, F7800

3134   Sancheti, D.C.

RURAL RECONSTRUCTION THROUGH COMMUNITY DEVELOPMENT
IN RAJASTHAN   (PH.D.)
Doct, Rajasthan U., 1964
(Prof. B.D. Bhargava)

3135   Sanghvi, P.S.

CRITICAL EVALUATION OF TENANCY POLICY OF THE
SUARASHTRA GOVERNMENT
in Rural Sociology in India
ed A.R. Desai
Bombay, Popular Prakashan, 1969, p. 430-433

3136   Santhanam, K.

HUMAN APPROACH IN AGRICULTURAL DEVELOPMENT
Kurukshetra, 1966, 15, 1, Oct, 24-26
SA, XVIII, 3, E2148

3137   Sarker, S.C.

RURAL INDUSTRIALISATION
KURUKSHETRA, 1966, 14, 6, Mar, 19-22
SA, XVII, 2, D6173

3138   Sarma, J.

A VILLAGE IN WEST BENGAL
in India's Village
ed. M.N. Srinivas
Dev. Dept. W. Bengal, 1955, 161-179

3139   Satin, L.R.

NEXT STEPS TO SUSTAIN THE AGRICULTURAL REVOLUTION
Int. Dev. Review, 1969, 11, 1, Mar, 20-21
SA, XVIII, 4, E3272

3140   Saxena, P.C.

PROFILE OF A VILLAGE IN A SEMI-ARID PART OF
RAJASTHAN
EAST ANTHROP. 1964, 17, 1, Jan-Apr 49-61
SA, XIV, 4, C0465

3141   Saxena, S.N.

RURAL RECONSTRUCTION IN THE POST-INDEPENDENCE ERA
IN UTTAR PRADESH   (PH.D.)
Agra U, 1962

3142   Schwartzberg, J.E.

AGRICULTURAL LABOR IN INDIA: A REGIONAL ANALYSIS WITH
PARTICULAR REFERENCE TO POPULATION GROWTH
Eco. Dev. Cult Change 1963, 11, 4, Jue, 337-352
SA, XIV, 5, C1363

3143   Sen, A.K.

SETTLEMENT PATTERNS IN RAJASTHAN
Man in India, 1966, 46, 3, Jul-Sep, 215-225
SA, XVI, 6, D3817

3144   Sen, Keshab C.

LE DEVELOPPEMENT RURAL EN INDE
(RURAL DEVELOPMENT IN INDIA)
Civilisations, 1963, 13, 4, 411-424 (Fr.)
SA, XII, 8, B3606

3145   Sengupta   T.

DEVELOPING JOB-CHART AND A RATING SCALE FOR
MEASURING EFFECTIVENESS OF VILLAGE LEVEL WORKING
IN THE INTENSIVE AGRICULTURAL DEVELOPMENT PROGRAMME
(PH.D.)
Doct, Indian Agricultural Research Instit, 1966
(Dr. K.N. Singh)

3146   Sengupta, T.

THE CHALLENGE OF AGRICULTURE
Kurukshetra, 1966, 15, 3, Dec, 9-10
SA, XVII, 6, E4990

3147   Shah, C.H.

CONDITIONS OF ECONOMIC PROGRESS OF FARMERS, AN
ANALYSIS OF THIRY-SIX CASE STUDIES, BOMBAY
Ind. Soc. Agri. Econ. 1960, 129 pp.
SA, XI, 4, A5257

3148   Shah, C.N. & A.V. Patel

CHARACTERISTICS RELATED WITH THE EFFECTIVENESS OF
FARM OPINION LEADERS IN TWO VILLAGES
Ind. Sociol. B. 1970, 7, 3-4, Apr-Jun 192-201
SA, XX, 5, F7319

3149   Shah, M.B.

THE SOCIAL AND ECONOMIC CONDITIONS OF KUMAON HILLS
(PH.D.)
Doct., Agra U., 1962

3150   Shah, S.A.

        THE AGRARIAN CRISIS IN INDIA
        J. Asian & African Studies, 1968, 3, 3-4
        Jul-Oct, 292-295
        SA, XVIII, 6, E4991

3151   Shah, V.

        BHUVEL: SOCIO-ECONOMIC SURVEY OF A VILLAGE
        Bombay: Vora, 1949, 154 pp

3152   Shaiza, W.

        AGRICULTURE IN TRIBAL AREAS
        Kurukshetra, 1966, 15, 3, Dec, 21-23
        SA, XVIII, 6, E4992

3153   Shantibhushan Nandi & D.S. Tyagi

        FORMS OF VILLAGES
        in Rural Sociology in India
        ed A.R. Desai
        Bombay Popular Prakashan, 1969, p. 206-219

3154   Sharma, H.P.

        FACTIONAL POLITICS IN A NORTH INDIAN VILLAGE
        Amer. Doct. Dissertations .(1968-69)
        Cornell U. (Sol.)

3155   Sharma, K.L.

        CASTE AND CLASS CONSCIOUSNESS IN RURAL RAJASTHAN:
        SOME SOCIAL AND PSYCHOLOGICAL EXPRESSIONS
        Sociology and Soc. Res. 1970, 54, 2, Apr, 378-387
        SA, XVIII, 1-2, E7443

3156   Sharma, K.N.

        URBAN CONTACTS AND CULTURAL CHANGE IN A LITTLE
        COMMUNITY
        Lucknow, PH.D. Dissert., 1956

3157   Sharma, M.D. & S.N. Ghosal

        INTEGRATION IN AGRICULTURAL COOPERATION
        Agri'al Situations In India, 1964, Jun 209-211
        SA, XV, 2, C4393

3158   Shea, T.

        AGRARIAN UNREST AND REFORM IN SOUTH INDIA
        Far East. Survey, 23, 81-8, June 1954

3159   Shelvankar, K.S.

        INDIAN FEUDALISM, ITS CHARACTERISTICS
        in Rural Sociology in India
        ed. A.R. Desai
        Part II Readings in Rural Sociology
        Bombay, Popular Prakashan, 1969 p 150-155

3160   Shingi, P.M.

        THE DYNAMICS OF COMMUNITY CHANGE IN RURAL INDIA:
        A CAUSAL MODEL   (PH.D.- Soc.)
        University of Illinois at Urbana--Champaign, 1972

3161   Shukla, R.C.

        SOCIO-ECONOMIC STUDY OF AGRICULTURISTS IN THE
        TRACTERISED AREAS OF BHOPAL REGION   (PH.D.)
        Doct. Agra U., 1959

3162   Siddiqi, N.A.

        THE CLASSIFICATION OF VILLAGES UNDER THE MUGHALS
        Ind. Econ. Soc. Hist. R. 1964, 1, 3, Jan-Mar 73-83
        SA, XV, 3, C5159

3163   Singh, A.

LEADERSHIP PATTERNS AND VILLAGE STRUCTURE:
A STUDY OF SIX INDIAN VILLAGES
Amer. Doctoral Dissertations '67-'68
Mississippi State U. (Soc.)

3164   Singh, B.S. & A.V. Patel

FARMER's CONCEPT OF GRAMSEVAK
Ind. J. Soc. Wrk. 1969, 30, 1, Apr, 65-72
SA, XVIII, 7, E6074

3165   Singh, Indera

A SIKH VILLAGE
in Traditional India;   Structure and Change
ED. M.B. Singer
Philadelphia American Folklore Society, 1959
p. 273-298

3166   Singh, I.

IMPACT OF POPULATION ON FARM HOUSEHOLD INCOMES
IN VILLAGE DARYAPUR RALAN OF THE UNION TERRITORY
OF DELHI
Paper Presented at the 3rd World Congress for Rural
Sociology
SA, XX, 5, Sup 24, F7805

3167   Singh, K.

REACTIONS TO THE SCHEME OF JOINT COOPERATIVE
FARMING
Ind. J. Soc. Res, 1964, 5, 2, Aug, 173-177
SA, XIV, 4, C0467

316⁹   Singh, Khushwant

        TWO VILLAGES: STORY OF CONTRASTS
        Kurukshetra, 1966, 14, 5, Feb, 9.
        SA,XVII, 2, D6175

3169   Singh, K.N.

        NEW AGRICULTURAL TECHNOLOGY
        Kurukshetra, 1966, 15, 1, Oct, 44-46
        SA, XVIII, 3, E2149

3170   *Singh, K. N. & P.N. Jha

        FACTORS ASSOCIATED WITH COMMUNICATION FIDELITY
        AS PERCEIVED BY PERSONS CONNECTED WITH HIGH-YIELDING
        VARIETIES PROGRAMME
        Behavioral Sciences and Community Development
        1971, 51, 1, Mar, 21-37
        SA, 21, 73 G0930

3171   Singh, K.N. & C. Shankariah

        DIFFERENTIAL CHARACTERISTEICS OF VEGETABLE AND
        NON-VEGETABLE GROWERS
        Ind. J. of Soc. Wrk., 167, 28, 2, Jul 160-178
        SA, XVII, 2, D6176

3172   Singh, N.P.

        DIFFERENT ATTITUDES OF AGRICULTURAL ENTREPRENEURS
        TOWARDS SOCIAL AND ECONOMIC GOALS
        Ind. J. Soc. Wrk, 1970, 31, 2, Jul, 177-182
        SA, XX 6, F8487

3173   Singh, N.P.; N.K. Jaiswal & B.N. Singh

        RELATIVE IMPORTANCE OF THE FACTORS INFLUENCING
        COORDINATION AMONG PERSONNEL WORKING IN THE
        INTENSIVE AGRICULTURAL DISTRICT PROGRAMME
        Behavioural Scist. C.D. 1969, 21, 1, Mar, 1-12
        SA, XIX, 4, E9924

3174   Singh, R. & T.S. Sohal

DIFFERENCES IN THE ASPIRATIONS OF FARMERS
Ind. Journal of Social Res, 1966, 7, 3,
Dec. 206-210
SA, XVII, 3, D7120

3175   Singh, R.P.

DIFFERENTIAL ATTITUDES OF FARMERS TOWARD SOME ASPECTS
OF THE COMMUNITY DEVELOPMENT PROGRAMME (PH.D.)
Doct., Indian Agricultural Research Instit, 1966
(Dr. K.N. Singh)

3176   Singh, S.K.

FARMER' VALUES IN RELATION TO COMMERCIALISATION IN
FARMS (PH.D.)
Doct., Indian Agricultural Research Institute, 1966
(Dr. K.N. Singh)

3177   *Singh, S.N. & A.S. Murthy

INFLUENCE OF NEED DISPOSITION OF THE FARMERS ON THEIR
COMMUNICATION BEHAVIOUR
Behavioral Sciences & Community Development, 1971,
5, 1, Mar, 59-63
SA, 21, 73G0931

3178   Singh, S.N. et. al.

A STUDY OF SOCIAL VALUES IN RELATION TO FARMING
Ind. J. Ext. Educ., 1965

3179   Singh, T.

THE COOPERATIVE VILLAGE
Econ. Wkly, 1958, 10, Annual, Jan 143-148
SA, VIII, 2, 7436

3180   Singh, Tariok

        TOWARDS ON INTEGRATED SOCIETY: REFLECTIONS ON
        PLANNING SOCIAL POLICY AND RURAL INSTITUTIONS
        Westport, Greenwood Pub. 1969

3181   Singh, V.B.

        CHANGING PATTERNS OF INDIAN VILLAGE COMMUNITY
        Agra U. J. of Res 3, 1955, 91-98

3182   Singh, V.B.

        LAND TENURE IN AN INDIAN STATE
        Sci. Soc. 1955, 19, 4, Fall, 303-319
        SA, Vol IV #3, 2520

3183   Singh, Y.

        THE CHANGING POWER STRUCTURE OF VILLAGE COMMUNITY--
        A CASE STUDY OF SIX VILLAGSES IN EASTERN U.P.
        in. Rural Sociology in India
        ed. A.R. Desai, Bombay, Popular, 1969, p 711-724

3184   Sinha, A.P.

        SOCIAL STRUCTURE OF A PINAR VILLAGE
        Man in India, 1967, 47, 3, Jul-Sep, 189-199
        SA, XVII, 2, D6177

3185   Sinha, D.

        INDIAN VILLAGES IN TRANSITION
        Intl. Pubns. Serv., 1972

3186   Sinha, N.K. & D.P. Yadav

        SUMMARY OF STUDY IN CROP DEMONSTRATIONS IN LUDHIANA
        DISTRICT
        India; State Gov't. of Punjab Operational Res.
        Report 1964

3187   Sinha, N.K. & D.P. Yadav

        SUMMARY OF A STUDY OF THE PREPARATION AND IMPLEMENTATION
        OF INTENSIVE AND EXTENSIVE FARM PLANS FOR KHARIF
        India; State Gov't of Punjab Operational Res.
        Report, 1964

3188   Sinha, P.R.R. and Acharjee, P.R.H.

        ROLE OF PREJUDICES IN AGRICULTURAL EXTENSION
        Ind. J. Soc. Res. 13, 3, Dec., 1972, 212-217

3189   Sinha, P.R.R. and S.S. Pawar

        DIFFERENTIAL CHARACTERISTICS OF SUCCESSFUL AND
        UNSUCCESSFUL RURAL YOUTH CLUBS
        Paper presented at the 3rd World Congress for Rural
        Sociology
        SA, XX, 5, Sup, 24, F7806

3190   Sinha, S.

        AGRICULTURAL CRAFTS AND WEEKLY MARKET, SOUTH MANBHUM
        J. of Anthrop. Survey, 1961, 10, 1

3191   Sinha, S. (ed.)

        PEASANT LIFE IN INDIA: A STUDY IN INDIAN UNITY AND
        DIVERSITY
        Memoi #8 Anthro. Survey of India, Calcutta, 1961

3192   Sinha, S.

        BADANIA NAD MOTYWACJA SPOLECZNOSI WIEJSKIEF W KRAJU
        ROZWIJAJACYM SIC (A STUDY OF THE HUMAN MOTIVATION
        OF THE RUAL POPULATION IN A DEVELOPING COUNTRY)
        Studia Socjologiczne, 1968, 28, 59-82 (Pol.)
        SA, XIX, 1-2, E7444

3193   Sinha, S. & R. Bhattacharya

BHADRALOK AND CHHOTOLOK IN A RURAL AREA OF WEST
BENGAL
Sociol. B. 1969, 18, 1, Mar, 50-66
SA, XIX, 1-2, E7445

3194   Sinha, S.P.

THE PROBLEM OF LAND ALIENATION OF THE TRIBALS IN AND
AROUND RANCHI
Bihar Tribal Welfare Research Institute Ranchi, 1968

3195   *Sirsikar, V.M.

THE RURAL ELITE IN A DEVELOPING SOCIETY
New Delhi, Orient Longmans, 1970

3196   Sisodia, G.S.

SOCIO-ECONOMIC FACTORS AFFECTING AGRICULTURAL
DEVELOPMENT. A STUDY IN TWO VILLAGES OF HISSAR
Ind. Soc. Bulletin, 1968, 6, 1, Oct, 71-81
SA, XVIII, 3, E2151

3197   Sisodia G.S. & A.S. Kahlon

A STUDY INTO THE VILLAGERS' REACTION TO THEIR ELECTED
LEADEERS
Ind. Sociol. B. 1966, 4, 1, Oct, 22-27
SA, XV, 7, C8448

3198   Sisson, R.

PEASANT MOVEMENTS AND POLITICAL MOBILIZATION: THE
JATS OF RAJASTHAN
Asian Survey, 1969, 9, 12, Dec, 946-963
SA, XX, 4, F6390

1116   rural sociology (village, agricult.)

   3199   Sivertsen, D.

            DASTER OG DOMMUNISTER I THYAGASAMUTHIRAM , EN SOR-
            INDISK HANDSBY (CASTE AND COMMUNISTS IN THYAGASAMUTHIRAM
            A SOUTH INDIAN AGRICULTURAL TOWN)

   3200   South Penn School Study Council

            PATTERNS OF VILLAGE LIFE IN SOUTHERN ASIA: INDIA
            PAKISTAN, INDONESIA, THAILAND
            Danville, Ill., 1965, p 6-23
            572,595,8072

   3201   Spate, O.H.K.

            THE INDIAN VILLAGE
            Georgraphy, 37, 1952, p. 142-52

   3202   Smith, M.W.

            MISAL: A STRUCTURAL VILLAGE--GROUP OF INDIA AND
            PAKISTAN
            Am. Anthrop. 54, 41-56, Jan, 1952

   3203   Spate, O.H.K.

            THE INDIAN VILLAGE
            in Rural Sociology in India
            ed A.R. Desai
            Bombay, Popular Prakashan, 1969, p. 193-201

   3204   Speight, J. T.

            COMMENTARY ON OOMMEN'S "RURAL COMMUNITY POWER STRUCTURE
            IN INDIA"
            Social Forces, Dec. 1971, 50, 2, p. 261-262

   3205   Srinivas, M.N. (ed.)

            INDIA's VILLAGES
            Bombay, Asia, 1955

3206   Srinivas, M.N.

REGIONAL DIFFERENCES IN CUSTOMS AND VILLAGE
INSTITUTIONS
Econ. Wkly. 1956, 8, 7, Feb. 215-221
SA, VIII, 1, 7009

3207   Srinivas, M.N.

THE STUDY OF DISPUTES IN AN INDIAN VILLAGE
Reg'l. Seminar on Techniques of Soc. Res.
New Delhi, UNESCO, Res. Center, 1959, 144-51

3208   Srinivas, M.N.

VILLAGE STUDIES AND THEIR SIGNIFICANCE
in Rural Sociology in India
ed. A. R. Desai
Bombay, Popular, 1969, p. 705-790

3209   Srinivasan, N.

VILLAGE GOVERNMENT IN INDIA
Far East. Quart, 1956, 15, 2, Feb, 201-213
SA, VI, 2, 4336

3210   Srivastava, D.

COOPERATIVE FINANCE AND AGRICULTURAL DEVELOPMENT IN
INDIA
Paper presented at the 3rd World Congress for Rural
Sociology
SA, XX, 5, Sup 24, F7813

3211   Srivastava, D.

AGRICULTURE COOPERATIVE ET ANIMATION RURALE INDE
(SOME IMPLICATION OF COOPERATIVE FARMING IN EXTENSION
WORK IN INDIA)
Archiv. In.t Sociol.. Coop. 1965, 18, Jul-Dec
200-205 (Fr.)
SA, XV, 4, C5914

3212   Srivastava, M.B.

THE SOCIO-ECONOMIC STUDY OF THE DOON VALLEY   (PH.D.)
Doct., Agra U., 1963

3213   *Srivastava, S.L.

STRATIFICATION AND ETIQUETTEE IN VILLAGE COMMUNITY
Man in India, 1970, 5, 3, Jul-Sep, 269-279
SA, 21, 73G3447

3214   Staub, W.J. & M.G. Blase

GENETIC TECHNOLOGY AND AGRICULTURAL DEVELOPMENT
Science, 1971, 173, 3992, Jul 9, 119-122
SA, XX, 7, F9527

3215   Subbarao, B.

GEOGRAPHICAL FACTORS IN INDIAN HISTORY
in. Rural Scoiology in India Part II--Readings in
Rural Sociology
ed. A.R. Desai
Bombay: Popular Prakashan, 1969, p. 126-131

3216   Subramaniam, C.

COOPERATIVE SECTOR IN RURAL ECONOMY
Kurkshetra, 1966, 15, 2, Nov, 8-11
SA, XVIII, 6; E4998

3217   Subramaniam, C.

MODERNIZAITON OF INDIAN AGRICULTURE
Kurukshetra, 1966, 14, 8, May 3-4
SA, XVII, 3, D7122

3218   Sudhakaran

COMMUNICATIONS FACILITIES IN VILLAGES
Kurukshetra, 1969, 17, 10, Jul, 29
SA, XIX, 4, E9925

3219   Supe, S.V. & P.L. Ganorkar

VALUES OF FARMERS AND AGRICULTURAL COLLEGE STUDENTS
TOWARDS FARMING
Beh. Scis. & C.D. 1970, 4, 1, Mar, 33-40
SA, XIX, 6, F1708

3220   Sussman, G.

THE VILLAGE LEVEL WORKERS: INDIA'S EXPLRIMENT IN
RURAL RECONSTRUCTION
Int. Dev. Rev. 1968, 10, 1, Mar, 40-42
SA, XVII, 6, D9571

3221   Tennant, Rev. W.

DESCRIPTION OF A VILLAGE IN THE BENARES DISTRICT
Man in India, 1963, 43, Jan-Mar, 35-41
SA, XII, 6, B1910

3222   Thirumalai, S.

TRENDS IN RURAL CHANGE
in Rural Sociol. in India
ed. A.R. Desai
Bombay, Popular, 1969, p 691-693

3223   Thorner, D.

LES COOPERATIVES AGRICOLES AUX INDES RAPPORT D'ENQUETE
(AGRICULTURAL COOPERATIVES IN INDIA SURVEY REPORT)
Archiv. Int. Sociol. Coop. 1963, 13, Jan-Jun, 95-131
(Fr.)   SA, XV, 2, C4416

3224   Thorner, D.

LES COOPERATIVES AGRICOLES AUX INDES, RAPPORT D'ENQUETTE
2 Partie, (AGRICULTURAL COOPERATIVES IN INDIA: A REPORT
OF AN INQUIRY , PART 2)
Archiv. Int. Sociol. Coop 1964, 15, Jan-Jun, 129-197
(Fr.)   SA, XV, 2, C4395

3225   Thorner, Daniel

LAND REFORM
in Rural Soc. in India
ed. A.R. Desai
Bombay, Popular Prakashan, 1969 p 476-481

3226   Thorner, D.

CONTEXT FOR COOPERATIVES IN RURAL INDIA
in. Rural Sociology in India
ed. A.R. Desai
Bombay, Popular Prakashan, 1969, 491-518

3227   Thorner, D. & A. Thorner

TYPES OF EMPLOYER--LABORER RELATIONSHIP IN INDIAN
AGRICULTURE
Ind. J. Agri. Econ. 1957, 12, 2, Apr-June 84-96
SA, VIII, 1, 7010

3228   Tinker, H.

AUTHORITY AND COMMUNITY IN VILLAGE INDIA
Pacific Aff., 1959, 32, 4, Dec, 354-375
also in J. Afr. Adm. 1960, 12, 4, Oct., 193-210
SA, IX, 3, 9991,; SA, X, 2, A1791

3229   Tirupathi, Naidu, U.

AGRICULTURAL CREDIT COOPERATIVES IN INDIA--A STUDY OF
THE FARMING CREDIT COOPERATIVE SOCIETIES (PH.D.)
Doct. Sri Venkateswara U., 1966
(Dr. D.L. Narayana)

3230   Trent, S.

IMPACT OF MONEY ECONOMY AND ADULT SUFFRAGE ON A MYSORE
VILLAGE
Econ.Wkly,   Annual, 1956, 8, 314 & 5, Jan 101-104
SA, VIII, 1, 7011

3231   Trivedi, D.N.

OPINION LEADERSHIP AND ADOPTION OF AGRICULTURAL
INNOVATIONS IN EIGHT INDIAN VILLAGES
Amer. Doct. Dessert ('68-'69)
Pennsylvania State U. (Soc.)

3232   Trivedi, G. J.

MEASUREMENT AND ANALYSIS OF SOCIO-ECONOMIC STATUS OF
RURAL FAMILIES   (PH.D.)
Doct., Indian Agricultural Research Inst. 1965
(Dr. V. Pareek)

3233   Varma, Baidyanath

COMMUNICATION AND SOCIAL CHANGE IN RURAL INDIA
American Doctoral Dissertations, 1958-1959
Columbia U., (Sociology)

3234   Venkatarayappa, K.N.

A STUDY OF CUSTOMS IN RURAL MYSORE
Sociol. B. 1962, 11, 1, 2, Mar-Sep, 208-220
SA, XI, 7, A7334

3235   Vepa, R.K.

PROBLEMS OF RURAL INDUSTRIALIZATION
Kurukshetra, 1964, 12, 10, Jul, 19-21
SA, XIV, 2-3, B9369

3236   Vidyarthi, L.P.

GHAGHRA: A VILLAGE OF TRIBAL BIHAR
Delhi, Census Operation, 1965

3237   Vyas, K.C.

AVIDHA -A NARRATIVE OF CHANGING LIFE IN A
GUJARAT VILLAGE
Sociol. B. V2, 1953, p. 18-34

3238   *Wanamali, Sudhir

ZONES OF INFLUENCE OF CENTRAL VILLAGES IN MIRYALGUDA
TALUKA: A THEORETICAL APPROACH
Behavioral Sciences & Community Development, 1972, 6, 1,
Mar 1-10
SA, 21, 73G2631

3239   Whitcombe, Eliz.

AGRARIAN CONDITIONS IN NORTHERN INDIA VOL I.   THE
UNITED PROVINCES UNDER BRITISH RULE, 1860-1900
Berkeley, U. of Calif. Press, 1972

3240   Wurzbacher, G; Siegfried, S & B. Sengupta

(INSTITUT FOR SIZIOLOGIE UND SOZIALANTHROPOLOGIE
FRIEDRICH-ALEXANDER-UNIVERSITAT EXLANGEN, NURNBERG
GERMANY)
SOZIOKUTURELLE DISKREPANZEN ALS GRUNDLAGE FUR
HYPOTHESEN ZUR ERKLARING VON WINDLUNG-SPROZESSEN-
UBERPONFT AN DEUTSCHEN DORFSTIDIEN UND AU FOLLOW-UP-
FORSCHUNGEN ZU T.S. EPSTEINS UNTERSUCHUNG ZWEIR
SUDINDISCHER DORFER (SOCIOCULTURAL DISCREPANCY AS THE
BASIS FOR HYPOTHESES EXPLAINING CHANGE PROCESSES-AS
TESTED THROUGH STUDIES OF GERMAN VILLAGES AND FOLLOW-
UP RESEARCH ON T.S. EPSTEINS STUDY OF TWO SOUTH INDIAN
VILLAGES
Sociologia Internationalis, 1972, 10, 1, 69-90 (Ger.)
SA, 21, 73G3448

3241   Yadava, J.S.

A DELHI VILLAGE IN TRANSITION: A STUDY OF CHANGING
FAMILY, CASTE AND POWER PATTERN (PH.D.)
Doct. Delhi U., 1969 (prof. P.C. Biswas) (Dr.J.D.Mehra)

3242   *Zagoria, Donald S.

A NOTE ON LANDLESSNESS, LITERACY AND AGRARIAN
COMMUNISM IN INDA
Archives Eurpiennes de Sociologie
1972, 13, 2, 326-334
SA, 21, 73G4409

3243   -----

VILLAGE IN INDIA
New Statesman and Nation 42, 428 Oct. 20, 1951

3244   -----

TWO VILLAGES OF EASTERN UTTAR PRADESH
Amer. Anthrop., V54, 1952, p. 179-90

1200   Urban Structures and Ecology

1218   urban structures and ecology

    3245   Acharya, H.

            URBANIZING ROLE OF A ONE-LAKH CITY
            Social. B. 1956, 5, 2, Sep. 89-101
            SA, VI, I, 3969

    3246   Antia, F.P.

            INDIA'S URBAN POPULATION
            Popul. R. 1963, 7, 1, Jan 17-32
            SA, XIII, 2, B5338

    3247   Bogue, D.J. & K. C. Zachariah

            URBANIZATION & MIGRATION IN INDIA
            in India's Urban Future
            ed. R. Turner
            Berkeley; U of Calif. Press, 1962, p 27-57

    3248   Bhowmik, K.K.

            A STUDY OF RURAL URBAN COMMUNITY IN AN INDUSTRIAL CITY
            WITH SPECIAL REFERENCE TO KANPUR (PH.D.)
            Doct. St., Agra U., 1969
            (Dr. R.N. Saxena)

    3249   Banerji, P.C.

            LABOUR AND INDUSTRIAL HOUSING IN KANPUR
            (D.PHIL.)
            Doct., Allhabad U., 1948
            (Prof. S.K. Rudra)

3250   Bopegamage, A.

     ECOLOGY OF BUSINESS IN POONA CITY
     Popul. R. 1963, 7, 1, Jan 57-68
     SA, XIII, 2, B5342

3251   Bopegamage, A.

     NEIGHBORHOOD RELATIONS IN INDIAN CITIES--DELHI
     Sociol. B. 1957, 6, 1, Mar, 34-43
     SA, VIII, i, 7020

3252   Bopegamage, A.

     ECOLOGICAL STUDY OF DELHI CITY (PH.D.)
     Doct., Bombay U., 1957
     (Prof. G.S. Ghurye)

3253   Bopegamage, A.

     A METHODOLOGICAL PROBLEM IN INDIAN URBAN SOCIOLOGICAL
     RESEARCH
     Sociol. Soc. Res., 1966, 50, 2, Jan 236-240
     SA, XIV, 5, C1397

3254   Baptista, (Miss) E.W.

     THE INDIAN CHRISTAIN COMMUNITY, WITH PARTICULAR REFERENCE
     TO THE EAST INDIANS OF BOMBAY, SALSETTE AND BASSEIN (PH.D.)
     Doct., Bombay U., 1957
     (Prof. K.M. Kapadia)

3255   Barve, S.G.

     URBANIZATION IN MAHARASHTRA STATE: PROBLESM AND A PLAN
     OF ACTION
     In. India's Urban Future
     ed. R. Turner
     Berkeley; U. of Calif. Press, 1962, p. 347-361

3256   Beech, M.H.

SEX ROLE DEVELOPMENT AND AGE GROUP PARTICIPATION
IN CALCUTTA
Paper presented at the 67th Annual Meeting of the
Amer. Sociol. Assoc.
SA, XX, 7, Sup. 28., G0008

3257   Bose, A.

A NOTE ON THE DEFINITION OF "TOWN" IN THE INDIAN
CENSUSES: 1901-1961
Ind. Econ. Soc. Hist. R. 1964, 1, 3, Jan-Mar, 84-94
SA, XV, 3, C5177

3258   Bose, A.

SIX DECADES OF URBANIZATION IN INDIA: 1901-1961
Ind. Econ. Soc. Hist. R. 1965, 2, 1, Jan, 23-41
SA, XV, 3, C5178

3259   Bose, A.B.

THE INDIGENONS SYSTEM OF COMMUNICATION IN AN INDUSTRIAL
CITY
J. Soc. Res. 1965, 8, 1, Mar, 71-75
SA, XIV, 5, C1398

3260   *Bose, N.K.

A SOCIAL PROBLEM OF CALCUTTA
Man in India, 1971, 51, 3, Jul-Sep, 175-181
SA, 21, 73G3451

3261   Bose, N.K.

SOME PROBLEMS OF URBANIZATION
Man in India, 1962, 42, 4, Oct-Dec, 255-262
SA, XII, 6, B1940

3262   Bose, N.K.

        CALCUTTA 1964:   A SURVEY
        Bombay, Lalvani Pub. House, 1968

3263   Brush, J.E.

        THE MORPHOLOGY OF INDIAN CITIES
        in. India's Urban Future
        ed. R. Turner
        Berkeley; U. of Calif. Press, 1962, p 57-71

3264   Bulsara, J.F.

        PROBLEMS OF RAPID URBANIZATION IN INDIA
        Bombay, Popular, 1964

3265   Burman, R.

        A SOCIO-ECONOMIC APPRAISAL OF THE UNREST IN CALCUTTA
        Ind. J. of Sociol. 1971, 2, 1, Mar, 20-37
        SA, XX, 3, F5112

3266   Chakravarty, B.C.

        ARTISAN COMMUNITIES IN CHHOTANAGPUR
        Doct. St., Ranchi U., 1969

3267   Chanekar, V.V.

        COOPERATIVE HOUSING (PH.D.)
        Doct., Poon U., 1970
        (Dr. M.R. Dhekney)

3268   *Chatterjee, Mary

        STABILIZATION OF IMMIGRANTS IN INDIAN TOWNS: THE CASE
        OF BOMBAY,
        Sociological Bulletin, 1971, 20, 2, Sep, 145-158
        SA, 21, 73G5801

3269   Chaudhuri, S.

CENTRALIZATION AND THE ALTERNATE FORMS OF
DECENTRALIZATION: A KEY ISSUE
in India'sUrban Future
ed. R. Turner
Berkeley; U. of Calif. Press, 1962 p 213-240

3270   Chauhan, B.R.

TOWNS IN THE TRIBAL SETTING
Intl. Pulns. Serv., 1972

3271   Chauhan, D.S.

TRENDS OF URBANIZATION IN AGRA
Bombay, Allied Publishers, 1966, 459 p.

3272   Chekki, D.A.

KINSHIP AND MODERNIZATIONS: TWO STUDIES IN URBAN
INDIA   (PH.D.)
Doct., Karnatak U., 1966
(DR. K. ISHWARAN)

3273   Chekki, D.A.

PROBLEMS OF URBAN HOUSING
Social Welfare, Dec., 1967

3274   *Chekki, Dan A.

COMMUNITY RESEARCH IN INDIA: SOME TRENDS
Paper presented at the 8th World Congress of Sociology,
Toronto, August 19-24, 1974

3275   Cherukupalle, M.D.

URBANIZATION IN SOUTH   ASIA: A CRITICAL OVERVIEW OF
THE LITERATURE
Paper presented at the CSAS Meeting Winnipeg, 1970

3276   Cherukupalle, M.D.

URBAN SOCIAL STRUCTURE AND ECONOMIC DEVELOPMENT
POLICY: SOME HYPOTHESES AND EMPIRICAL RESULTS
Man in India, 1972, 52, 2, 131-150

3277   Clinard,M.B.

SLUMS AND COMMUNITY DEVELOPMENT
New York, The Free Press, 1966

3278   Crane, Robert I.

URBANISM IN INDIA
Amer. J. Soc. 1955, 60, 5, Mar, 463-470
SA, Vol III, #4, 1781

3279   Das, A.K.

INFLUENCE OF CITY LIFE ON EDUCATED TRIBALS
B. of Cult. Res. Inst. 1962, 1, 2, 69-78

3280   Davis, K.

URBANIZATION IN INDIA: PAST AND FUTURE
India's Urban Future
ed. R. Turner
Berkeley;   U. of Calif. Press, 1962, p 3-27

3281   Desai, A.R. and S.D. Pillai

SLUMS AND URBANIZATION
Bombay, Popular, 1970

3282   Doshi, H.C.

ORGANIZATION OF TRADITION IN THE WESTERN INDIAN CITY
(PH.D.)
Doct., Rajasthan U., 1968
(Dr. B.R. Chauhan)

3283   Dowling, J.H.

        A RURAL INDIAN COMMUNITY IN AN URBAN SETTING
        Hum. Org. 1968, 27, 3, Fall, 236-240
        SA, XVII, 4, D7898

3284   D'Souza , V.L.

        SOCIO-ECONOMIC FACTORS IN URBAN PLANNING
        Urban Rur. Plan. Thought, 1959, 2, 3, Jul, 109-113
        SA, XII, 5, B1199

3285   D'Souza, V.S.

        SOUCIAL STRUCTURE OF A PLANNED CITY, CHANDIGARH
        Bombay, Orient Longmans, 1968, XV-408 p

3286   Eames, E. & W.B. Schwab

        URBAN MIGRATION IN INDIA AND AFRICA
        Hum. Org. 1964 23 1 Spring 24-27
        SA, XII, 8, B3639

3287   Eames, E.

        CORPORATE GROUPS AND INDIAN URBANIZATION
        Anthropological Quart., 1970, 43, 3, Jul, 168-186
        SA, XX, 6, F8505

3288   Echeverria, E.

        HOW MUCH LAND DO INDIAN CITIES NEED
        Urban Rur. Plans Thought, 1958, 1, 40 Oct, 253-262
        SA, XII, 5, B1200

3289   Ellefsen, R.A.

        CITY-HINTERLAND RELATIONSHIPS IN INDIA
        in. India's Urban Future
        ed. R. Turner
        Berkeley; U. of Calif Press, 1962, p 94-117

3290   Evenson, Norma

        CHANDIGARH: A STUDY OF THE CITY AND ITS MONUMENTS
        Berkeley, U. of Calif. Press, 1966

3291   Fernandes (Mrs.) P.A.

        PROBLEMS IN URBAN SOCIETY
        Doct. St., Bombay U., 1969
        (Dr. D. Narain)

3292   Fox, G. (ed.)

        URBAN INDIA: SOCIETY, SPACE.IMAGE
        Durham, N.C.: Duke U. Press, 1970

3293   Gadgil, D.R.

        POONA: A SOCIO-ECONOMIC SURVEY
        Poona; (2 vols.) Gokhale Institute of Politics and
        Economics, publications, n. 12, 25, 1945-52

3294   Gadgil, D.R.

        SOCIAL SURVEY OF KOLHAPUR CITY
        Poona; Gokhale Institute of Politics and Economics
        publications n. 18, 23, 24, 1952

3295   Geddes, P.

        PATRICK GEDDES IN INDIA
        (Ed. by J. Trywhitt)
        London; L. Humphries, 1947, 103 pp

3296   Ghosh, B.N.

        TRIBAL FAMILIES IN AN URBAN AND INDUSTRIAL SETTING
        Doct. St. Ranchi U., 1969

3297   Ghurye, G.S.

        ANATOMY OF A RURURBAN COMMUNITY
        Bombay, Popular Prakashan, 1963

3298   Ghurye, G.S.

        CITIES OF INDIA
        Sociol. B. V 2, May 1953, p 47-71

3299   Ghurye, G.S.

        PROLEGOMENA TO TOWN AND COUNTRY PLANNING
        Sociol. B. 1960, 9, 2, Sep, 73-91
        SA, XI, 6, A6543

3300   Ghurye, G.S.

        CITIES AND CIVILIZATION
        New York, Humanities, 1962

3301   Ghurye, G.S.

        BOMBAY, SUBURBANITIES: SOME ASPECTS OF THEIR
        WORKING LIFE (II)
        Sociol. B. 1965, 14, 2, Sep 1-8
        SA, XIV, 5, C1403

3302   Gillion, K.L.

        AHMEDABAD: A STUDY IN INDIAN URBAN HISTORY
        Berkeley, U. of Calif. Press, 1968

3303   Gist, N.P.

        THE ECOLOGICAL STRUCTURE OF AN ASIAN CITY: AN
        EAST-WEST COMPARISON
        Popul. R. 1958, 2, 1, Jan, 17-25
        SA, XII, 5, B1203

3304   Gist, N.P.

THE ECOLOGY OF BANGALORE, INDIA: AN EAST-WEST
COMPARISON
Soc. Forces, 1957, 35, 4, May 356-365
SA, VI, 4, 5035

3305   Gopalkrishan, C.G.

RANKING OF CITIES ACCORDING TO COSTLINESS
Ind. Eco. J. 1968, 15, 5, Apr-Jun, 618-623
SA, XIX, 5, F0803

3306   *Gore, M.S.

IMMIGRANTS AND NEIGHBORHOODS,
Bombay, Tata Institute of Social Sciences, 1970

3307   Guha, M.

CONCENTRATION OF COMMUNITIES IN BURRABAZAR
CALCUTTA
Man in India, 1964, 44, 4, Oct-Dec, 289-297
SA, XIV, 1, B8704

3308   Guha, M.

THE DEFINITION OF AN INDIAN URBAN NEIGHBORHOOD
Man in India, 1966, 46, 1, Jan-Mar, 59-65
SA, XVI, 6, D3489

3309   Guha, S.

SOCIO-ECONOMIC IMPACT OF URBANIZATION
AICC Econ. Rev. 1958, 10, 3, Jun, 16-18
SA, VIII, 2, 7448

3310   Gupta, H.C.

THE SOCIAL CONSEQUENCES OF INDUSTRIALISATION AND
URBANISATION IN FARIDABAD (PH.D.)
Doct. St. Agra U., 1969
(Dr. B. R. Chauhan)

3311   Gupta, R.P.

A SOCIOLOGICAL STUDY OF INDIAN METHODIST CHRISTIAN
COMMUNITY (METHODIST CHURCH IN SOUTHERN ASIA) IN
UTTAR PRADESH WITH PARTICULAR REFERENCE TO LUCKNOW,
KANPUR, ALLAHABAD, AGRA AND VARANASI
(PH.D.)
Doct., Lucknow U., 1969
(Prof. S.K. Sarah)

3312   Gupta, R.S.

URBAN COMMUNITY DEVELOPMENT IN INDIA: SOME
ADMINISTRATIVE ASPECTS
C.D. Journal, 1970, 5, 2, Apr, 94-97
SA, XX, 7, F9549

3313   Gupta, S.C. & B.G. Prasad

A NOTE ON THE LIVING AND WORKING CONDITIONS OF THE
SWEEPER COMMUNITY IN LUCKNOW
East. Anthrop. 1965, 18, 3, Sep-Dec, 177-185
SA, XIV, 6, C2403

3314   Harris, Britton

URBAN CENTRALIZATION AND PLANNED DEVELOPMENT
in India's Urban Future
ed. R. Turner
Berkeley, U. of Calif. Press, 1962, p. 261-277

3315   Hirt, H.F.

SPATIAL ASPECTS OF THE HOUSING PROBLEM IN ALIGARH
Popul. R. 1958, 2, 1, Jan., 37-45
SA, XII, 5, B1205

3316   Hoselitz, B.F.

URBANIZATION IN INDIA
Kyklos, 1960, 13, 3, 361-370
SA, XII, 8, B3645

3317   Hoselitz, Bert F.

THE ROLE OF URBANIZATION IN ECONOMIC DEVELOPMENT:
SOME INTERNATIONAL COMPARISONS
in India's Urban Future
ed. R. Turner
Berkeley; U. of Calif. Press, 1962, p 157-182

3318   Hoselitz, Bert F.

A SURVEY OF LITERATURE ON URBANIZATION IN INDIA
in India's Urban Future
ed R. Turner
Berkeley, Calif. U. Press, 1962, p 425-444

3319   India, Ministry of Home Affairs

AN APPROACH TO URBAN CITIES IN INDIA
Delhi, 1972

3320   Iyer, P.N.

ECONOMY AND SOCIETY AMONG THE ARTISAN OF SADAR SUB-
DIVISION OF RANCHI DISTRICT
Doct. St. Delhi U., 1969
(M.S.A. RAO)

3321   Jakobson, L.

URBANIZATION AND REGIONAL PLANNING IN INDIA
Urban Affairs Quart, 1967, 2, 3, Mar, 36-35
SA, SVI, 2, D0162

3322   Jethwa, P.S.

BHIL COMMUNITY OF RAJKOT   (PH.D.)
Doct., Gujarat U., 1963
(Prof. (Miss) T.N. Patel)

3323   Joshi, P.

TRADITION, VIE URBANE ET VIE RURALE DANS L'INDE DU
NORD. ETUDE COMPARATIVE DE QUELQUES ATTITUDES DANS
L'UTTAR-PRADESH (TRADITION, URBAN LIFE AND RURAL LIFE
IN NORTH INDIA.   COMPARATIVE STUDY OF ATTITUDES IN UTTAR
PRADESH) (Fr.)
R. Franc. Sociol., 1966, 7, 4, Oct-Dec, 485-490
SA, XV, 5, C6706

3324   Joshi, V.H.

SOCIAL CONSEQUENCES OF INDUSTRIALISATION AND URBANISA-
TION IN A VILLAGE IN SOUTH GUJARAT WITH SPECIAL REFERENCE
TO TENSIONS BETWEEN GROUPS AND CLASSES   (PH.D.)
Doct., Maharaja Sayajraao, U. of Baroda, 1962
(Dr. I. P. Desai)

3325   Kaldate, S.

URBANIZATION AND DISINTEGRATION OF RURAL JOINT FAMILY
·Sociol. B. 1962, 11, 1-2, Mar-Sep, 103-111
SA, XI, 7, A7351

3326   Kapadia, K.M.

THE GROWTH OF TOWNSHIPS IN SOUTH GUJARAT
Sociol. B. 1969, 10, 2, Sep, 69-87
SA, XI, 6, A6548

3327   Kapadia, K.M.

INDUSTRIAL EVOLUTION OF NAVSARI
Social. B. 1966, 15, 1, Mar, 1-24
SA, XIV, 6, C2409

3328   Kapoor, S.

       FAMILY AND URBANIZATION: A STUDY OF TWO SOCIAL GROUPS
       IN AN URBAN SETTING
       Doct. St., Delhi U., 1969
       (K.A. Uma)

3329   Karimi, S.M.

       URBANIZATION OF BIHAR PLAINS   (PH.D.)
       Doct. Aligarh Muslim U, 1967
       (Prof. M. Shafi)

3330   Karkal, G.L.

       PROBLEMS OF URBAN HOUSING AND SLUMS
       Ind. J. Soc. Wrk., 1970, 31, 1, Apr, 35-41
       SA, XX, 1-2, F3986

3331   Kesavaiyegar, S.

       A SOCIO-ECONOMIC SURVEY OF HYDERABAD-SECUNDERBAD   CITY
       AREA
       Hyderabad;   The Indian Institute of Economics, 1952,
       390 pp

3332   Khan, N.G.

       A SOCIO-ECONOMIC SURVEY OF THE MUSLIMS OF POONA
       (PH.D.)
       Doct., Bombay, U., 1952
       (Prof. D.R. Gadgil)

3333   Khandelkar, M.

       SOCIAL HOUSING IN INDIA WITH PARTICULAR REFERENCE TO
       INDUSTRIAL HOUSING
       Ind. J. Soc. Wrk. 1970, 31, 3, Oct., 229-242
       SA, XX, 6, F8513

3334   Kandekar, M.

LEVELS OF DEVELOPMENT AND HOUSING IN MAHARASHTRA
Ind. J. Soc. Wrk., 1971, 31, 4, Jan, 417-429
SA, XX, 6, F8512

3335   Koenigsherger, O.H.

NEW TOWNS IN INDIA
Town Planning Review, V. 23, July, 1952, pp 94-132

3336   Kolb, William L.

THE SOCIAL STRUCTURE AND FUNCITON OF CITIES
Econ. Develop. & Cult. Change 1954, 3, 1, Oct, 30-46
SA, Vol III, #2, 1263

3337   Krishna, R.

A SOCIOLOGICAL STUDY OF THE GROWTH OF A NEW INDUSTRIAL
TOWN (PH.D.)
Doct. St., Agra U., 1969
(R.N. Saxena)

3338   Kulkarni, M.R.

SMAL INDUSTRY IN TWO BIG CITIES: DELHI AND BOMBAY
Indian Eco. J. 1965, 12, 4, Apr-Jun, 452-458
SA, XVII, 1, D5264

3339   Lakdawala, D.T.

AN ENQUIRY INTO THE CONDITIONS OF THE REFUGEES IN
BOMBAY CITY
J. Univ. Bombay, 20, 4, Jan 1952, 62-69

3340   Lakdawala, D.T.

BOMBAY SURVEY
Regional Seminar on Research Techniques of Social
Research, Delhi, UNESCO Res. Center, 1959, 122-24

3341   Lal, S.K.

URBAN ELITE   (PH.D.)
Doct., Jodhpur U., 1968
(Dr. Indra Deva)

3342   Mohan, R.P.

URBANIZATION: CASE STUDY OF A VILLAGE IN UTTAR PRADESH
Jour. of Soc. Res., 1967, 10, 1, Mar, 14-17
SA, SVI, 5, D2656

3343   Majumdar, D.N.

SOCIAL CONTOURS OF AN INDISTRIAL CITY
Bombay; Asia Publ House, 1960

3344   Malhotra, P.C.

SOCIO-ECONOMIC SURVEY OF BHOPAL CITY AND BAIREGARH
New York, Asia, Publ, House, 1964, 404 pp

3345   Mathur, B.P.

A SOCIO-ECONOMIC STUDY OF URBAN MIDDLE CLASSES
(BASED ON A SURVEY SAMPLE OF KAVAL TOWNS)   (PH.D.)
Doct., Agra U., 1962

3346   Mayer, Albert

SOME OPERATIONAL PROBLEMS IN URBAN AND REGIONAL
PLANNING AND DEVELOPMENT
in India's Urban Future
ed. R. Turner, Berkeley, Calif. U. Press
1962, p. 397-413

3347   Mayer, Albert

NATIONAL IMPLICATIONS OF URBAN-REGIONAL PLANNING
in India's Urban Future
ed. R. Turner
Berkeley: U. of Calif. Press, 1962, p 335-347

3348   Mehta, Asoka

THE FUTURE OF INDIAN CITIES: NATIONAL ISSUES AND
GOALS
in India's Urban Future
ed   R. Turner
Berkeley, Calif U. Press, 1962 p 413-425

3349   Mehta, S.K.

PATTERNS OF RESIDENCE IN POONA (INDIA) BY INCOME,
EDUCATION, AND OCCUPATION (1937-1965)
Amer. Jour. of Sociol. 1968; 73, 4, Jan, 496-508
SA, XVI, 6, D3498

3350   Meier, Richard L.

RELATIONS OF TECHNOLOGY TO THE DESIGN OF VERY
LARGE CITIES
in India's Urban Future
ed. R. Turner
Berkeley; U. of Calif. Press, 1962, p 299-327

3351   Menon, V.K.

INDIA'S REPORT ON CITY ADMINISTRATION AND CITIZEN'S
PARTICIPATION
Europa R., 1962, 2, 1, Jun, 105-108
SA, XIII, 1, B4507

3352   Misra, J.

STRUCTURE OF URBANIZATION IN INDIA, 1961
(PH.D. in SOC.)
University of Chicago, 1969-70

3353   Misra, J.P.

INTELLEGINTSIA OF A METROPOLIS: THE WAY OF LIFE AND
OUTLOOK OF EDUCATED WORKERS IN THE CITY OF LUCKNOW
Doct. St. Lucknow U., 1969

3354   *Misra, P.K.

NOMADS IN A CITY SETTING,
Man in India, 1971, 51, 4, Oct-Dec, 317-333
SA, 21, 73G3468

3355   *Mishra, V.M.

COMMUNICATION AND MODERNIZATION IN URBAN SLUMS
New York, Asia, 1972

3356   Mody, (Miss) M.S.H.

WORLI: A STUDY IN CITY DEVELOPMENT   (PH.D.)
Doct., Bombay U., 1951
(Dr. N.A. Thoothi)

3357   Mohsin, M

SOCIO-ECOLOGICAL STUDY OF A WORKSHOP TOWN, WITH
PARTICULAR REFERENCE TO CHITTARANJAN, (PH.D.)
Doct, Bombay U., 1963
(Prof. G.S. Ghurye)

3358   Mohsin, M.

CHITTARANJAN: A STUDY IN URBAN SOCIOLOGY
New York, Humanities,1964

3359   Mohsin, M.

THE TENOR OF INDIAN URBANISM: WITH PARTICULAR
REFERENCE TO CHITTARANJAN
Sociol. B. 1963, 12, 2, Sep, 50-65
SA, XII, 8, B3651

3360   Mukherjee, R.

URBANIZATION AND SOCIAL TRANSFORMATION IN INDIA
Int. J. Comp. Sociol. 1963, 4, 2, Sep, 178-210
SA, XII, 8, B3652

3361   Mythile, (Miss) K.L.

A SOCIO-ECOLOGICAL STUDY ON AN IMMIGRANT COMMUNITY
(PH.D.)
Doct., Bombay U, 1959
(Prof. G. S. Ghurye)

3362   Naqui, H.K.

URBANIZATION AND URBAN CENSUS UNDER THE GREAT
MUGHALS
Simla, 1971

3363   Nav Nihar, Singh

THE URBAN HOUSING PROBLEM IN POST-WAR PERIOD IN
WESTERN U.P. (PH.D.)
Doct., Agra U., 1965

3364   Nayak, P.R.

THE CHALLENGE OF URBAN GROWTH TO INDIAN LOCAL
GOVERNMENT
in Indian's Urban Future
ed. R. Turner
Berkeley; U. of Calif. Press, 1962,. p. 361-382

3365   Neurath, P.

ON INTRODUCING INNOVATIONS IN AN URBAN SETTING
Mens en Maatschappij, 1968, 43, 1, jan-Feb. 127-139
SA, XVII, 2, D6201

3366   Nigam (Miss) M.

WORKING WOMEN IN INDIAN CITIES--A SOCIOLOGICAL STUDY
OF THEIR ATTITUDES AND THEIR WAY OF LIFE
Doct. St., Agra U., 1969
(R. N. Saksena)

3367   Pandey, V.K.

URBAN GROWTH AND SOCIAL CHANGE IN EASTERN U.P.
Gorakhpur U, 1969
(S.P. Nagendra)

3368   Pandeya, P.

IMPACT OF INDUSTRIALISATION ON URBAN GROWTH:
A CASE STUDY OF CHHOTANAGPUR
Allahabad, Central Book Depot, 1970, p 258

3369   Pant, Pitambar

URBANIZATION AND THE LONG RANGE STRATEGY OF ECONOMIC
DEVELOPMENT
in India's Urban Future
ed. R. Turner
Berkeley; U. of Calif. Press, 1962, p. 182-192

3370   Park, Richard L.

THE URBAN CHALLENGE TO LOCAL AND STATE GOVERNMENT:
WEST BENGAL, WITH SPECIAL ATTENTION TO CALCUTTA
in India's Urban Future
ed. R. Turner
Berkeley; U. of Calif Press, 1962, p. 382-397

3371   Patel, F.K.

POONA, A SOCIOLOGICAL STUDY   (PH.D.)
Doct., Poona U., 1955
(Dr. (Mrs.) I. Karve)

3372   Patel, S.D.

PATTERNS OF URBAN DEVELOPMENT IN SOUTH GUJARAT
(PH.D.)
Doct., Bombay U., 1965,
(Prof. K.M. Kapadia)

3373   Pethe, V.P.

ECONOMIC FUNCTTONS OF THE CITIES OF INDIA
Sociol. B. 1965, 14, 1, Mar, 1-12
SA, XIV, 4, C0517

3374   Pothen, K.P.

IMDUSTRIALIZATION AND URBANIZATION
Ind. Sociol. 1961, 3, 4, Mar, 16-24
SA, XIII, L, B4510

3375   Pothen, K.P.

A SOCIO-ECONOMIC SURVEY OF THE CHRISTIAN COMMUNITY IN
MALWA   (PH.D.)
Doct., Vikram U., 1968
(Dr. C.M. Abraham)

3376   Prabhu, P.N.

A STUDY ON THE EFFECTS OF URBANIZATION
in Social Implication of Industrialization and
Urbanization
Calcutta, UNESCO Res. Center, 1956

3377   Prakash, V.

NEW TOWNS IN INDIA
Detroit; The Cellar Book Shop, 1969, x-149 p

3378   Prasad, L.

THE GROWTH OF A SMALL TOWN: A SOCIOLOGICAL ANALYSIS
OF THE FACTORS IN THE GROWTH OF BALLIA
Doct. St., Gorakhpur U., 1969
(S.P. Nagendra)

3379   *Punekar, Vijaya, B.

NEIGHBORHOOD RELATIONS AMONG REGIONAL GROUPS IN INDIA
Sociology and Social Research, 54, 1, Oct., 1969

3380   Pusalker, A.D.

BOMBAY, STORY OF THE ISLAND CITY, BOMBAY: ALL INDIA
ORIENTAL CONFERENCE, 1949, 125 p.

3381   Rajagopalan, C.

THE HOUSING PROBLEM IN BOMBAY
Ind. J. Soc. Wk. 1964, 25, 1, Apr. 59-71
SA, XIII, 2, B5360

3382   Rajagopalan, C.

SUBURBAN ECOLOGY, WITH SPECIAL REFERENCE TO BOMBAY
(PH.D.)
Doct., Bombay U., 196
(Prof. G. Ghurye)

3383   Rajagopalan, C.

BOMBAY: A STUDY IN URBAN DEMOGRAPHY AND ECOLOGY
Sociol. B. 1960, 9, 1, Mar, 16-38
SA, XI, 6, A6556

3384   Rajwade, K.

HOUSING IN INDORE
Ind. Sociol. 1963, 5, 6, Mar, 13-14
SA, XIII, 3-4, B6312

3385   Ramu, G.N.

FAMILY AND CASTE IN A SOUTH INDIAN CITY
(PH.D.- Soc. Family)
University of Illiniois at Urbana-Champaign, 1972

3386   *Rao, M.S.A.

URBANIZATION AND SOCIAL CHANGE: A STUDY OF A RURAL
COMMUNITY ON A METROPOLITAN FRINGE
New Delhi, Orient Longmans, 1970

3387   Redfield, & M. Singer

        THE CULTURAL ROLE OF CITIES
        Eco. Dev. & Cult. Change, 1954, 3, 53-73

3388   Rosenthal, D.B.

        FACTIONS AND ALLIANCES IN INDIAN CITY POLITICS
        Midwest J. of Pol. Sci, 1966, 10, 3, Aug, 32-349
        SA, XVI, 2, D0171

3389   Saksena, (Miss) U.K.

        HOUSING PROBLEM UNDER SECOND FIVE-YEAR PLAN (PH.D.)
        Doct., Agra U., 1962

3390   Sangave, V.A.

        JAIN COMMUNITY: A SOCIAL SURVEY   (PH.D.)
        Doct. Bombay U., 1950
        (Prof. G. S. Ghurye)

3391   Sanikwal, R.C.

        A SOCIOLOGICAL STUDY OF A GROWING TOWN AND ITS RELATION
        TO SURROUNDING AREA: A STUDY OF GHAZIABAD
        Doct. St. Agra U., 1969
        (R.N. Saxena)

3392   Sarupria, S.L.

        ATTITUDES TOWARDS FAMILY PLANNING IN A SMALL URBAN
        COMMUNITY
        Ind. J. Soc. Wrk, 1964, 25, 1, Apr., 79-87
        SA, XIII, 2, B5364

3393   Saxena, (Mrs.) S.

        RECENT TRENDS OF URBANIZATION IN UTTAR PRADESH
        (PH.D.)
        Doct. Agra U., 1967

3394   Saxena, S.

TRENDS OF URBANIZATION IN UTTAR PRADESH
Agra, Satish Book Enterprise, 1970, xii-275 pp

3395   Shekhar, R.

REGIONAL CULTURES IN A METROPOLIS: A PROBLEM OF
COMMUNICATION AND INTEGRATION
Doct., St. Agra, U, 1969
(R.N. Saxena)

3396   Shete, M.K.

COOPERATIVE HOUSING: A CASE STUDY OF MADHYA PRADESH
(PH.D.)
Doct., Saugar U., 1968
(Dr. R.P. Roy)

3397   Siddiqui, M.K.A.

THE SLUMS OF CALCUTTA: A PROBLEM AND ITS SOLUTION
Ind. J. Soc. Wrk. 1968, 29, 2, Jul, 173-182
SA, XVIII, 4, E3294

3398   Siddique, M.M.

SOME ASPECTS OF URBANIZATION IN EAST U.P.
Doct. St. Gorakhpur U., 1969
(S.M. Dubey)

3399   Simmons, R.E.; K. Kent & V.M. Mishra

MEDIA AND DEVELOPMENTAL NEWS IN SLUMS OF ECUADOR AND
INDIA
Journalism Quart. 1968, 45, 4, Win, 698-705
SA, XVII, 7 E0448

3400   Singer, M.

THE GREAT TRADITION IN A METROPOLITAN CENTER: MADRAS
in Traditional India: Structure & Change
ed. M.B. Singer,
Philadelphia; Amer. Folklore Society, 1959, p 141-183

3401   Singh, R.L.

GORAKHPUR: A STUDY IN URBAN MORPHOLOGY
National Geographic Journal of India, v I, Sept, 1953
p 1-10

3402   Singh, T.

ALGUNAS IMPLICACIONES DE RECIENTES TENDENCIAS RURAL-
URBANAS EN LA INDIA (SOME IMPLICATIONS OF RECENT RURAL-
URBAN TENDENCIES IN INDIA)
R. Mexic. Sociol. 1958, 20, 3, Sep-Dec, 713-724
SA, XI, 2&3, A4728

3403   Singh, Tarlok

PROBLEMS OF INTEGRATING RURAL INDUSTRIAL AND URBAN
DEVELOPMENT
in India's Urban Future
ed R. Turner
Berkeley; Calif U. Press, 1962, p 327-335

3404   Sinha, B.

SIRSI: AN URBAN STUDY IN APPLICATION OF RESEARCH
MODELS
Dharwar, Karnatak University, 1970

3405   Sovani, N.V.

URBANIZATION AND URBAN INDIA
Bobmay, Asia, 1972

3406   Spate, O.H.K.

FIVE CITIES OF THE GANGETIC PLAIN: A CROSS-SECTION
OF INDIAN CULTURAL HISTORY
Geographical Review, V40, 1950, p 260-278

3407   Stizower,   S.

THE BENE ISRAEL OF BOMBAY: A STUDY OF JEWISH COMMUNITY
Schocken, 1971, 176 p.

3408   Subbash Chandra

URBAN SOCIAL PARTICIPATION: A COMPARATIVE STUDY OF
THREE RESIDENTIAL AREAS OF KANPUR METROPOLIS   (PH.D.)
Doct., Ind. Inst of Technology, Kanpur
(dr. K.N. Sharma)

3409   Tangri, Shanti

URBANIZATION, POLITICAL STABILITY, AND ECONOMIC GROWTH
in India's Urban Future
ed. R. Turner
Berkeley; U. of Calif Press, 1962, p 192-213

3410   Trivedi, H.R.

THE "SEMI-URBAN POCKET" AS CONCEPT AND REALITY IN INDIA
Human Organ. 1969, 28, 1, Spr 72-77,
SA, XVIII, 1-2-, E1264

3411   Roy Turner (ed.)

INDIA'S URBAN FUTURE
Seminar on Urbanization in India
Berkeley, University of California Press, 1962

3412   Vagale, L.R. et. al.

        FARIDABAD: A CRITICAL STUDY OF THE NEW TOWN
        Urban Rur Plan Thought, 1949, 2, 3, Jul, 84-108
        SA, XII, 5, B1213

3413   Vakil, C.N. and K. Ray

        GROWTH OF CITIES AND THEIR ROLE IN THE DEVELOPMENT
        OF INDIA
        Civilisations, 1965, 15, 3, 326-359
        SA, XVI, 2, D0175

3414   Van Huyck, A.P. & K.C. Rosser

        AN ENVIRONMENTAL APPROACH TO LOW-INCOME HOUSING
        International Development Rev., 1966, 8, 3, Sep, 15-17
        SA, XVII, 2, D6208

3415   Venkatrayappa, K.N.

        SOCIAL ECOLOGY OF PROVINCIAL TOWNS, WITH SPECIAL
        REFERENCE TO BANGALORE   (PH.D.)
        Doct., Bombay U., 1953
        (Prof. G.S. Ghurye)

3416   Venkatarayappa, K.N.

        URBAN LAND VALUE AND LAND UTILIZATION TRENDS IN INDIA
        Sociol. B. 1960, 9, 2, Sep, 34-47
        SA, XI, 6, A6563

3417   Venkatarayappa, K.N.

        SLUMS: A STUDY IN URBAN PROBLEM
        New Delhi, 1972

3418   Verma, B.K.

ANTRHOPOMETRY APPLIED TO ARCHITECTURE AND TOWN
PLANNING
J. of Soc. Res., 1969, 12, 1, Mar, 78-92
SA, XIX, 6, F1742

3419   Verma, (Mrs.) M.

WORKING WOMEN IN METROPOLITION CITY
Doct. St., Agra U., 1969
(R.N. Saxena)

3420   Verman, S.C.

THE STRUCTURE AND COMPOSITION OF URBAN MIDDLE CLASSES
IN THE CITY OF LUCKNOW
Doct. St., Lucknow U., 1969

3421   Vidyarthi, L.P. & R.B. Lal.

CULTURAL CONFIGURATION OF RANCHI: SURVEY OF AN
EMERGING INDUSTRIAL CITY OF TRIBAL INDIA 1960-62
Calcutta, J.N. Basu, Bookland, 1969, X-412 p.

3422   Vidyarthi, L.P.

INDUSTRIALISATION AND URBANIZATION IN TRIBAL AREA
Paper presented at Indian Sociological Conference,
Bombay, 1967

3423   Vyas, N.N.

KHERWARA: A TOWN IN A TRIBAL SETTING
Man in India, 1965, 45, 4, Oct-Dec, 246-301
SA, XVI, 5, D2661

3424   Wiebe, P.D.

SMALL TOWN IN MODERN INDIA
Amer. Doct. Dissert, 1968-1969
University of Kansas, (Soc.)

3425   Wurster, Catherine B.

URBAN LIVING CONDITIONS, OVERHEAD COSTS, AND THE
DEVELOPMENT PATTERN
in. India's Urban Future
ed. R. Turner
Berkeley; U. of Calif. Press, 1962p 277-296

1300   Sociology of the Arts

1330   sociology of language & literature

    3426   Bandyopadhyay, S. & A.D. Ross

            THE ATTITUDES TO AND USE OF ENGLISH BY STUDENTS OF
            THREE DIFFERENT MOTHER TONGUES: Hindi, Kannada,
            and Tamil
            Paper presented at the CSAA Meetings, Winnipeg, 1970

    3427   Bardis, P.D.

            SOCIOLINGUISTIC CONFLICT IN INDIA AND OTHER SOCIETIES
            J. of Soc. Res. 1967, 10, 2, Sep, 51-62
            SA, XVII, 2, D6211

    3428   Barnabas,A.P.

            SANKRITISATION
            Economic Wkly, 1961, 13, 15, 613-618

    3429   Beck, B.E.

            A COMPARISON OF WRITTEN AND ORAL VERSIONS OF A GREAT
            SOUTH INDIAN EPIC
            Paper presented at the 1971 Annual Meeting of the Cdn.
            Sociol. and Anthrop. Assoc.
            SA, XIX, 3, Sup. 16, E9330

    3430   Bhagwat, P.

            THE RIDDLE IN INDIAN LIFE, LOVE AND LITERATURE
            Bombay, 1968

    3431   Bhattacharjee, Mihir

            CREATION OF THE GANGA: JAIN STORY AND ITS PARALLEL
            HINDU STORY
            Folklore, India, 5, 1964

3432   Biswas, D.K.

CONTENT ANALYSIS OF THE MAJOR BENGALI NOVELS
PUBLISHED DURING 1920-1960
(PH.D.)
Doct., Patna U., 1968
Dr. Z. Ahmad (Dept. of Soc.)

3433   Bopegamage, A. & R.N. Kulahalli

SANSKRITIZATION AND SOCIAL CHANGE IN INDIA
Archives, Europeennes de Sociologie, 1971,
12, 1, 123-132
SA, XX, 4, F6423

3434   William Bright

SOCIAL DIALECT AND SEMANTIC STRUCTURE IN SOUTH ASIA
in Structure and Change in Indian Society
ed. B.S. Cohn and M.B. Singer
Chicago; Aldine, 1968, p 455-461

3435   Bright, Wm.

LINGUISTIC CHANGE IN SOME INDIAN CASTE DIALECTS
Int. J. of Amer. Linguistics, 1969, 26, 19-26

3436   Bright, Wm. & A.K. Ramanujan

SOCIAL-LINGUISTIC VARIATION AND LANGUAGE CHANGES
Proceedings of the Ninth International Congress of
Linguistics
The Hague, 1964

3437   Chaudhari, Rama

ANCIENT INDIAN FOLK LITERATURE
Indian Folklore, 1964, 26-28
(Also, in studies in Indian Folk Culture; Indian Pub.,
Calcutta)

3438   Clark, T.W. (ed.)

       NOVEL IN INDIA: ITS BIRTH AND DEVELOPMENT
       Berkeley, U. of Calif. Press, 1970

3439   Coomaraswami, A.K.

       THE BUGBEAR OF LITERACY
       London, 1949

3440   Dasgupta, A.K.

       THE LANGUAGE PROBLEM
       Man in India, 1968, 48, 1, Jan-Mar, 18-28
       SA, XVII, 7, E0457

3441   *Das Gupta, Jyotirindra, & Joshua A. Fishman

       INTER-STATE MIGRATION AND SUBSIDIARY LANGUAGE
       CLAIMING: AN ANALYSIS OF SELECTED INDIAN CENSUS
       DATA
       International Migration Review, 1971, 5, 2,
       Sum, 227-249
       SA, 21, 73G2652

3442   Dasgupta, J.

       LANGUAGE CONFLICT AND NATIONAL DEVELOPMENT:
       GROUP POLITICS AND NATIONAL LANGUAGE POLICY IN INDIA
       Berkeley; U. of Calif. Press, 1970

3443   Derrett, M.E.

       THE MODERN INDIAN NOVEL IN ENGLISH.   A COMPARATIVE
       APPROACH
       Bruxelles, Belgium: Universite Libre de Bruxelles
       Institut de Sociologie, Collection du Centre d'Etide
       du Sud-Est Asiatique, No. 3, 1966, 195 pp
       SA, XV, 2, C4436

3444   Deva, Indra

THE SOCIOLOGY OF BHOJPURI FOLD-LITERATURE: EASTERN
U.P. AND WEST. BIHAR
Doct., Lucknow .U., 1953

3445   Dumont, L.

LE VOCABULAIRE DE PARENTE DANS L'IND DU NORD
(KINSHIP VOCABULARY IN NORTHERN INDIA)
L'Homme, 1962, 2, 2, May-Aug, 5-48
SA, XII, 4, B0245

3446   Friedrich, P.

LANGUAGE AND POLITICS IN INDIA
Daedalus, 1962, 91- 3, Sum, 543-559
SA, XIII, 2, B5371

3447   Fromm, Erich

THE FORGOTTEN LANGUAGE
New York, 1951

3448   Gould, H.H.

SANSKRITISATION AND WESTERNIZATION: A DYNAMIC VIEW
Eco. Weekly, 1961, 13, 25, 245-50

3449   Goswami, Prafulladatta

FOLK LITERATURE OF ASSAM
Gouhati, 1954

3450   Gumperz, J.J.

DIALECT DIFFERENCES AND SOCIAL STRATIFICATION IN A
NORTH INDIAN VILLAGE
Amer. Anthrop, 1958, 60, 4, Aug, 668-682
SA, IX, 2, 9615

3451   Harrison, S.S.

        LEADERSHIP AND LANGUAGE POLICY IN INDIA
        in Leadership and Political Institutions In India
        ed R.L. Park & I. Tinker
        New York, Greenwood Press, 1969, p 151-167

3452   Ishwaran, K.

        MULTILINGUALISM IN INDIA
        in Studies in Multilingualism
        ed. Nels Anderson
        Leiden: E.J. Brill, 1969, p 122-150

3453   Jamil, M.

        INDIAN AND PAKISTANI WRITERS OF ENGLISH FICTION
        University Studies, 1964, 1, 1, Apr, 61-68
        SA, XVI, D1017

3454   Kalia, S.L.

        SASKRITISATION AND TRIBALISATION
        Bulletin of the Tribal Research Inst. (India)
        April, 1959, 33-43
        also in T.B. Naik (ed.) Changing Tribe
        Chindwara, Tribal Res. Inst. 1961

3455   Kloss, H.

        PROBLEMES LINGUISTIQUES DES INDES ET DE LEURS MINORITES
        (LINGUISTIC PROBLEMS OF THE INDIANS AND OF THEIR
        MINORITIES)
        R. Psychol. Peuples, 1966, 21, 3, Oct, 310-348 (Fr.)
        SA, XV, 6, C7591

3456   Kumar, D.

        LE PROBLEME LINGUISTIQUE EN INDE
        (THE LINQUISTIC PROBLEM IN INDIA)
        Anal. Prev. 1967, 3, 3, Mar, 213-220 (Fr.)
        SA, XV, 7, C8498

3457   Kunte, (Miss) U.Y.

IDEA OF REBIRTH: A SURVEY THROUGH THE MAIN STREAM
OF SANSKRIT LITERATURE (PH.D.)
Doct., Poona U., 1964
(Dr. (Mrs.) I. Karve)

3458   Lafont, P.

LE PROBLEM DE L'HINDI VU DU SUD DE L'INDE
(THE PROBLEM OF HINDI SEEN IN SOUTH INDIA)
R. Psychol. Peuples, 1966, 21, 4, Dec, 423-429
(Fr.)
SA, XV, 6, C7592

3459   Lal, P.

INDIAN WRITING IN ENGLISH
Harvard Educ. R. 1964, 34, 2, Spr, 316-319
SA, XII, 8, B3674

3460   Majumdar, D.N. (Jr.)

A STUDY OF SANKRITISATION AMONG THE BADO SPEAKING
TRIBES OF GARO HILLS.
(The Seminar on Tribal Situation in India, Indian Inst.
of Advance Study, Simila, 1969)

3461   Madan, T.N.

KINSHIP TERMS USED BY THE PANDITS OF KASHMIR:
A PRELIMINARY ANALYSIS
Eastern Anthropologist , V 7, 1953

3462   Malik, B.

LANGUAGE OF THE UNDER WORLD OF WEST BENGAL
Calcutta, 1972

3463   Naik, T.B.

SOME NOVELS THAT SHOULD INTEREST THE SOCIAL SCIENTIST
Lecture delivered before the Anthrop. Seminar, Utkal U,
1970

3464   Ranganathan, A.

THE LANGUAGE CRISIS IN INDIA
Civilisations, 1965, 15, 4, 534-541
SA, XVI, 2, D0190

3465   Rao, M.S.A.

SANKRITISATION AMONG THE TIYAS OF NORTH MALABAR
in B. Ratnam (ed.) Anthropology on the March
Madras, Soc. Sci. Assoc, 1963, p 320-324

3466   Roy, G.

CHARACTERISTIC FEATURES OF KONDH KINSHIP TERMINOLOGY
Eastern, Antrhop. V.3, 1950, p 151-157

3467   Sahay, K.N.

TRENDS OF SANSKRITISATION AMONG THE ORAON
B. of Bihar Tribal Res. Inst., 1962, 4, 2,

3468   Sen, Sukumar

FOLKLORE & BENGALI LITERATURE
Indian Folklore, 1956, 1, 44-49

3469   Shah, (Miss) N.S.

SOCIAL IDEALISM AND REALISM IN GUJARAT AS REFLECTED
IN GUJARATI LITERATURE   (PH.D.)
Doct., Bombay U., 1964, (Prof K.M. Kapadia)

3470   Srivastava, S.K.

THE PROCESS OF DE-SANKRITISATION IN VILLAGE INDIA
in. Antrhopology on the March
ed. B. Ratnam
Madras, Soc. Sci. Assoc. 1963, p 263-267

3471   Staal, J.K.

SANSKRIT AND SANKRITISATION
J. of Asian Studies, 1963, 22

3472   Tyler, S.A.

KOYA LANGUAGE MORPHOLOGY AND PATTERNS OF KINSHIP
BEHAVIOUR
Amer. Antrhop 1965, 67, 6, Part I, Dec, 1428-1440
SA, XIV, 6, C2432

3473   Tyler, Stephen, A.

KOYA: AN OUTLINE GRAMMAR
Berkeley, U. of Calif Press, 1969

3474   Uribe Villegas,O.

EL PROBLEMA SOCIOLINGUISTICO EN ENDIA
(THE SOCIOLINGUISTIC PROBLEM OF INDIA)
Revista Mexicana de Sociologia, 1968, 39, 2, Apr-Jun,
153-370, (Sp.)
SA, XVIII, 1-2, E1282

3475   Van Buitenen, J.A.B.

TALES OF ANCIENT INDIA
U. of Chicago Press, 1959

3476   Vidyarthi, L.P.

THE CULTURAL LINGUISTIC REGIONS OF INDIAN FOLKLORE
Indian Folklore, 1959, 2, 182-195

3477   Wilkinson, T.S.

THE FUNCTIONAL SIGNIFICANCE OF GHOTUL NOMENCLATURE
in. Anthropology on the March
ed. Balaratnam
Madras, Soc. Sci, Assocl, 1953, p 315-319

3478

LANGUAGE AND SOCIETY IN INDIA
Indian Instit. of Advanced Study
Transactions, No. 8, 1969

3479

MYTHS OF MIDDLE INDIA
Bombay, Oxford University Press, 1949, 532 p

1331   sociology of art (creative and performing)

3480   Adhikari (Mrs.) K.

SOCIOLOGICAL THOUGHT IN RECENT AESTHETICS: A SOCIO-
PSYCHOLOGICAL ANALYSIS   (PH.D.)
Doct., Lucknow U., 1960
(Prof. K. Prasad)

3481   Desai, (Mrs.) D.J.

SOCIAL BACKGROUND OF SEXUAL REPRESENTATION ON
MEDIEVAL HINDU TEMPLES (PH.D.)
Doct., Bombay U., 1970
(Prof. G.S. Ghurye)

3482   Deva, Indra

MODERN SOCIAL FORCES IN INDIAN FOLK-SONGS
Diogenes, 15, 1956

3483   Elwin, V.

TRIBAL ART FACES EXTINCTION
Illustrated Wkly of India, Sept. 14, 1952

3484   Fisher, A.J.

THE ALL INDIA HANDICRAFTS BOARD AND THE DEVELOPMENT
OF HANDICRAFTS IN INDIA   (PH.D. SOC.)
Syracuse U., 1972

3485   Kotal, (Mrs.) S.C.

INDIAN MUSIC AND ITS SOCIAL BEARINGS   (PH.D.)
Doct., Bombay U., 1950
(Dr. N.A. Thoothi)

3486   Maury, C.

FOLK ORIGINS OF INDIAN ART
New York: Columbia U. Press, 1969, 245 p

3487   Mehta, R.C.

VALUE OF FOLK-MUSIC
in Studies in Indian Folk Culture
ed S.S. Gupta & K.P. Upadhyaya
Calcutta, Indian Publications, 1964

3488   Mukerjee, R.

THE SOCIAL FUNCTIONS OF ART: SOCIAL STRUCTURE OF
VALUES
New York, MacMillan, 1948

3489   Poovalah, (Miss) S.C.

        THE ART AND SCIENCE OF INDIAN CLASSICAL DANCING AND
        ITS SOCIAL BEARING (PH.D.)
        Doct., Bombay U., 1951
        (Dr. N.A. Thothi)

3490   Saran, A.K.

        ART AND RITUAL AS METHODS OF SOCIAL CONTROL AND
        PLANNING
        Ethics, 1952-1953, 13

3491   Tewari, (Mrs.) G.R.

        SOCIAL IMPLICATIONS OF TRIBAL ARTS   (PH.D.)
        Doct, Agra U., 1963

3492   Virian, D'Souza, S.

        TRIBAL DANCE IN INDIA
        Doct. St., Bombay U., 1969
        (Dr. J.V. Ferriera)

1400   Sociology of Education

1432   sociology of education

   3493   Agarhar, A.J.

           SOCIAL BACKGROUND OF PHYSICAL EDUCATION WITH SPECIAL
           REFERENCE TO THE FOLK DANCES OF MAHARASHTRA--FOLK
           DANCE AND PHYSICAL EDUCATION   (PH.D.)
           Doct., Bombay U., 1947
           (Prof. G.S. Ghurye)

   3494   Aggarwal, J.C.

           PROGRESS OF EDUCATION IN FREE INDIA: CURRENT PROBLEMS
           OF INDIAN EDUCATION
           New Delhi; Arya Book Depot, 1966, vii-555 p

   3495   Aggarwal, J.C.

           EDUCATIONAL ADMINISTRATION: SCHOOL ORGANIZATION AND
           SUPERVISION
           Delhi, Arya Book Depot,   1967, viii-548 pp

   3496   Ahmad, S.M.F.

           EDUCATION AND SOCIAL CHANGE AMONG MUNDA TRIBE OF
           RANCHI DISTRICT
           Doct. St., Ranchi, U., 1969

   3497   *All India Report

           FIELD STUDIES IN THE SOCIOLOGY OF EDUCATION
           Bombay, New Jack Printing, 1972

   3498   *Altbach, Phillip G.

           BOMBAY COLLEGES
           Minerva, 1970, 8, 4, 520-541
           SA, 21, 73G1012

3499   Altbach, P.G.

THE TRANSFORMATION OF THE INDIAN STUDENT MOVEMENT
Asian Surv. 1966, 6, 8, Aug, 448-460
SA, XVI, 1, C9311

3500   Altbach, P.G.

STUDENT POLITICS AND HIGHER EDUCATION IN INDIA
Daedalus, 1968, 97, 1, Win, 254-273
SA, XVII, 2, D6228

3501   Altbach, P.G.

PROBLEMS OF UNIVERSITY REFORM IN INDIA
Comp. Educ. Rev., 16, 2, Jun 1972

3502   Albornoz, O.

LA EDUCACION SUPERIOR EN INDIA Y EN VENEZUELA
(HIGHER EDUCATION IN INDIA AND IN VENEZUELA)
Cicncias Sociales, 1967, 3, 1, Mar, 80-112 (Sp.)
XA, XVI, 7, D4445

3503   Ambasth, N.K.

A CRITICAL STUDY OF TRIBAL EDUCATION   (PH.D)
Doct., Ranchi U., 1966
(Prof. L. P. Vidyarthi)

3504   Ambasth, N.K.

A CRITICAL STUDY OF TRIBAL EDUCATION (RANCHI DISTRICT)
Doct. St., Ranchi U., 1969

3505   Anjaneyulu, B.S.R.

A STUDY OF JOB SATISFACTION IN SECONDARY SCHOOL TEACHERS
AND ITS IMPACT ON THE EDUCATION OF PUPILS, WITH SEPCIAL
REFERENCE TO THE STATE OF ANDHRA PRADESH   (PH.D.)
Doct., M.S.U. of Baroda, 1970
(dr. S.M. Divekar)

3506   Awasthi, D.

PROFESSIONAL AND TECHNICAL EDUCATION IN THE UNITED
PROVINCES
Int. R. Hist. Polit. Sci, 1965, 2, 2, Dec, 74-78
SA, XV, 4, C5978

3507   Bannerji, S.K.

SOME DIFFERENTIAL EFFECT ON PRIMARY EDUCATION OF THE
TRIBAL STUDENTS OF WEST BENGAL
B. of the Cult. Res. Inst. 1962, 1, 2, 46-53

3508   Bapat, N.V.M.

TRIBAL EDUCATION ON PROBLEM
Vanyajati, 1961, 2, 1, p 37-39

3509   Bapat, N.V.M.

A FEW THOUGHTS ON TRIBAL EDUCATION
Vanyajati, 1964, 12, 4, p 190-194

3510   Bastedo, T.G.

LAW COLLEGES AND LAW STUDENTS IN BIHAR
Law and Society Review 1968-1969, 3, 2-3, Nov-Feb,
269-294
SA, XVIII, 4, E3321

3511   Basu, M.N.

THE ROLE OF ANTHROPOLOGY IN THE EDUCATION OF ABORIGINAL
IN INDIA
Adivasi, 1958, 3, 2, 1-8

3512   Basu, M.N.

SUGGESTIONS FOR THE EDUCATIONAL PLAN OF THE ABORIGINAL
PEOPLE OF INDIA
Vanyajati, 1961, 9, 3, 123-126

3513   Basu, M.N.

        ANTHROPOLOGY IN TRIBAL EDUCATION
        B. of the Cult. Res. Inst., 1963, 2, 1, 22-27

3514   Basu, M.N.; B.B. Ghosh & M.K. Chowdhuri

        LEVEL OF TRIBAL LITERACY IN INDIA
        Society & Cult. 1970, 1, 1, Jul, 71-80
        SA, XX, 7, F9928

3515   Behari, R.R.

        EVALUATION OF UNIVERSITY EXAMINATION
        (IN TERMS OF WASTAGE AND ACHIEVEMENT AT THE POST-
        GRADUATE STAGE) (PH.D.)

3516   Belok, M.V.

        SCHOOLBOOKS' IMAGES OF INDIA AND INDIANS--CHANGE AND
        PERMANANCY
        Int. Rev. of Hist. & Poli. Sci., 1968, 5, 1, Feb,
        111-721
        SA, XVII, 3, D7175

3517   Bhattacharya, A.P.

        THE EDUCATIONAL PATTERN AND THE EMPLOYMENT STRUCTURE OF
        MADHYA PRADESH (PH.D.)
        Doct., Saugar U., 1966
        (Prof. J.N. Mishra)

3518   Bhatnager, J.K.

        THE VALUES AND ATTITUDES OF SOME INDIAN AND BRITISH
        STUDENTS
        Race, 1967, 9, 1, Jul, 27-35
        SA, XVI, 6, D3533

3519   Bhogle (Mrs.) S.

ORGANISATION AND PSYCHOLOGICAL CORRELATES OF ACCEPTANCE
OF INNOVATIONS BY HIGH SCHOOLS   (PH.D.)
Doct., Osmania U., 1970
(Dr. E.G. Parameshwaran)

3520   Biswas, P.C.

ANTHROPOLOGY & TRIBAL EDUCATION
Vanyajati, 1965, 3, 2, 81-83

3521   Biswas, P.C.

TRIBAL EDUCATION
Report of the Symposium on Problems of Education of
the Tribal People of India
Delhi, NCERT, 1966,3-5

3522   *Bose, A.B.

PROBLEMS OF EDUCATIONAL DEVELOPMENT OF SCHEDULED TRIBES
Man in India, 1970, 50, 1, Jan-Mar, 26-50
SA, 2, 73G3494

3523   *Bose, A.B.

EDUCATIONAL DEVELOPMENT AMONG SCHEDULED CASTE
Man in India, 1970, 50, 3, Jul-Sept, 209-239
SA, 21, 73G3493

3524   Bose, S.K.

TECHNOLOGICAL INSTITUTES: A NEW DIMENSION IN
EDUCATION IN INDIA
Impact. Sci. Soc. 1965, 15, 3, 187-194
SA, XIV, 7, C3147

3525   Chatterjee, P.K.

THE GROWTH AND DEVELOPMENT OF COMMUNITY ORGANIZATION
EDUCATION IN SCHOOLS OF SOCIAL WORK IN INDIA, 1936-
1969:   AN HISTORICAL ANALYSIS
(PH.D.-SOC. WRK.)
Bryn Maur Coll, 1972

3526   Chattopadhyaya, K.P.

TRIBAL EDUCATON
Man in India, 1953, 23, 1, 1-18

3527   Chattopadhyaya, K.P.

EDUCATION
Adivasi, 1960, 121-125

3528   Chaturvedi, P.P.

ROLE OF APPROVED SCHOOLS IN THE PROTECTION, TREATMENT,
AND REHABILITATION OF DEVIANT AND NEGLECTED CHILDREN
IN U.P.
Doct. St., Lucknow U., 1969

3529   Chaturvedi, S.C.

IMPACT OF SOCIAL EDUCATION ON THE LIFE AND LIVING OF
THE PEOPLE IN BLOCK AREAS   (PH.D.)
Doct., Lucknow U, 1970
(Dr. S. Chandra)

3530   *Chitra, M.N.

HIGHER EDUCATION AND SOCIETY IN MYSORE UNDER BRITISH RULE
Sociological Bulletin, 21, 2, Sept, 1972

3531   Chithra, M.N.

THE SOCIAL BACKGROUND OF SOME UNDER-GRADUATE WOMEN
STUDENTS IN MYSORE CITY   (PH.D.)
Doct., Delhi U., 1970
(Prof. M.S.A. Rao)

3532   Chitnis, S.

EDUCATION AND MODERNIZATION IN INDIA
Paper presented at the 7th World Congress of the
Int. Sociological Assoc., 1970
SA, XVIII, 5, Supp. 9, E3795

3533   Chopra, S.L.

RELATIONSHIP OF CASTE SYSTEM WITH MEASURED INTELLIGENCE
AND ACADEMIC ACHIEVEMENT OF STUDENTS IN INDIA
Soc. Forces, 1966, 44, 4, Jun, 573-576
SA, XIV, 7, C3151

3534   Chopra, S.L.

MEASURED INTELLIGENCE AND ACADEMIC ACHIEVEMENT AS
RELATED TO URBAN-RURAL RESIDENCE
Rural Sociology, 1968, 33, 2, Jun, 214-217
SA, XVII, 3, D7182

3535   Cormack, Margaret, L.

SHE WHO RIDES A PEACOCK: INDIAN STUDENTS AND SOCIAL
CHANGE, A RESEARCH ANALYSIS
Bombay; Asia Publ. House, 1961

3536   Das, A.K., B.B. Ghosh & S.K. Dey

ECONOMIC STATUS OF TRIBAL FAMILY AND ADOPTION OF
MODERN EDUCATION
Society & Cult. 1970, 1, Special Number, 33-42
SA, XX, 17, F9935

3537   Das, N.

GLIMPSES OF ABORIGENES' EDUCATION
Vanyajati, 1958, 6, 3, Jul, 122-129.
SA, VIII, 2, 7552

3538   *Das, M.S.

BRAIN DRAIN CONTROVERSY AND INTERNATIONAL STUDENTS
Lucknow, Lucknow Publishing House, 1972

3539   Das, Man Singh, Donald E. Allen, & F. Gene Acuff

BRAIN DRAIN AND STUDENTS FROM LESS DEVELOPED AND
DEVELOPING COUNTRIES
Paper presented at 7th World Congress of Sociology
1970, Varna, Bulgaria

3540   Dasgupta, N.K.

PROBLEMS OF TRIBAL EDUCATION AND THE SANTALS
New Delhi, Bharatiya Adimjati Sevak Sangh, 1964

3541   Dasgupta, Sujata

RURAL EDUCATION THROUGH RURAL RECONSTRUCTION
Indi. J. Soc. Wrk. 1954, 15, 2, Sep, 100-109
SA, VOL III, #3, 1521

3542   Deo, (Mrs.) K.

TRADITIONALISM TO NON-TRADITIONALISM: A SOCIO-
CULTURAL STUDY OF THE CHANGING NORMS AND VALUES OF
UNIVERSITY STUDENTS OF UJJAIN CITY
196, Doct. St., Indore (Pothen)

3543   Desai, B.G.

SOCIAL BACKGROUND OF HIGH SCHOOL STUDENTS IN BARODA
DISTRICT   (PH.D.)
Doct., Maharaja Sayajrao, U. of Baroda, 1962
(Dr. I.P. Desai)

3544   Desai, I.P.

HIGHT SCHOOL STUDENTS IN POONA
Poona, Deccan College Postgraduate and Research
Institute, Bulletin, 12, 1952, p 271-393

3545   Dholakia, J.L.

WORKERS" EDUCATION IN INDIA: AN APPRAISAL
Vidya, 1964, 7, 2, Aug, 46-54
SA, XIV, 2-3, B9649

3546   *Di Bona, J.E.

CHANGE AND CONFLICT IN THE INDIAN UNIVERSITY
Durham, Duke University, 1969

3547   Doshi, S.L.

THE DESTUDENTISATION OF ALIENATION: A PROBLEM OF
DISTURBED CAMPUS
J. of Soc. Res., 1969, 12, 1, Mar 67-77
SA, XIX, 6, F1755

3548   Dutta, (Miss) M.

MODERNISATION AND EDUCATION: A SOCIOL. STUDY OF
SELECTED GROUPS IN RAJASTHAN
Doct. St., Rajasthan U., 1969

3549   *Eakin, T.C.

STUDENTS AND POLITICS: A COMPARATIVE STUDY
Bombay, Popular, 1972

3550   Gautam, M.L.

STUDENT POLITICS AND HIGHER EDUCATION (SOCIOL. STUDY
OF POLIT. BEHAV. OF UNIV. STUDETNS)
Doct. St. Rajasthan, U., 1969

3551   Gajendragadkar, P.B.

THE MEDIUM OF INSTRUCTION IN INDIAN HIGHER EDUCATION,
THE LANGUAGE QUESTION
Minerva, 1968, 6, 2, Win, 257-262
SA, XVIII, 6, E5080

3552   *Gandhi, R.S.

SOME CONTRASTS IN THE FOREIGN STUDENT LIFE STYLES
International Journal of Contemporary Sociology,
1972, 9, 1, Jan, 34-43
SA, 21, 73G5828

3553   Gandhi, R.S.

CONFLICT AND COHESION IN AN INDIAN STUDENT COMMUNITY
Hum Org. 1970, 29, 2, Sum, 95-102
SA, XIX, 5, F0853

3554   Gandhi, R.S.

LITTLE INDIA: LOCALISM AND COSMOPOLITANISM IN AN INDIAN
STUDENT COLONY
American Doctoral Dissertations (1966-1967)
Un. of Minnesota (Soc.)

3555   Gargi (Miss)

SOCIAL BACKGROUND, VALUES AND ASPIRATIONS OF STUDENTS
IN AN INDIAN TOWN
Doct. St., Saugar U., 1969

3556   George, E.I., R.G. Pillay & K.S. Nair

A STUDY OF OCCUPATIONAL CHOICES AND VALUES OF HIGH
SCHOOL PUPILS
Ind. J. of Soc. Wrk, 1967, 28, 2, Jul, 213-220
SA, XVII, 2, D6246

3557   Ghatage, A.V.

PRIMARY EDUCATION IN POONA CITY AREA AND ITS BACKGROUND
Doct. St., Poona U., 1969

3558   Ghildyal, S.

INNOVATIONS IN EDUCATIONAL METHODOLOGY
Behavioural Sciencest C.D., 1967, 1, 2, Sep, 114-134
SA, XVIII, 7, E6184

3559   Ghosh, S.K.

EDUCATION AND SOCIAL CHANGE, NEFA
J. of Soc. Res., 1969, 12, 1, Mar, 27-37
SA, XIX, 6, F1761

3560   Gist, N.P.

EDUCATIONAL DIFFERENTIALS IN SOUTH INDIA
J. Educ. Sociol., 1955, 28, 7, Mar, 315-324
SA Vol IV #3, 2565

3561   Gore, M.S.; Desai, I.P. & Suma Chitnis (eds.)

        PAPERS IN THE SOCIOLOGY OF EDUCATION IN INDIA
        New Delhi, N.C.E.R.T., 1967

3562   Gosal, G.S.

        LITERACY IN INDIA: AN INTERPRETATIVE STUDY
        Rur. Sociol. 1964, 29, 3, Sep, 261-277
        SA, XII, 1, B4544

3563   Govil (Miss) M.

        CHANGING SOCIAL ATTITUDES AND BEHAVIOUR PATTERNS
        AMONG THE POST-GRADUATE STUDENTS IN UTTAR PRADESH
        (PH.D.)
        Doct. Agra U., 1967

3564   Grimshaw, A.D.

        UNIVERSITY EDUCATION IN INDIA: A TRANS-ATLANTIC VIEW
        J. Univ. Educ. (India), 1963, 2, 1, Sep.,
        SA, XIV, 1, B8744

3565   Gupta, A.K.D.

        REFLECTIONS ON HIGHER EDUCATION IN INDIA IN THE LIGHT
        OF THE ROBBINS REPORT
        Minerva, 1964, 2, 2, Win, 160-168
        SA, XIII, 2, B5397

3566   Gurman, Saran

        IMPACT OF EDUCATION ON THE SOCIAL STRUCTURE OF SOME
        PUNJAB VILLAGES (PH.D.)
        Doct., Panjab U., 1970
        (Dr. V.S. D'Souza)

3567   Hallen, G.C.

EDITORIAL: SOCIOLOGY OF STUDENT UNREST
Ind. Jorn. of Soc. Res. 1966, 7, 2, Aug, i-iv
SA, XVII, 2, D6252

3568   Hans, N.

EXPORTATION OF EDUCATIONAL IDEAS
J. Educ. Sociol. 1956, 29, 7, Mar, 274-281
SA, VOL. VII, 3, 6211

3569   Hooda, S.S.

THE BOMBAY COLLEGION: A STUDY IN SOCIAL BACKGROUND
(PH.D.)
Doct., Bombay U., 1969
(Dr. A.R. Desai)

3570   Hass, Marry R.

THE APPLICATION OF LINGUISTICS TO LANGUAGE TEACHING
in Anthropology Today
ed. A.L. Kroeber
U. of Chicago Press

3571   Hilda, Raj

EDUCATION OF ADIVASIS
East. Anthrop., 1952, 5, 4, 174-178

3572   India (Republic) Ministry of Education

ALL INDIA REPORT OF SOCIAL EDUCATION 1947-1951, Delhi
Gov't. of India, 1953, chi 251

3573   India, University Education Commission

REPORT DECEMBER 1948 -- AUGUST 1949
Delhi: Manager of publication, 1949

3574   Kahave, R.

HIGHER EDUCATION AND INTEGRATIVE ENTREPRENEURSHIP:
THE CASE OF INDIA
(PH.D. IN SOC.)
U. of Calif, Berkeley, 1970-1971

3575   Kahkar, N.K.

WORKER'S EDUCATION IN INDIA (PH.D.)
Doct. Agra. U., 1967

3576   Kapadia, K.M.

PROGRESS OF EDUCATION IN NAVSARI TALUKA
Sociol. B. 1959, 8, 1, Mar, 16-68
SA, XI, 6, A6783

3577   Kar, L.N.

PATTERN OF TRIBAL EDUCATION: A PSYCHOLOGICAL APPROACH
J. of the U. of Gauhati, 1957, 8, 59-72

3578   Kar, L.N.

THE ROLE OF TEACHERS IN A TRIBAL COMMUNITY
J. of U. of Gauhati, 1962, 13, 1, 57-63

3579   Karve, D.D.

THE UNIVERSITIES AND THE PUBLIC IN INDIA
Minerva, 1963, 1, 3, Spr, 263-284
SA, XII, 8, B3710

3580   Karve, Irawati

SOCIAL EDUCATION OF SCHEDULED TRIBES
Vanyajati, 1957, 5, 4,

3581   Kaul, S.K.

        EXISTING FACILITIES, COVERAGE, WASTAGE, STAGNATION AND
        UTILISATION OF FINANCIAL ASSISTANCE IN RESPECT OF
        TRIBAL EDUCATION
        in Tribal Education In India
        New Delhi, N.C.E.R.T. 1967

3582   Kopikar, G.K.

        THE EDUCATION OF THE ADIVASIS
        New Delhi, Manager of Publications
        Gov't. of India, 1956

3583   King, E.J.

        OTHER SCHOOLS AND OURS
        New York, Holt, Rinehart & Co. 1958
        SA, VII, 3, 6212

3584   Leuwa, K.K.

        SOCIAL EDUCATION: THE SHEET ANCHOR OF TRIBAL WELFARE
        Report of the Fourth Conference for Tribes and Tribal
        Areas
        New Delhi, 1967, 73-74

3585   Madan, T.N.

        EDUCATION OF TRIBAL INDIA
        Eastern Anthrop., 1952, 5, 4, 179-182

3586   Mahapatra, L,K.

        EDUCATION OLD & NEW
        Orissa Tribes Res. J.,
        (Inaugural #), 1955, 23-33

3587   Mahapatra, L.K.

        CURRICULA METHODS AND TEXT-BOOKS IN TRIBAL EDUCATION
        Tribal Education in India, New Delhi, N.C.E.R.T.,
        1967, 109-120

3588   Mallick, A.K.

        A STUDY OF SOCIO-ECONOMIC CONDITIONS OF REFUGEE STUDENTS
        Ind. J. Soc. Wrk., 1962, Apr. 23, 1, 31-34
        SA, XII, 1, A8412

3589   Mani, R.S.; Raja, K.C.R. & Subramanian, R.

        GANDHIGRAM RURAL INSTITUTE AND STUDENTS
        Ind. J. Soc. Work, 1961, 22, 2, Sep., 73-75
        SA, XI, 7, A7610

3590   Mehta, (Mrs.) K.

        EFFECTS OF SOCIO-ECONOMIC STATUS ON THE ACHIEVEMENT AND
        BEHAVIOUR OF HIGHER SECONDARY STUDENTS   (PH.D.)
        Doct., Agra, U., 1964

3591   Mehta, R.

        THE WESTERN EDUCATED HINDU WOMAN
        Bombay, Asia Pub., 1970

3592   Morgan, Thomas Bruer

        FRIENDS AND FELLOW STUDENTS
        New York, Crowell, 1956

3593   Mukerji, P.K.

        THE AIM OF TRIBAL EDUCATION
        Vanyajati, 1960, 9, 1, 26-28

3594   Mukerji, P.K.

        THE AIM OF TRIBAL EDUCATION
        Vanyajati, 1960, 9, 1, 26-28

3595   Mukhopadhyay, P.K. and J. Banerjee

        A PSYCHO-SOCIAL SURVEY OF THE PROCESS OF COHESION OF
        THE STUDENTS OF UNDERGRADUATE AND POSTGRADUATE LEVELS
        Ind. J. Soc Wrk., 1961, 22, 2, Sep, 89-95
        SA, XI, 7 A7612

3596   Munjal, B.M.

        A STUDY OF MAJOR SOCIOLOGICAL ASPECTS OF TRUANCY
        AMONG THE MALE COLLEGE-GOING STUDENTS OF INDORE CITY
        Doct. St. Indore, 1969

3597   Mysore, Committee for Education Reform

        REPORT OF THE COMMITTEE FOR EDUCATIONAL REFORM
        Bangalore; the Gov't Press, 1953, 500 pp

3598   Nag, D.S.

        EDUCATION FOR PRIMITIVES
        Vanyajati, 1954, 2, 4, 117-120

3599   Nagpaul, H.

        STUDY OF INDIAN SOCIETY: A SOCIOLOGICAL ANALYSIS OF
        SOCIAL WELFARE AND SOCIAL WORK & EDUCATION
        Verry, 1972

3600   Naik, T.B.

        HOW TO EDUCATE ABORIGINALS
        Ind. J. Soc. Wrk., 1959, 11, 2, 172-180

3601   Naik, T.B.

IMPACT OF EDUCATION ON THE BHILS
New Delhi, Planning Commission, 1969

3602   Naik, J.P.

EDUCATION OF SCHEDULED CASTES AND SCHEDULED TRIBES
Report of the Seminar on Employment of Scheduled
Castes and Scheduled Tribes
New Delhi, Manager of Publications, Gov't. of India
1965

3603   Naik, K.C.

THE SCHOOL & COMMUNITY: BASED ON THE STUDY OF THE
HIGHER SECONDARY SCHOOLS IN SADAR TEHSIL OF BASTI
DISTRICT
Doct. St. Gorakhpur U, 1969
(S.D. Nagendra)

3604   *Nandi, P.K.

TOWARD A MODERN INTELLECTUAL TRADITION: THE CASE
OF INDIA,
in Social Problems in a Changing World: A Comparative
Reader
ed. W.M. Gerson, New York, T.Y. Growell, 1969,
pp 472-480

3605   National Seminar on Tribal Education in India

TRIBAL EDUCATION IN INDIA
New Delhi, National Council of Educational Research
and Training, 1967, 221 pp
SA, XVI, 7, D4470

3606   Nikore, A. & P.N. Singh & M.V. Deshpande

DIFFERENTAIL NEED -- HIERARCHY OF UNIVERSITY STUDENTS:
A CRITICAL STUDY
Ind. J. Soc. Wrk., 1965, 26, 3, Oct., 231-238
SA, XVI, 4, D1872

3607   Narendra, K. & J. Chandiram

EDUCATIONAL TELEVISION IN INDIA
New Delhi, Arya Book Depot, 1967, viii-392 pp

3608   Pakrasi, K.

SOME ASPECTS OF TRIBAL EDUCATION
Vanyajati, 1956, 4, 4, 127-133

3609   Panchmukhi, P.R.

EDUCATIONAL CAPITAL IN INDIA
Indian Eco. J. 1965, 12, 3, Jan-Mar, 306-314
SA, XVII, 1, D5335

3610   Pandey, M.S.

BLOCK EXTENSION EDUCATION: A STUDY OF ROLE PERCEPTION
AND THE UTILIZATION OF THEIR TRAINING
Doct. St., Lucknow U., 1969

3611   Patel, A.S.

SOCIAL BACKGROUND OF THE HIGH SCHOOL STUDENTS IN
KAIRA DISTRICT (PH.D.)
Doct., Maharaja Sayajirao, U. of Barado, 1960
(Dr. I.P. Desai)

3612   Patnaik, N.

EDUCATION IN THE AREA OF BHAUPAL
Man in India, 1954, 34, 1, 20-39

3613   Paul, Gurbachan S.

THE STAY OR RETURN DECISION OF INDIAN STUDENTS (A
SPECIAL CASE OF INTERNATIONAL MIGRATION)
(PH.D. SOC.)
U. of Oregon, 1972

3614   Patnaik, N.

AN APPRAISAL OF ASHRAM SCHOOL EDUCATION
Report of the Fourth Conference of Tribes and Tribal
Areas, 1957

3615   Prasad, N.

PRIMARY EDUCATION AMONG THE ADIVASIS
Vanyajati, 1961, 9, 4, 161-162

3616   *Prasad, S.

MODERN EDUCATION AMONG THE TRIBALS OF BIHAR IN THE
SECOND HALF OF THE 19TH CENTURY
Man in India, 1971, 51, 4, Oct-Dec., 364-393
SA, 21, 73G3519

3617   Puri, B.

RECREATION AND SOCIAL EDUCATION
Verry, 1963

3618   Rahudkar, W.B.

PROBLEMS AND CONCERNS OF AGRICULTURAL COLLEGE STUDIES
Ind. J. of Soc. 1965, 26, 1, Apr, 49-55
SA, XVI, 4, D1877a

3619   ·Rahudkar, W.B.

MORAL NORMS OF AGRICULTURAL COLLEGE STUDENTS
Ind. J. of Soc. Wrk. 1966, 26, 4, Jan 429-431
SA, XVI, 5, D2731

3620   Rama Devi, (Miss) B.

WOMEN'S EDUCATION AND TRADITIONAL VALUES (PH.D.)
Doct., Madras U., 1962
(Dr. G. D. Boaz)

3621   Ramachandran, P.

MODERN--TRADITIONAL SOCIAL VALUES: ANALYTICAL PROCEDURE
Ind. J. Soc. Wrk, 1970, 31, 1, Apr, 63-73
SA, XX, 1-2, F4089

3622   Ram Swarup Pal

A CRITICAL STUDY OF FARMERS' TRAINING AND EDUCATION
PROGRAMME IN RELATION TO THE CHANGES IN THEIR
BEHAVIOURAL COMPONENTS (PH.D.)
Doct., Ind. Agri. Research Inst.,
(Dr. S.N. Singh)

3623   Randev, (Miss) M.

OCCUPATION, EDUCATION AND FAMILY STATUS AMONG TWO
LOWER CLASS GROUPS IN AN URBAN CENTER
Doct. St., Agra U., 1969

3624   Rao, M.S.A.

EDUCATION, SOCIAL STRATIFICATION AND MOBILITY
in Papers on Sociology of Education in India
eds. M.S. Gore, I.P. Desai, & S. Chitnis
Delhi, N.C.E.R.F., 1967, pp 126-146

3625   Rao, S.N.

WORKER'S EDUCATION IN INDIA
Doct. St., Andhra U., 1969
(Prof. M.V. Moorthy)

3626   Ray, N.

ADULT EDUCATION IN INDIA AND ABROAD
Delhi, S. Chand, 1967, viii-1972 pp

3627   Reddy, P.H.

        EDUCATION IN A CROSS-CULTURAL SETTING (PH.D.)
        Doct. Poona U., 1968
        (Dr. Y.B. Damle)

3628   Rettig, S.

        INVARIANCE OF FACTOR STRUCTURE OF ETHICAL
        JUDGEMENTS BY INDIAN AND AMERICAN COLLEGE STUDENTS
        Sociometry, 1964, 27, 1, 96-113
        SA, XII, 5, B1256

3629   Ross, A.D.

        STUDENT UNREST IN INDIA
        Montreal, McGill-Queen's University Press, 1969,
        XIV-301 pp

3630   Ross, Aileen D.

        THE SILENT SUFFERERS: THE LECTURER's ROLE IN STUDENT
        UNREST IN INDIA
        in Institutions and the Person
        ed. H.S. Becker, et al
        Chicago: Aldine Publishing Co. 1968

3631   Roy Burman, B.K.

        A NOTE ON THE PROGRESS OF SECONDARY EDUCATION AMONG
        SCHEDULED CASTES AND SCHEDULED TRIBES OF WEST BENGAL
        B. of Cult. Res. Inst., 1966, 5, 1-2, 59-66

3632   Roy Burman, B.K.

        RELATIVE ROLES OF GOVERNMENT AND VOLUNTARY AGENCIES
        IN EDUCATION OF TRIBAL PEOPLE
        in Report of Natl. Seminar on Tribal Education
        New Delhi, N.C.E.R.T. 1967, 121-32

3633   Roy Burman, B.K.

FACTORS RETARDING TRIBAL EDUCATION IN WEST BENGAL
B. of the Cult. Res. Inst., 1964, 3, 2, 36-40

3634   Roy Burman, B.K.

COLLECTION OF EDUCATIONAL DATA IN THE SECONDARY STAGE
THROUGH MAIL QUESTIONNAIRE
B. of Cult. Res. Inst. 1962, 1, 2, 32-39

3635   Roy Burman, B.K.

COMPARATIVE STUDY OF THE PROGRESS OF SECONDARY
EDUCATION AMONG THE SCHEDULED CASTES AND SCHEDULED
TRIBES OF WEST BENGAL
B. of the Cult. Res. Inst., 1963, 2, 1, 40-52

3636   Roy Burman, B.K.

PROBLEMS OF TRIBAL LANGUAGE IN EDUCATION
Vidyapith, Oct. 18, 1965, 18-22

3637   Ruhela, S.P.

SOME EDUCATIONAL PROBLEMS OF SCHEDULED TRIBES IN
RAJASTHAN
Jana Jagriti, 1964, 2, 1,

3638   Sachchidananda, A.N.

EDUCATION AND CHANGES IN SOCIAL VALUES
Man in India, 1968, 48, 1, Jan-Mar, 71-85
SA, XVII, 7, E0504

3639   Sachidananda

TRIBAL EDUCATION IN INDIA
Vanyajati, 1964, 12, 1, 3-6

3640   Sachidananda

SOCIO-ECONOMIC ASPECTS OF TRIBAL EDUCATION
Report of the National Seminar on Tribal Education
in India
New Delhi, N.C.E.R.T., 1967, 99-108

3641   Sah, Vimal

TRIBAL EDUCATION IN GUJARAT
Vanyajati, 1966, 14, 3, 109-112

3642   Sahai,S.N.

LIBRARY AND THE COMMUNITY   (PH.D.)
Doct., Patna, 1969
(Dr. Sachdhidanand)

3643   Sareen, (Miss) S.

WOMEN'S EDUCATION IN UTTAR PRADESH: A SOCIOLOGICAL
STUDY   (PH.D.)
Doct., Agra U, 1959

3644   Sarkar, K.K.

RURAL ADULT EDUCATION
Kurukshetra, 1966,   14, 10, Jul, 18-20
SA, XVII, 4, D7955

3645   Sarkar, S.N.

STUDENT UNREST IN BIHAR: FACTORS UNDERLYING IT (PH.D.)
Doct., Ranchi U., 1966
(Dr. A.K. Singh)

3646   Sen, G.N.

THE PRIMARY EDUCATION FOR TRIBALS
Report of the Second Conference for Tribes and Tribal
(Sehi) Areas
Delhi, Baratiya Adimjati Sevak Sangh, 1953, 135-136

3647   Seth, (Mrs.) K.D.

IDEALISTIC TRENDS IN INDIAN PHILOSOPHY OF EDUCATION
(D.PHIL.)
Doct., Allahabad U., 1953
(Prof. P.S. Naidu)

3648   Shah, B.V.

THE SOCIAL BACKGROUND OF THE STUDENTS OF THE M.S.
UNIVERSITY OF BARODA   (PH.D.)
Doct., M.S. U. of Baroda, 1960,
(Dr. I. P. Desai)

3649   Shah, B.V.

STUDENT'S UNREST: A SOCIOLOGICAL HYPOTHESIS
Sociol. B., 1968, 17, 1, Mar, 55-68
SA, XVII, 5, D8598

3650   Shah, V.P., T. Patel, and William H. Sewell

SOCIAL CLASS AND EDUCATIONAL ASPIRATIONS IN AN
INDIAN METROPOLIS
Sociol. B. XX, 2, 1971

3651   Shanthamani, V.S. & A. Hafeez

VOCATIONAL INTEREST PATTERN OF STUDENTS LEAVING
HIGH SCHOOL
Ind. J. Soc. Wrk., 1970, 30, 4, Jan, 291-302
SA, XIX, 6, F1785

3652   Sharma, K.D.

THE INDIAN STUDENTS IN THE UNITED STATES: A PORTRAIT
Ind. J. of Sociology, 1971, 2, 1, Mar, 92-115
SA, XX, 3,F5224

3653   Sharma, T.R.

PRIMARY EDUCATION IN RANCHI TRIBAL VILLAGE
B. of Bihar Tribal Res. Inst., 1962, 1, 76-89

3654   Sharma, V.D.

TRIBAL EDUCATION IN RAJASTHAN
J. of Tribal Res. Inst. and Training Centre, 1966,
2, 1-2, 1-4

3655   Shaw, J.H.

ADULT EDUCATION IN INDIA
Kurukshetra, 1966, 14, 7, Apr, 11-15
SA, XVII, 3, D7213

3656   Shils, E.

THE INTELLECTUAL BETWEEN TRADITION AND MODERNITY:
THE INDIAN SITUATION
The Hague, Mouton, 1961

3657   Shils, E.

INDIAN STUDENTS: RATHER SADHUS THAN PHILISTINES
J. Sociol. 1962, 33-52
SA, XII, 5, B1258

3658   Singh, A.K.

THE IMPACT OF FOREIGN STUDY: THE INDIAN EXPERIENCE
Minerva, 1962, 1, 1, Aut, 43-53
SA, XII, 3, A9611

3659   Shrikant, L.M.

EDUCATION OF THE BACKWARD CLASSES
Ind. Yearbook of Educ., N.C.E.R.T., New Delhi, 1964,
173-194

3660   Skrikant, L.M.

MEASURES PROPOSED FOR THE SPREAD OF EDUCATION AMONG
THE SCHEDULED TRIBES
Vanyajati, 1966, 15, 3, 133-138

3661   Skrikant, L.M.

EDUCATION COMMISSION AND BACKWARD CLASSES
Vanyajati, 1966, 15, 3, 128-130

3662   Singh, A.K.

INDIAN STUDENTS IN BRITAIN
New York, Asia, 1963

3662a   Singh, A.K.

THE FOREIGN-EDUCATED INDIANS: THEIR PROBLEMS AND
CONFLICTS
in Conflict, Tension and Cultural Trend in India
ed. Vidyarti, L.P.
1969

3663   Singh, (Miss) B.Q.

THE COMMUNICATION OF IDEAS THROUGH ADULT EDUCATION
IN INDIA   (PH.D.)
Doct., Bombay U., 1957
(Prof. G.S. Ghurye)

3664   *Singh, Inderjit & N.S. Gupta

ASPECTO SOCIOECONOMICOS DE LA EDUCACION SUPERIOR EL
CASE DE LA UNIVERSIDAD DE JAMMU, INDIA (SOCIO-ECONOMIC
ASPECTS OF HIGHER EDUCATION. THE CASE OF THE
THE UNIVERSITY OF JAMMU, INDIA)
Revista, Mexicana de Sociologia, 1971, 33, 1, Jan-Mar,
137-181, (Sp.)
SA, 21, 73G2695

3665   Singh, K.N. & K.N. Rao

        EDUCATIONAL PLANS AND ASPIRATIONS OF RURAL BOYS
        Kurukshetra, 1966, 15, 3, Dec, 13-14
        SA, XVIII, 6, E5112

3666   Sinha, A.K.P. & O.P. Upadhyay

        STEROTYPES OF MALE AND FEMALE UNIVERSTIY STUDENTS IN
        INDIA TOWARD DIFFERENT ETHNIC GROUPS
        J. Soc. Psychol. 1960, 51, Feb, 93-102
        SA, XI, 5, A5721

3667   Srinivasa Iyengar, K.R.

        A NEW DEAL FOR OUR UNIVERSITIES
        Calcutta; Orient Longmans, 1951, 134 pp

3668   Srivastava, L.R.N.

        SOME BASIC PROBLEMS OF TRIBAL EDUCATION
        Report of the Nat'l. Sem. on Tribal Educ. in India,
        N.C.E.R.T., New Delhi, 1967, 77-97

3669   Srivastava, L.R.N.

        WORKING PAPER--TRIBAL EDUCATION IN INDIA
        Report of the National Seminar on Tribal Education in
        India
        N.C.E.R.T., New Delhi, 1967, 17-32

3670   Srivastava, L.R.N.

        EDUCATION AND MODERNIZATION AMONG THE MUNDA AND ORAON
        OF RANCHI (PH.D.)
        Doct., Patna U., 1968
        (Dr. Sachchidanand)

3671   Tangri, S.S.

INTELLECTUALS AND SOCIETY IN NINETEENTH CENTURY INDIA
Comp. Stud. Soc. Hist. 1961, 3, 4, Jul, 368-394
SA, XI, 7, A7617

3672   *Taylor, J.H.

NEW CASTLE UPON TYNE: ASIAN PUPILS DO BETTER   THAN
WHITES
British Journal of Sociology, 24, 4, Dec, 1973

3673   Thirtha, N.V.

NATIONAL INTEGRATION: STUDY IN SOCIAL FOUNDATIONS
OF EDUCATION
Verry, 1964

3674   Thomas, P.T.

PROBLEMS OF SOCIAL WORK EDUCATION IN INDIA
Ind. J. of Social Work, 1967, 28, 1, Apr, 41-54
SA, XVI, 6, D3581

3675   Thomas, T.

INDIAN EDUCATIONAL REFORMS IN CULTURAL PERSPECTIVE
Delhi, S. Chand, 1978, XV-312 pp

3676   Tiwari, J.G. & P. Gautam

PERSONALITY CHARACTERISTICS OF SOCIALLY ACCEPTED AND
SOCIALLY NEGLECTED JUNIOR HIGH SCHOOL PUPILS
Ind. Jour. Soc. Wrk., 1966, 27, 2, Jul, 211-217
SA, XVI, 5, D2739

3677   Useem, J.

THE WESTERN EDUCATED MAN IN INDIA
New York, Dryden Press, 1955

3678   Upal, R.L.

PROGRESS OF EDUCATION FOR TRIBAL PEOPLE IN INDIA
Tribal Res. & Training Inst. Gujarat
Special Tribal #13-17, 1966

3679   Van Der Kroef, Justus M.

THE U.S. AND THE WORLD'S BRAIN DRAIN
Int. J. of Comp. Soc., XI, 3, 1970, p 220-239

3680   Verma, I.B.

BASIC EDUCATION: A REINTERPRETATION
Agra, Sri Ram Mehra, 1969, viii & 374 p.

3681   Verma, M.

SOCIO-ECONOMIC STUDY OF UNDER-GRADUATE GIRL STUDENTS
Ind. J. Soc. Wrk. 1960, 21, 3, Dec, 283-286
SA, XI, 7, A7619

3682   Verma, R.M.P.

A STUDY OF THE ACADEMIC AND NON-ACADEMIC CHARACTERISTICS
OF THE RURAL SCHOOL PUPILS AND THE SOCIOLOGICAL CORRELATES
OF THOSE CHARACTERISTICS   (PH.D.)
Doct. Bihar U., 1965
(Dr. A. Hazari)

3683   Vidyarthi, L.P.

EDUCATION IN TRIBAL BIHAR
Man in India, 1955, 35, 1, 39-45

3684   Vyas, A.N.

TRIBAL EDUCATION IN ORISSA
Report of the Second Confer. for Tribes & Tribal
(Scheduled)Areas
Delhi, 1953, p 129-134

3685   Vyas, A.N.

TEN YEARS PROGRESS OF ASHRAM EDUCATION IN ORISSA
Vanyajati, 1958, 6, 4, 157

3686   Vyas, A.N.

WHY THIS EMPHASIS ON VOCATIONAL BIAS IN EDUCATION IN
ASHRAM?
Adivasi, 1957, 45-49

3687   Vyas, A.N.

FIFTEEN YEARS OF PROGRESS OF TRIBAL EDUCATION IN
ORISSA
Vanyajati, 1963, 11, 2, 51-64

3688   Wilson,Stewart

THE ROLE OF FOLK MUSIC IN EDUCATION
in Music in Education, UNESCO, 1955

3689   Windhausen, J.D.

THE VERNACULARS, 1835-1839: A THRID MEDIUM FOR
INDIAN EDUCATION
Sociol. Educ., 1964, 37, 37 Spr, 254-270
SA, XII, 8, B3723

3690   Wood, Glynn

NATIONAL PLANNING & PUBLIC DEMAND IN INDIAN HIGHER
EDUCATION: THE CASE OF MYSORE
Minerva, X, 1, Jan, 1972, 83-107

3691   Wood, G.

PLANNING UNIVERSITY REFORM: AN INDIAN CASE STUDY
(MYSORE)
Comp. Educ. Rev., 16, 2, June, 1972

3692   Yajnik, K.S.

THE TEACHING OF SOCIAL STUDIES IN INDIA
Bombay, Orient Longmans, 1966, xii-174 p

3693   Yelaja, S.A.

SCHOOLS OF SOCIAL WORK IN INDIA: HISTORICAL
DEVELOPMENT, 1939-1966
Ind. J. of Soc. Wrk. 1969, 29, 4, Jan, 361-378
SA, XVIII, 6, E5123

3694   Yelaja, S.A.

SCHOOLS OF SOCIAL WORK IN INIDA: AN OVERVIEW OF
THEIR PRESENT STATUS
Ind. J. Soc. Wrk, 1969, 30, 1, Apr, 9-22
SA, XVIII, 7 E6221

3695   Zachariah, Mathew

POSITIVE DISCRIMINATION IN EDUCATION FOR INDIA'S
SCHEDULED CASTES: A REVIEW OF THE PROBLEMS, 1950-1970
Comp. Educ. Rev. 16, 1, 1972, p 16-29

1500   Sociology of Religion

1535   sociology of religion

3696   Acharya, B.T.

        HARIDASA SAHITYA: THE KARNATAK MYSTICS AND THEIR
        SONGS
        Bagalore; Indian Institute of Culture, 1953, 16 pp

3697   Agrawal, B.C.

        RELIGIO-ECONOMIC NETWORKS IN THE INTEGRATION OF
        HINDU UNIVERSE IN INDIA
        Abstract of Papers on South Asia, 28th International
        Congress of Orientalists, Canberra, 1971

3698   Aggarwal, P.C.

        CASTE, RELIGION AND POWER: AN INDIAN CASE STUDY
        New Delhi, ShriRam Centre for Industrial Relations,
        1971

3699   *Alexander, K.C.

        CASTE AND CHRISTIANITY IN KERALA, SOCIAL COMPASS,
        1971, 18, 4, 551-560
        SA, 21, 73G3533

3700   Alexander, K.C.

        THE PROBLEM OF THE NEW-CHRISTIANS OF KERALA
        Man in India, 1967, 47, 4, Oct-Dec, 317-330
        SA, XVII, 3, D7218

3701   Anant, S.S.

        STEROTYPES OF HINDUS ABOUT DIFFERENT RELIGIOUS
        GROUPS OF INDIA
        Man in India, 52, 2, 1972, 123-131

3702   Apte, V.M.

SOCIAL AND RELIGIOUS LIFE IN THE GRIHYA SUTRAS
Bombay; Popular Book Depot, 1954, 275 pp

3703   Baago, K.

RELIGIONS IN INDIA ACCORDING TO THE LAST CENSUS
Int. Rev. Miss. 1964, 53, 169-172
SA, XV, 6, C7641

3704   Bennet, J.C.

SOCIAL ISSUES AT NEW DELHI
Theo. Life, 1961, 4, 219-227
SA, XV, 6, C7642

3705   *Bereman, G.D.

HINDUS OF THE HIMALAYAS
Berkeley, U. of Calif. Press,1972

3706   Berreman, G.D.

BRAHMINS AND SHAMANS IN PAHARI RELIGION (U.P.)
in Religion in South Asia
ed. E.B. Harper
Seattle: U. of Washington Press, 1964, p 53-71

3707   *Beteille, A.

CASTE, CLASS, AND POWER
Berkeley, U. of California Press, 1971

3708   Bhagwat, Durga

BARADEO: THE HIGH GOD OF THE GONDS
J. of Anthrop. Survey of Bombay, 1953, 7, 60-71

3709   Bhagwat, Durga

THE FATE UNDERSTANDING
Folklore (India), 4, 392-6, 1963

3710   Bhatt, G.S.

BRAHMO SAMAJ, ARYA SAMAJ, AND THE CHURCH-SECT
TYPOLOGY
Review of Rel. Res.,   1968, 10, 1, Fall, 23-32
SA, XX, 1-2, F4120

3711   Bose, N.K.

RELIGION AND SOCIETY
Man in India, 1966, 46, 1, Jan-Mar, 1-13
SA, XVI, 6, D3593

3712   *Bougle, C. (Tr. D.F. Pocock)

ESSAYS ON THE CASTE SYSTEM
Cambridge U. Press, 1971

3713   *Brent, P.

GOD MEN OF INDIA
New York, Quadrangle, 1972

3714   Brown, W. Norman

MAN IN THE UNIVERSE: SOME CONTINUITES IN INDIAN
THOUGHT
Berkeley, U. of Calif. Press, 1966

3715   Brush, J.E.

DISTRIBUTION OF RELIGIOUS COMMUNITIES IN INDIA
Assoc. of Amer. Georgraphers, Annals, 29, 81-98
Jun 1949

3716   Caillat, C.

L'ASCETISME CHEZ LES JAINA (ASCETICISM AMONG THE
JAINA)
Archives de Sociologie des Religions, 1964, 18, Jun-Dec
45-54 (Fr.)
SA, XVI, 7, D4494

3717   Carman, J.B.

THE PRESENT ENCOUNTER BETWEEN CHRISTIANITY AND
HINDUISM IN INDIA
Rev. Exp. 1961, 58, 67-90
SA, X, 5, A3556

3718   Chandran, J.R.

CHURCH IN AND AGAINST ITS CULTURAL ENVIRONMENT
Int. Rev. of Missions 41, 257-72, Jul 1952

3719   Chattopadhyaya, K.R.

DIFFUSION OF A RELIGIOUS CULT
in Anthropology on the March ed. B. Ratnam
Madras, Social Sciences Association, Madras, 1963,
p. 325-33

3720   Cohen, S.P.

RULES AND PRIESTS: A STUDY IN CULTURAL CONTROL
Comp. Stud. Soc. Hist. 1964, 6, 2, Jan, 199-216
SA, XII, 7, B2531

3721   *Conlon, F.F.

CASTE BY ASSOCIATION: THE GAUDA SARASRATA BRAHMANA
UNIFICATION MOVEMENT
Journal of Asian Studies, XXIII, 3, May, 1974,
pp 351-365

3722   Coulborn, Rushton

        THE STATE AND RELIGION: IRAN, INDIA AND CHINA
        Comp. Stud. Soc. Hist., 1958, 1, 1, Oct, 44-59
        SA, XI, 2&3, A4890

3723   Das, N.

        SOCIO-RELIGIOUS LIFE IN GUDVELLA AREA BOLANGIR
        DISTRICT (ORISSA)
        Adivasi, 1967-1968

3724   Das, S.R.

        A STUDY OF THE URATA RITES OF BENGAL
        Man in India, 32, 1952, p 207-245

3725   Das, S.R.

        FOLK RELIGION OF BENGAL
        Calcutta: S.C. Kar, 1953

3726   de Heusch, L.

        INTRODUCTION (A REVIEW OF THE WORK OF THE CENTRE
        D'ETUDE DES RELIGIOUS 1960-1961)
        A. Cent. Et. Rel. 1962, 2, 11-26
        SA, XI, 6, A6813

3727   *Delfendahl, Bernard

        LA MULTIPLICATION DES DIEUX: ENGUETE A KUNJE (INDE)
        (THE MULTIPLICATION OF GODS: FIELDWORK AT KUNJE
        (INDIA))
        Annales, 1970, 25, 6, Nov-Dec, 1523-1546 (Fr.)
        SA, 21, 73G1058

3728   Derrett, J. Duncan

        RELIGION, LAW AND THE STATE IN INDIA
        New York, The Free Press of Glencoe, 1968

1535   sociology of religion

3729   Desai, A.R.

         NATIONAL INTEGRATION AND RELIGION
         Sociol. B. 1963, 12, 1, Mar, 53-65
         SA, XI, 7, A7646

3730   Devanandan, P.D.

         CHRISTIAN MESSAGE IN RELATION TO THE CULTURAL HERITAGE
         OF INDIA
         Ecumenical Review, 2, 3, 241-9, 1950

3731   Dingre, G.V.

         A STUDY OF TEMPLE TOWN AND ITS PRIESTHOOD (PH.D)
         Doct., Poona U., 1969,
         (Dr. (Mrs.) I. Karve)

3732   Diwangi, P.C.

         RELIGIOUS PREJUDICES AS A CLOG IN NATIONAL UNITY
         in Group Prejudices in India
         eds. M.B. Nanavati & C.N. Vakil
         Bombay, Vora, 1951, p 78-85

3733   Dixit, V.S.

         INVESTIGATION OF THE ROLE OF RELIGION IN CONTROLLING
         CRIMINAL BEHAVIOUR
         Doct. St. Saugar U., 1969

3734   Dube, Leela

         MATRILINY AND ISLAM
         Delhi; Nat'l. Publ House, 1969

3735   Dumont, L.

RELIGION, POLITICS & HISTORY IN INDIA: COLLECTED
PAPERS IN INDIAN SOCIOLOGY
The Hague: Mouton, 1970, vii, 166 pp

3736   Dumont, L.

LE RENONCEMENT DANS LES RELIGIONS DE L'INDE
(RENUNCIATION IN THE RELIGIONS OF INDIA)
Archiv. Sociool. Relig. 1959, 7, Jan-Jun, 45-69 (Fr.)
SA, XII, 5, B1281

3737   Dumont, L. & D.Pocock

A.M. HOCART ON CASTE-RELIGION AND POWER
Cont. Ind. Sociool. 1958, 2, Apr, 45-63
SA, XIV, 2-3, B9685

3738   Dumont, L. & D. Pocock

PURE AND IMPURE
Contri. Ind. Sociol. 1959, 3, Jul, 9-39
SA, XIV, 2-3, B9689

3739   Dumont, L. & D. Pocock

POSSESSION AND PRIESTHOOD
Contrib. Ind. Sociol. 1959, 3, Jul, 55-74
SA, XIV, 2-3, B9688

3740   Dumont, L. & D. Pocock

THE DIFFERENT ASPECTS ON LEVELS OF HINDUISM
Contrib. Ind. Sociol, 1959, 3, Jul, 40-54
SA, XIV, 2-3, B9687

3741   Dumont, L. & D. Pocock

APPENDIX: A STRUCTURAL DEFINITION OF A FOLK DEITY
OF TAMIL NAD: AIYANAR: THE LORD
Contr. Ind. Sociol. 1959, 3, Jul, 75-87
SA, XIV, 2-3, B9686

3742   Elder, Joseph, B.

RELIGIOUS BELIEFS AND TRADITIONAL ATTITUDES
1965, p. 1-35

3743   Elder, Joseph W.

FATALISM IN INDIA: A COMPARISON BETWEEN HINDUS
AND MUSLIMS
Anthropol. Quart. 39, July 1966. #3, p 227-243

3744   Elwin, V.

TRIBAL RELIGION & Magic In Middle India
Geographical Magazine, Feb, 1950, 22

3745   Elwin, V.

PURITANISM SEEPING INTO TRIBAL LIFE
Times of India, Aug, 21, 1952

3746   Fiski, A.M.

Religion and Buddhism Among India's New Buddhists
Soc. Res. 1969, 36, 1, Sp, 123-157
SA, XVIII, 3, E2297

3747   Freed, R.S. & S.A. Freed

TWO MOTHER GODESS CEREMONIES OF DELHI STATE IN THE
GREAT AND LITTEL TRADITIONS
Southw. J. Anthrop. 1962, 18, 3, Aut, 246-277
SA, XI, 7, A7647

3748   Fyzee, A.A.A.

ISLAMIC LAW AND CUSTOM
in. Group Prejudices in India
ed. M.B. Nanavati & C.N. Vakil
Bombay, Vora, 1951, p 85-90

3749   Galanter, Marc

SECULARISM, EAST AND WEST
Comp. Stud. Soc. Hist, VII, 2, 1965 (4), p. 133-159

3750   George, S.K.

RELATION OF CHRISTIANITY WITH OTHER RELIGIONS SPECIALLY
(A) HINDUISM (W) ISLAM (E) OTHERS
in Group Prejudices In India
ed. by M.B. Nanavati & C.N. Vakil
Bombay, Vora, 1951, p 90-96

3751   Ghurye, G.S.

ASCETIC ORIGINS
Social. B., VI, 1952, p 162-184

3752   Ghurye, G.S.

INDIAN SADHUS
Bombay; Popular Book Depot, 1953, 300 p.

3753   Gnanamble, K.

THE KANIKKARS OF TRANVANCORE , THEIR RELIGIOUS AND
MAGICAL PRACTICES
B. of the Dept. of Anthrop., 1954, 3, 2,

3754   Gnanamble, K.

RELIGIOUS BELIEFS OF THE URALI
B. of the Dept. of Anthrop., 1955, 4, 2,

3755   Gnanamabal, (Miss) K.

RELIGION OF THREE TRANVANCORE TRIBES (PH.D.)
Doct., Maharaja Sayajirao, U. of Baroda, 1961
(Dr. I.P. Desai)

3756   Gumperz, J.J.

RELIGION AND SOCIAL COMMUNICATION IN VILLAGE NORTH
INDIA
87-97, Chpt. in Religion in South Asia
ed. E.B. Harper
Seattle, Wash.: U. of Washington Press, 1964, 199 pp
SA, XIII, 5, B7133

3757   *Hardy, P.

THE MUSLIMS OF BRITISH INDIA
Cambridge U. Press, 1972

3758   Harper, E.B.

SHAMINISM IN SOUTH INDIA
Southw. J. Antrhop. 1957, 13, 3, Aut. 267-287
SA, VIII, 3, 8021

3759   Harper, E.B.

RITUAL POLLUTION AS AN INTEGRATOR OF CASTE & RELIGION
in Religions in South Asia
ed E.B. Harper
Seattle; U. of Washington, 1964, pp 151-199

3760   Hein, Nornin

THE RAM LILA
in Traditional India; Structure & Change
ed M.B. Singer
Philadelphia, American Folklore Society, 1959, p 73-99

3761   Izikowitz, Karl Gustav

THE GOTRA CEREMONY OF THE BORA GADABA
in Primitive view of the world
ed. Stanley Diamond
New York, Columbia U. Press, 1964

3762   Jhirad, J.A.

THE RELEVANCE OF INDIAN JUDAISM TO MODERN LIFE
India Cultures Quarterly, 27, 3-4, 1971, 98-100

3763   Kellock, James

CHRISTIANITY IN INDIA
in Group Prejudices in India
ed. M.B. Navati & C.N. Vakil
Bombay, Vora, 1951, p 96-108

3764   Kolenda, Pauline M.

RELIGIOUS ANXIETY AND HINDU FATE
in Religion in South Asia
ed G.B. Harper
Seattle; U. of Washington, 1964, p. 71-83

3765   Loomis, C.P.; Loomis, Z.K.

SOCIO-ECONOMIC CHANGE AND THE RELIGIOUS FACTOR IN
INDIA
New Delhi; Affliated East West Press, 1969, XX-140 p

3766   Mahar, Pauline

CHANGING RELIGIOUS PRACTICES OF AN UNTOUCHABLE CASTE
Eco. Dev. & Cult. Change, 1960, 8, 279-87

3767   Majumdar, R.C.

HINDUISM, A RETROSPECT AND REVIEW
in Group Prejudices in India
eds. M.B. Nanavati & C.N. Vakil
Bombay, Vora, 1951, p 71-78

3768   Mandelbaum, D.G.

INTRODUCTION: PROCESS & STRUCTURE IN SOUTH ASIA
RELIGION
in Religion in South Asia
ed. E.B. Harper
Seattle: U. of Washington, Press, 1964, p. 5-21

3769   Mandelbaum, D.G.

TRANCENDENTAL AND PRAGMATIC ASPECTS OF RELIGION
Amer. Anthrop. 1966, 68, 5, Oct, 1174-1191
SA, XV, 5, C6811

3770   McCormack, Wm.

THE FARMS OF COMMUNICATION IN VIRASARVA RELIGION
in. Traditional India: Structure & Change
ed. M.B. Singer
Philadelphia; American Folklore Society, 1959,
p 119-130

3771   *McCormack, William

LINGAYATS AS A SECT
Journal of the Royal Anthropological Institute
93: 59-71, 1963

3772   Mishra, K.K.

THE CONTRIBUTION OF RELIGIOUS MOVEMENTS AND
INSTITUTIONS IN INDIAN NATIONALISM (in Hindi)
(PH.D.)
Doct, Vikram U, 1968
(Dr. P.K. Bhattachanya)

3773   Misra, S.

RELIGION IN A POLYANDROUS SOCIETY (PH.D.)
Doct. Lucknow U., 1967
(Dr. K.S. Mathur)

3774   Misra, V.B.

A HISTORICAL STUDY OF RELIGIOUS BELIEFS AND PRACTICES
OF NORTH INDIA DURING THE EARLY MEDIEVAL PERIOD
(D.Phil)
Doct., Gauhati U., 1970

3775   Mujeeb, M.

ISLAMIC INFLUENCE ON INDIAN SOCIETY
Meerat, 1972

3776   Naik, T.B.

RELIGION OF THE ANAVILS OF SURAT
Traditional India: Structure and Change
Journal of Amer. Folklore, 71 (281) 1958, 389-96

3777   *Nevaskar, B.

CAPITALISTS WITHOUT CAPITALISM: THE JAINS OF INDIA
AND THE QUAKERS OF THE WEST
Westport, Greenwood, 1971

3778   Nichols, J.H., J. van Buitenen, R. Coulborn

DEBATE: THE STATE AND RELIGION
Comp. Stud. Soc. Hist. 1959, 1, 4, Jun 383-393
SA, XI, 4, A5459

3779   Opler, M.E.

THE PLACE OF RELIGION IN A NORTH INDIAN VILLAGE
Southw. J. Anthrop. 1959, 3, Aut, 219-226
SA, IX, 4, A0690

3780   Orenstein, H.

TOWARD A GRAMAR OF DEFILEMENT IN HINDU SACRED LAW
in Structure & Change in Indian Society
ed B.S. Cohn & M.B. Singer Chicago; Aldine, 1968
p 115-133

3781   Pandey, R.B.

HINDU SAMSKARAS, A SOCIO-RELIGIOUS STUDY OF THE
HINDU SACRAMENTS
Bhaidini: Vikrama Publication, 1949, 546 pp

3782   Parganika, B.L.

THE SATNAMI MOVEMENT
Jour. of Soc. Res. 1967, 10, 1, Mar, 1-16
SA, XVI, 5, D2758

3783   Parratt, S.N.

THE REGION OF GARIB   NIWAZ AND HINDUISATION OF MANIPUR
Abstract of Papers 28th Int'l. Congress of Orientalists,
Canberra, 1971

3784   Patterson, Maureen L.

CHITPAVAN BRAHMAN FAMILY DIETIES
paper presented to the first meeting of the
maharashtra Mandal
Philadelphia, 21 March 1968

3785   *Pothen, K.P.

LA SITUATION SOCIO-ECONOMIQUE DES CHRETIENS DE MALWA
(MP) INDE (THE SOCIO-ECONOMIC SITUATION OF CHRISTIANS
OF MALWA (MP) INDIA)
Social Compass, 1971, 18, 4, 561-574 (Fr.)
SA, 21, 73G3566

3786   Pradhan, M.C.

DEGREE OF RELIGIOUS CHANGE IN A PEASANT SOCIETY OF
SOUTH INDIA--THE VOKKALIGA
paper presented at the CSAS meetings, Winnipeg, 1970

3787   Prasad, N.

THE GAYAWALS OF BIHAR
Amer. Antrhop, V54, 1952, p 279-83

3788   Presler, H.H.

SOCIOLOGY OF RELIGION IN INDIA
Rev. Relig. Res. 1962, 3, 97-113
SA, XV, 6, C7677

3789   Pundalik, V.G.

SOCIOLOGY OF RELIGION
Doct. St. Poona U., 1969

3790   Puri, G.S.P.N.

THE ORIGIN AND GROWTH OF DASHNAMI SANYASI MOVEMENT
IN INDIA--SOCIOLOGY OF RELIGOUS ORGANIZATION
(PH.D.)
Doct., Patna U., 1966
(Dr. N. Prasad)

3791   Radhakrishanan, S.

RELIGION AND SOCIETY
London; G. Allen and Unwin, 1947, 242 p.

3792   Raghavan, V.

METHODS OF POPULAR RELIGOUS INSTRUCTION IN SOUTH INDIA
in Traditional India: Structure and Change
Philadelphia, American Folklore Society, 1959
p. 130-141

3793   Raha, M.K.

A NOTE ON CHANGES IN THE MAGICO-RELIGIOUS BELIEFS AND
PRACTICES OF THE ORAONS
B. of the Cultural Res. Inst., 1962, 1, 2

3794   *Ramanujan, A.K. (Translated)

SPEAKING OF SIVA
Harmondsworth, Penguin, 1973

3795   Rao, K.R. & K.R. Murty

CULTURAL MATRIC AND REFERENCE GROUP BEHAVIOUR: A CASE
OF DESANSKRITIZATION AND ISLAMIZATION OF THE TELANGANA
BRAHMINS
East. Anthrop, 25, 3, Sept-Dec, 1972, 241-249

3796   Rocher, L. & R. Rocher

LA SACRALITE DU POUROIR DANS L'INDE ANCIENNE D'APRES
LES TEXTES DE DHARMA (SARCREDNESS OF POWER IN ANCIENT
INDIA ACCORDING TO THE TEXTS OF DHARMA) LE POUVOIR ET
LE SACRE (POWER AND THE SACRED)
A. Cent. Et. Relig. 1961, 1, 123-139
SA, XI, 5, A5896

3797   Srinivas, M.N.

RELIGION AND SOCIETY AMONG THE COORGS OF SOUTH INDIA
Oxford, Clarendon Press, 1952

3798   Stern, H.

RELIGION ET SOCIETE EN INDE SELON MAX WEBER: ANALYSE
CRITIQUE DE HINDOUSME ET BOUDDHISME (RELIGION AND
SOCIETY IN INDIA ACCORDING TO MAX WEBER: A CRITICAL
ANALYSIS OF HINDUISM AND BUDDHISM)
Social Science Information, 1971, 10, 6,Dec 69-112
(French)
SA, XX, 7, F9647

3799   Subramanian, (Miss) K.

THE BRAHMIN PRIEST OF TAMILNAD: A STUDY OF THE SMARTA
BRAHMIN DOMESTIC PRIEST   (PH.D)
Doct., Saugar U., 1969
(Dr. L. Dube)

3800   Sur, S.K.: S. Gupta, & S.K. Santra

SOCIO-CULTURAL CHARACTERISTICS OF THE ZEMI NAGAS AND
THEIR ADOPTION OF CHRISTIANITY
Society & Cult. 1970, 1, Special Number, 65-71
SA, XX, 7, F9676

3801   Swamy, R.N.

SOUTH INDIAN TEMPLE--AS AN EMPLOYER
Ind. Eco. Soc. Hist. R., 1965, 2, 4, Oct, 367-372
SA, XV, 3, C5271

3802   Swart, W.R.

CHRISTIAN CONVERSION AND CULTURAL CHANGE
The India Cultures Quart, 27, 3-4, 1971, 96-98

3803   Taylor, R.W.

MISSIONARY SOCIETIES AND THE DEVELOPMENT OF OTHER
FORMS OF ASSOCIATIONS IN INDIA
Chapt. in Voluntary Associations, 189-206
ed. D.B. Robertson
Richmond, Va: John Knox Press, 1966, 448 pp
SA, XVI, 1, C9382

3804   Thomas, P.

HINDU RELIGION, CUSTOMS AND MANNERS
Bombay, D.B. Taraporevala, 1957, 161 pp

3805   Thomas, P.T.

SOME OBSERVATION ON THE RELIGION OF MUTHUVANS
J. of M.S.U. of Baroda, 3, 1, 1954

3806   Tripathi, B.D.

THE RELIGIONS MENDICANTS OF UTTAR PRADESH: A
SOCIOLOGICAL STUDY   (PH.D.)
Doct., Lucknow U., 1967
(Dr. S. Chandra)

3807   Upadhyaya, V.

SOCIO-RELIGIOUS CONDITION OF NORTH INDIA
Varanasi, 1968

3808   Van Buitenen, J.A.B.

THE INDIAN HERO AS A VIDYADHARA
in Traditional India: Structure & Change
ed. M.B. Singer
Philadelphia, American Folklore Society, 1959, p 99-106

3809   Venkatarama Aiyer, K.R.

HISTORY OF SRINGERI, 168 pp

3810   *Verba, Ahmed & Bhatt

CASTE, RACE AND POLITICS: A COMPARATIVE STUDY OF
INDIA AND THE U.S.A.
Berverley Hills, Calif. Sage, 1971

3811   Vidyarthi, L.P.

ASPECTS OF RELIGION IN INDIAN SOCIETY
Meerut, Kedar Nath Ram Nath, 1962, x & 410 pp
SA, XI, 7, A7654a

3812   Vidyarthi, L.P.

THE MALER: A STUDY IN NATURE-MAN-SPIRIT COMPLEX OF A
HILL TRIBE
Bookland, 1963

3813   Vora, (Mrs.) D.P.

EVOLUTION OF MORALS IN THE EPICS: THE MAHABHARATA
AND THE RAMAYANA   (PH.D.)
Doct,Bombay U., 1956
(Prof. K.M. Kapadia)

3814   Weber,M.

THE RELIGION OF INDIA: THE SOCIOLOGY OF HINDUISM
AND BUDDHISM
Tr. & ed. by Hans H. Girth & Don Martindale
Glencoe, Ill: The Free Press, 1958
SA, VII, 1, 5445

3815   Welty, Paul T.

BUDDHISM
in The Asians: Their Heritage and Destiny
ed. P.T. Welty
Philadelphia, J.B. Lippincott Co., 1962, p. 71-78

3816   Welty, Paul Thomas

HINDUISM
in The Asians; Their Heritage and Destiny
ed P.T. Welty
Philadelphia, J.B. Lippincott Co., 1962, p 61-71

3817   Wertheim, W.F.

RELIGIOUS REFORM MOVEMENTS IN SOUTH AND SOUTHEAST
ASIA
Archiv. Sociol. Relig. 1961, 12, 6, Jul-Dec. 53-62
SA, XII, 7, B2910

3818   Wiebe, P.D. & S. John-Peter

THE CATHOLIC CHURCH & CASTE IN RURAL TAMIL NADU
East. Antrhop., 25, 1, Jan-April 1972, 1-13

3819   Rangaswami Aiyangar, K.V.

SOME ASPECTS OF THE HINDU VIEW OF LIFE ACCORDING
TO DHARMASASTRA
Baroda Oriental Institute, 1952

3820.   Reddy, G.P.

CHRISTIANITY AND REDDIS: SOME OBSERVATIONS
J. Soc. Res., 1968, 11, 2, Sep, 109-120
SA, XVIII, 6, E5152

3821   Rodhe, S.

DELIVER US FROM EVIL: STUDIES ON THE VEDIC IDEAS
OF SALVATION
Amer. Oriental Society J. 67-219-20, July 1947

3822   Roy, P.

CHRISTIANITY AND THE KHASIS
Man in India, 1964, 44, 2, Apr-Jun, 105-116
SA, XII, 1, B4590

3823   Sadashivaiah, H.M.

COMPARATIVE STUDY OF TWO VIRASHARVA MONASTERIES (PH.D.)
Doct., Mysore U., 1960
(Prof. N.A. Nikkam)

3824   Sahay, K.N.

IMPACT OF CHRISTIANITY ON THE ORAONS OF THE THREE
VILLAGES IN CHHOTANAGPUR   (PH.D.)
Doct., Ranchi U., 1964
(Prof. L. P. Vidyarathi)

3825   Sahay, K.N.

IMPACT OF CHRISTIANITY ON THE URAON OF THE CHAINPUR
BELT IN CHOTANAGPUR: AN ANALYSIS OF ITS CULTURAL
PROCESSES
Amer. Anthrop, 1968, 70, 5, Oct., 923-942
SA, XVII, 6, D9686

3826   Saiyidain, K.G.

        EDUCATION, CULTURE AND SOCIAL ORDER
        New York, Asia, 1963

3827   Saraswati, B.

        TEMPLE ORGANIZATION IN GOA
        Man in India, 1963, 43, 2, Apr-Jun, 131-140
        SA, XII, 7, B2903

3828   Sarikwal, R.C.

        INDUSTRIALIZATION AND RELIGIOUS ORGANIZATION--A
        SOCIOLOGICAL ANALYSIS
        Ind. J. Soc. Res. 13, 2, Aug, 1972, 127-130

3829   Scott, R.W.

        SOCIAL ETHICS OF MODERN HINDUISM
        Calcutta; YMCA Publishing House, 1953, 243 pp

3830   Sharma, S.L.

        APPROACH TO THE STUDY OF SOCIO-CULTURAL OUTCOME OF
        CONVERSION
        Ind. J. Of Soc. Res. 1966, 7, 3, Dec, 194-197
        SA, XVII, 3, D7235

3831   Sharma, S.L.

        COMPARATIVE STYLES OF CONVERSION ON MAJORE RELIGIONS
        IN INDIA
        J. Soc. Res. 1968, 11, 2, Sep, 141-150
        SA, XVII, 6, E5155

3832   Sharma, S.L. & R.N. Srivastava

        INSTITUTIONAL RESISTANCE TO INDUCED ISLAMIZATION IN A
        CONVERT COMMUNITY: AN EMPIRIC STUDY IN SOCIOLOGY OF
        RELIGION
        Sociological B. 1967, 16, 1, Mar, 69-80   SA,XVII,2,D6309

3833   Shastri, D.R.

ORIGIN AND DEVELOPMENT OF THE RITUALS OF ANCESTOR
WORSHIP IN INDIA
Calcutta; Bookland Put. Ltd., 1963

3834   Sher Singh

THE SAINTS OF PUNJAB
Delhi, 1965

3835   Singer, M. (ed.)

KRISHNA: MYTHS, RITES AND ATTITUDES
U. of Chicago Press, 1966

3836   Singer, Milton

RELIGION AND SOCIAL CHANGE IN INDIA: THE MAX WEBER
THESIS, PHASE THREE
Econ. Dev.Cult. Change, 1966, 14, 4, Jul, 497-505
SA, XV, 2, C4506

3837   Singer, M.

REVIEW OF MAX WEBER'S RELIGION IN INDIA
Amer. Anthrop. IXIII, 1961

3838   Singh, T.R.

SOME ASPECTS OF RITUAL PURITY AND POLLUTION
East. Anthrop. 1966, 19, 2, May-Aug, 131-143
SA, XV, 3, C5269

3839   Smith, D.E.

INDIA AS A SECULAR STATE
Princeton: University Press, 1963

1535   sociology of religion

3840

SOME ASPECTS OF CHANGES IN BHUMIJ RELIGION
Man in India, V. 33, 1953, p 148-64

1600   Social Control

1636   sociology of law

  3841   Abraham, C.M.

            POLICE IN WELFARE STATE
            Ind. Soc. 1960, 2, 2, Feb, 64-72
            SA, XII, 6, B2054

  3842   Aryamane, (Miss) R.

            BACKWARD CLASSES IN INDIAN CONSTITUTION (PH.D.)
            Doct., Karnatak U., 1968
            (Prof. G.S. Hallappa)

  3843   Banningan, J.A.

            HINDU CODE BILL WOULD CODIFY AND MODERNIZE HINDU LAW
            GIVING GREATER RIGHTS TO WOMEN
            Far Eastern Survey, V 21, 1952, p 173-6.

  3844   Billore, S.

            IMPACT OF SOCIAL LEGISLATION ON RURAL COMMUNITY IN
            INDORE DISTRICT
            Doct. St. Indore U., 1969,
            (C.M. Abraham)

  3845   *Cartwright, B.C. & Schwartz, R.D.

            LITIGATION IN INDIA: STRUCTURAL DIVERSITY AND
            NORMATIVE INTEGRATION
            Paper presented at the ASA Annual Meetings, Montreal
            August 25-29, 1974

  3846   Cartwright, B.C. & R.D. Schwartz

            THE SALIENCE OF LEGAL NORMS IN CONFLICT RESOLUTION:
            THE ROLE OF NORMATIVE COMMUNICATION, PREDICTABILITY,
            AND POWER EQUALIZATION
            Paper presentd at the 66th Annual Meeting of the
            American Sociological Assoc.
            SA, XIX, 7, Sup. 20, F2935

3847   Chatterjee, B.B.

        IMPACT OF SOCIAL LEGISLATION ON SOCIAL CHANGE
        Calcutta, 1971

3848   Chekki, D.A.

        SOCIAL LEGISLATION AND KINSHIP IN INDIA: A
        SOCIO-LEGAL STUDY
        J. of Marriage and the Family, 1969, 31, 1,
        Feb, 165-172
        SA, XVII, 7, E0545

3849   Cohn,B.S.

        SOME NOTES ON LAW AND CHANGE IN NORTH INDIA
        Eco. Dev.Cult. Change, 1959, 8. 1, Oct, 79-93
        SA, XI, 7, A7658

3850   Cohn, B.

        ANTHROPOLOGICAL NOTES ON DISPUTES AND LAW IN INDIA
        Amer. Anthrop. 1965, 67, 6, Part, 2, Dec, 82-122
        SA, XIV, 6, C2513

3851   Derrett, J.D.M.

        THE ADMINISTRATION OF HINDU LAW BY THE BRITISH
        Comp. Stud. Soc. Hist, 1961, 4, 1, Nov, 10-52
        SA, XII, 1, A8450

3852   Derrett, G.D.M.

        ASPECTS OF MATRIOMONIAL CAUSES IN MODERN HINDU LAW
        Revue du Sud-Est Asiatique, 1964, 3, 203-241
        SA, XVI, 7, D4541

3853   Gafoor, S.K.A.

LEGISLATION FOR CATEGORIES OF UNDER PRIVILEGED
Ind. J. Soc. Wrk., 1960, 20, 4, Mar, 62-69
SA, XI, 6, A6854

3854   Galanter, Marc

THE MODERNIZATION OF LAW
in Modernization
ed Myron Weiner
New York, Basic Books, 196, p 153-165

3855   Galanter, Marc

THE USES OF LAW IN INDIAN STUDIES
in Languages and Areas: Studies Presented to
Geroge V. Bobrinskoy
Divison of the Humanities, U. of Chicago, 1967, p 37-44

3856   Galanter, M.

GROUP MEMBERSHIP AND GROUP
PREFERENCES IN INDIA
J. of Asian & African Studies, 1967, 2, 1-2, Jan-Apr,
91-924   SA, XVII, 1, D5392

3857   Galanter, M.

THE DISPLACEMENT OF TRADITIONAL LAW IN MODERN INDIA
J. of Social Issues, 1968, 24, 4, Oct., 65-92
SA, XVII, 5, D8630

3858   Galanter, Marc

THE ABORTED RESTORATION OF INDIGENOUS LAW IN INDIA
Comp. Stud. Soc. Hist. 14, 1, 1972, p 53-70

3859   Galanter, Marc

        UNTOUCHABILITY AND THE LAW
        Paper presented at conference on "The Untouchable in
        Contemporary India"
        U. of Arizona, Nov, 1967
        also Eco. & Polit. Weekly, Annual, Jan. 1969

3860   Gupta, M.G.

        POLICE IN A WELFARE STATE
        Ind. Sociol. 1960, 2, 2, Feb, 34-37
        SA, XII, 6, B2059

3861   Igbal, Nath

        SOCIAL LEGISLATION IN PUNJAB SINCE 1849   (PH.D.)
        Doct., Panjab U., 1959
        (Prof. B.R. Sharma)

3862   Ishwaran, K.

        CUSTOMARY LAW IN VILLAGE INDIA
        Int. J. Comp. Sociol. 1964, 5, 2, Sep 228-243
        SA, XIV, 1, B8815

3863   Jennings, Sir W.I.

        SOME CHARACTERISTICS OF THE INDIAN CONSTITUTION
        Madras; Oxford University Press, 1953, 86 pp

3864   Kalra, M.L.

        IMPACT OF SOCIAL LEGISLATION ON SOCIAL CONTROL IN
        RURAL HARYANA
        Doct. St., Indore U., 1969
        (Pothen)

3865   Khan, M.A.

        IMPACT OF RURAL SOCIAL LEGISLATION ON A MYSORE
        VILLAGE
        Social Welfare, 19, 6, 1972, 9-10

3866   Kidder, R.L.

        THE DYNAMICS OF LITIGATION: A STUDY OF CIVIL
        LITIGATION IN SOUTH INDIAN COURTS   (PH.D. SOC)
        Northwestern U., (70-71)

3867   Klappa, O.E.

        HEROES, VILLAINS & FOOLS, AS AGENTS OF SOCIAL CONTROL
        American Soc. Rev., 1954, 19, 56-62

3868   Mathur, A.S.

        THE LABOUR JUDICIARY IN INDIA
        J. of Ind. Re., 1964, 6, 3, Nov.239-255
        SA, XVI, 2, D0277

3869   McCormack, W.C.

        CASTE AND THE BRITISH ADMINISTRATION OF HINDU LAW
        J. of Asian and African Stud. 1966, 1, 1, Jan, 27-34
        SA, XVI, 2, D0278

3870   Mitra, P.

        LIFE ASSURANCE: LAW AND PRACTICE IN INDIA
        Calcutta, 1972

3871   Morrison, C.

        LAWYERS AND LITIGANTS IN A NORTH INDIAN DISTRICT:
        NOTES ON INFORMAL ASPECTS OF THE LEGAL SYSTEM
        LAW & Soc. Review, 1968-69, 3, 2-3, Nov.-Feb., 301-302
        SA, XVII, 4, E3423

3872   Morrison, Charles

        MUNSHIS AND THEIR MASTERS: THE ORGANIZATION OF
        AN OCCUPATIONAL RELATIONSHIP IN THE INDIAN LEGAL
        SYSTEM
        Journal of Asian Stud. XXXI, 2, 1972, p. 309-328

3873   Morrison, C.

        SOCIAL ORGANIZATION AT THE DISTRICT COURTS: COLLEAGUE
        RELATIONSHIPS AMONG INDIAN LAWYERS
        Law & Society Rev. 1968-69, 3, 2-3, Nov-Feb, 251-268
        SA, XVIII, 4, E3424

3874   Nimbkar, K.V.

        THE PRINCIPALS OF REHABILITATION APPLIED TO RECIDIVISM
        IN WOMEN
        Ind. Sociol. 1960, 2, 2, Feb, 38-41
        SA, XII, 6, B2063

3875   Pathak, (Miss) K.B.

        SOCIAL LEGISLATION IN INDIA   (PH.D)
        Doct., Agra U., 1959

3876   Pawar, K.S.

        POLICE IN A WELFARE STATE
        Ind. Sociol. 1960, 2, 2, Feb, 10-14
        SA, XII, 6, B2064

3877   Ray, R.

        BACKGROUND OF THE HINDU CODE BILL
        Pacific Affairs, V. 25, 1952, p 268-77

3878   Revankar, R.G.

THE INDIAN CONSTITUTION: A CASE STUDY OF BACKWARD
CLASSES
Fairleigh Dickinson, 1971

3879   Rowe, P.

INDIAN LAWYERS AND POLITICAL MODERNIZATION:
OBSERVATIONS IN FOUR DISTRICT TOWNS
Law & Society Rev., 1968-69, 3, 2-3, Nov-Feb, 219-250
SA, XVIII, 4, E3427

3880   Rudolph, L.I. & S.H. Rudolph

BARRISTERS AND BRAHMANS IN INDIA: LEGAL CULTURES AND
SOCIAL CHANGE
Comp. Stud. Soc. Hist, 1965, 8, 1, Oct, 24-49
SA, XIV, 5, C1519

3881   Sabnis, M.S.

LEGISLATION FOR THE PROTECTION OF CHILDREN
Ind. J. Soc. Wrk. 1960, 20, 4, Mar, 51-60
SA, XI, 6, A6859

3882   Sarkar, U.C.

CHARACTER AND SCOPE OF SOCIAL LEGISLATION IN INDIA OF
TODAY
International Journal of Legal Research, 1966, 1, 1,
Jun, 51-56
SA, XVII, 4, D7812

3883   Schwartz, Richd. D.

REFLECTIONS ON THE ROLE OF THE INDIAN LAWYER
in. Impact of Land Legislation (preface)
ed. C.K. Jayasimharao
Bangalore; Bharadwaja Publication, 1955

3884   Shastri, V.

        LEGISLATION FOR THE PROTECTION OF WOMEN
        Ind. J. Soc. Wrk., 1960, 20, 4, Mar, 69-71
        SA, XI, 6, A7056

3885   Singh, B.

        LAW AND LAW COURTS AS INSTRUMENTS OF SOCIAL JUSTICE
        AND SOCIAL TRANSFORMATION
        Int. J. of Legal Res, 1966, 1, 1, Jun, 3-8
        SA, XVII, 4, D7989

3886   Singh, B.

        EVOLUTION OF JUDICIAL SYSTEM IN INDIA
        Int. J. of Legal Res, 1966, 1, 1, Jun, 113-122
        SA, XVII, 4, D7990

3887   Singh, S.C.

        LAW OF PROBATION IN INDIA WITH SPECIAL REFERENCE TO
        UTTAR PRADESH
        Ind. J. Soc. Wrk, 1959, 20, 1, Jun, 13-32
        SA, XI, 6, A6861

3888   Singh, V.P.

        INTELLIGENCE IN CRIMINALS
        Ind. Jour. Soc. Wrk. 1966,27, 3, Oct., 269-274
        SA, XVI, 5, D2781

3889   Vatuk, V.P.

        THE POSITION OF WOMEN IN HITTITE LAWS AND MANUSMRITI
        J. of Asian & African Studies, 1967, 2, 3-4, Jul-Oct,
        251-265
        SA, XVII, 2, D6349

1636   sociology of law

    3890   Venkatarangayya, M.

            THE NEW CONSTITUTION AND THE REMOVAL OF GROUP PREJUDICES
            in Group Prejudices in India
            eds. M.B. Nanvati & C.N. Vakil
            Bombay, Vora, 1951, p 176-183

    3891
            THE REPUBLIC OF INDIA: THE DEVELOPMENT OF ITS LAWS
            AND CONSTITUTIONS
            London, Stevens, 1951, 309 p

    3892
            SOCIAL REFORM IN INDIA: THE HINDU CODE BILL
            World Today, V7, 1952, p 123-32

1653   penology and correctional problems

    3893   Agarwal- (Mrs.) S.K.

            PROBATION SYSTEM IN UTTAR PRADESH (PH.D)
            Doct., Agra U., 1964

    3894   Chandorkar, S.M.

            THE STUDY OF INDIAN PRISONS IN M.P.
            Doct. St., Saugar U., 1969

    3895   Chandra, D.

            OPEN AIR PRISONS AND THEIR INMATES: A SOCIOLOGICAL
            STUDY
            Lucknow, U., 1969

1653   penology and correctional problems

3896   Choudhary, M.

        THE PROBATION SYSTEM IN BIHAR
        Doct. St., Bhagalpur U., 1969
        (Prof. I. Prasad)

3897   Goyal, C.P.

        PRISON ADMINISTRATION IN INDIA   (PH.D:)
        Doct. St., Agra U., 1969

3898   Gupta, A.S.

        CRIME & POLICE IN INDIA
        Agra, 1972

3899   Haikerwal, B.S.

        A COMPARATIVE STUDY OF PENOLOGY (D.LITT.)
        Doct., Agra U., 1959

3900   Kulkarni, R.A.

        PROBATION OF OFFENDERS IN INDIA
        India, 1968

3901   Mukherjee, S.K.

        ADMINISTRATION OF JUVENILE CORRECTIONAL INSTITUTIONS:
        A COMPARATIVE STUDY IN DELHI&MAHARASHTRA
        Doct. St., Delhi U., 1969
        (V.Jagannadhan)

3902   Nair, (Mrs.) I.M.

        THE ROLE OF PRISON INDUSTRIES IN THE REHABILITATION
        OF THE DISCHARGED PRISONERS (PH.D.)
        Doct., Agra U., 1969
        (Dr. R.N. Saksena)

3903   Pandey, R.K.

PSYCHO-SOCIAL STUDY OF STAR CLASS PRISONERS IN MODEL
PRISON, LUCKNOW   (PH.D.)
Doct., Lucknow U., 1967
(Dr. S. Chandra)

3904   Rai, K.K.

PUNISHMENT OF CRIMINALS IN INDIA SINCE 1870
Doct. St., Agra U., 1969
(S.P. Varma)

3905   Raj Rami, A.

WOMEN LEGISLATIVE ELITE IN RAJASTHAN, 1962-1965
Polit. Sci. R. 6 (1), Jan-Mar, 1967, 39-57

3906   Reckless, W.C.

ROLE OF THE EXPERT ON CORRECTIONAL ADMINISTRATION
TO A REQUESTING COUNTRY
Am. Sociol. Rev. 19, 211-13, April. 54

3907   Reddy, G. Ram & K. Seshadri

DEVELOPING SOCIETY AND POLICE
Hyderabad, 1972

3908   Sandhu, H.S.

STUDY MEASURING THE IMPACT OF SHORT-TERM INSTITUTION-
ALISM ON PRISON INMATES (PH.D.)
Doct., Panjab U., 1962
(Dr. S. Jalota)

3909   Sandhu, H.S.

THE IMPACT OF SHORT-TERM INSTITUTIONALISM ON PRISON
INMATES
Brit.J. Criminal. 1964, 4, 5, Jul, 461-474
SA, XV, 2, C4519

3910   Sandhu, H.S.

PERCEPTION OF PRISON GUARDS: A CROSS-NATIONAL
STUDY OF INDIA AND CANADA
Intern'l. Rev. of Modern Sociology, 2, 1, Mar, 1972
26-33

3911   Sandhu, H.S.

A STUDY ON PRISON IMPACT
Chandigarh, 1968

3912   Sandhu, H.S. & D.E. Allen

THE PRISON GUARD: JOB PERCEPTIONS AND IN-SERVICE
TRAINING IN INDIA
Ind. J. Soc. Wrk. 1971, 32, 2, Jul, 115-120
SA, XX, 7, F9721

3913   Sangar, S.P.

CRIME AND PUNISHMENT IN MUGHAL INDIA
Delhi, Sterling Publisher, 1967, xii-249 pp

3914   Sharda, R.

LEGIŚLATORS AS ELITES: A SOCIOLOGICAL STUDY OF
LEGISLATORS OF UTTAR PRADESH
Doct. St., Lucknow U., 1969

3915   Shastree, (Mrs.) T.S.

A STUDY OF WOMEN PRISONERS
Doct. St., Poona U., 1969

3916   Srivastava, S.P.

CORRECTION IN INDIA: SOME ISSUES
Ind. J. Soc. Wrk. 1969, 30, 2, Jul, 117-122
SA, XIX, 1-2, E7646

1653   penology and correctional problems

3917   Trivedi, V.K.

        THE INDIAN LAWYER
        (ref. to Lucknow)
        Doct. St. Lucknow U., 1969

3918   Yadav, R.K.

        HUMAN RELATIONS IN PRISON COMMUNITY: A SOCIOLOGICAL
        STUDY (WITH PARTICULAR REFERENCE TO CENTRAL PRISON
        VARANASI)
        Doct. St., Agra U., 1969
        (Dr. S. Chandra)

3919   Vidya Bhushan

        PRISON ADMINISTRATION IN INDIA, WITH SPECIAL
        REFERENCE TO UTTAR PRADESH
        New Delhi, 1970

1700   **Sociology of Science**

1734   sociology of science & technology

    3920   Agarwal, (Miss) U.

SOCIAL CONSEQUENCES OF TECHNOLOGICAL CHANGE IN A
COMMUNITY DEVELOPMENT BLOCK (PH.D.)
Doct., Agra U.,
(Dr. R.N. Saksena)

    3921   Bali, R.

FARIDABAD: AN INDUSTRIAL TOWNSHIP: A STUDY OF SOME
SOCIAL IMPLICATIONS OF INDUSTRIALIZATION (PH.D.)
Doct., Bombay U., 1967
(Prof. K.M. Kapadia)

    3922   Baranwal, J.P.

SOCIAL EFFECTS OF URBANIZATION AND TECHNOLOGICAL
CHANGES IN VARANASI CITY (PH.D.)
Doct. St., Agra U., 1969
(Dr. B. S. Haikerwal)

    3923   Bhatnagar, S.S. and S.D. Mahant

PLACE OF SCIENCE IN BUILDING OF A UNITED INDIA
in Group Prejudices in India
ed M.B. Nanavatti & C.N. Vakil
Bombay, Vora, 1951, p 219

    3924   Bhatt, V.V.

ACCELERATING TECHNICAL CHANGE
Inter. Dev. Rev. 1967, 9, 1, Mar, 25-26
SA, XVII, 3, D7273

    3925   Bhattacharya, S.

CULTURAL AND SOCIAL CONSTRAINTS ON TECHNOLOGICAL
INNOVATION
Ind. Eco. & Soc. Hist. Rev., 1966, 3, 3, Sep, 240-267
SA, XVII, 1, D5426

3926   Bose, N.K.

        IMPACT OF CHANGING TECHNOLOGY ON SOCIETY
        Eco. Weekly, 1961

3927   Foster, G.M.

        TRADITIONAL CULTURES AND THE IMPACT OF TECHNOLOGICAL
        CHANGE
        New York, Harper, 1962

3928   Kuthiala, S.K.

        IMPACT OF FACTORY PRODUCTION ON TRADITIONAL SOCIETIES:
        MODERNIZATION, SOME ALTERNATIVE VIEWS ON INDIA
        Paper presented at the 7th World Congress of the Int.
        Soc. Assoc., 1970
        SA, XVIII, 5, Sup, 9, E3935

3929   Mahalanobis, P.C.

        STATISTICS AS A KEY TECHNOLOGY
        Amer. Statistician, 1965, 19, 2, Apr, 43-46
        SA, XIV, 1, B8828

3930   Marriott, McKim

        TECHNOLOGICAL CHANGE IN OVERDEVELOPED RURAL AREAS
        Eco. Dev. & Cult, change, V. I, 1952, p 261-72

3931   Mehrotra, R.c.

        LESSONS FROM INDIA IN INTRODUCING SCIENCE TO ANCIENT
        CIVILIZATIONS
        Science Forum 5, 1968, 1, 5, Oct, 6-10
        SA, XVIII, 1-2, E1420

3932   Meier, Richard L.

RELATIONS OF TECHNOLOGY TO THE DESIGN OF VERY LARGE
CITIES
in India's Urban Future
ed. R. Turner
Berkeley; U. of Calif. Press- 1962, p 299-327

3933   Morehouse, W.

CONFRONTING A FOUR-DIMENSIONAL PROBLEM: SCIENCE,
TECHNOLOGY, SOCIETY AND TRADITION IN INDIA AND
PAKISTAN
Technology & Culture, 1967, 8, 3, Jul, 363-374
SA,XVI, 6, D3642

3934   Patel, (Miss) K.M.

EFFECTS OF BOMBAY COTTON MILL INDUSTRY ON RATNAGIRI'S
RURAL POPULATION (PH.D.)
Doct. Bombay U, 1963
(Prof. G.S. Ghurye)

3935   Poddar, Arakinda, (ed.)

MAN, SCIENCE & SOCIETY
Simla, 1969

3936   Prasad, B.

FOREIGN TECHNOLOGY AND INDIA'S ECONOMIC DEVELOPMENT
Int. Dev. Rev., 1968, 10, 2, Jun, 18-20
SA, XVII, 7, E0587

3937   *Seshachar, B.R.

PROBLEMS OF INDIAN SCIENCE SINCE NEHRU
Impact of Science on Society, 1972, 22, 1-2, Jan-Jun,
133-141
SA, 21, 73G4560

1800   Demography and Human Biology

1835   family planning

   3938   Agarwal, R.P.

          A CRITICAL STUDY OF FAMILY PLANNING PROGRAMME IN U.P.
          (PH.D.)
          Doct., Agra U., 1970
          (Dr. P.N. Tandon)

   3939   Agarwala, S.N.

          A FAMILY PLANNING SURVEY IN FOUR DELHI VILLAGES
          Pop. Stud. 1961, 15, 2, Nov. 110-120
          SA, X, 3, A2572

   3940   Allen L.R.

          A FAMILY PLANNING STUDY AS A PART OF A COMPREHENSIVE
          HEALTH SERVICE IN A RURAL AREA
          Popul. R., 1957, 1, 1, Jan, 19-21
          SA, XII, 4, B0614

   3941   Apte, J.S.

          COMMUNICATION AND MOTIVATION IN FAMILY PLANNING
          Ind. J. Soc. Wrk. 1965, 26, 2, Jul, 133-138
          SA, XVI, 4, D1961

   3942   Balakrishna, S.

          FAMILY PLANNING: KNOWLEDGE, ATTITUDE & PRACTICE
          Hyderabad, 1968

   3943   Banerji, D.

          FAMILY PLANNING IN INDIA: A CRITIQUE AND PERSPECTIVE
          Delhi, 1968

1835   family planning

3944   Berelson, B.

NATIONAL PROGRAMMES IN FAMILY PLANNING
Meerut, 1968

3945   Bhatia, B. et al.

A STUDY IN FAMILY PALLING COMMUNICATION: DIRECT
MAILING
India; Central Family Planning Institute, 1966

3946   Balakrishna, S.S. & B. Radhaiyer

CHARACTERISTICS OF ADOPTERS OF FAMILY PLANNING METHODS
IN PUNJAB: A DISCRIMINANT FUNCTION APPROACH
Behavioural Scis. & C.D. 1968, 2, 1, Mar, 14-25
SA, XIX, 1-2, E7661

3947   Bishwas, D.K.

SOCIAL BARRIERS TO FAMILY PLANNING IN INDIA
Doct. St., Bhagalpur U., 1969
(Prof. I. Prasad)

3948   Bose, A.

ELEVEN MYTHS OF FAMILY PLANNING
South Asian R. 3 (4) Jul 1970, 323-330

3949   Burman, B.K.R.

FAMILY PLANNING FROM THE POINT OF VIEW OF CULTURAL
ANTHROPOLOGY
Ind. J. Soc. Wrk., 1970, 30, 4, Jan, 343-355
SA, XIX, 6, F1861

3950   Chandra, R.

CULTURAL BARRIERS TO FAMILY PLANNING AMONG BRAHMINS
OF LUCKNOW CITY
Doct. St. Lucknow U., 1969

3951   Chandrasekarahan, G.

CULTURAL FACTORS AID THE PROPAGATION OF FAMILY
PLANNING IN THE INDIAN SETTING
J. of Family Welfare, 1959, 5, 3, 43-51

3952   Chandrasekhar, S.

THE PROSPECT FOR PLANNED PARENTHOOD IN INDIA
Pacific Affairs, 26, 4, Dec, 1953, 318-328

3953   Chandrasekhar, S.

POPULATION AND PLANNED PARENTHOOD IN INDIA
(intro. by J. Huxley)
London; G. Allen & Unwin, 1955, XII & 108 pp

3954   Chandrasekhar   S.

FAMILY PLANNING IN AN INDIAN VILLAGE: MOTIVATIONS
AND METHODS
Popul. R. 1959, 3, 1, Jan, 63-71
SA, XII, 6, B2090

3955   Chandrasekhar,S.

FAMILY PLANNING IN RURAL INDIA
Ant. Rev. 1959, 19, 3, Fall, 399-411
SA, X, 3, A2578

3956   Chandrasekhar, S.

CULTURAL BARRIERS TO FAMILY PLANNING IN UNDER-
DEVELOPED COUNTRIES
Pop. Rev., 1957

3957　Chatterjee, B.

SOCIAL ASPECTS, OF FAMILY PLANNING IN INDIA
Ind. J. Soc. Wrk, 1971, 32, 2, Jul, 137-150
SA, XX, 7, F9831

3958　Chattopadhyay, (Miss) I.

THE POPULATION PROBLEM AND ATTITUDE STUDY TOWARDS
FAMILY PLANNING IN INDIA　(D.PHIL.)
Doct., Calcutta U., 1964

3959　Dandekar, K.

COMMUNICATION IN FAMILY PLANNING:　REPORT ON AN
EXPERIMENT
London;　Asia Publ. House, 1967, xii-109 pp

3960　Ganguli, H.C.

A PSYCHOLOGICAL ANALYSIS OF THE FAMILY PLANNING
SITUATION IN INDIA
Ind. J. Soc. Wrk. 1968, 29, 3, Oct, 233-242
SA, XVIII, 4, E3523

3961　Gopalaswami, R.A.

FAMILY PLANNING AND NATIONAL PLANNING
Popul. R. 1957, 1, 1, Jan,1-6
SA, XII, 4, B0621

3962　Gopalaswami, R.A.

FAMILY PLANNING:　OUTLOOK FOR GOVERNMENT ACTION IN
INDIA,
67-84, Chapt. in Research in Family Planning,
ed. C.V. Kiser
Princeton, Princeton U. Press,1962, xvi & 664 pp
SA, XIII, 2, B5619

3963   Gopalaswami, S.R.A.

ADMINISTRATIVE IMPLEMENTATION OF FAMILY PLANNING
POLICY
Pop. R. 1959, 3, 1, Jan 43-62
SA, XII, 6, B2102

3964   Gore, S.

FAMILY PLANNING TRAINING AND RESEARCH CENTER
Pop. R. 1960, 4,2, July, 58-63
SA, XII, 7 B3020

3965   Gupta, P.S.

FAMILY PLANNING FOR THE HOME WORKING WIVES & MOTHERS
Social Welfare, 19, 7, 1972, 8-16

3966   Hallen, G.C.

SOCIOLOGICAL IMPLICATIONS OF FAMILY PLANNING
Social Welfare, 1967, 14, 6, 5-6 & 27

3967   Hanif, W.

ATTITUDES TOWARDS FAMILY PLANNING
Ind. J. Soc. Res., 1962, 3, 2, Jul, 66-69
SA, XI, 6, A6934

3968   Hendre, S.S.

HINDUS & FAMILY PLANNING
Bombay, 1971

3969   Jackson, M.C.N.

FAMILY PLANNING IN ENGLAND AND INDIA
Journal of Sex Research, 1967, 3, 4, Nov, 269-271
SA, XVI, 7 D4560

3970   Jamnejai, Krishna

SOCIO-ECONOMIC ASPECTS OF FAMILY PLANNING WORK IN
HOSPITAL
Family Planning News, 8, 1968

3971   Jorapur, P.B.

PROGRESS IN FAMILY PLANNING: A STUDY OF SOCIAL AND
ECONOMIC CORRELATION
Ind. J. Soc. Wrk. 1971, 32, 1, Apr, 77-81
SA, XX, 7, F9841

3972   Kapil, K.K.

PROMOTION OF INTERSPOUSAL COMMUNICATION ON FAMILY
PLANNING AS A RESULT OF EDUCATIONAL SESSIONS IN THE
POST-NATAL CLINICS
Ind. Soc. Bu., 1968, 5, 4,Jul, 215-220
SA, XVII, 7, E0651

3973   Karr, B.B.

CULTURAL DETERMINANTS OF COGNITIVE GAP AND THE
PROBLEM OF PLANNED CHANGE IN FAMILY PLANNING IN INDIA
Ind. J. of Public Health, 1968, 12, 1, 30-35

3974   Khare, R.S.

A STUDY OF INTRA-FAMILY PROBLEMS OF MOTIVATION IN
RELATION TO FAMILY PLANNING IN INDIA
East. Anthrop. 1965, 18, 2, May-Aug., 73-79
SA, XIV, 6, C2591

3975   Kishore, R.

VALUE SYSTEM AND FAMILY PLANNING IN LUCKNOW CITY
Doct. St., Lucknow U., 1969

3976   Kivlin, J.E.

CORRELATES OF FAMILY PLANNING IN EIGHT INDIAN VILLAGES
Mich. State. U., Research Report, 1968

3977   Kumar, V.K. & S. Raghbir

ORGANISATIONAL IMPEDIMENTS TO FAMILY PLANNING: A
CASE STUDY
Ind. J. of Soc. Wrk, 1970, 30, 4, Jan, 357-360
SA, XIX, 6, F1958

3978   Lakshminarayana, H.B.

ANALYSIS OF FAMILY PATTERNS THROUGH A CENTURY
(PH.D.)
Doct., Poona U., 1965
(Dr. (Mrs.) I. Karte)

3979   Lloyd,R.

PROPOSAL FOR A WORLD FAMILY PLAN
International Development Rev., 1965, 7, 4, Sep. 21-23
SA, XVII, 1, D5521

3980   Mahajan, V.S.

POPULATION, EMPLOYMENT AND FAMILY PLANNING IN INDIA
Ind. J. Soc. Wrk. 1961, 22, 3, Dec, 253-257
SA, XI, 7, A7688

3981   Malhotra, P. & L. Khan

FACTORS FAVOURING ACCEPTANCE OF FAMILY PLANNING AMONG
WOMEN ATTENDING THE NEW DELHI, N.C.W. CENTER
J. of Family Welfare, 1961, 8, 1, 18 & 3, 4, 1-18

3982   Man, B.S.

FAMILY PLANNING AMONG THE TRIBES
Family Planning News, 1968, 9, 3, 15-17

3983   Marshall, J.F.

        A NEGLECTED AREA OF FAMILY PLANNING RESEARCH
        Pop. Rev., 1967, 11, 1, 30-37

3984   Mathew, C.

        THE POPULATION DILEMA AND FAMILY PLANNING PROGRAMME
        IN INDIA
        Ind. J. Soc. Wrk.,1961, 22,3, Dec, 233-238

3985   Mehta, S.R. & Advani, M.

        SOCIOLOGY OF FAMILY PLANNING
        Ind. J. Soc. Res, 12, 2, Aug 1971, 123-127

3986   Misra, B.D.

        CORRELATES OF MALES'ATTITUDES TOWARDS FAMILY
        PLANNING
        In. Sociological Contributions to FAmily Planning
        Research
        ed. D.J. Bogue
        U. of Chicago Press, 1967

3987   Misra, B.P.

        THE CASE FOR AND AGAINST FAMILY PLANNING WITH SPECIAL
        REFERENCE TO INDIA
        Mysore Eco. R. 41, 5, May 1955, 9-12

3988   Morrison, W.A.

        THE RELATIONSHIP OF FAMILY SIZE AND SOCIO-CULTURAL
        VARIABLES TO ATTITUDES TOWARD FAMILY PLANNING IN A
        VILLAGE OF INDIA
        American Doctoral Dissertations
        The University of Connecticut, 1956-57 (Sociology)

3989   Morrison, W.A.

FAMILY PLANNING ATTITUDES OF INDUSTRIAL WORKERS OF
AMBARNATH, A CITY OF WESTERN INDIA: A COMPARATIVE
ANALYSIS
Pop. Stud, 1961, 14, 3, Mar. 235-248
SA, IX, 4, A0769

3990   Morrison, Wm. A.

ATTITUDES OF MALES TOWARD FAMILY PLANNING IN A
WESTERN INDIAN VILLAGE
Mil. Mem. Fd. Quart., 1956, 34, 3, Jul,272-286

3991   Morrison, W.A.

ATTITUDES OF FEMALES TOWARDS FAMILY PLANNING IN A
MAHARASHTRIAN VILLAGE
Mil. Mem. Fd. Quart., 1957, 35, 1, Jan, 67-81
SA,VII, 1, 5494

3992   Morrison, W.A.

FAMILY PLANNING ATTITUDE PREDICTION, THE SOCIAL
WORKER AND THE VILLAGER
Ind. J. Soc. Wrk, 1959, 20, 3, Dec, 137-156
SA, XI, 5, A6164

3993   Mukerjee, R.

MOTIVATIONS AND VALUES
539-550, Chapter in Research In Family Planning
ed. C.V. Kiser
Princeton, Princeton U. Press, 1962, xvi & 664 pp
SA, XIII, 2, B5624

3994   Opler, M.E.

CULTURAL CONTEXT AND POPULATION CONTROL PROGRAMMES
IN VILLAGE INDIA
in Fact & Theory   in Social Science
ed. E.W. Count & G.T. Bowles

3995   Pandey, J.P.

THE IMPACT OF THE FAMILY PLANNING PROJECT ON THE
RURAL POPULATION WITH SPECIAL REF. TO CHOGGAWA BLOCK,
GORAKHPUR DISTRICT
Doct. St., Gorakhpur U., 1969

3996   Pandit, T.P.

FAMILY PLANNING IN THE PUNJAB
Jullundur City, Putta Maternity Hospital, 1952, 9 p

3997   Pareek, U. & V. Kothandapani

MODERNIZATION AND ATTITUDE TOWARD FAMILY SIZE AND
FAMILY PLANNING: ANALYSIS OF SOME DATA FROM INDIA
Social Biology, 1969, 16, 1, Mar, 44-48
SA, XVII, 1-2, E1511

3998   Patel, H.G.

RESISTING FACTORS TO MOVIVATION TOWARDS STERILIZATION:
METHODS OF FAMILY PLANNING
Ind. J. Soc. Wrk, 1966, 27, 1, 71-74

3999   Pathare, (Miss) R.M.

FAMILY PLANNING: ITS ACCEPTANCE AND LIMITATION   (PH.D.
Doct., Bombay U., 1966
(Prof. K.M. Kapadia)

4000   Pathare, R.

THE FAMILY PLANNING PROGRAMME: A SOCIOLOGICAL ANALYSIS
Sociol. B. 1966, 15, 2, Sep, 44-63
SA, XV, 6, C7747

1835   family planning

4001   Poffenberger, Thomas

        RESEARCH NEEDS IN FAMILY PLANNING AND POPULATION
        CONTROL
        Ind. J. Soc. Res, 1966, 7, 2, Aug, 94-100
        SA, XVII, 2, D6397

4002   Poffenberger, T.

        HUSBAND-WIFE DIFFERENCES IN ATTITUDE TOWARD FERTILITY
        CONTROL INNOVATIONS IN RURAL INDIA
        Ind. J. Soc. Res, 1968, 9, 1, Apr, 36-42
        SA, XVIII, 6, E5332

4003   Poffenberger, T. & S.B. Poffenberger

        HUSBAND-WIFE COMMUNICATION AND MOTIVIATIONAL ASPECTS
        OF POPULATION CONTROL IN AN INDIAN VILLAGE
        New Delhi, Central Family PLANNING INSTITUTE, 1969,
        117 pp

4004   Prasad, I, G.S. Prasad, & A. Sinha

        OPINION AND ATTITUDE TOWARDS FAMILY PLANNING AMONG
        WOMEN OF PRIMARY SCHOOL TEACHERS
        Ind. J. Soc. Wrk. 1962, 23, 2, Jul, 179-183
        SA, XII, 1, A8557

4005   Prasad, L.

        ATTITUDES TOWARDS FAMILY PLANNING
        Ind. J. Soc. Wrk., 1956, 17, 3, Dec, 184-188
        SA, VIII, 1, 7203

4006   Raina, B.L.

        INDIA
        in Family Planning & Population Programs
        ed. B. Berelson et al
        U. of Chicago Press, 1966

4007   Ramu, G.N.

GOLD MINERS AND FAMILY PLANNING
Ind. J. Soc. Wrk., 1967, 27, 4, Jan, 337-342
SA, XVI,6, D3717

4008   Rao, Kamala G.

AN EXPLORATORY STUDY OF IUD ACCEPTORS
New Delhi; Central Family Planning Institute, 1966

4009   Rao, K.G.

PROBLEMS IN THE ASSESSMENT OF BEHAVIORAL INDICES OF
THE IMPACT OF FAMILY PLANNING PROGRAMMES
Ind. J. Soc. Res., 1968, 9, 1, Apr, **28-35**
SA, XVIII, 6 E5335

4010   Rao, M.K.

FAMILY PLANNING: A NATIONAL OBLIGATION
Kurukshetra, 1967, 15, 5, Feb, 11-13
SA, XVIII, 6, E5244

4011   Rau, D.R.

FAMILY PLANNING IN INDIA
Jour. of Sex Research, 1967, 3, 4, Nov, 272-274
SA, XVI, 7, D4566

4012   Reeder, L.G. & G.B. Krishnamurty

FAMILY PLANNING IN RURAL INDIA: A PROBLEM IN SOCIAL
CHANGE
Soc. Prob. 1964, 12, 2, Fal, 212-223
SA, XIII, 2, B5625

4013   Royburman, B.K.

PROBLEM OF FAMILY PLANNING AMONG THE SCHEDULED TRIBES
OF WEST BENGAL
Vanyajati, 1958, 6, 4, Oct., 161-164
SA, VIII, 2, 7619

4014   Saksena, D.N.

A WORKING HYPOTHESIS UNDERLYING FAMILY PLANNING
COMMUNICATION WORK
Ind. Sociological B. 1967, 5, 1, Oct, 71-74
SA, XVII, 3, D7378

4015   Salunkhe,G.R.

FAMILY PLANNING AS UNDERSTOOD AND PRACTISED IN THE
CITY OF INDORE
Ind. Sociol. 1959, 1, 1, Mar, 59-65
SA, XII, 5, B1445

4016   Samuel, T.J.

FAMILY PLANNING AND HOW TO MAKE IT EFFECTIVE
Ind. J. Soc. Wrk. 1960, 21, 3, Dec,223-227
SA, XI, 7, A7781

4017   Sanyal, S.N.

ATTITUDE TOWARDS CONTRACEPTIVE METHODS
Man in India, 1962, 42, 2, Apr-Jun, 126-138
SA, XII, 5, B1446

4018   Sanyal, S.N.

FAMILY PLANNING PROBLEMS
Man in India, 1967,47, 4, Oct-Dec., 331-337
SA, XVII, 3, D7310

4019   Sarupia, S.L.

ATTITUDES TOWARDS FAMILY PLANNING IN A SMALL URBAN
COMMUNITY
Ind. J. Soc. Wrk., 1964

4020   Satyanarayana, V.

SOCIAL STRUCTURE AND FAMILY PLANNING: A STUDY OF
CULTURAL MILIEU AND SOCIAL COMMUNICATION
Doct. St., Andhra U., 1969
(Prof. N.S. Reddy)

4021   Sengupta, A.

EVALUATION OF FAMILY PLANNING PROGRAMME
Ind. J. Soc. Res., 1968, 9, 1, Apr, 43-49
SA, XVIII, 6, E5339

4022   Sengupta, A.

A STUDY OF THE PROMOTION OF KNOWLEDGE OF CONTRACEPTIVES
BY EDUCATION PROGRAMME IN FAMILY PLANNING, 1970
Ind. J. Soc. Wrk., 1968, 28, 4, Jan, 427-452
SA, XVII, 5, D8677

4023   Sethi, (Miss) N.

SOCIO-ECONOMIC FACTORS IN FAMILY LIMITATION IN AN URBAN
AREA, LUCKNOW, (PH.D.)
Doct., Lucknow U., 1970
(Dr. M.D. Joshi)

4024   Sharma, R.G.

A STUDY OF SOCIAL ATTITUDES OF MALE AND FEMALE
POPULATION TOWARDS FAMILY PLANNING MEASURES, WITH
REFERENCE TO INTRA-UTERIN CONTRACEPTIVE DEVICE
(PH.D.)
Doct., Ranchi U., 1970
(Dr. K. Bhaskaran)

4025   Shrivastava, R.C.

INDUSTRIALISATION AS A FACTOR IN ATTITUDES TOWARDS
FAMILY PLANNING (PH.D.)
Doct., Saugar U., 1966
(Dr. Jai Prakash)

4026   Siddh, K.K.

FERTILITY VALUES AND FAMILY PLANNING IN TWO RELIGIOUS
GROUPS IN A METROPOLITAN TOWN
Doct. St., Agra U., 1969
(Dr. R.N. Saxena)

4027   Siddique, M.K.A.

ATTITUDE TOWARDS FAMILY PLANNING IN THE SLUMS OF
CALCUTTA
Pop. Rev., 1965, 9, (1-2), 86-91

4028   Simmons, G.B.

THE INDIAN INVESTMENT IN FAMILY PLANNING
New York; The population Council, 1971, X & 213 pp

4029   Singh, B.

FIVE YEARS OF FAMILY PLANNING IN THE COUNTRYSIDE
Lucknow, Lucknow U., J.K. Inst. of Sociology and
Human Relations, 1958, 118 pp

4030   Singh, K.K. & H.B. Pardasani

EFFECTIVENESS OF SHORT DURATION CONTACTS IN
POPULARISING FAMILY PLANNING IN RURAL INDIA
Behav. Scis. & C.D., 1967, 1, 2, Sep, 135-149
SA, XVIII, 7, E6387

4031   Sinha, (Mrs.) P.

BARRIERS IN FAMILY PLANNING (PH.D.)
Doct. Patna U., 1968
(Dr. Z. Ahmad)

4032   Sinha, R.K.

FAMILY PLANNING AND ITS CULTURAL IMPLICATIONS IN
A CHHOTANAGPUR TRIBE: A STUDY IN THE ORIENTATION
OF THE CULTURAL VALUES
Doct. St., Ranchi U., 1969

4033   Sinha, V.C.

FERTILITY ATTITUDE TOWARDS FAMILY PLANNING OF OROANS
OF RANCHI
Doct.St. Ranchi U., 1969

4034   Thapar, Savitri

FAMILY PLANNING IN INDIA
Pop. Stud. 1963, 17, 1, Jul, 41-19
SA, XII, 4, B0641

4035   Thorat, S.S. & F.C. Fliegel

SOME ASPECTS OF ADOPTION OF HEALTH AND FAMILY PLANNING
PRACTICES IN INDIA
Behavioural Scis. & C.D. 1968, 2, 1, Mar, 1-13
SA, XIX, 1-2, E7703

4036   Verma, (Miss) S.

ATTITUDES OF EDUCATED MOTHERS TOWARDS FAMILY PLANNING
IN AGRA (PH.D.)
Doct. Agra U., 1970
(Dr. R.N. Saksena)

4037

FAMILY PLANNING
Mthly publ. Opin. Surv., 9, (6-7) Mar-Apr., 1964, 1-60

1835   family planning

4038

        POPULATION TRENDS AND FAMILY PLANNING
        Hyderabad, Gov't. Economic Affairs, 7, 5-6,
        May-Jun, 1954, 170-179

4039

        URBAN AND RURAL ATTITUDES TOWARDS FAMILY PLANNING:
        A NORTH INDIA SURVEY
        Mthly publ. Opin. Surv., 14 (7), April, 1969, 3-34

1837   demography (population study)

   4040   Agarwal, B.L.

        SAMPLE REGISTRATION IN INDIA
        Pop. Stu. 23, 3, Nov, 1969, 379-394

   4041   Agarwala, S.N.

        AGE AT MARRIAGE IN INDIA AS ASCERTAINED FROM CENSUS DATA
        American Doctoral Dissertations
        Princeton U., 1957-58
        (Sociology)

   4042   Agarwala, S.N.

        A METHOD FOR CORRECTING REPORTED AGES AND MARRIAGE
        DURATIONS
        Indian Pop. B. 1, 1, April 1960, 129-164

   4043   Agarwala, S.N.

        SOCIAL AND CULTURAL FACTORS AFFECTING FERTILITY IN
        INDIA
        Pop. R. 1964, 8, 1, Jan, 73-78
        SA, XIII, 3-4, B6501

1837   demography (population study)

    4044   Agarwala, S.N.

            IMPACT OF POPULATION GROWTH ON SOCIETY
            Ind. J. Soc. Wrk., 1965, 26, 2, Jul, 118-125
            SA, XVI, 4, D1960

    4045   Agarwala, S.N.

            SOME PROBLEMS'S OF INDIA'S POPULATION
            Bombay, Vora, 1966, iii-151-2 pp

    4046   Agarwala, S.N.

            THE ARITHMETIC OF STERILIZATION IN INDIA
            Eugenics Quart., 1966, 13, 3, Sep, 209-213
            SA, XV, 2, C4531

    4047   Agarwala, S.N.

            A DEMOGRAPHIC STUDY OF SIX URBANIZING VILLAGES
            Bombay; Asia Publ. House, 1970, 195 p.

    4048   Agarwala, S.N.

            INDIA'S POPULATION PROBLEMS
            New Delhi, 1972

    4049   Aird, J.S.

            FERTILITY LEVELS AND DIFFERENTIALS IN TWO BENGALI VILLAGES
            American Doctoral Dissertations (1956-1957)
            University of Michigan(Sociology)

    4050   Amundson, R.H.

            POPULATION PROBLEMS AND POLICIES IN PUERTO RICO,
            INDIA AND JAPAN
            American Doctoral Dissertations (1955-1956)
            Notre Dame University (Sociology)

1837   demography (population study)

    4051   Anand, K.

           AN ANALYSIS OF INTER-GENERATION FERTILITY
           Ind. J. of Soc. Wrk., 1967, 27, 4, Jan, 361-366
           SA, XVI, 6, D3648

    4052   Aparanji, N.R.

           A STUDY OF DEMOGRAPHIC TRENDS IN BAGALKOT   (PH.D.)
           Doct., Karnatak U, 1964
           (Dr. D.M. Nanjundappa)

    4053   Babu Ram

           FERTILITY PATTERNS IN ALLAHABAD CITY (D.PHIL)
           Doct., Allahabad U., 1970
           (Dr. A.D. Sharma)

    4054   Bagley, C.

           A SURVEY OF PROBLEMS REPORTED BY INDIAN AND
           PAKISTANI IMMIGRANTS IN BRITAIN
           Race, 1969, 11, 1, Jul, 65-76
           SA, XIX, 3, E9002

    4055   Bansil, P.C.

           THE FUTURE POPULATION OF INDIA
           Ind. J. Agric. Econ. 1958, 13, 3, Jul-Sep, 25 -43
           SA, VIII, 2, 7587

    4056   Basu, A.

           SELECTION INTENSITY IN THE PAHIRAS
           Eugenic Quart, 1967, 14, 3, Sep, 241-243
           SA, XVI, 2, D0301

    4057   Basu, A.

           INTRINSIC RATE OF NATURAL INCREASE AMONG THE PAHIRAS
           Sociol. Biology, 1971, 18, 2, Jun, 195-199
           SA, XX, 6, F867

1837   demography (population study)

    4058   Bebarta, P.C.

            RECENT STUDIES IN FERTILITY
            Sociol. B. 1961, 10, 2, Sep, 27-41
            SA, XI, 6, A6866

    4059   Bhatnagar, (Mrs. V.)

            DEMOGRAPHIC STUDY OF KAVAL CITIES OF UTTAR PRADESH,
            WITH SPECIAL REFERENCE TO KANPUR: A STUDY IN POPULATION
            OF KAVAL CITIES FROM 1901 TO 1961 (PH.D.)

    4060   *Bhattacharya, D.K.

            INDIANS OF AFRICAN ORIGIN
            Cahiers d'Etudes Africaines, 1970, 10, 4, 40, 579-582
            SA, 21, 73G3625

    4061   Bopegamage, A.

            INDIA'S POPULATION GROWS YOUNG
            Sociol. B. 1959, 8, 1, Mar. 69-85
            SA, XI, 6, A6870

    4062   Bose, A. (compiler)

            STUDIES IN DEMOGRAPHY
            North Carolina U.P., 1971

    4063   Bose, S.R.

            BIHAR POPULATION PROBLEMS
            Calcutta, 1968

    4064   Bottelier, P.

            EEN NOTTITIE OVER DEMOGRAFISCHE POLITIEK IN
            NIETWESTERSE LANDEN (A NOTE ABOUT DEMOGRAPHIC POLICY
            IN NON-WESTERN COUNTRIES)
            Sociologische Gids, 1965, 12, 3, May-Jun, 175-178
            (Dutch)
            SA, XVII, 6, D9731

1837   demography (population study)

4065   Chand, G.

        SOME ASPECTS OF THE POPULATION PROBLEM OF INDIA
        Patna, Patna U., 1957, 167 pp

4066   Chand, S. and A.N. Kapoor

        PEOPLE AND POPULATION OF INDIA: A CULTURO-DEMOGRAPHIC
        STUDY
        Delhi; Metropolitan Book Company, 1957, 142 pp

4067   Chander, R.

        PATTERN OF INTERNAL MIGRATION OF SCIENTIFIC AND
        TECHNICAL MANPOWER IN INDIA
        Manpower J., 4 (1), Apr.-Jun. 1968, 111-154

4068   Chandrasekaran, C. & M.V. George

        MECHANISMS UNDERLYING THE DIFFERENCES IN FERTILITY
        PATTERNS OF BENGALEE WOMEN FROM THREE SOCIO-ECONOMIC
        GROUPS
        Milbank Memor. Fund Quart., 1962, 40, 1, Jan, 59-89
        SA, XI, 7, A7672

4069   Chandrasekaran, C.

        SURVEY OF THE STATUS OF DEMOGRAPHY IN INDIA
        in The Study of Population
        ed. P.M. Hauser & O.D. Duncan
        U. of Chicago Press, 1959

4070   Chandrasekaran, C.

        INDIAN DEMOGRAPHIC TRENDS WITH A PROJECTION INTO THE
        NEXT TWENTY-FIVE YEARS AND THEIR SIGNIFICANCE FOR
        SOCIAL WELFARE
        Ind. J.S. Work, 1965, 26, 2, Jul, 126-128
        SA, XVI, 4, D1966

1837   demography (population study).

4071   Chandrasekaran, C. & P.P. Talwar

        FORMS OF AGE: SPECIFIC BIRTH RATES BY ORDERS OF
        BIRTH IN AN INDIAN COMMUNITY
        Eugenics Quart. 1968, 15, 4, Dec, 264-272
        SA, XIX, 7, F2676

4072   Chandrasekaran, K.S.

        LABOUR FORCE CHANGES AND EMPLOYMENT IN INDIA IN
        RELATION TO POPULATION GROWTH, 1951-66   (PH.D.)
        Doct., Bombay U., 1962
        (Prof. D.T. Lakdawala)

4073   Chandrasekhar, S.

        POPULATION TRENDS AND HOUSING NEEDS IN INDIA
        Popul. R. 1957, 1, 1, Jan, 12-18
        SA, XII, 4, B0556

4074   Chandrasekhar, S.

        MANGADU: DEMOGRAPHY OF AN INDIAN VILLAGE, PART I
        Pop. R. 1957, 1, 2, Jul, 57-70
        SA, XII, 5, B1351

4075   Chandrasekhar, S.

        THE COMPOSITION OF INDIA'S POPULATION ACCORDING TO
        THE 1951 CENSUS-I
        Pop. R. 1958, 2, 1, Jan, 63-78
        SA, XII, 5, B1352

4076   Chandrasekhar, S.

        THE COMPOSITION OF INDIA'S POPULATION ACCORDING TO
        THE 1951 CENSUS-II
        Pop. R. 1958, 2, 2, Jul, 59-64
        SA, XII, V, B1353

1837   demography (population study)

    4077   Chandrasekhar, S.

            INFANT MORTALITY IN INDIA 1901-1955: A MATTER OF
            LIFE AND DEATH
            London, G. Allen and Unwin, 1959,175 pp

    4078   Chandrasekhar, S.

            POPULATION GROWTH AND FOOD SUPPLY IN INDIA
            Pop. R., 1959, 3, 1, Jan, 79-84
            SA, XII, 6, B2091

    4079   Chandrasekhar, S.

            A NOTE ON DEMOGRAPHIC STATISTICS IN INDIA
            Pop. R. 1960, 4, 1, Jan 40-45
            SA, XII, 7, B2944

    4080   Chandrasekhar, S.

            POPULATION GROWTH AND ECONOMIC DEVELOPMENT IN INDI.
            Popul. R. 5, 1, Jan, 1961, 22-26

    4081   Chandrasekhar, S.

            MANGADU: VITAL STATICS IN AN INDIAN VILLAGE
            Popul. R., 1962, 2, Jul, 147-166
            SA, XII, 2, B5284

    4082   Chandrasekhar, S.

            INDIA'S POPULATION: FACTS, PROBLEM AND POLICY
            Meerut, Meenakshi Prakashan, 1967, 76 pp

1837   demography (population study)

    4083   Chandrasekhar, S. (ed.)

            ASIA'S POPULATION PROBLEM
            New York, Frederic A. ra ger, 1967, 311 pp
            SA, XV, 6, C7730

    4084   Chandrasekhar, S.

            HOW INDIA IS TACKLING HER POPULATION PROBLEM
            Foreign Affairs 47, 1, Oct 1968, 138-150,
            Also Demographia 1969, 12, 3, 251-262 (Hungarian)
            SA, XX, 1-2, F4212

    4085   Chattopadhyaya, K.P.

            ANCIENT INDIAN CULTURE CONTACTS AND MIGRATIONS
            Calcutta Sankrit College, Res. #XI, Calcutta, 1965

    4086   Chauhan, D.S.

            SOCIAL COSTS OF MIGRATION
            J. Soc. Sci., 1958, 1, 2, Jul, 29-59
            SA, VIII, 2, 7592

    4087   Chosh, A.K.

            SELECTION INTENSITY IN THE KOTA OF NILGIRI HILLS,
            MADRAS
            Social Biology, 1970, 17, 3, Sep, 224-225
            SA, XX, 3, F5315

    4088   Choudry, N.K.

            A NOTE ON THE DILEMMA OF PLANNING POPULATION IN INDIA
            Eco. Dev. & Cult, Change, 1955, 4, 1, Nov, 68-81
            SA, VI, 2, 4440

4089   Coale, A.J. and E.M. Hoover

POPULATION GROWTH AND ECONOMIC DEVELOPMENT IN LOW-
INCOME COUNTRIES: A CASE STUDY OF INDIA'S PROSPECTS
Princeton, Princeton U. Press, 1958, 389 pp
SA, X, 3, A2517

4090   Cumpston, I.M.

A SURVEY OF INDIAN IMMIGRATION TO BRITISH TROPICAL
COLONIES TO 1910
Pop. Stud. 1956, 10, 2, Nov. 158-165
SA, VIII, 1, 7157

4091   Dandekar, K.

STERILIZATION PROGRAMME: ITS SIZE AND EFFECTS ON
BIRTH RATE
Artha Vignana, 1, 3, Sept, 1959, 220-232

4092   Dandekar, K.

ANALYSIS OF BIRTH INTERVALS OF A SET OF INDIAN
WOMEN
Eugenics Quart. 1963, 10, 2, Jun, 73-78
SA, XII, 4, B0559

4093   Dandekar, K. & V. Bhate

PROSPECTS OF POPULATION CONTROL
Poona, 1971

4094   Dandekar, V.M. & K.

SURVEY OF FERTILITY AND MORTALITY IN POONA
DISTRICT
Poona, Gokhale Instit. of Politics and Economics
Publication #27, 1953, xii & 191 pp

4095   Das, A.K.

DEMOGRAPHIC STUDY: ITS APPLICATIONS IN AN ORAON
VILLAGE
Vanyajati, 1960, 8, 4, Cot, 132-139
SA, XII, 5, B1354

4096   *Das Gupta

ESTIMATION OF DEMOGRAPHIC MEASURES FOR INDIA,
1881-1961, BASED ON CENSUS AGE DISTRIBUTIONS
Population Studies, 1971, 25, 3, Nov, 395-414
SA, 21, 73G3633

4097   Datta, J.M.

PROPORTION OF BRAHMANS IN INDIA'S POPULATION IS
DECREASING
Mod. Rev., 1958, 103, 3, Mar, 230-236
SA, VIII, 2, 7593

4098   Datta, J.M. & H.K. Saha

INFLATION OF THE NUMBER OF KAYASTHAS IN CHITTAGONG
Man in India, 1962, 42, 3, Jul-Sep, 217-222
SA, XII, 5, B1355

4099   Datta, J.M.

ON THE SUBARNABANIKS
Man in India, 1963, 43, 2, Apr-Jun, 141-146
SA, XII, VII, B2946

4100   Davis, K.

THE POPULATION OF INDIA AND PAKISTAN
Princeton: Princeton U Press, 1951,263 pp

1838   demography (population study)

4101   Datta, J.M.

         POPULATION OF INDIA ABOUT 320 BC
         Man in India, 1962, 42, 4, Oct-Dec. 277-291
         SA, XII, 6, B2095

4102   De, A.K. & R.K. Som

         ABRIDGED LIFE TABLES FOR RURAL INDIA, 1957-1958
         Milbank Memor. Fund. Quart, 164, 42, 2, Apr, 96-106
         SA, XIII, 1, B4616

4103   Demeny, P.

         THE ECONOMICS OF GOVERNMENT PAYMENTS TO LIMIT
         POPULATION: A COMMENT
         Eco. Dev. Cult. Change, 1961, 9, 4, 1, Jul, 641-644

4104   Demereth, N.J.

         CAN INDIA REDUCE ITS BIRTH RATE? A QUESTION OF
         MODERNIZATION AND GOVERNMENTAL CAPACITY
         Journal of Social Issues, 1967, 23, 4, Oct, 179-194
         SA, XVI, 7, D4554

4105   Desai, R.C.

         STANDARD OF LIVING IN INDIA AND PAKISTAN, 1931-32 to
         1941
         Varansi, 1968

4106   Desai, S.F.

         TOWARD A NATIONAL POPULATION POLICY
         Ind. J. Soc. Wrk. 1965, 26, 2, Jul, 129-132
         SA, XVI, 4, D1969

4107   Dey, M.K.

         THE INDIAN POPULATION IN TRINIDAD AND TOBAGO
         Int. J. Comp. Socio. 1962, 3, 2, Dec, 245-253
         SA, XII, 5, B1356

1837   demography (population study)

4108   Driver, E.D.

DIFFERENTIAL FERTILITY IN CENTRAL INDIA
Princeton: Princeton U. Press, 1963, xx & 152 pp
SA, XII, 1 A8475

4109   D'Souza, S.

SOME DEMOGRAPHIC CHARACTERISTICS OF CHRISTIANITY
IN INDIA
Social Compass, 1966, 13, 5-6, 415-430
SA, XVII, 6, E5217

4110   Dubey,D.C.

INDIAN SOCIOLOGY AND THE POPULATION PROBLEM
Ind. Soc. Bulletin, 5 (4), July '68, 209-214

4111   *Dutta, J.M.

POPULATION OF INDIA IN 1360 A.D.
Man in India, 1971, 51, 4, Oct-Dec, 334-363
SA, 21, 73G3635

4112   El Badry, M.A.

AN EVALUATION OF THE PARITY DATA COLLECTED ON BIRTH
CERTIFICATES IN BOMBAY CITY
Milbank Memor. Fund Quart. 1962, 40, 3, Jul 328-355
SA, XI, 7, A7676

4113   El Badry, M.A.

HIGHER FEMALE THAN MALE MORTALITY IN SOME COUNTRIES OF
SOUTH ASIA: A DIGEST
J. of the Amer. Stat. Assoc. 1969, 64, 328, Dec.
1234-1244
SA, XIX, 5, F0949

4114   Etienne, G.

LA POPULATION DE L'INDE (THE POPULATION OF INDIA)
Popul. 1957, 12, 4, Oct-De., 661-678 (Fr.)
SA, IX, 3, A0205

4115   Etienne, G.

PRESSION DEMOGRAPHIQUE ET DONNEES DE BASE SUR
L'ECONOMIE AGRICOL DE L'INDE (DEMOGRAPHIC PRESSURE
AND BASIC DATA ON THE AGRICULTURAL ECONOMY OF INDIA)
Population, 1967, 22, 2, Mar-Apr., 287-296 (Fr.)
SA, XVI, 6, D3654

4116   *Freed, S.A. & Ruth S. Freed

THE RELATIONSHIP OF FERTILITY AND SELECTED SOCIAL
FACTORS IN A NORTH INDIAN VILLAGE
Man in India, 1971, 51, 4, Oct-Dec., 274-289
SA, 21, 73G3640

4117   Freymann, M.W.

POPULATION CONTROL IN INDIA
Marriage & Family Living, 1963, 25, 1, Feb, 53-61
SA, XI, 7, A7679

4118   Freyman, (Mrs.) M.

SOCIO-ECONOMIC FACTORS AND FERTILITY IN AN URBAN
POPULATION: RELEVANCE OF DEMOGRAPHIC TRANSITION
THEORY TO THE INDIAN SITUATION
Doct. St., Delhi   U., 1969
(M.N. Srinivas)
(S.N. Agarwal)

4119   Gowda, K.S.M.

THE NEED FOR THE LIMITATION OF POPULATION
Rural India, 19, 4, April, 1956, 140-146

1837   demography (population study)

4120   Gayet, G.

IMMIGRATIONS ASIATIQUES A MADAGASCAR
(ASIATIC IMMIGRATION IN MADAGASCAR)
Civilisations, 1955, 5, 1, 54-64
SA, vol II, #4, 1859

4121   Geddes, A.

THE SOCIAL AND PSYCHOLOGICAL SIGNIFICANCE OF
VARIABILITY IN POPULATION CHANGE, WITH EXAMPLE FROM
INDIA, 1871-1941
Human Relations, V 1, 1947, p 181-205

4122   Ghosh, A.

THE TREND OF THE BIRTH RATE IN INDIA 1911-1950
Pop. Stud. 1956, 10, 1, Jul, 53-68
SA, VII, 4, 6641

4123   Gideon, H.

A BABY IS BORN IN PUNJAB
Amer. Anthrop, 1962, 64, 6, Dec, 1220-1234
SA, XI, 7, A7680

4124   Gillion, K.L.

THE SOURCES OF INDIAN EMIGRATION TO FIJI
Pop. Stud, 1956, 10, 2, Nov. 139-157
SA, VIII, 1, 7161

4125   Gist, N.P.

SELECTIVE MIGRATION IN SOUTH INDIA
Sociol. B. 1955, 4, 2, Sep. 147-160
SA, V, 1, 2997

1837   demography (population study)

4126   Goel, S.C.

A PLEA FOR POPULATION CONTROL
Rur. India, 1955, 18, 1, Jan, 17-22
SA, VI, I, 4093

4127   Gooch, C.R.L.

TEN YEARS IN EXILE: AN APPRAISAL OF THE
RESETTLEMENT OF TIBETAN REFUGEES IN INDIA
C.D. Journal, 1969, 4, 4, Oct, 198-203
SA, XIX, 4, F0130

4128   Gopalaswami, S.R.A.

HOW JAPAN HALVED HER BIRTH RATE IN TEN YEARS:
THE LESSON FOR INDIA
Pop. R. 1959, 3, 2, Jul, 52-57
SA, XII, 7, B2949

4129   Gosal, G.S.

THE REGIONALISM OF SEX COMPOSITION OF INDIA'S
POPULATION
Rural Sociol., 1961, 26, 2, Jun, 122-137
SA, IX, 3, A0207

4130   Gosal, G.S.

REGIONAL ASPECTS OF POPULATION GROWTH IN INDIA,
1950--1961
Pacific Viewpoint 3 (2), Sept.,1962, 87-99

4131   *Gould, Ketayun H.

PARSIS AND URBAN DEMOGRAPHY: SOME RESEARCH
POSSIBILITIES
Journal of Marriage and the Family, 1972, 34, 2,
May, 345-352
SA, 21, 73G1133

1837   demography (population study)

4132   Guha, M.'

        SOCIAL INSTITUTION IN A MUNICIPAL WARD IN CALCUTTA
        Man in India, 1962, 42, 3, Jul-Sep, 181-194
        SA, XII, 5, B1360

4133   Gupta, B.G.

        WANTED A POLICY FOR POPULATION
        Rural India, 17, 1, Jan, 1954, 9-15

4134   Gurtu, A. & K.G. Rao

        A STUDY OF IUD USERS IN FOUR VILLAGES OF
        KANJHAWALA BLOCK
        Behavioral Scis, & C.D., 1968, 2, 2, Sep, 154-161
        SA, XIX, 3, E9015

4135   Gyan, Chand

        POPULATION IN PERSPECTIVE
        Delhi, 1972

4136   Hauser, P.M. & O.D. Duncan (eds.)
        THE STUDY OF POPULATION
        Chicago; U. of Chicago Press, 1959, xvi & 864 pp
        SA, VIII, 1, 7162

4137   Hillery, G.A. Jr.

        FELT POPULATION PRESSURES IN INDIA: METHODS OF
        IDENTIFICATION
        Pop. R. 1961, 5, 2, Jul, 41-49
        SA, XII, 8, B3764

4138   Hu, C.T.

        DEMOGRAPHIC STUDY OF VILLAGE CHANDANPUR
        East. Anthrop. 1955, 9, 1, Sep-Nov 4-20
        SA, V, 2, 3166

1837   demography (population study)

4139   Husain, I.Z.

        EDUCATIONAL STATUS AND DIFFERENTIAL FERTILITY IN
        INDIA
        Social Biology, 1970, 17, 2, Jun, 132-139
        SA, XX, 3, F5321

4140   India's Planning Commissions' Five Year Pland And
        The Population Problem
        EUGENICS REVIEW,
        44, 122 -5, Sep-Oct., 1952

4141   International Catholic Migration Congress

        SHORT SUMMARIES OF NATIONAL REPORTS (ON IMMIGRATION
        AND EMIGRATION)
        Soc. Compas, 1955-1956, 4, 3, 81-193
        SA, VIII, 4, 8719

4142   Jai, M.N.

        THE POPULATION OF INDIA--A STATISTICAL ANALYSIS
        Econ. Weekly, 1955,(Annual #), 26, Jan., 164-169
        SA, VI, 1, 4095

4143   Jain, A.J.

        PREGNANCY OUTCOME AND THE TIME REQUIRED FOR NEXT
        CONCEPTION
        Pop. Studies, 1969, 23, 3, Nov, 421-433
        SA, XIX, 1-2, E7680

4144   Jambunathan, M.V.

        FERTILITY MORES IN MYSORE: A PILOT STUDY
        Ind. J. Soc. Wrk., 1960, 21, 1, Jun, 47-53
        SA, XI, 6, A6884

4145   Jayaraman, (Mrs.) J.

THE IMPACT OF CHANGING POSITION OF WOMEN ON POPULATION
Doct. St., Bagalore U., 1969
(Dr. C. Rajagopalan)

4146   Jorapur, P.B.

A COMPARATIVE PICTURE OF THE DEMOGRAPHIC CHARACTERISTICS
OF WORKING AND NON-WORKING WOMEN
Ind.J. of Soc. Wrk., 1968, 29, 2, Jul, 183-192
SA, XVIII, 4, E3474

4147   Kamat, A.R.

THE DECLINE IN DEATH RATE AND ITS EFFECT ON THE
EXTENT OF WIDOWHOOD
Sociol. B. 1963, 12, 1, Mar, 18-31
SA, XI, 7, A7685

4148   Khan, N.A.

SOME REFLECTIONS ON THE CENSUS OF 1961--II
Ind. Econ. J. 1963, 10, 4, Apr, 419-431
SA, XIV, 5, C1563

4149   Kohli, K.L.

SPATIAL   VARIATIONS OF MORTALITY IN INDIA, 1951-1961
(PHD.D.--Soc. & Demog.)
U. of Pennsylvania, 1971

4150   Krishnamurty, K.

ECONOMIC DEVELOPMENT AND POPULATION GROWTH IN LOW
INCOME COUNTRIES: AN EMPIRICAL STUDY FOR INDIA
Eco. Dev. Cult. Change, 1966, 15, 1, Oct, 70-75
SA, XV, 3, C5311

4151   *Kumar, Joginder

A COMPARISON BETWEEN CURRENT INDIAN FERTILITY
AND LATE NINETEENTH CENTURY SWEDISH AND FINISH
FERTILITY
Population Studies, 1971, 25, 2, Jul, 269-282
SA, 21, 73G2043

4152   Kuriyan, G.

DEMOGRAPHY IN INDIA
Soc. Sci. Information, 1963, 2, 1, Jan, 103-116
SA, XV, 6, C7740

4153   *Kushner, G.

IMMIGRANTS FROM INDIA IN ISRAEL
Tucson, University of Arizona, Press, 1973

4154   Kuthiala, S.K.

DEMOGRAPHIC CHARACTERISTICS OF TRIBAL POPULATION
IN INDIA
Ind. Sociol. B. 1969, 7, 1, Oct, 57-68
SA, XX, 5, F7501

4155   *Lakshmalah, T.

A STUDY IN MIGRATION WITH SPECIAL REFERENCE TO
MIYALGUDE TALUKA
Behavioral sciences and Community Development, 1972,
6, 1, Mar, 135-142
SA, 21, 73G2808

4156   Lance, LM.

INDUSTRIALIZATION AND URBANIZATION OF KANPUR:
AN ECOLOGICAL AND DEMOGRAPHIC ANALYSIS
(Ph.d.-Soc.)
PURDUE U. ('69-'70)

1837   demography (population study)

4157   *Learmonth, A.T.A.

        SELECTED ASPECTS OF INDIA'S POPULATION GEOGRAPHY
        Australian Journal of Politics and History, 1966,
        12, 2, Aug. 146-154
        SA, 21, 73G2809

4158   Loebner, H.G.

        A PATH ANALYSIS OF FERTILITY IN CENTRAL INDIA
        (PH.D.-Soc-Demo)   U. of Massachusetts 1972

4159   Mahalingam, N.

        INDIA'S POPULATION PROBLEM AND INTERNAL MIGRATION
        Popul. R. 1964, 8, 2, Jul, 45-49
        SA, XIV, 1, B8871

4160   Malhotra, S.P.; L.P. Bharara, F.C. Patwa

        POPULATION RESOURCES AND FOOD SITUATION IN VARIOUS
        TRACTS WITHIN THE ARID ZONE OF RAJASTHAN
        Ind. Soc. B. 1969, 6, 4, Jul, 213-221
        SA, XIX, 1-2, E7684

4161   Mamoria, C.

        INDIA'S POPULATION PROBLEM (PH.D.)
        Doct. Agra U., 1958

4162   Mandelbaum,D.G.

        HUMAN FERTILITY IN INDIA
        Berkeley, University of Calif. Press, 1974

4163   Mathur, P.C.

        INTERNAL MIGRATION IN INDIA 1941- to 1951

        American Doctoral Dissertations
        University of Chicago, 1961-1962 (Soc.)

4164   Mathur, S.N.

        DEMOGRAPHIC TRENDS IN RAJASTHAN (PH.D.)
        Doct. Poona U., 1959
        (Prof. N.V. Sovani)

4165   May, D.A. and D.m. Heer

        SOME SURVIVORSHIP MOTIVATION AND FAMILY SIZE IN
        INDIA: A COMPUTER SIMULATION
        Population Studies, 1968, 22, 2, Jul, 199-210
        SA, XVII, 6, D9741

4166   Mazumdar, J. & A. Strommer

        VAESTONKESITYKSESTA JA VAESTOPALITISHASTA INTIASSA
        (POPULATION DEVELOMPMENT AND POPULATION POLICY IN
        INDIA)
        Chapter in Eripainos Vaestontukimuksen Vaiosikorjasta
        (Yearbook of Population Research in Finland)
        Helsinki, Finland, Pop. Res. Instit, 1961, to 1962,
        7, 9-18 (Fin)
        SA, XV, 5, C6867

4167   McCleary, G.F.

        INDIA'S POPULATION PROBLEM
        Contemp. R. 1038, July 1952, 37-40

1837   demography (population study)

4168   Meer Dink, J. & K. Ramachandran

        INFANT MORTALITY ACCORDING TO SOCIAL STATUS IN
        GREATER BOMBAY
        J. of Indian Medicine, 1962, 33, 9, 477-482

4169   Mehrotra, G.K.

        UNDER-REGISTRATION OF BIRTHS IN INDIA
        Artha Vignana, 10, 2, Jun, 1968, 213-228

4170   Mehta, B.H.

        HISTORICAL BACKGROUND OF TRIBAL POPULATION
        Indi, J. Soc. Wrk., 1953, 14, 3, Dec, 236-244
        SA, Vol. II, #4, 815

4171   Mitra, S.

        THE FUTURE OF POPULATION, URBANIZATION AND WORKING
        FORCE IN INDIA
        American Doctoral Dissertations (1960-61)
        University of Chicago (Soc.)

4172   Morrison, W.A.

        SOME THOUGHTS AND PROPOSALS RELATING TO EDUCATIONAL
        PROGRAMME FOR POPULATION CONTROL IN INDIA
        Ind. J. Soc. Wrk, 1961, 21, 4, Mar, 321-336
        SA, XI, 7, A7694

4173   Muntendam, P.

        THE WORLD POPULATION PROBLEM AND HUMAN RIGHTS
        Higher Education and Res. In the Netherlands,   1968,
        12, 2, 3-13

1837   demography (population study)

    4174   Murty, V.S.

            THE PROBLEMS OF INCREASING POPULATION AND ITS
            CONTROL IN INDIA (PH.D.)
            Doct., Nagpur U., 1958

    4175   Muthusubramanian, A.

            INFANT MORTALITY AND POPULATION GROWTH
            Ind. J. Soc. Wrk., 1962, 23, 1, Apr, 79-82
            SA, XII, 1, A8489

    4176   Nag, M.K.

            A DEMOGRAPHIC STUDY OF THE KANIKHARS OF TRANVANCORE
            B. Dept. Anthropology
            Gov't. of India, 1956

    4177   Nag, M.

            SEX, CULTURE AND HUMAN FERTILITY: INDIAN AND THE
            UNITED STATES
            Current Anthropology, U. of Chicago, April, 1972,
            13, 2, P. 231-238

    4178   National Conference on Population Policy & Programmes

            NEW DELHI, 1969; ASPECTS OF POPULATION POLICY IN INDIA
            New Delhi, 1971

    4179   Nayak, V.T.

            BIRTH CONTROL AND GANDHIAN MORALITY
            Ind. J. Soc. Wrk., 1961, 21, 4, Man, 373-386
            SA, XI, 7, A7695

    4180   Nirmala Devi, C.

            DEMOGRAPHIC CORRELATES OF URBAN SIZE IN INDIA: A
            DISCRIMINANT ANALYSIS
            Amer. Doctoral Dissertations 1966-1967
            Harvard U., (Soc. Regional and City Planning)

4181   Ogburn, W.F.

THE BIRTH-RATE AND THE LEVEL OF LIVING IN INDIA
Sociologist, 1956-1957, 1, 1, 10-14
SA, VIII, 1, 7166

4182   Ogburn, W.F.

A DESIGN FOR SOME EXPERIMENTS IN THE LIMITATION OF
POPULATION GROWTH IN INDIA
Chicago, 1952, 14 pp (mimeo)

4183   Opler, M.E.

CULTURAL CONTEXT AND POPULATION CONTROL PROGRAMS
IN VILLAGE INDIA
201-221   Chapt. in Fact and Theory in Social Science,
ed. E.W. C ount and G.T. Bowles
Syracuse, Syracuse U. Press, 1964, xvi & 253 pp
SA, XIV, 2-3, B9736

4184   Pakrasi, K.

A STUDY OF SOME ASPECTS OF STRUCTURAL VARIATION AMONG
IMMIGRANTS IN DURGAPUR, WEST BENGAL
Man in India, 1962, 42, 2, Apr-June, 114-125
SA, XII, 5, B1366

4185   Pakrasi, K.

A NOTE ON DIFFERENTIAL SEX-RATIOS AND POLYANDROUS
PEOPLE IN INDIA
Man in India, 1964, 44, 2, Apr-Jun, 161-174
SA, XIII, 1, B4636

4186   Pakrasi, K.

CASTE, FAMILY STRUCTURE AND MODE OF MIGRATION AMONG
THE REFUGEES OF WEST BENGAL, 1947-1948
Ind. J. Soc. Res., 1966, 7, 2, Aug, 145-154
SA, XVII, 2, D6394

1837   demography (population study)

4187   Pakrasi, Kanti

        SOME SOCIAL ASPECTS OF FERTILITY AND FAMILY IN INDIA
        Ind. J. Soc. Wrk., 1966, 27, 2, 153-161

4188   Pakrasi, K.

        OCCUPATION, CLASS, MIGRATON, AND FAMILY STRUCTURE
        AMONG THE REFUGEES OF WEST BENGAL, 1947-1948
        Man in India, 1967, 47, 3, Jul-Sep, 200-213
        SA, XVII, 2, D6395

4189   *Pakrasi, K. & B. Mukherjee

        THE SANTALS OF WEST BENGAL: SOME SOCIAL AND
        DEMOGRAPHIC CHARACTERS
        Man in India, 1971, 51, 2, Apr-Jun, 92-110
        SA, 21, 73G3660

4190   Peter, K.C.

        POPULATION AND CULTURE IN INDIA, TODAY
        Careers and Courses 5 (10) Oct. 1953, 902-906

4191   Pethe, V.P.

        POPULATION AND FERTILITY IN SHOLAPUR CITY: A SURVEY
        (PH.D.)
        Doct., Poona U., 1957,
        (Prof. N.V. Sovani)

4192   Phadke, M.V.

        POPULATION AND ITS RELATED PROBELSM TO SOCIETY AS A
        WHOLE
        Doct. St. Poona U., 1969

4193   Poti, S.J.B.C. & C.R. Malaker

RELIABILITY OF DATA RELATIONS TO CONTRACEPTIVE
PRACTISES
51-66 Chapter in Research in Family Planning
ed. C.V. Kiser
Princeton, N.J.: Princeton U. Press, 1962
xvi & 66r pp
SA, XIII, 2, B5538

4194   Potter, R.G.; Gordon, J.E.; Parker, M. & Wyon, J.B.

A CASTE STUDY OF BIRTH INTERVAL DYNAMICS
Popul. Stud. 1965, 19, 1, Jul, 81-96
SA, XIV, 4, C0668

4195   Potter, R.G. Jr. & M.L. New; J.B. Wyon; J.E. Gordon

A FERTILITY DIFFERENTIAL IN ELEVEN PUNJAB VILLAGES
Milbank Memor. Fund Quart. 1965, 43, 2, Part I,
Apr. 185-201
SA, XIV, 1, B8878

4196   Prabhu, J.C.

SOCIAL AND CULTURAL DETERMINANTS OF FERTILITY IN
INDIA: A CODIFICATION OF RESEARCH FINDINGS
PH.D. 1960
U. of Massachusetts

4197   Prasad, H.N.

THE POPULATION PROBLEM OF BIHAR (WITH SPECIAL REFERENCE
TO THE POST-WAR PERIOD)   (PH.D.)
Doct. Patna U., 1968
(Dr. K.N. Prasad)

4198   Prasada Rao, C.R.

RURAL-URBAN MIGRATION: A CLUE TO RURAL-URBAN RELATIONS
IN INDIA
Ind. J. Soc. Wrk., 1970, 30, 4, Jan, 335-342
SA, XIX, 6, F1889

4199   Raja, K.C.K.E.

        POPULATION CROWTH IN INDIA.
        J.Family Welfare, 1957, 3, 4, May 109-121.
        SA, VIII, 1, 7169

4200   Rakshit, H.K.

        BIRTH ORDER, SIBSHIP SIZE, AND SEX RATIO
        East. Anthrop. 1960, 13, 3, Mar. May 95-104
        SA, Xl, 4 A5493

4201   Rakshit, S.

        REPRODUCTIVE LIFE OF SOME MAHARASHTRIAN
        BRAHMAN WOMEN.
        Man in India, 1962, 42, 2, Apr.-June 139-159,
        SA, Xll, 5, B1371

4202   Ramachandran, K.V. & V.A. Deshpande

        THE SEX RATIO AT BIRTH IN INDIA BY REGIONS.
        Milbank Memor. Fund Quart. 1964 42, 2, Part 1,
        Apr. 84-95
        SA, Xlll, 1, B4639

4203   Ramu, G.N.

        MIGRATION, ACCULTURATION AND SOCIAL MOBILITY AMONG
        THE UNTOUCHABLE GOLD MINERS IN SOUTH INDIA:
        A CASE STUDY.
        Hum. Org. 1971, 30, 2, Jun, 170-178
        SA, XX6, F8705

4204   Reed, F.W.

        MIGRATION & MODERNIZATION,
        Ind. J. of Sociol. 1970, 1, S, Sep. 104-129
        SA, XlX, 5, F0960

1837   demography (population study)

    4205   Rees, E.

            THE REFUGEE PROBLEM: JOINT RESPONSIBILITY
            Annals Amer. Acad. Pol. Soc. Sci. 1960, 329,
            May, 15-22
            SA, VIII, 4, 8483

    4206   Reitz, J.G.

            USE OF RESEARCH IN POPULATION PROGRAME.
            Paper presented at the 67th Annual Meeting of the
            Amer. Sociol. Assoc.
            SA, XX, 7, Sup 28, C 0301

    4207   Rele, J.R.

            FERTILITY DIFFERENTIALS IN INDIA.
            Milbank Memor. Fund Quart. 1963 41, 2, Apr. 183-199
            SA,XX1, 7, A7698

    4208   Robinson, W.C.

            URBAN-RURAL DIFFERENCES IN INDIAN FERTILITY
            Pop. Stud. 1961, 14, 3, Man, 218-234,
            SA, 1X, 4, A0726

    4209   Roy Burman, B.K.

            TRIBAL DEMOGRAPHY IN INDIA - A PRELIMINARY
            APPRAISAL
            (Read in a Seminar on Tribal Situation in India,
            II.A.S.)
            Simla, 1969

    4210   Roy Burman, B.K.

            DEMOGRAPHIC & SOCIO-ECONOMIC PROFILES OF THE HILL
            AREA OF NORTH EAST INDIA,
            New Delhi, Office of the Registrar General of
            India, 1970

4211   Samuel, T.J.

CULTURE & HUMAN FERTILITY IN INDIA,
J. of Family Welfare, 1963, 9, 4, 45-53

4212   Samuel, T.J.

SOCIAL FACTORS AFFECTING FERTILITY IN INDIA
Eugenics R. 1965, 57, 1, Mar, 5-14,
SA, XlV, 2-3, B9740

4213   Samuel, T.J.

THE DEVELOPMENT OF INDIA'S POPULATION CONTROL.
Milbank Memor. Fund Quart.
1966, 44, 1, Part 1, Jan, 49-68
SA, XlV, 6, C2560

4214   Samuel,T.J.
POPULATION CONTROL IN JAPAN: LESSONS FOR INDIA
Eugenics R. 1966, 58, 1, Mar, 15-22
SA, XlV, 6, C2559

4215   Sanyal, S.N.

FACTORS AFFECTING FERTILITY
Man in India, 1957, 37, 4, Oct.-Dec. 268-279
SA, Vlll, 1, 7204

4216   Sanyal, S.N.

THE APPROACH TO THE PROBLEM OF POPULATION AND
TO ITS SOLUTION IN INDIA,
Man in India, 1960, 40, 3, Jul-Sep, 233-246
SA, Xll, 5, B1372

4217   Sarkar, J.

COMPARATIVE ANALYSIS OF DEATH RATES AMONG THE
SANTALS OF THE BIHAR VILLAGES,
Man in India, 1971, 51, 2, Apr. Jun. 142-150,
SA, 21, 73C, 3668

4218   Saxena, G.S.B.

DIFFERENTIAL FERTILITY AND MORTALITY IN DIFFERENT
CASTES AND COMMUNITIES IN THE RURAL UTTAR PRADESH
(INDIA) (Ph.D.),
Doct, Lucknow U, 1961 (Dr. R.K.Mukerjee)

4219   Saxena, P.C.

HUMAN FERTILITY AND STOHASTIC MODELS (Ph.D.)
Doct, Banaras Hindu U, 1970 (dr. S.N. Singh)

4220   Sen, T.

A DEMOGRAPHIC STUDY OF SOUTHEAST ASIA
Man in India, 1956, 36, 4, Oct-Dec, 247-260
SA, Vlll, 1, 7175

4221   Sharma, O.P.

TRENDS OF POPULATION, EMPLOYMENT AND SOCIAL
STANDARDS IN UTTAR PRADESH (Ph.D.)
Doct. Agra U. 1962

4222   Sidhu, R.S. & Anand, S.

SECONDARY SEX RATIO IN PUNJABI POPULATION,
East-Anthrop. 25, 1, Jan-Apr. 1972 29-39

4223   Singh, R.P. & Nagar, D.M.

A STUDY ON THE GROWTH OF POPULATION IN RAJASTHAN,
Sankhya, 1953, 13, 39-42,
SA, Vol. 111, #3, 1608

4224   Singh, S.N.

A CHANCE MECHANISM OF THE VARIATION IN THE NUMBER
OF BIRTHS PER COUPLE
J. of Amer. Statistical Association, 1968, 63, 321,
Mar, 209-213.
SA, XVll, 4, D8029

1837   demography (population study)

4225   Singhal, (Miss) M.

        DEMOGRAPHIC FACTORS IN URBANIZATION IN INDIA (Ph.D.)
        Doct. Agra U, 1967

4226   Smith, T.E.

        POPULATION CHARACTERISTICS OF SOUTH AND SOUTH-EAST
        ASIA
        Women in The New Asia (ed. B.E.Ward) Unesco,
        Paris, 1965, p. 500-523

4227   Spencer, D.L.

        POPULATION GROWTH AND FOREIGN AID,
        Pop. R. 1959, 3, 1, Jan, 72-78
        SA, Xll, 6, B2124

4228   Srivastava, A.R.N. & K.R.Verma

        DEMOGRAPHIC ASPECTS OF MARRIAGE AMONG THE
        KORWAS OF PALAMAUR
        Jour. of Soc. Res. 1967, 10, 1, Mar, 53-63
        SA, XVl, 5, D2819

4229   Srivastava, R.N.

        SOCIO-ECONOMIC CAUSES AND CONSEQUENCES OF POPULATION
        GROWTH IN EASTERN U.P. (Ph.D.)
        Doct, Gorakhpur U, 1965, (Dr. I. Deo.)

4230   Srivastava, S.C.

        INDIAN CENSUS IN PERSPECTIVE
        New Delhi, 1968

4231   Srivastava, S.C.

        CENSUS OF INDIA
        New Delhi, 1971

1837   demography (population study)

    4232   Subbarao, B.

            REGIONS AND REGIONALISM IN INDIA
            Econ. Wkly. 1958, 10, 38, 20, Sep 1215-1220
            SA, Vol. Vlll, 2, 7602

    4233   Subbiah, B.V.

            THE WORLD POPULATION CRISIS: A CASE STUDY OF INDIA
            Allahabad, 1972

    4234   Taliti, K.M.

            TRENDS IN FERTILITY AND MORTALITY, WITH SPECIAL
            REFERENCE TO SURAT CITY (ph.D.),
            Doct, Gujarat U, 1964 (Prof. D.R.Samant)

    4235   POPULATION TRENDS IN AN INDIAN VILLAGE (Punjab)
            Scientific American, July, 1970, 223, 1, pp. 106-114

    4236   United Nations

            FUTURE POPULATION ESTIMATES BY SEX AND AGE:
            REPORT IV - THE POPULATION OF ASIA AND THE FAR
            EAST: 1950-1980,
            New York, Columbia U. Press 1959 Vlll, 110 pp.,
            SA, Vlll, 4, 8490

    4237   Vaidyanathan, K.E.

            POPULATION REDISTRIBUTION & ECONOMIC CHANGE, INDIA,
            Amer. Doct. Dissertation (67-68)
            University of Pennsylvania (Soc.).

    4238   Vaidyanathan, K.E.

            A COMPARISON OF THE CSR ESTIMATES OF NET MIGRATION,
            1950-60 AND THE CENSUS ESTIMATES, THE UNITED STATES
            Social Forces, 1969, 48, 2, Dec. 233-242,
            SA, XVlll, 7, E6345

4239   Varma, K.N.

POPULATION PROBLEM IN THE GANGES VALLEY
Agra, Shiva Lal Agarwala, 1967, lX-164 p.

4240   Verma, K.K.

AN ANTHRO-DEMOGRAPHIC STUDY OF THE SANTHAL
BIHOR (Ph.D.)
Doct, Ranchi U, 1970
(Dr. L.P.Vidyarthi)

4241   Vig, O.P.

ESTIMATION OF INTRINSIC RATE OF GROWTH OF POPULATION
FOR INDIA 1901 - 1961,
Artha Vijnana, 10, 2, Jun, 1968, 183-198

4242   Visaria, L.

RELIGIOUS AND REGIONAL DIFFERENCES IN MORTALITY
& FERTILITY IN THE INDIAN SUBCONTINENT.
(Ph.D.) (Soc), Princeton U, 1972

4243   Visaria, P.M.

THE SEX RATIOS OF THE POPULATION OF INDIA
American Doctoral Dissertations
Princeton U. Soc.(63-64)

4244   Visaria, P.M.

MORTALITY AND FERTILITY IN INDIA, 1951-61
Milbank Memorial Fund Quart, 1969, 47, 1, 1,
1, Jan. 91-116
SA, xVlll, 6, E5256

4245   Viswanathan, G.

A DEMOGRAPHIC & ECOLOGICAL STUDY OF HYDERABAD (Ph.D.)
Doct, Andhra U, 1970, (Prof. M.V. Moorthy)

1837   demography (population study)

    4246   Wyon, J.B. & Gordon, J.E.

             A LONG-TERM PROSPECTIVE - TYPE FIELD STUDY OF POPULATIC
             DYNAMICS IN THE PUNJAB, INDIA 17-32, CHAPTER IN
             RESEARCH IN FAMILY PLANNING, C.V. KISER (ed.),
             Princeton N.J. : Princeton U. Press, 1962
             Xvii 664 pp.
             SA, Xlll, 2, B5555

    4247   Yankaur, Alfred

             AN APPROACH TO THE CULTURAL BASE OF INFANT
             MORTALITY IN INDIA
             Pop. Rev., 1959, 3, 2, 39-51

    4248   Zachariah, K.C.

             HISTORICAL STUDY OF INTERNAL MIGRATION IN THE
             INDIAN SUB-CONTINENT, 1901-31
             American Doctoral Dissertations (1961-62)
             U. of Pennsylvania (soc.)

    4249   Zachariah, K.C.

             THE MAHARASHTRIAN AND GUJARATI MIGRANTS IN GREATER
             BOMBAY
             Sociol. B. 1966, 15, 2, Sep, 68-88
             SA, XV, 6, C7758

4250   Das, P.B. & Das, B.M.

AGE AT MENARCHE OF KALITA GIRLS IN ASSAM
Man in India, 1967, 47, 2, Apr-Jun 173-117
SA, XVII, 1, D5478

4251   Pattnaik, B.

AGE AT MENARCHE AMONG URBAN CASTE WOMEN OF ORISSA
Man in India, 1971, 51, 3, Jul-Sep, 217-222
SA, 21, 73G3682

4252   Rastogi, (Mrs.) S.

HUMAN BIOLOGY OF THE RASTOGIS OF LUCKNOW
Doct. St, Lucknow U, 1969

4253   Ray, A.K.
COLOR BLINDNESS, CULTURE, AND SELECTION
Social Biology, 1969, 16, 3, Sep, 203-208,
SA, X1X, 1-2, E7712

1900   THE FAMILY AND SOCIALIZATION

1938   sociology of the child & socialization

4254   Alvares, (Miss) L.

        A STUDY OF PROBLEM CHILDREN IN THE CITY OF
        BOMBAY (Ph.D.)
        Doct. Bombay U, 1961 (Prof. K.M.Kapadia)

4255   Aphale, (Miss) C.A.

        CHILD IN HOME AND SCHOOL: A STUDY OF UPBRINGING OF
        CHILDREN IN MAHARASHTRIAN HINDU FAMILIES IN
        POONA (Ph.D.)
        Doct, Poona U, 1962 (Dr. I.Karve)

4256   Bildhaiya & Demeld, C.

        A STUDY OF SOME PREVALENT CUSTOMS & BELIEFS
        FOR THE HEALTH AND WELLBEING OF CHILDREN IN
        JABALPUR AREA
        Ind.J. of Public Health, 1968, 12, 4,
        215-218

4257   Broacha, (Miss) M.F.

        SOME SOCIAL AND RELIGIOUS LIKES AND DISLIKES
        OF SCHOOL-GOING GIRL STUDENTS IN AGRA (Ph.D.)
        Doct, Agra U, 1960

4258   Chaturvedi, P.P.

        ROLE OF APPROVED SCHOOLS IN THE PROTECTION,
        TREATMENT, AND REHABILITATION OF DEVIANT
        AND NEGLECTED CHILDREN IN U.P.
        Doct. St, Lucknow U, 1969

4259   Chauhan, N.S.

        TRUANCY AMONG SCHOOL-GOING CHILDREN OF AGRA
        (Ph.D.) Doct., Agra U, 1963

4260   Gupta, B.

        UPBRINGING OF AN INDIAN CHILD
        in: B.N.Verma CONTEMPORARY INDIA, Bombay, Asia
        Pub. House, 1964

1938   sociology of the child & socialization

4261   Hitchcock, J.T. & Leigh, M.

        THE RAJPUTS OF KHALAPUR, INDIA
        in: SIX CULTURES: STUDIES IN CHILD REARING,
        ed. B.B.Whiting, New York, John Wiley & Sons,
        1963

4262   Kapadia, K.M. & Pillai, S.D.

        YOUNG RUNAWAYS
        Bombay, 1968

4263   Kar, (Mrs.) P.

        UPBRINGING OF CHILDREN IN U.P. VILLAGE
        AND TOWN (Ph.D.)
        Doct, Lucknow U, 1961 (Dr.R.K.Muherjee)

4264   Khandekar, M.

        REPORT ON THE SITUATION OF CHILDREN AND YOUTH
        IN GREATER BOMBAY
        Bombay, 1970

4265   Maharaja Sayajirao University of Baroda

        SOCIAL CHANGE AND PERCEPTION OF CHANGE IN CHILD
        REARING IN A SUBURBAN INDIAN VILLAGE
        Baroda, 1970

4266   Majumdar, D.N.

        CHILDREN IN A POLYANDROUS SOCIETY
        East, Anthrop., 1953, 6, 3-4, Mar-Aug.
        177-189,
        SA, Vol II # 4, 745

4267   Mathur, S. & Mathur S.I.

        ATTITUDE TOWARDS CHILD REARING PRACTICES
        IN TWO CULTURES
        J. of Family Welfare, 1963, 10, 1, 64

4268   Melta, K.

        EFFECTS OF MARTIAL DISHARMONY ON CHILDREN
        Child Guidance Clinic, Gujarat Research Soc.
        1964

4269   Mencher, J.P.

        GROWING UP IN SOUTH MALABAR
        Hum. Org. 1963, 22, 1 Spr, 54-65
        SA, X11, 5, B1390

4270   Minturn, L. & Lambert, W.W.

        MOTHERS OF SIX CULTURES: ANTECEDENTS OF
        CHILD REARING
        New York: John Wiley & Sons, 1964, Xiit 351 pp.
        SA, X111, 3-4, B6488

4271   Mistry, (Miss) D.K.

        THE CHILD IN SOCIETY (Ph.D.)
        Doct. Bombay U, 1954
        (Prof. G.S.Ghurye)

4272   Mistry, (Miss) D.K.

        THE INDIAN CHILD AND HIS PLAY,
        Sociol. B. 1958, 7, 2, Sep, 137-147,
        SA, V111, 2, 7565

4273   Muthayya, B.C.

        CHILD WELFARE
        Hyderabad, 1968

4274   Narain, D.

        GROWING UP IN INDIA
        Fam. Process, 1964, 3, 1, Mar, 127-154,
        SA, X11, 8, B 3787

4275   Patel, (Miss) K.

        AN INVESTIGATION OF SOCIOMETRIC VARIABLES
        AND THEIR CORRELATES IN MULTI-LINGUAL
        NURSERY CHILDREN ATTENDING ANGLO-INDIAN SCHOOLS
        (D.Phil.), Doct, Calcutta U, 1965

4276   Phadke, S.

        CHILDREN IN URBAN AREAS OF INDIA
        Carnets de l'Enfance, 11, Jan. 1970
        109-124

4277   Poffenberger, T.

        CHILD DEVELOPMENT AND FAMILY RELATIONS
        AS A SCIENTIFIC FIELD
        Ind.J.of Soc.Work, 1963, 24, 2, Jul,
        110-114
        SA, Xll, 5, B1441

4278   Poffenberger, T.

        A PRELIMINARY SURVEY OF INDIAN INSTITUTIONS
        TEACHING AND CONDUCTING RESEARCH IN CHILD
        DEVELOPMENT AND FAMILY RELATIONSHIPS
        Baroda, Dept. of Child Dev., Faculty of
        Home Science, U. of Baroda, 1964

4279   Rao, P.T.

        A REVIEW OF THE METHODS OF UPBRINGING OF
        INFANTS AND CHILDREN IN INDIA AND THE NEED
        OF IMMEDIATE PARENTAL EDUCATION,
        J. of Indian Radiations Society, 1962, 1,
        373-379

4280   Ray, J.C.

        THE CHILDREN OF THE ABOR AND THE GALLONG
        Educ. & Psy. Delhi, 1959

4281   Raz, S.M.

GROWING UP IN A CHOTANAGPUR VILLAGE (A STUDY
OF SOCIALIZATION OF A MULTI-ETHNIC COMMUNITY)
(Ph.D.), Doct. Patna U, 1968 (Dr. Sachchidanand)

4282   Saxena, G.C.

THE PROBLEM OF NEGLECTED CHILDREN IN A SLUM
AREA, WITH SPECIAL REFERENCE TO KANPUR
(Ph.D.), Doct. Agra U, 1964

4283   Sen, (Miss) S.

CHILD REARING PRACTICES AND SOCIALIZATION:
A CASE STUDY OF SELECTED FAMILIES
Doct. st, Rajasthan U, 1969

4284   Singh, (Mrs.) U.S.

A SOCIOLOGICAL STUDY OF PROBLEM CHILDREN
IN INDORE CITY
Doct. st, Indore U, 1969

4285   Singh,(Miss) U.

INSTITUTIONAL CASE OF ORPHANS (A STUDY OF
ORPHANS IN KAVAL TOWNS OF UTTAR PRADESH)
Doct. st, Lucknow U, 1969

4286   Srivastava, J.P.

AGGRESSIVENESS IN SCHEDULED CASTE CHILDREN
Education (Lucknow), 33 (4 & 5), Apr. & May
1954, 16-19 & 10-13

4287   Straus, J.H. & Straus, M.A.

FAMILY ROLES AND SEX DIFFERENCES IN CREATIVITY·
OF CHILDREN IN BOMBAY AND MINNEAPOLIS
J. of Marriage and the Family 1968, 30,1, Feb,
46-53,
SA, XVll, 1, D5488

4288   Ahluvalia, S.

        YOUTH IN REVOLT
        New Delhi, 1972

4289   Awasthi, D.S.

        THE EMOTIONAL CRISIS AMONG THE TEENAGERS
        (PSYCHO-SOCIAL STUDY OF TEENAGERS IN THE
        CITY OF LUCKNOW)
        Doct.st. Lucknow U, 1969

4290   Basu, S.

        A SOCIO-PSYCHOLOGICAL STUDY OF THE ADOLESCENT
        TRIBAL CHILDREN OF WEST BENGAL HIMALAYAN
        REGION FOR THE PURPOSE OF NATIONAL INTEGRATION
        THROUGH CO-CURRICULAR PARTICIPATION (D.Phil.)
        Doct, Calcutta U, 1963, (Dr.S.C.Sinha)

4291   Bhatt, I.D.

        AN INVESTIGATION TO STUDY ADOLESCENT BOYS
        AND GIRLS IN BARODA DISTRICT - WITH REFERENCE
        TO BEHAVIOUR, INTERESTS AND GROUP LIFE
        (Ph.D.), Doct. M.S.U. of Baroda, 1970
        (Dr. N.S.Pathak)

4292   Guha, B.S.

        THE ABOR MOSHUK AS TRAINING CENTER FOR YOUTH
        Vanyajati, 1953, 1, 83-95

4293   Gupta, (Miss) S.

        ASPIRATIONS OF RURAL YOUTH: FACTORS
        WORKING FOR THEIR INHIBITION AND RELEASE
        Doct. st, Agra U, 1969 (R.N.Saxena)

4294   Kakar, S. & Chowdhry, K.

        CONFLICT AND CHOICE - INDIAN YOUTH IN A CHANGING
        SOCIETY,
        Verry, 1970

1939   adolescence and youth

4295   Kamleshkumar

A STUDY OF VOCATIONAL AND PERSONAL INTERESTS -
PROJECTS, PREFERENCES AND ATTITUDES OF THE
RURAL YOUTH TOWARDS THE YOUTH CLUB WORK (Ph.D.),
Doct, Indian Agricultural Research Institute
1966 (Dr. K.N.Singh)

4296   Kashappagoudar, N.B.

YOUTH CULTURE AND ITS STRUCTURAL ANALYSIS
Ind. Sociol. Bull. 1967, 4, 2, Jan. 127-132,
SA, XV1, 7, D4581

4297   Khanna, R.N.

JUVENILE TRUANCY AND THE SCHOOL (Ph.D.)
Doct, Lucknow U, 1960 (Dr.R.K.Mukerjee)

4298   Kuriakose, P.T.

AN APPROACH TO YOUTH WORK IN INDIA
New Delhi, 1972

4299   Mehandale, Y.S.

ADOLESCENT CRIMINAL (Ph.D.),
Doct. Poona U, 1951 (Dr. I. Karve)

4300   Mehra, L.S.

YOUTH IN MODERN SOCIETY   (A SOCIOLOGICAL
STUDY OF 500 MALE STUDENTS IN UNDER-GRADUATE
CLASSES AT LUCKNOW UNIVERSITY AND AFFILIATED
COLLEGES) (Ph.D.)
Doct. Lucknow U, 1969 (Dr.S.R.Sharma)

4301   Mehta, P. (ed.)

INDIAN YOUTH: EMERGING PROBLEMS AND ISSUES
Verry, 1971

4302   Mohan, R.P.

SEX DIFFERENCES IN ADOLESCENT ADJUSTMENT AND
PROBLEMS
Ind. Sociol. B., 1970, 7, 2, Jan, 91-96,
SA, XX, 5, F7538

4303   Manjal, B.M.

A STUDY OF MAJOR SOCIOLOGICAL ASPECTS OF
TRUANCY AMONG THE MALE COLLEGE-GOING STUDENTS OF
INDORE CITY
Doct. st, Indore, 1969

4304   Nair, S.P.

YOUTH CLUBS AND AGRICULTURAL PRODUCTION
Kurukshetra, 1966, 15, 3, Dec, 11-12
SA XVlll, 6, E4982

4305   Nanavatty, M.C.

YOUTH ORGANIZATION IN RURAL AREAS
Kurukshetra, 1964, 12, 12, Sep, 20-22,
SA XIV, 2-3, B9571

4306   Pathak, R.D.

SEX DIFFERENCES IN THE AREAS OF ADJUSTMENT
OF POPULAR, REJECTED AND ISOLATED ADOLESCENTS
Ind.J.of Soc.Work, 1971, 32, 1, Apr, 83-86
SA, XX, 7, F 9815

4307   Prasad, C.

PERSONAL AND SOCIAL GROWTH OF YOUTH CLUB MEMBERS
Ind. J. Soc. Res. 1966, 7, 2, Aug. 128-136
SA, XVll, 2, D6169

4308   Roy, M.

FRUSTRATION AMONG INDIAN YOUTHS
in: Vidyarthi L.P. (ed.) CONFLICT, TENSION AND
CULTURAL TREND IN INDIA, 1969

1939   adolescence and youth

4309   Salahuddin

IMPACT OF GANDHIAN SOCIAL THOUGHT UPON THE
YOUTH AFTER INDEPENDENCE
Doct. st, Lucknow U, 1969

4310   Salvi, P.V. & Rade, V.M.

ACTIVITIES OF RURAL YOUTH
Ind. J. of Soc. Work, 1967, 28, 2, Jul, 207-212
SA, XV11, 2, D6171

4311   Schiamberg, L.

SOME SOCIO-CULTURAL FACTORS IN ADOLSCENT-
PARENT CONFLICT: A CROSS-CULTURAL COMPARISON
OF SELECTED CULTURES
Adolescence, 1969, 4, 15, Fall, 333-360
SA, X1X, 1-2, E7728

4312   Sengupta, T.

YOUTH ORGANISATIONS
Kurukshetra, 1966, 14, 7, Apr. 16-18,
SA, XV11, 3, D7337

4313   Shah, B.V.

GURARATI COLLEGE STUDENTS AND SELECTION
OF BRIDE
Sociol. B. 1962, 11, 1-2, Mar, Sep, 121-140,
SA, X1, 7, A7736

4314   Shahani, (Mrs.) S.J.

HIGH SCHOOL STUDENTS OF BARODA - A SOCIOGRAPHIC
STUDY OF THE X AND XI CLASSES OF GUJARATI AND
MARATHI HIGH SCHOOLS IN BARODA (Ph.D.)
Doct, M.S. U of Baroda, 1962,(Dr. U.P.Desai)

4315   Shukla, V.N.

ADOLESCENTS' SUICIDES
Social Welfare, 19, 8, Nov. 1972, p.6-7

4316   Singh, K.N. & Prasad, C.

EDUCATIONAL IMPACT OF YOUTH CLUB ACTIVITIES ON
RURAL PARTICIPANTS
Ind. J. Soc. Work, 1966, 26, 4, Jan, 381-384
SA, XVl, 5, D2620

4317   Singh, S.N.

STUDY OF PROBLEMS OF ADJUSTMENT OF PREADOLESCENT
(JUNIOR HIGH SCHOOL) (Ph.D.)
Doct. Magadh U, 1970, (Dr.M.C.Joshi)

4318   Sinha, P.R.R. & Pawar, S.S.

DIFFERENTIAL CHARACTERISTICS OF SUCCESSFUL AND
UNSUCCESSFUL RURAL YOUTH CLUBS
Paper presented at the 3rd World Congress for
Rural Sociology
SA, XX, 5, Sup. 24, F7806

4319   Sundberg, N., Sharma, V., Wodtli, T. & Rohila, P.

FAMILY COHESIVENESS AND AUTONOMY OF ADOLESCENTS
IN INDIA AND THE UNITED STATES
J. of Marriage & the Family, 1969, 31, 2, May
403-407, SA, XVlll, 3, E2424

4320   Talwar, P.O.

ADOLESCENT STERILITY IN AN INDIAN POPULATION
Hum. Biol. 1965, 37, 3, Sep, 256-261,
SA, XlV, 5, C1601

4321   Varma, (Mrs.) M.

SOME PROBLEMS OF HINDU ADOLESCENT GIRLS (Ph.D.)
Doct, Agra U, 1964

1939   adolescence and youth

    4322   Warti, (Mrs.) M.S.

            A STUDY OF THE ATTITUDES OF THE YOUNG TOWARDS
            THE AGED (Ph.D.)
            Doct, M.S. U. of Baroda, 1967, (Dr. H.Fernandez)

4323   Agarwala, S.N.

A FOLLOW-UP OF INTRAUTERINE CONTRACEPTIVE
DEVICES: AN INDIAN EXPERIENCE
Eugenics Quart. 1968, 15, 1, Mar. 41-49
SA, XVll, 3, D7343

4324   Banerjee, G.R.

PROSTITUTION REQUIRES PROHIBITION
Ind. J. Soc. Work, 1958, 19, 1, Jun 11-17
SA, Vlll, 2, 7626

4325   *Bhatnagar, V.

ATTITUDES OF TEENAGE GIRLS TOWARDS SEX
Eastern Anthropologist, 26, 4, Oct-Dec.
1973, pp. 339-342

4326   Cadbury, (Mrs.) B.

FAMILY PLANNING IN SOUTH & SOUTH-EAST ASIA
in: WOMEN IN THE NEW ASIA, ed. B.E.Ward,
Paris, Unesco, 1965, p. 523-527

4327   Dandekar, K.

VASECTOMY CAMPS IN MAHARASHTRA
Pop. Stud. 1963, 17, 2, Nov. 147-154,
SA, Xll, 4, B603a

4328   Grovla, (Mrs.) U.

SOCIAL EFFECTS OF STERILIZATION ON WOMEN IN
INDORE CITY
Doct. st. Indore U, 1969 (Pothen)

4329   Hooja, S.L.

PROSTITUTION IN RAJASTHAN: THEN AND NOW
Ind. J.Soc. Work 1970, 31, 2, Jul, 183-190
SA, XX, 6, F8760

4330   Kapil, K. & Saxena, D.N.

         STERILIZATION AND K.A.P. STUDIES IN INDIA
         1969

4331   *Kapur, P.

         SEX IN MARITAL MALADJUSTMENT IN INDIA
         International Journal of Sociology of the
         Family, 1972, 2, 2, Sep, 159-167
         SA, 21, 73 G4622

4332   *Karkal, Malini

         CULTURAL FACTORS INFLUENCING FERTILITY: POST
         PARTUM ABSTENTION FROM SEXUAL INTERCOURSE
         Man in India, 1971, 51, 1, Jan-Mar, 15-26
         SA, 21, 73G3705

4333   Kumar, P.

         PROSTITUTION: A SOCIO-PSYCHOLOGICAL ANALYSIS
         Ind. J. Soc. Work 1961, 21,4,Mar, 425-430,
         SA, Xl, 7, A7742

4334   Meyer, J.J.

         SEXUAL LIFE IN ANCIENT INDIA
         Delhi, 1968

4335   Mohan, B.

         SEXUALITY OF MENTAL PATIENTS
         East Anthrop. 1968, 21, 1, Jan-Apr, 59-72
         SA, XVlll, 4, E3511

4336   Mohan, R.P.

         FACTORS TO MOTIVATION TOWARD STERILIZATION IN
         TWO INDIAN VILLAGES
         Family Life Coordinator, 1967, 16, 1-2, Jan-Apr,
         35-38, SA, XVll, 1, D5501

4337   Mukerji, N.

        SEXUAL DELINQUENCY
        Indian J. Soc.Work 1955, 16, 1, Jun 19-26,
        SA, Vol. V, # 2, 3314

4338   Nag, M.

        ATTITUDES TOWARDS VASECTOMY IN WEST BENGAL
        Pop.Rev., 1966, 10c, 61-64

4339   Pakrasi, K. & Halder, A.

        POLYGYNISTS OF URBAN INDIA, 1960-61,
        Ind. J. Soc. Work 1970, 31, 1. Apr, 49-62,
        SA, XX, 1-2, F4307

4340   Poffenberger, T. & Patel, H.G.

        THE EFFECT OF LOCAL BELIEFS ON ATTITUDES TOWARD
        VASECTOMY IN TWO INDIEN VILLAGES IN GUJARAT STATE
        Popul. R. 1964, 8, 2, Jul, 37-44,
        SA, X1V, 1, B8918

4341   Poffenberger, T. & Poffenberger, S.B.

        A COMPARISON OF FACTORS INFLUENCING CHOICE
        OF VASECTOMY IN INDIA AND THE U.S.
        Ind. J. Soc. Work 1965, 25, 4, Jan, 339-352,
        SA, XV, 5, C6927

4342   Punekar, S.D. & Rao, A.K.

        A STUDY OF PROSTITUTES IN BOMBAY WITH REFERENCE
        TO FAMILY BACKGROUND (2nd ed.)
        Bombay, Lalvani Pub. House, 1967, xvi & 244p.

4343   Sengupta, A.

        SOCIO-SEXUAL ASPECTS OF ORAL CONTRACEPTION
        Ind. J. Soc. Work 1970, 31, 3, Oct, 319-334,
        SA, XX, 6, F8762

4344   Shanmugham, T.E.

        SEX DELINQUENCY AND EMOTIONAL INSTABILITY IN WOMEN
        Ind. J.Soc. Work, 1956, 17, 1, Jun, 12-19,
        SA, Vlll, 1, 7211

4345   Shanmugan, T.E.

        SEX DELINQUENT WOMEN AND THEIR FANTASIES
        J. Psychol. Res. 1958, 2, 2, May, 77-82
        SA, Vlll, 2, 7631

4346   Sharma, K.K., Dubey, P.S. & Bhatia, R.S.

        PROSTITUTION
        Ind. Sociol. 1961, 3, 4, Mar 33-19,
        SA, Xlll, 1, B4697

4347   Sinha, A.P.

        PROCREATION AMONG THE EUNUCHS
        East. Anthropologist 1967, 20, 2, May-Aug 168-176,
        SA, XVll, 6, D9782

4348   Sinha, S.

        A NOTE ON THE CONCEPT OF SEXUAL UNION FOR SPIRITUAL
        QUEST AMONG THE VAISHNAVA PREACHERS IN THE BHUMIG BELT
        OF PAMLIA AND SINGBHUM ·
        East. Anthrop. 1961, 14, 2, May-Aug. 194-196
        SA, Xll, 8, B3811

4349   Singhi, N.K.

        THE PROBLEM AND PREVENTION (PROSTITUTION)
        Social Welfare, 19, 3, 1972, 8-10

4350   *Srivastava, S.P.

        SOCIAL PROFILE OF HOMOSEXUALS IN AN INDIAN MALE
        PRISON
        Eastern Anthropologist, 26, 4, Oct-Dec, 1973,
        pp. 313-322

1940   sociology of sexual behaviour

4351   Tongia, V.C.

        SOCIOLOGICAL ASPECTS OF STERILIZATION OF HUMAN
        MALES (A STUDY OF 250 CASES OF MALE STERILIZATION
        FROM INDORE CITY)
        Doct. st, Indore U, 1969

1941   sociology of the family

4352   Abraham, C.M.

CHANGING PATTERN OF FAMILY LIFE OF POLYANDROUS
COMMUNITY (NAIRS) OF CENTRAL TRAVANCORE
(PH.D.) Doct, Lucknow U, 1966 (Dr.N.K.Devaraja)

4353   Agarwala, B.R.

NATURE AND EXTENT OF SOCIAL CHANGE IN A MOBILE
COMMERCIAL COMMUNITY (ASTUDY OF CHANGE AND MARRIAGE
PATTERNS)
Sociol. B. 1962, 11, 1, 2, Mar-Sep, 141-145,
SA, Xl, 7, A7745

4354   Agrawal, B.C. & Agrawal, M.

A NOTE ON NATRA: THE SO-CALLED REMARRIAGE AMONG
THE HINDUS OF MALWA
East Anthrop. 25, 1, Jan-Apr, 1972, 73-81

4355   Agarwala, S.N.

REMARRIAGE RATES IN SOME DELHI VILLAGES
Medical Digest, Bombay, 1962

4356   Agarwala, S.N.

SOCIAL AND CULTURAL FACTORS AFFECTING FERTILITY
IN INDIA
Pop. R. 1964, 8, 1, Jan, 73-78,
SA, Xlll, 3-4, B6501

4357   Agarwala, S.N.

AGE AT MARRIAGE IN INDIA AS ASCERTAINED FROM
CENSUS DATA,
American Doctoral Dissertations Princeton U,
1957-57 (Sociology)

4358   Agarwal, (Mrs.) S.P.

STATUS AND ROLE PERCEPTION OF EDUCATED
MIDDLE-CLASS MARRIED HINDU WOMEN (Ph.D.)
Doct. st, Agra U, 1969, (Dr.R.N.Saxena)

4359   Ahluwalia, H.

MATRIMONIAL ADVERTISEMENTS IN PUNJAB
Ind. J. Soc. Work, 1969, 30, 1, Apr, 55-64,
SA, XV111, 7; E6368

4360   Ahmad, M.R.

FAMILY IN AN URBAN COMMUNITY: A SOCIAL WORK-STUDY IN
THE CITY OF LUCKNOW (Ph.D.)
Doct. Lucknow U, 1966 (Dr.S.Z.Hasan)

4361   Ahuja, R.

MARRIAGE AMONG THE BHILS
Man in India, 1966, 46, 3, Jul-Sep, 233-240,
SA, XV1, 6, D3707

4362   Ahuja, R.

FAMILY PATTERNS AMONG BHILS
East Anthrop. 1966, 19, 1, Jan-Apr 29-42,
SA, XV, 2, C4594

4363   Anand, K.

ATTITUDES OF PUNJAB UNIVERSITY WOMEN
STUDENTS TOWARDS MARRIAGE AND FAMILY
Ind. J. Soc. Work, 1965, 26, 1, Apr, 87-90,
SA, XV1, 4, D2027

4364   Anand, K.

AN ANALYSIS OF MATRIMONIAL ADVERTISEMENTS
Sociol. B. 1965, 14, 1, Mar, 59-71
SA, X1V, 4, C0712

4365   Anant, S.S.

THE CHANGING TRENDS IN INTER-CASTE MARRIAGES
IN INDIA: AN ANALYSIS OF MATRIMONIAL COLUMN IN
AN ENGLISH LANGUAGE DAILY
J. of Psychological Res., 1972, 16, 1, p.1-5

1941   sociology of the family

4366   Aschenbrenner, J.

POLITICS AND ISLAMIC MARRIAGE PRACTICES IN THE
INDIAN SUBCONTINENT
Anthropological Quart. 1969, 42, 4, Oct, 305-315,
SA, XX, 5, F7548

4367   Avasthi, (Miss) A.

THE CHANGING PATTERNS OF HINDU MARRIAGE - A
SOCIOLOGICAL STUDY OF THE CHANGING PATTERNS
OF MARRIAGE AMONG THE UPPER CASTE HINDUS IN
A METROPOLITAN CITY (Ph.D.)
Doct, Lucknow U, 1969 (Dr. S. Chandra)

4368   Banerjee, H.

A SANTAL MARRIAGE
Bulletin of the Cultural Res. Inst.
2,2,1964, 78-80

4369   Bardis, P.D.

DATING AMONG FOREIGN STUDENTS
Alpha Kappa Deltan, 1959, 29, 2, Spr. 48-51
SA, Vlll, 4, 8497

4370   Basavarajappa, K.G.

CHANGES IN AGE AT MARRIAGE OF FEMALES AND
THEIR EFFECT ON THE BIRTH RATE IN INDIA:
A REPLY
Eugenics Quart. 1968, 15, 4, Dec, 293-295
SA, XlX, 7, F2736

4371   Basavarajappa, K.G. & Belvalgidad, M.I.

CHANGES IN AGE AT MARRIAGE OF FEMALES AND
THEIR EFFECT ON THE BIRTH RATE IN INDIA
Eugenics Quart., 1967, 14, 1, Mar, 14-26,
SA, XV, 6, C7790

1941   sociology of the family

    4372   Basu, S.K. & Ray, S.

            CHANGE AND THE FREQUENCY OF CONSANGUINEOUS
            MARRIAGES AMONG THE DELHI MUSLIMS AFTER
            PARTITION
            East. Anthrop. 26, 1, Jan-Apr, 1972, 21-29

    4373   Beharta, P.C.

            FAMILY TYPE AND FERTILITY IN SIX INDIAN VILLAGES
            Eco. & Pol. Wkly, 1966, 1, 15, 633-634

    4374   Berreman, G.D.

            VILLAGE EXOGAMY IN NORTHERN MOST INDIA
            Southw. J. Anthrop. 1962, 18, 1, Spr. 55-58,
            SA, X1, 2 & 3, A 4966

    4375   Bharadwaj, L.K.

            FAMILY STRUCTURE AND GOALS AS RELATED TO
            ACHIEVEMENT IN FARMING (Ph.D.-Soc.) (69-70)
            U of Wisconsin

    4376   Bhowmik, A., Chowdhuri, M.K. & Ghosh, T.N.

            ATTITUDE OF THE TIYARS IN LIMITING FAMILY
            SIZE AND THEIR SOCIO-CULTURAL CHARACTERISTICS
            Society & Culture, 1970, 1, Special Number, 43-50,
            SA, XX, 7, F9501

    4377   Bose, A.B.

            THE STRUCTURE AND COMPOSITION OF RURAL FAMILIES
            Ind. J. Soc. Work, 1963, 23, 4, Jan, 351-358,
            SA, X11, 4, B0615

    4378   Bose, A.B. & Saxena, P.C.

            COMPOSITION OF RURAL JOINT HOUSEHOLDS IN
            RAJASTHAN (STUDIES IN HOUSEHOLDS III)
            Ind. J. Soc.Res., 1964, 5, 3, Dec, .299-308,
            SA, XIV, 5, C1607

                        - 667 -

4379   Bose, A.B. & Saxena, P.C.

        SOME CHARACTERISTICS OF NUCLEAR HOUSEHOLDS
        Man in India, 1965, 45, 3, Jul-Sep, 195-200
        SA, XVl, 5, D2347

4380   Bose, N.K.

        MARRIAGE AND KINSHIP AMONG THE JUANGS
        in: Bose, N.K., CULTURAL ANTHROPOLOGY AND
        OTHER ESSAYS, Calcutta: Indian Associated
        Pub., 1953, p. 136-146

4381   Chakrabarti, P.

        SOME TENANT FAMILIES IN CALCUTTA - A PILOT STUDY
        Ind. J.Soc. Work, 1968, 28, 4, Jan, 471-476,
        SA, XVll, 5, D8704

4382   Chakravarty, U.

        CONDITIONS OF BENGALI WOMEN AROUND THE 2ND HALF
        OF THE 19TH CENTURY
        Calcutta, 1968

4383   Chainrai, (Miss) U.R.

        TRADITION AND CHANGE IN URBAN FAMILY
        Doct. st, Rajasthan U, 1969

4384   Chambard, J.

        MARRIAGES SECONDAIRES ET FOIRES AUX FEMMES
        EN INDE CENTRALE (SECOND AND FAIR MARRIAGE
        OF WOMEN IN CENTRAL INDIA) (Fr.)
        L'Homme, 1961, 1, 2, May-Aug, 51-88,
        SA, Xll, 1, A8539

4385   Chandrasekhar, S.

        THE FAMILY IN INDIA
        Marriage & Family Living 1954, 16, 4, Nov. 336-342,
        SA, Vol. III, #3, 1616

4386   Chatterjee, H.N.

STUDIES IN THE SOCIAL BACKGROUND OF THE FORMS
OF MARRIAGE IN ANCIENT INDIA,
Varanasi, 1972

4387   Chatterjee, K. N.

HINDU MARRIAGE PAST AND PRESENT
Varanasi, 1972

4388   Chaturvedi, S.K.

FAMILY BUDGET OF SOME LOWER CASTE FAMILIES
IN FARRUKHABAD DISTRICT (D.Phil.)
Doct, Allahabad U, 1950 (Prof. Tompson)

4389   Chauhan, B.R.

FAMILY AND HOUSEHOLD IN A RAJASTHAN VILLAGE
Ind. Sociol. 1960, 2, 3, Mar, 36-40
SA, Xll, 7, B3017

4390   Chekki, D.A.

NAMING CHILDREN AMONG THE LINGAYAT FAMILIES
J. of Karnatak U. (Soc.Sci.)4,1968

4391   Chekki, D.A.

SOME ASPECTS OF MARRIAGE AMONG THE LINGAYATS,
Man in India, 1968, 48, 2, Apr-Jun, 124-132,
SA, XVlll, 1-2, E0939

4392   Chekki, D.A.

MATE SELECTION, AGE AT MARRIAGE, AND PROPINQUITY
AMONG THE LINGAYATS OF INDIA
J. of Marriage & the Family, 1968, 30, 4, Nov,
707-711
SA, XVll, 6, D9790

1941   sociology of the family

4393   *Chekki, D.A.

        MODERNIZATION AND KIN NETWORK
        Leiden, E.J.Brill, 1974

4394   Das, R.K.

        MARRIAGE AND KINSHIP AMONG THE KABUI NAGAS OF
        MANIPUR
        Man in India, 52, 3, 1972, 228-235

4395   Chetty, (Mrs.) B.S.

        MARRIAGE AND KINSHIP AMONG THE GANGADIKARA
        VOLKKALIGAS OF MYSORE (Ph.D.),
        Doct, Poona U, 1958 (Dr. I. Karve)

4396   Chowdhury, B.

        MARRIAGE CUSTOMS AMONG THE BARENG JADIAPOORJA OF
        KORAPUT
        Adibasi 1, 1963-64, 27-32

4397   Choudhary, K.M.

        A MARRIAGE AMONG BHILIA ABORIGINALS
        Vanyajati, 12, 1964, 25-31

4398   Choudhury, R.D.

        JOINT FAMILY SYSTEM - ITS PRESENT AND FUTURE
        Econ. Wkly, 1957, 9, 38, Sep. 1233-1236
        SA Vlll, 1, 7190

4399   Chowdhury, V.

        MARRIAGE CUSTOMS OF THE SANTALS
        Bulletin of the Dept. of Anthrop.,
        (Delhi) 1, Jan 1953, 86-112

4400   Collver, A.

THE FAMILY CYCLE IN INDIA AND THE UNITED STATES
Amer. Sociol. R., 1963, 28, 1, Feb, 86-96,
SA, Xl, 65, A6150

4401   *Conklin, G.H.

EMERGING CONJUGAL ROLE PATTERNS IN A JOINT
FAMILY SYSTEM: CORRELATES OF SOCIAL CHANGE
IN DHARWAR, INDIA
Journal of Marriage and the Family, 35, 4,
Nov. 1973

4402   Cormack, M.L.

THE HINDU WOMAN
New York, Bureau of Publications, Teachers
College, Columbia University, 1953, 207p.

4403   Cottrell, A.B.

INTERPERSONAL DIMENSIONS OF CROSS-CULTURAL
RELATIONS: INDIAN - WESTERN MARRIAGES IN
INDIA (Ph.D.-Soc.) Michigan State U. (69-70)

4404   Cottrell, A.B.

CROSS - CULTURAL MARRIAGES AS LINKAGES BETWEEN
SOCIETIES - INDIAN - WESTERN MARRIAGES IN
INDIA
1969 Annual Meeting of The American Sociological
Association, Session 93,
SA, XVll, 5, Supp 5, D 8954

4405   Damle, Y.B.

THE HINDU FAMILY IN ITS URBAN SETTING: A REVIEW
ARTICLE
Ind. J. Soc. Work, 1964, 25, 1, Apr. 89-93,
SA, Xlll, 2, B5612

1941   sociology of the family

4406   Dandekar, V.M. & Pethe, V.

        SIZE AND COMPOSITION OF RURAL FAMILIES
        Artha Vignana, 2, 1960, 189-199

4407   Darbari, (Miss) P.

        CHANGING SOCIAL ATTITUDES AMONG MODERN EDUCATED
        HINDU WOMEN (Ph.D.)
        Doct., Agra U, 1960

4408   Das, M.A.

        FEMALE INFANTICIDE AMONG THE BEDEES AND THE
        CHAUHANS: MOTIVES AND MODES
        Man in India 1956, 36, 4, Oct-Dec, 261-266
        SA, Vlll, 1, 7192

4409   Das, M.N.

        FEMALE INFANTICIDE AMONG THE KHONDS OF ORISSA
        Man in India, 1960, 40, 1, Jan-Mar 30-35,
        Xll, V, B1422

4410   Das, M.S.

        A COMPARATIVE STUDY OF INTERCASTE MARRIAGE IN
        INDIA AND THE UNITED STATES
        Paper presented at the 7th World Congress of the
        Int. Sociol. Assoc. 1970,
        SA, XVlll, 5, Sep p.9, E381

4411   Das, M.S.

        AN EXPLORATORY STUDY OF TOUCHABLE - UNTOUCHABLE
        INTERCASTE MARRIAGE IN INDIA
        Ind. J. of Sociol. 1970, 1, 2, Sep, 130-138
        SA, XlX, 5, F1010

4412   Das, N.

        ECONOMY OF PAUDI BHUIAN MARRIAGE
        Adibasi, 2, 1957-58, 40-44

1941   sociology of the family

4413   Das, N.

BHATARA MARRIAGE
Adivasi, 3, 2, 1958, 22-25

4414   Dasgupta, M.

CHANGES IN THE JOINT FAMILY IN INDIA
Man in India, 1965, 45, 4, Oct-Dec, 283-288
SA, XVl, 5, D2858

4415   Dass, J.P.

AUTHORITY PATTERNS AND FAMILY RELATIONSHIP
IN TWO PRIMITIVE TRIBES OF ORISSA
East. Anthrop. 1963, 16, 3, Sep-Dec, 208-212,
SA, X111, 3-4, B6510

4416   Desai, I.P.

THE JOINT FAMILY IN INDIA - AN ANALYSIS
Sociol. B. 1956, 5, 2, Sep, 144-156,
SA, Vl, No. 1, 4124

4417   Desai, I.P.

SOME ASPECTS OF FAMILY IN MAHUVA: A SOCIOLOGICAL
STUDY OF JOINTNESS IN A SMALL TOWN
Bombay, Asia Publ.House, 1964, 239p.

4418   Deshpande, C.G.

A COMPARATIVE STUDY OF CASTE AND INTER-CASTE MARRIED
COUPLES IN MAHARASHTRA, WITH SPECIAL REFERENCE TO THE
SOCIETAL, MARITAL AND PERSONAL ADJUSTMENT (Ph.D.)
Doct, Poona U, 1970, (Prof. V.K.Kothurkar)

4419   Devanadan, P.D. & Thomas, M.M.

THE CHANGING PATTERN OF FAMILY IN INDIA
Bangalore, Christian Inst. for the Study of Religion
& Society, 1960, 166p.

- 673 -

4420   Dronamraju, K.R.

        LE SYSTEME DES CASTES ET LES MARRIAGES CONSANGUINS
        EN ANDHRA PRADESH (INDE) (THE CASTE SYSTEM AND
        INTERMARRIAGES IN ANDHRA PRADESH (INDIA)) (Fr.)
        Population, 1964, 19, 2, Apr-May, 291-308
        SA, Xlll, 1, B4711

4421   Driver, E.D.

        FAMILY STRUCTURE AND SOCIO-ECONOMIC STATUS IN
        CENTRAL INDIA
        Sociol. B. 1962, 11, 1-2, Mar-Sep, 112-120,
        SA, Xl, 7, A7754

4422   D'Souza, V.S.

        MOTHER-RIGHT IN TRANSITION
        Sociol. B. V.2, 1953, p.135-142

4423   Dube, (Mrs.) L.

        THE GOND WOMAN (Ph.D.)
        Doct, Nagpur U, 1957

4424   Dubey, B.R.

        WIDOW REMARRIAGE IN MADHYA PRADESH
        Man in India 1965, 45, 1, Jan-Mar, 50-56
        SA, XlV, 2-3, B9814

4425   Dubey, B.R.

        MARRIAGE, WIDOWHOOD AND WIDOW-REMARRIAGE IN
        SELECTED VILLAGES OF M.P. AND RAJASTHAN - A
        COMPARATIVE STUDY
        Doct. st, Rajasthan U, 1969

4426   Dumont, L.

        MARRIAGE IN INDIA: THE PRESENT STATE OF THE QUESTION
        Contrib. Ind. Sociol. 1961, 5, 75-95,
        SA, XlV, 5, C1614

4427   Dumont, L.

        LES MARRIAGES NAYAR COMME FAITS INDIEN
        (NAYAR MARRIAGES AS INDIAN PHENOMENA) (Fr.)
        L'Homme 1961, 1, 1, Jan-Apr, 11-36,
        SA, X11, A8545

4428   Dumont, L.

        MARRIAGE IN INDIA: THE PRESENT STATE OF THE
        QUESTION: PROSTSCRIPT TO PART I - II
        NAYAR AND NEWAR
        Contrib. Ind. Sociol. 1964, 7, Mar, 77-98,
        Comment, 99-102,
        SA, X1V, 6, C2585

4429   Dumont, L.

        MARRIAGE IN INDIA - THE PRESENT STATE OF THE
        QUESTION: III. NORTH INDIAN IN RELATION TO
        SOUTH INDIAN
        Contr. to Ind. Soc. 1966, 9, Dec, 70-114,
        SA, XV1, 5, D2860

4430   *Ehrenfels, U.R. von

        MATRILINEAL JOINT FAMILY PATTERNS IN INDIA
        Journal of Comparative Family Studies, 1971,
        2, 1, Spr. 54-66, SA, 21, 73G2872

4431   Ehrenfels, U.R. von

        MATRILINEAL FAMILY BACKGROUND IN SOUTH INDIA
        J. Educ. Sociol., 1953, 26, 8, Apr. 356-361,
        SA, Vol. II, #2, 276

4432   Epstein, S.

        ECONOMIC DEVELOPMENT AND PEASANT MARRIAGE IN
        SOUTH INDIA
        Man in India, 1960, 40, 3, Jul-Sep, 192-232,
        SA, X11, 5, B1425

4433   Fonseca, M.B.

FAMILY DISORGANIZATION AND DIVORCE IN INDIAN
COMMUNITIES
Sociol.B. 1963, 12, 2, Sep, 14-33
SA, Xll, 8, B3821

4434   Fonseca, M.B.

COUNSELLING FOR MARTIAL HAPPINESS (Ph.D.)
Doct, Bombay U, 1965 (Prof. G.S.Ghurye)

4435   Fox, R.G.

FAMILY, CASTE, AND COMMERCE IN A NORTH
INDIAN MARKET TOWN
Eco. Dev. Cult. Change, 1967, 15, 3, Apr. 297-314
SA, XV, 6, C7799

4436   *Freed, S.A. & Freed, (Mrs.) R.S.

STATUS AND THE SPATIAL RANGE OF MARRIAGES IN
A NORTH INDIAN AREA
Anthrop. Quart. 46, 2, Apr, 1973

4437   Freire-Maia, N.

INBREEDING LEVELS IN DIFFERENT COUNTRIES
Eug.Quart, 1957, 4, 3, Sep, 127-138,
SA, Vlll, 1, 8193

4438   Gallagher, O.R.

ENDOGAMOUS MARRIAGE IN CENTRAL INDIA
Ethnol. 1965, 4, 1, Jan, 72-76,
SA, XlV, 2-3, B9819

4439   Gangopadhyay, (Miss) B.

MARRIAGE REGULATIONS AMONG CERTAIN CASTES OF BENGAL
(Ph.D.), Doct. Poona U, 1957 (Dr. (Mrs.) I. Karve)

4440   Gangrade, K.D. & Sinha, M.P.

        INTER-GENERATIONAL CONFLICT IN INDIA
        Verry, 1971

4441   Geldens, M.

        TWO RURAL FAMILIES IN UTTAR PRADESH
        New Delhi, Directorate of Extension Ministry
        of Food and Agriculture, 1960

4442   Ghosh, D.

        NOTES ON THE FAMILY AMONG THE DIMASA KACHARI
        Man in India, 1965, 45, 1, Jan-Mar, 17-26,
        SA, XlV, 2-3, B9821

4443   *Ghurye, G.S.

        TWO BRAHMANICAL INSTITUTIONS: GOTRA AND CHARANA
        Bombay, Popular, 1972

4444   Ghurye, G.S.

        FAMILY AND KIN IN INDO-EUROPEAN CULTURE (2nd.Ed.)
        New York,Humanities, 1962

4445   Giri, N.

        CHANGING PATTERN OF URBAN FAMILY: A STUDY IN THE
        TOWNS OF BALLIA, GHAZIPUR, JAUNPUR AND VARANASI
        Doct. st, Gorakhapur U, 1969 (D.P.Saxena)

4446   Gist, N.P.

        MATE SELECTION AND MASS COMMUNICATION IN INDIA
        Public Opinion Quart. 53/54, 17, 4, winter 481-495
        SA, Vol. II, #4, 829

4447   Goode, Wm. J.

        CHANGING FAMILY PATTERNS IN INDIA
        in: WORLD REVOLUTION AND FAMILY PATTERNS
        by W.J.Goode, New York, The Free Press, 1963,
        p. 203-268

1941   sociology of the family

4448   *Goldstein, R.L.

        INDIAN WOMEN IN TRANSITION: A BANGALORE CASE STUDY
        Metuchen, Scarecrow Press, 1972

4449   Goldstein, R.L.

        ATTITUDES ABOUT MARRIAGE AMONG COLLEGE-EDUCATED
        INDIAN WOMEN
        65th Annual Meeting of the American Sociological
        Association (1970),
        SA, XV111, 5, Sup. 11, E4374

4450   Gore, M.S.

        THE HUSBAND - WIFE AND MOTHER - SON RELATIONSHIPS
        Sociol. B. 1962, 11, 1-2, Mar-Sep, 91-102,
        SA, X1, 7, A7760

4451   Gore, M.S.

        URBANIZATION AND FAMILY CHANGE
        Bombay, Popular Prakashan, 1968

4452   Goswami, B.B.

        A NOTE ON THE LUSHAI FAMILY
        East Anthrop. 1963, 16, 3, Sep-Dec, 201-207
        SA, X111, 3-4, B6518

4453   Goswami, M.C. & Kamkhenthary, H.

        MOTHER'S BROTHER IN PAITE SOCIETY
        Man in India, 52, 1, 1972, 21-39

4454   Gough, E.K.

        CHANGING KINSHIP USAGES IN THE SETTING OF
        POLITICAL AND ECONOMIC CHANGE AMONG THE NAYARS
        OF MALABAR
        Royal Anthropological Institute of Gt.Brit.&
        Ireland, Journal, V. 82, 1952, 71-88

1941   sociology of the family

4455   Gould, H.A.

        THE MICRO-DEMOGRAPHY OF MARRIAGES IN A NORTH INDIAN
        AREA
        Southw. J. Anthrop. 1960, 16, 4, win, 476-491
        SA, X, 2, A2007

4456   Gould, H.A.

        A FURTHER NOTE ON VILLAGE EXOGAMY IN NORTH INDIA
        Southw. J. Anthrop. 1961, 17, 3, Aut, 297-300
        SA, X, 3, A2325

4457   Goyal, (Mrs.) S.L.

        MARITAL RITES AND PRACTICES AMONGST BAURIAL WOMEN
        IN U.P. (Ph.D.)
        Doct. st, Agra U, 1969, (R.N.Saxena)

4458   Gulati, S.C.

        IMPACT OF LITERACY, URBANIZATION, AND SEX-RATIO
        ON AGE AT MARRIAGE IN INDIA
        Artha Vignana, 11, 4, Dec, 1969, 685-697

4459   Gulati, J.S. & Gulati, K.S.

        THE UNDIVIDED HINDU FAMILY: A STUDY OF ITS TAX
        PRIVILEGES
        New York, Asia, 1962

4460   *Gupta, G. R.

        RELIGIOSITY, ECONOMY AND PATTERNS OF HINDU
        MARRIAGE IN INDIA
        International Journal of Sociology of the
        Family, 1972, 2, 1, Mar, 43-53

4461   Gupta, J.

        MARRIAGE RITUAL AND SOCIAL STRUCTURE IN A RAJASTHAN
        VILLAGE (Ph.D.),
        Doct, Rajasthan U, 1967, (Dr.B.R.Chauhan)

4463   Gupta, M.

STATUS AND ROLE OF HINDU WIDOWS -
A SOCIOLOGICAL STUDY OF 400 WIDOWS IN THE
CITY OF LUCKNOW
Doct. st, Lucknow U, 1969

4464   Gupta, (Miss) N.

CHANGING STATUS OF WOMEN IN HINDU MIDDLE
CLASS SOCIETY
Doct. st, Agra U, 1969, (R.N.Saxena)

4465   Hallen, G.C.

DOWRY SYSTEM IN INDIA
J.Soc.Res. (India) 1960, 1, 1, Jul, 77-92,
SA, X1, 2&3, A4977

4466   Hallen, G.C.

DOWRY: A SOCIAL EVIL
Ind.Sociol. B. 1963, 1, 1, Oct, 1-7,
SA, X11, 7, B3022

4467   Hallen, G.C.

THE FUTURE OF THE FAMILY
Soc.Sci.1967, 42, 3, Jun, 168-175,
SA, XV1, 2, D0373

4468   Hallen, G.C. & Theodorson, G.A.

CHANGE AND TRADITIONALISM
IN THE INDIAN FAMILY
Ind.J.Soc.Res.1963, 4, 1,
Jan, 105-110,
SA, X11, 4, B0622

4469   Hallen, G.C. & Theodorson, G.A.

THE FUTURE OF THE FAMILY
Ind. J. Soc. Res., 1966, 7, 2, Aug, 89-93,
SA, XV11, 2, D6444

4470   Handa, (Miss) S.B.

MARITAL CONFLICT IN SOCIOLOGICAL PERSPECTIVE
(A STUDY OF M.C. AMONG THE LOWER CASTES IN
LUCKNOW)
Doct. st, Lucknow U, 1969

4471   Hanumantharayappa, P. & Saxena, D.N.

STUDY OF HOUSEHOLD COMPOSITION: A NEW APPROACH
Ind. J. Soc. Work 1966, 27, 2, Jul, 197-205,
SA, XV1, 5, D2865

4472   Hitchcock, J.T.

TRADITIONAL INDIA: STRUCTURE AND CHANGE
J. of Amer. Folklore, 71, 281, 1958, 216-223

4473   Hoch, E.M.

"RELUCTANT HUSBANDS": PROBLEMS OF EMANCIPATION
FROM TWO TYPES OF INDIAN JOINT FAMILIES
Paper presented at the 7th World Congress of
the Int. Sociol. Assoc. 1970,
SA, XV111, 5, E 3869, Supp. 9

4474   Hooja, J.

DOWRY SYSTEM AMONG THE HINDUS IN NORTH INDIA:
A CASE STUDY
Ind. J. Soc. Work, 1968, 28, 4, Jan, 411-426,
SA, XV11, 5, D8709

4475   Husain, S.A.

MARRIAGE CUSTOMS OF THE SHIA MUSLIMS IN U.P.
(BASED ON A STUDY OF THE MARRIAGE CUSTOMS OF THE
SHIAS OF MAJOR CITIES OF UTTAR PRADESH) (Ph.D.)
Doct, Lucknow U, 1967 (Dr. S. Chandra)

4476   India, Cabinet Secretariat

AGE PATTERN OF MARRIAGE AND FERTILITY OF COUPLES
19th Round, July 1964-June 1965, Delhi, 1971

4477   Indian Social Institute

THE INDIAN FAMILY IN THE CHANGE AND CHALLENGE
OF THE SEVENTIES
New Delhi, 1972

4478   Iyer, L.A.Krishna

MATRIARCHY IN KERALA
J. of Mythic Society of Bangalore, 1960-61, 51

4479   Jamal, (Mrs.) K.

THE CHANGING STATUS OF MUSLIM WOMEN, BASED ON A
STUDY OF MIDDLE CLASS M.W. IN THE CITY OF GORAKHPUR
Doct, st, Gorakhpur U, 1969, (S.P.Nagendra)

4480   Jha, J.C.

CHANGING FAMILY IN A POLYANDROUS COMMUNITY
East. Anthrop., 1965, 18, 2, May-Aug, 64-72
SA, XIV, 6, C2590

4481   Joseph, J. Rev. Fr. P.

MARRIAGE AND FAMILY IN KERALA (Ph.D.)
Doct. Bombay U, 1964 (Prof. K.M.Kapadia)

4482   Kaldate, S.

URBANIZATION AND DISINTEGRATION OF RURAL JOINT
FAMILY
Sociol. B. 1962, 11, 1-2, Mar-Sep, 103-111,
SA, X1, 7, A7351

4483   Kannan, C.T.

INTERCASTE MARRIAGE IN BOMBAY
Sociol. B. 10, 2, Sep, 53-68,
SA, X1, 6, A6937

4484   Kapadia, K.M.

CHANGING PATTERNS OF HINDU MARRIAGE AND FAMILY (II)
Sociol. B. 1954, 3, 2, Sep, 131-157,
SA, Vol. III, #4, 1867

4485   Kapadia, K.M.

CHANGING PATTERNS OF HINDU MARRIAGE AND FAMILY (III)
Sociol. B. 1955, 4, 2, Sep. 161-192,
SA, Vol. V, #1, 3023

4486   Kapadia, K.M.

MARRIAGE AND FAMILY IN INDIA
Bombay, Oxford U. Press, 1955

4487   Kapadia, K.M.

RURAL FAMILY PATTERNS: A STUDY OF URBAN-RURAL
RELATIONS
Sociol. B. 1956, 5, 2, Sep. 11-126,
SA, V1, 1, 3983

4488   Kapadia, K.M.

MARRIAGE AND FAMILY IN INDIA (3rd Ed.)
Bombay, Oxford U. Press, 1966

4489   Kapoor, (Miss) B.

SOCIO-CULTURAL PRACTICES ASSOCIATED WITH CHILD-
BEARING IN A CONTEMPORARY URBAN INDIAN SETTING
Doct. st, Lucknow U, 1969

4490   Kapur (Mrs.) P.

FAMILY AND URBANIZATION - A STUDY OF TWO SOCIAL
GROUPS IN AN URBAN SETTING
Doct. st, Delhi U, 1969 (K.A.Uma)

4491   Kapur, (Mrs.) P.

A SOCIO-PSYCHOLOGICAL STUDY OF THE CHANGE IN
ATTITUDES OF YOUNG EDUCATED HINDU WOMEN (Ph.D.)
Doct, Agra U, 1960

4492   Kapur, (Mrs.) P.

THE STUDY OF MARITAL ADJUSTMENT OF EDUCATED
WORKING WOMEN IN INDIA
Doct. Agra U, 1968

4493   Kapur, (Mrs.) P.

MARRIAGE AND THE WORKING WOMAN IN INDIA
New York, Humanities Press, 1971

4494   Kapur, (Mrs.) P.

SEX IN MARITAL MALADJUSTMENT IN INDIA
Int. J. Soc. of the Family 2, 2, Sep. 1972, 159-168

4495   Karve, D.D. & McDonald, E.E.

NEW BRAHMANS: FIVE MAHARASHTRIAN FAMILIES
Berkeley, U. of Calif. Press, 1963

1941   sociology of the family

4496   Karve, I.

        KINSHIP USES OF KARNATAK
        Poona, Deccan College Research Institute, Bulletin
        V.10, N.1, 1950, p. 49-60

4497   Kennedy, B.C.

        RURAL URBAN CONTRASTS IN PARENT - CHILD RELATIONS
        IN INDIA
        Ind. J. Soc. Work 1954, 15, 3, Dec, 162-174
        SA, Vol. IV, #2, 2243

4498   Khan, A.U.

        MARRIAGE AND FAMILY AMONG SUNNI MUSLIMS
        Doct. st, Gorakhpur U, 1969 (S.M.Dubey)

4499   Khan, N.A.

        THE CHANGING PATTERN OF MARRIAGE IN UTTAR PRADESH
        - A PSYCHO-SOCIAL STUDY OF MARRIAGES UNDER THE
        SPECIAL MARRIAGES ACT, 1954 (Ph.D.)
        Doct, Lucknow U, 1963, (Dr.S.Z.Hasan)

4500   Khan, N.A.

        A NEW PATTERN IN INDIAN MARRIAGE
        Ind. J. Soc. Res. 1963, 4, 2, Jul, 83-96
        SA, XlV, 2-3, B9827

4501   Khanna, R.M.

        A SOCIO-PSYCHOLOGICAL STUDY OF MIDDLE CLASS WORKING
        MOTHERS OF U.P. WITH SPECIAL REFERENCE TO KAVAL TOWNS
        Doct. st. Agra U, 1969, (P.N.Tandon)

4502   Khanna, O.P.

        PROBLEMS OF LOVE AND SEX IN MARRIAGE
        Delhi, 1968

4503   Khanna, O.P.

        COURTSHIPS AND LOVE MARRIAGES
        Delhi, 1968

4504   Khare, P.N.

        A STUDY OF THE FAMILY LIFE OF WOMEN EARNERS
        OF INDORE CITY (Ph.D.)
        Doct, Vikram U, 1964 (Prof. C.M.Abraham)

4505   *Khare, R.S.

        ON HYPERGAMY AND PROGENY RANK DETERMINATION
        IN NORTHERN INDIA
        Man in India, 1970, 50, 4, Oct-Dec, 350-378
        SA, 21, 73 G3718

4506   Khatri, A.A.

        SOME NEGLECTED APPROACHES AND PROBLEMS IN THE
        STUDY OF FAMILY IN INDIA
        Sociol. B. 1961, 10, 1, Mar, 75-81
        SA, X1, 6, A6939

4507   Khatri, A.A.

        THE INDIAN FAMILY: AN EMPIRICALLY DERIVED
        ANALYSIS OF SHIFTS IN SIZE AND TYPES
        J. Marri& Family 34, 4, Nov. 72, 725-735
        also: paper presented at 7th World Congress
        of the Int. Soc. Assoc., 1970,
        SA, XV1ll, 5, Sup 9, E3905

4508   Khatri, A.A.

        SOCIAL CHANGE IN THE CASTE HINDU FAMILY AND ITS
        POSSIBLE IMPACT ON PERSONALITY AND MENTAL HEALTH
        Sociol. B. 11, 1-2, 1962, Mar-Sep, 146-165,
        SA, X1, 7, A7765

4509   Khatri, A.A.

        SOCIAL CHANGE IN THE HINDU FAMILY AND ITS POSSIBLE
        IMPACT ON MENTAL HEALTH
        Vidya, 1963, 6, 1, Mar, 65-77
        SA, X1V, 2-3, B9828

4510   Khatri, A.A.

CHANGING FAMILY AND PERSONALITY OF HINDUS
- A FEW BROAD HYPOTHESES
Vidya, 7, 2, Aug. 1965

4511   Khatri, A.A.

MANUAL OF THE SCALE TO MEASURE JOINTNESS OF
FAMILIES IN INDIA
Ahmedabad, 1970

4512   Khwaja, B.A.

ATTITUDE TOWARDS PURDAH AMONG MUSLIM GIRL STUDENTS
OF KANPUR
Man in India, 1965, 45,3, Jul-Sep, 223-227
SA, XVl, 5, D2869

4513   Kolenda, P.M.

REGION, CASTE AND FAMILY STRUCTURE: A COMPARATIVE
STUDY OF THE INDIAN "JOINT" FAMILY
in: STRUCTURE AND CHANGE IN INDIAN SOCIETY
ed. B.S. Cohn and M.B.Singer, Chicago, Aldine, 1968
p. 339-397

4514   Krishnan, P.

A NOTE ON CHANGES IN AGE AT MARRIAGE OF FEMALES
AND THEIR EFFECT ON THE BIRTH RATE IN INDIA
Social Biology, 1971, 18, 2, Jun, 200-202
SA, XX, 6, F8793

4515   Kulkarni, M.G.

FAMILY PATTERNS IN GOKAK TALUKA
Sociol. B. 1960, 9, 1, Mar, 60-81,
SA, Xl, 6, A6940

4516   Kumari, (Miss) R.

DIVORCE IN HINDU SOCIETY - A SOCIOLOGICAL ANALYSIS
OF DIVORCE CASES IN THE CITY OF LUCKNOW SINCE 1954
Doct. st, Lucknow U, 1969

4517   Kurian, G.

THE INDIAN FAMILY IN TRANSITION: A CASE STUDY OF
KERALA SYRIAN CHRISTIANS
The Hague, Mouton & Co, 1961, 140p.

4518   Kutty, T.M.A.R.

SOCIO-ECONOMIC LIFE AND CHANGE IN LACCADIVES
- MARRIAGE AND KINSHIP IN AN ISLAND SOCIETY (Ph.D.)
Doct, Saugar U, 1966 (Dr. (Mrs.) L.Dube)

4519   Lakshminarayana, H.B.

RHYTHM IN JOINT FAMILY
Ind. J.Soc.Res. 1963, 4, 2, Jul 97-98,
SA, X1V, 2-3, B9830

4520   Lakshminarayana, H.B.

PARENTAL ASPIRATIONS FOR EDUCATION AND OCCUPATION
TO THEIR CHILDREN IN A SOUTH INDIAN COMMUNITY
Ind. J. Soc. Res. 13, 2, Aug. 1972, 136-143

4521   Lemelin, B.

NOTES DE RECLERCHE SUR LA FAMILLE ET LE MARIAGE
A SEMERI (RESEARCH NOTES ON THE FAMILY AND MARRIAGE
IN SEMERI) (Fr.)
Anthropologica, 1968, 10, 1, 67-80
SA, XV111, 3, E1820

4522   Lokeshwari (Miss)

URBANIZATION AND CHANGING STRUCTURE OF JOINT FAMILY
Doct. st. Agra U, 1969 (R.N.Saxena)

4523   Luchinsky, M.S.

THE LIFE OF WOMEN IN A VILLAGE OF NORTH INDIA:
A STUDY OF ROLE AND STATUS
American Doctoral Dissertations (61-62)
Cornell U, (Soc.)

4524   Madan, T.N.

FAMILY AND KINSHIP: A STUDY OF THE PANDITS OF RURAL
KASHMIR
Bombay, Asia Publishing House, 1965, 265p.

4525   Mahar, J.M.

MARRIAGE NETWORKS IN THE NORTHERN GANGETIC PLAIN
American Doctoral Dissertations (1966-67)
Cornell U, (Soc.-Family)

4526   Majumdar, A.K. & Das, K.K.

SOME ASPECTS OF MARRIAGE IN WEST BENGAL
Man in India, 52, 3, 1972, 235-239

4527   Majumdar, D.N.

HIMALAYAN POLYANDRY
Bombay: Asia Publishing House, 1960

4528   Majumdar, D.N.

FAMILY AND MARRIAGE IN A POLYANDROUS SOCIETY
East Anthrop. 1954-1955, 8, 2, Dec.-Feb, 85-110
SA, Vol. IV, #2, 2369

4529   Majumdar, M.

AGE AT MARRIAGE AND MARRIAGE RATES IN INDIA
in: Int. Pop. Union Conference Paper # 69,
New York, 1967

4530   Mokashi, P.R.

SOME SOCIAL ASPECTS OF MARRIAGES IN POONA DISTRICT
1955 - 1956 (Ph.D.)
Doct, Poona U, 1963, (Dr. (Mrs.) I. Karve)

1941   sociology of the family

4531   Mamoria, C.B.

        TRIBES IN INDIA - THEIR CIVIL AND SOCIAL CONDITIONS
        Ind. J. Soc. Work, 1957, 18, 2, Sep, 115-125
        SA, V111, 1, 7199

4532   Mamoria, C.B.

        MARRIAGE AND FAMILY IN INDIA
        Ind. J. Soc. Work, 1962, 23, 2, Jul, 199-208,
        SA, X11, 1, A8554

4533   Mandelbaum, D.G.

        TEH FAMILY IN INDIA
        Southwestern J. of Anthrop. V. 4, 1948, p. 123-39

4534   Mann, R.S.

        STATUS OF WOMEN IN A DELHI VILLAGE
        Social Welfare, 19, 2, 1972, 7-9

4535   Martin, M.E.R.

        WOMEN IN ANCIENT INDIA
        Varanasi, 1968

4536   Mathur, S.

        MARRIAGE AMONG THARUS OF CHANDANCHOWSKI
        East Anthrop. 1967, 20, 1, Jan-Apr, 33-46,
        SA, XV1, 2, C9821

4537   Mencher, J.P.

        CHANGING FAMILIAL ROLES AMONG SOUTH MALABAR NAYARS
        Southw. J. Anthrop. 1962, 18, 3, Aut. 230-245
        SA, X1, 7, A7770

4538   Mistry, (Miss) J.P.

        FAMILY AS A UNIT OF SOCIETY (Ph.D.)
        Doct. Bombay U. 1955, (Prof. G.S. Ghurye)

1941   sociology of the family

4539   Mogey, J.

        FAMILY AND MARRIAGE
        Leiden, E.J. Brill, 1963

4530a   Morrison, W.A.

        FAMILY TYPES IN BADLAPUR: AN ANALYSIS OF A
        CHANGING INSTITUTION IN A MAHARASHTRIAN VILLAGE
        Sociol. B. 1959, 8, 2,
        SA, Xl, 6, A6945

4531a   Mukherjee, B.B.

        MARRIAGE CUSTOMS AND KINSHIP ORGANIZATION OF THE
        URALI OF TRAVANCORE
        B. Dept. Anthrop. Gov't of India, 1952, 1, 2

4532a   Mukherjee, B.B.

        MARRIAGE AMONG THE KANIKKARS OF TRAVANCORE
        B. Dept. of Anthrop. Gov't of India, 1956, 5, 1

4533a   Mukherjee, B.B.

        GARO FAMILY
        East Anthrop, 1957, 11, 1, 25-30

4534a   Mukerji, D.P.

        THE STATUS OF INDIAN WOMEN
        Int. Soc. Sci. J. v.3, 1951, P 793-801

4535a   Mukherjee, R.

        A NOTE ON VILLAGE AS UNIT OR VARIABLE FOR STUDIES
        OF RURAL SOCIETY
        East Anthrop. XlV, 1, 3-29, 1961
        SA, Xl, V, A5825

4536a   Mukherjee, R.

        ON CLASSIFICATION OF FAMILY STRUCTURES: DIMENSION -
        KINSHIP COMPOSITION
        Indian Anthropology: Essays in Memory of D.N.
        Majumdar, eds. Madan & Saran, Bombay, Asia, 1962

1941   sociology of the family

4537a   Mukherjee, R.

          FAMILY: ITS STRUCTURAL CLASSIFICATION
          Calcutta, 1966

4538a   Mukherjee, R.

          FAMILY IN INDIA: A PERSPECTIVE
          The Indian Journal of Public Administration
          XlVlll, 1971

4539a   Mukherjee, R.

          CONCEPTS AND METHODS FOR THE SECONDARY ANALYSIS OF
          VARIATIONS IN FAMILY STRUCTURES
          Current Anthropology, 13, 3-6, Jun-Oct, 1972

4540   Mukerji, D.P.

          THE INDIAN WOMEN AND MODERN FAMILY
          UNESCO, Seminar on the Status of Women in South Asia,
          New Delhi, 1952, 10p. mimeo.

4541   Murdiraj, G.N.R.

          ILLERIKAM: A MODE OF MARITAL ALLIANCE AND FAMILY
          ORGANIZATION
          Ind. J. of Sociol. 1970, 1, 1, Mar, 29-43
          SA, XlX, 4, F0196

4542   Murickan, S.J. Rev. Jose Varkey

          FAMILY SYSTEMS IN INDIA AND THE UNITED STATES:
          A CROSS - CULTURAL COMPARISON OF EDUCATIONAL ADEQUACY
          American Doctoral Dissertations (65-66), St. Louis U.

4543   Muthal, (Miss) S.

          DIFFERENTIAL FERTILITY IN WOMEN AND CONSEQUENT
          DOMESTIC CHANGES
          Doct. st, Saugar U, 1969

1941   sociology of the family

4544   Nag, M.K.

        FAMILY STRUCTURE OF THE KANIKKARS AND URALIS OF
        TRAVANCORE
        B.J. Dept. of Anthrop., Gov't of India, 1954, 3,3

4545   Nag, N.G.

        FAMILY AND MARRIAGE IN LAHAUL VALLEY
        East Anthrop., 1960, 8, 8

4546   Naik, T.B.

        FAMILY IN GUJARAT
        J. of Gujarat Res. Society, 15, July-Oct, 1953,
        117-137

4547   Naik, T.B.

        THE MATERNAL UNCLE OF GUJARAT
        J. of Gujarat Res. Society 6, Jan. 1954, 62-75

4548   Nakane, C.

        "AN ANALYSIS OF HINDU FAMILIES"
        Memoirs of the Inst. of oriental Culture (Tokyo)
        43, 1967, 1-82 (Japanese)

4549   Narain, D.

        INTERPERSONAL RELATIONSHIP IN THE HINDU FAMILY
        in: FAMILIES IN EAST AND WEST, ed. by Reuben Hill
        and Rene Koenig, Paris & The Hague, Mouton, 1970
        p. 454-481

4550   Nayar, (Miss) C.

        MATERNITY BEHAVIOUR IN URBAN UTTAR PRADESH
        - A SAMPLE SURVEY CONDUCTED IN THE CITY OF LUCKNOW
        (PH.D.), Doct, Lucknow U, 1964 (Dr. R.K. Mukerjee)

4551   Niehoff, A.

        A STUDY OF MATRIMONIAL ADVERTISEMENTS IN NORTH INDIA
        East. Anthrop. 1958-1959, 12, 2, Dec.-Feb., 73-86
        SA, X, 6, A3951

1941   sociology of the family

4552   Nimkoff, M.F.

SOME PROBLEMS CONCERNING RESEARCH ON THE CHANGING
FAMILY IN INDIA
Sociol. B. 1959, 8, 2, Sep, 32-38
SA, Xl, 6, A6948

4553   *Norr, K.

LOW-CASTE EMULATION OF HIGH CASTE MARRIAGE PATTERNS
Paper presented at the ASA Annual Meetings, New York,
August 27-30, 1973

4554   Orenstein,H.

THE RECENT HISTORY OF THE EXTENDED FAMILY IN INDIA
Soc. Problems, 1961, 8, 4, Spr. 341-350,
SA, X, 3, A2597

4555   Owens, R.

INDUSTRIALIZATION AND THE INDIAN JOINT FAMILY
Ethnology, 1971, 10, 2, Apr, 223-250,
SA, XX, 5, F7567

4556   Pakrasi, K.

A STUDY OF SOME ASPECTS OF HOUSEHOLD TYPES AND
FAMILY ORGANIZATION IN·RURAL BENGAL, 1946-47
East. Anthrop. 1962, 15, 3, Sep-Dec, 55-63,
SA, Xlll, 1, B4731

4557   Pakrasi, K.

ON SOME SOCIAL ASPECTS OF FERTILITY AND
FAMILY IN INDIA
Ind. J. Soc. Work, 1966, 27, 2, Jul, 153-162,
SA, XVl, 5, D2876

4558   Pakrasi, K.

SOME SOCIAL ASPECTS OF FERTILITY AND FAMILY
IN INDIA
Ind. J. Soc. Work, 1966, 27, 2, 153-161

1941   sociology of the family

4559   Pakrasi, K. & Malaker, C.

        THE RELATIONSHIP BETWEEN FAMILY TYPE AND
        FERTILITY
        Milbank Memorial Fund Quart. 1967, 45, 4,
        Oct, 451-460,
        SA, SV11, 1, D5528

4560   Panigrahi, R.

        BRITISH SOCIAL POLICY AND FEMALE INFANTICIDE IN
        INDIA
        Delhi, 1968

4561   Pandey, (Miss) N.

        WORKING MOTHERS IN THE MIDDLE CLASS FAMILY
        Doct. st, Gorakhpur U, 1969 (S.M.Dubey)

4562   Patel, H.G.

        THE CHANGE IN STRUCTURAL UNIT AND ATTITUDES TOWARD
        MARRIAGE BY EXCHANGE
        Sociol. B. 1966, 15, 2, Win. 63-68,
        SA, SV, 6, C7813

4563   Patel, N.

        FAMILY DISPERSAL AMONG INDIAN IMMIGRANTS
        Int. J. Soc. of Family 2,2, Sep, 1972,
        168-179,
        SA, 73 G 4656, 21

4564   Patel, T. & Shah, V.

        FAMILY IN INDIA
        in: MARRIAGE AND THE FAMILY: A COMPREHENSIVE READER
        ed. J.K.Hadden & M.L. Borgatta Itasca,
        F.E. Peacock Publishers, Inc., 1969, p. 81-93

4565   Patio, G.C.S.

        INTER-CASTE MARRIAGES
        Social Welfare, 19, 2, 1972, 24

1941   sociology of the family

4566   Patterson, M.L.P.

CHITPAVAN BRAHMAN FAMILY HISTORICAL SOURCES FOR
A STUDY OF SOCIAL STRUCTURE AND SOCIAL CHANGE IN
MAHARASHTRA
in: STRUCTURE AND CHANGE IN INDIAN SOCIETY
Eds. B.S. Cohn & M.B. Singer, Chicago, Aldine,
1968, P.397-413

4567   Patterson, M.L.P.

INTERCASTE MARRIAGE IN MAHARASHTRA
The Eco. Weekly Annual, Jan. 1958, p.139-142

4568   Pethe, V.P.

LIFE CYCLE OF FAMILIES IN AN URBAN COMMUNITY
Sociol. B. 1963, 12, 1, Mar, 39-46,
SA, X1, 7, A7775

4569   Pillai, S.D.

THE STUDY OF AGE AT MARRIAGE: SOME NEGLECTED ISSUES
Ind. J. Soc. Res. 12, 3, Dec. 1971, 194-197

4570   Pimpley, P.N. & Anand, K.

ROLE OF OCCUPATION IN MARITAL ALLIANCE
Ind. J. Soc. Work, 1965, 25, 4, Jan, 381-388
SA, XV, 5, C6945

4571   Prasad, K.

SOCIAL POSITION OF WOMEN IN INDIA IN RECENT TIMES
Doct. st, Bhagalpur U, 1969, (Prof. I.Prasad)

4572   Puthenkalam, Fr.J.

THE FAMILY ORGANIZATION IN THE SOUTH WEST OF INDIA
Sociol. B. 1966, 15, 2, Sep, 1-27,
SA, XV, 6, C7814

4573   *Rakshit, H.K. & Jayasri Dasgupta

ASPECTS OF MARRIAGE PATTERN IN NINE POPULATION
GROUPS OF MAHARASHTRA
Man in India, 1971, 51, 2, Apr-Jun, 83-91
SA, 21, 73G3726

4574   Ram, B.

A NOTE ON THE CHANGE IN MARITAL STATUS
DISTRIBUTION AND ITS IMPACT ON FERTILITY:
A CASE STUDY OF INDIA
Int. J. of Soc. of the Family, 2, 1, Mar, 1972,
54-64, SA, 21, 73G4656

4575   Ramu, G.N.

GEOGRAPHIC MOBILITY, KINSHIP AND THE FAMILY
IN SOUTH INDIA
J. of Marriage and the Family, 1972, 34, 1, Feb, 147-152
SA, XX, 6, F8805

4576   Ramu, G.N.

RESEARCHES ON THE FAMILY IN INDIA
Man in India, 1972, 52, 3, 212-228

4577   Ramu, G.N.

CASTE SERVICE IN RURAL MARRIAGES: A CASE STUDY
FROM MYSORE
East. Anthrop. 1968, 21, 1, Jan-Apr, 1-10,
SA, XVlll, 4, E3270

4578   Ranadive, J.S.

FAMILY IN URBAN AND RURAL AREAS (Ph.D.)
Doct, Poona U, 1961, (Dr. (Mrs.) I. Karve)

4579   Rao, B.S.S.

A STUDY OF MATRIMONIAL ADVERTISEMENT,
Ind. J. Soc. Work, 1969, 29, 4, Jan, 379-388,
SA, XVlll, 6, E5334

1941   sociology of the family

4580   Rao, G.R.S.

EMERGING ROLE PATTERN OF WOMEN IN FAMILY
Ind. J. Soc. Work, 1965, 26, 3, Oct, 239-242,
SA, XV1, 4, D2046

4581   Rao, N.P.

ROLE CONFLICT OF EMPLOYED MOTHER IN HYDERABAD,
INDIA (Ph.D. Soc.)
Mississippi State U. (70-71)

4582   Reddy, N.S.

RITES AND CUSTOMS ASSOCIATED WITH MARRIAGE IN
A NORTH INDIAN VILLAGE
East. Anthrop. 1955-56, 9, 2, Dec.-Feb, Part I
78-91, Part II, 9, 3 & 4, 178-190

4583   Rege, B.S.
HINDU MARRIAGE (Ph.D.)
Doct, Bombay U., 1952 (Dr.N.A.Thoothi)

4584   Rele, J.R.

SOME ASPECTS OF FAMILY AND FERTILITY IN INDIA
Popul. Stud. 1962, 15, 3, Mar, 267-278,
SA, X1, 1 & 2, A4992

4585   Reyes-Hockings, A.

THE NEWSPAPER AS SURROGATE MARRIAGE BROKER
IN INDIA
Sociol. B. 1966, 15, 1, Mar, 25-39,
SA, XiV, 6, C2601

4586   Ross, A.D.

EDUCATION AND FAMILY CHANGE
Sociol. B. 1959, 8, 2, Sep, 39-44,
SA, X1, 6, A6951

4587   Ross, A.D.

SYMPOSIUM ON CASTE AND JOINT FAMILY:
AN APPROACH
Sociol. B, 1955, 4, 2, Sep, 85-96,
SA, V, 1, 3028

4588   Ross, A.D.

THE HINDU FAMILY IN ITS URBAN SETTING
Toronto, U of Toronto Press, 1961, xit 325 pp.
SA, X, 1, A1523

4589   Ross, M.H.

FAMILY ORGANIZATION AND THE DEVELOPMENT OF
AGRARIAN CAPITALISM IN A NORTH INDIAN VILLAGE
Amer. Doct. Dissertation (68-69)
U of Wisconsin

4590   Rowe, W.L.

THE MARRIAGE NETWORK AND STRUCTURAL CHANGE IN
A NORTH INDIAN COMMUNITY
Southw. J. Anthrop. 1960, 16, 3, Aut, 299-311,
SA, X, 2, A2027

4591   Queen, S.A. & Habenstein, R.W.

THE POLYANDROUS TODA FAMILY
in: THE FAMILY IN VARIOUS CULTURES
New York, J.B. Lippincott Co, 1967, 346 pp.,
SA, Xv11, 1, D5529

4592   Saksena, S.N.

BOUNDARY EXPLANATION BETWEEN HOUSEHOLD AND
FAMILY IN THE CONTEXT OF HINDU SYSTEM OF
FAMILY AND KINSHIP
J. of Gujarat Res. Soc. 27, 4, 1965

4593   Sanghvi, L.B.

INBREEDING IN INDIA
Eugenics Quart. 1966, 13, 4, Dec, 291-301,
SA, XV, 3, C5318

4594   Sarma, J.

THREE GENERATIONS IN MY CALCUTTA FAMILY
in: WOMEN IN THE NEW ASIA, ed. B.E.Ward,
Paris, Unesco, 1965, p. 216-2230

4595   Sarkar, S.S.

BIJAY CHANDRA MEMORIAL LECTURES 1967
Man in India, 1969, 49, 4, Oct-Dec, 313-360
SA, XlX, 5, F1021

4596   Sarma, J.

FORMAL AND INFORMAL RELATIONS IN THE HINDU
JOINT HOUSEHOLD OF BENGAL
Man in India, V.31, 1951, p.51-71

4597   Savita

SOCIAL CHANGE AND THE PARENT - CHILD RELATIONSHIP
IN MIDDLE CLASS HINDU FAMILIES
J. Soc. Sci., 1958, 1, 1, Jan 87-92,
SA, Vlll, 2, 7620

4598   Schlesinger, B.

THE CHANGING PATTERNS IN THE HINDU JOINT FAMILY
SYSTEM OF INDIA
Marriage & Family Living 1961, 23, 2, May, 170-175
SA, X, 5, A3672

4599   Sen, D.K.

SOME NOTES ON THE FERTILITY OF JANUSARI WOMEN
East Anthrop. 1956, 10, 1, Sep-Nov, 60-67,
SA, Vlll, 1, 7203

4600   Sen, L.K.

FAMILY IN FOUR INDIAN VILLAGES
Man in India, 1965, 45, 1, Jan-Mar, 1-16,
SA, XlV, 2-3, B9845

4601   Sen, S.

THE HINDU MARRIAGE ACT, 1955
Mod. Rev. (Calcutta) 1955, 98, 2, Aug, 120-124,
SA, Vl, 1, 4134

4602   Sengupta, N.

EVOLUTION OF HINDU MARRIAGE
Bombay, 1965

4603   Sengupta, S.

FAMILY ORGANIZATION IN WEST BENGAL : ITS
NATURE AND DYNAMICS
Econ. Wkly, 1958, 10, 11, 15, Mar, 384-389,
SA, Vlll, 2, 7621

4604   Shah, A.M.

BASIC TERMS AND CONCEPTS IN THE STUDY OF
THE FAMILY IN INDIA
Ind. Econ. Soc. Hist. R. 1964, 1, 3, Jan-Mar, 1-36,
SA, XV, 3, C5369

4605   Shah, A.M.

FAMILY AND KINSHIP AMONG THE PANDITS OF RURAL
KASHMIR: A REVIEW
East. Anthrop., 1968, 21, 3, Sep-Dec, 305-317
SA, XVlll, 7, E6386

4606   Shah, A.M.

THE HOUSEHOLD DIMENSION OF THE FAMILY IN INDIA
Berkeley, U of California Press, 1974

4607   Shah, V.P.

ATTITUDINAL CHANGE AND TRADITIONALISM IN THE
HINDU FAMILY
Sociol. B. 1965, 14, 1, Mar, 72-89,
SA, XlV, 4, C0757

4608   Sharma, S.L.

MARRIAGE AND FAMILY IN MEO COMMUNITY
- A STUDY IN THE SYNTHESIS OF HINDU AND
MUSLIM CULTURES (Ph.D.)
Doct.,Agra U, 1966

4609   Sharma, S.P.

STUDY OF CHANGING FAMILY STRUCTURE OF ORAONS OF
CHHOTANAGPUR
Doct. st, Ranchi U, 1969

4610   *Singer, M.

WHEN A GREAT TRADITION MODERNIZES
New York, Praeger, 1972

4611   Singer, M.

THE INDIAN JOINT FAMILY IN MODERN INDUSTRY
in: STRUCTURE AND CHANGE IN INDIAN SOCIETY
ed. M.B.Singer & B.S.Cohn,
Chicago, Aldine, 1968, p. 423-455

4612   Singh, N.R.

TIBETO - BURMAN FAMILY ORGANIZATION (Manipur Data)
Doct. st, Poona U, 1969

4613   Singh, R.D.

FAMILY ORGANIZATION IN A NORTH INDIAN VILLAGE:
A STUDY IN CULTURE CHANGE
American Doctoral Dissertation (61-62),
Cornell U. (Soc.)

4614   Singh, S.

MARRIAGE RATES OF THE SONSI TRIBE
Vanyajati, 8, 3, 1960, 104-111, 8, 4, 1960,155-162

4615   Sinha, D.K.

THE IMPACT OF URBANIZATION ON FAMILY AND
MARRIAGE: A SOCIOLOGICAL STUDY OF GORAKHPUR
Doct. st, Gorakhpur U, 1969 (D.P.Saxena)

4616   Sinha, S.N.

MEN AND WOMEN OF INDIA TODAY
in: SEX ROLES IN CHANGING SOCIETY
ed. H.Seward & R.C.Williamson,
New York, Random House, 1970, p. 321-334

4617   Sirsalkar, P.

MARRIAGE AND FAMILY LIFE AMONG THE RAJGONDS
OF ADILABAD DISTRICT (Ph.D.),
Doct, Osmania U, 1954 (Dr. S.C.Dube)

4618   Srinivas, M.N.

A JOINT FAMILY   DISPUTE IN A MYSORE VILLAGE
J. of M.S.U. of Baroda, 1952

4619   Srivastava, B.K.

THE FAMILY ORGANIZATION AND MARRIAGE AMONG
ORAONS: A STUDY IN CHANGE
Doct. st, Ranchi U, 1969

4620   Srivastava, J.P.

PARENT - CHILD RELATIONSHIP IN THE URBAN
MIDDLE CLASS: A SOCIOL. STUDY OF 500 FAMILIES
IN THE CITY OF SITAPUR
Doct. st, Lucknow U, 1969

4621   Srivastava, R.N.L.

MARRIAGE AMONG THE KORKA GALONGS
NEFA Research Bulletin, 1, 1, 1958, 36-58

1941   sociology of the family

4622   Srivastava, S.C.

MARITAL PREFERENCES AND CHOICE AMONG THE
MIDDLE-CLASS PEOPLE IN THE CITY OF LUCKNOW
(A STUDY BASED ON 500 CASES) (Ph.D.)
Doct, Lucknow U, 1968 (Dr.S.R.Sharma)

4623   Strauss, M.A.

HUSBAND - WIFE INTERACTION IN MIDDLE AND WORKING
CLASS NUCLEAR AND JOINT HOUSEHOLDS IN BOMBAY
Studies in Honour of K.M.Kapadia, Bombay,
University of Bombay, 1970

4624   Strauss, M.A.

COMMUNICATION, CREATIVITY, AND PROBLEM-SOLVING
ABILITY OF MIDDLE AND WORKING-CLASS FAMILIES IN
THREE SOCIETIES,
American J. of Soc., 73, 4, 1868

4625   Strauss, M.A. & Winkelman, (Mrs.) D.

SOCIAL CLASS, FERTILITY, AND AUTHORITY IN NUCLEAR
AND JOINT HOUSEHOLDS IN BOMBAY
J. of Afr. & Asian Stud., 9, 1969, pp. 61-74

4626   Strauss, M.A. & Vasquez, M.M.

ADOLESCENT - PARENT CONFLICT IN BOMBAY AND
MINNEAPOLIS IN REALTION TO SOCIAL CLASS AND
PERSONALITY
1969 Annual Meeting of the Amer. Sociol. Assoc.,
Session 52,
SA, XVll, 5, Sup 5, 09115

4627   *STRODTBECK, F.L. et al

DOMINANT DYADS IN HINDU AND CONFUCIAN FAMILIES:
THE UNEASY CASE RELATING UNCONSCIOUS MASCULINITY
AND PRAGMATISM
Paper presented at the ASA Annual Meeting, New York,
27-30, 1973

4628   Suryanarayana, N.

FAMILY AND KINSHIP AMONG THE SAVARAS
Doct. st, Ardhra U, 1969 (Prof. N.S.Reddy)

4629   Talwar, P.P.

A NOTE ON CHANGES IN AGE AT MARRIAGE OF FEMALES
AND THEIR EFFECT ON THE BIRTH RATE IN INDIA,
Eugenics Quart., 1967, 14, 4, Dec, 291-295,
SA, XVll, 2, D6458

4630   Theodorson, G.A.

ROMANTICISM AND MOTIVATION TO MARRY IN THE
UNITED STATES, SINGAPORE, BURMA AND INDIA
Soc. Forces, 1965, 44, 1, Sep, 17-27,
SA, XlV, 4, C0761

4631   Thusu, K.N. & Jha, M.

CLAN AND FAMILY AMONG THE OLLAR-GADBA OF
KORAPUT (ORISSA)
East Anthrop. 25, 2, May-Aug, 1972, 161-169

4632   Tripathi, K.P.

THE JOINT FAMILY IN THE RURAL SETTING - A STUDY
OF THE CHANGES IN THE STRUCTURE OF THE JOINT
FAMILY IN SELECTED VILLAGES OF A BLOCK IN GORAKHPUR
DISTRICT
Doct. st, Gorakhpur U, 1969, (S.P.Nagendra)

4633   Trivedi, (Mrs.) S.

A STUDY OF THE CHILD - REARING PRACTICES IN
NUCLEAR AND EXTENDED FAMILIES IN A SMALL TOWN
Doct. st, Indore U, 1969, (Abraham)

4634   Upadhyaya, H.S.

THE ORGANIZATION OF THE HINDU JOINT FAMILY AS
DEPICTED IN THE BHOJPURI FOLKSONGS OF INDIA
Phillipine Sociological Review, 1968, 16, 1-2,
Jan-Apr, 61-65,
SA, XVlll, 7, E6393

1941   sociology of the family

4635   Upadhyaya, H.S.

        FAMILIAL PATTERNS OF BEHAVIOR BETWEEN BROTHER AND
        SISTER IN THE HINDU JOINT FAMILY STRUCTURE: A STUDY
        BASED UPON THE ANALYSIS OF BHOJPURI FOLKSONGS OF INDIA
        Ind. Sociol.B. 1969, 6, 3, Apr, 197-206,
        SA, XVlll, 6, E5344

4636   Upadhyaya, H.S.

        PATTERNS OF MOTHER - SON BEHAVIOUR IN THE HINDU FAMILY
        AS DEPICTED IN THE BHOJPURI FOLKSONGS OF INDIA
        Anthropologica, 1969, 11, 2, 203-214,
        SA, X1X, 4, F0205

4637   Useem, R.H.

        THE AMERICAN FAMILY IN INDIA
        A. Amer. Acad. Polit.Soc. Sci. 1966, 368, Nov,
        132-145,
        SA, XV, 3, C5372

4638   Vaerting, M.T.

        DIE AUFLOESOESUNG DER FAMILIE DURCH UEBERVOELKERUNG
        IN CHINA UND INDIA (THE DISSOLUTION OF THE FAMILY
        THROUGH OVERPOPULATION IN CHINA AND INDIA) (Ger.)
        L.Staatssoz., 62, 9, 2, 1966, 10-20,
        SA, SV, 3, C5373

4639   *Vatuk, S.

        KINSHIP AND URBANIZATION
        Berkeley, u of California Press, 1973

4640   Venkatarayappa , K.N.

        FEMININE ROLES
        Bombay, Popular, 1967

4641   Viswananathan, N. & Desai, M.M.

        HOUSING AND FAMILY LIFE
        Ind. J.Soc.Work, 1966, 26, 4, Jan, 393-405,
        SA, XVl, 5, D2882

1941   sociology of the family

4642   Vreede-de Stuers, C.

        HUWELIJKSADVERTENTIES IN INDIA (MATRIMONIAL
        ADVERTISEMENTS IN INDIA) (Dut.)
        Mens en My. 1962, 37, 1, Jan-Feb, 11-23,
        SA, X1, 1&2, A998

4643   Vreede-de Stuers, C.

        HUWELIJKSADVERTENTIES IN INDIA (MATRIMONIAL
        ADVERTISEMENTS IN INDIA) (Dut.)
        Mens en Maatschappij, 1966, 41, 5, Sep-Oct, 378-385
        SA, XVL, 2, D0231

4644   Vreede-de Stuers, C.

        GIRL STUDENTS IN JAIPUR. A STUDY OF ATTITUDES TOWARDS
        FAMILY LIFE, MARRIAGE AND CAREER
        New York, Humanities, 1970

4645   Vreede-de Stuers, C.

        PARDA: A STUDY OF MUSLIM WOMEN'S LIFE IN NORTHERN
        INDIA
        New York, Humanities, 1968

4646   Wadia, A.B.

        SOME ASPECTS OF FAMILY WELFARE IN INDIA
        Marriage & Family Living 1955, 17, 3, Aug, 226-230,
        SA, Vol. IV, #3, 2629

4647   Welty, P.T.

        THE FAMILY IN INDIA
        in: THE ASIANS: THEIR HERITAGE AND DESTINY,
        ed. P.T.Welty, Phil, &   NY: J.B.Lippincott Co.,
        1962, p. 93-99

4648   Welty, P.T.

        THE WOMEN OF INDIA
        in: THE ASIANS: THEIR HERITAGE & DESTINY
        ed. P.T.Welty, Philadelphia, J.P.Lippincott Co.,
        1962, pp. 99-108

1941   sociology of the family

  4649   *Wiebe, P.D. & Ramu, G.N.

          MARRIAGE IN INDIA: A CONTENT ANALYSIS OF MATRIMONIAL
          ADVERTISEMENTS,
          Man in India, 1971, 51, 2, Apr-Jun, 111-120,
          SA, 21, 73G3731

  4650   Y.M.C.A., India

          THE EDUCATED WOMAN IN INDIAN SOCIETY TODAY
          Bombay, 1971

  4651   ------

          A COMPARISON OF INCEST PROHIBITIONS AND THE RULES
          OF EXOGAMY IN THREE MATRILINEAL GROUPS OF THE MALABAR
          COAST
          International Archives of Ethnography, V. 46, 1952,
          p. 82-105

2000   SOCIOLOGY OF HEALTH AND MEDICINE

2045   sociology of medicine (public health)

    4652   Advani, M.

            SOCIAL SCIENCE STUDIES ON HEALTH IN INDIA:
            A BRIEF BIBLIOGRAPHICAL ANALYSIS
            Conference on Review of Behavioural Research
            in Health and Extension Education,
            New Delhi, Central Health Education Bureau, 1967

    4653   Ahluwalia, A.

            SOCIOLOGY AND MEDICINE IN INDIA: AN APPROACH
            Eco. & Polit. Wkly, 1967, 2, 22, 1007-1012

    4654   Ahluwalia, A.

            SOME ASPECTS OF THE SOCIAL SYSTEM OF THE INDIAN
            HOSPITAL
            Doct, st, Delhi U, 1969 (Dr. A.M.Shah)

    4655   Aurora, G.S.

            TOWARDS SOCIOLOGY OF FOODS AND NUTRITION IN INDIA
            Soc. Action 19, 2, Apr-Jun, 1969, 124-135

    4656   Babusenan, G.

            PATTERN OF DISABILITY IN ULLOOR PANCHAYAT
            OF KERALA: A SURVEY REPORT
            Ind. J. Soc. Work, 1969, 29, 4, 411-416,
            SA, XVlll, 6, E5347

    4657   Bagchi, S.C., Prasad, B. & Mathew, G.B.

            STUDY OF SOME SOCIO-ENVIRONMENTAL FACTORS OF
            HOOKWORM INFECTION IN THE AREAS OF RURAL HEALTH
            TRAINING CENTER, SAROJINI NAGAR
            L.K.O. Indian J. of Medical Res., 1964, 418-424

    4658   Baijal, D.K.

            INCIDENCE AND SOCIAL COST OF SICKNESS AMONG THE
            TEXTILE WORKERS WITH SPECIAL REFERENCE TO KANPUR
            (Ph.D.), Doct., Agra U, 1964

4659   Balan, K.

SOCIOLOGY OF LEPROSY
Social Welfare, 19, 10, 1972, 1-3

4660   Banerjee, G.R.

SOME MEDICO - SOCIAL ASPECTS OF TUBERCULOSIS CONTROL
Ind.J.Soc.Work, 1954, 15, 2, Sep, 93-99,
SA, Vol. III, No. 3, 1674

4661   Banerjee, G.R.

TRAINING FOR MEDICAL AND PSYCHIATRIC SOCIAL WORK
Ind. of Soc. Work, 1967, 28, 1, Apr, 79-88,
SA, XV1, 6, D3725

4662   Berg, A.D. & Levinson, F.J.

COMBATTING MALNUTRITION: A WORKING MODEL
Int. Dev.Rev., 1968, 10, 2, Jun, 15-17,
SA, XV11, 7, E0668

4663   Bhatt, (Miss) V.G.

CRIPPLES IN BOMBAY STATE (Ph.D.)
Doct, Bombay U, 1959 (Prof. K.M.Kapadia)

4664   Carstairs, G.M.

MEDICINE AND FAITH IN RURAL RAJASTHAN
in: HEALTH, **CULTURE** AND COMMUNITY
ed. B.D.Paul, New York, Russell Sage Foundation, 1955

4665   Croizier, R.C.

MEDICINE, MODERNIZATION, AND CULTURAL CRISIS
IN INDIA AND CHINA
Comp. Studies in Society and Hist., 1970, 12,3,
Jul, 275-291,
SA, XX, 3, F5430

4666   Dhillen, H.S. & Yadav, I.R.

DIETARY HABITS AND BELIEFS IN PREGNANCY:
A BENGAL STUDY
Swasth Hindi, 1966, 33-35 & 37

4667   Elwin, V.

TRIBAL MEDICINE IN INDIA
Statesman, March 22, 1953

4668   Elwin, V.

A GREAT TRIBAL MEDICINE MAN
Statesman, March 29, 1953

4669   Elwin, V.

FOLKLORE OF DISEASE (1) THE DEMON OF CHOLERA
Statesman, April 5, 1953

4670   Elwin, V.

FOLKLORE OF DISEASE (2) SMALL POX: THE OLD MOTHER
Statesman, April 12, 1953

4671   Elwin, V.

FOLKLORE OF DISEASE (3) LEPROSY: SCOURGE OF THE
SUNGOD
Statesman, April 19, 1953

4672   Elwin, V.

FOLKLORE OF DISEASE (4) RABIES: THE INEXPLICABLE
SPORT OF FATE
Statesman, April 26, 1953

4673   Foranoff, S.L. & Harnaroof, A.

THE CULTURAL ENVIRONMENT OF MEDICAL GEOGRAPHY IN
RURAL INDIA
Pacific View, Pt, 1966, 7, 67-84

4674   Freeman, H.E. & Reeder, G.G.

        MEDICAL SOCIOLOGY: A REVIEW OF LITERATURE
        Amer. Soc. Rev, 1957, 2, 73-81

4675   Freidson, E.

        THE SOCIOLOGY OF MEDICINE: A TREND REPORT AND
        BIBLIOGRAPHY
        Current Sociology, 1961-62, 10-11

4676   Freidson, E.

        THE HOSPITAL IN MODERN SOCIETY
        Glencoe: The Free Press, 1963

4677   Gopalan, C., Pillai, K.M. & Raman, S.

        HEALTH SURVEY OF KUDUMBIS: A CLOSED COMMUNITY
        IN KERALA
        Indust. J. of Public Health, 1968, 10, 3,
        115-120, 128

4678   Gould, H.A.

        THE IMPLICATIONS OF TECHNOLOGICAL CHANGE FOR
        FOLK AND SCIENTIFIC MEDICINE
        Amer. Anthrop. 1957, 59, 3, Jun, 507-516
        SA, Vlll, 3, 8123

4679   Gupta, V.C.

        THOUSANDS CAN BE SAVED FROM GOING BLIND
        Pop.R.1962, 6, 2, Jul, 143-146,
        SA, Xlll, 2, B5637

4680   Hall, O.

        SOCIOLOGICAL RESEARCH IN THE FIELD OF
        MEDICINE: PROGRESS AND PROSPECTS
        Amer. Socio. Rev., 1951, 16, 639-44

4681   Hasan, K.A.

         SOCIAL AND CULTURAL FACTORS AFFECTING HEALTH
         IN A RURAL COMMUNITY (Ph.D.)
         Doct, Lucknow U, 1961, (Prof. D.K.Sen)

4682   Hasan, K.A.

         CULTURAL FRONTIER OF HEALTH IN VILLAGE INDIA
         Paragon, 1967

4683   Hirmes, J.S. & Watson, V.

         SOCIAL VALUE AS A FACTOR AFFECTING CHANGE OF
         MEDICAL PRACTICE IN A NORTHERN INDIAN VILLAGE
         1969 Annual Meeting of The American Sociological
         Association, Session 88,
         SA, XVll, 5, Sup. 5, D8998

4684   Hira, Singh

         THE CRIPPLED CHILD - PROBLEMS AND HIS RECOVERY
         AND REHABILITATION IN A SOCIAL WORK PROGRAMME (Ph.D.)
         Doct, Lucknow U, 1963 (Dr. R.K.Mukerjee)

4685   Hussain, S.K.M.

         MEDICINE AMONG THE GONDS, KOLAMS, AND CHENCHUS
         Man in India, 1950, 30, 23-31

4686   Junghare, Y.N. & Roy, P.

         THE RELATION OF HEALTH-PRACTISE INNOVATIONS TO
         SOCIAL BACKGROUND CHARACTERISTICS AND ATTITUDES
         Rur. Soc. 1963, 28, 4, Dec, 394-400,
         SA, Xll, 4,B0448

4687   Kahar, D.N.

         THE HEALTH CENTER DOCTOR AND SPIRIT MEDIUM IN A
         NORTH INDIAN WILLAGE
         East Anthrop. 25, 3, Sep-Dec, 1972, 249-259

4688   Kapoor, J.M.

LEPERS IN THE CITY OF LUCKNOW
Ind.J.Soc.Work, 1961, 22, 3, Dec, 239-246
SA, Xl, 7, A7803

4689   Kapoor, J.M.

A STUDY OF THE HOSPITALISED PATIENTS IN UTTAR PRADESH
(Ph.D.), Doct, Lucknow U, 1965, (Dr.S.K.Khindaka)

4690   Khandelwal, (Miss), S.K.

A SOCIOLOGICAL STUDY OF LEPERS IN HOSPITALS
IN UTTAR PRADESH (Ph.D.),
Doct, st, Agra U, 1969, (Prof. R. Prasad)

4691   Khare, R.S.

A PLEA FOR CULTURAL DIMENSION IN MEDICINE
East Anthrop. 1959, 12, 3, p.196-201

4692   Khare, R.S.

FOLK MEDICINE IN A NORTH INDIAN VILLAGE
Hum. Org. 1963, 22, 1, Spr, 36-40,
SA, Xll, 5, B1454

4693   Mahadevan, I.

SOCIAL FACTORS IN SOME NUTRITIONAL DEFICIENCY
DISEASES
Ind. J. Soc. Work, 1962, 23, 41-52

4694   Malhotra, M.

AN INVESTIGATION INTO THE ACCEPTANCE OF THE APPLIED
NUTRITION PROGRAMME IN A SELECTED VILLAGE OF PUNJAB
M.S.Thesis, India, 1966

4695   Mamoria, C.B.

        PUBLIC HEALTH IN INDIA
        Ind. J. Soc. Work, 1959, 19, 4, 291-308,
        SA, Xl, 6, A6888

4696   Mann, R.S.

        CONCEPTS OF DISEASES AND CHANGE IN A DELHI VILLAGE
        Ind. J. Soc. Work, 1967, 27, 4, Jan, 353-360
        SA, XVl, 6, D3729

4697   Mann, R.S.

        SOCIO - CULTURAL MILIEU AS BARRIER TO APPLIED
        NUTRITION PROGRAMME
        in: CONFLICT, TENSION AND CULTURAL TREND IN INDIA
        ed. Vidyarthi, L.P., 1969

4698   Marriot, M.

        THE HINDU VILLAGE AND SCIENTIFIC MEDICINE
        New York, Russell Sage Foundation, 1953

4699   Marriot, M.

        WESTERN MEDICINE IN A VILLAGE OF NORTHERN INDIA
        in: HEALTH, CULTURE AND COMMUNITY, ed. B.D.Paul,
        New York, 1955

4700   Mathur, (Mrs.) J.

        HUMAN ORGANIZATION OF A RAJASTHAN HOSPITAL
        - INTER-PERSONNEL RELATIONS IN A HOSPITAL
        ATTACHED TO A MEDICAL COLLEGE
        Doct. st., Rajasthan U, 1969

4701   Menon, V. & Nayar, S.B.

        A SOCIO - MEDICAL SURVEY OF MATERNAL AND CHILD
        HEALTH IN THE MARKET AREA OF VILLAGE BANTHRA IN
        LUCKNOW DISTRICT
        Ind. J. Soc.Work 1968, 28, 4, Jan, 389-398,
        SA, XVll, 5, D8725

4702   Mohanty, A.K.

SOCIAL FACTORS IN LEPROSY: A STUDY ON
ADJUSTMENT OF VICTIMS TO DISEASE AND HANDICAP
33rd Annual Meeting of the Southern Sociological
Society, Session 17,
SA, XV111, 3, Supp. 7, E2635

4703   Motalhar, R.K.

CULTURAL FACTORS IN URBAN HEALTH
Ind. J. of Public Health, 1968, 7, 2, 102

4704   Narde, A.D.

HEALTH SURVEY OF SILKMILL WORKERS
Ind. J. Soc.Work 1954, 15, 1, Jun, 41-47
SA, Vol. III, #3, 1678

4705   Nayar, (Mrs.) S.B.

A STUDY OF REACTIONS OF SURGICAL PATIENTS ON
HOSPITALIZATION AND THE NEED OF MEDICAL SOCIAL
WORK IN SURGICAL WARDS (Ph.D.)
Doct, Agra U, 1970 (Dr. R.N.Saxena)

4706   Opler, M.E.

THE CULTURAL DEFINITION OF ILLNESS IN VILLAGE INDIA
Hum.Org. 1963, 22, 1, Spring, 32-35,
SA, X11, 5, B1455

4707   Parthasarathy, N.L. & Gupta, C.K.

INFLUENCE OF SOME OF THE SOCIO-ECONOMIC FACTORS
ON THE PREVALENCE OF TRACHOMA
Ind. J. Soc. Work, 1962, Apr, 23, 1, 127-130
SA, X11, 1, A8569

4708   Parvathamma, C. & Shardamma, L.S.

        MEDICAL SOCIOLOGY: SOME PROBLEMS FOR STUDY
        Eco. Wkly, 1965, 17, 49, 1793-1796

4709   Paul, B.D.

        HEALTH, CULTURE AND COMMUNITY
        New York, Russel Sage Foundation, 1955

4710   Pillai, K.M.

        PRIMARY HEALTH CENTRE - A SOCIOLOGICAL ANALYSIS (Ph.D.)
        Doct., Bombay U, 1970, (Dr.A.R.Desai)

4711   Prasad, B.G., Rao, A.R. & Nayar, S.B.

        A STUDY OF BELIEFS AND CUSTOMS IN A LUCKNOW
        VILLAGE IN RELATION TO CERTAIN DISEASES,
        MENSTRUATION, CHILD BIRTH AND FAMILY PLANNING
        Ind. J.Soc.Work, 1969, 30, 1, Apr, 45-54,
        SA, XVlll, 7, E6402

4712   Purushottam, N.

        MEDICAL ASPECTS OF UNDER-NUTRITION AND OVER-NUTRITION
        IN INDIA
        Pop.R. 1963, 7, 1, Jan, 69-72,
        SA, Xlll, 2, B5640

4713   *Ray, J. & Basu, S.

        SOCIAL ASPECTS OF LEPROSY
        Man in India, 1971, 51, 2, Apr-Jun, 130-141
        SA, 21, 73G3750

4714   Roemer, M.I. & Mackintosh, J.M.

        HENRY E. GIGERIST ON THE SOCIOLOGY OF MEDICINE
        New York, MD Publications, 1960, xiiit 397 pp.,
        SA, lX, 1, 9254

4715   Roy, S.C.

       CULTURAL CONTACT AS A DYNAMIC OF SOCIAL CHANGE
       - A STUDY OF THE TREATMENT OF THE BLIND IN INDIA
       American Doctoral Dissertations (New York U.),
       1960-61, (Soc.)

4716   Sanghri, L.D.

       ANTHROPOLIGICAL DIMENSION IN MEDICAL EDUCATION
       1966, 5, 3, 203-205

4717   Sanhar, K.

       A STUDY OF THE SOCIAL ENVIRONMENTAL AND HEALTH
       CONDITIONS OF SOME NILGIRI TRIBES
       Ind.J.Soc.Work, 1958, 179-187

4718   Saran, P.

       MEDICAL CASE AND ITS DETERMINING FACTORS
       AT AN INDIAN HOSPITAL
       Ind.Soc.B. 1968, 5, 4, Jul, 197-208,
       SA, XV11, 7, D6681

4719   Saxena, V.B. & Prasad, B.G.

       AN EPIDEMIOLOGICAL STUDY OF YAWER
       IN M.P., CULTURAL ASPECTS   `
       Ind. J. of Medical Res., 1963, 51, 768-820

4720   Srivastava, A.L.

       MEDICAL SOCIOLOGY IN THE INDIAN SETTING
       Ind.J.Soc. Work, 1970, 31, 2, Jul, 169-176
       SA, XX, 6, F8832

4721   Srivastava, (Mrs.) P.

       INCIDENCE AND SOCIO-ECONOMIC EFFECTS OF
       INDUSTRIAL DISEASES IN UTTAR PRADESH, WITH
       SPECIAL REFERENCE TO KANPUR (Ph.D.)
       Doct, Agra U, 1959

4722   Subba-Reddy, D.V.

        FOLK MEDICINE AND MODERN MEDICINE IN PRESENT
        SOCIETY, ITS RELEVANCE TO MEDICAL EDUCATION
        Ind. J. Med.Educ., 1966, 5, 3, 206-213

4723   Tewari, A.S.

        THE INDIAN DOCTOR - A STUDY OF THE STATUS,
        ROLE, AND VALUES OF PRACTITIONERS OF
        ALLOPATHY IN THE CITY OF LUCKNOW,
        Doct. st, Lucknow U, 1969

4724   Thorat, S.S.

        INFLUENCE OF TRADITIONAL AND NON-TRADITIONAL
        STATUS ON THE ADOPTION OF HEALTH PRACTICES
        Behavioral Scis. & C.D., 1969, 3, 1, Mar, 38-50
        SA, X1X, 4, F0220

4725   Tomar, (Miss) N.

        THE INDIAN NURSE
        Doct. st, Lucknow U, 1969

4726   Verma , (Miss), M.R.

        FEMALE NURSES
        Doct. st, Gorakhpur U, 1969 (D.P.Saxena)

4727   Verma, P.L.

        PROBE INTO THE ADJUSTMENT PROBLEMS OF THE
        BLIND
        Ind.J.Soc.Work, 1971, 32, 1, Apr, 53-62
        SA, XX, 7, F9874

4728   Vyas, R.T.

        THE VISUALLY HANDICAPPED IN BOMBAY STATE:
        THEIR SOCIAL BACKGROUND AND PRESENT STATUS (Ph.D.)
        Doct, Bombay U, 1958 (Prof.G.S.Ghurye)

2045   sociology of medicine (public health)

4729   -----

        SANIDAD (HEALTH) (Sp.)
        Revista Espanda de la Opinion Publica, 1966, 6,
        Oct-Dec, 432-436
        SA, XVl, 6, D3736

2046   social psychiatry (mental health)

    4730   Amesur, C.A.

        EDUCATION AND REHABILITATION OF THE MENTALLY
        RETARDED IN INDIA
        Ind.J.Soc.Work 1962, 23, 2, Jul, 167-172,
        SA, Xll, 1, A8573

    4731   Chandra, R.

        SOCIOLOGICAL FACTORS IN MENTAL ILLNESS (Ph.D.),
        Doct, st, Agra U, 1969, (Dr.R.N.Saxena)

    4732   Ganguli, H.C.

        MENTAL HEALTH, STUDY OF AN INDIAN INDUSTRIAL
        POPULATION
        Ind.J.Soc.Work, 1969, 30, 2, Jul, 123-132,
        SA, XlX, 1-2, E7787

    4733   Gupta, S.P.

        A STUDY OF SOCIAL ADJUSTMENT AND REHABILITATION
        OF MENTALLY SUBNORMAL CHILDREN (Ph.D.)
        Doct st., Agra U, 1969, (Dr.R.N.Saxena)

    4734   Jain,(Miss) C.D.

        PSYCHIATRIC-SOCIAL WORK PRACTICE WITH ANXIETY
        NEUROTIC PATIENTS
        Doct. st, Lucknow U, 1969

4735   Marfatia, J.C.

CULTURAL AND SOCIAL FACTORS CONTRIBUTING TO
CHILD'S MALADJUSTMENT
Ind.J.Soc.Work, 1958, 19, 2, Sep, 115-118,
SA, Vlll, 2, 7416

4736   Marfatia, J.C. & Batiwalla, B.M.

MENTAL HEALTH SERVICES AND THE FIVE-YEAR
PLAN IN INDIA
Int.J.Soc.Psychiatry, 1956, 2, 4, Sum, 58-61
SA, XV, IV, C6172

4737   Nigam, K.P.

A SOCIOLOGICAL STUDY OF PSYCHOSIS (Ph.D.·)
Doct., Agra U, 1963

4738   Obeyesekere, G.

AYURVEDA AND MENTAL ILLNESS
Comp. Studies in Society and History
1970, 12, 3, Jul, 292-296,
SA, XX, 3, F5455

4739   Opler, M.K.

CULTURE AND MENTAL HEALTH
New York, Macmillan Co, 1959, xxi & 533 pp.
SA, X, 6, A 3828

4740   Rao, S.

CULTURE AND MENTAL DISORDER: A STUDY
IN AN INDIAN MENTAL HOSPITAL
Int.J.Soc.Psychiat.1966, 12, 2, Spr.139-148
SA, XV, 7, C8105

4741   Robins, A.J.

PSYCHIATRIC INSTITUTIONAL SERVICES IN INDIA
Pop.R.1958, 2, 1, Jan, 46-62,
SA, Xll, 5, B1475

2046   social psychiatry (mental health)

4742   Roy, A.M.

TRAINING OF SOCIAL SERVANTS
Ind. J.Soc.Work, 1964, 24, 4, Jan, 235-346,
SA, X111, 2, B5658

4743   Shardamba, (Miss) H.R.

SOCIO-ECONOMIC AND EDUCATIONAL FACTORS IN
MENTAL DISORDER (Ph.D.)
Doct, Ranchi U, 1964 (Dr. L.P.Verma)

2100   SOCIAL PROBLEMS AND SOCIAL WELFARE

2101   social problems (general)

    4744   Bhatnagar, C.P.

        THE CRISIS IN INDIAN SOCIETY
        Delhi, 1971

    4745   Bondurant, J.V. & Fisher, M.W.

        ETHICS IN ACTION: CONTRASTING APPROACHES TO
        SOCIAL AND POLITICAL PROBLEMS IN MODERN INDIA
        Austral.J.Polit.Hist.1212 Aug 1966, 177-193

    4746   Bose, D.

        PROBLEMS OF INDIAN SOCIETY
        New York, Humanities, 1968

    4747   Brij, Mohan

        INDIA'S SOCIAL PROBLEMS
        Allahabad, 1968

    4748   Kumarappa

        SOCIAL PROBLEMS OF INDIA
        National Conference of Social Work, 1948, 74-78

    4749   Madan, G.R.

        INDIAN SOCIAL PROBLEMS (2 Vols.)
        Paragon, 1966-67

    4750   Mamoria, C.B.

        SOCIAL PROBLEMS AND SOCIAL DISORGANIZATION
        IN INDIA
        Allahabad: Kitab Mahal, 1960, 432 pp.
        SA, 1X, 2, 9812

2101   social problems (general)

    4751   Murphy, G.

        IN THE MINDS OF MEN: THE STUDY OF
        HUMAN BEHAVIOUR AND SOCIAL TENSIONS
        IN INDIA
        New York, Basic Books, 1953

    4752   Raj, R.C.

        FUNCTIONS AND DISFUNCTIONS OF SOCIAL CONFLICT (Ph.D.)
        Doct, Rajasthan U, 1968 (Dr.T.K.N.Unnithan)

    4753   *Rose, A.M.
        HINDU VALUES AND INDIAN SOCIAL PROBLEMS
        Sociological Quarterly, VIII (summer), 1967,
        329-39

2143   social gerontology

    4754   Bryce, L.W.

        EMERGING PROBLEMS
        Ind. Sociol. 1962, 4, 5, Mar, 29-32,
        SA, Xlll, 2, B5673

    4755   D'Souza, V.S.

        CHANGES IN SOCIAL STRUCTURE AND CHANGING
        ROLES OF OLDER PEOPLE IN INDIA
        Sociol. & Soc.Res. 1971, 55, 3, Apr, 297-304,
        SA, XX, 3 F4713

    4756   Kumar, G.

        THE DESTITUTE AGED: A SOCIAL WORK STUDY
        OF OLD AGE PENSIONERS IN THE KAVAL TOWNS
        OF U.P.
        Doct st, Lucknow U, 1969

2143   social gerontology

    4757   *Marulasiddaiah, H.M.

            OLD PEOPLE OF MAKUNTI,
            Dharwar, Karnatak U, 1969

    4758   Marulasiddaiah, H.M.

            THE DECLINING AUTHORITY OF OLD PEOPLE
            Ind.J.Soc.Work, 1966, 27, 2, Jul, 175-185,
            SA, XVl, 5, D2905

    4759   Raj, B. & Prasad, B.G.

            A STUDY OF RURAL AGED PERSONS IN SOCIAL PROFILE
            Ind.J.Soc.Work, 1971, 32, 2, Jul, 155-162,
            SA, XX, 7, F9893

    4760   Rastogi, R.S.

            SOCIAL SECURITY
            Ind.Sociol. 1959, 1, 1, Mar, 53-58,
            SA, Xll, 5, B1480

    4761   Srivastwa, R.C.

            THE SOCIO-ECONOMIC PROBLEM OF OLD AGE
            Doct. st, Gorakhpur U, 1969 (D.P.Saxena)

2147   social disorganization (crime)

    4762   Advani, (Miss) N.H.

            SOCIAL FACTORS IN CRIME AND CORRECTION
            Doct.st, Rajasthan U, 1969

    4763   Ahuja, R.

            FEMALE OFFENDERS IN INDIA
            Meerut, Meenakshi Prakashan
            1969, xi, 131p.

4764   Ahuja, R.

        FEMALE MURDERERS IN INDIA - A SOCIOLOGICAL
        STUDY
        Ind.J.Soc.Work, 1970, 31, 3, Oct, 271-284,
        SA, XX, 6, F8848

4765   Aiyar, R.P.

        IN THE CRIMELIGHT
        Bombay, India Book House, 1967, 173 p.

4766   Agnihotri, H.N.

        CULPABLE HOMICIDE IN SAGAR DISTRICT
        Doct. st, Saugar U, 1969

4767   Ali, S.A.

        INCIDENCE OF CRIME AMONG THE TRIBES OF MADHYA PRADESH
        in: VIDYARTHI (ed), APPLIED ANTHROPOLOGY IN INDIA,
        Allahabad, Kitab Mahal, 1961

4768   Ayyangar, M.A.

        CONFLICTS AND TENSION IN THE NATIONAL PEERSPECTIVE
        in: CONFLICT, TENSION AND CULTURAL TREND IN INDIA
        ed: Vidyarthi, 1967

4769   Basu, M.N.

        CONFLICTS AND TENSION IN HUMAN SOCIETY
        in: CONFLICT, TENSION AND CULTURAL TREND IN INDIA
        ed: Vidyarthi, Calcutta, Punthi Pustak, 1969

4770   Bayley, D.H.

        THE EFFECTS OF CORRUPTION IN A DEVELOPING NATION
        in: A SOCIOLOGICAL READER ON COMPLEX ORGANIZATIONS
        (2nd ed.) Amitai Etzioni (ed.), New York,
        Holt, Rinehart & Winston, Inc. 1969, pp. 463-479

4771   Bhaskaran, K.

SOCIAL TENSION AND CONFLICTS IN CONTEMPORARY
INDIAN SOCIETY: FROM A PSYCHIATRIC POINT OF
VIEW
in: CONFLICT, TENSION AND CULTURAL TREND IN INDIA
ed. Vidyarthi, 1969

4772   Bose, N.K.

SOCIAL TENSIONS IN INDIA
Man in India, 1963, 43, 1, 1-8,
SA, X11, 6, B1667

4773   Carstains, G.M.

THE CASE OF THAKUR KHUMAN SINGH: A CULTURE
CONDITIONED CRIME
Br. J. Of Delinquency, 1953, 4, 19-25

4774   Chandra, S.

SOCIOLOGY OF DEVIATION IN INDIA
Bombay -Allied Publishers, 1967, xii-264 p.

4775   Charanlal, A.A.

HABIT,ECONOMY AND CRIME IN CHHOTANAGPUR
Doct.st, Ranchi U, 1969

4776   Chatterjee, B.B.

TENSION, CONFLICT AND DEVELOPMENT IN SMALL
RURAL COMMUNITIES: A BEHAVIOUR THEORETIC CRITIQUE
in: CONFLICT, TENSION AND CULTURAL TREND IN INDIA
ed. Vidyarthi, 1969

4777   Chekki, D.A.

SOCIOLOGICAL APPROACH TO CRIME CAUSATION
Government Law College Magazine, Bombay, 1959

4778   Dasgupta, L.

OUR SOCIETY: CONFLICT AND COHESION
Calcutta, 1971

4779   Dastur, R.N.

DRUG POISONING AND ATTEMPTED SUICIDE:
A SOCIAL INQUIRY
Ind.J.Soc.Work, 1966, 26, 6, 365-375

4780   Deb, R.S.

PRINCIPLES OF CRIMINOLOGY, CRIMINAL LAW AND
INVESTIGATIONS
Calcutta, 1968-72

4781   Driver, E.D.

INTERACTION AND CRIMINAL HOMICIDE IN INDIA
Soc. Forces. 1961, 40, 2, Dec, 153-158
SA, X, 5, A3704

4782   Hallen, G.C.

SOCIAL ALIENATION IN MODERN INDIAN SOCIETY
(PROCESSES, CONDITION AND SOCIAL RESPONSES)
(D.Litt.),
Doct.st, Agra U, 1969

4783   Ghosal, P.

PSYCHOLOGICAL AND SOCIAL ASPECTS OF
INDIAN CRIMINOLOGY (D.Phil.)
Doct, Calcutta U, 1959

4784   Ghurye, G.S.

SOCIAL TENSIONS IN INDIA
Bombay, Popular Prakashan, 1968, xi, 552p.

4785   Gowriswarudu, V.

THE PHENOMENON OF ANOMIE (Ph.D.),
Doct, Poona U, 1968 (Dr.Y.B.Damle)

4786   Gupta, B.K.D.

RECIDIVISM IN INDIA - ITS PREVENTION AND
TREATMENT
Ind. Sociol. 1960, 2, 2, Feb, 18-26,
SA, Xll, 6, B2231

4787   Gupta, (Miss) M.

CRIME AND MENTAL ILLNESS
Doct st, Bombay U, 1969 (Dr.M.J.Sethna)

4788   Hitchcock, J.T.

FATALISTIC SUICIDE RESULTING FROM
ADAPTION TO AN ASSYMMETRICAL SEX RATIO
Eastern Anthropologist, 1967, 20, 2, May-
Aug, 133-142,
SA, XVll, 6, D9262

4789   Jayakar, R.B.

PROSTITUTION IN THE CITY OF BOMBAY   (Ph.D.)
Doct, Bombay U, 1950 (Dr.N.A.Thoothi)

4790   Katore, S.S.

PATTERNS OF DACOITY IN M.P. (Ph.D.)
Doct, Saugar U, 1969,   (Prof. D.P.Jatar)

4791   Kerawalla, (Miss) P.C.

NATURE AND VOLUME OF CRIME IN BOMBAY STATE (Ph.D.)
Doct, Bombay U, 1956, (Prof. K.M.Kapadia)

4792   Majumdar, D.N. & Others

INTER-CASTE TENSIONS
in: RURAL SOCIOLOGY IN INDIA,
ed. A.R.Desai, Bombay, Popular, Prakashan,
1969, pp. 398-403

2147   social disorganization (crime)

4793   Mamoria, C.B.

        THE CRIMINAL TRIBES IN INDIA
        AICC Econ. R. 1959, 11, 8, 1, Sep, 19-23,
        SA, X11, 5, B1491

4794   Mehta, B.H.

        FORESTRY AND TENSIONS IN TRIBAL AREA
        in: CONFLICT, TENSION AND CULTURAL TREND IN
        INDIA,
        ed. Vidyarthi, 1969

4795   Mehendale, Y.S.

        CRIME AND ENVIRONMENT
        Ind.J.Soc. Work, 1955, 16, 3, Dec, 146-152
        SA, V111, 1, 7234

4796   Mehta, B.H.

        EX-CRIMINAL GROUPS IN INDIA
        Indian J.of Soc.Work, 1955, 16, 1, Jun, 10-18,
        SA, Vol. V, #2, 3313

4797   Murphy, J.

        IN THE MINDS OF MEN, THE STUDY OF HUMAN
        BEHAVIOUR AND SOCIAL TENSIONS IN INDIA
        New York, Basic Books, 1953, 306p.

4798   Naik, T.B.

        A STUDY OF BHIL CRIMES IN M.P.
        1969 (unpublished)

4799   Nandi, S.

        RESOLUTION OF CONFLICTS IN BENGAL VILLAGE
        in: CONFLICT, TENSION AND CULTURAL TREND
        IN INDIA
        ed. Vidyarthi, 1969

2147   social disorganization (crime)

   4800   Nigam, D.P.

           SOCIAL TENSIONS IN U.P.
           (DEVA BLOCK, DISTRICT BARABANKI, U.P.)
           Doct.st, Lucknow U, 1969

   4801   Pandey, N.L.

           SOCIAL DISORGANISATION IN KAVAL TOWNS OF U.P. (Ph.D.)
           Doct, Agra U, 1962

   4802   Paras, Ram

           A UNESCO STUDY OF SOCIAL TENSION IN ALIGARH
           Ahmedabad, 1955

   4803   Pandey, R.E.

           THE SUICIDE PROBLEM IN INDIA
           Int.J.of Social Psychiatry 1968, 14, 3,
           Sum, 193-200,
           SA, XVll, 6, D9271

   4804   Patrick, C.H.

           THE CRIMINAL TRIBES OF INDIA WITH SPECIAL
           EMPHASIS ON THE MANG GARUDI: A PRELIMINARY
           REPORT
           Man in India, 1968, 48, 3, Jul-Sep, 244-257
           SA, XVlll, 3, E2497

   4805   Pundir, (Miss) S.

           SLUM CULTURE AND CRIMINAL BEHAVIOUR
           Doct. st, Agra U, 1969, (R.N.Saxena)

   4806   Raj, A.S.

           NEW GOALS FOR OLD
           Sociologist, 1956-57, 1, 1, 34-37
           SA, Vlll, 1, 7238

4807   Ramachandran, P.

        RESEARCH REPORTS AND NOTES ON THE PROBLEMS
        OF BEGGARS AND PROSTITUTES
        Ind.J.Soc.Work, 1963, 24, 1, Apr.35-30,
        SA, Xll, 4, B0718

4808   Ramachandran, P.

        RECENT RESEARCH ON CRIME AND CORRECTIONS IN
        INDIA
        Ind.J.Soc.Work, 1963, 24, 2, Ju, 99-102,
        SA, Xll, 5, B1497

4809   Ramanujam, T.

        PREVENTION AND DETECTING CRIMES
        Madras, Madras Book Agency, 1966, xxi-464p.

4810   Rangiah, N.C.B.

        CRIME IN MYSORE STATE (Ph.D.),
        Doct, Poona U, 1951, (Dr. (Mrs.) I.Karve)

4811   Rastogi, P.N.

        FACTIONALISM, POLITICS AND CRIME IN
        A UTTAR PRADESH VILLAGE
        East Anthrop. 1964, 17, 3, Sep-Dec, 168-182,
        SA, XlV, lV, C0630

4812   Raval, I.B.

        A STUDY OF CRIME AMONG THE BHILS
        Man in India, 1964, 44, 3, Jul-Sep, 221-232,
        SA, Xlll, 3-4, B6572

4813   Ray, P.C.

        STEREOTYPES AND TENSIONS AMONG THE MUSLIMS
        AND HINDUS IN A VILLAGE IN BENGAL
        in: CONFLICT, TENSION AND CULTURAL TREND IN INDIA,
        ed. Vidyarthi, 1969

4814   Roy Burman, B.K.

         CONFLICT AND TENSION IN RURAL INDIA
         in: CONFLICT, TENSION AND CULTURAL TREND IN INDIA
         ed. Vidyarthi, 1969

4815   Roy Choudhary, P.C.

         ALIENATION OF THE ADIBASI LANDS
         in: CONFLICT, TENSION AND CULTURAL TREND IN INDIA
         ed. Vidyarthi, 1969

4816   Sahay, K. N.

         CHRISTIANITY AS A FACTOR OF TENSION AND
         CONFLICT AMONG THE TRIBALS OF CHOTANAGPUR
         in: CONFLICT, TENSION AND CULTURAL TREND IN INDIA
         ed. Vidyarthi, 1969

4817   Rose, A.M.

         HINDU VALUES AND INDIAN SOCIAL PROBLEMS
         Sociol. Quart, 1967, 8, 3, Su, 329-339,
         SA, XVl, 2, D0422

4818   Sachchidananda

         CASTE AND CONFLICT IN A BIHAR VILLAGE
         in: CONFLICT, TENSION AND CULTURAL TREND IN INDIA
         ed. Vidyarthi, 1969

4819   Sandhu, H.S.

         VALIDATION OF SOCIALIZATION SCALE (OR
         DELINQUENCY SCALE) IN INDIA
         Ind. J.Soc.Work, 1960, 21, 2. Sep, 155-165,
         SA, Xl, 6, A7035

4820   Saran, A.B.

         MURDER AND SUICIDE AMONG THE TRIBES OF CHHOTANAGPUR
         (Ph.D.), Doct, Ranchi U, 1962, (Prof.Sachchiananda)

4821   Saran, A.B.

MURDER AMONG THE MUNDA: A CASE STUDY
Ind.J.Soc.Work, 1962, 23, 1, Apr, 1-7,
SA, X11, 1, A8597

4822   Saran, A.B.

SOCIAL CONFLICT AND TRIBAL TENSION
in: CONFLICT, TENSION AND CULTURAL TREND IN INDIA
ed. Vidyarthi, 1969

4823   Saxena, S.C.

WHITE COLLAR CRIME IN UTTAR PRADESH (Ph.D.),
Doct, Agra U, 1969 (Dr.R.N.Saksena)

4824   Sen, S.

ASPECTS OF CONFLICTS AND TENSION IN
CENTEMPORARY INDIAN SOCIETY
in: CONFLICT, TENSION AND CULTURAL TREND IN INDIA
ed. Vidyarthi, 1969

4825   Sethna, M.J.

SOCIETY AND THE CRIMINAL
Doct, Bombay U, 1947 (Dr.N.A.Thoothi)

4826   Shah, J.H.

CAUSES AND PREVENTION OF SUICIDES
Ind.J.Soc.Work, 1960, 21, 2, Sep, 167-176
SA, X1, 6, A7037

4827   Shandilya, (Mrs.)S.

A SOCIOLOGICAL STUDY OF SUICIDES IN CITIES
OF UTTAR PRADESH (Ph.D.)
Doct, Agra U, 1967

2147   social disorganization (crime)

4828   Shankar, G.

WEARING AWAY FROM CRIME: A STUDY OF TWO
EX-CRIMINAL TRIBES IN TRANSITION (Ph.D.),
Doct, Patna U, 1964 (Dr.Z.Ahmad)

4829   Sharma, (Mrs.) R.K.

WOMEN OFFENDERS OF UTTAR PRADESH
- A PSYCHO-SOCIAL STUDY OF WOMEN CONVICTS
AND UNDER-TRIAL PRISONERS IN UTTAR PRADESH
JAILS (Ph.D.)
Doct, Lucknow U, 1963, (Prof. S. Chandra)

4830   Sherry,A.S.

PSYCHO - SOCIAL FACTORS IN HOMICIDE IN
UTTAR PRADESH (PH.D.)
Doct, Lucknow U, 1969 (Dr.S.Chandra)

4831   Shukla, B.C.K.

SOCIO - CULTURAL ASPECTS OF THE USE
OF ADDICTIVE DRINKS AND DRUGS IN A
NORTH INDIAN VILLAGE (Ph.D.)
Doct, Lucknow U, 1969, (Dr.K.S.Mathur)

4832   Shukla, K.S.

SOCIO - ECONOMIC STUDY OF 300 CASES
OF OFFENDERS AGAINST PROPERTY LAW 16-24 YEARS
IN THE CITY OF BHOPAL,
Doct. st, SaugarU, 1969

4833   Sinha, M.P. & Gangrade, K.D.

INTER-GENERATIONAL CONFLICT IN INDIA
Bombay, 1968

4834   Singh, I.P.

THE EX - CRIMINAL TRIBE OF DELHI STATE
Delhi,U of Delhi, 1960

4835   Srivastava, L.R.N.

INTER - VILLAGE AND INTRA - VILLAGE
CONFLICT IN TRIBAL SOCIETY
in: CONFLICT, TENSION AND CULTURAL TREND IN INDIA
ed. Vidyarthi, 1969

4836   Srivastava, S.P.

SOCIAL - PSYCHOLOGICAL STUDY OF BANVARSAN
EX-CRIMINAL TRIBE OF U.P. (Ph.D.)
Doct, Lucknow U, 1970 (Prof. R.N.Loomba)

4837   Sushil, Chaudra

SOCIAL DEVIATION AND DEFENCE IN INDIA (Ph.D.)
Doct, Agra U, 1964

4838   Thakur, U.

THE HISTORY OF SUICIDE IN INDIA
Delhi, 1963

4839   UNESCO, **Social** Sciences Department

"UNESCO STUDIES OF SOCIAL TENSIONS IN INDIA"
Int.Soc.Sci. B. 3, 1, Spring 1951, 133-34

4840   Varma, P.

PATHOLOGY OF CRIME AND DELINQUENCY
Agra, 1972

2147   social disorganization (crime)

   4841   Varma, S.C.

           SOME FEATURES OF SUICIDE IN INDIA
           East Anthrop. XXV, 3, Sep-Dec, 1972, 227-235

   4842   Verma, R.K.

           PATTERN IN CRIMINAL HOMICIDE STUDY OF
           CASES REGISTERED IN THE NAGPUR CITY FROM
           1950 TO 1963,
           Doct. st, Saugar U, 1969

   4843   Vidyarthi, L.P.

           INTER-GROUP CONFLICTS IN INDIA
           - TRIBAL, RURAL AND INDUSTRIAL
           in: CONFLICT, TENSION AND CULTURAL TREND IN INDIA
           ed. Vidyarthi, 1969

   4844   Vidyarthi, L.P.

           CONFLICT, TENSION AND CULTURAL TREND IN INDIA
           Calcutta, Punthi Pustak, 969, viii-312p.

   4845   Wandrekar, D.N.

           TENSION AND CONFLICTS IN THE TRIBAL
           REGIONS OF CENTEMPORARY INDIA
           in: CONFLICT, TENSION AND CULTURAL TREND IN INDIA
           ed. Vidyarthi, 1969

2148   applied sociology (social work)

   4846   Agarwal, (Mrs.) K.

           A CRITICAL STUDY OF WOMEN AND CHILDREN'S WELFARE
           IN INDIA (Ph.D.)
           Doct, Agra U, 1967

4847   Agarwal, R.D.

        ECONOMIC ASPECTS OF WELFARE STATE IN INDIA
        Intl. Subns. Serv., 1967

4848   Agarwala, A.N.

        INSURANCE IN INDIA - A STUDY OF INSURANCE
        ASPECT OF SOCIAL SECURITY (D.Litt.)
        Doct. Allabad U, 1957 (Prof. M.K.Ghosh)

4849   Aiyappan, A.

        APPLIED ANTHROPOLOGY
        Adivasi, 1959, 3

4850   Aiyappan, A.

        ANTHROPOLOGY AND TRIBAL WELFARE
        Second All India Seminar on Tribal Welfare
        Bhubaneswar, 1964

4851   Anderson, R.T.

        VOLUNTARY ASSOCIATIONS IN HYDERABAD
        Anthrop. Quart. 1964, 37, 4, Oct, 175-190
        SA, Xlll, 3-4, B6174

4852   Aptekar, H.H.

        SOCIAL WORK IN CROSS-CULTURAL PERSPECTIVE
        Ind.J.Soc.Work, 1963, 24, 2, Jul, 85-98,
        SA, Xll, 5, B1501

4853   Arora, S.

        SOCIAL SECURITY IN INDIA (Ph.D.)
        Doct, Banaras Hindu U, 1955

4854   Banerjee, G.R.

        KARMA YOGA AND SOCIAL CASE WORK PRACTICE IN
        INDIA
        Ind.J.Soc.Work, 1964, 24, 4, Jan, 229-234,
        SA, Xlll, 2, B5645

4855   Banerjee, G.R.

        CONCEPTS OF SOCIAL WORK IN THE GITA
        Ind.J.Soc.Work 1964, 25, 1, Apr, 29-34,
        SA, Xlll, 2, B5689

4856   Banerjee, U.

        SOCIAL SERVICE ADMINISTRATION OF AN
        URBAN METROPOLIS - A STUDY OF DELHI MUNICIPAL
        CORPORATION, WITH SPECIAL REFERENCE TO HEALTH
        AND FAMILY PLANNING
        Doct.st. Delhi U, 1969 (Dr.V.Jagannadhan)

4857   Bharal, G.P.

        CHILD WELFARE AND FIVE YEAR PLANS
        Kurukshetra, 1967, 15, 4, Jan, 5-7,
        SA, SVlll, 6, E5393

4858   Bhattacharya, V.R.

        SOME ASPECTS OF SOCIAL SECURITY MEASURES
        IN INDIA (Ph.D.),
        Doct, Delhi U, 1968 (Prof.A.Dasgupta)

4859   Bheri, L.N.

        SOCIAL WELFARE AND VOLUNTARY AGENCIES
        Doct.st, Andhra U, 1969, (Prof.M.V.Moorthy)

4851a   Biswas,P.C.

        THE UTILITY OF RESEARCH FOR THE TRIBAL PEOPLE
        Vanyajati, 1964, 2, 1, 8-9

4852a   Bose, A.B.

CENTRAL AND STATE RESPONSIBILITY FOR THE
DEVELOPMENT OF SOCIAL WELFARE SERVICES
Ind.J.Soc.Work, 1970, 31, 1, Apr, 25-34,
SA, XX, 1-2, F4367

4853a   Budhraja, M.A.M.

A SOCIOLOGICAL STUDY OF VOLUNTARY
ASSOCIATIONS IN ONE PARTICULAR AREA
OF DELHI
Doct.st, Delhi U, 1969, (A.M.Shah)

4854a   Cabinetmaker, (Miss) P.H.

SOCIAL SERVICES IN INDIA, WITH SPECIAL
REFERENCE TO THE CITY OF BOMBAY (Ph.D.)
Doct, Bombay U, 1950 (Dr.N.A.Thoothi)

4855a   Chandrasekhar, S.

A COMMENT ON DR. ENKE'S ARTICLE
Pop.R.1960, 4, 2, Jul, 51-54,
SA, Xll, 7, B3105

4856a   Chansarkar, M.A.

SOCIAL INSURANCE FOR INDIAN WORKING CLASS
Bombay, 1968

4857a   Chatterjee, B.

INTERNATIONAL CONSULTANCY IN SOCIAL WORK
Ind.J.Soc.Work, 1970, 31, 1, Apr, 75-85,
SA, XX, 1-2, F4368

4858a   Chatterjee, P.

SOCIAL WORK AND COMMUNITY DEVELOPMENT
Ind.J.Soc.Work, 1961, 21, 4, Mar, 417-423,
SA, Xl, 7, A7845

4859a   Chaudhari, K.S.

THE VERTICES OF SOCIAL WELFARE
Ind.J.Soc.Work, 1958, 19, 2, Sep, 127-131
SA, Vlll, 2, 7682

4860   Chekki, D.A.

SOCIAL REFORMERS IN KARNATAK
J. of the U of Bombay, 1958
(Post-graduate Department)

4861   Chhajed, S.

PROBLEMS OF WELFARE OF THE INSTITUTIONALIZED
CHILDREN
Doct.st, Indore U, 1969, (Abraham)

4862   Chowdhry, D.P.

SOCIAL WELFARE PROGRAMMES SINCE INDEPENDENCE
Social Welfare, 19, 5, 1972, 2-4

4863   Chowdhury, D.P.

VOLUNTARY SOCIAL WELFARE IN INDIA
Delhi, Sterling Pubs., 1971

4864   Das, T.C.

A SCHEME FOR TRIBAL WELFARE
in: APPLIED ANTHROPOLOGY IN INDIA,
ed. Vidyarthi, Allahabad, Kitab Mahal, 1968

4865   Dasgupta, S.

TOWARDS A PHILOSOPHY OF SOCIAL WORK IN INDIA
New York, Humanities

4866   Das Gupta, S.

RURAL WELFARE THROUGH COMMUNITY PROJECTS
Ind.J.Soc.Work, 1954, 14, 4, Mar 338-345,
SA, Vol.III, #3, 1681

4867   Dasgupta, S.

ASOKA'S CONCEPT OF SOCIAL WELFARE
Ind.J.Soc.Work, 1958, 19, 3, Dec, 197-201
SA, Vlll, 2, 7683

4868   Dasgupta, S.

GANDHIAN CONCEPT OF NON-VIOLENCE AND ITS
RELEVANCE TODAY TO PROFESSIONAL SOCIAL WORK
Ind. J. Soc.Work, 1968, 29, 2, Jul, 113-122,
SA, XVlll, 4, E3572

4869   Dasgupta, S.

SOCIAL WORK AND SOCIAL CHANGE
Boston, Extending Horizons Books, 1968, pp.222

4870   Dayal, P.

GANDHIAN APPROACH TO SOCIAL WORK (Ph.D.),
Doct, Agra U, 1968, (Dr.R.N.Saxena)

4871   Desai, M.M.

TRAINING FOR FAMILY AND CHILD WELFARE
Ind.J.Soc.Work, 1967, 28, 1, Apr, 115-120,
SA, XVl, 6, D3766

4872   Deshmukh, D.

SOCIAL WELFARE AND ECONOMIC DEVELOPMENT
Kurukshetra, 1965, 13, 4, Jan 26, 16-17,
SA, XlV, 5, C1681

4873   Din, P.

EXPLORATION OF MEDICAL SOCIAL WORK POTENTIAL
IN AN URBAN COMMUNITY ₍(A SOCIAL WORK STUDY
IN THE MAJOR MEDICAL SETTING OF LUCKNOW
Doct, st, Lucknow U, 1969

4874   Dube, S.C.

APPROACHES TO TRIBAL PROBLEMS IN INDIA
in: APPLIED ANTHROPOLOGY IN INDIA
ed. Vidyarthi, Allahabad, Kitab Mahal, 1968

4875   Gangrade, K.D.

CONFLICTING VALUE SYSTEM AND SOCIAL CASE WORK
Ind.J.Soc.Work, 1964, 24, 4, Jan, 247-256,
SA, Xlll, 1, B4778

4876   Gangrade, K.D.

FAMILY CENTERED APPROACH AND SOCIAL CASE WORK
Ind.J.Soc.Work, 1968, 29, 3, Oct, 277-288
SA, XVlll, 4, E3574

4877   Gupta, B.L.

A CRITICAL ESTIMATE OF SOCIAL WELFARE IN
UTTAR PRADESH (Ph.D.)
Doct, Agra U, 1963

4878   Gupta, B.L.

EXISTING PATTERNS OF SOCIAL WELFARE ADMINISTRATION
IN INDIA (D.Litt.)
Doct. st, Agra U, 1969

4879   Hasan, N.

THE SOCIAL SECURITY SYSTEM IN INDIA
New Delhi, 1968

4880   Herlekar, A.

THE ARTICLES ON SOCIAL WORK IN THE INDIAN
JOURNAL OF SOCIAL WORK
Ind.J.Soc.Work, 1965, 25, 4, Jan, 299-308
SA, XV, 5, C7009

4881   Hersey, E.W.

SOCIAL AND ECONOMIC FACTORS IN INDIA'S
WELFARE PROGRAM
Social Casework, 32, 300-6, July 1951

4882   Hooja, S.L.

SOCIAL WELFARE LEGISLATION AND ADMINISTRATION
AFFECTING CHILDREN IN DELHI (Ph.D.),
Doct. Delhi U, 1965 (Prof.V.K.N.Menon),
(Dr.V.Jagananathan)

4883   Indian Conference of Social Work

SOCIAL WORK IN INDIA AND A DIRECTORY
OF NATIONAL SOCIAL WELFARE AGENCIES
Bombay, 1952, ii & 50p.

4884   International Resources for Social Welfare

Ind.J.Soc.Work, 1962, 22, 4, Mar, 422-443,
SA, Xl, 7, A7848

4885   Jagannadhan, V.

SOCIAL POLICY IN A WELFARE STATE
- ADMINISTRATIVE ASPECTS
Ind.J.Soc.Work, 1961, 22, 1, Jun, 39-48,
SA, Xl, 7, A7849

4886   Jagannadhan, V.

SOCIAL WELFARE ORGANIZATION
New Delhi, 1968

4887   Jay, E.J.

THE ANTHROPOLOGISTS AND TRIBAL WELFARE
HILL MARIAS - A CASE STUDY
in: ANTHROPOLOGY AND TRIBAL WELFARE IN INDIA,
ed. Vidyarthi, 1968

4888   Joshi, V.R.

WAGE, EMPLOYMENT AND THE PROBLEMS OF SOCIAL
SECURITY OF AGRICULTURAL LABOUR IN EASTERN
UTTAR PRADESH (Ph.D.)
Doct. Lucknow U, 1965 (Dr.V.B.Singh)

4889   Keshari, J.P.

CO-ORDNATION: ITS ROLE IN SOCIAL WELFARE
ADMINISTRATION
Ind.J.Soc.Work, 1962, 23, 2, Jul, 185-198,
SA, Xll, 1, A8607

4890   Khan, I.H.

WELFARE PROGRAMME UNDER PANCHAYATI RAJ,
Doct.st, Delhi U, 1969 (S.N.Ranade)

4891   Koppell, G.O.

LEGAL AID IN INDIA
J.of the Indian Law Instit. 8, 224-51, 1966

4892   Kulkarni, P.D.

SOCIAL POLICY IN A WELFARE STATE
Ind.J.Soc.Work, 1961, 22, 1, Jun, 25-32,
SA, Xl, 7, A7850

4893   Maas, W.

TRIBAL UPLIFT
Sociologus, 1954, 4, 2, 146-160
SA, Vol. III, #3, 1686

4894   Majumdar, D.N.

INDIAN ANTHROPOLOGISTS IN ACTION
in: ANTHROPOLOGY AND TRIBAL WELFARE
ed. Vidyarthi, 1959

4895   Malhotra, S.P. & Bose, A.B.

PROBLEMS OF REHABILITATION OF NOMADIC BANJARA
Annals of Arid Zone, 1963, 2, 1,

4896   Marulasiddaiah, H.M.

SOCIAL WELFARE SERVICES IN BANGALORE
CORPORATION AREA
Doct. st, Delhi U, 1969, (S.N.Ranade)

4897   Maurya, M.R.

FIELD WORK TRAINING IN SOCIAL WORK
Ind.J.Soc.Work, 1962, Ap, 23, 1, 9-14,
SA, Xll, 1, A8609

4898   Maurya, M.R.

MODERN SOCIAL WORK PRACTICES IN INDIAN CITY
- A STUDY OF METHODS AND TECHNIQUES IN SOCIAL
WORK PRACTICES IN THE SOCIAL WELFARE AGENCIES
IN LUCKNOW (Ph.D.)
Doct, Lucknow U, 1970 (Dr.S.Chandra)

4899   Mehta, B.H.

HOMELESS CHILDREN AND THEIR REHABILITATION
Ind.J.Soc.Work, 1953, 14, 2, Sep, 123-131,
SA, Vol.II, #3, 602

4900   Mehta, B.H.

SOCIAL POLICY IN A WELFARE STATE
Ind.J.Soc.Work, 1958, 18, 4, Mar, 244-250
SA, Vlll, 2, 7686

4901   Mehta, U.B.

THE IMPACT OF WELFARE MEASURES ON RURAL
SOCIETY (Ph.D.)
Doct, Bombay U, 1967 (Dr.A.R.Desai)

4902   Menon, A.K.

MAHATMA GANDI'S CONTRIBUTION TO SOCIAL
WELFARE IN INDIA - A STUDY OF THREE MAJOR
PROGRAMMES,
American Doctoral Dissertations (1959-60)
Columbia U (Sociology)

4903   Moorthy, B.M.L.

SOCIAL SECURITY IN INDIA
1954

4904   Moorthy, M.V.

CONTEMPORARY FIELDS OF PROFESSIONAL SOCIAL
WORK IN INDIA
Ind.J.Soc.Work, 1961, 22, 1, June, 65-68,
SA, X1, 7, A7851

4905   Muggeridge, M.

SOMETHING BEAUTIFUL FOR GOD
New York, Harper & Row, 1971

4906   Nagpaul, H.

THE STUDY OF INDIAN SOCIETY: A SOCIOLOGICAL
ANALYSIS OF SOCIAL WELFARE AND SOCIAL WORK
EDUCATION
New Delhi, 1968

4907   Mukundrao, K.V.

THE BHAGAVAD GITA: A STUDY OF ITS VALUE CONTENT WITH
REFERENCE TO SOCIAL WORK IN INDIA
American Doctoral Dissertations (1963-64)
U of Pennsylvania (Social Work)

4908   Nagpaul, H.

DILEMMAS OF SOCIAL WORK EDUCATION
IN INDIA
Indian J.of Soc.Work, 1967, 28, 3, Oct, 269-284,
SA, XV11, 4, D8116

4909   Nagpaul, H.

SOCIOLOGICAL ANALYSIS OF SOCIAL WELFARE
IN INDIAN SOCIETY: A BIBLIOGRAPHICAL ESSAY
Ind.J.Soc.Work, 1970, 31, 3, Oct, 303-318,
SA, XX, 6,8862

4910   Nagpaul, H.

PATTERNS OF SOCIAL ADMINISTRATION IN INDIA:
NEED FOR SPECIALIZED TRAINING IN SOCIAL WORK
Ind.J.Soc.Res. 12, 3, Dec, 1971, 221-224

4911   Nanavatty, M.C.

SOCIAL POLICY IN A WELFARE STATE
Ind.J.Socol.Work, 1961, 22, 1, Jun, 33-37,
SA, X1, 7, A7853

4912   Naravane, T.R.

SOCIAL POLICY IN A WELFARE STATE
Ind.J.Soc.Work, 1961, 22, 1, Jun, 19-24,
SA, X1, 7, A7854

4913   Natarajan, S.

A CENTURY OF SOCIAL REFORM IN INDIA (2nd Ed.)
London; Asia Pub. House, 1962, 223p.

4914   National,Council of Applied Economic Research

REHABILITATION AND DEVELOPMENT OF BASTI DISTRICT
New Delhi, 1959

4915   National Social Service for Youth

Ind.J.Soc.Work, 1962, 22, 4, Mar, 353-369,
SA, X1, 7, A7855

4916   Nayar, (Mrs.) K.

LABOUR WELFARE WORK AMONG INDUSTRIAL
WORKERS IN U.P. (Ph.D.)
Doct, Agra U, 1959

4917   New Social Welfare Progammes in The Third Plan

Ind.J.Soc.Work, 1962, 22, 4, Mar, 370-391,
SA, X1, 7, A7856

4918   Non-Institutional Services for Children

Ind.J.Soc.Work, 1962, 22, 4, Mar, 394-420
SA, X1, 7, A7857

4919   Orenstein, H.

VILLAGE, CASTE, AND THE WELFARE STATE
Human Org., 1963, 22, 1

4920   Pareek,U. & Kergey, S.N.

WORKSHOP   IN ACTION RESEARCH
1960

4921   Pattanaik, P.K.

ASPECTS OF WELFARE ECONOMICS (Ph.D.),
Doct, Delhi U. 1968 (Prof.A.K.Sen)

4922   Paul, D.

VOLUNTARY EFFORT IN SOCIAL WELFARE (Ph.D.)
Doct, Agra U, 1968 (Dr.R.N.Saxena)

4923   Prabhat, C.

PLANNING OF SOCIAL SECURITY LABOUR WELFARE IN
INDIA (Ph.D.),
Doct. Agra U, 1954

4924   Prasad, C.

IMPLICATIONS OF PSYCHOLOGICAL THEORIES
FOR SOCIAL WORK PRACTICE (Ph.D.),
Doct, Agra U, 1969 (Dr.R.N.Saksena)

4925   Peter, K.D.

FIELD WORK PRACTICES IN MADRAS SCHOOL FOR
SOCIAL WORK, MADRAS, INDIA AND SYRACUSE UNIVERSITY,
SCHOOL OF SOCIAL WORK, SYRACUSE, NEW YORK
American Doctoral Dissertations (1960-61)
Syracuse U , (Soc.)

4926   Ponsioen, J.A. (editor), de Schlippe,P.,
Karve, D.G. & Pusie, E.

SOCIAL WELFARE POLICY I; CONTRIBUTIONS TO
THEORY
The Hague: Mouton & Co., 1962, 287pp
SA, XlV, 1, B9017

4927   Punekar, S.D.

SOCIAL INSURANCE FOR INDUSTRIAL WORKERS
IN INDIA
Bombay, U of Bombay & Oxford U Press,
1951, 228p

4928   Qader, S.A.

ASSESSMENT OF NEED IN THE PRESENT SETUP
Ind.J.Soc.Work, 1960, 20, 4, Mar, 97-102
SA, Xl, 6, A7053

4929   Raje, G.M.

COMMUNICATION AND SOCIAL WELFARE (Ph.D.)
Doct, Bombay U, 1967 (Prof.G.S.Ghurye)

4930   Ramachandran, P. & Padmanabha, A.

PROFESSIONAL SOCIAL WORKERS IN INDIA
United Asia Pub., 1969

4931   Sankhala, (Miss) T.

EVOLUATION AND ORGANIZATION OF WELFARE
PROGRAMME FOR WOMEN IN RAJASTHAN (Ph.D.)
Doct, Agra U, 1968, (Dr.R.N.Saxena)

4932   Sankhala, (Miss) T.

SOCIAL WELFARE PROGRAMMES AND SOCIAL
CHANGE IN RAJASTHAN (D.Litt)
Doct. st., Agra, 1969

4933   Saxena, R.N.

APPLICATION OF SOCIOLOGY IN SOCIAL
WELFARE PLANNING IN INDIA
Presidential Address, 4th Indian Sociology
Conference, Calcutta, 1954

4934   Schlesinger, B.

AMERICAN TRAINING FOR INDIAN SOCIAL WORKER:
CURE OR CURSE?
Ind.J.Soc.Work, 1960, 21, 3, Dec, 261-265,
SA, Xl, 7, A7858

4935   Sen, A.C. (ed.)

TRAINING IN VOLUNTARY ACTION Vol. I
Intl.Pubns.Serv. 1967

4936   Sen, A.C.

INTRODUCING VOLUNTARY AGENCIES IN INDIA
Delhi, 1971

4937   Sharma, G.B.

SOCIAL ADMINISTRATION: TOWARDS THEORETICAL
STANDARDISATION AND TERMINOLOGICAL CLARIFICATION
Ind.J.Soc.Work, 1970, 31, 1, Apr, 11-24
SA, XX, 1-2, F4377

4938   Shiva, Kumar

EX-CRIMINAL TRIBE AND THEIR REHABILITATION
IN UTTAR PRADESH (Ph.D.)
Doct, Agra U, 1964

4939   Shrikant, L.M.

TRIBAL SOCIAL WELFARE
Ind.J.Soc.Work, 1953, 14, 3, Dec, 292-295
SA, Vol. II, #4, 923

4940   Singh, D.V.

SOCIAL AND ECONOMIC WELFARE SERVICES IN
UTTAR PRADESH SINCE INDEPENDENCE (Ph.D.)
Doct, Agra U, 1968 (Dr.J.N.Singhal)

4941   Singh, D.

THE IDEA OF SOCIALISTIC PATTERN OF SOCIETY
AND SARVODAYA IN INDIA (Ph.D.)
Doct, Agra U, 1966

4942   Singh, D.

WEALTH AND WELFARE OF SHEKHAWATI (Ph.D.)
Doct, Rajasthan U, 1957 (Dr.B.S.Agrawal)

4943   Singh, G.

GROWTH AND DEVELOPMENT OF SOCIAL WELFARE
ORGANISATION IN PUNJAB: A SOCIOLOGICAL
ANALYSIS (Ph.D.)
Doct, Panjab U, 1966 (Dr.V.S.D'Souza)

4944   Singh, R.R.

WELFARE OF THE AGED
Ind.J.Soc.Work, 1970, 30, 4, Jan, 327-334,
SA, XlX, 6, F2015

4945   Sinha, (Mrs.) A.

SOCIAL AND POLITICAL PHILOSOPHY OF
SARVODAYA
Doct. st, Bhagalpur U, 1969 (Dr.P.S.Muhar)

4946   Srivastava, K.N.

SOCIAL INSURANCE IN INDIA
Doct, Bihar U, 1965 (Dr.S.B.Singh)

4947   Srivastava, M.N.

THE IMPACT OF WELFARE MEASURES ON THE EMPLOYEES
OF NORTH-EASTERN RAILWAY
Doct.st, Lucknow U, 1969

4948   Thangavelu, R.

METHODS AND TECHNIQUES OF SOCIAL WORK AND
SOCIAL WELFARE AND SAFEGUARDING OF HUMAN RIGHTS
Ind.J.Soc.Work, 1968, 29, 1, Apr, 53-66,
SA, XVlll, 102, E1578

4949   Upadhyay, V.S.

TRIBAL REHABILITATION SCHEMES (Ph.D.)
Doct, Ranchi U, 1966 (Prof.Sachchidananda)

2148   applied sociology (social work)

4950   Varma, H.S.

         OF HUMAN ELEMENT IN ACTION RESEARCH
         Ind.J.Soc.Work, 1969, 29, 4, 389-97

4951   Venkateswarlu, J.S.

         THE IMPLICATIONS OF MORTALITY IN SOCIAL SECURITY
         Ind.J.Soc.Work, 1969, 30, 3, Oct, 234-250
         SA, X1X, 4, F0249

4952   Verma, M.

         A SOCIO-ECONOMIC SURVEY OF 500 FAMILIES OF THE
         PHYSICALLY HANDICAPPED IN KANPUR
         Ind.J.Soc.Work, 1961, 21, 4, 447-450
         SA, X1, 7, A7859

4953   Vidyarthi, L.P.

         ANTHROPOLOGY, AUTHORITY AND TRIBAL WELFARE
         IN INDIA
         East. Anthrop. 1957, 11, 1, Sep-Nov, 14-25,
         SA, V111, 1, 7250

4954   Viswanathan, N.

         SCHOOLS OF SOCIAL WORK AND SOCIAL POLICY IN INDIA
         Ind.J.Soc.Work, 1964, 25, 3, Oct, 233-242

4955   Wilkinson, T.S.

         SOCIAL WORK
         Ind.Sociol. 1962, 4, 5, Mar, 26-28,
         SA, X111, 2, B5706

4956   Workshops

         INDIAN CONFERENCE OF SOCIAL WORK 11th NATIONAL
         SESSION
         Ind.J.Soc.Work, 1960, 20, 4, Mar, 122-132,
         SA, X1, 6, A7058

2148   applied sociology (social work)

4957   Yasas, F.M.

        GANDHIAN VALUES AND PROFESSIONAL SOCIAL
        WORK VALUES, WITH SPECIAL EMPHASIS ON THE
        DIGNITY OF MAN
        American Doctoral Dissertations (1961-62)
        (The Catholic University of America) (Soc.Work)

4958   Yasas, F.M.

        GANDHIAN VALUES IN PROFESSIONAL SOCIAL WORK
        EDUCATION IN INDIA
        Ind.J.Soc.Work, 1964, 25, Apr, 1-28,
        SA, X111, 2, B5709

4959   Zutshi, G.L.

        PRELIMINARIES REGARDING APPLIED RESEARCH
        AMONG BACKWARD CLASSES
        Vanyajati, 1959, 6, 3,

4960   -----

        LABOUR WELFARE IN MADHYA PRADESH
        Ind.Sociol. 1963, 5, 6, Mar, 9-12,
        SA, X111, 304, B6576

4961   -----

        REHABILITATIONS AND RESETTLEMENT OF DISPLACED
        PERSONS IN THE INDIAN UNION
        Int.Labour Rev., 61, 410-26, April 1950

2151   delinquency

4962   Abraham, C.M.

        JUVENILE DELINQUENCY
        Ind.Sociol.1963, 5, 6, Mar, 15-37
        SA, X111, 3-4, B6590

4963   Attar, A.D.

        JUVENILE DELINQUENCY: A COMPARATIVE STUDY
        Bombay, 1968

4964   Brar, H.S. (alias Chanda Singh)

        A STUDY MEASURING THE IMPACT OF REFORMATORY
        EDUCATION ON THE MANIFEST BEHAVIOUR AND SOME
        PSYCHO-SOCIAL ASPECTS OF THE YOUNG DELINQUENTS
        Doct, Panjab U, 1969 (Dr. P.S. Hundal)

4965   Cavan, R.S. & Davan, J.T.

        DELINQUENCY AND CRIME
        Philadelphia, Pa: J.B. Lippincott Co.,
        1968, 244 pp.,
        SA, XV11, 4, D8119

4966   Chattopadhyay, K.P.

        PATTERN OF JUVENILE DELINQUENCY IN CALCUTTA
        Int. J. Comp. Sociol. 1962, 3,2, Dec. 221-228,
        SA, X11, V, B1397

4967   Chattopadhayaya, S.K.

        SOCIAL FORMS IN DELINQUENT (D.Phil.)
        Doct, Calcutta U, 1966, (Dr. S.Sinha)

4968   Desai, A.N.

        THE PROBLEM OF JUVENILE DELINQUENCY (Ph.D.)
        Doct, Gujarat U, 1959, (Dr. A.K.Trivedi)

4969   Devi, (Mrs.) S.

        ENVIRONMENTAL AND EMOTIONAL FACTORS
        INVOLVED IN JUVENILE DELINQUENCY
        (A SOCIOLOGICAL STUDY WITH SPECIAL
        REFERENCE TO JUVENILE DELINQUENCY IN
        AGRA CITY (Ph.D.)
        Doct st., Agra U, 1969, (R.N.Saxena)

2151   delinquency

4970   Ganguly, D. & Maitra, A.K.

        RESEARCH REPORTS AND NOTES: SOME
        ENVIRONMENTAL CORRELATES OF JUVENILE
        DELINQUENCY
        Ind.J. Soc. Work, 1966, 27, 2, Jul, 205-210
        SA, XVl, 5, D2928

4971   Goyal, C.P.

        STUDY OF FIVE HUNDRED JUVENILE DELINQUENTS
        IN RELATION TO HOME AND SOCIAL SITUATIONS (Ph.D.)
        Doct, Agra U, 1965

4972   Kakar, D.N.

        ROLE OF PROBATION IN THE TREATMENT OF
        DELINQUENCY IN U.P., WITH SPECIAL
        REFERENCE TO AFTER-CONDUCT OF PROBATIONERS
        (Ph.D.), Doct, Agra U, 1967

4973   Kumar, B.

        JUVENILE AND ADOLESCENT DELINQUENCY IN AN
        INDIAN CITY
        Doct, Lucknow U, 1969 (Dr. S. Chandra)

4974   Mukhopadhyay, S.

        JUVENILE DELINQUENCY IN CALCUTTA
        Man in India, V. 33, Dec. 1953, P.315-322

4975   Panakal, J.J.

        JUVENILE DELINQUENCY
        Ind.J.Soc.Work, 1961, 22, 3, Dec, 263-266
        SA, Xl, 7, A7833

4976   Panakal, J.J.

        SPECIAL TRAINING OF POLICE FOR PREVENTION
        OF JUVENILE DELINQUENCY
        Ind.J.Soc.Work, 1961, 22, 2, Sep, 139-141,
        SA, Xl, 7, A7832

4977   Pathak, (Miss) S.B.

SOCIAL BACKGROUND OF THE DELINQUENT CHILD
(Ph.D.), Doct, Agra U, 1960

4978   Pati, G.

A COMPARATIVE STUDY OF SOCIO-CULTURAL AND
PERSONALITY FACTORS OF JUVENILE DELINQUENTS (Ph.D.),
Doct, Utkal U, 1963 (Dr. R. Rath)

4979   Seth, V.B.

AN ETIOLOGICAL INVESTIGATION OF JUVENILE
DELINQUENCY (Ph.D.),
Doct, Patna U, 1969, (Dr. A.K.P. Sinha)

4980   Sharma, (Mrs.) C.P.

REFORMATION OF JUVENILE OFFENDERS
Doct. st. Agra U, 1969, (R.N.Saxena)

4981   Sheth, (Miss) H.B.

JUVENILE DELINQUENCY IN BOMBAY STATE (Ph.D.)
Doct, Bombay U, 1958 (Prof. K.M.Kapadia)

4982   Shewak, D.

GROUP SENTIMENT AND DELINQUENCY
Kurukshetra, 1966, 14, 8, May, 30-31,
SA, XVll, 3, D7448

4983   Shukla, K.S.

ADOLESCENT THIEVES - A CRIMINO-SOCIOLOGICAL
STUDY OF TWO HUNDRED OFFENDERS IN GWALIOR
INDORE (Ph.D.),
Doct, Saugar U, 1970, (Dr. S.S.Shrivastava)

2151   delinquency

4984   Singh, (Mrs.) P.K.

EMOTIONAL FACTORS IN JUVENILE DELINQUENCY
IN THE AGE GROUP ELEVEN TO TWENTY-ONE YEARS
IN THE KAVAL TOWNS OF U.P. (Ph.D.)
Doct, Agra U, 1970, (Dr. R.N.Saksena)

4985   Sivanandam, C.

A STUDY OF FRUSTRATION - REACTION IN
DELINQUENT AND NON-DELINQUENT CHILDREN
Ind.J.Soc.Work, 1971, 32, 2, Jul, 151-154,
SA, XX, 7, F9902

4986   Srivastava, V.S.

DELINQUENCY CONTROL AND PROBATION.
Ind.J.Soc.Work, 1960, 21, 3, Dec, 267-270,
SA, Xl, 7, A7841

4987   Tandon, (Miss) S.

FAMILY BACKGROUND OF JUVENILE DELINQUENTS
IN AN URBAN AREA
Doct, st, Agra U, 1969, (R.N.Saxena)

4988   Varma, S.C.

THE YOUNG DELINQUENTS: A SOCIOLOGICAL
INQUIRY
Lucknow, Pustak Kendra 1970, V-105p

4989   Verma, S.C.

THE SOCIAL AND ECONOMIC BACKGROUND
AND JUVENILE AND ADOLESCENT
DELINQUENCY IN KANPUR AND LUCKNOW (Ph.D.)
Doct, Lucknow U, 1960 (Dr. R.K.Mukerjee)

2200   SOCIOLOGY OF KNOWLEDGE

2233   sociology of knowledge

4990   Adhaide, R.V.

        THE EXTENT OF RATIONAL THOUGHTS IN
        EDUCATED INDIA (Ph.D.),
        Doct, Bombay U, 1951 (Prof. G.S. Ghurye)

4991   Bhambri, R.S.

        MYTH AND REALITY ABOUT PRIVATE
        ENTERPRISE IN INDIA
        Wrld. Polit. 1960, 12, 2, Jan, 186-200
        SA, IX, A0169

4992   Broomfield, J.H.

        THE REGIONAL ELITES: A THEORY OF MODERN
        INDIAN HISTORY
        Ind.Eco. & Social History Rev, 1966, 3, 3,
        Sep, 275-291,
        SA, XVll, 1, D5598

4993   Clinard, M.B. & Elder, J.W.

        SOCIOLOGY IN INDIA: A STUDY IN THE
        SOCIOLOGY OF KNOWLEDGE
        Amer. Sociol. R., 1965, 30, 4, Aug, 581-587
        SA, XlV, 4, C0027

4994   *Das, M.S.

        BRAIN DRAIN CONTROVERSY AND INTERNATIONAL·
        STUDENTS
        Lucknow, Lucknow Publishing, 1972

4995   Embree, A.T.

        THE HINDU TRADITION: READINGS IN ORIENTAL
        THOUGHT
        New York, Random House, 1972

4996   Ghurye, G.S.

        VIDYAS: INDIAN CONTRIBUTION TO SOCIOLOGY
        OF KNOWLEDGE
        Sociol. B. 1957, 6, 2, Sep. 29-71
        SA, Vlll, 1, 7103

4997   Mukerjee, R.

        HUMANISM, EAST AND WEST
        Ind.J.of Soc.Res., 1966, 7, 3, Dec, 178-185
        SA, XVll, 3, D7454

4998   Mukerjee, R.

        WHERE INDOLOGY AND HISTORY MEET SOCIAL
        RESEARCH "ON INDIA"
        Berlin, Akademie-Verlag, 1970, 307-322

4999   *Nandi, P.K.

        TOWARD A MODERN INTELLECTUAL TRADITION:
        THE CASE OF INDIA,in:SOCIAL PROBLEMS IN A
        CHANGING WORLD: A COMPARATIVE READER
        (ed.) W.M. Gerson, New York, T.Y. Crowell,
        1969, pp. 472-480

5000   Pelaya, M.G.

        THE HAPPY KINGDOM OF THE END OF TIME
        Rev. Cie. Soc. 1958, 2,2, Jun, 157085,
        SA, Vlll, 2, 7535

5001   *Prasad, R. Hallen, G.C. & Pathak, K. (eds)

        CONSPECTUS OF INDIAN SOCIETY
        Agra, Satish Book, 1971

5002   Rahman, A.

        SCIENTISTS IN INDIA: THE IMPACT OF
        ECONOMIC POLICIES AND SUPPORT IN
        HISTORICAL AND SOCIAL PERSPECTIVE
        Int.Social Science J. 1970, 22, 1, 54-79,
        SA, X1X, 7, F2823

5003   Raychaudhuri, T.

THE SOCIAL SCIENCES AND THE STUDY OF INDIAN
ECONOMIC HISTORY, 1600-1947
Int.Soc.Sci, J., 1965, 17, 4, 635-643,
SA, XV, 6, C7188

5004   Rose, A.M.

HINDU VALUES AND INDIAN SOCIAL PROBLEMS
Sociological Quart., Vlll (Summer), 1967, 329-39

5005   Saran, A.K.

SOCIOLOGY OF KNOWLEDGE AND TRADITIONAL THOUGHT
Soc. B., 1964, 13, 1, 33-46 &
14, 1, 41-58

5006   *Satyamurthy, T.V.

THE AMERICAN SCIENCE OF INDIAN POLITICS:
AN ESSAY IN SOCIOLOGY OF KNOWLEDGE
Economic & Political Weekly, 1971,
6, 23, Jun, 1133-1136,
SA, 21, 73G4738

5007   *Shils, E.

THE INTELLECTUAL BETWEEN TRADITION AND
MODERNITY: THE INDIAN SITUATION
The Hague, Mouton, 1961

5008   *Thapar, Romila

THE IMAGE OF THE BARBARIAN IN EARLY INDIA
Comparative Studies in Society and History
1971, 13, 4, Oct, 408-436,
SA, 21, 73 G2141

5009   Voight, J.H.

BRITISH POLICY TOWARDS INDIAN HISTORICAL
RESEARCH AND WRITING, 1870-1930
Ind.Eco. & Social His.Rev., 1966, 3, 2,
Jun, 137-149,
SA, XVll, 1, D5605

5010   Ahmad, Z.

        SOCIAL PHILOSOPHY OF L.T.HOBHOUSE   (Ph.D.)
        Doct, Patna   U, 1962, (Dr. N. Prasad)

5011   Atraya, S.P.

        A CRITICAL STUDY OF ANCIENT HINDU SOCIAL THOUGHT
        Doct. st, Gorakhapur U, 1969 (V.P.Upadhyaya)

5012   Daya, K.

        SOCIAL PHILOSOPHY, PAS/T AND FUTURE
        Simla, 1969

5013   Heiji, N.

        THE DEBATABLE ISSUES IN THE STUDY OF THE
        STUDY OF THE CONTEMPORARY HISTORY OF INDIA
        Developing Economics, .1968, 6, 2, Jun, 158-175,
        SA, XV111, 3, E2532

5014   Majumdar, B.

        HISTORY OF INDIAN SOCIAL AND POLITICAL
        IDEAS FROM RAMMOHAN TO DAYANANDA (2nd ed.)
        Intl. Pubns. Serv., 1967

5015   Malik, S.C.

        ARCHAEOLOGY AS A SOURCE IN WRITING
        SOCIO-CULTURAL AND SOCIO-ECONOMIC HISTORY
        East Anthrop, 1968, 21, 3, Sep-Dec, 291-304
        SA, XV111, 7, E6466

5016   Motwani, K.

        MANU: THE ORIGINS OF SOCIAL THOUGHT
        Bombay, Bhartiya Vidya Bhawan, 1970, 100pp

5017   Prasad, N.

SOCIAL THOUGHT: THE BEGINNINGS
Meerut, 1968

5018   Sahay, K.

SOCIAL PHILOSOPHY OF ANCIENT INDIA,
WITH SPECIAL REFERENCE TO MAURYA, SUNGA
AND GUPTA PERIODS (D.Litt.)
Doct, Patna U, 1965

5019   Shukla, S.V.N.

INDIVIDUAL AND SOCIETY IN THE HINDU TRADITION
(A SOCIOLOGICAL STUDY BASED ON THE EPICS)
Doct. st, Lucknow U, 1969

2300   COMMUNITY DEVELOPMENT

2317   community development

5020   Abrahamson, J.

INVOLVING PEOPLE IN COMMUNITY DEVELOPMENT:
THE BARODA PROJECT
C.D.Journal 1970, 5, 1, Jan, 17-25,
SA, XlX, F2847

5021   Abraham, M.F.

C.D. AND COMMUNITY ORGANIZATION
Kurukshetra, 1966, 15, 3, Dec, 5-8,
SA, XVlll, 6, E5438

5022   Agarwal, A.L.

AN INDIAN RURAL COMMUNITY -   A CASE
STUDY (Ph.D.),
Doct, Agra U, 1967

5023   Agarwal, R.D.

HUMAN ASPECTS OF COMMUNITY DEVELOPMENT
Kurukstetra, 1964, 12, 9, Jun, 11-13,
SA, XlV, 1, B8673

5024   Agarwal, (Miss) U.

SOCIAL CONSEQUENCES OF TECHNOLOGICAL CHANGE
IN A COMMUNITY DEVELOPMENT BLOCK (Ph.D.)
Doct, Agra U, (Dr. R.N.Saksena)

5025   Amin, D.K.

SOCIAL WORK IN COMMUNITY DEVELOPMENT
Social Welfare, 19, 7, 1972, 4

5026   Annual Conference on CD and Panchayat Raj
(New Delhi, India)

COMMUNITY DEVELOPMENT IN OUR PLAN STRATEGY
Krukshetra, 1964, 12, 11, Aug, 6-10,
SA, XlV, 2-3, B9603

5027   Badgaiyan, S.D.

SOCIOLOGICAL APPROACH TO COMMUNITY DEVELOPMENT
Kurukshetra, 1968, 16, 12, Sep, 9-10,
SA, XlX, 4, F0279

5028   Balraj, S.

SUPERVISION IN C.D. PROGRAMME
Kurukshetra, 1967, 15, 5, Feb, 5-6 & 8,
SA, XVlll, 6, E5440

5029   Balraj, S.

TRAINING C.D. PERSONNEL FOR NEW TASKS
Kurukshetra, 1967, 15, 7, Apr. 14-16,
SA, XVlll, 7, E6471

5030   Barnabas, A.P.

RELATIONSHIP BETWEEN AREA OF ASSIGNMENT AND
ACCOMPLISHMENT OF INDIVIDUAL ESTENSION WORKERS
Allahabad, 1955

5031   Basal, S.C.

THE ROLE OF CO-OPERATION IN COMMUNITY
DEVELOPMENT IN MADHYA PRADESH (Ph.D.)
Doct, Jabalpur U, 1966

5032   Basu, M.N., Ghosh, B.B. & Chowdhuri, M.K.

LEVEL OF TRIBAL LITERACY IN INDIA
Society & Cult., 1970, 1, 1, Jul, 71-80,
SA, XX, 7, F9928

5033   Beers, H.W.

PROGRAM EVALUATION IN INDIA
Rural Sociol. 1960, 25, 4, Dec, 430-441,
SA, lX, 2, 9441

5034   Beers, H.W.

        EVALUATION IN COMMUNITY DEVELOPMENT
        - THE INDIAN EXPERIENCE
        Int. R.Com.Dev. 1960, 5, 203-219,
        SA, Xll, 6, B1914

5035   Berreman, G.

        CASTE AND COMMUNITY DEVELOPMENT
        Hum.Org. 1963, 22, 1, Spring, 90-94,
        SA, Xll, 5, B1164

5036   Bhalerao, C.N.

        DEVELOPMENT ADMINISTRATION IN THE DISTRICT
        Kurukshetra, 1967, 15, 4, Jan, 19-22,
        SA, XVlll, 6, E5441

5037   Bharal, G.P.

        DENOTIFIED COMMUNITIES AND THEIR PROBLEMS
        OF REHABILITATION
        Ind.J.Soc.Work, 1968, 28, 4, Jan, 353-362,
        SA, XVll, 5, D8761

5038   Bharara, L.P. & Bose, A.B.

        SOCIO - ECONOMIC INVESTIGATIONS IN A COMMUNITY
        DEVELOPMENT BLOCK - POPULATION, LAND AND ECONOMY
        IN A DESERT TRACT
        Annals of Arid Zone, 1964, 2, 2, Mar, 101-113,
        SA, XlV, 5, C1372

5039   Bhattacharya, S.N.

        COMMUNITY DEVELOPMENT IN DEVELOPING COUNTRIES
        Calcutta, 1972

5040   Bhattacharjee, B.B.

        CONCEPT OF COMMUNITY DEVELOPMENT IN ANIMAL
        HUSBANDRY
        Kurukshetra, 1967, 15, 6, Mar, 13-14,
        SA, XVlll, 7, E6473

5041   Brown, R.H.

        INTERMINISTERIAL CO-OPERATION FOR NATIONAL AND
        COMMUNITY DEVELOPMENT
        Kurukshetra, 1966, 14, 10, Jul, 14-17,
        SA, XVll, 4, D8137

5042   Bridgland, (Mrs.) K.

        MOBILE CRECHES IN INDIA: A NEW BASIS FOR C.D.
        IN DELHI
        C.D. Jour. 7, 2, April 1972

5043   Bulsara, J.F.

        COMMUNITY DEVELOPMENT PROGRAM IN INDIA
        - THE SOCIAL IMPACT OF COMMUNITY DEVELOPMENT
        AND OTHER PROJECTS ON RURAL LIFE
        Sociol. B. 1958, 7, 2, Sep, 81-97
        SA, Vlll, 2, 7428

5044   Chakravarti , S.S.

        COMMUNITY DEVELOPMENT PLANNING AND ADMINISTRATION
        AT LOCAL LEVEL INDIA
        J.Loc. Adm.Overseas, 1963, 2, 4, Oct, 212-221,
        SA, Xlll, 5, B7152

5045   Chakravarti, S.

        PLANNING AND ADMINISTRATION IN COMMUNITY DEVELOPMENT
        Kurukshetra, 1964, 12, 7, Apr, 8-11,
        SA, XlV, 1, B8676

5046   Chakravarty, (Miss) I.

COMMUNITY DEVELOPMENT PROJECT AS A TECHNIQUE
OF DEVELOPMENT (Ph.D.)
Doct, Patna U, 1964, (Prof.D.Jha)

5047   Chapekar, L.N.

COMMUNITY DEVELOPMENT PROJECT BLOCKS IN BADLAPUR
Sociol. B. 1958, 7, 2, Sep. 111-122,
SA, Vlll, 2, 7681

5048   Chatterjee, B.

RURAL COMMUNITY DEVELOPMENT IN INDIA
Civilisations, 1957, 7, 2, 187-197
SA, X, 2, A1780

5049   Chatterjee, B.

SOME ISSUES IN URBAN COMMUNITY DEVELOPMENT
Int.R.Com.Dev. 1962, 9, 113-124,
SA, Xlll, 1, B4485

5050   Chatterjee, B.B.

MICRO-STUDIES IN COMMUNITY DEVELOPMENT,
PANCHAYATI RAJ, AND CO-OPERATION
Delhi, Sterling Pubs. 1969

5051   Chattopadhyay, B.

COMMUNITY DEVELOPMENT IN THE SADAR SUB-DIVISION
OF MURSHIDABAD DISTRICT, WEST BENGAL (Ph.D.)
Doct, Calcutta U, 1969 (Dr. N.C. Ray)

5052   Chawdhari, T.P. (ed.)

SELECTED READINGS ON COMMUNITY DEVELOPMENT
Intl.Pubns.Serv.1967

5053   Cheema, A.S.

COMMUNITY DEVELOPMENT IN INDIA WITH PARTICULAR
REFERENCE TO THE BHADSON PROJECT
American Doctoral Dissertations (1959-60)
Cornell U. (Sociology)

5054   Choukidar, V.V.

JOB RELATED PRE-SERVICE TRAINING NEEDS OF
VILLAGE LEVEL WORKERS IN COMMUNITY DEVELOPMENT
BLOCKS OF POONA DISTRICT (Ph.D.)
Doct, Indian Agricultural Research Inst. 1969,
(Dr.S.K.Sharma)

5055   Clinard, M.B.

SLUMS AND COMMUNITY DEVELOPMENT
New York, The Free Press, 1966

5056   Clinard, M.B. & Chatterjee, B.

URBAN COMMUNITY DEVELOPMENT IN INDIA:
THE DELHI PILOT PROJECT
in: INDIA'S URBAN FUTURE,
ed. R. Turner, Berkeley U. of Calif. Press, 1962,
p.71-94

5057   Community Development and Economic Development
Part IIA: A CASE STUDY OF THE GHOSHI COMMUNITY
DEVELOPMENT BLOCK, UTTAR   PRADESH, INDIA
ECAFE/FAO Agrl. Division, 1960, 100p.
SA, X1, 5, A5835

5058   Damiens, J.

BHUDAN, GRAMDAN ET COOPERATION AUX INDES
(THE BHUDAN, THE GRAMDAN AND CO-OPERATION IN INDIA)
Archives Internationales de Sociologie de la
Cooperation et de la Developpement,
1969, 25, Jan-Jun, 16-48 (Fr.)
SA, XV1ll, 6, E5445

5059   Das, A.K.

ON SOCIO-ECONOMIC ACHIEVEMENTS OF SCHEDULED TRIBE
IN WEST BENGAL
Socioty & Cult. 1970, 1, 1, Jul, 25-36
SA, XX, 7, F9934

5060   Das, G.N.

C.D. PROGRAMME - SOME PROBLEMS
Kurukshetra, 1967, 15, 4, Jan, 16-17,
SA, XVlll, 6, E5446

5061   Dasgupta, S.

COMMUNITY FACTORS IN AGRICULTURAL DEVELOPMENT:
A CASE STUDY OF SIX INDIAN VILLAGES
Int.Rev.of Com.Dev. 1968, 19-20,285-308,
SA, XVlll, 3, E2542

5062   Dasgupta, S.

SOCIAL WORK AND SOCIAL CHANGE:
A CASE STUDY OF INDIAN VILLAGE DEVELOPMENT
Boston, Porter Sargent, 1968

5063   Deb, P.C.

SOCIO-CULTURAL CORRELATES OF COMMUNITY PARTICIPATION
Man in India, 1969, 49, 3, Jul-Sep, 259-266
SA, XlX, 4, F0282

5064   Desai, A.R.

COMMUNITY DEVELOPMENT PROJECTS
- A SOCIOLOGICAL ANALYSIS -
in: RURAL SOCIOLOGY IN INDIA,
ed. A.R.Desai, Bombay, Popular, 1969, 611-622

5065   Desai, M.B. & Mehta, R.S.

CHANGE AND ITS AGENCIES IN COMMUNITY DEVELOPMENT
BLOCK IN GUJARAT
Ind.J.Agri.Econ. 1964, 19, 3-4, 147-166,
SA, XlV, 6, C2376

5066   Desal, (Miss) M.W.

         COMMUNITY PROJECT IN GREATER BOMBAY AND
         THANA DISTRICT
         Doct. st., Bombay U., 1969 (Dr.J.V.Ferriera)

5067   Dey, S.K.

         COMMUNITY DEVELOPMENT AND RURAL PROJECTS
         Ind.J.Soc.Work, 1954, 14, 4, Mar, 333-338
         SA, Vol. III, # 3, 1682

5068   Dey, S.K.

         COMMUNITY DEVELOPMENT:A BIRD'S EYE VIEW
         Bombay, Asia Publishing House, 1964, 94 pp.
         SA, XlV, 4, C0476

5069   Dey, S.K.

         COMMUNITY PROJECTS IN ACTION IN INDIA
         in: LEADERSHIP AND POLITICAL INSTITUTIONS IN
         INDIA
         ed. R.L. Park & I.Tinker, New York,
         Greenwood Press, 1969, p. 347-358

5070   Dhillen, H.S. & Mukerji

         NEED OF KNOWLEDGE OF GROUP STRUCTURE IN A
         VILLAGE FOR ACTION PROGRAMMES
         Ind.Sociol.Confer., Calcutta, 1959

5071   Dibona, J.

         FAIR COMMUNITIES AND FOUL CITIES: THE
         ETHNIC FACTOR IN URBAN COMMUNITY DEVELOPMENT:
         THE INDIAN CASE
         Ind.J.Soc.Work, 1969, 30, 1, Apr, 23-32,
         SA, XVlll, 7, E6478

5072   Digarsey, P.

A STUDY OF THE COMMUNITY DEVELOPMENT PROGRAMME
IN M.P. STATE - ITS ACHIEVEMENTS, PROBLEMS AND
SUGGESTIONS (Ph.D.)
Doct, Jabalpur U, 1969, (Dr. R.K.Gupta)

5073   Doshi, S.L.

NON-CLUSTERED TRIBAL VILLAGES AND COMMUNITY
DEVELOPMENT
Hum.Org. 1969, 28, 4, Win, 297-302,
SA, XVlll, 8, E6480

5074   Dube, L.

LEADERSHIP IN C.D. AND DECENTRALIZED DEMOCRACY
Kurukshetra, 1966, 14, 9, Jun, 5-10,
SA, XVll, 4, D8139

5075   Dube, S.

ORGANIZATIONAL STRAINS IN THE COMMUNITY
DEVELOPMENT BLOCKS IN INDIA
Ind.J.of Soc.Work, 1968, 29,2,Jul, 135-146
SA, XVlll, 4, E3617

5076   Dube, S.C.

INDIA'S CHANGING VILLAGES: HUMAN FACTORS
IN COMMUNITY DEVELOPMENT
New York, Humanities, 1958

5077   Dube, S.C.

INSTITUTION BUILDING FOR COMMUNITY DEVELOPMENT
Kurukshetra, 1966, 14, 6, Mar, 2-4,
SA, XVll, 2, D6536

5078   Dube, S.C.

COMMUNITY DEVELOPMENT - A CRITICAL REVIEW
in: RURAL SOCIOLOGY IN INDIA,
ed. A.R. Desai, Bombay, Popular 1969, p.622-627

5079   Dubey, D.C. et al

VILLAGE LEVEL WORKERS: THEIR WORK AND
RESULT DEMONSTRATIONS
Hyderabad, Nat'l. Inst. Of C.D. 1962

5080   Dubey, D.C. & Sutton, W.

A RURAL "MAN IN THE MIDDLE": THE
INDIAN VILLAGE LEVEL WORKER IN
COMMUNITY DEVELOPMENT
Hum Org. 1965, 24, Summer, 2, 148-151
SA, XlV, 2-3, B9553

5081   Dubey, S.N.

ORGANIZATIONAL TENSION IN THE COMMUNITY
DEVELOPMENT BLOCKS OF INDIA
Human Org. 1969, 28, 1, Spr., 64-71,
SA, XVlll, 1-2, E1604

5082   Dubey, S.N.

COMMUNITY ACTION PROGRAMS AND CITIZEN
PARTICIPATION: ISSUES AND CONFUSIONS
Social Work, 1970, 15, 1, Jan, 76-84,
SA, XlX, 4, F0283

5083   Dumont, R.

LE PROJET DE DEVELOPPEMENT COMMUNAUTAIRE
EN INDE (THE PROJECT OF COMMUNITY DEVELOPMENT
IN INDIA) (Fr.)
Int.R.Com.Dev. 1962, 10, 33-46,
SA, Xlll, 1, B4457

5084   Dutta, V.R.

LOCAL PLANNING AWARENESS OF ZILA PARISHAD MEMBERS
Kurukshetra, 1969, 17, 6, Mar, 8-9
SA, XlX, 4, F0284

5085   Dwivedi, R.C.

THE WORKING OF THE COMMUNITY DEVELOPMENT
PROJECTS IN U.P., WITH SPECIAL REFERENCE TO PILOT
PROJECT AT ETAWAH (Ph.D.)
Doct, Agra U, 1956

5086   Elwin, V. (ed.)

REPORT OF THE COMMITTEE ON SPECIAL
MULTI-PURPOSE TRIBAL BLOCKS
New Delhi, Ministry of Home Affairs, 1960

5087   Ensminger, D.

A GUIDE TO COMMUNITY DEVELOPMENT
New Delhi, Ministry of C.D., 1956

5088   Ensminger, D.

ASSESSING PROGRESS IN COMMUNITY DEVELOPMENT
Kurukshetra, 1965, 13, 4, Jan, 26, 6-7
SA, XlV, 5, C1377

5089   Estimates Committee's Findings

COMMUNITY DEVELOPMENT UNDER THE MICROSCOPE
Kurukshetra, 1966, 14, 8, May, 13-19,
SA, XVll, 3, D7468

5090   Evaluation Report on Working of Community
Projects & N.E.S.

COMMUNITY DEVELOPMENT PROJECTS -
AN EVALUATION
in: RURAL SOCIOLOGY IN INDIA,
ed. A.R.Desai,
Bombay, Popular, 1969, p. 607-611

5091   Fox, R.G.

FROM ZAMINDAR TO BALLOT BOX; COMMUNITY
CHANGE IN A NORTH INDIAN MARKET TOWN
Ithaca, N.Y., Cornell U Press, 1969

5092   Fraser, Thomas, M.J.

BARPALI: CASE STUDIES IN COMMUNITY
DEVELOPMENT
(mss) New Delhi, n.d.

5093   Gaikwad, V.R. & Verma, G.L.

EXTENT OF PEOPLE'S INVOLVEMENT IN C.D.
PROGRAMME
Behavioural Scis. & C.D. 1968, 2, 2, Sep, 143-153
SA X1X, 3, E9216

5094   Gandhi, P.K.

COMMUNITY DEVELOPMENT FACES CHALLENGE
Kurukshetra, 1966, 14, 6, Mar, 8-9,
SA, XV11, 2, D5639

5095   Gangrade, K.D.

SOCIAL WELFARE FOR THE COMMUNITY AND
THE PROBLEM OF ITS RELATIONS WITH INDIVIDUAL RIGHTS
Ind.J.Soc.Work, 1968, 29, 1, Apr, 43-50,
SA, XV111, 1-2, E1607

5096   Gangrade, K.D.

THE CHANGE AGENT IN COMMUNITY DEVELOPMENT:
INDIA'S VILLAGE LEVEL WORKER
Int.Rev.of Com.Dev.1968, 19-20, 309-326,
SA, XV111, 3, E2544

5097   Gangrade, K.D.

COMMUNITY ORGANIZATION IN INDIA
Bombay, Popular Prakashan, 1971, pp. 200

5098   Goodall, M.R.

THE CORNELL - LUCKNOW EVALUATION STUDIES OF
THE COMMUNITY DEVELOPMENT PROGRAMME
East. Anthrop. 1955, 8, 3-4, Mar-Aug,
243-245, SA, Vol. IV, #2, 2344

5099   Gray, J.D.

COMMUNITY DEVELOPMENT AS PREPARATION
FOR ECONOMIC GROWTH IN DEVELOPING
COUNTRIES WITH PARTICULAR REFERENCE
TO THE SAKTIGAR PROGRAM IN INDIA
American Doctoral Dissertations (1959-60)
Cornell U, (Sociology)

5100   Gupta, R.K.

IMPACT OF COMMUNITY DEVELOPMENT IN
RURAL LIFE (Ph.D.)
Doct, Jabalpur U, 1967

5101   Gupta, R.S.

URBAN COMMUNITY DEVELOPMENT IN INDIA
- SOME ADMINISTRATIVE ASPECTS
C.D. Journal, 1970, 5,2, Apr, 94-97
SA, XX, 7, F95'49

5102   Hojela, T.N.

RURAL CO-OPERATIVES AND COMMUNITY
DEVELOPMENT IN UTTAR PRADESH (Ph.D.)
Doct, Agra U, 1960

2317   community development

5103   Hunn, D.

        INKLINGS FROM INDIA
        Phalanx, 1967, 1, 3, Fall, 89-94,
        SA, XV11, 2, D6540

5104   Iyer, H.R.S.

        GENERALIST - SPECIALIST RELATIONS IN
        COMMUNITY DEVELOPMENT ADMINISTRATION
        Social Welfare, 19, 7, 1972, 1-3

5105   Jacob, P.E., Teune, H. & Watts, T.

        VALUES, LEADERSHIP AND DEVELOPMENT:
        A FOUR NATION STUDY
        Soc.Sci. Information, 1968, 7, 2, Apr, 49-92
        SA, XV11, 3, D7473

5106   Jain, S.C.

        COMMUNITY DEVELOPMENT ADMINISTRATION IN
        RAJASTHAN (Ph.D.)
        Doct, Rajasthan U, 1963, (Dr. S.P.Varma)

5107   Jain, S.C.

        COMMUNITY DEVELOPMENT AND PANCHAYATI RAJ
        IN INDIA
        Bombay, Allied Publishers, 1967

5108   Kaikobad, N.F.

        TRAINING FOR COMMUNITY DEVELOPMENT
        Ind.J.of Soc.Work, 1967, 28, 1, Apr, 95-108
        SA, XV1, 6, D3810

5109   Kantowsky, D.

        COMMUNITY DEVELOPMENT AND PANCHAYATI RAJ
        Interdiscipline, 1967, 4, 1, Spr, 43-57,
        SA, XV11, 3, D7474

5110   Kaufman, H.F.

        RURAL COMMUNITY DEVELOPMENT IN INDIA,
        Int.R.Com.Dev. 1962, 9, 77-94,
        SA, Xlll, 1, B4430

5111   Kaul, M.L.

        DELHI URBAN COMMUNITY DEVELOPMENT PILOT
        PROJECT: CITIZEN DEVELOPMENT COUNCILS IN
        PROCESS
        Int.Rev.of C.D. 1970, 23-24, Dec, 233-246
        SA, XlX, 5, Fl120

5112   Kaushal, M.P.

        A STUDY OF COMMUNITY DEVELOPMENT AS A PROCESS
        OF SOCIAL CHANGE IN THE PUNJAB (Ph.D.)
        Doct, Panjab U, 1967 (Dr. M.L.Sharma)

5113   Khan, I.H.

        COMMUNITY PROJECTS IN INDIA (Ph.D.)
        Doct, Aligarh Muslim U, 1960, (Prof.M.Sultan)

5114   Khare, V.P.

        COMMUNITY DEVELOPMENT ADMINISTRATION IN THE
        TRIBAL BLOCKS OF MANDLA DISTRICT (M.P.) (Ph.D.),
        Doct, Jabalpur U, 1969, (Dr. T.G.Dugbekar)

5115   Kivlin, J.E.

        MIGRANTS AS CHANGE AGENTS
        Behavioral Sciences & C.D. 1967, 1, 2, Sep, 100-106
        SA, XVlll, 7, E6488

5116   Kothari, C.R.

        C.D. IS STILL VALID
        Kurukstetra, 1969, 17, 8, May, 13
        SA, XiX, 4, F0289

5117   Lavania, B.K.

THE IMPACT OF THE COMMUNITY DEVELOPMENT
PROGRAMMES ON THE SOCIAL STRUCTURE OF THE
BHILS IN SOUTHERN RAJASTHAN - A STUDY IN
SOCIAL CHANGE (Ph.D.)
Doct, Agra U, 1969, (Dr. R.N.Saksena)

5118   Mani, R.S.

ECONOMIC AND NON-ECONOMIC FACTORS IN C.D.
Kurukshetra, 1964, 13, 1, Oct, 23-26,
SA, XlV, 4 C0480

5119   Mann, H.S.

ANALYSIS OF SOME PROBLEMS OF COMMUNITY
DEVELOPMENT IN INDIA
Delhi, Atma Ram, 1967, xii-103p.

5120   Mann, R.S.

CASTE AND COMMUNITY DEVELOPMENT
Ind.J.Soc.Work, 1962, 23, 1, Apr, 131-132,
SA, Xll, 1, A8352

5121   Man, M.

COMMUNITY PROJECTS IN INDIA, WITH SPECIAL
REFERENCE TO MADHYA PRADESH (Ph.D.)
Doct, Saugar U, 1966, (Dr. R.P.Roy)

5122   Mathur, V.K.

THE TRADITIONAL CONTINUUM - AN ASSUMPTION
IN TRIBAL DEVELOPMENT
J. of Soc. Res., 1967, 10, 2, Sep, 11-25,
SA, XVll, 2, D6542

5123   Mayer, A.

PILOT PROJECT INDIA
Berkeley, California, U. of Calif. Press,
1958, xxiv & 367 pp,
SA, Vll, 3, 6096

5124   Mayer, A.C.

SOME POLITICAL IMPLICATIONS OF COMMUNITY
DEVELOPMENT IN INDIA
Eur.J.Sociol. 1963,4, 1, 86-106
SA, Xll, 7, B2800

5125   Mathur, J.S.

COMMUNITY DEVELOPMENT PROJECTS
AND NATIONAL EXTENSION SERVICE
BLOCKS IN DELHI AND PUNJAB (Ph.D.)
Doct, Agra U, 1961

5126   Mehta, B.H. (ed.)

A PRELIMINARY SURVEY OF THE TAIMA
DEVELOPMENT PILOT PROJECT)
(mimeographed), 1967

5127   Mehta, C.

CITIZENS' PARTICIPATION IN URBAN
COMMUNITY DEVELOPMENT
C.D.Journal 1969, 4, 3, Jul, 133-136
SA, XlX, 1-2, E7873

5128   Mehta, R.S.

SOCIAL EXPERIMENTS IN EXTENSION PROJECTS
Ind.J.Soc.Work, 1962, 23, 1, Apr, 53-56,
SA, Xll, 1, A8353

5129   Menon, R.S.

APPLIED ANTHROPOLOGY AND COMMUNITY
DEVELOPMENT
March, August, 15, 1964

5130   *Misra, G.K.

        THE CENTRALITY ORIENTED CONNECTIVITY OF ROADS
        IN MIRYALGUD TALUKA   - A CASE STUDY
        also: Behav.Sci. & C.D.
        1972, 6, 1, Mar, 76-88,
        SA, 21, 73G2979

5131   Moulik, T.K. & Pareek, U.

        GROUP FACTORS IN PARTICIPATION
        Ind.J.Soc.Work, 1963, 24, 2, Jul, 79-84,
        SA, Xll, 5, B1150

5132   Mukerji, B.

        COMMUNITY DEVELOPMENT IN INDIA (rev.ed.)
        Intl.Pubns. Serv. 1967

5133   Nagpaul, H.

        SVILUPPO DI DOMUNITA IN ZONE URBANE
        DELL INDIA (COMMUNITY DEVELOPMENT IN
        URBAN ZONES IN INDIA), (It.)
        Int.R.Com. Dev.1962, 9, 95-111,
        SA, Xlll, 1, B4509

5134   Nanavatty, M.C.

        SOME PROBLEM-AREAS OF COMMUNITY DEVELOPMENT
        Kurukshetra, 1966, 15, 1, Oct, 13-17,
        SA, XVLLL, 3, E2552

5135   *Narayan, J.P.

        COMMUNITARIAN SOCIETY AND PANCHAYATI RAJ
        New Delhi, Indraprastha Press, 1970

5135   Nath, S.

        WHITHER COMMUNITY DEVELOPMENT?
        Kurukshetra, 1966, 14, 5, Feb, 2-4,
        SA, XVll, 2, D6543

5136   Nat'l Inst. of C.D.

THE VILLAGE LEVEL WORKERS, THEIR WORK AND
RESULT DEMONSTRATION
New Delhi, Gov't of India Press, 1962

5137   Panda, B.

COMMUNITY AND DEVELOPMENT
Kurukshetra, 1969, 17, 7, Apr, 9 & 11
SA, XlX, 4, F0294

5138   Panda, B.M.

DEVELOPMENT SCHEMES AS FACTORS OF CHANGE
IN TRIBAL AREAS
J. of Soc.Res. 1968, 11, 2, Sep, 33-57,
SA, XVlll, 6, E5452

5139   Pande, V.

VILLAGE COMMUNITY PROJECTS IN INDIA:
ORIGIN, DEVELOPMENT AND PROBLEMS
Bombay, Asia Pub. House, 1967,
x, 258p.

5140   Panikkar, K.K.

COMMUNITY DEVELOPMENT ADMINISTRATION
IN KERALA (Ph.D.),
Doct, Kerala U, 1968, (Dr. V.K.S.Nayar)

5141   Patil, R.K.

COMMUNITY DEVELOPMENT ACHIEVEMENTS AND
FAILURES
Kurukshetra, 1965, 13, 4, Jan, 5-6,
SA, XlV, 5, C1387

5142   Patnaik, N.

POLITICAL CHANGES AND ECONOMIC STAGNATION
IN A TRIBAL BLOCK IN ORISSA
Behav.Sciences & C.D. 1969, 3, 1, Mar, 13-22,
SA, XlX, 4, F0296

5143   Panda, B.M.

THE DIMENSIONS OF TRAINING: A STUDY
OF THE IMPACT OF TRAINING OF C.D. PERSONNEL
Doct. st, Ranchi U, 1969

5144   Pothen, K.P.

COMMUNITY PROJECTS AND N.E.S. BLOCKS
Ind.Sociol. 1962, 4, 5, Mar, 33-39
SA, Xlll, 2, B5327

5145   Prasad, J.

IMPACT OF C.D. PROJECTS ON THE PATTERN
OF RURAL LEADERSHIP POWER STRUCTURE
Doct. st, Gorakhpur U, 1969,
(S.P.Nagendra)

5146   Prasad, L.

MOBILIZING COMMUNITY INTO ACTION
Ind.J.Soc.Res.1961, 2, 1, Jan., 69-77
SA, Xl, 6, A7052

5147   Rahudkar, W.B.

THE RELATIONSHIP OF CERTAIN PERSONAL ATTRIBUTES
TO THE SUCCESS OF VILLAGE LEVEL WORKERS
Ind.J.Soc.Work, 1963, 23, 4, Jan, 319-326,
SA, Xll, 4, B0450

5148   Rajamani, A.N.

LOGIC OF COMMUNITY DEVELOPMENT EXPENDITURE
PATTERN
Kurukshetra, 1968, 17, 2, Nov, 5-7
SA, X1X, 4, F0301

5149   Raman, K.S.V.

FUTURE OF COMMUNITY DEVELOPMENT
Kurukshetra, 1966, 15, 1, Oct, 9-11,
SA, XV111, 3, E2553

5150   Ramaswamay, A.S.

BLOCK DEVELOPMENT ADMINISTRATION AT
CROSS ROADS
Kurukshetra, 1969, 17, 9, Jun, 3-5,
SA, X1X, 4, F0302

5151   Ramavtar L.

COMMUNITY DEVELOPMENT OF BIHAR (Ph.D.)
Doct, Patna U, 1959 (Prof.B.R.Mishra)

5152   Rastogi, P.N.

POLARIZATION AT THAKURPUR: THE PROCESS
AND THE PATTERN
Sociol. B., 1966, 15, 1, 61-74,
SA, X1V, 6, C2387

5153   Roy, P., Kivlin, J., Sen, L. & Fliegel, F.

TWO BLADES OF GRASS
Hyderabad, N.I.C.D., 1968

5154   Sancheti, D.C.

RURAL RECONSTRUCTION THROUGH COMMUNITY
DEVELOPMENT IN RAJASTHAN (Ph.D.),
Doct, Rajasthan U, 1964,
(Prof.B.D.Bhargava)

5155   Sangave, V.A.

COMMUNITY DEVELOPMENT PROGRAM IN
KOLHAPUR DISTRICT
Sociol. B. 1958, 7, 2, Sep, 97-111,
SA, Vlll, 2, 7687

5156   Saxena, S.K.

COOPERATION IN INDIA
Archiv. Int. Sociol. Coop. 1957, 1, 1, Jan-Jun, 88-95,
SA, Xlll, 2, B5331

5157   Sen, B.R.

THE ROLE OF COMMUNITY DEVELOPMENT
Kurukshetra, 1766, 15, 1, Oct, 5-7,
SA, XVlll, 3, E2554

5158   Sen, (Miss) J.

COMPARATIVE STUDY OF DEVELOPMENT METHODS
AS EMPLOYED BY CHRISTIAN MISSIONS AND
OFFICIAL AGENCIES (D.Phil.)
Doct, Calcutta U, 1965, (Prof. N.K.Bose)

5158   Sen, K.C.

WORKING OF COMMUNITY PROJECTS IN INDIA
Kerul du Sud-Est Asiatique, 1964, 1, 11-26
SA, XVl, 5, D2971

5159   Sen, L.K. & Roy, P.

AWARENESS OF C.D. IN VILLAGE INDIA
Hyderabad, Nat'l Inst. of C.D., 1966

5160   Shah, C.H. & Shukla, T.

IMPACT OF A COMMUNITY DEVELOPMENT PROJECT
J.Univ. Bombay, 1958, 26, 4, Jan, 18-31,
SA, Vlll, 2, 7688

5161   Shanker, P.

ATTITUDE CHANGES IN SOME COMMUNITY
PROJECT AREAS OF U.P. AND BIHAR (Ph.D.)
Doct, Lucknow U, 1960 (Prof. K.Prasad)

5162   Shiwalkar, R.S.

PROBLEMS OF C.D. WORKERS
Kurukshetra, 1964, 12, 7, Apr, 16-18
SA, XlV, 1, B8692

5163   Singh, A.

A REASSESSMENT OF ACTION APPROACH TO
COMMUNITY LEADERSHIP
Sociologia Ruralis, 1970, 10, 1, 3-20,
SA, XlX, 4, F0305

5164   *Singh, B.

A TRIBAL EXPERIMENT IN DANDAKARANAYA
Eastern Anthropologist, 26, 4, Oct,-Dec.
1973, pp. 343-348

5165   Singh, B.N.

THE IMPACT OF THE COMMUNITY DEVELOPMENT
PROGRAMME ON RURAL LEADERSHIP
in: LEADERSHIP AND POLITICAL INSTITUTIONS
IN INDIA
R.Park & I.Tinker (eds.)
Oxford U Press, 1960, 358-371

5166   Singh, B.N.

INDIVIDUAL AND COMMUNITY DEVELOPMENT IN A
MORMON COMMUNITY IN UTAH WITH IMPLICATIONS
FOR COMMUNITY DEVELOPMENT IN INDIA
American Doctoral Dissertations (1958-1959)
(Sociology) Cornell U.

5167   Singh, B.N.

ADMINISTRATION OF COMMUNITY DEVELOPMENT
BLOCK IN BIHAR (Ph.D.)
Doct, Magadh U, 1967, (Dr.H.Singh)

5168   Singh, D.N.

COMMUNITY DEVELOPMENT IN WESTERN U.P.:
A STUDY OF ADMINISTRATION (Ph.D.)
Doct, Lucknow U, 1967, (Dr.R.B.Das)

5169   Singh, R.P.

DIFFERENTIAL ATTITUDES OF FARMERS TOWARDS
SOME ASPECTS OF THE COMMUNITY DEVELOPMENT
PROGRAMME (Ph.D.)
Doct, Indian Agricultural Research Instit, 1966,
(Dr. K.N.Singh)

5170   Singh, U.

EVALUATION AND STATISTICAL ANALYSIS OF
COMMUNITY DEVELOPMENT AND NATIONAL EXTENSION
SERVICE IN UTTAR PRADESH (Ph.D.)
Doct, Agra U, 1959

5171   Sinha, D.P.

INNOVATION, RESPONSE AND DEVELOPMENT IN BANARI
Man in India, 1968, 48, 3, Jul-Sep, 225-243,
SA, XV111, 3, E2555

5172   Singhai, G.C.

IMPACT OF COMMUNITY DEVELOPMENT PROGRAMME ON
THE RURAL ECONOMY OF NORTHERN MAHAKOSHAL, M.P. (PH.D.)
Doct, Saugar U, 1969, (Prof.J.N.Mishra)

5173   *Sinha, P.R.R.

       ATTITUDE OF EXTENSION PERSONNEL TOWARDS IACP AND
       CD APPROACHES IN AGRICULTURAL DEVELOPMENT IN
       PUNJAB
       Behavioural Sciences & Community Development
       1971, 5, 1, Mar, 1-13,
       SA, 21, 73G1311

5174   Sreekantiah, K.N.

       TRAINING IN COMMUNITY DEVELOPMENT
       Kurukshetra, 1964, 12, 9, Jun, 14-15
       SA, XlV, 1, B8695

5175   *Srinivasan, V.

       LEADERSHIP TRAINING COURSE FOR SLUM WOMEN TO
       PREPARE THEM TO RUN NUTRITION EDUCATION
       CLASSES FOR OTHER WOMEN IN THEIR NEIGHBOURHOOD
       Community Development Journal, 1971, 6, 1,
       Win. 19-22,
       SA, 21, 73G1367

5176   Srivastava, R.N.

       THE SOCIAL IMPACT OF COMMUNITY DEVELOPMENT
       PROGRAMME OF TRIBAL LIFE IN DUDHI (Ph.D.)
       Doct, Agra U, 1960

5177   Srivastava, R.N.

       IMPACT OF C.D. PROGRAM ON TRIBAL LIFE
       Kurukshetra, 1965, 13, 5, Feb, 11-12,
       SA, XlV, 6, C2390

5178   Srivastava, S.K.

       THE ROLE OF SOCIAL PSYCHOLOGIST IN THE
       NATIONAL DEVELOPMENT PROGRAM IN INDIA
       WITH SPECIAL REFERENCE TO C.D. PROJECTS
       Paper read at Sociology Conference Calcutta, 1959

5179   Stibbe, T.

QUELQUES ASPECTS DU FONCTIONNEMENT DES
"COMMUNITY DEVELOPMENT PROJECTS" ET
DES COOPERATIVES EN INDE (SOME ASPECTS
OF THE FUNCTIONING OF THE COMMUNITY
DEVELOPMENT PROJECTS AND THE COOPERATIONS
IN INDIA) (Fr.)
Archiv. Int.Sociol.Coop. 1961, 9, Jan-Jun,
63-82,
SA, XV, 2, C4415

5180   Subramaniam, C.

FUTURE WORKING OF COMMUNITY DEVELOPMENT
KEY ROLE FOR PANCHAYATI RAJ
Kurukshetra, 1966, 15, 2, Nov. 18-20,
SA, XVlll, 6, E5457

5181   Subramaniam, C.

NEW APPROACHES TO COMMUNITY DEVELOPMENT
Kurukshetra, 1966, 14, 11, Aug, 2-4,
SA, XVlll, 1-2, E1614

5182   Sussman, G.

THE VILLAGE LEVEL WORKERS: INDIA'S
EXPERIMENT IN RURAL RECONSTRUCTION
Int'.Dev.Rev. 1968, 10, 1, Mar, 40-42,
SA, XVll, 6, 09571

5183   Taylor, C.C.

CRITICAL ANALYSIS OF INDIA'S C.D. PROGRAMMES
New Delhi, n.d.

5184   Taylor, C.C. & Ensminger, D.

ROLE AND STATUS RELATIONSHIPS IN
PROGRAM ADMINISTRATION
Int.R.Com.Dev. 1963, 12, 88-108
SA, Xlll, 2, B5334

5185   Taylor, C.C. et al

INDIA'S ROOTS OF DEMOCRACY
Bombay, Orient Longmans, 1965

5186   Tewari, G.C.

THE IMPACT OF COMMUNITY DEVELOPMENT
PROJECTS ON THE SOCIAL ECONOMY OF
KUMAON HILLS (Ph.D.)
Doct, Agra U, 1965

5187   Thoppil, J.J.

IMPACT OF DEVELOPMENT PROGRAMME ON
RATIONALITY (Ph.D.)
Doct, Poona U, 1968,
(Dr.Y.B.Damle)

5188   Udeshi, J.J.

AN EVALUATION OF COMMUNITY DEVELOPMENT
PROJECT IN THE PURANDHAR TALUKA OF POONA
DISTRICT OF MAHARASHTRA STATE (Ph.D.)
Doct, Bombay U, 1965, (Dr.C.H.Shah)

5189   Ulrey, O.

COMMUNITY DEVELOPMENT IN INDIA
Kurukshetra, 1964, 12, 11, Aug, 18-19,
SA, XlV, 2-3, B9602

5190   Unnithan, T.K.N. & Singh, K.B.

STORY OF LALGARH: AN EXPERIMENT IN
SELF-HELP AND COMMUNITY PLANNING
Urban Rer. Plan. Thought, 1960, 3, 4, Oct,
163-202
SA, Xll, 5, B1183

5191   Ussem, J. & Useem, R.

THE INTERFACES OF A THIRD CULTURE
J.Soc.Issues, 1967, 23, 1, Jan, 130-143,
SA, XV, 6, C7554

5192   Valsan, E.H.

COMMUNITY DEVELOPMENT PROGRAMS AND RURAL
LOCAL GOVERNMENT: COMPARATIVE CASE
STUDIES OF INIDA AND THE PHILIPPINES
(Special Studies in International Economics
and Development)
New York, Praeger, 1970

5193   Varma, H.C.

A SOCIOLOGICAL ANALYSIS OF RURAL RECONSTRUCTION
AND COMMUNITY DEVELOPMENT PROGRAMME IN UTTAR
PRADESH, WITH SPECIAL REFERENCE TO GORAKHPUR
DIVISION (Ph.D.)
Doct, Lucknow U, 1970, (Dr.S.Chandra)

5194   Varughese, M.T.

AN EVALUATION OF THE TRAINING PROGRAM
FOR THE VILLAGE LEVEL WORKER IN INDIA
American D.ctoral Dissertations (1957-58)
The Claremont Graduate School (Sociology)

5195   Vepa, R.K.

SOME UNCONVENTIONAL THOUGHTS ON C.D.
PROGRAMME
Kurukshetra, 1966, 15, 1, Oct, 11-13,
SA, XV111, 3, E2559

5196   Vijayakumar, C.

LABOUR COMMUNITY DEVELOPMENT
Doct, St, Andhra U, 1969,
(Prof.M.V.Moorthy)

5197   Waring, P.A.

AN EXPERIMENT IN DEVELOPMENT:
RURAL INDIA
Man in India, 1966, 46, 2, Apr-Jun, 108-113,
SA, XV1, 6, D3821

2317   community development

5198   Wiebe, P.

RELIGIOUS TRADITIONS AND THE PROBLEM OF
COMMUNITY DEVELOPMENT IN INDIA
Kansas J.of Sociol. 1967, 3, 1, Win, 29-44,
SA, XVl, 3, D1311

5199   Yadav, M.M.K.

SOCIOLOGY OF URBAN COMMUNITY DEVELOPMENT
IN INDIA: A STUDY OF DELHI PROJECT
Doct. St, Agra U, 1969, (Dr.R.N.Saxena)

5200   Zealey, P.

TRAINING LOCAL LEADERS FOR COMMUNITY DEVELOPMENT
Int.R.Com.Dev. 1959, 3, 117-123
SA, Xll, 5, B1188

5201   -----

COMMUNITY DEVELOPMENT - A CONTINUING STRATEGY
Kurukshetra, 1966, 14, 5, Feb, 5-6,
Comment, 7-8
SA, XVll, 2, D6547

5202   -----

OBJECTIVES OF COMMUNITY DEVELOPMENT
AND ITS ROLE IN NATIONAL DEVELOPMENT
Behavioural Sciences & C.D. 1967, 1, 1, Mar, 56-59,
SA, XVlll, 6, E5459

5203   -----

ACTION FOR RURAL CHANGE: READINGS IN
INDIAN COMMUNITY DEVELOPMENT
Delhi, 1970

2400   PLANNING, FORECASTING & SPECULATION

2454   planning, forecasting & speculation

5204   Adhikari, B.P.

CONSTRUCTION OF SOCIO-ECONOMETRIC MODELS
FOR PLANNING
East Anthrop. 1960, 13, 3, Mar-May 84-94
SA, Xl, 4, A5054

5205   Agarwalla, S.N.

A METHOD FOR ESTIMATING DECADE INTERNAL
MIGRATION IN CITIES FROM INDIAN CENSUS
DATA
Ind.Econ.Rev.1958, 4, 1, 59-76
SA, Vlll, 2, 7585

5206   Alatas, S.H.

THE CAPTIVE MIND IN DEVELOPMENT PLANNING
11th World Conference of the Society
for International Development,
New Delhi, 1969

5207   Balakrishna, R.

REGIONAL PLANNING IN INDIA
Bangalore, Bangalore Printing & Publishing,
1948, 458p.

5208   Bettelheim, C.

SOME BASIC PLANNING PROBLEMS
Bombay, Asia

5209   Bulsara, J.F.

THE CONCEPT OF SOCIAL PLANNING
Ind.J. Soc.Work, 1964, 25, 3, Oct, 187-192
SA, Xlll, 6-7, B7712

5210   Chandrasekaran, C.

        INDIAN DEMOGRAPHIC TRENDS WITH A
        PROJECTION INTO THE NEXT 25 YEARS AND
        THEIR SIGNIFICANCE FOR SOCIAL WELFARE
        Ind.J.S.Work, 1965, 26, 2, Jul, 126-128,
        SA, XVl, 4, D1966

5211   Chandrasekhar, M.

        SOCIAL CHANGE IN INDIA (PLANNING PERIOD)
        (Ph.D.)
        Doct, Poona U, 1964, (Dr.Y.B.Damle)

5212   Dandekar, K.

        POSSIBLE TARGETS AND THEIR ATTAINMENT
        IN THE FIELD OF FAMILY PLANNING IN
        INDIA DURING 1966-1976
        Artha Vijnana, 8, 3, Sep, 1966, 239-248

5213   *Das Gupta, A.K.

        A FRAMEWORK OF PLANNING FOR INDIA
        Indian Economic Journal, 1969, 16, 3,
        Jan-Mar, 265-8276

5214   Dinesh, C.

        SOCIAL VALUES AND RURAL PLANNING
        Kurukshetra, 1966, 14, 10, Jul, 22-23,
        SA, XVll, 4, D7869

5215   Dube, S.C.

        COMMUNICATION INNOVATION AND PLANNED CHANGE
        IN INDIA
        in: COMMUNICATION AND CHANGE IN DEVELOPING
        COUNTRIES
        eds. D. Lerner & W. Schramm, Honolulu, 1967

5216   Harris, B.

        URBAN CENTRALIZATION AND PLANNED DEVELOPMENT
        in: INDIA'S URBAN FUTURE,
        ed. R. Turner, Berkeley, U of Calif. Press,
        1962, p.261-277

5217   Kraft, P.N.

        THE DEVELOPMENT OF PLANNING: CLASS AND
        STATE IN INDIA (Ph.D.-Soc.)
        Washington U, 1971

5218   Krishnamachari, V.T.

        PLANNING IN INDIA
        Intl. Pubns. Serv. 1961

5219   Malenbaum, W.

        WHO DOES THE PLANNING?
        in: LEADERSHIP AND POLITICAL INSTITUTIONS
        IN INDIA
        Ed. R.L.Park & I.Tinker, New York,
        Greenwood, 1969, p. 301-314

5220   Mandelbaum,D.G.

        PLANNING AND SOCIAL CHANGE IN INDIA
        Hum.Org. 1953, 12, 3, Fall, 4-12,
        SA, Vol.II, #4, 746

5221   Mayer, A.

        NATURAL IMPLICATIONS OF URBAN-REGIONAL
        PLANNING
        in: INDIA'S URBAN FUTURE
        ed. R. Turner, Berkeley: U of Calif. Press, 1962,
        p.335-347

5222   Mukerjee, R. (ed.)

        SOCIAL SCIENCES AND PLANNING IN INDIA
        Bombay, Asia, 1971

5223   Myrdal, G.

        INDIAN ECONOMIC PLANNING
        Pop. R. 1959, 3, 1, Jan, 17-32,
        SA, X11, 6, B1752

5224   Nair, M.N.V.

        SOCIAL IMPACT OF PLANNING IN INDIA (Ph.D.)
        Doct, Bombay U, 1969, (Prof.G.S.Ghurye)

5225   Nath, V.

        PLANNING FOR URBAN GROWTH
        Ind.J.of Social Work, 1966, 27, 2, Jul, 119-146,
        SA, XV1, 5, D2657

5226   Nayar, B.R.

        THE MODERNIZATION IMPERATIVE AND INDIAN
        PLANNING
        Delhi, Vikas Publications, 1972, 246 pp.

5227   Pafola, T.S.

        THE CRISIS OF INDIAN PLANNING
        East Anthrop. 1969, 22, 2, May-Aug, 229-246

5228   *Pandey, R.S.

        AN INTER-ORGANIZATIONAL ANALYSIS OF PLANNING
        FOR SOCIAL DEVELOPMENT IN INDIA
        International Review of Community Development,
        n.s., 29-30, Summer, 1973

5229   Premi, M.K.

        IMPLICATIONS OF POPULATION TRENDS FOR PLANNING
        EDUCATIONAL PROGRAMS IN INDIA
        Amer. Doctoral Dissertations (1967-68)
        Univeristy of Chicago (Soc.)

5230   Price, R.B.

IDEOLOGY AND INDIAN PLANNING
Amer. J. Econ. & Sociol. 1967, 26, 1, Jan, 47-64,
SA, XV, 4, C5740

5231   Sathyarmurthy, T.V.

L'ORDER MONDIAL EN L'AN 2000,
PERSPECTIVES ASIATIQUES (THE
WORLD ORDER IN THE YEAR 2000
ASIAN PROSPECTS) (Fr.)
Analyse & Prevision, 1969, 8, 1-2,
Jul-Aug, 487-502,
SA, X1X, 102, $7882

5232   Sen, L.K., Wanmali, S., Bose, S.,
Misra , G.K. & Ramesh, K.S.

PLANNING RURAL GROWTH CENTERS FOR INTEGRATED
AREA DEVELOPMENT: A STUDY OF MIRYALGUDA TALUKA
Hyderabad, Nat'l Instit. of C.D. 1971, xiv,
245 pp.

5233   Sen, S.R.

PLANNING MACHINERY IN INDIA
Ind.J.Publ.Admin.1961, 7, 3, Jul-Sep, 215-235,
SA, X11, 1, A8112

5234   Shah, A.B.

PLANNING FOR DEMOCRACY AND OTHER ESSAYS
Paragon, 1967

5235   Siddiqi, A.A.

PLANNING AND SOCIAL CHANGE
Agra U J.Res. (Lett.) 1955, 3, Dec, 118-121
SA, V1, 1, 4190

5236   Singh, Tarlok

TOWARDS AN INTEGRATED SOCIETY: REFLECTIONS
ON PLANNING, SOCIAL POLICY AND RURAL INSTITUTIONS
Westport, Greenwood,Pub. 1969

5237   Singh, T.

ON PLANNING TECHNOLOGICAL CHANGE IN
INDIAN AGRICULTURE
Int.Soc.Sci. J. 1969, 21, 2, 265-271
SA, XVlll, 6, E4995

5238   Sinha, D.P.

PRINCIPLES AND PROBLEMS OF PLANNED CULTURAL
CHANGE
in: APPLIED ANTHROPOLOGY IN INDIA
Ed. L.P.Vidyarthi, Allahabad, Kitab Mahal,
1968, pp. 72-83

5239   Sovani, N.V.

POPULATION PLANNING IN INDIA
India J. of Economics 27, Jan, 1947, 299-315

5240   Sovani, N.V.

PLANNING AND PLANNERS IN INDIA
Ind.Eco.J.1966, 13, 4, Jan-Mar, 477-497
SA, XVll, 3, D6948

5241   Subbiah, B.V.

A NATIONAL PLANNING POLICY FOR INDIA:
(TO MEET THE PRESSURES OF POPULATION)
American Doctoral Dissertations (1964-65)
New York U (Soc.-Family)

5242   Suri, G.K.

SOME ASPECTS OF SOCIO-CULTURAL ENVIRONMENT
AND ECONOMIC PALNNING IN INDIA
Calcutta R. 1960, 134, 3, Mar, 265-269,
SA, Xll, 6, B1758

5243   *Wanmali, S. & Waheeduddin, K.

ROLE OF LOCATION IN REGIONAL PLANNING WITH
PARTICULAR REFERENCE TO THE PROVISION OF
SOCIAL FACILITIES
Behavioural Sciences & Community Development,
1970, 4, 2, Sep, 65-91,
SA, 21, 73G1313

2454   planning, forecasting & speculation

5244   -----

ECONOMIC AND SOCIAL PLANNING IN INDIA
Int.Labour Rev. 55, 419-25, May 1947

2500   RADICAL SOCIOLOGY

2555   radical sociology

2656   .environmental interactions

5245   Allchin, B., Hedge, K.T.M. & Goudil, A.

PREHISTORY AND ENVIRONMENTAL CHANGE IN
WESTERN INDIA: A NOTE ON THE BUDHA PUSHKAR
BASIN, RAJASTHAN
Man, 7, 4, Dec 1972, 541-565

5246   Mukerjee, R.

MAN AND HIS HABITATION
Bombay, 1968

5247   *Odend'hal, S.

ENERGETICS OF INDIA CATTLE IN THEIR
ENVIRONMENT
Human Ecology, 1972, 1, 1, Mar, 3-22,
SA, 21, 73G3007

5248   Rai, B.K.

NATURE AND MAN: A STUDY OF INTERACTION
BETWEEN MAN AND FOREST IN CHHOTANAGPUR (Ph.D.)
Doct, Ranchi U, 1967, (Prof.Sachchidananda)

5249   Saran, A.K.

THE NATURAL SCIENCES AND THE STUDY OF MAN:
THE PROBLEM OF THEIR SYNTHESIS IN CONTEMPORARY
CULTURES
East. Anthrop., 1961, 14, 2, 122-35

5250   Singh, R.N.P.

A CRITICAL ANALYSIS OF LE PLAY'S THEORY OF
ENVIRONMENTAL DETERMINISM
Ind.J.Soc.Res. 13, 3, Dec, 1972, pp.172-178

2700   STUDIES IN POVERTY

2757   studies in poverty

    5251   Bhatnagar, (Mrs.)S.R.

            SOCIO-ECONOMIC CONDITIONS OF BEGGARS IN
            UTTAR PRADESH (Ph.D.)
            Doct, Agra U, 1959

    5252   Bopegamage, A.

            CASTE AND POVERTY
            Sociology and Social Research, 57, 1, Oct. 1972,
            62-69

    5253   Fonseca, A.J. (ed.)

            CHALLENGE OF POVERTY IN INDIA
            Intl.Pubns.Serv. 1972

    5254   Gore, M.S.

            SOCIETY AND THE BEGGAR
            Sociol. B. 1958, 7, 1, Mar, 23-48,
            SA, Vlll, 2, 7661

    5255   Mehta, A.

            THE PROBLEM OF POVERTY IN UNDERDEVELOPED
            COUNTRIES: THE INDIAN EXPERIENCE
            Revue du Sud-Est Asiatique 1964, 1, 1-10,
            SA, XVl, 5, D2444

    5256   Myrdal, G.

            THE CHALLENGE OF WORLD POVERTY
            New York, Vintage Books, 1970

5257   Myrdal, G.

ASIAN DRAMA: AN INQUIRY INTO THE POVERTY
OF NATIONS (3 Vols.)
New York, 20th Century Fund and Pantheon Books,
1968

5258   Naoroji, D.

POVERTY AND UN-BRITISH RULE IN INDIA
Verry, 1962

5259   Patel, T.

SOME REFLECTIONS ON THE BEGGAR PROBLEM IN
AHMEDABAD
Sociol.B. 1959, 8, 1, Mar, 5-15,
SA, X1, 6, A7031

5260   Rao, T.S. & d.Bogaert, M.V.

THE BEGGAR PROBLEM IN RANCHI
Ind.J.Soc.Work, 1970, 31, 3, Oct, 285-302
SA, XX, 6, F8925

5261   Rao, V.V.P.

TOWARD THE DEVELOPMENT OF A TYPOLOGY
OF LOW INCOME FAMILIES (Ph.D.-Soc.)
Mississippi State U (1970-71)

5262   Singh, T.

POVERTY AND SOCIAL CHANGE, WITH A REAPPRAISAL
(2nd ed.), Bombay, Orient Longmans, 1969

2800   STUDIES IN VIOLENCE

2858   studies in violence

   5263   Roy Burman, B.K.

            SOCIAL PROFILE OF AHMEDABAD AND THE COMMUNAL
            DISTURBANCES
            Seminar, Gandhi Peace Foundation, 1969

   5264   Sunder, S.

            A SOCIOL. STUDY OF COMMUNAL RIOTS IN
            THE STATE OF U.P.
            Doct.St, Lucknow U, 1969

   5265   Bondurant, J.

            CONQUEST OF VIOLENCE: THE GANDHIAN
            PHILOSOPHY OF CONFLICT
            Berkeley, U of Calif Press, 1965

ADDENDUM
===============

103   methodology (social science & behavioural)

5266 *Bharati, A.
      THE HIMALAYAS AS A CULTURAL AREA:
      A NOVEL METHODOLOGICAL PERSPECTIVE
      in: MAIN CURRENTS IN INDIAN SOCIOLOGY
      Vol.I (ed.) G.R.Gupta, Delhi, Vikas, 1975

5267 *Indra Deva

      METHODOLOGICAL PERSPECTIVES FOR THE STUDY
      OF SOCIETY IN INDIA
      in: MAIN CURRENTS IN INDIAN SOCIOLOGY,
      Vol. I, (ed.) G.R.Gupta, Delhi, Vikas,1975

5268 *Weinstein, J.A.

      MADRAS: THEORETICAL, TECHNICAL AND EMPIRICAL
      ISSUES
      in: MAIN CURRENTS IN INDIAN SOCIOLOGY
      Vol. I, (ed.) G.R.Gupta, Delhi, Vikas, 1975

104   research technology

5269 Adhikari, B.P.

      CONSTRUCTION OF SOCIO-ECONOMETRIC MODELS
      FOR PLANNING
      East. Anthrop. 1960, 13, 3, Mar-May, 84-94,
      SA, Xl, 4, A5054

5270 Chekki, D.A.

      MEASURING KINSHIP ORIENTATION
      Ind. J.Soc.Res. Xl, 1970, 1. pp. 47-50

5271 Khatri, A.A.

      MANUAL OF THE SCALE TO MEASURE
      JOINTNESS OF FAMILIES IN INDIA
      Ahmedabad, 1970

5272 Lakdawala, D.T.

      BOMBAY SURVEY
      Regional Seminar on Research Techniques
      of Social Research
      Delhi, UNESCO Res. Center, 1959, 122-24

5273 Sinha, B.

      SIRSI: AN URBAN STUDY IN APPLICATION OF
      RESEARCH MODELS
      Dharwar, Karnatak University, 1970

202   of professional interest

5274 *Beteille, A.

      THE TEACHING OF SOCIOLOGY IN INDIA
      Sociological Bulletin, 22, 2, 1973,
      216-233

5275 *Chowdhury, A.

      SOCIOLOGY IN BANGLADESH: THE NEED FOR
      EMPIRICAL RESEARCH
      Sociological Bulletin, 22, 1, 1973, 112-119

5276 *Khare, R.S.

      "INSIDE" APROPOS OF "OUTSIDE" SOME
      IMPLICATIONS OF A SOCIOLOGICAL DEBATE
      in: MAIN CURRENTS IN INDIAN SOCIOLOGY,
      Vol. I, (ed.) G.R.Gupta, Delhi, Vikas, 1975

5277 *Lambert, R.D.

      LANGUAGE AND AREA STUDIES REVIEW
      Monograph 17, Philadelphia, The Annals. AAPSS, 1973

202   of professional interest

5278 *Lambert, R.D.

   RESOURCES FOR SOUTH ASIAN AREA STUDIES
   IN THE UNITED STATES
   Philadelphia, University of Pennsylvania
   Press, 1962

5279 *Mukherjee, R. et al

   DATA INVENTORY ON SOCIAL SCIENCES: INDIA,
   FIRST PHASE: 1967-68
   Calcutta, Statistical Publishing Society, 1971
   pp. 160

5280 Srivasthava, S.K.

   THE ROLE OF SOCIAL PSYCHOLOGIST IN
   THE NATIONAL DEVELOPMENT PROGRAM IN
   INDIA WITH SPECIAL REFERENCE TO
   C.D. PROJECTS
   Paper read at Sociology Conference Calcutta, 1959

206   history and present state of sociology

5281 *Chekki, D.A.

   SOCIOLOGICAL RESEARCH IN INDIA: SOME TRENDS
   IN COMMUNITY RESEARCH
   in: MAIN CURRENTS IN INDIAN SOCIOLOGY
   Vol. I (ed.) G.R.Gupta, Delhi, Vikas, 1975

5282 *Crane, R.I.

   REGIONS & REGIONALISM IN SOUTH ASIAN STUDIES
   Durham, Duke University, 1969

5283   Dubey, D.C.

       INDIAN SOCIOLOGY AND THE POPULATION PROBLEM
       Ind. Soc. Bulletin, 5(4), Jul 68, 209-214

5284   *Indian Council of Social Science Research

       A SURVEY OF RESEARCH IN SOCIOLOGY AND SOCIAL
       ANTHROPOLOGY, Vol. III
       Bombay, Popular Prakashan, 1972, pp. xv & 335

5285   *Indian Council of Social Science Research

       A SURVEY OF RESEARCH IN SOCIOLOGY AND SOCIAL
       ANTHROPOLOGY, Vols. I & II
       Bombay, Popular Prakashan, 1974

5286   *Mukherjee, R.

       INDIAN SOCIOLOGY: HISTORICAL DEVELOPMENTS
       AND PRESENT PROBLEMS
       Sociological Bulletin, 22, 1, 1973, 29-58

5287   *Srinivas, M.N. & Panini, M.N.

       THE DEVELOPMENT OF SOCIOLOGY AND SOCIAL
       ANTHROPOLOGY IN INDIA
       Sociological Bulletin, 22, 2, 1973, 179-215

207   theories, ideas and systems

5288   Broomfield, J.H.

       THE REGIONAL ELITES: A THEORY OF
       MODERN INDIAN HISTORY
       Ind. Eco. & Social History Rev. 1966, 3, 3,
       Sep, 275-291,
       SA, XVll, 1, D5598

5289 *Hallen, G.C. & Prasad, R. (eds.)

SOROKIN AND SOCIOLOGY
Agra, Satish Book, 1972

5290 *Nagendra, A.P.

THE CONCEPT OF RITUAL IN MODERN SOCIOLOGICAL
THEORY
New Delhi, Academic Journals, 1971

5291 *Rastogi, P.N.

STRUCTURE, FUNCTION AND PROCESS:
A CYBERNETIC APPROACH TO SOCIAL PHENOMENA
Sociological Bulletin, 22, 2, 1973, 309-320

5292 Saxena, P.C.

HUMAN FERTILITY AND STOCHASTIC MODELS (Ph.D.)
Doct, Banaras Hindu U, 1970, (Dr.S.N.Singh)

5293 Shingi, P.M.

THE DYNAMICS OF COMMUNITY CHANGE IN RURAL INDIA:
A CAUSAL MODEL (Ph.D.-Soc.)
University of Illinois at Urbana-Champaign, 1972

5294 Singh, R.N.P.

A CRITICAL ANALYSIS OF LE PLAY'S THEORY
OF ENVIRONMENTAL DETERMINISM
Ind.J.Soc.Res., 13, 3, Dec, 1972, pp. 172-178

5295 *Srivastava, R.N.

SOME ANTECEDENT AND CURRENT IDEAS OF
DEVELOPMENT AND LIMITATIONS OF
DEVELOPMENT THEORY
Sociological Bulletin, 22, 2, 1973, 283-296

5296 *Anant, S.S.

      CHANGING CASTE HINDU ATTITUDES TOWARDS HARIJANS
      in: MAIN CURRENTS IN INDIAN SICIOLOGY
      Vol. III (ed) G.R.Gupta, Delhi, Vikas, 1975

5297 Darbari, (Miss) P.

      CHANGING SOCIAL ATTITUDES AMONG MODERN
      EDUCATED HINDU WOMEN (Ph.D.)
      Doct, Agra U, 1960

5298 Sinha, A.K.P. & Upadhyay, O.P.

      STEREOTYPES OF MALE AND FEMALE UNIVERSITY
      STUDENTS IN INDIA TOWARD DIFFERENT ETHNIC GROUPS
      J.Soc.Psychol. 1960, 51, Feb, 93-102,
      SA, X1, 5, A5721

5299 Sinha, S.

      BADANIA NAD MOTYWACJA SPOLECZNOSCI WIEJSKIEJ
      W KRAJU ROZWIJAJACYM SIC (A STUDY OF THE HUMAN
      MOTIVATION OF THE RURAL POPULATION IN A DEVELOPING
      COUNTRY) (Pol.)
      Studia Socjologiczne, 1968, 28, 59-82,
      SA, X1X, 1-2, E7444

309   interaction within (small) groups

5300 *Shrivastava, R.S.

      FORMATION AND FUNCTIONING OF FRIENDSHIP GROUPS:
      A SOCIOLOGICAL STUDY AMONG PRISON INMATES
      Sociological Bulletin, 22, 1, 1973, 98-111

5301 *Erickson, E.C.

STRUCTURAL DIMENSIONS OF COMMUNITY LEADERSHIP
IN INDIA
in: MAIN CURRENTS IN INDIAN SOCIOLOGY
Vol. III (ed.) G.R. Gupta, Delhi, Vikas, 1975

5302 Katju, K.N.

LACK OF LEADERSHIP IN INDIAN VILLAGES
Kurukshetra, 1964, 12, 9, Jun, 8-10,
SA, XlV, 1, B8659

5303 Prasad, J.

IMPACT OF C.D. PROJECTS ON THE PATTERN OF
RURAL LEADERSHIP POWER STRUCTURE
Doct. st, Gorakhpur U, 1969 (S.P.Nagendra)

5304 Shah, C.N. & Patel, A.V.

CHARACTERISTICS RELATED WITH THE EFFECTIVENESS
OF FARM OPINION LEADERS IN TWO VILLAGES
Ind.Sociol. B. 1970, 7, 3-4, Apr-Jul, 192-201
SA, XX, 5, F7311

410   interaction between (large) groups
       (race relations, group relations, etc.)

5305 *Brookman, L.M.

HINDUS AND MUSLIMS: COMMUNAL RELATIONS AND
CULTURAL INTEGRATION
in: MAIN CURRENTS IN INDIAN SOCIOLOGY
Vol.III (ed.) G.R.Gupta, Delhi, Vikas, 1975

410   interaction between (large) groups
       (race relations, group relations, etc.)

    5306 Das Gupta, J.

          LANGUAGE CONFLICT AND NATIONAL DEVELOPMENT:
          GROUP POLITICS AND NATIONAL LANGUAGE POLICY
          IN INDIA
          Berkeley, U of Calif. Press, 1970

    5307 *Khan, M.F. (ed.)

          NATIONAL INTEGRATION: ITS MEANING AND RELEVANCE
          Navachetna Prakashan, 1970

    5308 *Pereira, C.P.

          EAST INDIANS IN WINNIPEG: A STUDY OF THE
          CONSEQUENCES OF IMMIGRATION FOR AN ETHNIC
          GROUP IN CANADA
          Thesis, University of Manitoba, 1971, xi & 201

    5309 *Schaefer, R.T.

          ENCOUNTERS IN A FOREIGN LAND: INDIAN
          COMMUNITIES IN GREAT BRITAIN
          in: MAIN CURRENTS IN INDIAN SOCIOLOGY
          Vol. III (ed.) G.R.Gupta, Delhi, Vikas, 1975

    5310 *Vaid, K.N.

          THE OVERSEAS INDIAN COMMUNITY IN HONG KONG
          Hongkong, Centre of Asian Studies, University
          of Hong Kong, 1972, iv & 108

    5311 *Wright, T.P. Jr.

          INDIAN MUSLIMS, BANGLA DESH SECESSION AND
          INDO-PAKISTAN WAR OF 1971
          in: MAIN CURRENTS IN INDIAN SOCIOLOGY,
          Vol. III (ed.) G.R. Gupta, Delhi, Vikas, 1975

5312 Bhagwat, D.

      THE RIDDLE IN INDIAN LIFE, LOVE AND LITERATURE
      Bombay, 1968

5313 Ghurye, G.S.

      FAMILY AND KIN IN INDO-EUROPEAN CULTURE (2nd ed.)
      New York, Humanities, 1962

5314 *Gist, N.P.

      THE ANGLO-INDIANS OF INDIA
      in: MAIN CURRENTS IN INDIAN SOCIOLOGY
      Vol. III (ed.) G.R.Gupta, Delhi, Vikas, 1975

5315 Mukherjee, B.B.

      MARRIAGE CUSTOMS AND KINSHIP ORGANIZATION OF
      THE URALI OF TRAVANCORE
      B.Dept.Anthrop. Gov't of India, 1952, 1, 2

5316 *Wright, R.D. & Wright, Susan A.

      THE ANGLO-INDIAN COMMUNITY IN CONTEMPORARY INDIA
      Midwest Quarterly, 1971, 12, 2, Jan, 175-185
      SA, 21, 73G3830

513   culture (evolution)

5317 *Basham, A.L.

      THE WONDER THAT WAS INDIA
      London, Sidgwick & Jackson, 1954

513   culture (evolution)

5318 *Brown, W. Norman

        THE CONTENT OF CULTURAL CONTINUITY IN INDIA
        The Journal of Asian Studies, 20, 1961, 427-434

5319 *Embree, A.T. (ed.)

        THE HINDU TRADITION: READINGS IN ORIENTAL THOUGHT
        New York, Vintage, 1966

5320 *Gokak, V.K.

        INDIA AND THE WORLD CULTURE
        Delhi, Vikas, 1972

5321 Lewis, O.

        PEASANT CULTURE IN INDIA AND MEXICO:
        A COMPARATIVE ANALYSIS
        in: VILLAGE INDIA
        ed. M. Marriott, U of Chicago Press, 1956
        p.145-171

5322 *Misra, S.N.

        SURPLUS CATTLE IN INDIA: A CRITICAL SURVEY
        Sociological Bulletin, 22, 2, 1973, 297-308

5323 Paul, B.D.

        HEALTH, CULTURE AND COMMUNITY
        New York, Russel Sage Foundation, 1955

5324 Vidyarthi, L.P.

        THE CULTURAL LINGUISTIC REGIONS OF
        INDIAN FOLKLORE
        Indian Folklore, 1959, 2, 182-195

5325   Aiyappan, A.

       APPLIED ANTHROPOLOGY
       Adivasi, 1959, 3

5326 *Aurora, G.S.

       TRIBE-CASTE-CLASS ENCOUNTERS: SOME ASPECTS
       OF FOLK-URBAN RELATIONS IN ALIRAJPUR TEHSIL
       Hyderabad, Administrative Staff College of
       India, 1972, pp. ii & 293

5327   Dube, S.C.

       APPROACHES TO TRIBAL PROBLEMS IN INDIA
       in: Vidyarthi (ed), APPLIED ANTHROPOLOGY IN INDIA
       Allahbad, Kitab Mahal, 1968

5328   Dumont, L.

       LE VOCABULAIRE DE PARENTE DANS L'INDE
       DU NORD (KINSHIP VOCABULARY IN NORTHERN
       INDIA) (Fr.)
       L'Homme, 1962, 2, 2, May-Aug., 5-48,
       SA, Xll, 4, B0245

5329 *Furer-Haimendorf, C. von

       A CENTRAL INDIAN TRIBAL PEOPLE: RAJ GONDS
       in South Asia: SEVEN COMMUNITY PROFILES,
       ed. C.Maloney, New York, Holt, Rinehart &
       Winston, 1974

5330 *Gardner, P.M.

       INDIA'S CHANGING TRIBES: IDENTITY AND INTERACTION
       IN CRISES
       in: MAIN CURRENTS IN INDIAN SOCIOLOGY
       Vol. III, (ed.) G.R.Gupta, Delhi, Vikas, 1975

5331 *Hockings, P.

      THE LAST DRY FUNERAL OF TODA
      in: MAIN CURRENTS IN INDIAN SOCIOLOGY
      Vol. I, (ed.) G.R.Gupta, Delhi, Vikas, 1975

5332 *Maloney, C.

      PEOPLES OF SOUTH ASIA
      New York, Holt, Rinehart & Winston, 1974

5333 *Maloney, C. (ed.)

      THE EVIL EYE
      New York, 1974

5334 *Vatuk, V.P. & S.

      SOCIAL CONTEXT OF GIFT EXCHANGE IN NORTH INDIA
      in: MAIN CURRENTS IN INDIAN SOCIOLOGY
      Nol. II (ed.) G.R.Gupta, Delhi, Vikas,1975

621   industrial sociology (labour)

5335 *Bellwinkel, M.

      RAJASTHAN: CONTRACT LABOUR IN DELHI: A CASE
      STUDY OF THE RELATIONSHIP BETWEEN COMPANY,
      MIDDLE-MAN AND WORKER
      Sociological Bulletin, 22, 1, 1973, 78-97

5336 Dugal, B.S.

      THE VILLAGE CHIEF IN THE INDIAN CONSTRUCTION
      INDUSTRY
      Hum. Org. 1959-60, 18,4,Win, 174-176,
      SA, X, 3, A2278

5337   Gupta, H.C.

THE SOCIAL CONSEQUENCES OF INDUSTRIALISATION
AND URBANISATION IN FARIDABAD (Ph.D.)
Doct. st, Agra U, 1969, (Dr.B.R.Chauhan)

5338   *Ramaswamy, E.A.

THE ROLE OF THE TRADE UNION LEADER IN INDIA
Hum.Org. 33, 2, Summer, 1974

5339   Singh, Tarlok

PROBLEMS OF INTEGRATING RURAL, INDUSTRIAL
AND URBAN DEVELOPMENT
in: INDIA'S URBAN FUTURE
ed. R.Turner, Berkeley, Dalif. U Press, 1962,
p. 327-335

5340   Vidyarthi, L.P.

INDUSTRIALISATION AND URBANIZATION IN TRIBAL AREA
Paper presented at Indian Sociological Conference,
Bombay, 1967

715   social change and economic development

5341   Ahmad, S.M.F.

EDUCATION AND SOCIAL CHANGE AMONG MUNDA
TRIBE OF RANCHI DISTRICT
Doct. st, Ranchi U, 1969

5342   Bulsara, J.F.

THE CONCEPT OF SOCIAL PLANNING
Ind.J.Soc.Work, 1964, 25, 3, Oct, 187-192,
SA, X111, 6-7, B7712

5343 Chauhan, S.S.

      AGRICULTURAL PRODUCTION PROGRAMMES AND
      SOCIAL CHANGE IN UTTAR PRADESH (Ph.D.)
      Doct. st, Agra U, 1969 (A.S.Mathur)

5344 Cherukupalle, M.D.

      URBAN SOCIAL STRUCTURE AND ECONOMIC DEVELOPMENT
      POLICY: SOME HYPOTHESES AND EMPIRICAL RESULTS
      Man in India, 1972, 52, 2, 131-150

5345 *Cohn, B.S.

      SOCIETY AND SOCIAL CHANGE UNDER THE RAJ
      South Asian Review, 4, 1970, 27-49

5346 Cormack, (Mrs.) M.L.

      SHE WHO RIDES A PEACOCK: INDIAN STUDENTS
      AND SOCIAL CHANGE, A RESEARCH ANALYSIS
      Bombay, Asia Pub. House, 1961

5347 *Crane, R.I.

      INDIA: PAST AND PRESENT
      in: ASIA IN THE MODERN WORLD
      ed. H.G.Matthew, New York, New American
      Library, 1963, pp. 155-191

5348 Ensminger, D.

      RURAL INDIA IN TRANSITION
      New Delhi, All India Panchayat Parishad, 1972,
      115 pp.

5349 *Epstein, S.

      SOUTH INDIA: YESTERDAY, TODAY AND TOMORROW:
      MYSORE VILLAGES REVISITED
      New York, Holmes & Meier, 1973,
      xvlll & 273

5350   Gomathinayagam, V.

      RURAL SOCIAL CHANGE: ITS CORRELATION TO
      CASTE RANKING, ECONOMIC POSITION, AND
      LITERACY LEVEL
      Ind.J.Soc.Res. 13,3, Dec, 1972, 224-230

5351 *Gore, M.S.

      SOME ASPECTS OF SOCIAL DEVELOPMENT,
      Bombay, Tata Institute of Social Sciences,
      1973, pp. vi & 118

5352 *Gough, K. & Sharma, H.P.

      IMPERIALISM AND REVOLUTION IN SOUTH ASIA
      New York & London, Monthly Review Press
      1973, pp. viii & 470

5353 *Gusfield, J.R.

      TRADITION AND MODERNITY: MISPLACED
      POLARITIES IN THE STUDY OF SOCIAL CHANGE
      American Journal of Sociology, 1966, pp.351-62

5354 *Hale, M.L.

      BARRIERS TO FREE CHOICE OF DEVELOPMENT IN INDIA
      Paper presented at the 8th World Congress of
      Sociology, Toronto, August 19-24, 1974

5355 *Lambert, R.

   SOCIAL CHANGE IN INDIA SINCE INDEPENDENCE:
   PROBLEMS AND PROSPECTS
   in: MAIN CURRENTS IN INDIAN SOCIOLOGY,
   Vol. I, Contemporary India: Some Sociological
   Perspectives (ed.) G.R.Gupta, Delhi, Vikas, 1975

5356 *Mandelbaum, D.G.

   SOCIETY IN INDIA (2 Vols.)
   Berkeley, U of California Press, 1970

5357 Mandelbaum,D.G.

   PLANNING AND SOCIAL CHANGE IN INDIA
   Hum.Org. 1953, 12, 3, Fall, 4-12,
   SA, Vol. II,#4, 746

5358 Misra, D.N.

   CONTINUITY AND CHANGE IN VILLAGE COMMUNITY IN
   INDIA, WITH SPECIAL REFERENCE TO SELECTED
   GROUP OF VILLAGES IN DISTRICT GORAKHPUR OF
   EAST UTTAR PRADESH
   Doct st, Gorakhpur U, 1969 (S.P.Nagendra)

5359 *Moore, C.D. & Eldredge, D. (eds.)

   INDIA: YESTERDAY AND TODAY
   New York, Bantam, 1970

5360 Myrdal, Gunnar

   INDIAN ECONOMIC PLANNING
   Pop. R. 1959, 3, 1, Jan, 17-32,
   SA, Xll, 6, B1752

5361   Narayana, P.L.

       TRADITIONS AND CHANGE IN THE RURAL SOCIETY OF
       VISAKHAPATNAM DISTRICT
       Doct, st, Andhra U, 1969, (Prof.N.S.Reddy)

5362 *Oommen, M.A.

       DEVELOPMENT: PERSPECTIVES AND PROBLEMS
       Madras, The Christian Literature Society,
       1973, pp vii & 120

5363 *Oommen, T.K.

       CHARISMA, STABILITY AND CHANGE
       New Delhi, Thomson Press, 1972

5364   Pandey, V.K.

       URBAN GROWTH AND SOCIAL CHANGE IN EASTERN
       UTTAR PRADESH
       Gorakhpur U, 1969, (S.P.Nagendra)

5365   Pant, Pitambar

       URBANISATION AND THE LONG RANGE STRATEGY
       OF ECONOMIC DEVELOPMENT
       in: INDIA'S URBAN FUTURE
       ed.R.Turner, Berkeley, U of Calif. Press,
       1962, p. 182-192

5366   Pothen, K.P.

       INDUSTRIALIZATION AND URBANIZATION
       Ind.Sociol. 1961, 3, 4, Mar, 16-24,
       SA, X111, 1, B4510

5367   Siddiqi, A.A.

       PLANNING AND SOCIAL CHANGE
       Agra Univ.J.Res.(Lett.) 1955, 3, Dec, 118-121
       SA, V1, 1, 4190

5368 *Singer, M. (ed.)

    ENTREPRENEURSHIP AND MODERNIZATION OF OCCUPATIONAL
    CULTURES IN SOUTH ASIA
    Monograph 12, Program in Comparative Studies on
    Southern Asia,
    Durham, Duke University, 1973

5369 Tangri, Shanti

    URBANIZATION, POLITICAL STABILITY, AND
    ECONOMIC GROWTH
    in: INDIA'S URBAN FUTURE
    ed. R. Turner,
    Berkeley, U of Calif Press, 1962, p. 192-213

5370 Tewari, G.C.

    THE IMPACT OF COMMUNITY DEVELOPMENT PROJECTS
    ON THE SOCIAL ECONOMY OF KUMAON HILLS (Ph.D.)
    Doct, Agra U, 1965

5371 *Transactions

    TRENDS OF SOCIO-ECONOMIC CHANGE IN INDIA
    Simla, Indian Institute of Advanced Study, 1970

828   communication

5372 Bose, A.B.

    THE INDIGENOUS SYSTEM OF COMMUNICATION
    IN AN INDUSTRIAL CITY
    J.Soc.Res.1965, 8, 1, Mar, 71-75,
    SA, XlV, 5, C1398

5373   Malhotra, M.

AN INVESTIGATION INTO THE ACCEPTANCE OF THE
APPLIED NUTRITION PROGRAMME IN A SELECTED
VILLAGE OF PUNJAB
M.S.thesis, India, 1966

5374 *Mookherjee, H.N.

DIFFUSION OF AGRICULTURE INNOVATIONS IN INDIA
in: MAIN CURRENTS IN INDIAN SOCIOLOGY
Vol. I (ed.) G.R.Gupta, Delhi, Vikas, 1975

5375   Narendra, K. & Chandirain, J.

EDUCATIONAL TELEVISION IN INDIA
New Delhi, Agra Book Depot, 1967, viii-392p.

5376   Sahay, B.N.

REVIEW OF RESEARCHES DONE AT THE DIVISION
OF AGRICULTURAL EXTENSION
(Seminar on Extension Research and
Education,
Delhi, I.A.R.I., 1969

5377   Sudhakaran

COMMUNICATIONS FACILITIES IN VILLAGES
Kurukshetra, 1969, 17, 10, Jul, 29,
SA, X1X, 4, E9925

911   interactions between societies, nations and states

5378   Khare, R.S.

AN INDIAN VILLAGE'S REACTION TO CHINESE AGGRESSION
Asian Surv. 1964, 4, 11, Nov, 1152-1160,
SA, X1V, 4, C0449

5379 *Carras, Mary C.

THE DYNAMICS OF INDIAN POLITICAL FACTIONS
New York, Cambridge U Press, 1972

5380 *Cohen, S.P.

INDIA'S SECURITY: PROCESS AND POLICY
in: MAIN CURRENTS IN INDIAN SOCIOLOGY
Vol. III, (ed.) G.R.Gupta, Delhi, Vikas, 1975

5381 *Hardgrave, R.L.

CASTE, CLEAVAGE AND POLITICAL CONFLICT
in: MAIN CURRENTS IN INDIAN SOCIOLOGY,
Vol. III, (ed.) G.R.Gupta, Delhi, ·Vikas, 1975

5382 *Jay, E.J.

AUTHORITY STRUCTURE, FACTIONS AND SOCIAL CHANGE
IN CENTRAL INDIA
in: MAIN CURRENTS IN INDIAN SOCIOLOGY,
Vol. III, (ed.) G.R.Gupta, Delhi, Vikas, 1975

5383 *Kochanek, S.A.

BUSINESS AND POLITICS IN INDIA
Berkeley, University of California Press, 1974

5384 Marriott, M.

VILLAGE STRUCTURE AND THE PUNJAB GOVERNMENT:
A RESTATEMENT
Amer.Anthrop.V55, 1953, p. 137-43

5385 Nayak, P.R.

THE CHALLENGE OF URBAN GROWTH TO INDIAN
LOCAL GOVERNMENT
in: INDIA'S URBAN FUTURE,
ed.R.Turner,
Berkeley, U of Calif.Press, 1962,p.361-382

5386 *Pandey, U.S.

CONTEMPORARY INTERPRETATIONS OF COMMUNITY
POWER: A CRITICAL REVEIW OF THE MAJOR
THEORETICAL AND CONCEPTUAL ISSUES
Sociological Bulletin, 22, 2, 1973, 260-282

5387 Park, Richard L.

THE URBAN CHALLENGE TO LOCAL AND STATE GOVERNMENT:
WEST BENGAL, WITH SPECIAL ATTENTION TO CALCUTTA
in: INDIA'S URBAN FUTURE,
ed. R.Turner,
Berkeley, U of Calif.Press, 1962, 382-397

5388 *Reed, F.

THE SOCIAL ORIGINS OF DEMOCRACY - IS REVOLUTION
NECESSARY?
in: MAIN CURRENTS IN INDIAN SOCIOLOGY,
Vol. III (ed.) G.R.Gupta, Delhi, Vikas, 1975

5389 Sisson, R.

PEASANT MOVEMENTS AND POLITICAL MOBILIZATION:
THE JATS OF RAJASTHAN
Asian Survey, 1969, 9, 12, Dec, 946-963,
SA, XX, 4, F6390

5390 Sivertsen, D.

KASTER OG KOMMUNISTER I THYAGASAMUTHIRAM,
EN SOR-INDISH HANDSBY (CASTE AND COMMUNISTS IN
THYAGASAMUTHIRAM, A SOUTH INDIAN AGRICULTURAL
TOWN) (Nor.)
Iidss. Samfunnsj, 1960, 1, 3, Sep, 121-139,
XA, XlV, 1, B8693

5391 *Weiner, M.

PARTY BUILDING IN A NEW NATION
Chicago, Univ. of Chicago Press, 1967

5392   *Ahmed, I. (ed.)

        CASTE AND SOCIAL STRATIFICATION AMONG THE MUSLIMS
        Delhi, Manohar, 1973

5393   Anant, S.S.

        THE CHANGING TRENDS IN INTER-CASTE MARRIAGES
        IN INDIA: AN ANALYSIS OF MATRIMONIAL COLUMNS
        IN AN ENGLISH LANGUAGE DAILY
        J.of Psychological Res., 1972, 16, 1, 71-5

5394   *Beteille, A.

        INEQUALITY AND SOCIAL CHANGE,
        Delhi, Oxford University Press, 1972

5395   *Cohn, B.S.

        RECRUITMENT OF ELITES IN INDIA UNDER
        BRITISH RULE
        in: ESSAYS IN COMPARATIVE SOCIAL STRATIFICATION
        (eds.) L.Plotnicov & A. Tuden
        Pittsburgh, University of Pittsburgh Press, 1970

5396   Dasgupta, S.

        CASTE DOMINANCE AND AGRICULTURAL DEVELOPMENT
        IN VILLAGE INDIA
        Paper presented at the 1973 Annual Meeting of
        the Rural Sociol. Society,
        SA, XX, 5, Sup. 25, F7841

5397   Deshpande, C.G.

        A COMPARATIVE STUDY OF CASTE AND INTER-CASTE
        MARRIED COUPLES IN MAHARASHTRA, WITH SPECIAL
        REFERENCE TO THE SOCIETAL, MARITAL AND PERSONAL
        ADJUSTMENT (Ph.D.)
        Doct, Poona U, 1970 (Prof.V.K.Kothurkar)

5398   *Gartrell, J.W.

DEVELOPMENT AND SOCIAL STRATIFICATION IN SOUTH
INDIAN AGRARIAN COMMUNITIES
Paper presented at the 8th World Congress of
SociologyToronto, August 19-24, 1974

5399   Jaiswal, N.K. & Jha, V.C.

CASTE - A DISCRIMINATOR OF SOCIO-ECONOMIC
CHARACTERISTICS OF RURAL PEOPLE
Ind.J.Soc.Work, 1970, 30, 4, Jan, 361-367,
SA, X1X, 6, F1697

5400   *Johnson, M.G.

SOCIAL MOBILITY AMONG UNTOUCHABLES
in: MAIN CURRENTS IN INDIAN SOCIOLOGY,
Vol. III (ed.) G.R.Gupta, Delhi, Vikas, 1975

5401   Majumdar, A.K. & Das, K.K.

STUDY ON THE VALUES OF RURAL PEOPLE
IN RELATION TO OCCUPATIONAL STRATIFICATION
Society and Cult. 1970, 1, 1, Jul, 41-49,
SA, XX, 7, F9519

5402   Orenstein, H.

VILLAGE, CASTE, AND THE WELFARE STATE
Human Org., 1963, 22, 1

5403   Prasad, B.K.

VILLAGE LIFE IN SOUTH BIHAR - A STUDY IN
CASTE DOMINANCE
Doct. st, Ranchi U, 1969

5404   *Saberwal, S.

RECEDING POLLUTION: INTERCASTE RELATIONS
IN URBAN PUNJAB
Sociological Bulletin, 22, 2, 1973, 234-259

5405   Sachchidananda

CASTE AND CONFLICT IN A BIHAR VILLAGE
in:CONFLICT, TENSION AND CULTURAL TREND IN INDIA
(ed.) Vidyarthi, 1969

5406   *Schermerhorn, R.A.

SOCIAL MOBILITY OF THREE MINORITIES IN INDIA:
A QUALITATIVE APPROACH
in: MAIN CURRENTS IN INDIAN SOCIOLOGY
Vol. III, (ed.) G.R.Gupta, Delhi, Vikas, 1975

5407   *Sharma, K.L.

DOWNWARD SOCIAL MOBILITY: SOME OBSERVATIONS
Sociological Bulletin, 22, 1, 1972, 59-77

5408   Sharma, K.L.

CASTE AND CLASS CONSCIOUSNESS IN RURAL RAJASTHAN:
SOME SOCIAL AND PSYCHOLOGICAL EXPRESSIONS
Sociology & Soc.Res.1970,54,3,Apr,378-387
SA, XVlll, 1-2, E7443

5409   *Silverberg, J.

SOCIAL CATEGORIES VS. ORGANIZATIONS: CLASS
CONFLICT IN A CASTE STRUCTURED SYSTEM
in: MAIN CURRENTS IN INDIAN SOCIOLOGY
Vol. III (ed.) G.R.Gupta, Delhi, Vikas, 1975

1019   social stratification

5410   Sinha, S.N.

         MEN AND WOMEN OF INDIA TODAY
         in: SEX ROLES IN CHANGING SOCIETY
         ed. H.Seward & R.C.Williamson
         New York, Random House, 1970, p. 321-334

1020   sociology of occupations and professions

5411   Morrison, Charles

         MUNSHIS AND THEIR MASTERS: THE ORGANIZATION
         OF AN OCCUPATIONAL REALTIONSHIP IN THE INDIAN
         LEGAL SYSTEM
         Journal of Asian Studies, XXXl, 2, 1972, p.309-328

5412   Schwartz, R.D.

         REFLECTIONS ON THE ROLE OF THE INDIAN LAWYER
         in: IMPACT OF LAND LEGISLATION (preface)
         C.K.Jayasimha Rao
         Bangalore, Bharadwaja Publications, 1955

5413   *Van Groenou, W.

         SOCIOLOGY OF WORK IN INDIA
         in: MAIN CURRENTS IN INDIAN SOCIOLOGY
         Vol. I (ed.) G.R.Gupta, Delhi, Vikas, 1975

1116   rural sociology (village, agriculture)

5414   *Chekki, Dan A.

         COMMUNITY RESEARCH IN INDIA: SOME TRENDS
         8th World Congress of Sociology, Toronto,
         August 19-24, 1974

5415   *Epstein, S.

SOUTH INDIA: YESTERDAY, TODAY & TOMORROW:
MYSORE VILLAGES REVISITED
New York, Holmes & Meier, 1973, xviii & 273

5416   Gangte, T.S.

A SOCIOLOGICAL STUDY OF SOME KUKIS VILLAGES
IN MANIPUR
Doct, st, Delhi U, 1969, (A.M.Shab)

5417   *Ishwaran, K.

A VILLAGE IN KARNATAKA: MAPPING EVERYDAY
LIFE IN SIVAPUR
in: SOUTH ASIA: SEVEN COMMUNITY PROFILES
ed.C.Maloney,   New York, Holt, Rinehart &
Winston, 1974

5418   *Klass, Morton

COMMUNITY STRUCTURE IN WEST BENGAL
American Anthropologist, 1972, 74, 3, Jun, 610-610
SA, 21, 73G1301

5419   Kumarappa, J.C.

AN OVERALL PLAN FOR RURAL DEVELOPMENT (2nd ed.)
Wardha, M.P.: Maganvadi, 1948

5420   *Maloney, C. (ed.)

SOUTH ASIA: SEVEN COMMUNITY PROFILES
New York, Holt, Rinehart & Winston, 1974

5421   *Misra, Girish K.

A SERVICE CLASSIFICATION OF RURAL SETTLEMENTS
IN MIRYALGUDA
Behavioural Sciences & Community Development
1972, 6, 1, Mar, 64-75,
SA, 21, 73G2978

5422   *Reddy, V.S. & Jagannadha Rao, R. &
       Sharma, A.V.K.

       PACKING AREAS IN REGIONAL STUDIES
       Behavioural Sciences & Community Development
       1972, 6, 1, Mar, 127-134,
       SA, 73G2984

5423   Sen, L.K., Wanmali, S., Bose, S.,
       Misra , G.K. & Ramesh, K.S.

       PLANNING RURAL GROWTH CENTERS FOR INTEGRATED
       AREA DEVELOPMENT: A STUDY OF MIRYALGUDA TALUKA
       Hyderabad, Nat'l Instit. of C.D., 1971,
       xiv, 245 pp.

5424   *Sinha, Sachchidanand

       THE INTERNAL COLONY: A STUDY IN REGIONAL
       EXPLOITATION
       New Delhi, Sindhu Publications, 1973,
       pp. vi & 519

5425   *Wanamali, Sudhir

       CENTRAL PLACES AND THEIR TRIBUTORY POPULATION
       SOME OBSERVATIONS
       Behavioural Sciences & Community Development
       1972, 6, 1, Mar, 11-39
       SA, 21, 73G2988

5426   *Wanamali, Sudhir

       CLUSTERING OF SERVICES AS A FUNCTION OF
       'POPULATION DISTANCE' IN SETTLEMENT SYSTEMS
       Behavioural Sciences & Community Development
       1972, 6, 1, Mar, 40-47,
       SA, 21, 73G2989

5427   *Bopegamage, A. & Kulahalli, R.N.

        CASTE AND OCCUPATION IN RURAL INDIA:
        A REGIONAL STUDY IN URBANIZATION AND
        SOCIAL CHANGE
        Rural Sociology, 37, 3, Sept. 1972

5428   Doshi, H.C.

        INDUSTRIALIZATION AND NEIGHBORHOOD COMMUNITIES
        IN A WESTERN INDIAN CITY - CHALLENGE AND RESPONSE
        Sociol. B. 1968, 17, 1, Mar, 19-34
        SA, XV11, 5, D8320

5429   *Gould, H.

        CITIES ON THE NORTH INDIAN PLAIN: CONTRASTING
        LUCKNOW AND KANPUR
        in: SOUTH ASIA: SEVEN COMMUNITY PROFILES
        ed.C.Maloney
        New York, Holt, Rinehart & Winston, 1974

5430   Nirmala Devi, C.

        DEMOGRAPHIC CORRELATES OF URBAN SIZE IN INDIA:
        A DISCRIMINANT ANALYSIS
        Amer. Doctoral Dissertations (1966067)
        Harvard U. (Soc.-regional and city planning)

5431   Sinha, D.K.

        THE IMPACT OF URBANISATION ON FAMILY AND
        MARRIAGE: A SOCIOLOGICAL STUDY OF GORAKHPUR
        Doct. st, Gorakhpur U, 1969, (D.P.Saxena)

5432   Viswanathan, G.

        A DEMOGRAPHIC AND ECOLOGICAL STUDY OF
        HYDERABAD (Ph.D.)
        Doct, Andhra U, 1970, (Prof.M.V.Moorthy)

1218   urban sociology and ecology

  5433   *Wiebe, P.

           SOCIAL LIFE IN A MADRAS SLUM
           in: MAIN CURRENTS IN INDIAN SOCIOLOGY
           Vol. I, (ed.) G.R.Gupta, Delhi, Vikas, 1975

1330   sociology of language and literature

  5434   Hass, Marry R.

           THE APPLICATION OF LINGUISTICS TO LANGUAGE
           TEACHING
           in: ANTHROPOLOGY TODAY
           ed. A.L.Kroeber, U of Chicago Press

1331   sociology of art (creative and performing)

  5435   *Lannoy, R.

           THE SPEAKING TREE: A STUDY OF INIDAN CULTURE
           AND SOCIETY
           Delhi, Oxford University Press, 1973

  5436   Srivastava, (Miss) U.

           SOCIAL LIFE AS REFLECTED IN INDIAN ART FROM
           POST-MAURYAN TO GUPTA PERIOD (D.Phil.)
           Doct, Allahabad U, 1970 (Dr. S.Mukerji)

1432   sociology of education

  5437   *Altbach, P.

           HIGHER EDUCATION AND MODERNIZATION: THE
           INDIAN CASE
           in: MAIN CURRENTS IN INDIAN SOCIOLOGY
           Vol.I (ed.) G.R.Gupta, Delhi, Vikas, 1975

1432   sociology of education

5438   *Bhatnagar, G.S.

        EDUCATION AND SOCIAL CHANGE
        Calcutta, Minverva Associates, 1972

5439   *Dickinson, R.D.N.

        THE CHRISTIAN COLLEGE IN DEVELOPING INDIA:
        A SOCIOLOGICAL INQUIRY
        Bombay, Oxford University Press, 1972

5440   *Gusfield, J.R.

        EDUCATIONAL INSTITUTIONS IN THE PROCESS
        OF ECONOMIC AND NATIONAL DEVELOPMENT
        Journal of Asian and African Studies, 1-2,
        April, 1966, 129-146

5441   *Mazumdar, Vina

        EDUCATION AND SOCIAL CHANGE
        Simla, Indian Institute of Advanced Study, 1972

1535   sociology of religion

5442   *Spencer, R.F. (ed.)

        RELIGION AND CHANGE IN CONTEMPORARY ASIA
        Calcutta, Oxford University Press, 1972

5443   Visaria, L.

        RELIGIONS AND REGIONAL DIFFERENCES IN
        MORTALITY AND FERTILITY IN THE INDIAN
        SUBCONTINENT (Ph.D.-Soc.)
        Princeton U, 1972

1636   sociology of law

5444   *Derrett, D.M.

        SOCIOLOGY AND FAMILY LAW IN INDIA: THE
        PROBLEM OF THE HINDU MARRIAGE
        in: MAIN CURRENTS IN INDIAN SOCIOLOGY
        Vol. II (ed.) G.R.Gupta, Delhi, Vikas, 1975

1835   family planning

5445   Dandekar, K.

        POSSIBLE TARGETS AND THEIR ATTAINMENT IN THE
        FIELD OF FAMILY PLANNING IN INDIA DURING
        1966 - 1976
        Artha Vijnana, 8, 3, Sep, 1966, 239,248

1837   demography (population study)

5446   Agarwalla, S.N.

        A METHOD FOR ESTIMATING DECADE INTERNAL MIGRATION
        IN CITIES FROM INDIAN CENSUS DATA
        Ind.Econ.Rev.1958, 4, 1, 58-76,
        SA, Vlll, 2, 7585

5447   Beharta, P.C.

        FAMILY TYPE AND FERTILITY IN SIX INDIAN
        VILLAGES
        Eco. & Pol. Wkly, 1966, 1, 15, 633-634

5448   *Nag, M.

        DIFFERENTIAL FERTILITY PATTERNS IN INDIA
        in: MAIN CURRENTS IN INDIAN SOCIOLOGY
        Vol. I (ed.) G.R.Gupta, Delhi, Vikas, 1975

1939   adolescence and youth

  5449   *UNICEF

          STATISTICAL PROFILE OF CHILDREN AND YOUTH IN INDIA
          New Delhi, UNICEF, 1973, pp. 135

  5450   *UNICEF

          A WASTED ASSET: A SURVEY OF RURAL YOUTH IN TWO
          INDIAN DISTRICTS
          New Delhi, UNICEF, 1973, pp. x & 173

1940   sociology of sexual behaviour

  5451   *Sur, A.K.

          SEX AND MARRIAGE IN INDIA: AN ETHNO-HISTORICAL
          SURVEY
          Calcutta, Allied, 1973, pp. vii & 194

1941   sociology of the family

  5452   *Conklin, G.H.

          FAMILY STRUCTURE, CASTE AND ECONOMIC
          DEVELOPMENT: AN URBAN RURAL COMPARISON
          FROM DHARWAR
          in: MAIN CURRENTS IN INDIAN SOCIOLOGY
          Vol. II (ed.) G.R.Gupta, Delhi, Vikas, 1975

  5453   *Deshpande, Kamalabai

          DIVORSE CASES IN THE COURT OF POONA:
          AN ANALYSIS
          The Economic Weekly, 15, 1963, 1179-1183

1941   sociology of the family

5454   *Foss, D. & Strauss, M.

        CULTURE, CRISIS AND CREATIVITY OF FAMILIES
        IN BOMBAY, SAN JUAN AND MINNEAPOLIS
        Paper presented at 8th World Congress of
        Sociology, August 19-24, 1974

5455   *Freed, S.A.

        A NATURAL BARRIER, TRANSPORTATION NETWORKS, AND
        POPULATION MOVEMENT IN A NORTH INDIAN AREA
        in: MAIN CURRENTS IN INDIAN SOCIOLOGY
        Vol. II (ed.) G.R.Gupta, Delhi, Vikas, 1975

5456   *Inkeles, A. & Miller, (Mrs.) Karen

        FROM TRADITIONALISM TO MODERNISM:
        DEVELOPMENT OF A CROSS NATIONAL SCALE
        OF FAMILY MODERNISM
        8th World Congress of Sociology,
        Toronto, August 19-24, 1974

5457   *Jacobson, D.A.

        WOMEN AND FAMILY WEALTH IN RURAL INDIA
        in: MAIN CURRENTS IN INDIAN SOCIOLOGY
        Vol. II (ed.) G.R.Gupta, Delhi, Vikas, 1975

5458   *Kapur, P.

        STUDIES OF THE URBAN WOMEN IN INDIA
        in: MAIN CURRENTS IN INDIAN SOCIOLOGY
        Vol. II (ed.) G.R.Gupta, Delhi, Vikas, 1975

5459   *Khatri, A.A.

        UNDERSTANDING CHANGES IN THE HINDU FAMILY
        IN THE CONTEMPORARY WORLD
        8th World Congress of Sociology
        Toronto, August 19-24, 1974

1941   sociology of the family

5460   *Khatri, A.A.

        PARENTAL PREFERENCES FOR A BOY OR A GIRL AND
        THEIR RATIONALE AS PERCEIVED BY EAST INDIAN
        CHILDREN
        8th World Congress of Sociology
        Toronto, August 19-24, 1974

5461   *Khatri, A.A.

        THE JOINT FAMILY IN INDIA TODAY
        Paper presented at the ASA Annual Meeting,
        Montreal, August 25-29, 1974

5462   *Kurian, G.

        THE INDIAN FAMILY IN TRANSITION:
        SOME REGIONAL VARIATIONS
        in: MAIN CURRENTS IN INDIAN SOCIOLOGY
        Vol. II (ed.) G.R.Gupta, Delhi, Vikas, 1975

5463   *Liu, W.T.

        CULTURE, CRISIS AND CREATIVITY OF FAMILY
        IN BOMBAY, SAN JUAN AND MINNEAPOLIS
        8th World Congress of Sociology,
        Toronto, August 19-24, 1974

5464   *Patel, N.

        HINDUISM OUTSIDE INDIA: SELECTIVE
        RETENTION IN GUJARATI FAMILIES
        in: MAIN CURRENTS IN INDIAN SOCIOLOGY
        Vol. II (ed.) G.R.Gupta, Delhi, Vikas, 1975

5465   Poffenberger, T.

        CHILD DEVELOPMENT AND FAMILY RELATIONS
        AS A SCIENTIFIC FIELD
        Ind.J.Soc.Work, 1963, 24, 2, Jul, 110-114,
        SA, Xll, 5, B1441

5466   Poffenberger, T. (et al)

A PRELIMINARY SURVEY OF INDIAN INSTITUTIONS
TEACHING AND CONDUCTING RESEARCH IN CHILD
DEVELOPMENT AND FAMILY REALTIONSHIPS
Baroda, Dept. of Child Dev., Faculty of
Home Science, U of Baroda, 1964

5467   *Pothen, K.P.

INTER-RELIGIOUS MARRIAGES IN CENTRAL INDIA
Paper presented at the ASA Annual Meeting,
Montreal, August 25-29, 1974

5468   *Ramu, G.N.

FAMILY STRUCTURE AND ENTREPRENEURSHIP
AN INDIAN CASE
Journal of Comparative Family Studies,
4, 2, Autumn 1973, 239-256

5469   *Ross, A.D.

CHANGING ASPIRATIONS AND ROLES:
MIDDLE AND UPPER CLASS INDIAN WOMEN
ENTER THE BUSINESS WORLD
in: MAIN CURRENTS IN INDIAN SOCIOLOGY
Vol. II (ed.) G.R.Gupta, Delhi, Vikas, 1975

5470   *Sengupta, Padmini

WORKING WOMEN IN INDIA
Bombay, Asia, 1962

5471   *Ullrich, H.E.

WOMEN IN SELECTED KANNADA FOLKTALES
in: MAIN CURRENTS IN INDIAN SOCIOLOGY
Vol. II (ed.) G.R.Gupta, Delhi, Vikas, 1975

1941   sociology of the family

  5472   *Wakil, P.S. & Chevan, A.

          INDO-PAKISTANI FAMILY IN CANADA
          8th World Congress of Sociology
          Toronto, August 19-24, 1974

2045   sociology of medicine (public health)

  5473   Bildhaiya & Demeld, C.

          A STUDY OF SOME PREVALENT CUSTOMS AND BELIEFS
          FOR THE HEALTH AND WELL-BEING OF CHILDREN IN
          JABALPUR AREA
          Ind.J.of Public Health, 1968, 12, 4, 215-218

2101   social problems (general)

  5474   *Brij Mohan

          INDIA'S SOCIAL PROBLEMS: ANALYSING
          BASIC ISSUES
          Allahabad, Indian International Pub. 1972,
          pp. xv & 148

2143   social gerontology

  5475   Singh, R.R.

          WELFARE OF THE AGED
          Ind.J.Soc.Work, 1970, 30, 4, Jan, 327-334,
          SA, XlX, 6, F2015

2147   social disorganization (crime)

2147   social disorganization (crime)

5476   *Beals, A.R.

CRIME AND CONFLICT IN SOME SOUTH
INDIAN VILLAGES
mimeographed, 1965, 23pp.

5477   Mukerji, N.

SEXUAL DELINQUENCY
Ind. J. Soc.Work, 1955, 16, 1, Jun, 19-26,
SA, Vol. V, #2, 3314

5478   Shukla, V.N.

ADOLESCENTS' SUICIDES
Social Welfare, 19, 8, Nov, 1972, p.6-7

2148   applied sociology (social work)

5479   Amin, D.K.

SOCIAL WORK IN COMMUNITY DEVELOPMENT
Social Welfare, 19, 7, 1972, 4

5480   Dasgupta, S.

SOCIAL WORK AND SOCIAL CHANGE: A CASE
STUDY OF INDIAN VILLAGE DEVELOPMENT
Boston, Porter Sargent, 1968

5481   Singhi, N.K.

THE PROBLEM AND PREVENTION (PROSTITUTION)
Social Welfare, 19, 3, 1972, 8-10

5482   Wadia, A.B.

SOME ASPECTS OF FAMILY WELFARE IN INDIA
Marriage & Family Living 1955, 17, 3, Aug, 226-230
SA, Vol. IV, #3, 2629

2233   sociology of knowledge

  5483   *Dasgupta, S.

         ALTERNATIVE PERSPECTIVES ON THE GLOBAL SOCIETY
         Paper presented at the ASA Annual Meeting,
         Montreal, August 25-29, 1974

  5484   *Hiebert, P.G.

         INDIAN AND AMERICAN WORLD VIEWS:
         A STUDY IN CONTRASTS
         in: MAIN CURRENTS IN INDIAN SOCIOLOGY
         Vol. I, (ed.) G.R.Gupta, Delhi, Vikas, 1975

  5485   *Singh, Y.

         THE ROLE OF SOCIAL SCIENCES IN INDIA:
         A SOCIOLOGY OF KNOWLEDGE
         Sociological Bulletin, 22, 1, 1973, 14-28

2252   history of ideas

  5486   *Ganguli, B.N.

         NATURE AND SIGNIFICANCE OF IDEOLOGY
         Sociological Bulletin, 22, 1, 1973, 1-13

2454   planning and forecasting

  5487   Saxena, R.N.

         APPLICATION OF SOCIOLOGY IN SOCIAL WELFARE
         PLANNING IN INDIA
         Presidential Address, 4th Indian Sociology
         Conference, Calcutta, 1954